Principles of Supply Chain Management

A Balanced Approach | 5e

JOEL D. WISNER, PhD
University of Nevada, Las Vegas

KEAH-CHOON TAN, PhD
University of Nevada, Las Vegas

G. KEONG LEONG, PhD
*California State University,
Dominguez Hills*

Australia • Brazil • Mexico • Singapore • United Kingdom • United States

Principles of Supply Chain Management, **Fifth Edition**

Joel Wisner, Keah-Choon Tan, G. Keong Leong

Senior Vice President: Erin Joyner

Vice President, Business and Economics: Mike Schenk

Sr. Product Team Manager: Joe Sabatino

Sr. Product Manager: Aaron Arnsparger

Content Developer: Chris Valentine

Product Assistant: Renee Schnee

Sr. Marketing Manager: Nate Anderson

Digital Product Manager: Mark Hopkinson

Manufacturing Planner: Ron Montgomery

Production Service: Lumina Datamatics, Inc

Sr. Art Director: Michelle Kunkler

Intellectual Property

   Analyst: Brittani Morgan

   Project Manager: Nick Barrows

Cover Image: niroworld / Shutterstock

For product information and technology assistance, contact us at **Cengage Learning Customer & Sales Support, 1-800-354-9706**

For permission to use material from this text or product, submit all requests online at **www.cengage.com/permissions**
Further permissions questions can be emailed to **permissionrequest@cengage.com**

Library of Congress Control Number: 2017947976

ISBN: 978-1-337-40649-9

Cengage Learning
20 Channel Center Street
Boston, MA 02210
USA

Cengage Learning is a leading provider of customized learning solutions with employees residing in nearly 40 different countries and sales in more than 125 countries around the world. Find your local representative at **www.cengage.com.**

Cengage Learning products are represented in Canada by Nelson Education, Ltd.

To learn more about Cengage Learning Solutions, visit **www.cengage.com**

Purchase any of our products at your local college store or at our preferred online store **www.cengagebrain.com**

Printed in the United States of America
Print Number: 05   Print Year: 2019

To CJ, Hayley, Blake, Phyllis, and Sally.

—JOEL WISNER

To Shaw Yun, Wen Hui, and Wen Jay.

—KEAH-CHOON TAN

To Lin and Michelle.

—G. KEONG LEONG

Brief Contents

Preface   xvi
MindTap for Supply Chain Management   xvii
Acknowledgments   xix
About the Authors   xx

Part 1   Supply Chain Management: An Overview   1

Chapter   1   Introduction to Supply Chain Management   3

Part 2   Supply Issues in Supply Chain Management   35

Chapter   2   Purchasing Management   37
Chapter   3   Creating and Managing Supplier Relationships   81
Chapter   4   Ethical and Sustainable Sourcing   111
Chapter   5   Demand Forecasting   145

Part 3   Operations Issues in Supply Chain Management   181

Chapter   6   Resource Planning Systems   183
Chapter   7   Inventory Management   231
Chapter   8   Process Management—Lean and Six Sigma
             in the Supply Chain   275

Part 4   Distribution Issues in Supply Chain Management   329

Chapter   9   Domestic U.S. and Global Logistics   331
Chapter   10   Customer Relationship Management   383
Chapter   11   Global Location Decisions   413
Chapter   12   Service Response Logistics   449

Part 5   Integration Issues in Supply Chain Management   499

Chapter   13   Supply Chain Process Integration   501
Chapter   14   Performance Measurement Along Supply Chains   543

Appendix   1   Areas Under the Normal Curve   575
Appendix   2   Answers to Selected End-of-Chapter Problems   576

On the Companion Website

Student and Instructor Materials

Contents

Preface xvi
MindTap for Supply Chain Management xvii
Acknowledgments xix
About the Authors xx

Part 1 **Supply Chain Management: An Overview** 1

Chapter 1 Introduction to Supply Chain Management 3
Introduction 4
Supply Chain Management Defined 5
The Importance of Supply Chain Management 9
The Origins of Supply Chain Management
in the United States 11
The Foundations of Supply Chain Management 14
Supply Elements 14
Operations Elements 16
Logistics Elements 18
Integration Elements 20
Current Trends in Supply Chain Management 21
Use of Supply Chain Analytics 22
Improving Supply Chain Sustainability 22
Increasing Supply Chain Visibility 23
Summary 24
Discussion Questions 24
Essay/Project Questions 25
Cases 26

Appendix 1.1
The Beer Game 28
Additional Resources 31
Endnotes 32

Part 2 **Supply Issues in Supply Chain Management** 35

Chapter 2 Purchasing Management 37
Introduction 39
A Brief History of Purchasing Terms 39

The Role of Supply Management in an Organization   40
   The Financial Significance of Supply Management   41
The Purchasing Process   44
   The Manual Purchasing System   44
   Electronic Procurement Systems (e-Procurement)   47
   Small-Value Purchase Orders   50
Sourcing Decisions: The Make-or-Buy Decision   53
   Reasons for Buying or Outsourcing   53
   Reasons for Making   55
   Make-or-Buy Break-Even Analysis   56
Roles of the Supply Base   57
Supplier Selection   58
   The Total Cost of Ownership Concept   59
How Many Suppliers to Use   59
   Reasons Favoring a Single Supplier   62
   Reasons Favoring Multiple Suppliers   62
Purchasing Organization   63
   Advantages of Centralization   63
   Advantages of Decentralization   64
Global Sourcing   64
   Reasons for Global Sourcing   66
Procurement in Government and Nonprofit Agencies   67
   Characteristics of Public Procurement   68
   Summary   71
   Key Terms   71
   Discussion Questions   72
   Essay/Project Questions   73
   Spreadsheet Problems   73
   Cases   76
   Additional Resources   79
   Endnotes   79

Chapter   3   Creating and Managing Supplier Relationships   81
Introduction   82
Developing Supplier Relationships   83
   Building Trust   84
   Shared Vision and Objectives   84
   Personal Relationships   85
   Mutual Benefits and Needs   85
   Commitment and Top Management Support   85
   Change Management   85
   Information Sharing and Lines of Communication   86
   Relationship Capabilities   86

Performance Metrics   87
Continuous Improvement   89
Monitoring Supplier Relationships   89
Key Points   90

Supplier Evaluation and Certification   91
The Weighted Criteria Evaluation System   92
External Certifications   93

Supplier Development   95

Supplier Recognition Programs   97

Supplier Relationship Management   98
Summary   101
Key Terms   101
Discussion Questions   101
Problems   102
Essay/Project Questions   103
Cases   104
Endnotes   107

Chapter   4   Ethical and Sustainable Sourcing   111

Introduction   112

Ethical and Sustainable Sourcing Defined   113
Ethical Sourcing   113
Sustainable Sourcing   116

Developing Ethical and Sustainable Sourcing Strategies   120

Ethical and Sustainable Sourcing Initiatives   123
Ethical and Sustainable Supplier Certification Programs   123
Supply Base Rationalization Programs   124
Outsourcing Products and Services   124

Early Supplier Involvement   125
Vendor Managed Inventories   126

Strategic Alliance Development   127
Negotiating Win–Win Strategic Alliance Agreements   129

Rewarding Supplier Performance   130

Benchmarking Successful Sourcing Practices   131

Assessing and Improving the Firm's Sourcing Function   133
Summary   135
Key Terms   135
Discussion Questions   135
Essay/Project Questions   137
Cases   137
Additional Resources   141
Endnotes   141

Chapter 5 Demand Forecasting 145

Introduction 147

The Importance of Demand Forecasting 147

Forecasting Techniques 148
  Qualitative Methods 149
  Quantitative Methods 150
  Cause-and-Effect Models 156

Forecast Accuracy 159

Collaborative Planning, Forecasting, and Replenishment 161

Useful Forecasting Websites 164

Forecasting Software 165
  Cloud-Based Forecasting 167
  Summary 170
  Key Terms 170
  Discussion Questions 170
  Problems 171
  Essay/Project Questions 174
  Cases 174
  Endnotes 178

Part 3 Operations Issues in Supply Chain Management 181

Chapter 6 Resource Planning Systems 183

Introduction 185

Operations Planning 185

The Aggregate Production Plan 187
  The Chase Production Strategy 187
  The Level Production Strategy 189
  The Mixed Production Strategy 191

The Master Production Schedule 191
  Master Production Schedule Time Fence 192
  Available-to-Promise Quantities 192

The Bill of Materials 195

The Material Requirements Plan 198
  Terms Used in Material Requirements Planning 199

Capacity Planning 205
  Capacity Strategies 206

The Distribution Requirements Plan 206

The Legacy Material Requirements Planning Systems 208
  Manufacturing Resource Planning 208

The Development of Enterprise Resource Planning Systems   209
The Rapid Growth of Enterprise Resource Planning Systems   211
Implementing Enterprise Resource Planning Systems   213
*Advantages and Disadvantages of Enterprise
Resource Planning Systems   216*
Enterprise Resource Planning Software Applications   217
Summary   219
Key Terms   219
Discussion Questions   220
Essay/Project Questions   221
Spreadsheet Problems   221
Cases   225
Additional Resources   229
Endnotes   229

Chapter 7   Inventory Management   231
Introduction   233
Dependent Demand and Independent Demand   234
Concepts and Tools of Inventory Management   234
The Functions and Basic Types of Inventory   235
Inventory Costs   235
Inventory Investment   236
The ABC Inventory Control System   237
Radio Frequency Identification   242
Inventory Models   247
The Economic Order Quantity Model   247
The Quantity Discount Model   251
The Economic Manufacturing Quantity Model   253
The Statistical Reorder Point   257
*The Continuous Review and the Periodic Review
Inventory Systems   261*
Summary   264
Key Terms   264
Discussion Questions   264
Essay/Project Questions   265
Spreadsheet Problems   266
Cases   269
Additional Resources   273
Endnotes   273

Chapter 8   Process Management—Lean and Six Sigma in the Supply Chain   275

Introduction   276

Lean Production and the Toyota Production System   278

Lean Thinking and Supply Chain Management   281

The Elements of Lean   281

Waste Elimination   281

Lean Supply Chain Relationships   284

Lean Layouts   285

Inventory and Setup Time Reduction   287

Small Batch Production Scheduling   288

Continuous Improvement   291

Workforce Commitment   291

Lean Systems and the Environment   292

The Origins of Six Sigma Quality   292

Comparing Six Sigma and Lean   295

Lean Six Sigma   295

Six Sigma and Supply Chain Management   295

The Elements of Six Sigma   297

Deming's Contributions   297

Crosby's Contributions   298

Juran's Contributions   299

The Malcolm Baldrige National Quality Award   300

The ISO 9000 and 14000 Families of Management Standards   302

The DMAIC Improvement Cycle   303

Six Sigma Training Levels   304

The Statistical Tools of Six Sigma   305

Flow Diagrams   305

Check Sheets   305

Pareto Charts   305

Cause-and-Effect Diagrams   306

Statistical Process Control   307

Statistical Process Control and Supply Chain Management   315

Summary   316

Key Terms   316

Discussion Questions   316

Essay/Project Questions   318

Problems   319

Cases   321

Additional Resources   324

Endnotes   325

Part 4   Distribution Issues in Supply Chain Management   329

Chapter 9   Domestic U.S. and Global Logistics   331

Introduction   333

Transportation Fundamentals   334
- *The Objective of Transportation*   334
- *Legal Forms of Transportation*   335
- *The Modes of Transportation*   336
- *Intermodal Transportation*   341
- *Transportation Pricing*   342
- *Transportation Security*   344
- *Transportation Regulation and Deregulation in the United States*   345

Warehousing and Distribution   349
- *The Importance and Types of Warehouses*   350
- *Risk Pooling and Warehouse Location*   352
- *Lean Warehousing*   355

The Impacts of Logistics on Supply Chain Management   356
- *Third-Party Logistics (3PL) Services*   357
- *Other Transportation Intermediaries*   360

Environmental Sustainability in Logistics   361

Logistics Management Software Applications   362
- *Transportation Management Systems*   363
- *Warehouse Management Systems*   363
- *Global Trade Management Systems*   365

Global Logistics   365
- *Global Freight Security*   365
- *Global Logistics Intermediaries*   366
- *Foreign-Trade Zones*   367
- *The North American Free Trade Agreement*   368

Reverse Logistics   368
- *The Impact of Reverse Logistics on the Supply Chain*   369
- *Reverse Logistics and the Environment*   370
- *Summary*   371
- *Key Terms*   371
- *Discussion Questions and Exercises*   372
- *Essay/Project Questions*   373
- *Problems*   374
- *Cases*   374
- *Additional Resources*   377
- *Endnotes*   378

Chapter   10   Customer Relationship Management   383
Introduction   384
Customer Relationship Management Defined   385
Key Tools and Components of CRM   388
Segmenting Customers   388
Predicting Customer Behaviors   390
Customer Value Determination   391
Personalizing Customer Communications   392
Automated Sales Force Tools   392
Managing Customer Service Capabilities   394
Designing and Implementing a Successful CRM Program   398
Creating the CRM Plan   398
Involving CRM Users from the Outset   399
Selecting the Right Application and Provider   399
Integrating Existing CRM Applications   400
Establishing Performance Measures   401
Training for CRM Users   401
Trends in CRM   402
Summary   404
Key Terms   404
Discussion Questions and Exercises   404
Essay/Project Questions   406
Problems   406
Cases   406
Additional Resources   410
Endnotes   410

Chapter   11   Global Location Decisions   413
Introduction   414
Global Location Strategies   415
Critical Location Factors   416
*Regional Trade Agreements and the World Trade
   Organization   418*
Competitiveness of Nations   419
The World Economic Forum's 12 Pillars of Competitiveness   421
Government Taxes and Incentives   422
Currency Stability   422
Environmental Issues   423
Access and Proximity to Markets   424
Labor Issues   425
Access to Suppliers   425
Utility Availability and Cost   426

Quality-of-Life Issues   426
Right-to-Work Laws   427
Land Availability and Cost   428

Facility Location Techniques   428
The Weighted-Factor Rating Model   428
The Break-Even Model   429

Business Clusters   430

Sustainable Development and Facility Location   432

Additive Manufacturing and Its Impact on Facility Location   434
Summary   437
Key Terms   437
Discussion Questions   437
Essay/Project Questions   438
Problems   438
Cases   440
Endnotes   444

Chapter   12   Service Response Logistics   449
Introduction   450

An Overview of Service Operations   451
Service Productivity   452
Global Service Issues   455
Service Strategy Development   456
The Service Delivery System   457
Service Location and Layout Strategies   457

Supply Chain Management in Services   462
Service Quality and Customers   463

The Primary Concerns of Service Response Logistics   463
Managing Service Capacity   464
Managing Queue Times   469
Managing Distribution Channels   478
Managing Service Quality   483
Summary   486
Key Terms   486
Discussion Questions   486
Essay/Project Questions   488
Problems   488
Cases   491
Additional Resources   494
Endnotes   495

Part 5   Integration Issues in Supply Chain Management   499

Chapter   13   Supply Chain Process Integration   501

Introduction   502

The Supply Chain Management Integration Model   503

Identify Critical Supply Chain Trading Partners   503

Review and Establish Supply Chain Strategies   505

*Align Supply Chain Strategies with Key Supply
Chain Process Objectives   505*

*Develop Internal Performance Measures
for Key Process Effectiveness   510*

*Assess and Improve Internal Integration
of Key Supply Chain Processes   511*

*Develop Supply Chain Performance Measures
for the Key Processes   512*

*Assess and Improve External Process Integration
and Supply Chain Performance   512*

*Extend Process Integration to Second-Tier
Supply Chain Partners   513*

Reevaluate the Integration Model Annually   515

Obstacles to Process Integration Along the Supply Chain   515

The Silo Mentality   516

Lack of Supply Chain Visibility   516

Lack of Trust   517

Lack of Knowledge   518

Activities Causing the Bullwhip Effect   519

Managing Supply Chain Risk and Security   522

Managing Supply Chain Risk   522

Managing Supply Chain Security   526

Summary   531

Key Terms   531

Discussion Questions   531

Essay/Project Questions   533

Cases   533

Additional Resources   538

Endnotes   538

Chapter   14   Performance Measurement Along Supply Chains   543

Introduction   544

Viewing Supply Chains as a Competitive Force   546

Understanding End Customers   546

Understanding Supply Chain Partner Requirements   547

Adjusting Supply Chain Member Capabilities   547
Traditional Performance Measures   548
   *Use of Organization Costs, Revenue, and Profitability
     Measures   549*
   Use of Performance Standards and Variances   550
   Productivity and Utilization Measures   550
World-Class Performance Measurement Systems   552
   Developing World-Class Performance Measures   553
Supply Chain Performance Measurement Systems   555
   Supply Chain Environmental Performance   555
The Balanced Scorecard   557
   Web-Based Scorecards   559
The SCOR Model   560
   Summary   563
   Key Terms   563
   Discussion Questions   563
   Problems   565
   Essay/Project Questions   565
   Cases   566
   Additional Resources   571
   Endnotes   571

Appendix   1
Areas Under the Normal Curve   575

Appendix   2
Answers to Selected End-of-Chapter Problems   576

Glossary   579

Author Index   589

Subject Index   590

On the Companion Website

Student and Instructor Materials

Preface

Welcome to the fifth edition of *Principles of Supply Chain Management: A Balanced Approach*. The practice of supply chain management has become widespread in all industries around the globe today, and the benefits to firms of all sizes are being realized. We think this text is unique in that it uses a novel and logical approach to present discussions of this topic from four foundation perspectives: purchasing, operations, logistics, and process integration. We think this text is also somewhat different than the other supply chain management texts available, since we present a more balanced view of the topic—many of the texts available today concentrate primarily on just one of the three areas of purchasing, operations, or logistics.

The objective of the text is to make readers think about how supply chain management impacts all of the various areas and processes of the firm and its supply chain trading partners and to show how managers can improve their firm's competitive position by employing the practices we describe throughout the text. Junior- or senior-level business students, beginning MBA students, as well as practicing managers can benefit from reading and using this text.

There are several changes to this fifth edition that we hope you will find interesting and useful. Perhaps the biggest change are the three cases at the end of each chapter (Chapter 1 has just one case). The teaching notes for each case can be found in the Instructor's Manual. There is also a greater emphasis on technological advances throughout the text. Additionally, each chapter contains a number of SCM Profiles, beginning with a chapter-opening profile, and then other smaller company profiles throughout the chapters. All chapter references throughout the text have been updated, with new and interesting storylines, to keep readers engaged and informed. Additionally, new end-of-chapter discussion, essay and project questions, and exercises have been added. Other ancillary materials are described below.

As with the fourth edition, the fifth edition has a tie-in to a wonderfully engaging global supply chain simulation game called SCM Globe. A separate page dedicated to SCM Globe follows this preface. We are very excited about the simulation and hope instructors will take it for a test drive and then use it in their classes.

New to the fifth edition is MindTap for supply chain management. A separate page dedicated to MindTap follows this preface.

Finally, PowerPoint lecture slides are available for download. The online instructor resource center contains sample syllabi, case teaching notes, answers to all of the end-of-chapter questions and problems, and a test bank. In the Chapter 1 Appendix, there is a discussion of the Beer Game, with inventory tracking sheets to allow instructors to actually play the game with their students. There are also quantitative as well as qualitative problems and questions, essay/project exercises, and Excel problems spread throughout most of the chapters.

Part 1 is the overview and introduction to the topic of supply chain management. This chapter introduces the basic understanding and concepts of supply chain management and should help students realize the importance of this topic. Core concepts such as the bullwhip effect, supplier relationship management, forecasting and demand management, enterprise resource planning, transportation management, and customer relationship management are briefly discussed. There is also a closing section on current trends in supply chain management.

Part 2 presents supply issues in supply chain management. This very important topic is covered in three chapters, building from an introduction to purchasing management, to managing supplier relationships, and then finally to ethical and sustainable sourcing. Within these chapters can be found sections on government purchasing, global sourcing, e-procurement, software applications, supplier development, ethical purchasing, and green purchasing.

Part 3 includes four chapters regarding operations issues in supply chain management. This section progresses from forecasting, resource planning, and inventory management to lean production and Six Sigma in a supply chain setting. Topics in this section include the basics of forecasting; collaborative planning, forecasting, and replenishment; material requirements planning; enterprise resource planning; inventory models; lean thinking; Six Sigma concepts and tools; and statistical process control techniques.

Part 4 presents distribution issues in supply chain management and consists of four chapters. This section begins with a review of domestic U.S. and international logistics with sections on green transportation, international logistics security, and reverse logistics. This is followed by chapters on customer relationship management, global location decisions, and service response logistics. Content in these chapters includes new software application discussions, social media, and cloud computing in customer relationship management, sustainability in logistics, new location trends in the global economy, and cloud computing in services.

The final section is Part 5, which presents discussions of the integration issues in supply chain management and performance measurements along the supply chain. While cooperation and integration are frequently referred to in the text, this section brings the entire text into focus, tying all of the parts together, first by discussing internal and external process integration in detail, followed by a discussion of traditional and world-class performance measurement systems. The topics of supply chain risk management and expanded coverage of performance measurement models are also included.

We think we have compiled a very interesting set of supply chain management topics that will keep readers engaged and we hope you enjoy it. We welcome your comments and suggestions for improvement. Please direct all comments and questions to:

Joel D. Wisner: joel.wisner@unlv.edu (primary contact),

Keah-Choon Tan: kctan@unlv.edu, or

G. Keong Leong: gkleong@csudh.edu

MINDTAP FOR SUPPLY CHAIN MANAGEMENT

MindTap, new to this edition, features Excel Online integration powered by Microsoft, a complete digital solution for the supply chain course. It has enhancements that take students from learning basic supply chain concepts to actively engaging in critical thinking applications, while learning valuable software skills for their future careers.

MindTap is a customizable digital course solution that includes an interactive eBook and auto-graded exercises from the text. All of these materials offer students better access to understand the materials within the course. For more information on MindTap, please contact your Cengage representative.

SCM Profile | SCM Globe–A Supply Chain Simulation

SCM Globe is an engaging supply chain experience. Students can design supply chains from scratch or use the case studies to understand how different supply chains produce different operating results. It is an easy-to-use, map-based supply chain simulation application. As they work with the simulations, students get an intuitive feel and an analytical understanding for how supply chains work.

SCM Globe leverages capabilities of Google Maps and adds further functionality that enables the design of new supply chains and the modeling of existing real supply chains. Users define products used in a supply chain and drag-and-drop the facilities that make or consume those products on a map of the world. They specify the routes (road, rail, air, water) that connect the facilities, and define the vehicles that run on those routes. Then the simulations show how well these supply chains perform.

SCM Globe lets students simulate the operation of their supply chains while showing animated displays of vehicles moving on the map following the routes defined between facilities. There are also on-screen displays showing inventory levels and operating costs at facilities. Problem areas (where products accumulate or run out) are identified. Students can keep improving their supply chain designs until they get the results they want.

Everything students need to get started is in the online guide. In 15–30 minutes, students can scan the short videos and tutorials in the "Getting Started" section of the online guide and will have what they need to start using SCM Globe. They learn more as the need arises by referring to specific sections in the online guide. There is also a library of case studies. Each case study is a bit more challenging than the last and illustrates supply chain operating principles. These principles and other issues are presented in a section for each case study. For instructors there are also step-by-step study guides illustrated with screenshots so instructors can quickly come up to speed with these semester-length case studies and coach their students through exploring the issues and challenges in each case study.

For instructors using this text, we have created a sample course syllabus that shows how to combine readings from this text with interactive supply chain simulations. The simulations illustrate and reinforce the concepts students learn in the readings and lectures. For a copy of this course syllabus please send an e-mail to Michael Hugos at mhugos@scmglobe.com.

SCM Globe costs $64.95 per student per semester and is provided at no charge to the instructors, with classes of five or more students. To learn more about SCM Globe, go to www.scmglobe.com. Click on the short video on the home page or click on the blue "Start Here" button to see more about what SCM Globe can do. You can request a personal web demonstration by sending an e-mail to SCM Globe at info@scmglobe.com.

ACKNOWLEDGMENTS

We greatly appreciate the efforts of a number of fine and hard-working people at Cengage. Without their feedback and guidance, this text would not have been completed. The team members are Aaron Arnsparger, product manager; Nate Anderson, marketing manager; and Chris Valentine, our content developer and day-to-day contact person. A number of other people at Cengage also need to be thanked including Mark Hopkinson and Jenny Ziegler.

Additionally, we would like to thank all of the case writers who contributed their cases to this text. Their names, along with their contact information, are printed following each case in the text. Finally, we thank C. J. Wisner for all her help in preparing the MindTap quizzes, PowerPoints, and test bank. As with any project of this size and time span, there are certain to be a number of people who gave their time and effort to this text, and yet their names remain unknown and so were inadvertently left out of these acknowledgments. We apologize for this and wish to thank you here.

About the Authors

Joel D. Wisner is professor of supply chain management in the Lee Business School at the University of Nevada, Las Vegas. He earned his BS in mechanical engineering from New Mexico State University in 1976 and his MBA from West Texas State University in 1986. During that time, Dr. Wisner worked as an engineer for Union Carbide at its Oak Ridge, Tennessee, facility and then worked in the oil industry in the Louisiana Gulf Coast and West Texas areas. In 1991, he earned his PhD in supply chain management from Arizona State University. He holds certifications in transportation and logistics (CTL) and in purchasing management (CPM).

He is currently keeping busy teaching courses and writing texts in supply chain management and operations management at UNLV. His research and case writing interests are in process assessment and improvement strategies along the supply chain. His articles have appeared in numerous journals including *Journal of Business Logistics, Journal of Operations Management, Journal of Supply Chain Management, Journal of Transportation, Production and Operations Management Journal*, and *Business Case Journal*.

Keah-Choon Tan is professor of operations management in the Lee Business School at the University of Nevada, Las Vegas. He received a BSc degree and an MBA from the University of South Alabama and a PhD in operations management from Michigan State University. Prior to academia, Dr. Tan was a hospital administrator and an account comptroller of a manufacturing firm. He holds certifications in purchasing management (CPM) and production and inventory management (CPIM). Dr. Tan has served as the department chair of the marketing department and associate dean for academic affairs at the Lee Business School in UNLV.

Dr. Tan has published articles in the area of supply chain management, quality, and operations scheduling in academic journals and magazines including *Decision Sciences, Decision Support Systems, International Journal of Production Research, International Journal of Operations & Production Management, International Journal of Logistics Management, Journal of Supply Chain Management*, and *Omega*, among others. He has served as editor, coguest editor, and on the editorial boards of academic journals. Dr. Tan has received several research grants and teaching awards, including the UNLV Foundation Distinguished Teaching Award.

G. Keong Leong is a professor in the information systems and operations management department, in the College of Business Administration and Public Policy at California State University, Dominguez Hills. He received an undergraduate degree in mechanical engineering from the University of Malaya and an MBA and PhD from the University of South Carolina. He was previously a member of the faculty at the University of Nevada, Las Vegas and the Ohio State University and a clinical faculty member at the Thunderbird School of Global Management.

His publications appear in academic journals such as *Journal of Operations Management, Decision Sciences, Interfaces, Journal of Management, European Journal of Operational Research*, and *International Journal of Production Research*, among others. He has coauthored three books including *Operations Strategy: Focusing Competitive Excellence* and *Cases in International Management: A Focus on Emerging Markets* and received research, teaching, and service awards including an Educator of the Year award from the Asian Chamber of Commerce in Las Vegas, Dennis E. Grawoig Distinguished Service award from Decision Sciences Institute, and OM Distinguished Scholar award from the Operations Management Division, Academy of Management. He has been active in the Decision Sciences Institute, serving as president, editor of *Decision Line*, at-large vice president, associate program chair, chair of the Innovative Education Committee, chair of the Doctoral Student Affairs Committee, and Manufacturing Management Track chair. In addition, he served as president of the Western Decision Sciences Institute and chair of the Operations Management Division, Academy of Management.

PART 1

Supply Chain Management: An Overview

Chapter 1   Introduction to Supply Chain Management

Chapter 1
INTRODUCTION TO SUPPLY CHAIN MANAGEMENT

Companies increasingly must extend their supply chain's talent base beyond technical skills to bring more leadership and professional skills into more levels. This has the potential to empower and inspire employees at all levels to support constant innovation in fast-moving industries, and to generate new forms of leadership that can help create more engaged and effective supply chains.

— Kelly Marchese, principal, Deloitte Consulting[1]

World-class supply chain management is fundamentally about the uninterrupted, seamless flow of products and information. Integration of these elements is the foundation for an agile supply chain, but achieving this cohesion can be a challenge for companies.

— John Menna, vice president of Global Strategy, Healthcare Logistics, UPS[2]

Learning Objectives

After completing this chapter, you should be able to

- Describe a supply chain and define supply chain management.
- Describe the objectives and elements of supply chain management.
- Describe basic supply chain management activities.
- Describe a brief history and current trends in supply chain management.
- Understand the bullwhip effect and how it impacts the supply chain.

Chapter Outline

Introduction

Supply Chain Management Defined

The Importance of Supply Chain Management

The Origins of Supply Chain Management in the United States

The Foundations of Supply Chain Management

Current Trends in Supply Chain Management

Summary

SCM Profile	A Look at the Top Five Supply Chains

Connecticut-based research company Gartner published its 12th annual ranking of the world's leading supply chains in 2016. One of the objectives of the annual ranking is to increase the realization of the importance of supply chain management for corporate executives. The ranking focuses on supply chain leadership, operational and innovation excellence, corporate social responsibility, and the desire to improve the management of supply chains. The top five companies and their supply chains are summarized below:

1. Apple—Its supply chain strategy is the delivery of winning customer solutions. Historically, this was accomplished using a mixed ownership of the physical supply chain. Today, it is investing billions of dollars in manufacturing tooling and equipment for the production of its latest line of products. Apple has become more vertically integrated using acquisitions of key component technologies. It has also insourced its iPad and iPhone components.

2. Proctor & Gamble—It is a pioneer in demand management, incorporating a range of inputs, including consumer social data. P&G also collaborates well with retailers. To capitalize on emerging markets, P&G moved its personal care and cosmetics headquarters to Singapore. Now it has an advanced innovation center there, manufacturing rapid, small-scale products for consumer testing and creating innovations in packaging.

3. Unilever—It has ambitiously sought sustainable growth, with a goal of doubling its revenue using half its environmental footprint by 2020. Unilever's supply chain program is designed to determine the right level of services and marketing support each channel requires to enable profitable growth. Its cost-to-serve program is also driving improvements in its distribution network.

4. McDonald's—Two of its current strategies are further coordination along its supply chains and higher speed to market. Its "McDonald's System" clearly communicates operating principles for owner-operators, suppliers, and the corporate headquarters. McDonald's has created a culture emphasizing long-term strategic partnerships with key suppliers. McDonald's has created high-performing supply chains across its large global network.

5. Amazon—It continues a push to create innovative products and services. Using the latest technologies, Amazon manages its supply chains in a precise and efficient manner. Today, Amazon is experimenting with the management of the final mile of delivery in some markets, using small aerial drones to deliver shoebox-size packages from Amazon's fulfillment centers.[3]

INTRODUCTION

Global marketplaces and the number of competitors are growing, along with the prices of labor, material, real estate, and fuel. Successful organizations today must be heavily involved with their best suppliers and customers. Creating goods and services that customers want, at a price they are willing to pay, requires firms to be good at a number of things. Managers must pay closer attention to where materials come from; how suppliers' products are designed, produced, and transported; how their own products and services are produced and distributed to customers; and finally, what their direct customers and the end-product consumers really think of the firms' goods and services.

Thirty years ago, many large firms were vertically integrated, meaning they owned some of their suppliers and/or customers. Today, this practice is much less common due to the high cost and difficulty in managing such diverse business units. Instead, firms are focusing more of their resources on core capabilities, while trying to create alliances with suppliers, transportation and warehousing companies, and distributors. Thus, a collaborative approach to buying, making, and distributing goods and services has become the best way for firms to stay successful—and it is central to the practice of supply chain management (SCM).

Several factors are enabling firms to work together more effectively than ever before. Communication and information exchange using enterprise resource planning (ERP) system applications (discussed further in Chapter 6) have made global collaboration not only possible but also necessary for firms to compete. Communication technologies continue to change rapidly, making partnerships and teamwork much easier than ever before. Competition is also expanding rapidly in all industries and in all markets around the world, bringing new materials, products, people, and resources together, making it more difficult for many of the local, individually owned shops to keep customers. Additionally, the recent global recession made customers more cost-conscious while seeking higher levels of quality and service, which is requiring organizations to find even better ways to compete. Customers are also demanding more socially responsible and environment-friendly goods and services from organizations. Considering all of these changes to the environment, it is indeed an exciting time for companies to develop new products, find new suppliers and customers, and compete more successfully. Consequently, many job opportunities are opening up in the areas of purchasing, operations, logistics, and supply chain management.

As you read this textbook, you will be introduced to the many concepts of supply chain management and how to use these concepts to become better managers in today's global economy. Examples are used throughout the text to illustrate the topics discussed, and cases at the end of each chapter are provided to enable you to test your problem-solving and decision-making skills in supply chain management. It is hoped that by the end of the text you will have gained an appreciation of the value of supply chain management and will be able to apply what you have learned, both in your profession and in future courses in supply chain management.

In this chapter, the term *supply chain management* is defined, including a discussion of its importance, history, and developments to date. The chapter ends with a look at a few of the current trends in supply chain management.

SUPPLY CHAIN MANAGEMENT DEFINED

To understand supply chain management, one must first begin with a discussion of a **supply chain**; a generic one is shown in Figure 1.1. The supply chain shown in the figure starts with firms extracting raw materials from the earth—such as iron ore, oil, wood, and food items—and then selling these to raw material suppliers such as lumber companies, steel mills, and raw food distributors. These firms, acting on purchase orders and specifications they have received from component manufacturers, turn the raw materials into materials that are usable by their customers (materials such as sheet steel, aluminum, copper, lumber, and inspected foodstuffs). The component manufacturers, responding to orders and specifications from their customers (the final product manufacturers), make and sell intermediate components (electrical wire, fabrics, plumbing items, nuts and bolts, molded plastic components, component parts and assemblies, and processed foods). The

Figure 1.1	A Generic Supply Chain

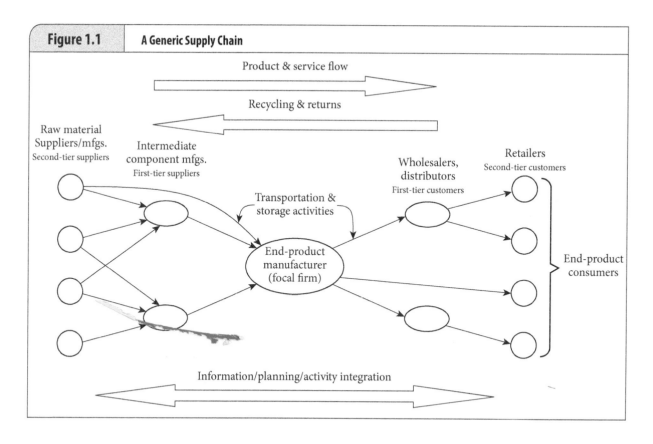

final product manufacturers (companies such as Boeing, General Motors, and Kraft) assemble the finished products and sell them to wholesalers or distributors, who then resell these products to retailers as their product orders are received. Retailers, in turn, sell these products to us, the end-product consumers.

Consumers purchase products based on a combination of cost, quality, availability, maintainability, and reputation factors, and then hope the purchased items satisfy their requirements and expectations. Companies, along with their supply chains, that can provide all of these desired things will ultimately be successful. Along the supply chain, intermediate and end customers may need to return products or obtain warranty repairs, or they may just throw products away or recycle them. These reverse logistics activities are also included in the supply chain and are discussed further in Chapter 9.

Referring again to Figure 1.1, the firm in the middle of the figure is referred to as the *focal firm* simply because it is the central firm being discussed; the direct suppliers and customers of the focal firm are first-tier suppliers and first-tier customers. The first-tier suppliers' suppliers are thus the focal firm's second-tier suppliers, and the first-tier customers' customers are the focal firm's second-tier customers. Not all supply chains look exactly like the one shown in Figure 1.1. Some raw material and end-product manufacturers, for example, may sell directly to end consumers. Some supply chains, such as an automobile supply chain, might have many tiers, while others such as a law office's supply chain might have very few tiers of suppliers and customers.

Thus, the series of companies eventually making products and services available to consumers, including all of the functions enabling the production, delivery, and recycling of materials, components, end products, and services, is called a supply chain. Companies with multiple products likely have multiple supply chains. All goods and services reach their customers via some type of supply chain—some much larger, longer, and more complex than others. Some may also involve foreign suppliers or markets.

With this idea of a supply chain in mind, there really is only one true source of income for all supply chain organizations—a supply chain's end customers. According to Manu Vora, the founder and president of Business Excellence Inc., a global management consulting services firm, high-performing supply chains are not only essential to delivering goods on time, but global companies also depend on their supply chain processes to manage the divergent expectations of customers, to stay one step ahead of the competition.[4] When companies make business decisions while ignoring the interests of end customers and other chain members, these decisions create additional risks, costs, and waiting time along the supply chain, ultimately leading to higher end-product prices, lower supply chain service levels, and eventually lower end-customer demand.

A number of other companies are also indirectly involved in most supply chains, and they play a very important role in the delivery of goods to customers. These are the many service providers, such as trucking and airfreight shipping companies, information system providers, public warehousing firms, freight forwarders, agents, and supply chain consultants. These service providers are extremely useful to the firms in most supply chains because they can help to get goods where they need to be in a timely fashion, allow buyers and sellers to communicate effectively, allow firms to serve outlying markets, enable firms to save money on domestic and global shipments, and in general allow firms to adequately serve their customers at the lowest possible cost.

Now that a general description of a supply chain has been provided, what is **supply chain management**? A number of definitions are available in the literature and among various professional associations. A few of these are provided here from various organizations connected to the practice of supply chain management:

- The Council of Supply Chain Management Professionals (CSCMP) defines supply chain management as:

  The planning and management of all activities involved in sourcing and procurement, conversion, and all logistics management activities. Importantly, it also includes coordination and collaboration with channel partners, which can be suppliers, intermediaries, third-party service providers, and customers.[5]

- The Institute for Supply Management (ISM) describes supply chain management as:

  The design and management of seamless, value-added processes across organizational boundaries to meet the real needs of the end customer.[6]

- The Association for Operations Management (APICS) defines supply chain management as:

  The design, planning, execution, control, and monitoring of supply chain activities with the objective of creating net value, building a competitive infrastructure, leveraging worldwide logistics, synchronizing supply with demand, and measuring performance globally.[7]

Consistent across these definitions is the idea of coordinating or integrating a number of goods- and services-related activities among supply chain participants to improve operating efficiencies, quality, and customer service. Thus, for supply chain management to be successful, firms must work together by sharing information on things like demand forecasts, production plans, capacity changes, new marketing strategies, new product and service developments, new technologies employed, purchasing plans, delivery dates, and anything else impacting the supply chain members' purchasing, production, and distribution plans. In a recent supply chain innovation survey conducted by MHI, a material handling association, and Deloitte, the top two strategic priorities for supply chain executives are supply chain analytics (tools that harness data from internal and external sources to produce breakthrough insights that can help supply chains reduce costs and risk) and multichannel fulfillment (allowing consumers to shop for what they want, where they want, and when they want, and then their purchases delivered quickly and consistently).[8]

In theory, companies in a supply chain work as a cohesive, singularly competitive unit, accomplishing what many large, vertically integrated firms tried and failed to accomplish in years past. The difference is that independent firms in a supply chain are relatively free to enter and leave supply chain relationships if these relationships are no longer proving to be beneficial; it is this free market alliance-building that allows supply chains to operate more effectively than vertically integrated conglomerates.

For example, when a particular item is in short supply accompanied by rising prices, a firm might find it beneficial to align itself with one of these suppliers to ensure a continued supply of the scarce item. This alignment may become beneficial to both parties—new markets for the supplier leading to new, future product opportunities, and long-term continuity of supply and stable prices for the buyer. Later, when new competitors start producing the scarce product or when demand declines, the supplier may no longer be valued by the buying firm; instead, the firm may see more value in negotiating with other potential suppliers for its purchase requirements and may then decide to dissolve the original buyer–supplier alignment. Unforeseen weather events and accidents can also create supply chain management problems.

For example, Indiana-based Zimmer Biomet, which makes artificial joints and dental devices, blamed its recently declining stock price on supply chain disruption problems. "Our current supply chain not being fully integrated did hamper our ability to respond effectively to this shifting product mix," said Daniel Florin, Zimmer Biomet's chief financial officer.[9] In China, in 2015, two blasts tore through a chemical warehouse containing 3,000 tons of hazardous chemicals, including sodium cyanide and explosive ammonium nitrate. Along with destroying buildings and infrastructure within a 1.2-mile radius and the loss of life, the blasts incinerated more than 10,000 new cars. Jaguar Land Rover, Volkswagen, Fiat Chrysler, Hyundai, and Renault, all reported significant vehicle losses, which hampered their supply chain effectiveness.[10] As can be seen from these examples, supply chains are often very dynamic, which can create problems in effectively managing them.

While supply chain management may allow organizations to realize the advantages of vertical integration, certain conditions must be present for successful supply chain management to occur. One important prerequisite is a melding of the corporate cultures of the supply chain participants so all parties are receptive to the requirements of successful supply chain management, such as sharing process information. More traditional organizational cultures that emphasize short-term, company-focused performance can conflict with the objectives of supply chain management. Supply chain management focuses on positioning organizations in such a way that all participants benefit. Successful supply chain management requires high levels of trust, cooperation, collaboration, and honest, accurate communications.

Boundaries of supply chains are also dynamic. It has often been said that supply chain boundaries for the focal firm extend from "the suppliers' suppliers to the customers'

customers." Today, most supply chain collaboration efforts do not extend beyond these boundaries. In fact, in many cases, firms find it very difficult to extend coordination efforts beyond a few of their most important direct suppliers and customers (in one survey, a number of firm representatives stated that most of their supply chain efforts were with the firm's *internal* suppliers and customers only!).[11] However, with time and successful initial results, many firms are extending the boundaries of their supply chains to include their **second-tier suppliers**, **second-tier customers**, and logistics services (transportation and warehousing) providers. Some of the firms considered to be the best at managing their supply chains have very recognizable names. Each year, for example, the business advisory company Gartner, Inc., announces the twenty-five companies that exhibit the best supply chain management business performance and leadership. The chapter-opening SCM Profile summarizes the five best from this list.

THE IMPORTANCE OF SUPPLY CHAIN MANAGEMENT

While all firms are part of a chain of organizations bringing products and services to customers (and most firms operate within a number of supply chains), certainly not all supply chains are managed in a coordinated fashion. Firms continue to operate independently in many industries (particularly small firms). It is often easy for managers to be focused solely on their immediate customers, their daily internal operations, their sales, and their costs. After all, with customers complaining, employees to train, late supplier deliveries, creditors to pay, and equipment to repair, who has time for relationship building and other supply chain coordination efforts? Particularly during times like the prolonged economic downturn starting in 2009, firms were struggling to just keep their doors open, and supply chain management efforts may have waned.

Many firms today, though, have worked through their economic problems and are encountering some value-enhancing benefits from their supply chain management efforts. Firms with large system inventories, many suppliers, complex product assemblies, and highly valued customers with large purchasing budgets have the most to gain from the practice of supply chain management. For these firms, even moderate supply chain management success can mean lower purchasing and inventory carrying costs, better product quality, and higher levels of customer service—all leading to more sales and better profits.

According to the U.S. Census Bureau's Annual Survey of Manufactures, the total cost of all materials purchased in 2014 exceeded $3.4 trillion among U.S. manufacturers, up $25 billion from 2013 and about $80 billion from 2012. The total 2014 end-of-year inventory value for all U.S. manufacturers was over $623 billion, up from $607 billion in 2012.[12] Thus, it can be seen that purchasing and inventory costs can be quite sizable for firms and represent areas where significant cost savings can be realized when using effective supply chain management strategies. In fact, in a 2013 survey of over 450 supply chain executives, conducted by MHI (the nation's largest material handling, logistics, and supply chain association) and consulting firm Deloitte, over 70 percent of the respondents said that controlling costs was a top priority, making it the number one focus area for supply chain executives. Additionally, most respondents expected to increase their supply chain investments over the next three years.[13]

Supply chain management efforts can start small—for instance, integrating processes with just one key supplier—and gather momentum over time to include more supply chain participants such as other important suppliers, key customers, and logistics or third-party services. Obviously, other behind-the-scenes activities must also be included such as getting stakeholder buy-in and use of an in-house or cloud IT solution. Finally, supply chain management efforts can include second-tier suppliers and customers. So why are these integration activities so important? As alluded to earlier, when a firm, its customers, and its suppliers all know each other's future plans and are willing to work together, the planning process is easier and much more productive in terms of cost savings, quality improvements, and service enhancements.

On the other hand, lack of effective supply chain management can cause problems for organizations. Using a fictitious setting, Example 1.1 illustrates some of the costs associated with independent planning and lack of supply chain information sharing and coordination.

Example 1.1   Grebson Manufacturing's Supply Chain

The Pearson Bearings Co. makes roller bearings for Grebson Manufacturing on an as-needed basis. For the upcoming quarter, it has forecasted Grebson's roller bearing demand to be 25,000 units. Since Grebson's demand for bearings from Pearson has been somewhat erratic in the past due to the number of bearing companies competing with Pearson and also the fluctuation of demand from Grebson's customers, Pearson's roller bearing forecast includes 5,000 units of safety stock. The steel used in Pearson Bearings' manufacturing process is usually purchased from CJ Steels, Inc. CJ Steels has, in turn, forecasted Pearson's quarterly demand for the high-carbon steel it typically purchases for roller bearings. Its forecast also includes safety stock of about 20 percent over what CJ Steels actually expects Pearson to buy over the next three months.

Since Pearson Bearings does not know with full confidence what Grebson's roller bearing demand will be for the upcoming quarter (it could be zero or it could exceed 25,000 units), Pearson will incur the extra costs of producing and holding 5,000 units of safety stock. Additionally, Pearson Bearings risks having to either scrap, sell, or hold onto any units not sold to Grebson, as well as losing current and future sales to Grebson if its demand exceeds 25,000 units over the next quarter. CJ Steels faces the same dilemma—extra materials, labor costs, and warehouse space for safety stock along with the potential stockout costs of lost present and future sales. Additionally, Grebson's historic demand pattern for roller bearings from its suppliers already includes some safety stock, since it uses roller bearings in other products it makes for a primary customer.

Grebson's safety stock, which it has built into its roller bearing purchase orders, has resulted in still additional safety stock production levels at the Pearson plant. In fact, some of the erratic purchasing patterns of Grebson are probably due to its leftover safety stocks causing lower purchase quantities during subsequent production cycles. This, in turn, creates greater demand variability, leading to a decision at Pearson to produce even higher levels of safety stock. This same scenario plays out between Pearson and CJ Steels, with erratic buying patterns by Pearson and further safety stock production by CJ. This magnification of safety stock, based on erratic demand patterns and forecasts derived from demand already containing safety stock and from lack of sharing information, continues to grow as orders pass to more distant suppliers up the supply chain.

The continuing cycle of erratic demand causing forecasts to include safety stock which in turn magnify supplier forecasts and cause production planning problems is known as the **bullwhip effect.** If Grebson Manufacturing *knew* its customers' purchase plans for the coming quarter along with how their purchase plans were derived, it would be much more confident about what the upcoming demand was going to be, resulting in little, if any, safety stock requirement, and consequently it would be able to communicate its own purchase plans for roller bearings to Pearson. If Grebson purchased its roller bearings from only Pearson and, further, told Pearson what its quarterly purchase plans were, and if Pearson did likewise with CJ Steels, safety stocks throughout the supply chain would be reduced considerably, driving down the costs of purchasing, producing, and carrying roller bearings at each stage. Trade estimates suggest that the bullwhip effect results in excess costs on the order of 12 to 25 percent for each firm in a supply chain, which can be a tremendous competitive disadvantage. This discussion also sets the stage for a supply chain management concept called collaborative planning, forecasting, and replenishment, discussed further in Chapter 5.

As working relationships throughout the supply chain mature, key trading partners will feel more comfortable investing capital in better facilities, better products, and better services for their customers. With time, customers will share more information with suppliers, and suppliers will be more likely to participate in their key customers' new product design efforts, for instance. These, then, become some of the more important benefits of a well-integrated supply chain. In the following chapters of the text, other associated benefits will also become apparent.

THE ORIGINS OF SUPPLY CHAIN MANAGEMENT IN THE UNITED STATES

During the 1950s and 1960s, U.S. manufacturers were employing mass production techniques to reduce costs and improve productivity, while little attention was typically paid to creating supplier partnerships, improving process design and flexibility, or improving product quality (see Figure 1.2). New product design and development was slow and relied exclusively on in-house resources, technologies, and capacity. Sharing technology and expertise through strategic buyer–supplier partnerships was essentially unheard of back then. Processes on the factory floor were cushioned with work-in-process inventories to keep machines running and maintain balanced material flows, products moving through the facility even when equipment broke down, resulting in large inventory carrying cost investments.

In the 1960s and 1970s, computer technologies began to flourish and material requirements planning (MRP) and manufacturing resource planning (MRPII) software applications were developed. These systems allowed companies to see the importance of effective materials management—they could now recognize and quantify the impact of high levels

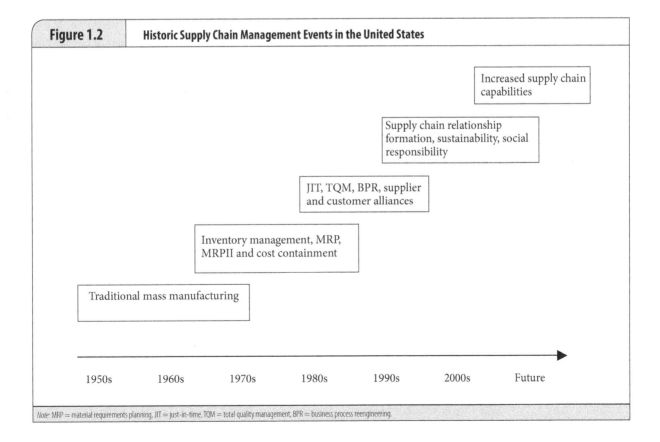

| Figure 1.2 | Historic Supply Chain Management Events in the United States |

Increased supply chain capabilities

Supply chain relationship formation, sustainability, social responsibility

JIT, TQM, BPR, supplier and customer alliances

Inventory management, MRP, MRPII and cost containment

Traditional mass manufacturing

1950s   1960s   1970s   1980s   1990s   2000s   Future

Note: MRP = material requirements planning, JIT = just-in-time, TQM = total quality management, BPR = business process reengineering.

of inventories on manufacturing, storage, and transportation costs. As computer capabilities grew, the sophistication of inventory-tracking software also grew, making it possible to further reduce inventory costs while improving internal communication of the need for purchased parts and supplies.

The 1980s were the breakout years for supply chain management. One of the first widely recorded uses of the term *supply chain management* came about in a paper published in 1982.[14] Intense global competition beginning in the 1980s (and continuing today) provided an incentive for U.S. manufacturers to make low-cost, high-quality products along with high levels of customer service. Manufacturers utilized just-in-time (JIT) and total quality management (TQM) strategies to improve quality, manufacturing efficiencies, and delivery times. In a JIT manufacturing environment with little inventory to cushion scheduling and/or production problems, firms began to realize the potential benefits and importance of strategic and cooperative supplier–buyer–customer relationships, which are the foundations of SCM. The concept of these partnerships or alliances emerged as manufacturers experimented with JIT and TQM.

As competition in the United States intensified further in the 1990s accompanied by increasing logistics costs and the trend toward market globalization, the challenges associated with improving quality, cost, customer service, and product design also increased. To deal with these challenges, manufacturers began purchasing from a select number of certified, high-quality suppliers with excellent service reputations and involved these suppliers in their new product design activities as well as in cost, quality, and service improvement initiatives. In other words, companies realized that if they started giving only their best suppliers most of their business, then they, in return, could expect these suppliers to provide continued benefits in the form of on-time deliveries; high-quality, low-cost products; and help with new product design efforts.

Interestingly, the general idea of supply chain management had been discussed for many years prior to the chain of events shown in Figure 1.2. In 1915, Arch W. Shaw of the Harvard Business School wrote the textbook *Some Problems in Market Distribution*, considered by many to be the first on the topic of what we now refer to as supply chain management (Shaw never used this term). The text included discussions of how best to purchase raw materials, transport products, locate facilities, and analyze productivity and waste. He recommended a "laboratory point of view" or what could now be termed a systematic study of supply chain issues.[15]

Business process reengineering (BPR), or just **reengineering**, described as the radical rethinking and redesigning of business processes to reduce waste and increase performance, was introduced in the early 1990s and was the result of a growing interest during this time in the need for cost reductions and a return to an emphasis on the key competencies of the firm to enhance long-term competitive advantage. Michael Hammer and James Champy's very popular book, *Reengineering the Corporation: A Manifesto for Business Revolution*, combined with the many statements from notable business experts like Peter Drucker along the lines of "Reengineering is vital to success and it has to be done," created a fervor at the time among managers seeking some sort of magic pill or easy method for making their businesses successful.[16] As this fad died down in the late 1990s (the term became synonymous with downsizing and thus fell out of favor), the practice of supply chain management rapidly increased in popularity as a source of competitive advantage.

Also during this time, managers, consultants, and academics began developing an understanding of the differences between logistics and supply chain management. Up until then, supply chain management was simply viewed as logistics outside the firm.

As companies began implementing supply chain management initiatives, they began to understand the need to integrate key business processes among the supply chain participants, enabling the supply chain to act and react as one entity. Today, logistics is viewed as one important element of the much broader supply chain management concept.

At the same time, companies also saw benefits in the creation of alliances or partnerships with their customers. Developing these long-term, close relationships with customers (referred to as **customer relationship management** or CRM) meant the need for less finished product safety stock (as discussed earlier in the bullwhip effect example) and allowed firms to focus their resources on providing better products and services to their best customers. In time, when market share improved for its customers' products, the result was more business for the firm.

Thus, supply chain management has evolved along two parallel paths: (1) the purchasing and supply management emphasis from industrial buyers at the focal firm and (2) the logistics and customer service emphasis from logistics personnel at the focal firm. The increasing popularity of alliances with suppliers and customers (and eventually suppliers' suppliers and customers' customers) has also meant a greater reliance on the inbound and outbound shipping, warehousing, and logistics services that provide transportation, storage, documentation, and customs clearing services to trading partners within a typical supply chain. Relationship building has also occurred increasingly with many of these **third-party logistics providers** (3PLs) to ensure a continuous, uninterrupted supply of goods. The need to periodically assess the performance of these relationships has also accompanied the growth of supply chain management. One of the challenges faced today by many firms involved in supply chain management is how to adequately assess overall end-to-end performance in often extremely complex, global supply chains. This idea of evaluating supply chain performance from numerous perspectives including financial, sustainability, speed, and risk is explored in Chapter 14.

For the wholesaling and retailing industries, the supply chain management focus is on location, logistics, and customer service issues more often compared to manufacturing. Supply chain management in these industries has often been referred to as quick response, service response logistics, or integrated logistics. The advancement of electronic data interchange (EDI) systems, bar coding, Internet systems, logistics software applications, and radio frequency identification (RFID) technologies over the past two decades has greatly aided the evolution of the integrated supply chain concept. Retailers utilize supply chain management to help quickly meet changing demands in the marketplace and to reduce inventories throughout their supply chains.

Most recently, the rapid development of client/server supply chain management software that typically includes integrated supply chain management and e-commerce components has aided in the evolution and adoption of supply chain management. These software applications are commonly referred to as **enterprise resource planning** (ERP) systems, and for years, the top two providers worldwide have been SAP and Oracle. Total worldwide ERP product sales in 2015 were over $80 billion, and sales growth has consistently averaged about 10 percent per year for the past ten years.[17] Sharing information with supply chain partners through the Internet has enabled firms to integrate stocking, logistics, materials acquisition, shipping, and other functions to create a more proactive and effective style of business management and customer responsiveness.

Today, an emphasis is being placed on the environmental and social impacts of supply chains. Customers are demanding that companies and their supply chains act in an ethically and socially responsible manner. This includes an attention on how suppliers hire and train employees, how they grow and harvest plants, how they manufacture parts, how their activities impact the environment, and what sorts of sustainability policies are being utilized. The term **sustainability** as applied to supply chains is a broad term that includes protecting the environment and some aspects of social responsibility, as well as financial performance (hence the linking of sustainability to what is termed the **triple bottom line**, or people, planet, and profits). Sustainability can be defined as the ability to meet the needs of current supply chain members without hindering the ability to meet the needs of future generations in terms of economic, environmental, and social challenges. Simply put, sustainability is doing the right things in ways that make economic sense. These topics are discussed further in Chapter 4. With these practices in mind, supply chain managers today must also cope with maintaining the most flexible supply chain possible to take advantage of new markets, new sources of supply, and new customer demands.

THE FOUNDATIONS OF SUPPLY CHAIN MANAGEMENT

The foundation elements of supply chain management are introduced in this section. These elements essentially make up the table of contents for this textbook and are shown in Table 1.1 along with the chapters where they are discussed.

Supply Elements

Traditional purchasing strategies typically emphasized the use of many suppliers, managed using hard bargaining, competitive bidding, and short-term contracts. This often created adversarial buyer–supplier relationships with a focus primarily on the product's purchase price instead of the capabilities of the suppliers and how they could contribute to the long-term competitiveness of the buying organization. In many cases, purchasing was performed by a clerk. Over the past twenty-five years, there has been a shift toward a more strategic approach to purchasing, and this broader approach is more commonly referred to as **supply management**. Supply management professionals now most often perform the purchasing function. Effective supply management has resulted generally in smaller supply bases and the development of more long-term, trusting, mutually beneficial supplier relationships (termed **supplier relationship management** or SRM) to achieve the competitive benefits described earlier.

Purchasing and the strategic concepts of supply management are one of the foundations of supply chain management, since incoming material quality, delivery timing, purchase price, product safety, and the impact of purchasing on the environment are all affected

Table 1.1	**The Foundations of Supply Chain Management**	
FOUNDATION ELEMENTS	**IMPORTANT ISSUES**	**CHAPTERS**
Supply	Supply base reduction, supplier alliances, SRM, global sourcing, ethical and sustainable sourcing	2, 3, 4
Operations	Demand management, CPFR, inventory management, MRP, ERP, lean systems, Six Sigma quality	5, 6, 7, 8
Logistics	Logistics management, CRM, network design, RFID, global supply chains, sustainability, service response logistics	9, 10, 11, 12
Integration	Barriers to integration, risk and security management, performance measurement, green supply chains	13, 14

by the buyer–supplier relationship and the capabilities of suppliers. "The issues today are more challenging and global," observes Mohan Ponnudurai, industry solution director at software provider Sparta Systems. "The challenge is to manage suppliers, ensuring the right type of suppliers from a brand risk perspective while meeting your mission regarding safety, regulatory compliance, costs and a global presence."[18] Chapters 2 through 4 cover the topics associated with supply management.

The economic downturn beginning in 2009 added another problem to the supply side of businesses, namely, how the focal firm could continue producing successfully, when several key suppliers went out of business. "One of the lessons learned was that we often do a very good job of looking at the creditworthiness of our customers and their ability to pay us, but we don't do as good a job looking at the financial wherewithal of our suppliers," says Tom Murphy, executive vice president of manufacturing and wholesale distribution at Georgia-based RSM McGladrey, a professional services firm.[19] Thus, supply chain managers today must build better visibility and security into their supply chains using software applications and frequent communications to spot these problems before they become unmanageable.

One of the more crucial issues within the topic of supply management is **supplier management**. Simply put, this means encouraging or helping the firm's suppliers to perform in some desired fashion, and there are a number of ways to do this. This involves assessing the suppliers' current capabilities and then deciding if and how they need to improve. Thus, one of the key activities in supplier management is **supplier evaluation,** or determining the current capabilities of suppliers. This occurs both when potential suppliers are being evaluated for a future purchase and when existing suppliers are periodically evaluated for ongoing performance purposes. A closely related activity is **supplier certification**. Supplier certification allows buyers to assume the supplier will meet certain product quality and service requirements covered by the certification, thus reducing duplicate testing and inspections and the need for extensive supplier evaluations. Farm implement manufacturer Deere & Company, for example, has its Achieving Excellence program wherein suppliers are evaluated annually across several performance categories. The idea is to reward high performers and provide feedback to promote continuous improvement. Norway-based Wallenius Wilhelmsen Logistics (WWL) earned recognition as a partner-level supplier for 2015 in Deere's Achieving Excellence Program. The partner-level status is Deere's highest supplier rating. WWL was selected for the honor due to providing high-quality products and services and its commitment to continuous improvement. WWL is a supplier of ocean transportation and logistics services to John Deere's operations globally.[20]

Over time, supplier management efforts allow firms to selectively screen out poor-performing suppliers and build successful, long-term, trusting relationships with fewer, but top-performing suppliers. These suppliers can provide tremendous benefits to the buying firm and the entire supply chain. As discussed in greater detail in Chapter 2, greater purchase volumes, using fewer suppliers, typically means lower per-unit purchase costs (causing a much greater impact on profits than a corresponding increase in sales) and in many cases higher quality and better delivery service. These characteristics are viewed as strategically important to the firm because of their impact on the firm's competitiveness. "To succeed in today's manufacturing ecosystem, we work with and rely on our suppliers to produce every part at affordable costs, on-time and in compliance with all of our quality, performance and compliance specifications," says Dave Emmerling, VP of Strategic Sourcing at jet engine maker Pratt & Whitney. "Our supply chain team, manufacturing experts and engineers are working closely with our suppliers to ensure they have the manufacturing technology and tools in place to increase engine production."[21]

Suppliers also see significant benefits from the creation of closer working relationships with customers in terms of long-term, higher-volume sales. These trading partner relationships have come to be termed **strategic partnerships** and are emphasized throughout this text as one of the more important aspects of supply chain management. In the trade publication *Industrial Distribution* the results of their 2015 survey of operations show that companies look to continue market share gains with strategic supplier partnerships. In the survey, product quality was considered the most important when evaluating strategic suppliers, followed by on-time delivery, service/support, and finally, price.[23] Chapter 3 explores strategic partnerships and other topics associated with supplier relationship management.

Recently, the supply management discipline has come to include a closer emphasis on **ethical and sustainable sourcing,** or purchasing from suppliers that are governed by environmental sustainability and social and ethical practices. Companies are realizing that suppliers can have a significant impact on a firm's reputation and carbon footprint, as well as their costs and profits. Supply chain managers must therefore learn how to develop socially responsible and environment-friendly sourcing strategies that also create a competitive advantage for the company. The nearby SCM Profile describes an initiative in the railroad industry trying to do just that. These topics along with other supplier management topics are discussed in detail in Chapter 4.

Operations Elements

Once materials, components, and other purchased items are delivered to the buying organization, a number of internal operations elements become important in assembling or processing the items into finished products, ensuring that the right amount of product is produced and that finished goods and services meet specific quality, cost, and customer

SCM Profile | **The Railsponsible Supplier Initiative**

Six railroad companies in Germany, the Netherlands, and France founded the Railsponsible initiative in 2015, with the goal of supporting sustainable sourcing practices throughout the railway industry's supply chains. Sustainable purchasing has become a priority for the industry, since it benefits the organization, the economy, and the environment. Additionally, supply chain practices must comply with industry regulations; to do this, it became necessary to establish formal industry standards that take into account social and environmental concerns.

The Railsponsible initiative brings together rail companies to formalize and implement responsible supply chain practices throughout the rail industry. Railsponsible has started a forum for exchange and discussion on the most ecologically and socially responsible procurement practices for the industry. The initiative is open to all rail companies that want to promote responsible supply chains. "This collaborative work will benefit the whole rail sector supply chain and contribute to increased productivity, a reduction in costs while promoting the development of more sustainable products and solutions," says Oliver Baril, chair of Railsponsible.

Railsponsible members gather regularly throughout the year, when they share their best practices and processes and work to extend the reach of corporate responsibility and sustainability. Since the launch of the initiative, more than 460 suppliers have been assessed for corporate social responsibility.[22]

service requirements. Along with supply management, operations management is also considered a foundation of supply chain management and is covered in Chapters 5 through 8.

During a calendar year, seasonal demand variations commonly occur. Firms can predict when these variations will occur based on historic demand patterns, through use of forecasting techniques that guide weekly or monthly production plans. If demand does not occur as forecasted, then the focal firm is left with either too much or too little inventory (or service capacity). Both situations are cost burdens to the firm (inventory-carrying costs and stock-out costs). As a matter of fact, in a recent survey, 63 percent of Americans admitted they would be somewhat to highly likely to look for an alternative brand if a product shortage affected their favorite electronics brand. Only 14 percent said they would stay loyal to their favorite brand in the event of a shortage.[24] To minimize lost sales and other costs, firms often rely on **demand management** strategies and systems, with the objective of matching available capacity to demand, either by improving production scheduling, curtailing demand, using a back-order system, or increasing capacity.

Managing inventories is one of the most important aspects of operations and is certainly value enhancing for the firm. Firms typically have some sort of **material requirements planning** (MRP) software system for managing their inventories, purchases, and production schedules. These systems can be linked throughout the organization and its supply chain partners using **enterprise resource planning** (ERP) systems, providing real-time purchase and sales data, inventory, and production information to all business units and to key supply chain participants. These system configurations vary considerably, based on the number and complexity of products, size of the firm, and design of the supply chain. Retailers like Walmart, for example, scan the bar codes of items when consumers make purchases, causing the local store's MRP system to deduct units from inventory until a preset reorder point is reached. When this occurs, the local computer system automatically contacts Walmart's regional distribution center's MRP system and generates an order. At the distribution center, the order is filled and sent along with other orders to the particular Walmart. Eventually, the inventory at the distribution center needs replenishing, and at that time, the distribution center's MRP system automatically generates an order with the manufacturer, who then delivers the product to the Walmart distribution center. This type of order communication and **inventory visibility** may extend farther up the supply chain, reducing the likelihood of stockouts, excess inventories, and long lead times. In 2015, about half of U.S. retail brands had real-time in-store inventory visibility (up from 36 percent in 2014), aided in part by the use of MRP and **radio frequency identification** (RFID) systems, which can scan incoming cartons and pallets for RFID tags, which describe the contents of the packages to the MRP.[25]

Another common form of inventory management is through use of a **lean production system** (lean production may also be referred to as just-in-time or the Toyota production system). Lean within a production system refers to operating with low inventory levels. Implementing a lean system takes time but usually results in faster delivery times, lower system inventory levels, fewer stockouts, and better quality. An important aspect of a lean production system is the quality of the incoming purchased items and the quality of the assemblies as they move through the various production processes. Higher quality means less need for safety stock.

Firms employing lean production concepts usually have a **Six Sigma quality management** strategy in place to ensure continued quality compliance among suppliers and with internal production facilities. Six Sigma was originally created at Motorola in the 1980s, and Motorola proved the program's value when it won the Baldrige Quality Award in 1988. Many organizations have reported large savings with use of Six Sigma including $1.7 billion at Ford, $17 billion at Motorola, $1.2 billion at 3M, and $8 billion at General Electric.[26] Lean and Six Sigma are discussed in detail in Chapter 8.

Logistics Elements

When goods are produced, they can be delivered to customers through a number of different modes of transportation. Delivering products to customers at the right time, quality, and volume requires a high level of planning and cooperation between the firm, its customers, and the various logistics elements or services employed (such as transportation, warehousing, and break-bulk or repackaging services). In contrast, services are produced and delivered to the customer simultaneously in most cases, so services are extremely dependent upon server capacity and successful service delivery to meet customer requirements. Logistics is the third foundation of supply chain management, and these topics are presented in Chapters 9 through 12.

Logistics decisions typically involve trade-offs between cost and delivery timing or customer service. Considering the five modes of transportation, motor carriers (trucks) are more expensive to use than rail carriers but offer more flexibility and speed, particularly for short routes. Air carriers are even more expensive but much faster than any other transportation mode. Water carriers are the slowest but are also the least expensive. Finally, pipelines are used to transport oil, water, natural gas, and coal slurry. Many transportation services offer various modal combinations, as well as warehousing and customs-clearing services.

In a typical integrated supply chain environment where JIT deliveries are the norm, **third-party logistics services** or 3PLs are critical to the overall success of supply chains. In many cases, these services are considered supply chain partners and are viewed as key value enhancers for supply chains. From earthquakes, to tornadoes, floods, and other risk-prone environments, companies are teaming up with 3PLs to improve visibility, flexibility, and delivery performance while reducing risk in their supply chains. "Globally, manufacturers and retailers are taking a renewed interest in redesigning and reengineering their supply chains in the wake of these events," says Jim McAdam, president of 3PL provider, APL Logistics.[27]

The desired goal of logistics is an appropriate level of customer service at a reasonable price. In order to provide the desired level of customer service, firms must identify customer requirements and then provide the right combination of transportation, warehousing, packaging, and information services to successfully satisfy those requirements. Through frequent contact with customers, firms develop customer relationship management strategies for meeting delivery due dates, resolving customer complaints, communicating with customers, and determining other logistics services required. From a supply chain management perspective, these customer activities take on added importance because second-tier, third-tier, and end-product consumers are ultimately dependent on the logistics performance at each stage within a supply chain. A recent survey finds the use of data analysis gaining popularity in logistics decisions. Among 3PLs, 71 percent said the greatest value data analysis provides is in improving process quality and performance, with 70 percent saying improving logistics optimization matters most and 53 percent pointing to improving integration across the supply chain as the key benefit. "Data-driven decision-making is certainly an increasing trend in the supply chain," noted Tom McKenna, senior vice president of engineering and technology for Penske Logistics.[28]

Designing and building an effective **distribution network** is one method of ensuring successful product delivery. Again, there is typically a trade-off between the cost of the distribution network's design and the level of customer service provided. For example, a firm may utilize a large number of regional or local warehouses in order to deliver products quickly to customers. In this case, the transportation cost from factory to warehouse, the inventory holding cost, and the cost to build and operate multiple warehouses would be quite high, but the payoff would be excellent customer service. On the other hand, a firm may choose to operate only a few, centralized warehouses, saving money on the inbound transportation costs from factories (since they would be delivering larger quantities to fewer locations) and the warehouse construction and operating costs, but then having to be content with limited customer service capabilities since the warehouses would be located farther from most customers. Today, the use of massive, efficient warehouses to serve large market areas is growing. For example, the Browning Investments/Duke Realty partnership has constructed a 900,000-square-foot warehouse at All Points Midwest industrial park in Plainfield, Indiana, and Missouri-based North Point Development is building a 741,000-square-foot warehouse near Lebanon Business Park in Indiana. Much of this building surge is driven by retailers opening e-commerce facilities at a dizzying pace as online shopping becomes more prevalent.[29]

When firms operate globally, their supply chains are more complex, making global location decisions (the topic of Chapter 11) a necessary aspect of supply chain management. The increasing demand for products in emerging global markets like Russia, the Philippines, Thailand, and China combined with growing foreign competition in domestic markets, along with comparatively low labor costs in many Asian countries, have made international business commonplace for many companies. Firms must understand both the risks and advantages of operating in foreign locations and the impact this may have on their **global supply chains**. Some of the advantages include a larger market for products, economies of scale in purchasing and production, lower labor costs, a supply base of potentially cheaper, higher-quality suppliers, and the generation of new product ideas from foreign suppliers and employees. Some of the risks include fluctuating exchange rates affecting production, warehousing, and purchasing and selling prices; government intervention or political instabilities causing supply disruptions; security concerns; and potential changes in subsidies, tariffs, and taxes.

Companies react to these problems by building flexibility into their global supply chains. This is accomplished by using a number of suppliers as well as manufacturing and storage facilities in various foreign locations. As product demand and economic conditions change, the supply chain can react to take advantage of opportunities or cost changes to maximize profits. "Obviously, those with production capability in multiple regions and/or countries present a lower risk than a single location or a cluster of facilities in a single region or country," says Mark Taylor, vice president at North Carolina-based Risk International Services. "Even if you source 90 percent from the primary, by maintaining a second or third qualified (supplier), you've substantially shortened your lead time in making a change."[30]

For service products, the physical distribution issue is typically much less complex. Making sure services are delivered in a timely fashion is a primary topic of Chapter 12. Services are, for the most part, delivered by a server when customers request service. For instance, consider an example in which a customer walks into an auto repair facility in search of service for her automobile. She may talk to two or three facility employees during this service but eventually will complete a repair form, wait for the service to be completed, and then receive her repaired automobile. She will leave, satisfied with the service she received, as long as a number of things occurred: she got what she came for (the repair job), she got the type of service she expected to get (a reasonable waiting period, knowledgeable servers, and a repaired auto), and she got the service at a reasonable price. Otherwise, she will most likely be dissatisfied.

Successful service delivery depends on service location (service providers must be close to the customers they are trying to serve), service capacity (customers will leave if the wait is too long), and service capability (customers must be able to trust what servers are saying or doing for them). The final requirement of successful service is knowing what customers want. Residence Inn, for example, offers a number of family-friendly amenities. It knows that about one-third of its customers remove minibar items to chill food and drink items, and about half will wash items in the sink. Its suites come equipped to handle these needs.[32] Canadian grocer Vince's Market has become successful in part, because it knows what its customers want. This company is discussed in the nearby SCM Profile.

Integration Elements

Thus far, three of the four foundations of supply chain management have been discussed: supply, operations, and logistics activities occurring among the firm and its tiers of customers and suppliers. The final foundation topic—and certainly the most difficult one—is to integrate these processes among the focal firm and its key supply chain trading partners. Supply chain **process integration** is discussed in detail in the final two chapters of the text.

Processes in a supply chain are said to be integrated when members of the supply chain work together to make purchasing, inventory, production, quality, logistics, and other decisions that impact the overall profits of the supply chain. If one key process activity fails or is performed poorly, then the flow of goods moving along the supply chain is disrupted, jeopardizing the effectiveness of the entire supply chain. Successful supply chain process integration occurs when the participants realize that effective supply chain management must become part of each member's strategic planning process, where objectives and policies are jointly determined based on the end consumers' needs and what the supply chain as a whole can do for them.

| SCM Profile | Vince's Market Knows Its Customers |

Vince's Market, in Ontario, Canada, has become a highly sought-after grocer of many developers. "We've been approached by a number of them to take over as an anchor tenant in their complexes," says store operator Giancarlo Trimarchi. In 2014, Vince's spent about $2 million on its Newmarket location to add 800 square feet and resize departments. The frozen food and grocery sections were shrunk, while the deli and bulk food sections expanded. "We increased space to the shopping patterns of today. So far, its meeting our expectations," says Trimarchi.

Nowadays, analytics plays a big part in the planning process. That can be as simple as matching weekly movement reports to production forms "so that we know where we overproduced or underproduced," says Giancarlo. But data can also pinpoint trends, such as organics (trending up) and frozen food (trending down).

In 2012, Vince's launched a healthy foods line under the Go Natural brand. And in 2014, it rebranded its private label, Vince's Own, adding several new lines. Vince's Own homestyle pasta sauce, created by co-owner Carmen Trimarchi, is now one of the chain's top-selling grocery products. Vince's Newmarket always had a butcher on-site, but was hidden from customers. During the store expansion, a wall was replaced with glass, so shoppers could see the butcher in action. Vince's customers wanted to know if the store had its own butcher. Vince's stocks 275 cheese varieties and holds an annual cheese festival to showcase products and educate consumers. The result—cheese is now a top selling item.[31]

Ultimately, trading partners act together to maximize total supply chain profits by determining optimal purchase quantities, product availabilities, service levels, lead times, production quantities, use of technology, and product support at each tier within the supply chain. These integration activities also require high levels of *internal* functional integration of activities within each of the participating firms, such that the supply chain acts as one entity. This idea of supply chain integration can run contrary to some potential supply chain participants' independent profit-maximizing objectives, making supply chain integration a tough sell in many supplier–buyer–customer situations. Thus, continued efforts are required to break down obstacles, change cultural norms and adversarial relationships, knock down corporate silos, reduce conflicts, and bridge functional barriers within and between companies if supply chain integration is to become a reality.

The need for and value of process integration has impacted the auto industry in particular. Michigan governor Rick Snyder and Ontario, Canada, premier Kathleen Wynne went on the offensive in August 2016, to counteract any potential oncoming recession in North America, by signing a memorandum of understanding to increase the region's competitiveness in the automotive industry. The agreement covers best practices, improved supply chain integration, and technology transfer agreements.

Ontario and Michigan account for more than 26 percent of vehicle production in the Great Lakes region. "Collaborating to improve the auto sector is a great use of resources that will lead to continued growth and job creation in both economies. Sharing best practices and integrating our supply chains will advance Michigan's and Ontario's positions as leaders in the auto industry," said Snyder.[33]

One additional integration topic is the use of a **supply chain performance measurement** system. Performance measurements must be utilized along supply chains to help firms keep track of their supply chain management efforts. It is crucial for firms to know whether certain strategies are working as expected—or not—before they become financial and customer drains on the organizations. Firms work together to develop long-term supply chain management strategies and then devise tactics to implement these strategies. Performance measurements help firms decide the value of these tactics and should be developed to highlight performances within the areas of purchasing, operations, logistics, and integration.

Performance measures should be designed around each important supply chain activity and should be detailed performance descriptors instead of merely sales or cost figures. High levels of supply chain performance occur when the strategies at each of the firms fit well with overall supply chain strategies. Thus, each firm must understand its role in the supply chain, the needs of the supply chain's end customer, the needs of each firm's immediate customers, and how these needs translate into internal operations requirements and the requirements being placed on suppliers. Once these needs and the products and services themselves can be communicated and transported through the supply chain effectively, successful supply chain management and its associated benefits can be realized.

CURRENT TRENDS IN SUPPLY CHAIN MANAGEMENT

The practice of supply chain management is a fairly recent phenomenon, and many organizations are beginning to realize both the benefits and the problems accompanying integrated supply chains. Supply chain management is a complex and time-consuming undertaking, involving cultural change among most or all of the participants, investment and training in new software and communication systems, the building of trust between supply chain members, and a change or realignment of the competitive strategies employed among at least some of the participating firms. Further, as competitors, products, technologies, economic conditions, and customers change, the priorities for supply chain trading partners also change. A look at the most recent industry surveys of executives reveals a number of supply chain issues that companies are addressing today, including the use of supply chain analytics, improving supply chain sustainability, and increasing supply chain visibility.[34] While these and other supply chain management issues are discussed in numerous places in this text, these newest trends are discussed below to give the reader a better sense of some of the issues facing executives and their companies' supply chains today.

Use of Supply Chain Analytics

Supply chain analytics refers to examining raw supply chain data and then reaching conclusions or making predictions with the information. It is used in many industries to allow supply chain managers to make better business decisions. The market for supply chain analytics solutions is growing at about 15 percent per year with 2018 global revenues expected to exceed $4.8 billion. The solutions include supply chain planning and procurement, sales and operations planning, forecasting, manufacturing analytics, transportation and logistics analytics, and visualization and reporting tools. The growth is being pushed by the enormous rise in computing capabilities and the huge volumes of data generated (hence the term **big data**) in business organizations including retail, healthcare, manufacturing, and electronics, and the rising awareness levels among executives regarding the benefits of these analytics solutions.[35]

Analytics can be used along the supply chain, for example, to schedule production according to expected supplier deliveries, to route delivery trucks through a distribution network, or to determine when a customer is most likely to be home to accept a delivery. Analytics solution provider Blue Yonder has developed forecasting methods for retailers, for instance, where 130,000 stock keeping units (SKUs) and 200 influencing variables generate 150,000,000 probability distributions every day to ensure the right products are replenished at each store. Increased forecast accuracy generates savings on inventory and other supply chain costs. In a transportation application, UPS has spent ten years developing its on-road integrated optimization and navigation system to optimize routes in real time according to traffic. While cost reduction is often the trigger of analytics initiatives, customers benefit from reduced stockouts and more accurate delivery slots.[36]

Improving Supply Chain Sustainability

As mentioned earlier in this chapter, **supply chain sustainability** refers to meeting the needs of current supply chain members without hindering the ability to meet the needs of future generations in terms of economic, environmental, and social challenges. In a 2016 report compiled from interviews of over 100 leading company executives, performed by Ernst & Young in collaboration with the UN Global Compact, the goal was to better understand how companies are managing their supply chains in ways that support sustainability. Overall, the study indicated that by improving environmental, social, and governance performance throughout the supply chain, companies can enhance processes, reduce costs, increase productivity, uncover product innovation, achieve market differentiation, and improve societal outcomes. The study found that most companies are trying to improve their supply chain sustainability performance.[37]

In 2016, Ford Motor Co. announced an effort to expand its environmental and resource conservation goals down its supply chain, unveiling what it calls its Partnership for a Cleaner Environment. Working with 25 suppliers representing 800 manufacturing plants in 40 countries, Ford's Partnership will share with these suppliers what it considers best practices around reducing water, energy, and carbon dioxide as well as materials reuse. Ms. Mary Wroten, Ford's senior manager of supply chain sustainability, said that by sharing what it has found that works in-house with its suppliers, Ford is able to multiply the reductions in water, energy use, and GHG emissions. "Climate is not a competitive space, and more that we can talk about this and share what we are doing, a stronger planet we can create," says Wroten.[38]

Increasing Supply Chain Visibility

Supply chain visibility can be defined as the ability of suppliers, manufacturers, business partners, and customers to know exactly where products are, at any point in the supply chain. This inventory visibility is obviously made easier by technology and can prove very advantageous when dealing with disruptive events such as floods, hurricanes, and political upheavals. UPS and Fedex tracking methods are good examples of visibility—shipments are tracked and monitored using technology, and alerts are sent to shippers as the item is in transit and then delivered. Today, more sophisticated software applications are being developed and offered to organizations for tracking orders, inventories, deliveries, returned goods, and even employee attendance.[39]

Automaker Renault is using a cloud platform to allow tracking of its spare parts to all export markets around the world. The company expects that its cloud platform will help it to better serve its international markets and customers while reducing inventory and transportation costs.[40] In another example, Colorado-based transportation management systems provider 10-4 Systems partnered with Anheuser-Busch to add visibility to all of its brewery shipments. "AB recognized an opportunity to improve their customer's product and shipment visibility experience. Our technology was able to help them achieve this goal through centralizing carrier visibility and modernizing the methods in which those events were communicated to their end-users," says 10-4's CEO, Travis Rhyan. According to James Sembrot, Anheuser-Busch's Sr. Director of Logistics Strategy, "We're committed to using technology to enhance our supply chain processes. Using 10-4's platform, we are now tracking all shipments from our U.S. breweries through customer delivery, enabling our logistics operations team to proactively address any transportation issues."[41]

SUMMARY

Supply chain management is the integration of key business processes from initial raw material extraction to the final or end customer, including all intermediate processing, transportation, storage activities, along with the final sale to the end-product customer and eventually product returns. It is working together to provide benefits to all stakeholders. Today, the practice of supply chain management is becoming extremely important to reduce costs and improve quality and customer service, with the end objective of improving competitiveness. Many firms are today becoming adept at managing at least some part of their supply chains. Supply chain management is an outgrowth and expansion of lean and Six Sigma activities and has grown in popularity since the 1980s. The foundations of supply chain management can be found in the areas of purchasing, production, logistics, and collaboration between trading partners. Finally, as markets, political forces, technology, and economic conditions change around the world, the practice of supply chain management must also change and grow. This chapter serves as an opening discussion of the topic of supply chain management and describes what the remaining chapters will cover.

KEY TERMS

big data, 22

bullwhip effect, 10

business process reengineering, 12

customer relationship management, 13

demand management, 17

distribution network, 18

enterprise resource planning, 13

ethical and sustainable sourcing, 16

global supply chains, 19

inventory visibility, 17

lean production system, 17

material requirements planning, 17

process integration, 20

radio frequency identification, 17

reengineering, 12

second-tier customers, 9

second-tier suppliers, 9

Six Sigma quality management, 17

strategic partnerships, 16

supplier certification, 15

supplier evaluation, 15

supplier management, 15

supplier relationship management, 14

supply chain, 5

supply chain analytics, 22

supply chain management, 7

supply chain performance measurement, 21

supply chain sustainability, 22

supply chain visibility, 23

supply management, 14

sustainability, 14

third-party logistics providers, 13

third-party logistics services, 18

triple bottom line, 14

DISCUSSION QUESTIONS

1. Define the term *supply chain management* in your own words, and list its most important activities.

2. Can a small business like a local sandwich or bicycle shop benefit from practicing supply chain management? What aspects would they most likely concentrate on?

3. Describe and draw a supply chain for a bicycle repair shop, and list the important supply chain members.

4. Can a bicycle repair shop have more than one supply chain? Explain.

5. What roles do "collaboration" and "trust" play in the practice of supply chain management?

6. Why don't firms just become more vertically integrated (e.g., buy out suppliers and customers), instead of trying to manage their supply chains?

7. What types of organizations would benefit the most from practicing supply chain management? What sorts of improvements could be expected?

8. What are the benefits of supply chain management?

9. Can nonprofit, educational, or government organizations benefit from supply chain management? How?

10. What does the term, "third-tier supplier" mean? What about "third-tier customer"? What about the "focal firm"? Provide examples.

11. What is the bullwhip effect and what causes it? How would you try to reduce the bullwhip effect?

12. When did the idea and term *supply chain management* first begin to be thought about and discussed? Which two operations management practices became the origin of supply chain management?

13. Do you think supply chain management is simply the latest trend in management thinking and will likely die out in a few years? Why or why not?

14. How has technology impacted supply chain management?

15. What are the four foundation elements of supply chain management? Describe some activities within each element.

16. Is the use of a large number of suppliers a good idea? Why?

17. Do you think the proper way to choose a supplier is to always find the one that will give you the lowest price? When might this not be a good idea?

18. What is supplier management? What are some of the activities of supplier management?

19. What is the difference between supply chain management and logistics?

20. What is demand management, and why is this an important part of supply chain management?

21. What is the difference between an MRP system and an ERP system?

22. What role do information systems play in supply chain management? Give some examples.

23. Briefly describe the terms *lean production* and *Six Sigma systems.*

24. What are 3PLs, and what role do they play in SCM?

25. What is logistics? What is the objective of logistics?

26. What is the triple bottom line and how would you describe it for Walmart?

27. What trade-offs must be considered in designing a distribution system?

28. What are the advantages and risks involved with global supply chains?

29. What does process integration mean? Can supply chain management succeed without it? Why, or why not?

30. Should companies require their suppliers to get certified if they are performing well?

31. At what point should a supplier be considered to have a *strategic partnership* with a firm?

32. Why are performance measurement systems important when trying to manage supply chains?

33. Does a global supply chain have more risk than a domestic supply chain? Why?

34. What are big data and data analytics? How might they be used in supply chains?

35. What are some things supply chain members could do to improve sustainability?

36. Describe supply chain visibility, and why supply chain managers like it.

ESSAY/PROJECT QUESTIONS

1. Visit the websites of companies like Walmart, Dell, and Home Depot and see if you can find discussions of their supply chain management activities. List information you can find on purchasing/supplier, logistics, information system, inventory management, quality, and customer service issues.

2. Search on the term *supply chain management.* How many hits did you get? Describe five of the websites found in your search.

3. Go to http://www.agrichain-centre.com/ (or a similar website found when searching on *New Zealand supply chain management*), and discuss the current state of supply chain (or value chain) management in New Zealand.

4. Search on the term *bullwhip effect*, and write a paper on the impacts of the bullwhip effect and the companies profiled in the papers you find.

5. Search on the term *supply chain management software applications*, and write a paper about how companies use these to improve their financial performance.

6. Search on the term *green supply chains* and write a paper regarding the global regulatory status of environmental legislation and how it is impacting supply chain management.

CASES

1. Supply Chain Management: The Big Picture*

Cyber Logic Systems is a successful regional company in the United States that specializes in cyber security. Because of the dramatic increase in the hacking of business and government databases, Cyber Logic Systems believes this is the moment to expand its operations. Elmer Armstrong, chief executive officer, met with the board of directors and explained his vision for the company. Elmer planned to aggressively expand into Europe and South America. The board of directors gave Elmer the go ahead.

Elmer called a meeting of his senior staff and explained his vision to them. He asked what major issues they saw that required immediate resolution before Cyber Logic Systems could proceed with such an aggressive expansion. Rhonda Mendoza, director of operations, said that the company's current supply chain structure would not be able to support such an expansion. She further stated that the supply chain structure would collapse under the strain, thus endangering their regional business, as well as the expansion. Elmer tasked Rhonda with developing a plan on how to get the supply chain structure robust enough to move forward with the expansion.

Rhonda began analyzing the company's supply chain management needs by reviewing the four foundation elements—supply, operations, logistics, and integration. As she performed her analysis, Rhonda realized that not all their current suppliers had the

*Written by Rick Bonsall, D. Mgt., McKendree University, Lebanon, IL. The people and institution are fictional and any resemblance to any person or institution is coincidental. This case was prepared solely to provide material for class discussion. The author does not intend to illustrate either effective or ineffective handling of a managerial situation.

capabilities to support Cyber Logic Systems' operations in Europe and South America. Rhonda decided to perform a detailed supplier evaluation on each supplier. Through this evaluation she determined that some suppliers could easily support European operations, while others were better suited for the South American operations. Furthermore, some suppliers, who were a tremendous asset to Cyber Logic Systems, would only be capable of supporting their current regional business.

Each market area, United States, Europe, and South America, had regulations with differing standards for cyber security. The technical specifications for the systems Cyber Logic Systems would install varied significantly between the three marketplaces. Rhonda decided this could be a considerable problem. Her solution was simple, yet elegant, supplier certification. Supplier certification would ensure that the suppliers supporting the specific operational markets would be qualified to meet the particular regulatory requirements.

Although the systems Cyber Logic Systems installed were primarily software, often new hardware was required to support the software. Rhonda understood that its current distribution network was insufficient. It needed to redesign and build a more self-sustaining distribution network in order to ensure timely product delivery. It truly needed to move from the mind-set of a regional distribution system to a global supply chain. This requirement would mean sourcing from suppliers who were close to the customers. When a customer has a cyber security issue, time is the enemy. The new systems must be in place as quickly as possible to avoid further damage to the customer's databases and to enable them to continue operating.

Rhonda believed she had identified the key elements that must be improved before they could move forward with the expansion. The last hurdle was how to guarantee that the three foundation elements—supply, operations, and logistics—worked as one smooth global supply chain and not as disjointed parts. This was the biggest challenge of all. If Cyber Logic Systems didn't solve this issue, the chance of failure was high.

Rhonda reflected on her studies in operations and supply chain management. The answer to the issue was process integration. She knew that it had a challenge ahead. The company must convince each supply chain partner that this supply chain management structure must be part of everyone's strategic planning process. Only then could it ensure that the individual pieces, purchasing, inventory, operations, logistics, quality, etc., would work together as a single well-oiled machine. Rhonda was ready to outline her plan to Elmer and the other members of his senior staff.

Discussion Questions

1. When analyzing the supply chain management foundation element "supply," what are some of the specific issues Cyber Logic Systems must address?

2. When analyzing the supply chain management foundation element "operations," what are some of the specific issues Cyber Logic Systems must address?

3. When analyzing the supply chain management foundation element "logistics," what are some of the specific issues Cyber Logic Systems must address?

4. When working on process integration, what type of issues must a company overcome for true integration to be achieved?

Appendix 1.1

The Beer Game

The Beer Game is a popular game played in operations management and supply chain management courses, and was developed by MIT in the 1960s.[42] The game simulates the flow of product and information in a simple supply chain consisting of a retailer, a wholesaler, a distributor, and a manufacturer. One person takes the role of each organization in a typical game. The objective is to minimize total supply chain inventory and back-order costs. In this way, a class can be separated into any number of four-person supply chains—each supply chain competing against the others. The game is used to illustrate the bullwhip effect and the importance of timely and accurate communications and information with respect to purchases along the supply chain (in this game, no one is allowed to share any information other than current order quantities, as might be found in unmanaged or unlinked supply chains).

Each supply chain participant follows the same set of activities:

1. The participant fills customer orders from current inventory and creates back orders if demand cannot be met.

2. The participant forecasts customer demand and then orders beer from the supplier (or schedules beer production if the participant is the manufacturer), which then takes several weeks to be delivered.

3. The participant attempts to manage inventories in order to minimize back-order costs (stockouts) and inventory carrying costs.

Figure A1.1 illustrates the beer supply chain, showing the transportation and information delays. There is no product transportation or order delay between the retailer and the end customers. For the other supply chain members, there is a one-week delay between customer order and supplier acceptance, and a two-week transportation delay from the time a customer's order is received until that order reaches the customer. It also takes two weeks to complete a production order at the factory, such that beer will be ready to fill customer orders.

Here is how the game progresses:

Starting conditions. At the start of the game (Week 0), each supply chain member (except the manufacturer) has twelve cases of beer in ending inventory (see Table A1.1), four cases in the second week of inbound transportation delay, four cases in the first week (updated) of inbound transportation delay, and four cases in the beginning of the first week of inbound transportation delay. The manufacturer has twelve cases of beer in ending inventory, four cases of beer in the second week of production lead time, four cases in the first week of production lead time, and four cases at the beginning of the first week of production lead time. Each player also has an *outgoing order* of four cases sitting in his or her outgoing order box (or production order box). The retailer must begin with twenty

Figure A1.1	**The Beer Game Supply Chain**

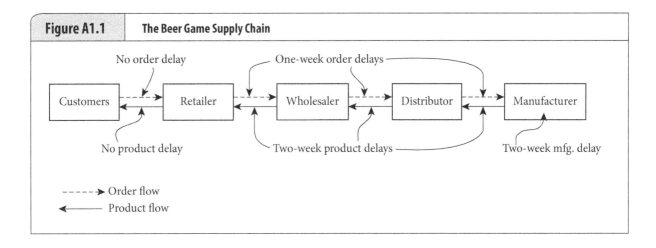

weeks of customer demand information provided by the game coordinator or instructor, such that the retailer can only view one week's demand at a time (these can be written on the underneath side of twenty sticky notepads for each retailer, for example).

Step 1. Each member *updates his or her beer inventories.*

- Move the cases of beer from the second week of inbound delay for the previous period and add to the ending inventory of the previous period, putting the total in the beginning inventory column of the current period (see Week 0/Week 1 of Table A1.1). For the manufacturer, this is a production delay.

- Move inventory from the first week of inbound delay (updated column) to the second week of delay (see Table A1.1).

- Move inventory from the first week of inbound delay (beginning column) to the first week of inbound delay (updated column) (see Table A1.1).

Step 2. Each member *fills his or her customer orders.*

- The retailer uncovers and reads the current week's customer demand slip, and then places the slip face down in the discard area, *such that it cannot be seen by the wholesaler.*

- The retailer then fills this order (after first satisfying any back orders) and subtracts demand from beginning inventory. This amount then becomes the ending inventory amount. If ending inventory is negative, then a back order of this amount is created, and ending inventory becomes zero.

- Next, the retailer places last week's outgoing order on the wholesaler's incoming demand order box.

- Finally, the retailer forecasts future demand and orders beer from the wholesaler by writing an order on the slip provided and places it face down in the retailer's outgoing order box, *such that it cannot be seen by the wholesaler.* (This order will go to the wholesaler next week—remember the one-week delay.)

The wholesaler follows the same steps as above: The wholesaler reads the incoming demand order slip, discards it, satisfies any back orders, and fills as much of the incoming order as possible from beginning inventory. At this point, the wholesaler must tell the retailer how much of the order it can satisfy, and the retailer records this amount in the first week beginning delay for the current period. The wholesaler then updates its ending

Table A1.1	**Inventory Record Sheet**

Your supply chain role:

Your name: Team name:

Incoming demand from supply chain customer	Discard area		Outgoing orders to supply chain supplier, OR production orders for manufacturer

Week	Ending Inventory	Beginning Inventory	Back Orders	Second Week Inbound Delay	First Week Inbound Delay	
					Updated	Beginning
0	12		0	4	4	4
1		16		4	4	
2						
3						
4						
5						
6						
7						
8						
9						
10						
11						
12						
13						
14						
15						
16						
17						
18						
19						
20						
Totals						

Amount of outgoing order received

Note: Ending inventories must be zero when you have a back order. If ending inventory is greater than zero, back orders must equal zero. Back orders equal previous period back orders plus the incoming order, minus current inventory. At end of game: Sum *ending inventory* column and *back-orders* column and determine total cost as—[Total ending inventories × $1] + [Total back orders × $2] = $_____. Then sum total costs for all supply chain members. Total supply chain costs = $_____.

inventory and back order quantities, it sends last week's outgoing order to the distributor's incoming demand, and then it decides how much to order and places the order sheet face down in the wholesaler's outgoing order box, *such that it cannot be seen by the distributor.*

The distributor goes through the same steps as the wholesaler when it gets an incoming order from the wholesaler.

The manufacturer also follows the same steps, except instead of sending last week's outgoing order somewhere, it reads the outgoing order and fills the production request by transferring that number of cases from its raw materials storage area to the first week's beginning production delay (it simply creates the cases needed for the order).

Step 3. Repeat Steps 1 and 2 until the game limit is reached. Calculate total costs at game's end.

A typical game progresses in this fashion for twenty weeks (this is usually sufficient to introduce the bullwhip effect into the game). The game is played with sticky notepads for beer orders, using Table A1.1 to keep track of inventories, orders, and back orders. Players must take care *not to talk* to the other players during the game *or to show what orders they are receiving or planning* for the next week. The retailer must *not look at future customer demand data,* provided by the instructor. Remember, this game is meant to illustrate what happens when *no communication* about future orders or order strategies occurs between supply chain members.

At the end of twenty weeks (or shorter if time does not permit), players determine the total cost of their inventories and back orders on the inventory record sheet (back-orders cost $2 per unit per week, and inventories cost $1 per unit per week). Given these costs, the basic strategy should be to attempt to avoid stockouts or back orders, while, to a lesser degree, trying to minimize total inventory carrying costs. This requires attempting to forecast future demand accurately (as time progresses, firms should use their inventory record sheet demand information for forecasting purposes). The winning team is the team with the lowest total supply chain costs.

Beer Game Questions and Exercises

1. All players but the retailer should answer this question—what do you think the retailer's customer demand pattern looked like? How did your customer orders vary throughout the game?

2. What happened to the current inventory levels, looking back up the supply chain from retailer to manufacturer? Why?

3. How could the supply chain members reduce total inventory and back-order costs in the future?

4. Go to http://www.beergame.lim.ethz.ch/, and try playing this Internet version of the game. Report on your experiences playing the game.

ADDITIONAL RESOURCES

Burgess, R. "Avoiding Supply Chain Management Failure: Lessons from Business Process Reengineering," *The International Journal of Logistics Management* 9(1), 1998: 15–24.

Chopra, S., and P. Meindl. *Supply Chain Management: Strategy, Planning, and Operation.* NJ: Prentice-Hall, 2001.

Frazelle, E. *Supply Chain Strategy: The Logistics of Supply Chain Management.* New York: McGraw-Hill, 2002.

Hammer, M., and J. Champy. *Reengineering the Corporation.* London: Nicholas Brealey, 1993.

Handfield, R. B., and E. L. Nichols. *Introduction to Supply Chain Management.* NJ: Prentice-Hall, 1999.

Lambert, D. M., M. C. Cooper, and J. D. Pagh. "Supply Chain Management: Implementation Issues and Research Opportunities," *The International Journal of Logistics Management* 9(2), 1998: 1–19.

Lee, H. L., V. Padmanabhan, and S. Whang. "Information Distortion in a Supply Chain: The Bullwhip Effect," *Management Science* 43(4), 1997: 546–558.

Simchi-Levi, D., P. Kaminsky, and E. Simchi-Levi. *Designing and Managing the Supply Chain.* New York: McGraw-Hill, 2000.

Stevens, G. C. "Integrating the Supply Chain," *International Journal of Physical Distribution and Logistics Management* 19(8), 1989: 3–8.

Tan, K. C. "A Framework of Supply Chain Management Literature," *European Journal of Purchasing and Supply Management* 7(1): 39–48.

Webster, S. *Principles & Tools for Supply Chain Management.* New York: McGraw-Hill/Irwin, 2008.

ENDNOTES

1. Blanchard, D., "A Supply Chain Investment That's Guaranteed to Pay Off," *Material Handling & Logistics,* June 9, 2015: 1.

2. Barlow, R., "Crises, Disasters Should Disrupt Supply Chain's Status Quo," *Healthcare Purchasing News* 39(2), 2015: 10,12–13.

3. Aronow, S., D. Hofman, M. Burkett, J. Romano, and K. Nilles, "The 2014 Supply Chain Top 25: Leading the Decade," *Supply Chain Management Review* 18(5), 2014: 8–17. Also see: https://www.rankingthebrands.com/The-Brand-Rankings.aspx?rankingID=94

4. Vora, M., "7 Steps to Link Quality Improvement to your Supply Chain," *Supply Chain Management Review* 19(4), 2015: 44–51.

5. Listed in the CSCMP Terms and Glossary at www.cscmp.org

6. Found in the ISM Glossary of Key Supply Management Terms at www.ism.ws

7. Found in the APICS dictionary at www.apics.org

8. Prest, G., and Sopher, S., "Innovations That Drive Supply Chains," *Supply Chain Management Review* 18(3), 2014: 42–49.

9. Dye, J., and A. Samson, "Zimmer Biomet Sinks After Supply Chain Problems," *FT.com,* October 31, 2016: 1.

10. McLeod, D., "Tianjin Blast Rocks Insurer Balance Sheets," *Business Insurance* 49(23), 2015: 1.

11. Tan, K., S. Lyman, and J. Wisner, "Supply Chain Management: A Strategic Perspective," *International Journal of Operations and Production Management* 2(6), 2002: 614–631.

12. U.S. Census Bureau information found at https://factfinder.census.gov/faces/tableservices/jsf/pages/productview.xhtml?pid=ASM_2014_31GS101&prodType=table

13. Prest, G., and S. Sopher, "Innovations That Drive Supply Chains," *Supply Chain Management Review* 18(3), 2014: 42–49.

14. Keith, O., and M. Webber, "Supply-Chain Management: Logistics Catches Up with Strategy," *Outlook,* 1982, cit. M. G. Christopher, *Logistics, The Strategic Issue.* London: Chapman and Hall, 1992.

15. Shaw, A., *Some Problems in Market Distribution*. Cambridge, MA: Harvard University Press, 1915.

16. See, for example, Burgess, R., "Avoiding Supply Chain Management Failure: Lessons from Business Process Re-engineering," *The International Journal of Logistics Management* 9(1), 1998: 15–23; Hammer, M., and J. Champy, *Re-engineering the Corporation: A Manifesto for Business Revolution*. New York, NY: Harper Business, 1993; and Morris, D., and J. Brandon, *Re-engineering Your Business*. New York, NY: McGraw-Hill, 1993.

17. See, for instance, https://www.appsruntheworld.com/top-10-erp-software-vendors-and-market-forecast-2015-2020

18. Dutton, G., "Is Your Supply Chain Safe?" *World Trade* 26(1), 2013: 35–40.

19. Cable, J., "What You Can't See Can Hurt You," *Industry Week* 259(1), 2010: 44.

20. See, for example, http://www.2wglobal.com/about-us/wwl/press-releases/wallenius-wilhelmsen-logistics-earns-recognition-as--john-deere-partner-level-supplier/#.WE8jOObzMa8

21. Anonymous, "Pratt & Whitney Notrs USD18BN in Supplier Long-Term Agreements," *Airline Industry Information,* April 6, 2015: 1.

22. Noureldin, A., "Railsponsible Encourages Responsible Procurement," *International Railway Journal* 56(9), 2016: 94–95.

23. Hockett, M., "Survey of Distributor Operations: Best Practices," *Industrial Distribution,* May 24, 2016: 1.

24. Anonymous, "Elementum: Holiday Shortage Fears Outweigh Brand Loyalty," *Wireless News*, December 15, 2016: 1.

25. Sanders, B., "RFID and Retail: The New Power Couple," *Customer* 32(6), 2014: 26–27 and Anonymous, "L2 Rolls out Intelligence Report: Omnichannel Retail Study Results," *Entertainment Close-Up*, September 17, 2015: 1.

26. Barsalou, M., and R. Perkin, "A Structured, Yet Flexible, Approach," *ASQ Six Sigma Forum Magazine* 14(4), 2015: 22–25, 3.

27. Walz, M., "Trends to Watch in 2012," *World Trade* 25(1), 2012: 24–28.

28. Anonymous, "Survey: Need for Big Data in Logistics Keeps Growing," *Fleet Owner,* September 27, 2016: 1.

29. Olson, S., "Lauth Planning Big Warehouse in Brownsburg," *Indianapolis Business Journal* 35(35), 2014: 6.

30. Phillips, Z., "Outsourcing Overseas Cuts Costs, Raises Risks," *Business Insurance* 44(31), 2010: 11–12.

31. Burns, G., "Where Meals and Math Make Sense," *Canadian Grocer* 128(9), 2014: 48–49.

32. Anonymous, "Lodging Companies: Residence Inn Helps Families," *Marketing Weekly News*, May 19, 2012: 1358.

33. Walsh, D., "Dual View of Auto Horizon: Fear of Recession Clouds Technology Excitement at Industry Conference," *Crain's Detroit Business* 32(32), 2016: 3.

34. See, for example, Blanchard, D., "Supply Chain & Logistics: The Competitive Advantage of a Supply Chain," *Industry Week*, July 11, 2014: 1; Prest, G., and S. Sopher, "Innovations That Drive Supply Chains," *Supply Chain Management Review* 18(3), 2014: 42–49; and Stank, S., P. Dornier, K. Petersen, and M. Srinivasan, "Global Supply Chain Operations: A Region-by-Region Assessment of Readiness," *Supply Chain Management Review* 19(1), 2015: 10–18.

35. Anonymous, "Global Supply Chain Analytics Market Solutions Report 2015-2019," *PR Newswire Europe Including UK Disclose*, April 1, 2015: 1.

36. Hoberg, K., and K. Alicke, "The Customer Experience," *Supply Chain Management Review* 20(5), 2016: 28–30, 32–37.

37. Anonymous, "How to Build a Responsible Supply Chain," *Material Handling & Logistics*, August 23, 2016: 1.

38. Anonymous, "How Auto Companies Are Saving the Environment and Making Money," *Material Handling & Logistics*, March 31, 2016: 1.

39. McCrea, B., "Supply Chain and Logistics Technology: Defining Visibility," *LogisticsManagement.com*, September 1, 2011: 1.

40. Anonymous, "Renault Expects Better Supply Chain Visibility from Cloud," *Material Handling & Logistics*, December 5, 2012: 1.

41. Anonymous, "10-4 Partners with Anheuser Busch," *Fleet Owner*, November 18, 2016: 1.

42. Copyright © 1994 President and Fellows of Harvard College (the Beer Game board version) and © 2002 The MIT Forum for Supply Chain Innovation (the Beer Game computerized version).

PART **2**

Supply Issues in Supply Chain Management

Chapter 2   Purchasing Management

Chapter 3   Creating and Managing Supplier Relationships

Chapter 4   Ethical and Sustainable Sourcing

Chapter 5   Demand Forecasting

Chapter 2

PURCHASING MANAGEMENT

State procurement offices are no longer the paper pushers of old but instead have become strategic visionaries, leveraging state spending capacity in new ways to meet these challenges. Government is using the power of procurement not only to react to changes, but as a cornerstone for long-term government financial stability.

— **Krista Ferrell, National Association of State Procurement Officials**[1]

The supply chain is the lifeblood that keeps the heart of most businesses beating in a volatile economy. The supply management role is growing in importance, as executives come to realize the holistic value of supply chain innovation and partnerships. No longer is the supply chain viewed as a place to cut costs. It's now a fundamental and carefully-valued piece of a healthy, long-term business strategy.

— **Lisa Arnseth, Inside Supply Management**[2]

Learning Objectives

After completing this chapter, you will be able to

- Describe the role of purchasing and its strategic impact on an organization's competitive advantage.
- Describe the traditional purchasing process, e-procurement, public procurement, and green purchasing.
- Recognize and know how to handle small-value purchase orders.
- Analyze and evaluate sourcing decisions and the factors impacting supplier selection, including outsourcing, make or buy, and break-even analysis.
- Analyze and compute total cost of ownership.
- Analyze the pros and cons of single sourcing versus multiple sourcing.
- Describe the key characteristics of centralized, decentralized, and hybrid purchasing organizations.
- Describe the opportunities and challenges of global sourcing.

Chapter Outline

Introduction

A Brief History of Purchasing Terms

The Role of Supply Management in an Organization

The Purchasing Process

Sourcing Decisions: The Make-or-Buy Decision

Roles of the Supply Base

Supplier Selection   Global Sourcing

How Many Suppliers to Use   Procurement in Government and Nonprofit Agencies

Purchasing Organization   Summary

SCM Profile · Develop World-Class Purchasing

In today's global market, purchasing managers must have the proper skills and tools to develop a world-class purchasing strategy. Although the purchasing function significantly impacts a firm's bottom line, most manufacturing purchasing departments are understaffed, with roughly less than 5 percent of the salaried personnel managing 65 percent of the firm's cost of goods sold. Fortunately, there are tools that can help purchasing managers to implement a world-class purchasing strategy.

For example, consider a component part supplier requests for a 5 percent price increase, despite raw material prices being stable. Assuming the annual volume is 5,000,000 units at $3 each, and the supplier's gross margin is 35%. The price increase adds $750,000 (5,000,000 units $\times$ $3 $\times$ 5%) to the material cost. While the average purchasing managers may concede to the price increase, a world-class purchasing manager with a solid supply base will consider shifting 25 percent of the volume elsewhere and inform the supplier that an increase that is not supported by market fundamentals will reduce profit by $750,000. Indeed, supplier's product cost is likely to be higher due to the lower volume from the price increase, resulting in even less profit and discouraging the supplier from raising price. Thus, a solid supply base is essential for world-class purchasing managers.

Profit at $3.00	5,000,000 units × $3/unit × 35% = $5,250,000
Profit at $3.15	(5,000,000 units × 75%) × ($3 unit × 35% + $.15/unit) = $4,500,000
Change in Profit	$5,250,000 − $4,500,000 = $750,000

Another necessary tool for world-class purchasing managers is that they must not appear as easy targets for suppliers to pass on margin increases, especially one that is not justified. Obviously, talented purchasing leaders are necessary to develop, execute, and follow up on world-class purchasing strategies. There is no one-size-fits-all purchasing strategy. Instead, managers should develop a custom purchasing strategy that capitalizes on its business strengths, and improves its weaknesses, which is part of the continuous improvement cycle when striving for world-class status.

Other skills and knowledge such as market intelligence, strategic planning, good project management, and good performance measures are necessary to ensure successful implementation and execution of world-class purchasing strategy. The four key parts of market intelligence are market pricing, market news, product supply and demand, and product forecast/cost models. Knowledge of marketing pricing is essential to ensure the firm is paying a fair price, whereas market news reduces the risk of unfavorable surprises. Product supply and demand affects market price and product availability. Lastly, product forecast/cost models are necessary for budgeting and prioritizing purchasing decisions.[3]

Now, let's assume that you are the world-class purchasing manager. A new supplier for a critical component part offers a multiyear, lower price contract. Will you accept the new multiyear contract? Clearly, market intelligence is needed to determine whether to accept the long-term contract.

INTRODUCTION

In the context of supply chain management (SCM), purchasing can be defined as the act of obtaining merchandise; capital equipment; raw materials; services; or maintenance, repair, and operating (MRO) supplies in exchange for money or its equivalent. Purchasing can be broadly classified into two categories: **merchant** and **industrial buyers**. The first category, merchant buyers, includes the wholesalers and retailers who primarily purchase for resale purposes. Generally, merchants purchase their merchandise in volume to take advantage of quantity discounts and other incentives such as transportation economy and storage efficiency. They create value by consolidating merchandise, breaking bulk, and providing the essential logistical services. The second category is the industrial buyers, whose primary task is to purchase raw materials for conversion purposes. Industrial buyers also purchase services, capital equipment, and MRO supplies. The typical industrial buyers are the manufacturers, although some service firms such as restaurants, landscape gardeners, and florists also purchase raw materials for conversion purposes.

An effective and efficient purchasing system is crucial to the success of a business. Indeed, the *Annual Survey of Manufactures*[4] consistently shows that the total cost of materials exceeds value added through manufacturing in the United States. Thus, it is not surprising that purchasing concepts and theories that evolved over the last three decades focused on industrial buyers' purchases of raw materials and how purchasing can be exploited to improve competitive success.

The primary focus of this chapter is the industrial buyer. The chapter describes the role of purchasing in an organization, the processes of a traditional purchasing system and the common documents used, how an electronic purchasing system works, various strategies for handling small-order problems, the advantages and disadvantages of centralized versus decentralized purchasing systems, purchasing for nonprofits and government agencies, sourcing issues including supplier selection, and other important topics affecting the role of purchasing and supply management in supply chain management.

A BRIEF HISTORY OF PURCHASING TERMS

Purchasing is a key business function that is responsible for acquisition of required materials, services, and equipment. However, acquisition of services is widely called *contracting*. The increased strategic role of purchasing in today's business setting has brought a need for higher levels of skill and responsibility on the part of purchasing professionals. Consequently, the term **supply management** is increasingly being used in place of purchasing to describe the expanded set of responsibilities of purchasing professionals. The traditional purchasing function of receiving requisitions and issuing purchase orders is no longer adequate; instead, a holistic and comprehensive acquisition strategy is required to meet the organization's strategic objectives.

The Institute for Supply Management (ISM) defines supply management as the "identification, acquisition, access, positioning, management of resources and related capabilities the organization needs or potentially needs in the attainment of its strategic objectives."[5] Key activities of supply management have expanded beyond the basic purchasing function to include negotiations, logistics, contract development and administration, inventory control and management, supplier management, and other activities. However, purchasing remains the core activity of supply management. Although *procurement* is frequently used in place of *purchasing*, procurement typically includes the added activities of specifications development, value analysis, negotiation, expediting, contract administration, supplier quality control, and some logistics activities; hence, it is widely used by government agencies due to the type of purchases and frequent service contracting they made with government suppliers. However, it is difficult to clearly distinguish where purchasing activities end and the supply management function begins. Moreover, many organizations use these terms interchangeably. In many parts of this book, we have retained the traditional term *purchasing* in place of *supply management* to emphasize the term's original meaning.

THE ROLE OF SUPPLY MANAGEMENT IN AN ORGANIZATION

Traditionally, purchasing was regarded as being a service to production, and corporate executives paid limited attention to issues concerned with purchasing. However, as global competition intensified in the 1980s, executives realized the impact of large quantities of purchased material and work-in-process inventories on manufacturing cost, quality, new product development, and delivery lead time. Savvy managers adopted new supply chain management concepts that emphasized purchasing as a key strategic business process rather than a narrow specialized supporting function to overall business strategy.

The *Annual Survey of Manufactures* (as shown in Table 2.1), conducted by the U.S. Census Bureau, shows that manufacturers spend more than 50 percent of each sales dollar (shown as "value of shipments") on raw materials (shown as "cost of materials"). Purchases of raw materials actually exceeded value added through manufacturing (shown as "manufacture"), which accounted for less than 50 percent of sales. Purchases as a percent of sales dollars for merchants are expected to be much higher since merchandise is primarily bought for resale purposes. Unfortunately, aggregate statistics for merchants are not readily available.

However, individual information can easily be obtained from the annual report, Form 10K, of publicly traded companies, either directly or from the U.S. Securities and Exchange Commission (SEC). For example, Walmart reported that its cost of sales ranged from 74.4 to 75.7 percent of its net sales for the seven most recent fiscal years ending January 31, 2011 to 2017. This ratio shows the potential impact of purchasing on a company's profits. Therefore, it is obvious that many successful businesses are treating purchasing as a key strategic process.

The primary goals of purchasing are to ensure uninterrupted flows of raw materials at the lowest total cost, to improve quality of the finished goods produced, and to maximize customer satisfaction. Purchasing can contribute to these objectives by actively seeking better materials and reliable suppliers, working closely with and exploiting the expertise of strategic suppliers to improve the quality of raw materials, and involving suppliers and purchasing personnel in product design and development efforts. Purchasing is the crucial link between the sources of supply and the organization itself, with support coming from overlapping activities to enhance manufacturability for both the customer and the supplier. The involvement of purchasing and strategic suppliers in concurrent engineering activities is essential for selecting components and raw materials that ensure that requisite quality is designed into the product and to aid in collapsing design-to-production cycle time.

Table 2.1	Cost of Materials as a Percent of the Value of Shipments						
	VALUE OF SHIPMENTS	COST OF MATERIALS		MANUFACTURE		CAPITAL EXPENDITURES	
YEAR	$ MILLIONS	$ MILLIONS	%	$ MILLIONS	%	$ MILLIONS	%
2015	$5,546,998	$3,117,562	56.2%	$2,430,098	43.8%	$175,388	3.2%
2014	$5,880,890	$3,486,762	59.3%	$2,400,063	40.8%	$173,310	2.9%
2013	$5,846,768	$3,456,983	59.1%	$2,398,392	41.0%	$172,992	3.0%
2012	$5,704,167	$3,384,339	59.3%	$2,348,112	41.2%	$166,458	2.9%
2011	$5,498,599	$3,240,477	58.9%	$2,295,220	41.7%	$146,652	2.7%
2010	$4,916,647	$2,763,128	56.2%	$2,185,326	44.4%	$127,952	2.6%
2009	$4,436,196	$2,438,427	55.0%	$1,978,017	44.6%	$130,081	2.9%
2008	$5,486,266	$3,213,708	58.6%	$2,274,367	41.5%	$168,505	3.1%
2007	$5,338,307	$2,975,906	55.7%	$2,390,643	44.8%	$159,422	3.0%
2006	$5,015,553	$2,752,904	54.9%	$2,285,929	45.6%	$135,801	2.7%
2005	$4,742,077	$2,557,601	53.9%	$2,210,349	46.6%	$128,292	2.7%
2004	$4,308,971	$2,283,144	53.0%	$2,041,434	47.4%	$113,793	2.6%
2003	$4,015,387	$2,095,279	52.2%	$1,923,415	47.9%	$112,176	2.8%
2002	$3,914,719	$2,022,158	51.7%	$1,889,291	48.3%	$123,067	3.1%
2001	$3,967,698	$2,105,338	53.1%	$1,850,709	46.6%	$142,985	3.6%
2000	$4,208,582	$2,245,839	53.4%	$1,973,622	46.9%	$154,479	3.7%
1999	$4,031,885	$2,084,316	51.7%	$1,954,498	48.5%	$150,325	3.7%
1998	$3,899,810	$2,018,055	51.7%	$1,891,266	48.5%	$152,708	3.9%
1997	$3,834,701	$2,015,425	52.6%	$1,825,688	47.6%	$151,510	4.0%
1996	$3,715,428	$1,975,362	53.2%	$1,749,662	47.1%	$146,468	3.9%
1995	$3,594,360	$1,897,571	52.8%	$1,711,442	47.6%	$134,318	3.7%
1994	$3,348,019	$1,752,735	52.4%	$1,605,980	48.0%	$118,665	3.5%
1993	$3,127,620	$1,647,493	52.7%	$1,483,054	47.4%	$108,629	3.5%
1992	$3,004,723	$1,571,774	52.3%	$1,424,700	47.4%	$110,644	3.7%
1991	$2,878,165	$1,531,221	53.2%	$1,341,386	46.6%	$103,153	3.6%

Source: Annual Survey of Manufactures, 1991–2015 U.S. Census Bureau.

The Financial Significance of Supply Management

Undoubtedly, purchasing has become more global and gained strategic corporate focus over the last two decades. The increasing use of outsourcing (discussed later in the chapter) of noncore activities has further elevated the role of purchasing in a firm. In addition to affecting the competitiveness of a firm, purchasing also directly affects profitability. Next, we discuss the financial significance of purchasing on a firm.

Profit-Leverage Effect

Purchase spend is the money a firm spends on goods and services. The **profit-leverage effect** of purchasing measures the impact of a change in purchase spend on a firm's profit before taxes, assuming gross sales and other expenses remain unchanged. The measure is commonly used to demonstrate that a decrease in purchase spend directly increases profits before taxes by the same amount. However, it is important to remember that a decrease in purchase spend must be achieved through better purchasing strategy, thus enabling the firm to acquire materials of similar or better quality and yield at a lower total acquisition cost. The profit-leverage effect example in Table 2.2 shows that if a firm manages to lower its purchase spend on materials by $20,000, profits before taxes increase by $20,000 because purchase spend on materials is a part of the cost of goods sold. Indeed, the reduction in purchase spend has an identical impact on gross profits. Table 2.2 shows that gross profits also increased by $20,000 from $500,000 to $520,000. The direct effect of purchasing on a firm's profitability is a key reason that drives business executives to continually refine the sourcing function. Boosting sales and cutting costs are not the only ways to increase profits. An often overlooked but very efficient means of improving profits is through smarter purchasing.

Return on Assets Effect

Return on assets (ROA) is a financial ratio of a firm's net income in relation to its total assets. The ratio is also referred to as **return on investment** (ROI). In the context of accounting, total assets consist of current and fixed assets. Current assets include cash, accounts receivable, and inventory, whereas fixed assets include equipment, buildings, and real estate. ROA indicates how efficiently management is using its total assets to generate profits. A high ROA suggests that management is capable of generating large profits with relatively small investments. The formula for ROA is:

$$\text{ROA} = \frac{\text{Net income}}{\text{Total assets}}$$

Assuming the firm in Table 2.2 has total assets of $500,000, its ROA is then 10 percent ($50,000 ÷ $500,000). If the firm reduces its purchase spend on materials by $20,000 through a more effective purchasing strategy, its ROA then increases to 14 percent ($70,000 ÷ $500,000). The $20,000 reduction in purchase spend on materials is also likely to result in a lower raw material inventory (and thus lower total assets). However, the effect on ROA from this potential change in inventory is difficult to quantify because the ratio of a firm's raw material inventory to its total assets and the ratio of raw materials cost to its total cost of goods sold vary widely depending on the firm and industry.

Inventory Turnover Effect

Inventory turnover shows how many times a firm's inventory is utilized and replaced over an accounting period, such as a year. There are numerous ways to compute the inventory turnover ratio, but a widely used formula is the ratio of the cost of goods sold to average inventory at cost. To compute a monthly ratio, it is a common practice to use the mean of beginning and ending monthly inventory as the average inventory. This monthly

Table 2.2	Profit-Leverage Effect	SIMPLIFIED PROFIT & LOSS STATEMENT	REDUCE MATERIAL COSTS BY $20,000
Gross Sales/Net Revenue		$1,000,000	$1,000,000
– Cost of Goods Sold (Materials + Manufacturing Cost)		$500,000	$480,000
Gross Profits		$500,000	$520,000
– General & Administrative Expenses (45% of Gross Sales)		$450,000	$450,000
Profits Before Taxes		$50,000	$70,000

inventory average is a good measure for computing the annual inventory turnover ratio. In general, low inventory turnover indicates poor sales, overstocking, and/or obsolete inventories. A firm must compare its inventory turnover ratio against the industry standard to judge how well the company is doing compared to competitors. We will discuss some company-specific examples of inventory turnover ratios in Chapter 7. Through a more effective sourcing strategy, purchasing can help to reduce inventory investment, and thus improve the firm's inventory turnover. Several inventory turnover formulas are shown here:

$$\text{Inventory turnover ratio} = \frac{\text{Cost of goods sold}}{\text{Average inventory}}$$

$$\text{Monthly inventor turnover ratio} = \frac{\text{Cost of goods sold for the month}}{(\text{Beginning inventory} + \text{Ending inventory})/2}$$

$$\text{Annual inventory turnover ratio} = \frac{\text{Cost of goods sold for the year}}{\text{Average monthly inventory}}$$

Consider a hypothetical example in which a firm has an ending inventory of $125,000 as of December 31, 2016 and the following accounting information. The monthly and annual inventory turnover ratios can be computed as follows:

MONTH (2017)	ENDING INVENTORY	COST OF GOODS SOLD	MONTHLY INVENTORY TURNOVER RATIO
January	$52,000	$85,000	$\frac{\$85,000}{(\$125,000 + \$52,000)/2} = 0.96$
February	$88,000	$1,250,000	$\frac{\$1,250,000}{(\$52,000 + \$88,000)/2} = 17.86$
March	$85,000	$950,000	$\frac{\$950,000}{(\$88,000 + \$85,000)/2} = 10.98$
April	$55,000	$750,000	$\frac{\$750,000}{(\$85,000 + \$55,000)/2} = 10.71$
May	$75,000	$950,000	$\frac{\$950,000}{(\$55,000 + \$75,000)/2} = 14.62$
June	$85,000	$850,000	$\frac{\$850,000}{(\$75,000 + \$85,000)/2} = 10.63$
July	$156,000	$555,000	$\frac{\$555,000}{(\$85,000 + \$156,000)/2} = 4.61$
August	$215,000	$1,325,000	$\frac{\$1,325,000}{(\$156,000 + \$215,000)/2} = 7.14$
September	$65,000	$985,000	$\frac{\$985,000}{(\$215,000 + \$65,000)/2} = 7.04$

MONTH (2017)	ENDING INVENTORY	COST OF GOODS SOLD	MONTHLY INVENTORY TURNOVER RATIO
October	$100,000	$850,000	$\dfrac{\$850,000}{(\$65,000 + \$100,000)/2} = 10.30$
November	$165,000	$1,250,000	$\dfrac{\$1,250,000}{(\$100,000 + \$165,000)/2} = 9.43$
December	$105,000	$1,050,000	$\dfrac{\$1,050,000}{(\$165,000 + \$105,000)/2} = 7.78$

Total cost of goods sold for the year = $85,000 + $1,250,000 + $950,000 + $750,000 + $950,000 + $850,000 + $555,000 + $1,325,000 + $985,000 + $850,000 + $1,250,000 + $1,050,000 = $10,850,000

Average monthly inventory = [($125,000 + $52,000)/2 + ($52,000 + $88,000)/2 + ($88,000 + $85,000)/2 + ($85,000 + $55,000)/2 + ($55,000 + $75,000)/2 + ($75,000 + $85,000)/2 + ($85,000 + $156,000)/2 + ($156,000 + $215,000)/2 + ($215,000 + $65,000)/2 + ($65,000 + $100,000)/2 + ($100,000 + $165,000)/2 + ($165,000 + $105,000)/2]/12 = $104,667

Thus, the annual inventory turnover ratio for 2017 is $\dfrac{\$10,850,000}{\$104,667} = 103.66$.

THE PURCHASING PROCESS

The traditional purchasing process is a manual, paper-based system. However, with the advent of information technology and the Internet, many companies are moving toward a more automated, electronic-based system. The goal of a proper purchasing system is to ensure the efficient transmission of information from the users to the purchasing personnel and, ultimately, to the suppliers. Once the information is transmitted to the appropriate suppliers, the system must also ensure the efficient flows of the purchased materials from the suppliers to the users and the flow of invoices from the suppliers to the accounting department. Finally, the system must have adequate operational or **internal control** to prevent abuse of purchasing funds. For example, purchase orders (POs) should be prenumbered and issued in duplicate, and buyers should not be authorized to pay invoices. Prenumbered purchase orders make it easier to trace any missing or unaccounted-for purchase orders. A duplicate purchase order should be issued to the accounting department for internal control purposes and to inform the department of a future payment or commitment of resources. The authority to approve payments should be different from the authority to approve purchase orders.

The Manual Purchasing System

Figure 2.1 shows a simplified traditional manual purchasing system. While some manual systems may look slightly different than what is shown in Figure 2.1, it captures the essential elements of a good purchasing system that is easy to use and yet exerts adequate internal control of the process. The manual purchasing system is slow and prone to errors due to duplication of data entries during various stages of the purchasing process. For example, similar information on the material requisition, such as the product description, is reproduced on the purchase order.

Figure 2.1	Traditional Manual Purchasing System

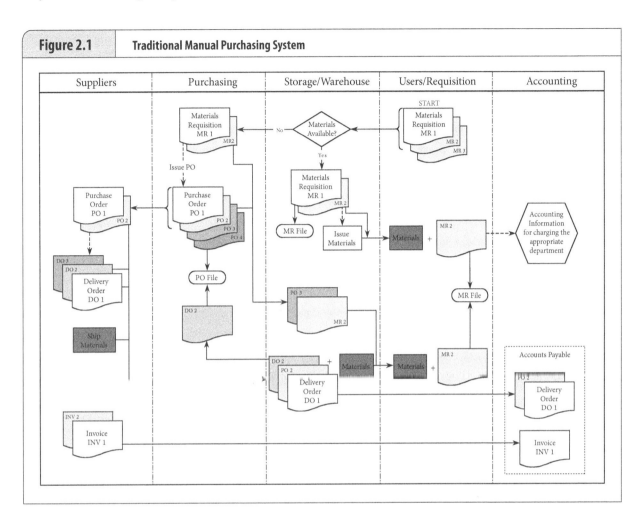

The Material Requisition

The purchasing process starts when the material user initiates a request for material by issuing a **material requisition** (MR) in duplicate. A **purchase requisition**, instead of a material requisition, is used in some firms. The product, quantity, and delivery due date are clearly described on the material requisition. The number of duplicates issued depends on the internal control system of the organization. Generally, the issuer retains a copy and the warehouse receives the original plus a duplicate. The duplicate accompanies the material as it moves from the warehouse to the user. This copy also provides the essential information for the accounting department to charge the appropriate user or department for the material.

While most requisitions are transmitted through the generic material requisition, a **traveling requisition** is used for materials and standard parts that are requested on a recurring basis. Instead of describing the product on the generic material requisition, the product description and other pertinent information, such as delivery lead time and lot size, are preprinted on the traveling requisition. When a resupply is needed, the user simply enters the quantity and date needed and submits it to the warehouse. Once the resupply information is recorded, the traveling requisition is returned to the user for future requests.

Figure 2.2	Sample Purchase Requisition

BabiHutan Inc.
523 Las Vegas Blvd
Las Vegas, NV 89154
Tel: 702-123-4567

Purchase Requisition

RX #: 6334554

Requestor: _____   Department: _____

Phone #: _____   Account #: _____   Date: _____

Suggested Vendor: _____

Address: _____   Phone: _____

No.	Description	Price	Quantity

Special instructions: _____
_____
_____

Approval Authority: _____   Date: _____

Distribution: White-Purchasing/Yellow-Purchasing (return to requestor)/Pink-Department

Planned order releases from the material requirements planning (MRP) system or a bill of materials (BOM) can also be used to release requisitions or to place orders directly with the suppliers. This approach is suitable for firms that use the same components to make standard goods over a relatively long period of time.

If the requested material is available in the warehouse, the material is issued to the user without going through the purchasing department. Otherwise, the requisition is assigned to a buyer who is responsible for the material. If there is a better substitute for the material, purchasing recommends and works with the user to explore whether it is a viable substitute. However, purchasing personnel should not change the specifications of the materials or parts without the user's knowledge and agreement. While it is the right and responsibility of purchasing personnel to select the appropriate supplier, the user in many cases may suggest a list of potential suppliers when requesting new material. A sample material requisition is shown in Figure 2.2.

The Request for Quotation and the Request for Proposal

If the material is not available in the warehouse, the material requisition is routed to the purchasing department. If there is no current supplier for the item, the buyer must identify a pool of qualified suppliers and issue a **request for quotation** (RFQ). A **request for proposal** (RFP) may be issued instead for a complicated and highly technical component part, especially if the complete specification of the part is unknown. An RFP allows suppliers to propose new material and technology, thus enabling the firm to exploit the technology and expertise of suppliers.

A growing trend among firms that practice supply chain management is **supplier development**. When there is a lack of suitable suppliers, firms may assist existing or new suppliers to improve their processing capabilities, quality, delivery, and cost performance by providing the needed technical and financial assistance. Developing suppliers in this manner allows firms to focus more on core competencies, while **outsourcing** noncore activities to suppliers.

The Purchase Order

When a suitable supplier is identified, or a qualified supplier is on file, the buyer issues a **purchase order** (PO) in duplicate to the selected supplier. Generally, the original purchase order and a duplicate are sent to the supplier. An important feature of the purchase order is the terms and conditions of the purchase, which is typically preprinted on the back. The purchase order is the buyer's offer and becomes a legally binding contract when accepted by the supplier. Therefore, firms should require the supplier to acknowledge and return a copy of the purchase order to indicate acceptance of the order. A sample purchase order is shown in Figure 2.3.

The supplier may offer the goods at its own terms and conditions, especially if it is the sole producer or holds the patent to the product. Then a supplier's **sales order** will be used. The sales order is the supplier's offer and becomes a legally binding contract when accepted by the buyer.

Once an order is accepted, purchasing personnel need to ensure on-time delivery of the purchased material by using a **follow-up** or by **expediting** the order. A follow-up is considered a proactive approach to prevent late delivery, whereas expediting is considered a reactive approach that is used to speed up an overdue shipment.

The **Uniform Commercial Code** (UCC) governs the purchase and sale of goods in the United States, except in the state of Louisiana. Louisiana has a legal system that is based on the Napoleonic Code.

Electronic Procurement Systems (e-Procurement)

Electronic data interchange (EDI) was developed in the 1970s to improve the purchasing process. However, its proprietary nature required significant up-front investments. The rapid advent of information technology in the 1990s spurred the growth of more flexible Internet-based e-procurement systems. Many e-commerce service providers surfaced in the late 1990s, but many are no longer in business after the dot-com bubble burst in 2000. Today, many well-managed e-commerce firms are thriving as users realize the benefits of their services.

Figure 2.4 describes the Internet-based electronic purchasing system used by the University of Nevada, Las Vegas. The database that drives the e-procurement system resides on a server, but the software is installed on workstations. The e-procurement system is

Figure 2.3	Sample Purchase Order

BabiHutan Inc.
523 Las Vegas Blvd
Las Vegas, NV 89154
Tel: 702-123-4567

Purchase Order

PO#: 885729

Date: _____

Vendor:

Required Delivery Date: _____
Payment Terms: _____
FOB Terms: _____
Price Agreement No.: _____

Ship To:

Include PO # in all packages, invoice,
shipping papers & correspondence.
Mail original and one copy of invoice
attached to second copy of Purchase
Order for payment.

No.	Description	Unit Price	Quantity	Total Price
			Total $ of Order	

Buyer: _____   Phone: _____ Fax: _____

Buyer Signature: _____   Requisition No.: _____

SEE REVERSE FOR TERMS & CONDITIONS

Distribution: White-Vendor/Yellow-Vendor(return with invoice)/Pink & Blue-Purchasing/Green-Fixed Assets

also accessible via the Internet. The e-procurement system allows users to submit their purchase requisitions to the purchasing department electronically and enables buyers to transmit purchase orders to suppliers over the Internet, fax, e-mail, or snail mail.

The material user initiates the e-procurement process by entering a purchase request and other pertinent information, such as quantity and date needed, into the purchase requisition module. The material user may recommend suppliers or potential sources for the requisition. Next, the purchase requisition is approved and transmitted electronically to a buyer at the purchasing department. The buyer reviews the purchase requisition for accuracy and appropriate approval level and determines the value of the requisition. If the amount is below $25,000, the buyer extracts details of the purchase requisition stored in the database to prepare an electronic purchase order. Next, the buyer assigns a preferred supplier from the e-procurement database, or uses a supplier from the purchase requisition. If the amount of the purchase requisition is between $25,000 and $50,000, two formal

| Figure 2.4 | Internet-Based Electronic Purchasing System |

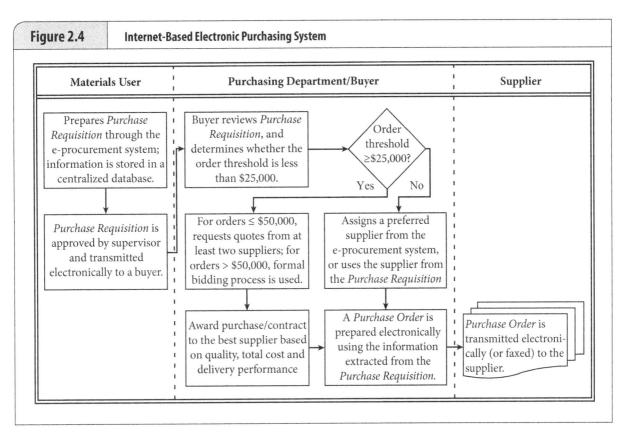

requests for quotation are needed before a purchase order can be released. However, if the amount exceeds $50,000, a supplier must be chosen by means of a formal bidding process. At the specified time and place, bids are opened publicly. The purchase is awarded to the lowest responsible bidder whose bid conforms to all requirements of the solicitation. Then an electronic purchase order (or formal contract for purchase of services) is prepared and transmitted (or mailed) to the selected supplier.

Advantages of the e-Procurement System

The traditional manual purchasing system is a tedious and labor-intensive task of issuing material requisitions and purchase orders. Although EDI solved some of these problems, its proprietary nature requires a high start-up cost, making it inaccessible to small firms with limited budgets. E-procurement systems have changed the infrastructure requirement, making it readily affordable to most firms. Benefits derived from implementing an e-procurement system include:

1. *Time savings*: E-procurement is more efficient when (a) selecting and maintaining a list of potential suppliers, (b) processing requests for quotation and purchase orders, and (c) making repeat purchases. Individual buyers can create preferred supplier lists for each category of products and services. For example, a small tools supplier group may consist of fifteen suppliers. The buyer uses this group to purchase small tools. The list can be edited and shared with all buyers in the firm. Supplier performance data can be updated quickly and made available online in real time. Collecting, sorting, reviewing, and comparing RFQs are labor-intensive and time-consuming processes. Using the manual purchasing system, a typical firm may have to sort and match hundreds of bids on a daily basis. E-procurement

eliminates these non-value-adding activities. Duplicate data entry on the purchase order is eliminated since the information can be extracted from the RFQ, originally entered by the user. Also, an e-procurement system minimizes the need for interdepartmental routing of paper purchase requisitions, streamlines the approval process, and automates purchase order issuance.

E-procurement systems can be programmed to handle automatic bidding of frequently ordered items on a fixed interval, such as daily or weekly—a commonly used practice. The ability to submit automatic bidding is invaluable for handling perishable goods, which must be ordered in small lot sizes, and other frequently purchased items where the specifications are known.

2. *Cost savings*: Buyers can handle more purchases, and the manual task of matching bids to purchase requisitions is reduced. Other cost savings include lower prices of goods and services (since more suppliers can be contacted), reduced inventory costs (due to the ability to purchase on a more frequent basis), use of fewer buyers, lower administrative costs, elimination of the need for preprinted purchase requisition forms, and faster order fulfillment.

3. *Accuracy*: The system eliminates double-key inputs—once by the material users and then once again by the buyers. The system also enhances the accuracy of communications between buyers and suppliers. More up-to-date information on suppliers, with goods and services readily available online, allows users to assess their options before preparing a purchase requisition.

4. *Real-time use*: Buyers have real-time access to the purchase requisition once it is prepared. Once the purchase requisition is processed, the buyer can post the bid instantly, instead of waiting to contact all the suppliers individually to alert them of the bids. The system enables buyers to initiate bids and suppliers to respond in real time on a 24/7 basis.

5. *Mobility*: The buyer can submit, process, and check the status of bids, as well as communicate with suppliers regardless of the buyer's geographical location and time of day. Thus, the e-procurement system is highly flexible.

6. *Trackability*: The e-procurement system allows submitters and buyers to track each purchase requisition electronically through the process—from submission, to approval, and finally conversion to a purchase order. Moreover, audit trails can be maintained for all transactions in electronic form. Tracing an electronic bid and transaction is much easier and faster than tracking paper trails. Buyers and suppliers can ask for additional information online, leave comments, or indicate whether they are interested in bidding.

7. *Management benefits*: The system can be designed to store important supplier information, including whether suppliers are minority or locally owned, thus allowing the buyers to support such businesses. Summary statistics and supplier performance reports can be generated for management to review and utilize for future planning.

8. *Supplier benefits*: Benefits include lower barriers to entry and transaction costs, access to more buyers, and the ability to instantly adjust to market conditions, thus making e-procurement attractive to most suppliers.

Small-Value Purchase Orders

The administrative costs to process an order can be quite substantial. It has been estimated that the cost of placing an order using the manual purchasing system can be as high as $175.[6] The figure could be higher when we consider the salary of senior purchasing personnel and other indirect costs incurred by purchasing personnel. It is not uncommon to find that the cost to process a purchase order exceeds the total dollar value of the order itself. While *small dollar value* is a relative term depending on the size of the firm, $500 to $1,000 can be considered a reasonable cutoff point.

Small-value purchases, particularly in a manual purchasing system, should be minimized to ensure that buyers are not overburdened with trivial purchases that may prevent them from focusing on more crucial purchases. Due to the efficiency of the e-procurement system, buyers are less likely to be overburdened by small-value purchases. Nevertheless, all firms should have a system in place to handle small-value purchases. To control unnecessary administrative costs and reduce order cycle time, purchasing managers have various alternatives to deal with small-value purchases. Generally, the alternatives are used for purchases of office supplies and other indirect materials. Let us review the alternatives.

Procurement Credit Card/Corporate Purchasing Card

Procurement credit cards or **corporate purchasing cards** (P-cards) are credit cards with a predetermined credit limit, usually not more than $5,000 depending on the organization, issued to authorized personnel of the buying organization to make low-dollar purchases. It is not uncommon that in many companies, more than half of their purchases are less than $500. American Express, MasterCard, Visa, and Diners Club are commonly used for this purpose. The P-card allows the material user to purchase the material directly from the supplier without going through purchasing. Usually, the user must purchase the needed materials from a list of authorized suppliers. Procurement credit cards have gained popularity over the last two decades, especially among government agencies, because of their ease of use and flexibility. In a 2012 P-card study, it was reported that P-card transactions for small-value purchases under $2,500 have exceeded paper checks since 2009.[7] A follow-up survey reported that P-card spending in North America has continued to grow from $196 billion in 2011 to $245 billion in 2013. The growth in the private sector (31 percent) slightly outpaced the public sector (29 percent). The average transaction size was $454, and the average monthly spend and number of monthly transactions per card were $2,767 and 6.1, respectively. P-card spending was predicted to increase to $318 billion by 2016, and $377 billion by 2018.[8]

When authorized, P-cards can also be used to pay for meals, lodging, and other traveling expenses, thus eliminating the need to process travel expenses in advance for the user. This type of P-card is commonly called **travel card**. At the end of the month, an itemized statement is sent to the purchasing department, the cardholder's department, or directly to the accounting department. Generally, the purchasing department is responsible for managing the overall program, but the individual unit is responsible for managing its cardholder accounts. To ensure appropriate internal control of the procurement credit card system, a supervisor should be assigned to review the monthly statement of each cardholder to prevent fraud. Cardholders should maintain proper supporting documents and records for each purchase.

Despite the success of the P-card program, there are unique challenges in expanding the program globally. P-card programs are more common in English-speaking regions, such as the United Kingdom, the United States, and Australia, and less common in France, Germany, and Italy, where automatic transfers are more common. In some Asian markets where employee turnover is high, employers are concerned about card fraud. Card-issuing banks may not have coverage in all countries to enable a corporation to expand its P-card program globally. There are also country-specific challenges. Germany, for instance, has complicated data protection laws, and new programs must be reviewed by each company's Workers Council. The same issues with data protection laws are also found in France, where direct debit is preferred. In Eastern Europe, the commercial card market is still in its infancy.[9]

Blanket or Open-End Purchase Orders

A **blanket purchase order** covers a variety of items and is negotiated for repeated supply over a fixed time period, such as quarterly or yearly. The subtle difference of an **open-end purchase order** is that additional items and expiration dates can be renegotiated. Price and estimated quantity for each item, as well as delivery terms and conditions, are usually negotiated and incorporated in the order. A variety of mechanisms, such as a **blanket order release** or production schedule, may be used to release a specific quantity against the order. Blanket or open-end purchase orders are suitable for buying MRO supplies and office supplies. At a fixed time interval, usually monthly, the supplier sends a detailed statement of all releases against the order to the buying firm for payment.

While blanket purchase orders are frequently used to handle small-value purchases, when used in conjunction with blanket order releases, cooperative supplier relationships, and single sourcing, blanket purchase orders are a formidable tool for handling the complex purchasing needs of a large, multidivision corporation.

Blank Check Purchase Orders

A **blank check purchase order** is a special purchase order with a signed blank check attached, usually at the bottom of the purchase order. Due to the potential for misuse, it is usually printed on the check that it is not valid for over a certain amount (usually $500 or $1,000). If the exact amount of the purchase is known, the buyer enters the amount on the check before passing it to the supplier. Otherwise, the supplier enters the amount due on the check and cashes it after the material is shipped. Nevertheless, purchasing managers are embracing the use of P-cards and phasing out blank check purchase orders.

Stockless Buying or System Contracting

Stockless buying or **system contracting** is an extension of the blanket purchase order. It requires the supplier to maintain a minimum inventory level to ensure that the required items are readily available for the buyer. It is stockless buying on the buyer's perspective because the burden of keeping the inventory is on the supplier. Some firms require suppliers to keep inventory at the buyer's facilities to minimize order cycle time.

Petty Cash

Petty cash is a small cash reserve maintained by a midlevel manager or clerk. Material users buy the needed materials and then claim the purchase against the petty cash by submitting the receipt to the petty cashier. A benefit of this system is that the exact reimbursement is supported by receipts. Nonetheless, petty cash is also being phased out in favor of P-cards.

Standardization and Simplification of Materials and Components

Where appropriate, purchasing should work with design, engineering, and operations to seek opportunities to standardize materials, components, and supplies to increase the usage of standardized items. For example, a car manufacturer could design different models of automobiles to use the same starter mechanism, thus increasing its usage and reducing storage space requirements while allowing for large quantity price discounts. This will also reduce the number of small-value purchases for less frequently used items.

Simplification refers to reduction of the number of components, supplies, or standard materials used in a product or process. For example, a computer manufacturer could integrate the video card directly onto the motherboard instead of using different video card modules for different models. Thus, simplification can further reduce the number of small-value purchases while reducing storage space requirements, as well as allowing for quantity purchase discounts.

Accumulating Small Orders to Create a Large Order

Numerous small orders can be accumulated and mixed into a large order, especially if the material request is not urgent. Otherwise, purchasing can simply increase the order quantity if the ordering cost exceeds the inventory holding cost. Larger orders also reduce the purchase price and unit transportation cost.

Using a Fixed Order Interval for a Specific Category of Materials or Supplies

Another effective way to control small orders is to group materials and supplies into categories and then set fixed order intervals for each category. Order intervals can be set to biweekly or monthly depending on usage. Instead of requesting individual materials or supplies, users request the appropriate quantity of each item in the category on a single requisition to be purchased from a supplier. This increases the dollar value and decreases the number of small orders.

SOURCING DECISIONS: THE MAKE-OR-BUY DECISION

The term **outsourcing** is commonly used to refer to buying materials or components from suppliers instead of making them in-house. In recent years, the trend has been moving toward outsourcing combined with the creation of supply chain relationships to replace the practice of backward or forward vertical integration. **Backward vertical integration** refers to acquiring upstream suppliers, whereas **forward vertical integration** refers to acquiring downstream customers. For example, an end-product manufacturer acquiring a supplier's operations that supplied component parts is an example of backward integration. Acquiring a distributor or other outbound logistics providers would be an example of forward integration.

The **make or buy decision** is a strategic one that can impact an organization's competitive position. It is obvious that most organizations buy their MRO and office supplies rather than make the items themselves. Similarly, seafood restaurants usually buy their fresh seafood from fish markets. However, the decision on whether to make or buy technically advanced engineering parts that impact the firm's competitive position is a complex one. For example, do you think the Honda Motor Company would rather make or buy the engines used for its automobile manufacturing? Why?

Traditionally, cost has been the major driver when making sourcing decisions. However, organizations today focus more on the strategic impact of the sourcing decision on the firm's competitive advantage. For example, the Honda Motor Company would not outsource the making of its engines because it considers engines to be a vital part of its automobiles' performance and reputation. However, Honda may outsource the production of brake rotors to a high-quality, low-cost supplier that specializes in brake rotors. Generally, firms outsource noncore activities while focusing on core competencies. Finally, the make-or-buy decision is not an exclusive either-or option. Firms can always choose to make some components or services in-house while buying the rest from suppliers.

Reasons for Buying or Outsourcing

Organizations buy or outsource materials, components, and/or services from suppliers for many reasons. Let us review these now:

1. *Cost advantage*: For many firms, cost is an important reason for outsourcing, especially for supplies and components that are nonvital to the organization's operations

SCM Profile — Keeping up with the Curve

Supply management professionals are constantly debating whether to outsource or insource complex information technologies, especially when legacy systems are unable to handle higher-level, data analytic functions, or to provide sufficient data storage. Information technology is evolving so rapidly that it is difficult for organizations to stay ahead of the curve. Outsourcing has the advantage of economies of scale of a third-party provider, but there are other potential impacts on the business that must be considered.

The primary advantage of outsourcing information technology is that third-party providers can provide a specialized process and low cost labor without the huge initial capital outlay. Instead of investing heavily in infrastructure and application software, buying firms can operationalize information technology and treat it as variable cost and pay for what they use. The provider's capability and expertise can provide a higher quality of service and allow the buying firm to focus on its business processes and core competencies. Moreover, third-party providers update their software regularly to ensure that the systems are up to date. For example, the procure-to-pay technology that integrates the purchasing department with the accounts payable department provides many small businesses with capabilities that they previously couldn't afford.

However, supply managers must analyze the cost, benefits, and risks of outsourcing information technology. A major risk of outsourcing information technology is the loss of control. A firm risks exposing confidential data to the third-party provider and competitors, even if the data are protected under a non-disclosure agreement. Another risk is that it may be difficult to coordinate operations with the third-party provider. An outsourced service tends to be more standardized than the customized in-house systems that are more aligned to the firm's operations.

When analyzing risk, supply managers should also evaluate whether the risk is real or perceived. It is not uncommon that the fear of change management has caused managers to make suboptimal decisions. If aerospace and defense companies are putting their data in the cloud, why should traditional manufacturing firms or service organizations worry about data security?

To make outsourcing a viable business strategy, supply managers should adopt a three-level framework that offers visibility, analytical tools, and execution capabilities to determine the needs and information technologies to outsource. First, outsourced software should have the visibility capability to pool information from suppliers, customers, and ERP systems into one place for data analysis. Second, outsourced software should have the appropriate analytical tools to analyze data such as cost analysis, sales forecast, and scenario modeling. Third, outsourced software should have the capability to execute corrective actions if something goes wrong.[10]

and competitive advantage. This is usually true for standardized or generic supplies and materials for which suppliers may have the advantage of **economies of scale** because they supply large quantities of the same item to multiple users. In most outsourcing cases, the quantity needed is so small that it does not justify the investment in capital equipment to make the item. Some foreign suppliers may also offer a cost advantage because of lower labor and/or materials costs.

2. *Insufficient capacity*: A firm may be running at or near capacity, making it unable to produce the components in-house. This can happen when demand grows faster than anticipated or when expansion strategies fail to meet demand. The firm buys parts or components to free up capacity in the short term to focus on vital operations. Firms may even subcontract vital components and/or operations under very strict terms and conditions in order to meet demand. When managed properly, **subcontracting** instead of buying is a more effective means to expand short-term capacity because the buying firm can exert better control over the manufacturing process and other requirements of the components or end products.

3. *Lack of expertise*: The firm may not have the necessary technology and expertise to manufacture the item. Maintaining long-term technological and economic viability for noncore activities may be affecting the firm's ability to focus on core competencies. Suppliers may hold the patent to the process or product in question, thus precluding the make option, or the firm may not be able to meet environmental and safety standards to manufacture the item.

4. *Quality*: Purchased components may be superior in quality because suppliers have better technologies, processes, skilled labor, and the advantage of economies of scale. Suppliers' superior quality may help firms stay on top of product and process technologies, especially in high-technology industries with rapid innovation and short product life cycles.

Reasons for Making

An organization also makes its own materials, components, services, and/or equipment in-house for many reasons. Let us briefly review them:

1. *Protect proprietary technology*: A major reason for the make option is to protect proprietary technology. A firm may have developed an equipment, product, or process that needs to be protected for the sake of competitive advantage. Firms may choose not to reveal the technology by asking suppliers to make it, even if it is patented. An advantage of not revealing the technology is to be able to surprise competitors and bring new products to market ahead of competition, allowing the firm to charge a price premium.

2. *No competent supplier*: If existing suppliers do not have the technology or capability to produce a component, the firm may be forced to make an item in-house, at least for the short term. The firm may use supplier development strategies to work with a new or existing supplier to produce the component in the future as a long-term strategy.

3. *Better quality control*: If the firm is capable, the make option allows for the most direct control over the design, manufacturing process, labor, and other inputs to ensure that high-quality components are built. The firm may be so experienced and efficient in manufacturing the component that suppliers are unable to meet its exact specifications and requirements. On the other hand, suppliers may have better technologies and processes to produce better-quality components. Thus, the sourcing option ensuring a higher quality level is a debatable question and must be investigated thoroughly.

4. *Use existing idle capacity*: A short-term solution for a firm with excess idle capacity is to use the excess capacity to make some of its components. This strategy is valuable for firms that produce seasonal products. It avoids layoff of skilled workers and, when business picks up, the capacity is readily available to meet demand.

5. *Control of lead time, transportation, and warehousing costs*: The make option provides better control of lead time and logistical costs since management controls all phases of the design, manufacturing, and delivery processes. Although raw materials may have to be transported, finished goods can be produced near the point of use, for instance, to minimize holding cost.

6. *Lower cost*: If technology, capacity, and managerial and labor skills are available, the make option may be more economical if large quantities of the component are needed on a continuing basis. Although the make option has a higher fixed cost due to initial capital investment, it has a lower variable cost per unit due to the lack of supplier profits.

Make-or-Buy Break-Even Analysis

The current sourcing trend is to buy equipment, materials, and services unless self-manufacture provides a major benefit such as protecting proprietary technologies, achieving superior characteristics, or ensuring adequate supplies. However, buying or outsourcing has its own shortcomings, such as loss of control and exposure to supplier risks. While cost is rarely the sole criterion in strategic sourcing decisions, **break-even analysis** is a handy tool for computing the cost-effectiveness of sourcing decisions when cost is the most important criterion. Several assumptions underlie the analysis: (1) all costs involved can be classified as either fixed or variable cost, (2) fixed cost remains the same within the range of analysis, (3) a linear variable cost relationship exists, (4) fixed cost of the make option is higher because of initial capital investment in equipment, and (5) variable cost of the buy option is higher due to supplier profits.

Consider a hypothetical situation (shown below) in which a firm has the option to make or buy a part. Its annual requirement is 15,000 units. A supplier is able to supply the part at $7 per unit. The firm estimates that it costs $500 to prepare the contract with the supplier. To make the part, the firm must invest $25,000 in equipment, and the firm estimates that it costs $5 per unit to make the part.

COSTS	MAKE OPTION	BUY OPTION
Fixed Cost	$25,000	$500
Variable Cost	$5	$7
Annual Requirement = 15,000 units		

Break-even Point

The break-even point, Q, is found by setting the total cost of the two options equal and solving for Q (see Figure 2.5):

Total Cost to Make	= Total Cost to Buy
$\Rightarrow$ \$25,000 + \$5Q	= \$500 + \$7Q
$\Rightarrow$ 7Q – 5Q	= 25,000 – 500
$\Rightarrow$ 2Q	= 24,500 units
$\Rightarrow$ Break-even point, Q	= 12,250 units

The total cost for both options at the break-even point is:

$$TC_{BE} = \$25,000 + (\$5 \times 12,250) = \$86,250$$

For the annual requirement of 15,000 units:

The total cost for the make option is:

$$TC_{Make} = \$25,000 + (\$5 \times 15,000) = \$100,000$$

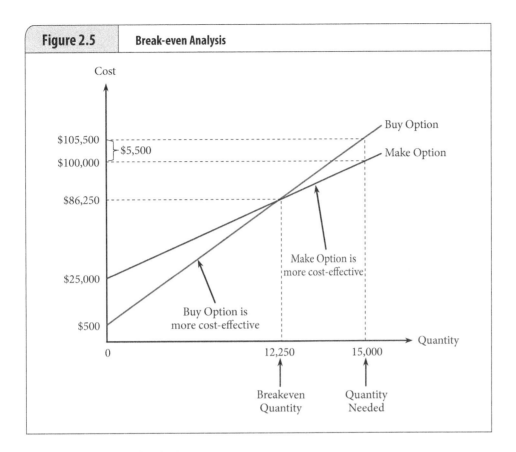

Figure 2.5   Break-even Analysis

The total cost for the buy option is:

$$TC_{Buy} = \$500 + (\$7 \times 15,000) = \$105,500$$

The cost difference is:

$$TC_{Buy} - TC_{Make} = \$105,500 - \$100,000 = \$5,500$$

The analysis shows that the break-even point is 12,250 units. The total cost at the break-even point is $86,250. If the requirement is less than 12,250 units, it is cheaper to buy. It is cheaper to make the part if the firm needs more than 12,250 units. With small purchase requirements (less than 12,250 units), the low fixed cost of the buy option makes it attractive. With higher purchase requirements (greater than 12,250 units), the low variable cost of the make option makes it more attractive. The analysis shows that the firm should make the item since the quantity is large enough to warrant the capital investment.

ROLES OF THE SUPPLY BASE

The **supply base** or **supplier base** refers to the list of suppliers that a firm uses to acquire its materials, services, supplies, and equipment. Firms engaging in supply chain management emphasize long-term strategic supplier alliances by reducing the variety of purchased items and consolidating volume into one or fewer suppliers, resulting in a smaller supply base. For example, both Xerox and Chrysler reduced their supply bases by about 90 percent in the 1980s. Similarly, Delphi Automotive, the world's largest auto parts supplier, cut its global supply base by about 75 percent in the 2000s.[11] An effective supply base that enhances a firm's competitive advantage is critical to its success.

Savvy purchasing managers develop a sound supply base to support the firm's overall business and supply chain strategies, based on an expanded role for suppliers. It is thus vital to understand the strategic role of suppliers.

Besides supplying the obvious purchased items, key or preferred suppliers also supply:

1. Product and process technology and expertise to support the buyer's operations, particularly in new product design and value analysis;

2. Information on the latest trends in materials, processes, or designs;

3. Information on the supply market, such as shortages, price increases, or political situations that may threaten supplies of vital materials;

4. Capacity for meeting unexpected demand; and

5. Cost efficiency due to economies of scale, since the supplier is likely to produce the same item for multiple buyers.

When developing the supply chain, preferred suppliers are developed to provide services to the firm. Supply base plays an important role in the success of the supply chain.

SUPPLIER SELECTION

The decision to select a supplier for office supplies or other noncritical materials is likely to be an easy one. However, the process of selecting a group of competent suppliers for important materials, which can potentially impact the firm's competitive advantage, is a complex one and should be based on multiple criteria. In addition to cost and delivery performance, firms should also consider how suppliers can contribute to product and process technology. Factors that firms should consider while selecting suppliers include:

1. *Process and product technologies*: Suppliers should have competent process technologies to produce superior products at a reasonable cost to enhance the buyer's competitive edge.

2. *Willingness to share technologies and information*: With the current trend that favors outsourcing to exploit suppliers' capabilities and to focus on core competencies, it is vital that firms seek suppliers that are willing to share their technologies and information. Suppliers can assist in new product design and development through **early supplier involvement** (ESI) to ensure cost-effective design choices, develop alternative conceptual solutions, select the best components and technologies, and help in design assessment. By increasing the involvement of the supplier in the design process, the buyer is free to focus more attention on core competencies.

3. *Quality*: Quality levels of the purchased item should be a very important factor in supplier selection. Product quality should be high and consistent since it can directly affect the quality of the finished goods.

4. *Cost*: While the unit cost of an item is not typically the sole criterion in supplier selection, total cost of ownership is an important factor. **Total cost of ownership** or **total cost of acquisition** includes the unit cost of the item, payment terms, cash discount, ordering cost, carrying cost, logistical costs, maintenance costs, and other more qualitative costs that may not be easy to assess. An example of a total cost of ownership analysis is provided in the following section. The total cost analysis demonstrates how other costs besides the unit cost can affect purchase decisions.

5. *Reliability*: Aside from a reliable product quality level, reliability can refer to other supplier characteristics. For example, is the supplier financially stable? Otherwise, it may not be able to invest in research and development or stay in business. Is the supplier's delivery lead time reliable? Otherwise, production may have to be interrupted due to a shortage of material.

6. *Order system and cycle time*: How easy to use is a supplier's ordering system, and what is the normal order cycle time? Placing orders with a supplier should be easy, quick, and effective. Delivery lead time should be short, so that small lot sizes can be ordered on a frequent basis to reduce inventory holding costs.

7. *Capacity*: The firm should also consider whether the supplier has the capacity to fill orders to meet requirements and the ability to fill large orders if needed.

8. *Communication capability*: Suppliers should possess a communication capability that facilitates communication between the parties.

9. *Location*: Geographical location is another important factor in supplier selection, as it impacts delivery lead time, transportation, and logistical costs. Some firms require their suppliers to be located within a certain distance from their facilities.

10. *Service*: Suppliers must be able to back up their products by providing good services when needed. For example, when product information or warranty service is needed, suppliers must respond on a timely basis.

There are numerous other factors—some strategic, others tactical—that a firm must consider when choosing suppliers. The days of using competitive bidding to identify the cheapest supplier for strategic items are long gone. The ability to select competent strategic suppliers directly affects a firm's competitive success. Strategic suppliers are trusted partners and become an integral part of the firm's design and production efforts.

A tiered supply chain model is widely used in the aerospace, automotive, and computer industries where the finished goods consist of many complex subassemblies that must comply with stringent quality standard and complex manufacturing process. **Original equipment manufacturers** (OEM) are the companies that make the final products. **Tier-1** suppliers provide parts or services directly to the OEM; **Tier-2** suppliers provide their outputs to Tier-1 suppliers, but not directly to the OEM; and **Tier-3 suppliers** sell their outputs to Tier-2 suppliers.

The Total Cost of Ownership Concept

The total cost of ownership concept extends the traditional break-even analysis beyond considering only the original purchase cost and capital equipment cost; other qualitative and quantitative factors, including freight and inventory costs, tooling, tariffs and duties, currency exchange fees, payment terms, maintenance, and nonperformance costs should be considered. Firms can use a total cost analysis to select the most cost-effective supplier or as a negotiation tool to inform suppliers regarding areas where they need to improve. Example 2.1 demonstrates a total cost of ownership analysis.

HOW MANY SUPPLIERS TO USE

The issue of how many suppliers to use for each purchased item is a complex one. While numerous references propose the use of a single source for core materials and supplies to

Example 2.1   Kuantan ATV Inc.: A Total Cost of Ownership Analysis

Kuantan ATV, Inc. assembles five different models of all-terrain vehicles (ATVs) from various ready-made components to serve the Las Vegas, Nevada, market. The company uses the same engine for all its ATVs. The purchasing manager, Ms. Jane Kim, needs to choose a supplier for engines for the coming year. Due to the size of the warehouse and other administrative restrictions, she must order the engines in lot sizes of 1,000 each. The unique characteristics of the standardized engine require special tooling to be used during the manufacturing process. Kuantan ATV agrees to reimburse the supplier for the tooling. This is a critical purchase, since late delivery of engines would disrupt production and cause 50 percent lost sales and 50 percent back orders of the ATVs. Jane has obtained quotes from two reliable suppliers but needs to know which supplier is more cost-effective. She has the following information:

Requirements (annual forecast)	12,000 units
Weight per engine	22 pounds
Order processing cost	$125 per order
Inventory carrying rate	20% per year
Cost of working capital	10% per year
Profit margin	18%
Price of finished ATV	$4,500
Back-order cost	$15 per unit backordered

Two qualified suppliers have submitted the following quotations:

UNIT PRICE	SUPPLIER 1	SUPPLIER 2
1 to 999 units/order	$510.00	$505.00
1,000 to 2,999 units/order	$500.00	$498.00
3,000+ units/order	$490.00	$488.00
Tooling Cost	$22,000	$20,000
Terms	2/10 net 30	1/10 net 30
Distance	125 miles	100 miles
Supplier Quality Rating (defects)	2%	3%
Supplier Delivery Rating (late delivery)	1%	2%

Jane also obtained the following freight rates from her carrier:

Truckload (TL ≥ 40,000 lbs):	$0.80 per ton-mile
Less-than-truckload (LTL):	$1.20 per ton-mile

Note: per ton-mile = 2,000 lbs per mile; number of days per year = 365

TOTAL COST OF OWNERSHIP COMPUTATION–SUPPLIER 1

Note that due to the size of the warehouse, order lot size, Q, is limited to 1,000 units. The total cost of ownership for supplier 1 can be computed as follows (see Figure 2.6):

(1) Total Engine Cost = Annual requirement × Unit cost
     = 12,000 units × $500/unit = $6,000,000.00

(2) Cash Discount (based on 365 days per year)
     A cash discount of *2/10 net 30* means the invoice must be paid within 30 days, but a 2% discount is given if the invoice is paid within 10 days of the invoice date. The calculation of the cash discount is done in two parts—whether the buyer pays the invoice on the 10th day (receives a 2% discount) or 30th day (pays the full amount). It is assumed that the buyer will take advantage of the largest discount.

   (A) Net 30 = Saving on the cost of capital by paying invoices on the 30th day
          = Total engine cost × cost of capital × 30/365
          = $6,000,000.00 × 10% × 30/365 = $49,315.07

   (B) 2/10 cash discount = Saving on the cost of capital and 2% discount by paying invoices on the 10th day
             = Total engine cost × (cost of capital + 2% discount)
             = $6,000,000.00 × (10% × 10/365 + 2%)
             = $136,438.36

   Hence, the buyer should pay invoices on the 10th day to take advantage of the $136,438.36 cash discount provided by the 2/10 term.

(3) Tooling Cost = $22,000.00

(4) Transportation Cost

Since the order size is 1,000 units, the total weight of each shipment is 22,000 pounds (1,000 units × 22 lbs/unit) Since it is less than 40,000 pounds, the buyer must use less-than-truckload shipment at $1.20 per ton-mile.

$$\text{Total Transportation Cost} = \text{distance} \times \text{quantity} \times \text{weight/unit} \times \text{rate/ton-mile}$$
$$= 125 \text{ miles} \times 12,000 \text{ units} \times 22 \text{ lbs/unit} \times \$1.20/2,000 \text{ lbs-mile}$$
$$= \$19,800.00$$

5) Since the number of orders = annual requirement /order size,

$$\text{Ordering Cost} = \text{number of orders} \times \text{order processing cost}$$
$$= (12,000 \text{ units}/1,000 \text{ units}) \times \$125 = \$1,500.00$$

(6) Since average inventory = order size/2,

$$\text{Carrying Cost} = \text{Average inventory} \times \text{price per unit} \times \text{inventory carrying rate}$$
$$= (\text{order size}/2) \times \text{price per unit} \times \text{inventory carrying rate}$$
$$= (1,000 \text{ units}/2) \times \$500/\text{unit} \times 20\% = \$50,000.00$$

(7) Quality Cost = Total engine cost × defect rate
$$= \$6,000,000.00 \times 2\% = \$120,000.00$$

(8) Delivery Rating

(A) Backorder Cost (50%) = Total quantity × late delivery rate × back order percentage × unit back order cost
$$= 12,000 \text{ units} \times 1\% \times 50\% \times \$15/\text{unit} = \$900.00$$

(B) Lost Sales (50%) = Total quantity × late delivery rate × lost sales percentage × price of ATV × profit margin
$$= 12,000 \text{ units} \times 1\% \times 50\% \times \$4,500/\text{unit} \times 18\%$$
$$= \$48,600.00$$

(9) Total Cost of Supplier 1 = $6,000,000.00 − $136,438.36 + $22,000.00 + $19,800.00 + $1,500.00 + $50,000.00 + $120,000.00 + $900.00 + $48,600.00 = $6,126,361.64

The total cost of ownership for supplier 2 can be computed using the same logic. The total cost analysis (see Figure 2.6) shows that Supplier 1 is more cost-effective, although its unit price and tooling costs are slightly higher than those of Supplier 2. The cash discount, quality cost, and delivery performance set Supplier 1 apart from Supplier 2. Using unit cost as the sole criterion to select a supplier would have ultimately cost the company $138,925.75 ($6,265,287.40 − $6,126,361.64).

Figure 2.6	Total Cost of Ownership Analysis	

Description	Supplier 1		Supplier 2	
1. Total Engine Cost	12,000 units × $500	$6,000,000.00	12,000 units × $498	$5,976,000.00
2. Cash Discount n/30 1/10 2/10 Largest discount	$6,000,000 × 10% × 30/365 $49,315.07 N/A $6,000,000 (10% × 10/365 + 2%) $136,438.36	$(136,438.36)	$5,976,000 × 10% × 30/365 $49,117.81 $5,976,000 (10% × 10/365 + 1%) $76,132.60 N/A	$(76,132.60)
3. Tooling Cost		$22,000.00		$20,000.00
4. Transportation Cost (22,000 lb LTL)	125 miles × 12,000 units × 22 lb × $1.20/2000	$19,800.00	100 miles × 12,000 units × 22 lb × $1.20/2000	$15,840.00
5. Ordering Cost	(12,000/1000) × $125	$1,500.00	(12,000/1000) × $125	$1,500.00
6. Carrying Cost	(1000/2) × $500 × 20%	$50,000.00	(1000/2) × $498 × 20%	$49,800.00
7. Quality Cost	$6,000,000 × 2%	$120,000.00	$5,976,000 × 3%	$179,280.00
8. Delivery Rating Backorder (50%) Lost Sales (50%)	12,000 × 1% × 50% × $15 12,000 × 1% × 50% × $4,500 × 18%	$900.00 $48,600.00	12,000 × 2% × 50% × $15 12,000 × 2% × 50% × $4,500 × 18%	$1,800.00 $97,200.00
TOTAL COST		$6,126,361.64		$6,265,287.40

facilitate cooperative buyer–supplier partnerships, single sourcing can be a very risky proposition. Although Xerox and Chrysler had substantially reduced their supply base in the 1980s, it was not documented that they resorted to single sourcing for their vital materials and components. The current trends in sourcing favor using fewer sources, although not necessarily a single source. Theoretically, firms should use single or a few sources, whenever possible, to enable the development of close relationships with the best suppliers. However, by increasing reliance on one supplier, the firm increases its risk that poor supplier performance will result in plant shutdowns or poor-quality finished products. Although **sole sourcing** and **single sourcing** are sometimes used interchangeably, sole sourcing typically refers to the situation when the supplier is the only available source, whereas single sourcing refers to the deliberate practice of concentrating purchases of an item with one source from a pool of viable suppliers. A comparison follows of some of the reasons favoring the use of a single supplier versus using two or more suppliers for a purchased item.

Reasons Favoring a Single Supplier

1. *To establish a good relationship*: Using a single supplier makes it easier for the firm to establish a mutually beneficial strategic alliance relationship with the supplier, as with well-managed supply chains, especially when the firm can benefit from the supplier's technologies and capabilities.

2. *Less quality variability*: Since the same technologies and processes are used to produce the parts when using a single source, variability in the quality levels is less than if the parts are purchased from multiple suppliers.

3. *Lower cost*: Buying from a single source concentrates purchase volume with the supplier, typically lowering the purchase cost per unit. Due to the large purchase volume, the supplier is more likely to ensure that it meets all of its performance goals to keep the business. Single sourcing also avoids duplicate fixed costs, especially if the part requires special tooling or expensive setups.

4. *Transportation economies*: Because single sourcing concentrates volume, the firm can take advantage of truckload (TL) shipments, which are cheaper per unit than the less-than-truckload (LTL) rate. By moving up to full truckloads, the firm has the option of using both rail and motor carriers. Rail carriers are more efficient for hauling heavy loads over long distances.

5. *Proprietary product or process purchases*: If it is a proprietary product or process, or if the supplier holds the patents to the product or process, the firm has no choice but to buy from the sole source.

6. *Volume too small to split*: If the requirement is too small, it is not worthwhile to split the order among many suppliers. Single sourcing is a good approach for acquiring supplies and services that do not contribute to the firm's core competencies.

Reasons Favoring Multiple Suppliers

1. *Need capacity*: When demand exceeds the capacity of a single supplier, the firm has no choice but to use multiple sources.

2. *Spread the risk of supply interruption*: Multiple sources allow the firm to spread the risk of supply interruptions due to a strike, quality problem, political instability, and other supplier problems.

3. *Create competition*: Using multiple sources encourages competition among suppliers in terms of price and quality. While modern supplier management philosophy

opposes the use of multiple sources simply to create competition, this may still be the preferred approach for sourcing nonvital items that do not affect the firm's competitive advantage. Using a single source to develop alliances for these types of purchases may not be cost-effective.

4. *Information*: Multiple suppliers usually have more information about market conditions, new product developments, and new process technologies. This is particularly important if the product has a short product life cycle.

5. *Dealing with special kinds of businesses*: The firms, particularly government contractors, may need to give portions of their purchases to small, local, or women- or minority-owned businesses, either voluntarily or as required by law.

The number of suppliers to use for one type of purchase has changed from the traditional multiple suppliers to the use of fewer, more reliable suppliers and even to the extent of using a single, highly rated, and trusted supplier. Relationships between buyers and suppliers traditionally were short-term, adversarial, and based primarily on cost, resulting in a mutual lack of trust. Buyer–supplier relationships, particularly in integrated supply chain settings, have evolved today into trusting, cooperative, and mutually beneficial long-term relationships. Firms today reduce their supply base to only the best suppliers.

PURCHASING ORGANIZATION

The purchasing department's organization within the firm has evolved over the years as the responsibilities of the purchasing function of firms changed from a clerical, supporting role to an integral part of corporate strategy that directly affects the competitiveness of the firms. In addition to the actual buying process, purchasing personnel are now involved in product design, production decisions, supplier relationship management, and other aspects of a firm's operations. The decision of how to organize purchasing to best serve its purpose is firm and industry-specific and dependent on many factors, such as market conditions and the types of parts and materials required. Purchasing structure can be viewed as a continuum, with centralization at one extreme and decentralization at the other. While there are few firms that adopt a pure centralized or decentralized structure, the benefits of each are worth a closer examination. The current trend is toward purchasing centralization for the vital materials where firms can take advantage of economies of scale and other benefits.

Centralized purchasing is where a single purchasing department, usually located at the firm's corporate office, makes all the purchasing decisions, including order quantity, pricing policy, contracting, negotiations, and supplier selection and evaluation. **Decentralized purchasing** is where individual, local purchasing departments, such as at the plant level, make their own purchasing decisions. A discussion of advantages and disadvantages to each of these purchasing structures follows.

Advantages of Centralization

1. *Concentrated volume*: An obvious benefit is the concentration of purchase volume to create quantity discounts, less-costly volume shipments, and other more favorable purchase terms. This is often referred to as **leveraging purchase volume**. A centralized system also provides the buying firm more clout and bargaining power. Suppliers generally are more willing to negotiate, give better terms, and share technology due to the higher volume.

2. *Avoid duplication*: Centralized purchasing eliminates the duplication of job functions. A corporate buyer can research and issue a large purchase order to cover the same material requested by all units, thus eliminating duplication of activities. This also results in fewer buyers, reducing labor costs.

3. *Specialization*: Centralization allows buyers to specialize in a particular product or group of items instead of being responsible for all purchased materials and services. It allows buyers to spend more time and resources to research items for which they are responsible, thus becoming specialized buyers.

4. *Lower transportation costs*: Centralization allows larger shipments to be made to take advantage of truckload or railcar shipments, and yet smaller shipments still can be arranged for delivery directly from suppliers to the points of use.

5. *No competition between units*: Under the decentralized system, when different units purchase the same material, a situation may be created in which units are competing among themselves, especially when scarce materials are purchased from the same supplier. Centralization minimizes this problem.

6. *Common supply base*: A common supply base is used, thus making it easier to manage and negotiate contracts.

Advantages of Decentralization

1. *Better knowledge of unit requirements*: A buyer at the individual unit is more likely to know its exact needs better than a central buyer at the home office.

2. *Local sourcing*: If the firm desires to support local businesses, it is more likely that a local buyer will know more about local suppliers. The proximity of local suppliers allows materials to be shipped more frequently in small lot sizes and is conducive to the creation of closer supplier relationships.

3. *Less bureaucracy*: Decentralization allows quicker response due to less bureaucracy and closer contact between the user and the buyer. Coordination and communication with operations and other divisions are more efficient.

Thus, while centralized purchasing may result in lower costs and better negotiating power, the centralized system may also be too rigid and even infeasible for large, multiunit organizations consisting of several unrelated business operations. For these reasons, a **hybrid purchasing organization** may be warranted. Large multiunit organizations may use a **decentralized/centralized purchasing structure** to decentralize purchasing at the corporate level, while centralizing the procurement function at the business unit level. Conversely, a firm may utilize a **centralized/decentralized purchasing structure** to negotiate national contracts at the corporate level, while decentralizing buying at the business unit level. These hybrid purchasing organizations allow firms to exploit the advantages of both the centralized and decentralized systems.

GLOBAL SOURCING

International agreements aimed at relaxing trade barriers and promoting free trade have provided opportunities for firms to expand their supply bases to participate in **global sourcing** (also occasionally referred to as international purchasing). Indeed, world merchandise exports and commercial services trade were $15.985 trillion and $4.755 trillion, respectively, in 2015.[12] In 2015, the United States was the world's largest importer ($2.308 trillion) and second largest exporter for merchandise trade ($1.505 tril-lion). In the same year, the United States was the world's largest importer and exporter for commercial services (imports were $469 billion; exports were $690 billion). The world's top three merchandise trade exporters were China ($2.275 trillion), the United States ($1.505 trillion), and Germany ($1.329 trillion). While global sourcing provides oppor-tunities to improve quality, cost, and delivery performance, it also poses unique chal-lenges for purchasing personnel. Engaging in global sourcing requires additional skills and knowledge to deal with international suppliers, logistics, communication, political, cultural, and other issues not usually encountered in domestic sourcing. The total cost of ownership illustration in Example 2.1 can also be used to compare the cost-effectiveness of domestic versus global sourcing. Various methods are employed for global sourcing. It is not merely limited to setting up an international purchasing office or using existing purchasing personnel to handle the transactions in-house. An **import broker** or **sales agent**, who performs transactions for a fee, can be used. Import brokers and sales agents do not take title to the goods. Instead, title passes directly from the seller to the buyer. International purchasers can also buy foreign goods from an **import merchant**, who buys and takes title to the goods and then resells them to the buyer. Purchasing from a **trading company**, which carries a wide variety of goods, is another option.

There are numerous international trade organizations designed to reduce tariff and non-tariff barriers among member countries. A **tariff** is an official list or schedule showing the duties, taxes, or customs imposed by the host country on imports or exports. **Nontariff barriers** are import quotas, licensing agreements, embargoes, laws, and other regulations imposed on imports and exports. A discussion of major international trade organizations follows.

1. The *World Trade Organization* (WTO) is the largest and most visible interna-tional trade organization dealing with the global rules of trade between nations. It replaced the General Agreement on Tariffs and Trade (GATT) on January 1, 1995. Its main goal is to ensure that international trade flows smoothly, predictably, and freely among member countries. The WTO Secretariat is based in Geneva, Switzer-land. It has 164 member countries as of March 2017.

2. The *North American Free Trade Agreement* (NAFTA) was implemented on January 1, 1994. Its goal is to remove trade and investment barriers among the United States, Canada, and Mexico. Under NAFTA, all nontariff agricultural trade barriers between the United States and Mexico were eliminated. Most tariffs affecting agricultural trade between the United States and Canada were removed by 1998. NAFTA was fully implemented as of January 1, 2008. The overall economic impact of NAFTA is difficult to measure because investment trends are influenced by many economic factors, such as economic growth, inflation, and unemployment rate. Since the agree-ment took effect, U.S. trade with Canada and Mexico has more than tripled. Trade with Mexico has increased more rapidly than trade with Canada. In 2016, Canada was the leading market for U.S. exports, and Mexico ranked second, accounting for 34 percent of U.S. exports. In imports, Canada and Mexico were the second and third largest exporters to the United States, accounting for 26 percent of U.S. imports.[13]

3. The *European Union* (EU) was set up on May 9, 1950, and comprised of Belgium, France, Luxembourg, Italy, the Netherlands, and Germany. The United Kingdom, Denmark, and Ireland joined the EU in 1973. As of March 2017, the EU has twenty-eight member countries. One of the primary goals of the EU is to create a single mar-ket without internal borders for goods and services, allowing member countries to better compete with markets like the United States. The EU's economy, measured by

the combined gross domestic product (GDP) of its member countries dropped from $18.574 trillion in 2014 to $16.312 trillion in 2015, whereas the GDP in the United States increased from $17.393 trillion in 2014 to $18.037 in 2015.[14] On June 23, 2016, United Kingdom voted to withdraw from the EU by March 2019.[15] The United Kingdom's referendum to withdraw from the EU is widely known as Brexit.

Reasons for Global Sourcing

Firms expand their supply bases to include foreign suppliers for many reasons. These can include lower price, better quality, an overseas supplier holding the patent to the product, faster delivery to foreign units, better services, and better process or product technologies.

A primary reason that many firms purchase from foreign suppliers is to lower the price of materials. As stated earlier, price generally is an important factor when purchasing standard materials and supplies that do not impact the competitive position of the firm. Many factors can contribute to cheaper materials from overseas suppliers—for example, cheaper labor costs and raw materials, favorable exchange rates, more efficient processes, or intentional dumping of products by foreign suppliers in overseas markets.

Additionally, the quality of overseas products may be better due to newer and better product and process technologies. Further, while foreign suppliers may be located farther away, they may be able to deliver goods faster than domestic suppliers due to more efficient transportation and logistical systems. Foreign suppliers may even maintain inventory and set up support offices in the host country to compete with domestic sources and to provide better services.

Firms may buy from foreign suppliers to support the local economy where they have subsidiaries, or they may be involved in **countertrade**, in which the contract calls for the exchange of goods or services for raw materials from local suppliers. While foreign purchasing may provide a number of benefits to the buyer, some problems may also be encountered.

Potential Challenges for Global Sourcing

Over the last few decades, global sourcing has surged due to many factors, such as the improvement of communication and transportation technologies, the reduction of international trade barriers, and deregulation of the transportation industry. However, global sourcing poses additional challenges that purchasing must know how to handle effectively. For example, the complexity and costs involved in selecting foreign suppliers and dealing with duties; tariffs; custom clearance; currency exchange; and political, cultural, labor, and legal problems present sizable challenges for the international buyer.

Unlike dealing with domestic suppliers, the costs involved in identifying, selecting, and evaluating foreign suppliers can be prohibitive. For a foreign supplier in a distant location, customs clearance, transportation, and other logistical issues may render delivery lead time unacceptable, especially for perishable goods. While many multinational corporations source globally for better quality materials and component parts, the opposite can also be true. It is not uncommon for multinational corporations to suffer irreparable damage to their reputations and incur expensive legal liabilities for unknowingly purchased tainted raw materials or faulty component parts from overseas suppliers.

In addition to the Uniform Commercial Code (UCC), which governs the purchase and sale of goods in the United States (except the state of Louisiana), global purchasers must also know the United Nations' **Contracts for the International Sale of Goods**(CISG). The CISG applies to international purchases and sales of goods, unless both parties elect to opt out. The UCC allows either party to modify the terms of acceptance for the purchase contract; however, the terms of acceptance cannot be modified under the CISG.

Global purchasers must also deal with more complex shipping terms than domestic buyers. The International Chamber of Commerce created a uniform set of rules, called **incoterms** (which is the commonly used term referring to the **International Commercial Terms**), to simplify international transactions of goods with respect to shipping costs, risks, and responsibilities of buyer, seller, and shipper. However, incoterms do not deal with transfer of title of the goods. Incoterms are often used in conjunction with a geographical location. *Incoterms 2010* revised the thirteen incoterms adopted in 2000, which were divided into four categories, to eleven rules. These eleven Incoterms 2010 are divided into two categories based on method of delivery. Seven of these eleven rules are applicable to sales that involve all method of delivery, whereas the remaining four rules are applicable to sales that involve transportation over water.[16]

Countertrade

Global sourcing may involve countertrade, in which goods and/or services of domestic firms are exchanged for goods and/or services of equal value or in combination with currency from foreign firms. This type of arrangement is sometimes used by countries where there is a shortage of hard currency or as a means to acquire technologies. Countertrade transactions are more complicated than currency transactions because goods are exchanged for goods.

The various forms of countertrade include barter, offset, and counterpurchase. **Barter** is the complete exchange of goods or services of equal value without the exchange of currency. The seller can either consume the goods or services or resell the items. **Offset** is an exchange agreement for industrial goods or services as a condition of military-related export. It is also commonly used in the aerospace and defense sectors. Most of the offset packages are divided into direct and indirect offsets. **Direct offset** usually involves coproduction, or a joint venture and exchange of related goods or services; whereas **indirect offset** involves exchange of goods or services unrelated to the initial purchase. **Counterpurchase** is an arrangement whereby the original exporter agrees to sell goods or services to a foreign importer and simultaneously agrees to buy specific goods or services from the foreign importer. Many developing countries mandate the transfer of technology as part of a countertrade or offset arrangement.

PROCUREMENT IN GOVERNMENT AND NONPROFIT AGENCIES

Public procurement or **public purchasing** refers to the management of the purchasing and supply management function in the government and nonprofit sectors, such as educational institutions; hospitals; and federal, state, and local governments. Although public procurement is subjected to political pressure and public scrutiny, its goals are similar to the private sector. However, public procurement is subjected to special rules and regulations that are established by the federal, state, and local governments. For example, all U.S. federal government purchases must comply with the **Federal Acquisition Regulation** (FAR)[18]. Consequently, the procedures for public procurement differ from the private sector—in addition to ensuring that purchases for goods and services are in strict compliance with statutes and policies, public procurement procedures are generally designed to **maximize competition**. The e-procurement system described in Figure 2.4 is an example of a public procurement system. In addition to the typical operations control, the e-procurement system in Figure 2.4 requires additional treatments of purchases exceeding $25,000.

In the United States, the **General Services Administration** (GSA), passed by the 81st Congress and signed into law by President Harry Truman in 1949, is responsible for most federal purchases. The GSA, based in Washington, D.C., has eleven regional offices in Boston, New York, Philadelphia, Atlanta, Chicago, Kansas City, Fort Worth, Denver, San Francisco, Auburn (Washington), and Washington, D.C. It is one of the world's largest purchasing entities. The **Department of Defense** (DOD) is the other major public procurement entity in the United States.

Characteristics of Public Procurement

A unique characteristic of public procurement is the preference to use competitive bidding to encourage competition among suppliers. For example, a government agency may implement procurement procedures that require a written quote for purchases that are more than $3,000 but less than $10,000, two written quotes for purchases that are less than $25,000, three written quotes for purchases less than $100,000, and competitive bids for purchases over $100,000.

In competitive bidding, the contract is usually awarded to the *lowest-priced bidder* determined to be *responsive* and *responsible* by the buyer. A responsive bid is one that conforms to the invitation to bid, and a responsible bid is one that is capable and willing to perform the work as specified.

The bidding process is usually very time-consuming and not cost-efficient for small purchases. On October 13, 1994, U.S. President Bill Clinton signed the **Federal Acquisition Streamlining Act** (FASA) to remove many restrictions on government purchases below $100,000. Instead of using full and open competitive bidding, government agencies can now use simplified procedures that require fewer administrative details, lower approval levels, and less documentation for soliciting and evaluating bids up to $100,000. **Micro-purchases**, government purchases of $3,000 (originally set at $2,500 but revised to $3,000 in 2006) and below, can now be made without obtaining competitive quotes. Additionally, all federal purchases between $2,500 and $100,000 are reserved for small businesses, unless the buyer cannot obtain offers from two or more small businesses that are competitive on price, quality, and delivery. In the United States, a small business is defined as one with fewer than 100 employees.

U.S. government agencies are required to advertise all planned purchases over $25,000. When the requirements are clear, accurate, and complete, the government agency usually uses an **invitation for bid** (IFB) to solicit **sealed bids**. The specifications for the proposed purchase; instructions for preparation of bids; and the conditions of purchase, delivery, and payment schedule are usually included with the IFB. The IFB also designates the date and time of bid opening. Sealed bids are opened in public at the purchasing office at the time designated in the invitation, and facts about each bid are read aloud and recorded. A contract is then awarded to the lowest responsible and responsive bidder.

Generally, bidders are also required to furnish bid bonds to ensure that the successful bidder will fulfill the contract as stated. There are three basic types of bid bond: **bid** or **surety bonds** guarantee the successful bidder will accept the contract; **performance bonds** guarantee the work of the successful bidder meets specifications and in the time stated; and **payment bonds** protect the buyer against any third-party liens not fulfilled by the bidder.

SCM Profile | The State of State Procurement

State government spending is one of the largest economic drivers in the United States. Similar to the private sector, state procurement professionals are continually revolutionizing the way goods and services are bought. Some of the major issues that state procurement professionals faced are emerging technology, state-wide centralization, contract management, and hiring and retaining talented staff.

Technology: The birth of the information age has changed the traditional technology procurement that used to focus on hardware, such as computers and printers, to highly complex information technology (IT) infrastructure, IT systems, and cloud services. State procurement professionals must now handle new challenges, including cyber security, data ownership, and liability limits. Traditional procurement methods cannot adequately handle these emerging needs to create enterprise-wide efficiencies and maximize the state's buying power. Fortunately, according to the 2015 National Association of State Procurement Officials (NASPO) survey, state procurement professionals considered procurement process reform and reengineering as their most important focus area for 2016.

Centralization: State procurement professionals are centralizing procurement authority to streamline processes and consolidate purchases. Centralized procurement increases visibility of solicitation opportunities to suppliers and streamline the procurement processes at the state level to maximize competition. Moreover, a centralized system avoids duplication of procurement functions, eliminates competition between units at the local level, and establishes a common supply base to allow local procurement professionals to develop strategic projects and manage contracts with key suppliers early in the process.

Contracts: In addition to manage cost overrun, states are exploring ways to evaluate technical merits, innovation, and life-cycle cost (i.e., the economic analysis used to select alternatives that affect the present and future costs) of contracts to acquire the highest quality goods and services. State contracts must now include well-defined key performance indicators (KPIs) to measure supplier performance. State procurement professionals must also focus on building lasting collaborative relationships with suppliers, and be aware of new procurement models such as the public-private partnerships (P3s), social impact bonds and category management. A P3s is a contractual arrangement between a public agency, such as federal, state or local government, and a private entity where the skills and assets of both entities are utilized to deliver goods or services to the public. A social impact bond is a public–private partnership used to fund social services through a performance-based contract where the investors provide the initial capital support and the government agrees to pay when the desired social outcomes are achieved.

Talent: State procurement offices must hire and retain highly qualified and talented procurement professionals who not only understand supply chain management and public contracting, but also must be knowledgeable in strategy, data management, leadership, and the legal framework of state government. The lucrative compensation package and career opportunity in the private sector make it more difficult for state procurement offices to hire or retain talented procurement professionals. Moreover, as state budgets continue to shrink, so does the availability of professional training and development opportunity for the current workforce.

Despite these challenges, state procurement professionals can shape the way in which tax dollars are spent for the betterment of the public. The public sector must look at procurement through a fresh lens and recognize the strategic value that it brings to serving citizens in ways that maximize value and reduce cost.[17]

Another characteristic of public procurement is the **Buy American Act** that mandates U.S. government purchases and third-party purchases that utilize federal funds to buy domestically produced goods, if the price differential between the domestic product and an identical foreign-sourced product does not exceed a certain percentage amount. However, the U.S. president has the authority to waive the Buy American Act.

While **green purchasing** is not a new sourcing concept, there is a push to expand green purchasing requirements in the public sector. There are at least five federal statutes and more than a dozen presidential executive orders requiring federal purchasing officials to include environmental considerations and human health when making purchasing decisions.[19] Public procurement advocates the purchase of more energy-efficient products, bio-based products, recycled content products, non-ozone-depleting substances, green power, and other environment-friendly products.[20]

SUMMARY

Over the last decade, the purchasing function has evolved into an integral part of supply chain management. Purchasing is an important strategic contributor to overall business competitiveness. It is the largest single function in most organizations, controlling activities and transactions valued at more than 50 percent of sales. Every dollar saved due to better purchasing impacts business operations and profits directly. Purchasing personnel talk to customers; users; suppliers; and internal design, finance, marketing, and operations personnel, in addition to top management. The information they gain from all this exposure can be used to help the firm to provide better, cheaper, and more timely products and services to both internal and external customers. Savvy executives are thus turning to purchasing to improve business and supply chain performance.

KEY TERMS

backward vertical integration, 53

barter, 67

bid, 68

blank check purchase order, 52

blanket order release, 52

blanket purchase order, 52

break-even analysis, 56

Buy American Act, 70

centralized purchasing, 63

centralized/decentralized
    purchasing structure, 64

contracts for the International
    Sale of Goods, 67

corporate purchasing cards, 51

counterpurchase, 67

countertrade, 66

decentralized purchasing, 63

decentralized/centralized
    purchasing structure, 64

Department of Defense, 68

direct offset, 67

early supplier involvement, 58

economies of scale, 54

expediting, 47

Federal Acquisition Regulation, 67

Federal Acquisition Streamlining
    Act, 68

follow-up, 47

forward vertical integration, 53

General Services
    Administration, 68

global sourcing, 64

green purchasing, 70

hybrid purchasing organization, 64

import broker, 65

import merchant, 65

incoterms, 67

indirect offset, 67

industrial buyers, 39

internal control, 44

International Commercial Terms, 67

inventory turnover, 42

invitation for bid, 68

leveraging purchase volume, 63

make or buy decision, 53

material requisition, 45

maximize competition, 68

merchant, 39

micro-purchases, 68

nontariff barriers, 65

offset, 67

open-end purchase order, 52

original equipment
    manufacturers, 59

outsourcing, 47

payment bonds, 68

performance bonds, 68

petty cash, 52

planned order releases, 46

procurement credit cards, 51

profit-leverage effect, 41

public procurement, 67

public purchasing, 67

purchase order, 47

purchase requisition, 45

purchase spend, 41

request for proposal, 47

request for quotation, 47

return on assets, 42

return on investment, 42

sales agent, 65

sales order, 47

sealed bids, 68

simplification, 52

single sourcing, 62

sole sourcing, 62

stockless buying, 52

subcontracting, 55

supplier base, 57

supplier development, 47

supply base, 57

supply management, 39

surety bonds, 68

system contracting, 52

tariff, 65

Tier-1, 59

Tier-2, 59

Tier-3 suppliers, 59

total cost of acquisition, 58

total cost of ownership, 58

trading company, 65

travel card, 51

traveling requisition, 45

Uniform Commercial Code, 47

DISCUSSION QUESTIONS

1. Describe the steps in a traditional manual purchasing system.

2. Describe the e-procurement system and its advantages over the manual system. Are there any disadvantages to the electronic system? Do you think the e-procurement system will ultimately replace the manual system? Why or why not?

3. How can purchasing help to improve the competitive edge of an organization?

4. What is the profit-leverage effect of purchasing? What is the return-on-assets effect of purchasing?

5. How does a merchant differ from an industrial buyer?

6. Describe the purpose of a material requisition, a purchase order, a request for quotation, and a request for proposal. Does the material requisition serve the same purpose as the purchase order?

7. Why are small-value purchase orders problematic? How can purchasing more effectively deal with this problem?

8. Should unit price be used as the sole criterion for selecting suppliers? Why?

9. Explain backward vertical integration. What are the advantages of outsourcing compared to backward vertical integration?

10. When should a firm outsource instead of making the items in-house?

11. What factors should be considered while choosing suppliers?

12. Describe the difference between sole source and single source.

13. What are the reasons to use a single supplier? Is this the most efficient way to purchase materials in general?

14. Describe centralized and decentralized purchasing and their advantages.

15. Describe how the hybrid purchasing organization works.

16. Describe how blanket orders and blanket order releases can be used to manage the procurement system of a business that owns a dozen large restaurants in a city.

17. How does public procurement differ from corporate purchasing?

18. Describe the different types of bid bonds.

19. What are micropurchases? How can they be used to improve public procurement?

20. Why do firms purchase from foreign suppliers? What are the risks involved in global sourcing?

21. What is countertrade? Describe the various types of countertrade.

22. Describe how a typical government bidding process is conducted.

23. How can global sourcing enhance a firm's competitiveness?

24. Describe the disadvantages of global sourcing and how it can adversely affect a firm's competitiveness.

25. Describe Tier-1, Tier-2, and Tier-3 suppliers.

ESSAY/PROJECT QUESTIONS

1. Go to the World Trade Organization's website, and use the information to write a report that includes (a) the functions of the WTO, (b) the latest number of membership countries, (c) its relationship with GATT, (d) the number of countries that had originally signed the GATT in 1994, and (e) the last five countries that became members of the WTO.

2. Utilize the Internet to search for "incoterms 2010." Write a report to (a) summarize the incoterms into two groups and (b) describe each of the eleven terms.

3. Go to the General Services Administration's website, and use the information to write a brief report to summarize the roles of GSA. Additionally, discuss the roles of the federal acquisition regulation (FAR), federal management regulation (FMR), and the federal travel regulation (FTR).

4. Use the Internet to research and describe "Brexit" and its latest developments.

SPREADSHEET PROBLEMS

1. If a firm's net income (profits before taxes) is $120,000 and it has total assets of $1.5 million, what is its return on assets?

2. If a firm's total assets is $2.5 million and its return on assets is 12 percent, what is its net income?

3. If a firm is able to sustain the same level of operations in terms of sales and administrative expenses but reduces its materials cost by $50,000 through smarter purchases, what is the profit-leverage effect on gross profits? What is the profit-leverage effect on profits before taxes?

4. If a firm's cost of goods sold is $2.5 million and its average inventory is $500,000, what is the inventory turnover?

5. If a firm's cost of goods sold is $5 million and its inventory turnover is ten times, what is the average inventory?

6. If a firm's inventory turnover is eight times and its average inventory is $160,000, what is the cost of goods sold?

7. A retailer in Las Vegas has an ending inventory of $250,000 as of December 31, 2016, and the following accounting information.

MONTH	ENDING INVENTORY	COST OF GOODS SOLD
January	$225,000	$1,200,000
February	$325,000	$1,250,000
March	$240,000	$1,350,000
April	$325,000	$1,500,000
May	$460,000	$950,000
June	$220,000	$850,000
July	$85,000	$1,650,000
August	$156,000	$1,325,000
September	$220,000	$1,750,000
October	$265,000	$850,000
November	$100,000	$2,200,000
December	$350,000	$3,500,000

a. Compute the monthly inventory turnover ratio for each of the twelve months.
b. What are the annual cost of goods sold and the average inventory for the year?
c. Compute the annual inventory turnover ratio. How is the retailer's performance compare to the industry standard, assuming its business is similar to Walmart's?

8. A small firm has an ending inventory of $52,000 as of December 31, 2016, and the following accounting information.

MONTH	ENDING INVENTORY	COST OF GOODS SOLD
January	$75,000	$225,000
February	$56,000	$325,000
March	$25,000	$240,000
April	$85,000	$325,000
May	$125,000	$460,000
June	$95,000	$220,000
July	$72,000	$85,000
August	$45,000	$156,000
September	$52,500	$220,000
October	$120,000	$265,000
November	$162,500	$100,000
December	$255,000	$350,000

a. Compute the monthly inventory turnover ratio for each of the twelve months.
b. What are the annual cost of goods sold and the average inventory for the year?
c. Compute the annual inventory turnover ratio. What can the purchasing department do to improve the firm's performance?

9. You are given the following information:

COSTS	MAKE OPTION	BUY OPTION
Fixed Cost	$125,000	$5,000
Variable Cost	$15	$17

a. Find the break-even quantity and the total cost at the break-even point.
b. If the requirement is 150,000 units, is it more cost-effective for the firm to buy or make the components? What is the cost savings for choosing the cheaper option?

10. You are given the following information:

COSTS	MAKE OPTION	BUY OPTION
Fixed Cost	$25,000	$3,000
Variable Cost	$8	$12

a. Find the break-even quantity and the total cost at the break-even point.
b. If the requirement is 4,500 units, is it more cost-effective for the firm to buy or make the components? What is the cost savings for choosing the cheaper option?
c. If the requirement is 6,000 units, is it more cost-effective for the firm to buy or make the components? What is the cost savings for choosing the cheaper option?

11. Ms. Jane Kim, purchasing manager of Kuantan ATV, Inc., is negotiating a contract to buy 20,000 units of a common component part from a supplier. Jane has done a preliminary cost analysis on manufacturing the part in-house and concluded that she would need to invest $50,000 in capital equipment and incur a variable cost of $25 per unit to manufacture the part in-house. Assuming the total fixed cost to draft a contract with her supplier is $1,000, what is the maximum purchase price that she should negotiate with her supplier? What other factors should she negotiate with the suppliers?

12. A Las Vegas, Nevada, manufacturer has the option to make or buy one of its component parts. The annual requirement is 20,000 units. A supplier is able to supply the parts for $10 each. The firm estimates that it costs $600 to prepare the contract with the supplier. To make the parts in-house, the firm must invest $50,000 in capital equipment and estimates that the parts cost $8 each.

a. Assuming that cost is the only criterion, use break-even analysis to determine whether the firm should make or buy the item. What is the break-even quantity, and what is the total cost at the break-even point?

b. Calculate the total costs for both options at 20,000 units. What is the cost savings for choosing the cheaper option?

13. Given the following information, use total cost analysis to determine which supplier is more cost-effective. Late delivery of raw material results in 60 percent lost sales and 40 percent back orders of finished goods.

Order lot size	1,000
Requirements (annual forecast)	120,000 units
Weight per engine	22 pounds
Order processing cost	$125/order
Inventory carrying rate	20% per year
Cost of working capital	10% per year
Profit margin	15%
Price of finished goods	$4,500
Back order cost	$15 per unit

UNIT PRICE	SUPPLIER 1	SUPPLIER 2
1 to 999 units/order	$50.00	$49.50
1,000 to 2,999 units/order	$49.00	$48.50
3,000 + units/order	$48.00	$48.00
Tooling cost	$12,000	$10,000
Terms	2/10, net 30	1/10, net 30
Distance	125 miles	100 miles
Supplier Quality Rating	2%	2%
Supplier Delivery Rating	1%	2%

Truckload (TL ≥ 40,000 lbs): $0.85 per ton-mile

Less-than-truckload (LTL): $1.10 per ton-mile

Note: per ton-mile = 2,000 lbs per mile; number of days per year = 365

14. A buyer received bids from three suppliers for a vital component part for its latest product. Given the following information, use total cost analysis to determine which supplier should be chosen. Late delivery of the component results in 70 percent lost sales and 30 percent back orders of finished goods.

Order lot size	2,000
Requirements (annual forecast)	240,000 units
Weight per engine	40 pounds
Order processing cost	$200/order
Inventory carrying rate	20% per year
Cost of working capital	10% per year
Profit margin	15%
Price of finished goods	$10,500
Back order cost	$120 per unit

UNIT PRICE	SUPPLIER 1	SUPPLIER 2	SUPPLIER 3
1 to 999 units/order	$200.00	$205.00	$198.00
1,000 to 2,999 units/order	$195.00	$190.00	$192.00
3,000 + units/order	$190.00	$185.00	$190.00
Tooling Cost	$12,000	$10,000	$15,000
Terms	2/10, net 30	1/15, net 30	1/10, net 20
Distance	120 miles	100 miles	150 miles
Supplier Quality Rating	2%	1%	2%
Supplier Delivery Rating	1%	1%	2%

Truckload (TL ≥ 40,000 lbs) $0.95 per ton-mile

Less-than-truckload (LTL): $1.20 per ton-mile

Note: per ton-mile = 2,000 lbs per mile; number of days per year = 365

CASES

1. 3 Bees Buttermilk Corporation—Supplier Selection*

Basil Brandenburg, Bernie Boatwright, and Buford Baumgartner own the 3 Bees Buttermilk Corporation. The 3 Bees Buttermilk Corporation is an international corporation that sources its supplies from around the globe. The company had expanded from its original business of selling buttermilk to selling a multitude of food products. The food industry is very competitive. Basil's, Bernie's, and Buford's principle business strategy is low-cost leadership. They are intent on keeping expenses as low as possible. They believe this is their chief sustainable competitive edge.

Because of the large number of items they source worldwide, supplier selection is a major activity for the 3 Bees. It is essential to cost management. Buck Baumgartner, Buford's son, is studying supply chain management and is doing an internship with the 3 Bees Buttermilk Corporation. This year Buford decided they would teach Buck what was involved in the supplier selection process.

Basil, chief executive officer, took the first turn. He explained to Buck that for him communication capability was the most critical factor when selecting suppliers. In the food industry, products have an expiration date. Getting the correct item to the correct locations in time was essential. Consequently, communication of schedules, deliveries, and any issues is a must in their business. Basil felt that reliability was another important factor to consider and that it complemented communication capability.

Bernie, chief financial officer, is big on the cost factor. He explained to Buck that they had to determine the total cost of ownership. This went beyond the price. Total cost of ownership also included payment terms, cash discount, ordering cost, carrying cost, and much more.

Buford, chief technology officer, emphasized the importance of supplier process and product technology. In addition, he focused on the supplier's willingness to share technologies. Because of Buford's stance on these factors, he ensured the 3 Bees Buttermilk Corporation engaged in early supplier involvement when deciding to procure a new product.

As Buck listened to them he knew that these weren't the only factors to consider. He planned to discover what other factors were necessary to consider and ask 3 Bees about them.

Discussion Questions

1. Name and explain two factors of the supplier selection process that were not mentioned in the case.

2. What are the advantages of early supplier involvement?

3. Identify qualitative and quantitative factors that are taken into consideration when looking at the total cost of ownership.

©2019 Cengage Learning

*Written by Rick Bonsall, D. Mgt., McKendree University, Lebanon, IL. The people and institution are fictional and any resemblance to any person or any institution is coincidental. This case was prepared solely to provide material for class discussion. The author does not intend to illustrate either effective or ineffective handling of a managerial situation.

2. Frank's Driving Appurtenances—A Make-or-Buy Decision*

Frank Ziegler is a car buff. From his early childhood days Frank loved to tinker with cars. As he grew older, Frank's interest in cars evolved into how to enhance the comfort, convenience, and enjoyment of driving. Frank always had an entrepreneurial spirit, so he decided to open his own business, Frank's Driving Appurtenances.

Frank investigated the industry of car accouterments. He discovered that, like himself, many people enjoyed adding accessories to their car that expressed their unique personalities. He had designed many unique items for himself and his friends such as cup holders, objects to hang from the mirror, as well as things to adorn the outside of the vehicle. Frank believes that there is an enormous market for these items.

Frank was confident in his skill to design, manufacture, and sell unique accessories. His research showed that there were many suppliers for the type of items Frank made for himself and his friends. Consequently, he didn't have to make things himself; he could purchase and then resell them. Therefore, Frank believed his first step in creating Frank's Driving Appurtenances was to complete a make-or-buy break-even analysis. Although his primary motivation was to share his own creations, Frank was a realist. He knew that initially the best approach was to ascertain which method, make or buy, was the best financial decision. If buying and reselling was more financially sound, he could later move to making the items himself once his reputation for quality and individuality was established.

Frank had to calculate the costs for both options. Frank had to determine what his fixed cost would be if he made the items. He would need additional tools and machinery and a place to work. His garage would not be sufficient space to make the volume of items he thought he needed.

As Frank evaluated the buy option, he discovered that one element of the variable cost was shipping. Most of the suppliers who sold the types of items Frank wanted were in foreign markets. Although their base price for the items varied slightly, the shipping cost added to the base cost was somewhat volatile.

As Frank prepared to calculate the make-or-buy break-even point, he understood that the one critical piece of data was the volume of sales. How much did Frank think he could sell? An inaccurate estimate of sales could result in the wrong break-even point and potential failure.

Discussion Questions

1. What is the purpose for using the break-even analysis?

2. What are the two types of cost Frank must consider when doing the break-even analysis?

3. Generally speaking, which type of cost is higher for the make option and which type of cost is higher for the buy option? Why?

*Written by Rick Bonsall, D. Mgt., McKendree University, Lebanon, IL. The people and institution are fictional and any resemblance to any person or any institution is coincidental. This case was prepared solely to provide material for class discussion. The author does not intend to illustrate either effective or ineffective handling of a managerial situation.

3. Middleton Fine Furniture—Supply Chain Savings Opportunities*

The furniture industry is a tough industry to complete in. It is a very price-driven business and every expense must be constantly reviewed and reduced as much as possible. Middleton Fine Furniture was feeling the pressure of the economic downturn and needed to cut expenses. If they could not accomplish this, the only alternative was to lay off employees.

Sally Sherman was the chief executive officer of Middleton Fine Furniture. In its 100 years of operations, Middleton Fine Furniture was extremely proud of the fact that its employees were like family and Sally didn't feel layoffs were an option. Sally knew that until the economy turned around, her company would need to tighten its belt. However, Sally wanted more than immediate financial relief, she want sustainable cost reductions.

Sally met with Kenisha Yost, chief financial officer, and Ellie Gomez, vice president of supply chain management to discuss Middleton's financial predicament. Sally emphasized that she wanted a solution that enabled Middleton Fine Furniture to manage expenses in a manner that potentially could result in recurring savings. She didn't just want to survive this current financial crisis, she wanted to avoid it happening again.

Kenisha and Ellie began brainstorming on what they could do to provide a long-term solution. Kenisha mentioned that inventory, while essential to their business, was money on the shelf. It did no good sitting there. How could they reduce inventory without endangering the business?

Ellie pointed out that the initial step to reducing inventory was to calculate their current inventory turnover ratio. Once they had that as a baseline, they could work on specific actions to reduce inventory. Furthermore, by analyzing their current inventory turnover ratio they could identify actions in other departments, other than just the supply department, that may be contributing to having too much money sitting on the shelf. Ellie explained that low inventory turnover can also be an indicator of poor sales, overstocking, and obsolete inventory. Issues that would need marketing's support to correct.

Ellie looked deeper into Middleton Fine Furniture's supply chain management processes. She discovered that Middleton had preferred to use multiple sourcing as its procurement method. Although multiple sourcing has many advantages, single sourcing can be advantageous as well. Although not all the parts they procured for the furniture could be single sourced, there were several that could. These were large-volume parts where quality was critical. Consequently, switching to single sourcing for these particular parts would ensure less quality variability and potentially less waste, a true cost reduction. Another advantage would be the opportunity to lower the cost of the parts because of the volume they would purchase from a single vendor. The increased volume for a single vendor would result in a lower purchase cost per unit for Middleton Fine Furniture.

As Ellie continued to ponder the problem, she reflected on the changes in Middleton's processes over the years. In its early years Middleton made all the parts for its furniture. As it grew, it sourced more and more pieces from suppliers. Ellie decided the time

*Written by Rick Bonsall, D. Mgt., McKendree University, Lebanon, IL. The people and institution are fictional and any resemblance to any person or any institution is coincidental. This case was prepared solely to provide material for class discussion. The author does not intend to illustrate either effective or ineffective handling of a managerial situation.

was right for a make-or-buy break-even analysis on the parts they still made in-house and the parts they bought. This would be a challenging task and it would take time; however, the potential benefit of reducing costs outweighed the effort required.

Kenisha and Ellie met with Sally. They outlined the three major initiatives they were pursuing, inventory turnover analysis, single versus multiple sourcing for specific parts, and an evaluation of whether to change from make or buy where applicable. Sally believed their solutions would generate the savings they needed and the processes put in place as a result would facilitate sustainable cost reductions.

Discussion Questions

1. Explain the reasoning of determining the inventory turnover ratio. What value does this action have for Middleton?

2. What are the two main ways single sourcing can help reduce expenses? What is the risk?

3. What are the two types of cost that Kenisha and Ellie must consider when reevaluating the company's make-or-buy decisions?

©2019 Cengage Learning

ADDITIONAL RESOURCES

Johnson, P. F., and A. E. Flynn. *Purchasing and Supply Management*, 15th ed. New York: McGraw-Hill Irwin, 2015.

Monczka, R., R. Handfield, L. C. Giunipero, and J. L. Patterson. *Purchasing and Supply Chain Management*, 6th ed. Boston, MA: Cengage Learning, 2016.

Prahalad, C. K., and G. Hamel. "The Core Competence of the Corporation," *Harvard Business Review* 68(3), 1990: 79–91.

Tan, K. C. "A Framework of Supply Chain Management Literature," *European Journal of Purchasing & Supply Management* 7(1), 2001: 38–48.

Tan, K. C., V. R. Kannan, and R. B. Handfield. "Supply Chain Management: Supplier Performance and Firm Performance," *International Journal of Purchasing and Materials Management* 34(3), 1998: 2–9.

Wisner, J. D., and K. C. Tan. "Supply Chain Management and Its Impact on Purchasing," *Journal of Supply Chain Management* 36(4), 2000: 33–42.

ENDNOTES

1. Ferrell, K. "The State of State Procurement," *Inside Supply Management* 27(5), June/July 2016: 32–33.

2. Arnseth, L. "The Evolution of Supply Management," *Inside Supply Management* 28(1), January/February 2017: 22–25.

3. Ray, J. "Develop World Class Purchasing," *ICIS Chemical Business* 290(5), August 15–21, 2016: 26–28.

4. "Annual Survey of Manufactures: Geographic Area Statistics: Statistics for All Manufacturing by State," *Annual Survey of Manufactures*, U.S. Census Bureau, January 19, 2017.

5. ISM Glossary of Key Supply Management Terms, www.ism.ws/glossary, accessed March 10, 2017.

6. Tan, K.C., and R. Dajalos. "Purchasing Strategy in the 21st Century: E-Procurement," *Practix: Best Practices in Purchasing & Supply Chain Management* 4(3), 2001: 7–12.

7. Palmer, R., and M. Gupta. "2012 Purchasing Card Benchmark Survey Results," RPMG Research Corporation.

8. Palmer, R., and M. Gupta. "2014 Purchasing Card Benchmark Survey Results," RPMG Research Corporation.

9. Hannon, D. "P-card Program Expansion Is a Global Challenge," *Purchasing* 138(12), December 19, 2009: 53–55.

10. Doerfler, S. "Keeping Up with the Curve," *Inside Technology Supplement to ISM*, July 2016: 4–7.

11. Sherefkin, R. "Delphi Aims for Smaller Global Supply Base," *Automotive News*, 78(6107), August 16, 2004: 4.

12. World Trade Organization. "International Trade Statistics 2016," WTO Publications, Geneva.

13. Villarreal, M.A., and Fergusson, I.F. "The North American Free Trade Agreement (NAFTA)," Congressional Research Service (R42965), February 22, 2017: 7–5700.

14. "European Union GDP," http://www.tradingeconomics.com/european-union/gdp, accessed March 12, 2017.

15. "The History of the European Union - 2016," http://europa.eu/european-union/about-eu/history/2010-today/2016_en, accessed March 12, 2017.

16. "Incoterms 2010," https://cdn.iccwbo.org/content/uploads/sites/3/2010/01/ICC-Intro-duction-to-the-Incoterms-2010.pdf, accessed March 12, 2017.

17. Ferrell, K. "The State of State Procurement," *Inside Supply Management* 27(5), June/July 2016: 32–33.

18. "Federal Acquisition Regulation (FAR)," https://www.acquisition.gov/?q=browsefar, accessed March 12, 2017.

19. Case, S., and D. Arnold. "Greening Federal Purchasing," *Government Procurement*, August 2005: 18–26.

20. "Green Procurement Compilation," https://www.gsa.gov/portal/content/198257, accessed March 12, 2017.

Chapter 3

CREATING AND MANAGING SUPPLIER RELATIONSHIPS

Ensuring the best prices through strategic sourcing is no longer perceived as a strategic capability of the procurement function. As a result of further outsourcing of non-core competencies, organizations are starting to realize that they have become more reliant on suppliers in terms of innovative power, security of supply, corporate social responsibility, and on-going cost savings. Strategic partnerships are at the top of the corporate agenda of many global organizations and Supplier Relationship Management (SRM) is seen as one of the few remaining procurement topics that can still make a significant difference.

— *PricewaterhouseCoopers website*[1]

As FCA continues to grow globally, we want to work with our top supplier partners to bring the highest quality vehicles to drivers across the world.

— **Scott Thiele, Global Purchasing Officer for FCA Group**[2]

The greatest change in corporate culture – and the way business is being conducted – may be the accelerated growth of relationships based … on partnership.

— **Peter F. Drucker**[3]

Learning Objectives

After completing this chapter, you should be able to

- Explain the importance of supplier partnerships.
- Understand the key factors for developing successful partnerships.
- Develop a supplier evaluation and certification program.
- Explain the importance of a supplier recognition program.
- Understand the capabilities of supplier relationship management.
- Explain the benefits of using SRM software to manage suppliers.

Chapter Outline

Introduction

Developing Supplier Relationships

Supplier Evaluation and Certification

Supplier Development

Supplier Recognition Programs

Supplier Relationship Management

Summary

SCM Profile   Supplier Relationship Management at Ford

After the financial crisis of 2008, Ford began to develop a collaborative working relationship with its suppliers. Earlier in 2007, Ford implemented its One Ford program, which reduced the number of global automobile platforms from 27 to 8. As such, there were economies of scale to be gained from this strategic move. This collaborative working model entailed long-term development and purchasing agreements with select suppliers. According to Thai-Tang, vice president of global purchasing at Ford, "It was modeled after some of the best practices in the industry. It's not about sourcing to the lowest-cost bidder on something that's very much a true commodity … It's more, 'Who are our long-term strategic partners that we want to align ourselves with, that we want to count on to help us innovate?'" Ford is actively pursuing supplier development when Ford starts manufacturing in new global markets. For example, in India, Ford found a supplier who was not already in the automotive industry and worked with the supplier to transfer their experience doing harness work for the appliance industry to producing parts for Ford. According to Ford, it takes three or more years to develop a supplier. Engaging suppliers early in the design process is key. Thai-Tang said, "Talk with them about what is the customer problem that we're trying to solve, and how do we collaborate to get to the best design cost and ensure that they make a fair margin. Then we're actually leveraging their knowledge, their expertise, and learning from their best practices based on all the customers they serve."[4]

According to a recent study by Planning Perspectives, Inc., on supplier relations "Ford, General Motors, FCA US [formerly Chrysler] and Nissan collectively would have earned $2 billion more in operating profit last year had their supplier relations improved as much as Toyota's and Honda's did during the year." Toyota and Honda are on top of the ranking based on a supplier relations index developed by Planning Perspectives. Ford recently regained third place over Nissan. The study finds that "Toyota and Honda are executing the foundational activities very well and continue working to improve them while they also focus on improving their relational activities. That's why we see the growing gap between them and Ford, Nissan, GM, and FCA, each of whom is struggling with the foundational activities."[5] Foundational activities involve two categories. One is related to the business practice of the purchasing function, while the other deals with the OEM buyers on issues such as knowledge of the job, trustworthiness, ability to resolve problems effectively, and open and honest communications.

INTRODUCTION

In today's competitive environment, as companies focus on their core competencies, the level of outsourcing will continue to rise. Increasingly, companies are requiring their suppliers to deliver innovative and quality products not only in just-in-time (JIT) fashion but also at a competitive price. In the last few decades, we have learned that good supplier relations can provide many benefits such as delivery flexibility, better quality, better information, and faster material flows between buyers and suppliers. Many companies believe strongly that better supplier partnerships are important for achieving competitive corporate performance. As such, companies are realizing the importance of developing win–win, long-term relationships with suppliers. It is critical that customers and suppliers develop stronger relationships and partnerships based on a strategic rather than a tactical perspective and then manage these relationships to create value for all participants. Successful partnerships with key suppliers can contribute to innovations and have the potential to create a competitive advantage for the firm. Selecting the right supply partners and successfully managing these relationships over time is thus strategically important; it is often stated "a firm is only as good as its weakest suppliers." As presented in the chapter-opening SCM Profile feature, Toyota and Honda continue to lead the way in supplier relations for North American automakers although General Motors and Ford have made significant improvement in building trust with suppliers. According to John Hedge, president of Planning Perspectives, Inc., "Going forward, automakers will have to invest heavily in new resources and training programs to improve their working relations with suppliers because suppliers have a significant impact on an automaker's profits."[6]

According to the Institute for Supply Management's glossary of terms, a supplier partnership is defined as:

> *A commitment over an extended time to work together to the mutual benefit of both parties, sharing relevant information and the risks and rewards of the relationship. These relationships require a clear understanding of expectations, open communication and information exchange, mutual trust and a common direction for the future. Such arrangements are a collaborative business activity that does not involve the formation of a legal partnership. The term strategic alliance is used in many organizations to mean the same thing as a supplier partnership. In some organizations, however, the term strategic alliance is used to describe a more inclusive relationship involving the planned and mutually advantageous joint utilization of additional operating resources of both organizations.[7]*

Ford Motor Company's Aligned Business Framework focuses on "collaborative and transparent work in areas such as ethical business practices, working conditions, global manufacturing and development footprints, and sourcing from minority-, veteran- and women-owned businesses."[8] This rigorous framework is beneficial to Ford since it enables the company to reduce costs and obtain suppliers' innovative technologies. To achieve Ford's goals in managing its supply chain, Ford fosters long-term relationships with their suppliers through active engagement and communication of its expectations on critical issues such as human rights, working conditions, and environmental sustainability, and ensuring that their suppliers have management systems in place to mitigate potential risks and safeguard continuity of supply.[9] The opening SCM Profile also shows the improvement of supplier relationship at Ford. Recently, Ford launched the Partnership for a Cleaner Environment program at the G7 Alliance Forum on Resource Efficiency workshop in Washington, DC in 2016. "We are committed to expanding our stewardship with our global suppliers to help minimize our environmental impact more broadly," said Hau Thai-Tang, Ford group vice president, global purchasing.[10] Good supplier relationships and collaboration are necessary for developing an end-to-end, integrated, sustainable supply chain.

DEVELOPING SUPPLIER RELATIONSHIPS

According to Kenichi Ohmae, global management consultant, and known as "Mr. Strategy" worldwide, "Companies are just beginning to learn what nations have always known: in a complex, uncertain world filled with dangerous opponents, it is best not to go it alone."[11] Building strong supplier partnerships requires a lot of hard work and commitment by both buyers and sellers. Developing true partnerships is not easily achieved, and much has to be done to get the partnership to work. An example is Raytheon, which has developed close supplier relationships with its suppliers (see nearby SCM Profile). Several key ingredients for developing successful partnerships are discussed below.

SCM Profile | Supplier Relationship Management at Raytheon[12]

Raytheon is a "technology and innovation leader specializing in defense, civil government, and cybersecurity solutions."[13] The company has 61,000 employees worldwide with sales in excess of $23 billion. The company realized that in the highly competitive U.S. defense industry, great technology alone is not sufficient to win orders. Factors such as purchase price and lifetime maintenance costs were becoming more critical. Consequently, Raytheon had to revamp how it collaborated with its suppliers. The thinking was that Raytheon had to move from a tactical relationship based on negotiated price to a more strategic one where suppliers participate early in the design of new products, where real cost reductions can be made. Raytheon had more than 10,000 suppliers and developing close relationships with that many suppliers was not possible. Raytheon needed to identify key suppliers to develop partnerships to compete successfully in the market place. Dave Nelson, a reputed leader in supply management, suggested a plan for Raytheon "… to earn preferential treatment from suppliers," which basically translates to "Customer of Choice." Getting there required a lot of hard work. One of the approaches recommended was to set up a Supplier Advisory Council (SAC) where a subset of suppliers representing a mix of large and small businesses were chosen to participate in the SAC. According to Mark Lee of Whitmor/Wirenetics, "As a supplier, we often find that there is a gap between what leadership wants to do and what procurement and engineering are doing. The SAC provides an opportunity for suppliers to discuss issues that management may not be aware of without fear of retaliation. In fact, if it's not candid, it won't work."[14] The real benefit is for Raytheon to reduce cost at the design stage and develop innovative technologies that are not only affordable but also have low lifetime maintenance cost.

Building Trust

Trust is critical for any partnership or alliance to work. It must be built not just at the senior management level but at all levels of the organization. Trust enables organizations to share valuable information, devote time and resources to understand each other's business, and achieve results beyond what could have been done individually. Jordan Lewis, in his book *Trusted Partners,* points out that "Trust does not imply easy harmony. Obviously, business is too complex to expect ready agreement on all issues. However, in a trusting relationship conflicts motivate you to probe for deeper understandings and search for constructive solutions. Trust creates goodwill, which sustains the relationship when one firm does something the other dislikes."[15] With trust, partners are more willing to work together; find compromise solutions to problems; work toward achieving long-term benefits for both parties; and in short, go the extra mile. In addition, there is goodwill developed over time between the partners. This can be beneficial when one partner gets into a difficult situation and the other partner is willing to help out.

Shared Vision and Objectives

All partnerships should state the expectations of the buyer and supplier, reasons and objectives of the partnership, and plans for the dissolution of the relationship. According to Lenwood Grant, sourcing expert with Bristol-Myers-Squibb, "You don't want a partnership that is based on necessity. If you don't think that the partnership is a good mix, but you do it because you have to—possibly because that supplier is the only provider of that material in the market, because you've signed an exclusive contract in the past, or for some other reason—it's not a true partnership and is likely to fail."[16] Both partners must share the same vision and have objectives that are not only clear but mutually agreeable. Many alliances and partnerships have failed because objectives are not well aligned or are overly optimistic. The focus must move beyond tactical issues and toward a more strategic path to corporate success. When partners have equal decision-making control, the partnership has a higher chance of success.

Personal Relationships

Interpersonal relationships in buyer–supplier partnerships are important since it is people who communicate and make things happen. According to Leonard Greenhalgh, author of *Managing Strategic Relationships,* "An alliance or partnership isn't really a relationship between companies, it's a relationship between specific individuals. When you are considering strategic alliances of any kind, the only time the company matters is in the status associated with it [strategic alliance]. Whoever is interfacing with the other company, they are the company."[17]

Mutual Benefits and Needs

Partnering should result in a win–win situation, which can only be achieved if both companies have compatible needs. Mutual needs not only create an environment conducive for collaboration but opportunities for increased innovation. When both parties share in the benefits of the partnership, the relationship will be productive and long lasting. An alliance is much like a marriage: if only one party is happy, the marriage is not likely to last. For example, highly qualified Toyota engineers who work as consultants on projects support Toyota's performance improvement programs with suppliers. Any cost savings arising from this program are shared with the suppliers. Toyota also ensures that their suppliers earn a reasonable return. An important recipe for success is when the buyer is respectful, fair, and trustworthy in its dealings with suppliers.

Commitment and Top Management Support

First, it takes a lot of time and hard work to find the right partner. Having done so, both parties must dedicate their time, best people, and resources to make the partnership succeed. According to author Stephen R. Covey, "Without involvement, there is no commitment. Mark it down, asterisk it, circle it, underline it. No involvement, no commitment."[18] Commitment must start at the highest management level. Partnerships tend to be successful when top executives are actively supporting them. The level of cooperation and involvement shown by the organization's top leaders is likely to set the tone for joint problem solving further down the line.

Successful partners are committed to continuously looking for opportunities to grow their businesses together. Management must create the right kind of internal attitude needed for alliances to flourish. Since partnerships are likely to encounter bumps along the way, it is critical that management adopt a collaborative approach to conflict resolution instead of assigning blame.

Change Management

With change comes stress, which can lead to a loss of focus. Companies must avoid distractions from their core businesses as a result of the changes brought about by the partnership. Companies must be prepared to manage change that comes with the formation of new partnerships. According to author Stephen Covey, "The key to successful change management is remaining focused on a set of core principles that do not change, regardless of the circumstances."[19] In a case study on delivering value through strategic supplier relationships, Hewlett Packard (HP) identified several key steps to ensure better change management[20]:

- Identify internal champions
- Secure executive buy-in
- Coordinate internal communication and support teams
- Train and survey impacted managers
- Conduct business reviews with key client groups

HP realized that having internal champions and coordination enabled better change management.

Information Sharing and Lines of Communication

Both formal and informal lines of communication should be set up to facilitate free flows of information. When there is high degree of trust, information systems can be customized to serve each other more effectively. Confidentiality of sensitive financial, product, and process information must be maintained. Any conflict that occurs can be resolved if the channels of communication are open. For instance, early communication to suppliers of specification changes and new product introductions are contributing factors to the success of purchasing partnerships. Buyers and sellers should meet regularly to discuss any change of plans, evaluate results, and address issues critical to the success of the partnerships. Since there is free exchange of information, nondisclosure agreements are often used to protect proprietary information and other sensitive data from leaking out. It is not the quantity but rather the quality and accuracy of the information exchanged that indicates the success of information sharing.

While collaboration has many positives, there is also the fear of the loss of trade secrets when sensitive information is shared between partners. According to the U.S. Economic Espionage Act of 1996, the definition of trade secrets is: "All forms and types of financial, business, scientific, technical, economic, or engineering information, including patterns, plans, compilations, programmed devices, formulas, designs, prototypes, methods, techniques, processes, procedures, programs, or codes, whether tangible or intangible, and whether or how stored, compiled, or memorialized physically, electronically, graphically, photographically, or in writing."[21] Trade secrets tend to be more critical in the high-technology sector where the unique technique or process used in the company's business can provide it with tremendous competitive advantage. Vendors have been known to steal or misappropriate trade secrets, terminate the partnership, and become competitors. One of the most basic and successful approaches for protecting trade secrets is to require employees and vendors to sign a nondisclosure agreement.

Relationship Capabilities

Organizations must develop the right capabilities for creating long-term relationships with their suppliers. In a study on world-class procurement organizations, the Hackett Group found that one of the two best practices for top-performing companies is using cross-functional teams to achieve common objectives.[22] Thus, companies aspiring to be world class must develop cross-functional team capabilities. In addition, the employees must not only be able to collaborate successfully within the company in a cross-functional team setting but also have the skills to do so externally. Key suppliers must have the right technology and capabilities to meet cost, quality, and delivery requirements. In addition, suppliers must be sufficiently flexible to respond quickly to changing customer requirements. Before entering into any partnership, it is imperative for an organization to conduct a thorough investigation of its suppliers' capabilities and core competencies. Organizations prefer working with suppliers who have the technology and technical expertise to assist in the development of new products or services that would lead to a competitive advantage in the marketplace.

Performance Metrics

The old adage "You can't improve what you don't measure" is particularly true for buyer–supplier alliances. Measures related to quality, cost, delivery, and flexibility have traditionally been used to evaluate how well suppliers are doing. Information provided by supplier performance will be used to improve the entire supply chain. Thus, the goal of any good performance evaluation system is to provide metrics that are understandable, easy to measure, and focused on real value-added results for both the buyer and supplier.

By evaluating supplier performance, organizations hope to identify suppliers with exceptional performance or developmental needs, improve supplier communication, reduce risk, and manage the partnership based on an analysis of reported data. Northrup Grumman rates their supplier performance using a scorecard format based on four categories: quality profile rating, late delivery, customer satisfaction, and process health/lean Six Sigma.[23] After all, it is not unusual that the best customers want to work with the best suppliers. Additionally, the best suppliers are commonly rewarded and recognized for their achievements. Supplier awards will be discussed later in this chapter.

Although price or cost is an important factor when selecting suppliers, other criteria such as technical expertise, lead times, environmental awareness, and market knowledge must also be considered. In the electronics industry, which pioneered the Six Sigma revolution, quality is the prime supplier selection criteria due to its strategic importance. Thus quality and the ability of suppliers to bring new technologies and innovations to the table, rather than cost, are often the key selection drivers. A multicriteria approach is therefore needed to measure supplier performance. Examples of broad performance metrics are shown in Table 3.1.

Over the past several years, **total cost of ownership** (TCO), a broad-based performance metric, has been widely discussed in the supply chain literature. As mentioned in Chapter 2, TCO is defined as "the combination of the purchase or acquisition price of a good or service and additional costs incurred before or after product or service delivery." Costs are often grouped into **pretransaction**, **transaction**, and **posttransaction costs**.[24] These three major cost categories are described as follows:

- *Pretransaction costs:* These costs are incurred prior to order and receipt of the purchased goods. Examples are the cost of certifying and training suppliers, investigating alternative sources of supply, and delivery options for new suppliers.

- *Transaction costs:* These costs include the cost of the goods/services and cost associated with placing and receiving the order. Examples are purchase price, preparation of orders, and delivery costs.

- *Posttransaction costs:* These costs are incurred after the goods are in the possession of the company, agents, or customers. Examples are field failures, company's goodwill/reputation, maintenance costs, and warranty costs.

Table 3.1	Examples of Supplier Performance Metrics

1. Cost/Price
- Competitive price
- Availability of cost breakdowns
- Productivity improvement/cost reduction programs
- Willingness to negotiate price
- Inventory cost
- Information cost
- Transportation cost
- Actual cost compared to: historical (standard) cost, target cost, cost-reduction goal, benchmark cost
- Extent of cooperation leading to improved cost

2. Quality
- Percent defect free
- Use of statistical process control
- Use of continuous process improvement
- Fitness for use
- Use of corrective action program
- Use of documented quality program such as ISO 9000
- Warranty characteristics
- Actual quality compared to: historical quality, specification quality, target quality
- Quality improvement compared to: historical quality, quality-improvement goal
- Extent of cooperation leading to improved quality

3. Delivery
- Delivery time
- Delivery reliability
- Percentage of defect-free deliveries
- Actual delivery compared to promised delivery window (i.e., two days early to zero days late)
- Extent of cooperation leading to improved delivery

4. Responsiveness and Flexibility
- Responsiveness to customers
- Accuracy of record keeping
- Ability to work effectively with teams
- Responsiveness to changing situations
- Participation/success of supplier certification program
- Short-cycle changes in demand/flexible capacity
- Changes in delivery schedules
- Participation in new product development
- Solving problems
- Willingness of supplier to seek inputs regarding product/service changes
- Advance notification given by supplier as a result of product/service changes
- Receptiveness to partnering or teaming

5. Environment
- Environmentally responsible
- Use of environmental management system such as ISO 14000
- Extent of cooperation leading to improved environmental issues

---

6. Technology
- Proactive improvement using proven manufacturing/service technology
- Superior product/service design
- Extent of cooperation leading to improved technology

7. Business Metrics
- Reputation of supplier/leadership in the field
- Long-term relationship
- Quality of information sharing
- Financial strength such as Dun & Bradstreet's credit rating
- Strong customer support group
- Total cash flow
- Rate of return on investment
- Extent of cooperation leading to improved business processes and performance

8. Total Cost of Ownership
- Purchased products shipped cost-effectively
- Cost of special handling
- Additional supplier costs as the result of the buyer's scheduling and shipment needs
- Cost of defects, rework, and problem solving associated with purchases

---

TCO provides a proactive approach for understanding costs and supplier performance leading to reduced costs. However, the challenge is to effectively identify the key cost drivers needed to determine the total cost of ownership.

Continuous Improvement

The process of evaluating suppliers based on a set of mutually agreed performance measures provides opportunities for continuous improvement. As discussed in Chapter 8, continuous improvement involves continuously making a series of small improvements over time, resulting in the elimination of waste in a system. Both buyers and suppliers must be willing to continuously improve their capabilities in meeting customer requirements pertaining to things like cost, quality, delivery, sustainability, and technology. Partners should not focus on merely correcting mistakes, but work proactively toward eliminating them completely. For continuous improvement to succeed, employees must first identify areas that are working to understand the improvements made. These improvements provide the basis for implementing improvements in other processes, which in turn will lead to even more success. In today's dynamic environment, staying ahead of change means that you have to practice continuous improvement. Companies must work with suppliers on continuous improvement programs to ensure that products and services are meeting customer requirements.

Monitoring Supplier Relationships

Unless an organization has a firm grasp of the key issues surrounding supplier relationships, it cannot reap the benefits of such relationships. An assessment of how the relationships with an organization's suppliers are doing will enable these relationships to be managed better. In a study of the food industry, five key performance indicators were identified to objectively measure supply chain relationship performance:[25]

- Creativity—promoting quality, innovation, and a long-term approach by encouraging high performance.
- Stability—investment, synchronization of objectives, and confidence building.
- Communication—frequent, open dialogue and information sharing.
- Reliability—concentrating on service and product delivery, lowering joint costs.
- Value—creating a win–win relationship in which each side is delighted to be a part.

In the same study, several intrinsic characteristics of relationship performance were also identified as follows:[26]

- Long-term Orientation—encouraging stability, continuity, predictability, and long-term joint gains.
- Interdependence—loss in autonomy is compensated through the expected gains.
- C^3 Behavior—collaboration, cooperation, coordination, jointly resourcing to achieve effective operations.
- Trust—richer interaction between parties to create goodwill and the incentive to go the extra mile.
- Commitment—the relationship is so important that it warrants maximum effort to maintain it.
- Adaptation—willingness to adapt products, procedures, inventory, management, attitudes, values, and goals to the needs of the relationship.
- Personal Relationships—generating trust and openness through personal interaction.

The assessment of key performance indicators should create a clear understanding of what the issues are, so that the problems can be resolved to further improve the relationship.

Key Points

It must be noted that developing supplier partnerships is not easy. All the factors mentioned above have to be in place for the supplier relationship to be successful. While there are numerous instances where supplier partnerships work well, there are also examples where the relationship did not turn out as expected. An example is the horsemeat scandal in the United Kingdom several years ago. Hamburgers containing horsemeat DNA were made by the Silvercrest factory of the ABP Group in Ireland. According to Ryan Finstad, director of operations at California-based supply chain solutions provider Cathay Solutions, "Companies that have long-standing relationships with their manufacturers have naturally become more lax over time. As these firms searched for ways to cut costs, they may have reduced or eliminated monitoring of manufacturers that had historically performed well."[27] As a result, without a good quality verification program, it is easy for suppliers to compromise on quality and to deliver substandard products. The importance of supplier relationships cannot be overstated, and cultivating these relationships is an essential part of doing business globally.

The recent emission scandal, outlined in the nearby SCM Profile, is considered one of the most expensive in automotive history and caused Volkswagen to pay $14.7 billion to settle with three federal agencies. Bosch, one of VW's major suppliers, is also part of the investigation. Transparency and communication are necessary to avoid problems like these in the supply chain.

SCM Profile | **The VW Diesel Emission Scandal**

The Volkswagen emission scandal hit the automotive market hard. The problems ultimately affected VW's supply chain, both upstream and downstream. Consumers have sued the company for loss in value of their cars. VW dealerships are also not immune from this problem. Sales were affected as a result of the scandal. What was shocking was the deliberate deception of customers and government agencies. A Volkswagen engineer pleaded guilty to "… helping the auto maker's admitted efforts to cheat on emissions tests, becoming the first person criminally convicted in the United States in a wide-ranging scandal that has cost the German giant billions of dollars."[28] VW had acknowledged earlier to installing illegal emissions-cheating software on about 600,000 diesel cars in the United States and 11 million vehicles globally. The conspiracy started in November 2006 and continued until the cheating was discovered in September 2015. This is the first case where the Justice Department had charged an individual in corporate investigations. VW will pay $14.7 billion as part of a settlement with three federal agencies who sued the company for excessive diesel emissions.[29]

The investigation of VW has been extended to its suppliers. Bloomberg News reported that the Justice Department is "… looking at whether industry suppliers also knew or contributed to VW's insertion of software into diesel-powered cars to allow them to cheat emissions tests."[30] In particular, Bosch, one of the world's largest manufacturers of components and systems to the auto industry, "… supplied diesel software to VW for test purposes but it ended up in vehicles on the road."[31] Bosch issued a statement saying: "As is usual in the automotive supply industry, Bosch supplies these components to the automaker's specifications. How these components are calibrated and integrated into complete vehicle systems is the responsibility of each automaker." Bosch has allocated €750 m for legal costs relating to this case.[32] This scandal has been very costly for both VW and Bosch.

SUPPLIER EVALUATION AND CERTIFICATION

Only the best suppliers are targeted as partners. Companies want to develop partnerships with the best suppliers to leverage their expertise and technologies to create a competitive advantage. Learning more about how an organization's key suppliers are performing can lead to greater visibility, which can provide opportunities for further collaborative involvement in value-added activities. Many organizations are tracking product and service quality, on-time deliveries, customer service efforts, and cost-control programs as part of the supplier rating system. This information can be used to develop supplier programs that will help eliminate problems or improve supply chain performance.

A supplier evaluation and certification process must be in place so that organizations can identify their best and most reliable suppliers. In addition, sourcing decisions are made based on facts and not perception of a supplier's capabilities. Providing frequent feedback on supplier performance can help organizations avoid major surprises and maintain good relationships.

One of the goals of evaluating suppliers is to determine if the supplier is performing according to the buyer's requirements. An extension of supplier evaluation is **supplier certification**, defined by the Institute of Supply Management as "an organization's process for evaluating the quality systems of key suppliers in an effort to eliminate incoming inspections."[33] The certification process implies a willingness on the part of customers and suppliers to share goals, commitments, and risks to improve their relationships. This would involve making visits to observe the operations at the supplier organizations. For example, dirty bathrooms and messy shop floors could indicate that an emphasis on quality is lacking in the production facility. A supplier certification program also indicates long-term mutual commitment. For example, a certification program might provide incentives for suppliers to deliver parts directly to the point of use in the buyer firm, thus reducing costs associated with incoming inspection and storage of inventory.

Implementing an effective supplier certification program is critical to reducing the supplier base, building long-term relationships, reducing time spent on incoming inspections, improving delivery and responsiveness, recognizing excellence, developing a commitment to continuous improvement, and improving overall performance. Supplier certification allows organizations to identify the suppliers who are most committed to creating and maintaining a partnership and who have the best capabilities. Listed below are several criteria generally found in certification programs:

- No incoming product lot rejections (e.g., less than 0.5 percent defective) for a specified time period
- No incoming nonproduct rejections (e.g., late delivery) for a specified time period
- No significant supplier production-related negative incidents for a specified time period
- ISO 9001/Q9000 certified or successfully passing a recent, on-site quality system evaluation
- ISO 14001 certified
- Mutually agreed upon set of clearly specified quality performance measures
- Fully documented process and quality system with cost controls and continuous improvement capabilities, and
- Supplier's processes are stable and in control.

The Weighted Criteria Evaluation System

One approach toward evaluating and certifying suppliers is to use the weighted criteria evaluation system described in the steps below:

1. Select the key dimensions of performance mutually acceptable to both customer and supplier.
2. Monitor and collect performance data.
3. Assign weights to each of the dimensions of performance based on their relative importance to the company's objectives. The weights for all dimensions must sum to one.
4. Evaluate each of the performance measures on a rating between 0 (fails to meet any intended purpose or performance) and 100 (exceptional in meeting intended purpose or performance).
5. Multiply the dimension ratings by their respective importance weights and then sum to get an overall weighted score.

6. Classify vendors based on their overall scores, for example:
- Unacceptable (less than 50)—supplier dropped from further business
- Conditional (between 50 and 70)—supplier needs development work to improve performance but may be dropped if performance continues to lag
- Certified (between 70 and 90)—supplier meets intended purpose or performance
- Preferred (greater than 90)—supplier will be considered for involvement in new product development and opportunities for more business

7. Audit and ongoing certification review.

An example of the above evaluation and certification process is shown in Example 3.1.

Federal-Mogul is a company that uses a weighted scorecard to evaluate its suppliers. The company has a SupplyNet Scorecard website[34] that provides its Supplier Rating Qualifications and rates suppliers on three main categories, with the weights shown in parentheses: delivery (40 percent), quality (40 percent), and supplier cost-saving suggestions (20 percent). The quality score is based on two equally weighted components: parts per million defective and the quantity of supplier corrective action requests issued. The on-time delivery score is computed as "the average percentage across using plants for the current month. On-time delivery percentage has a window of one day early and zero days late to the due date and ±5 percent of order quantity. The on-time delivery percentage is determined by line items received on time divided by the number of line items due by the supplier for the month." The *Overall Rating Weighted Point Score* ranges from 0 to 100. Suppliers are considered "preferred" if they score between 90 and 100. Preferred suppliers are those that Federal-Mogul will work with on new product development, approve for new business, and assist in maintaining a competitive position. An "acceptable" supplier rating is between 70 and 89. In this category, the supplier is required to provide a plan to Federal-Mogul on how to achieve preferred status. A score of 0 to 69 means that the supplier has a "developmental" supplier rating. Here, Federal-Mogul requires the vendor to take corrective action if the supplier is rated at this level for three consecutive months during the calendar year.

External Certifications

Today, external certifications such as ISO 9000 and ISO 14000 have gained popularity globally as natural extensions of an organization's internal supplier evaluation and certification program. These evaluation criteria are frequently used to evaluate suppliers and are briefly discussed next.

Example 3.1   Supplier Scorecard Used for the XYZ Company

PERFORMANCE MEASURE	RATING	×	WEIGHT	=	FINAL VALUE
Technology	80		0.10		8.00
Quality	90		0.25		22.50
Responsiveness	95		0.15		14.25
Delivery	90		0.15		13.50
Cost	80		0.15		12.00
Environmental	90		0.05		4.50
Business	90		0.15		13.50
Total score			1.00		88.25

Note: Based on the total score of 88.25, the XYZ Company is considered a certified supplier.

ISO 9000

In 1987, the global network of national standards institutes, called the International Organization for Standardization (ISO), developed **ISO 9000**, a series of management and quality assurance standards in design, development, production, installation, and service. There are many standards in the ISO 9000 family, including[35]:

- ISO 9000:2015—covers the basic concepts and language
- ISO 9001:2015—sets out the requirements of a quality management system
- ISO 9004:2009—focuses on how to make a quality management system more efficient and effective
- ISO 19011:2011—sets out guidance on internal and external audits of quality management systems.

The European Union in 1992 adopted a plan that recognized ISO 9001 as a third-party certification; the result is that many European companies (as well as companies outside Europe) prefer suppliers with ISO 9001 certifications. Thus, companies wanting to sell in the global marketplace are compelled to seek ISO 9001 certifications.

To date, more than 1 million ISO 9001 certificates have been awarded.[36] In the United States over 33,000 certificates have been issued. China, which has the largest number of ISO 9001 certificates, has issued over 292,000, representing 28.3 percent of the total certificates issued worldwide. Obtaining the ISO 9001 certification provides further verification that the supplier has an established quality management system in place. ISO certification will lead organizations to consistently deliver products that meet customer and applicable statutory and regulatory requirements. In addition, organizations seek to enhance customer satisfaction by continual improvement of their quality management system. A recent survey clearly showed that the primary reason for seeking ISO 9001 certification is improved customer satisfaction. The basic ISO 9000/9001 standards are discussed further in Chapter 8.[37]

ISO 14000

In 1996, **ISO 14000**, a family of international standards for environmental management, was first introduced. In 2004, it was revised to make the standards easier to understand and emphasized compliance and compatibility with ISO 9000 for businesses that wanted to combine their environmental and quality management systems. There are many standards in the ISO 14000 family and these are covered in ISO's publication, "Environmental Management—The ISO 14000 Family of International Standards."[38] Organizations can only be certified to ISO 14001:2004, which sets the criteria and framework for an organization to develop an effective environmental management system but does not state requirements for environmental performance.

The benefits of investing in an **Environmental Management System** (EMS) based on ISO 14000 standards include the following[39]:

- Demonstrate compliance with current and future statutory and regulatory requirements
- Increase leadership involvement and engagement of employees
- Improve company reputation and the confidence of stakeholders through strategic communication

- Achieve strategic business aims by incorporating environmental issues into business management
- Provide a competitive and financial advantage through improved efficiencies and reduced costs
- Encourage better environmental performance of suppliers by integrating them into the organization's business systems

As of 2015, there were 6,067 ISO 14001 certificates issued in the United States, representing 2 percent of the 319,324 certificates issued globally in 192 countries.[40] China and Japan are the top two countries with ISO 14001 certificates. Given the interest in sustainability, investments in environmental management systems and ISO 14001 are likely to increase in the future. Additionally, as more organizations are certified in ISO 14001, they are likely to pass this requirement on to their suppliers. ISO 14001 enables an organization's management, employees, and external stakeholders to measure and improve environmental impacts.

SUPPLIER DEVELOPMENT

Supplier development is defined as "any activity that a buyer undertakes to improve a supplier's performance and/or capabilities to meet the buyer's short- and/or long-term supply needs."[41] Supplier development requires financial and human resource investments by both partners and includes a wide range of activities such as training of the supplier's personnel, investing in the supplier's operations, and ongoing performance assessment. As companies outsource more and more parts, a larger portion of costs lies outside the company in a supply chain, and it becomes increasingly difficult to achieve further cost savings internally. One way out of this dilemma is for companies to work with their suppliers to lower the total cost of materials purchased. Companies that are able to leverage their supply base to impact their total cost structure will have a competitive advantage in their markets.

A seven-step approach to supplier development is outlined below:[42]

1. *Identify critical goods and services.* Assess the relative importance of the goods and services from a strategic perspective. Goods and services that are purchased in high volume, do not have good substitutes, or have limited sources of supply are considered strategic supplies.

2. *Identify critical suppliers not meeting performance requirements.* Suppliers of strategic supplies not currently meeting minimum performance in quality, on-time delivery, cost, technology, or cycle time are targets for supplier development initiatives.

3. *Form a cross-functional supplier development team.* Next, the buyer must develop an internal cross-functional team and arrive at a clear agreement for the supplier development initiatives.

4. *Meet with the top management of suppliers.* The buyer's cross-functional team meets with the suppliers' top management to discuss details of strategic alignment, supplier performance expectations and measurement, a time frame for improvement, and ongoing professionalism.

5. *Rank supplier development projects.* After the supplier development opportunities have been identified, they are evaluated in terms of feasibility, resource and time requirements, supply base alternatives, and expected return on investment. The most promising development projects are selected.

6. *Define the details of the buyer–supplier agreement.* After consensus has been reached on the development project rankings, the buyer and supplier representatives jointly decide on the performance metrics to be monitored such as percent improvement in quality, delivery, and cycle time.

7. *Monitor project status and modify strategies.* To ensure continued success, management must actively monitor progress, promote exchange of information, and revise the development strategies as conditions warrant.

Intel's Supplier Continuous Quality Improvement (SCQI) program is a "corporate wide program that utilizes critical Intel supplier management tools and processes to drive continuous improvements in a supplier's overall performance and business."[43] Their SCQI program was started in the 1980s with the objective of improving supplier quality and minimizing the time needed to inspect incoming products. Intel suppliers are rewarded with the company's prestigious SCQI Award if they demonstrate "industry-leading results and commitment across all critical focus areas on which they are measured: quality, cost, availability, technology, customer service, labor and ethics systems, and environmental sustainability."[44]

According to Intel, the SCQI program accomplishes the following:

- Establishes aligned goals, indicators, and metrics
- Enables benchmarking of supplier performance
- Identifies potential quality issues before they impact Intel
- Drives supplier agility and ability to provide leading-edge products and services
- Matures critical Intel–supplier relationships
- Encourages collaborative agreements, team problem resolution, and two-way continuous learning
- Encourages continuous improvement throughout the year
- Provides data to support supplier recognition

With the SCQI program, Intel was able to reap valuable benefits from their suppliers. Additionally, as the quality of the suppliers' products improves, greater opportunities exist for making further improvements.

By tracking supplier performance over time, Honeywell is able to observe trends and to catch problems early. Honeywell has implemented its Six Sigma Plus program aimed at eliminating variations in processes to meet required specifications with no more than 3.4 parts per million defective (or 99.9997 percent error free) and to apply lean manufacturing techniques to eliminate waste and to synchronize suppliers' activities. At Honeywell, "Six Sigma is a critical strategy to accelerate improvements in processes, products, and services, and to radically reduce manufacturing and/or administrative costs and improve quality. These outcomes are achieved by relentlessly focusing on eliminating waste and reducing defects and variation."[45] The ultimate aim of the Six Sigma strategy is to provide maximum value to customers through a logical and structured approach to all business processes.

In summary, it is critical that an organization has an active supplier development program. The program should be managed such that it can meet both current and future needs. With a proactive supplier development program, suppliers are forced to stay on top of today's dynamic environment so that customers are not stuck with products or services that are not leading edge.

SUPPLIER RECOGNITION PROGRAMS

While a large percentage of companies track supplier performance, only about half recognize excellent performance with supplier awards and appreciation banquets. Today, it is not sufficient just to reward your best suppliers with more business; companies need to recognize and celebrate the achievements of their best suppliers. As award-winning suppliers, they serve as role models for a firm's other suppliers. Boeing understands that *supplier performance excellence is critical to its success.* The company's Supplier of the Year Award is based on the "… high quality of their (supplier's) product or service and the value they create for Boeing and its global airline and United States and allied government customers."[46] Boeing realizes that they need excellent suppliers to keep the company at the leading edge of technology and innovation. "I've witnessed firsthand the critical role suppliers—and especially the best ones—play in Boeing's success," said Dennis Muilenburg, Boeing chairman, president, and CEO. "Our supply chain partners help us provide our customers with more capability for less cost in today's tough and dynamic business environment. We have ambitious goals for the future, and I know we will achieve them, in part, by working closely with our exceptional extended team."[47]

As part of Intel's SCQI Program, there are three recognition awards: Certified Supplier Award (CSA), Preferred Quality Supplier (PQS) Award, and Supplier Continuous Quality Improvement (SCQI) Award. The CSA is given to suppliers who consistently meet Intel's expectations and have a proven commitment to continuous improvement. Intel's PQS award is for outstanding commitment to quality, excellent performance, and excellence at meeting and exceeding high expectations and tough performance goals. The SCQI Award, which is the most prestigious of Intel's three recognition awards, is given to suppliers who have a score of at least 95 percent on performance and the capability to meet cost, quality, availability, delivery, technology, and environmental, social, and governance goals. In addition, suppliers must score 90 percent or greater on a challenging improvement plan and show outstanding quality and business systems. "Intel's SCQI award winners demonstrate a relentless pursuit of excellence and the highest standards of responsibility, service and professionalism," said Sohail Ahmed, senior vice president and general manager of Intel's Technology and Manufacturing Group. "These companies are truly world class, and we're honored to recognize their important role in helping Intel remain at the forefront of technology manufacturing and global supply chain leadership."[48] According to Jacklyn Sturm, vice president, Technology and Manufacturing Group and general manager of Global Supply Management at Intel, "The winners of the Preferred Quality Supplier and Achievement Award are an integral part of Intel's success. The absolute focus and rigorous attention to continuous improvement and time-to-market innovation are a testament to their world-class support, providing Intel with a critical part of the foundation to be a leader in computing innovations." [49]

Hormel Food Corporation's No. 1 Award program differs from other programs because they only give this award once every five years. Hormel gave out its first award in 1996, with the last award presented in 2016. To qualify for the No. 1 Award, a supplier must have met the following criteria:[50]

- Have a supplier rating index of 96 percent or better in the fourth calendar quarter of the reporting year. The average of the five-year supplier rating index must be equal to or greater than 96 percent.

- Must be a recipient of the Spirit of Excellence Award—an annual award given by Hormel Foods—for a minimum of four times over the last five consecutive years.

- Meet additional requirements in the areas of number of products sold by the supplier to Hormel Foods, dollars of exposure and deliveries to Hormel Foods, number of Hormel Foods locations serviced, and participation in continuous improvement processes.

Hormel also has a yearly Spirit of Excellence Award given to suppliers achieving a minimum supplier rating index score of 92 over a twelve-month period. The criteria for the Supplier Rating Index include an ability to meet requirements, make timely deliveries, provide accurate administrative support, and maintain inventories. Additional criteria such as customer support, awareness of environmental concerns, and sales representative performance are considered but are not a requirement for the award. "I would like to congratulate these suppliers on this special recognition," said Bryan D. Farnsworth, senior vice president of supply chain at Hormel Foods. "Thank you all for the outstanding contributions you make to our company in respect to the goods and services you provide us."[51] The Spirit of Excellence Award also recognizes the role these suppliers play in Hormel's continuous improvement process throughout the year.

SUPPLIER RELATIONSHIP MANAGEMENT

Supplier relationship management (SRM) has garnered increasing attention among firms actively practicing supply chain management. According to global consultant Accenture, SRM "… encompasses a broad suite of capabilities that facilitate collaboration, sourcing, transaction execution and performance monitoring between an organization and its trading partners. SRM leverages the latest technology capabilities to integrate and enhance supplier oriented processes along the supply chain such as design-to-source, source-to-contract and procure-to-pay."[52] In a nutshell, SRM involves streamlining the processes and communication between the buyer and supplier and using software applications that enable these processes to be managed more efficiently and effectively.

The success of e-procurement, which has a predominantly internal focus, created the need for SRM solutions for managing the supply side of an organization's supply chain. SRM software automates the exchange of information among several layers of relationships that are complex and too time-consuming to manage manually and results in improved procurement efficiency, lower business costs, real-time visibility, faster communication between buyer and seller, and enhanced supply chain collaboration. A list of some of the SRM software vendors is shown in Table 3.2.

Table 3.2	**Examples of Companies Offering SRM Software**
JDA Software Group, Inc. (www.jda.com)	
Customers: Airbus SAS, Finmeccanica SpA, Galileo Avionica SpA, GES International Limited, Honeywell International Inc., Lockheed Martin Integrated Systems & Solutions, Northrop Grumman Information Systems, Rafael Advanced Defense Systems Ltd., Rockwell Collins, Inc., Samsung SDS Co., Ltd., Sandia National Laboratories, Schneider Electric SA, The Tokyo Electric Power Company, Inc., Toshiba Semiconductor Company	
(Acquired Manugistics in July 2006, i2 Technologies in January 2010)	
Oracle (www.oracle.com)	
Customers: Dartmouth-Hitchcock Medical Center, Commonwealth Bank, Duke Energy, Foxwoods, City of Los Angeles	
(Acquired PeopleSoft in 2005)	
SAP (www.sap.com)	
Customers: British American Tobacco, Capgemini Procurement Services, Consol Energy Inc., Deloitte, Johnson Controls, Pitney Bowes Inc., Newell-Rubbermaid, envia Mitteldeutsche Energie AG, Swisscom	

Many organizations are investing in SRM software modules due to the wealth of information that can be derived from these systems. SRM software can organize supplier information and provide answers to questions such as:

- Who are our current suppliers? Are they the right set of suppliers?
- Who are our best suppliers, and what are their competitive rankings?
- What are our suppliers' performances with respect to on-time delivery, quality, and costs?
- Can we consolidate our buying to achieve greater scale economies?
- Do we have consistency in suppliers and performance across different locations and facilities?
- What goods/services do we purchase?
- What purchased parts can be reused in new designs?

SAP's Supplier Relationship Management application (SAP SRM) provides companies with innovative approaches to effectively coordinate business processes with key suppliers. SAP SRM enables companies to optimize their procurement strategy, to work more efficiently with their suppliers, and therefore gain long-term benefits from their supplier relationships. SAP SRM enables companies to examine and forecast purchasing behavior, shorten procurement cycles, and work with their partners in real time. As a result companies are able to develop long-term relationships with all those suppliers that have proven to be reliable partners. [53]

In general, SRM software varies by vendors in terms of capabilities offered. AMR Research has identified five key tenets of an SRM system:[54]

- Automation of transactional processes between an organization and its suppliers.
- Integration that provides a view of the supply chain that spans multiple departments, processes, and software applications for internal users and external partners.
- Visibility of information and process flows in and between organizations. Views are customized by role and aggregated via a single portal.
- Collaboration through information sharing and suppliers' ability to input information directly into an organization's supply chain information system.
- Optimization of processes and decision-making through enhanced analytical tools such as data warehousing and online analytical processing (OLAP) tools with the migration toward more dynamic optimization tools in the future.

There are two types of SRM: transactional and analytic. **Transactional SRM** enables an organization to track supplier interactions such as order planning, order payment, and returns. The volume of transactions involved may result in independent systems maintained by geographic region or business lines. Transactional SRM tends to focus on short-term reporting and is event driven, focusing on such questions as: What did we buy yesterday? What supplier did we use? What was the cost of the purchase? On the other hand, **analytic SRM** allows the company to analyze the complete supplier base. The analysis provides answers to questions such as: Which suppliers should the company develop long-term relationships with? Which suppliers would make the company more profitable? Analytic SRM enables more difficult and important questions about supplier relationships. Thus, we can see that transactional SRM addresses tactical issues such as order size, whereas analytic SRM focuses on long-term procurement strategies. With analytic SRM, an organization can assess where it was yesterday, where it stands today, and where it wants to go in the future to meet its strategic purchasing goals.

The challenges in any SRM software implementation are assembling all the data needed for an SRM application to work, and employee training. For example, analysis of supplier information requires access to applications containing data about suppliers, as well as enterprise resource planning, accounting and existing supplier information databases. Before SRM implementation, buyers typically spend 10 percent of their time on supplier relationship development, 40 percent on expediting, and 50 percent on order processing/ tracking. After SRM implementation, the buyer's time allocation is estimated to be 50 percent on collaborative planning, 30 percent on supplier relationship development, 10 percent on expediting, and 10 percent on exception management.

Until recent years, purchasing professionals did not have the right technologies to help them accomplish their jobs effectively. Automating procurement activities can lead to significant cost savings as buyers move toward managing processes by exception. This effectively frees buyers to focus on more strategic and value-added activities such as collaborative planning. In addition, purchasing professionals can work effectively on maximizing the return on their relationships with suppliers. Greater procurement visibility from using SRM software also translates into smoother processes, faster cycle times, reduced new product development, improved time to market, streamlined purchasing, and reduced inventory costs. The Toshiba Semiconductor Company used JDA's SRM software to reduce its list of suppliers to the most valuable suppliers only. In the process, Toshiba was able to get the best price, quality, and delivery performance from its suppliers.

SUMMARY

Over the past few decades, we have seen the buyer–supplier relationship evolves from an arm's-length/adversarial approach to one favoring the development of long-term partnerships. Significant competitive advantage can be achieved by organizations working closely with their suppliers. Without a shared vision, mutual benefits, and top management commitment, partnerships are likely to be short-lived. Other ingredients necessary for developing and managing lasting supplier relationships are trust, creating personal relationships, effective change management, sharing of information, and using performance metrics to create superior capabilities. Mutually agreeable measures to monitor supplier performance provide the basis for continuous improvement to enhance supplier quality, cost, and delivery. Supplier certification ensures that buyers continue to work with their best suppliers to improve cost, quality, delivery, and new product development to gain a competitive advantage. Finally, supplier relationship management software automates the exchange of information and allows for improved efficiency and effectiveness in managing supplier relationships and improving performance. Organizations that successfully implement supplier relationship management can improve quality, reduce cost, access new technologies from their suppliers, increase speed to market, reduce risk, and achieve high performance.

KEY TERMS

analytic SRM, 99

business metrics, 105

Environmental Management System, 94

ISO 14000, 94

ISO 9000, 94

posttransaction costs, 87

pretransaction, 87

supplier certification, 91

supplier development, 95

supplier relationship management, 98

total cost of ownership, 87

transaction, 87

transactional SRM, 99

DISCUSSION QUESTIONS

1. Explain the importance of supplier relationships to the performance of an organization.

2. Compare and contrast the arm's length or adversarial approach to the partnership approach to building customer–supplier relationships.

3. Explain how an organization can manage its suppliers more effectively.

4. What are the key factors that contribute to a lasting buyer–supplier partnership?

5. Explain how manufacturers can leverage their suppliers to gain a competitive advantage.

6. Describe the key performance indicators used to objectively measure the performance of supplier relationships.

7. Explain why the majority of strategic alliances fail.

8. What are the criteria used in evaluating a supplier?

9. Discuss how an organization develops a supplier evaluation and certification program.

10. What are the benefits and challenges of investing in supplier development programs?

11. Describe the steps needed to develop a successful supplier development program.

12. What are the benefits of ISO 9000 certification?

13. Do sustainability issues influence purchasing decisions? What are the benefits of ISO 14000 certification?

14. Research ISO's website (www.iso.ch), and discuss the growth of ISO 9000 and 14000 certifications by regions of the world such as Africa/West Asia, Central and South America, North America, Europe, Far East, and Australia/New Zealand.

15. Explain the key capabilities of supplier relationship management software.

16. Why do organizations have supplier awards programs?

17. What is supplier certification? Why do companies want to have a supplier certification program?

18. How can supplier development and relationships help in avoiding scandals such as product fraud and recalls, which are damaging to an organization's reputation and profitability?

19. List the similarities and differences in the capabilities of SRM software offered by JDA, Oracle, and SAP.

20. What are the advantages of using SRM solutions to manage suppliers?

21. What are the differences between transactional and analytic SRM?

PROBLEMS

1. The Dominguez Hills Manufacturing Company is performing an annual evaluation of one of its suppliers, the Carson Company. Bo, purchasing manager of the Dominguez Hills Manufacturing Company, has collected the following information on the Carson Company.

PERFORMANCE CRITERIA	SCORE	WEIGHT
Continuous improvement	90	0.10
Cost	85	0.20
Delivery	80	0.15
Quality	95	0.25
Responsive	90	0.15
Sustainability	80	0.05
Technology	90	0.10
Total score		

A score based on a scale of 0 (unsatisfactory) to 100 (excellent) has been assigned for each performance category considered critical in assessing the supplier. A weight is assigned to each of the performance criteria based on its relative importance. Vendors are classified based on their overall scores as follows:

- Unacceptable (less than 50)—supplier dropped from further business

- Conditional (between 50 and 70)—supplier needs development work to improve performance but may be dropped if performance continues to lag

- Certified (between 70 and 90)—supplier meets intended purpose or performance

- Preferred (greater than 90)—supplier will be considered for involvement in new product development and opportunities for more business

What is the Carson Company's score and how would you evaluate their performance as a supplier?

2. The Michelle Equipment Company is in the process of ranking its suppliers for one of its key components. To assist in the evaluation process, the information on their four suppliers is shown in the following table.

PERFORMANCE CRITERIA	WEIGHT	SCORES			
		TOROS	SUN DEVILS	GAMECOCKS	BUCKEYES
Price	0.10	85	95	90	90
Payment terms	0.20	90	80	95	85
Quality	0.10	95	80	85	90
Delivery	0.10	95	90	90	85
Suggestions for quality improvement	0.20	85	90	90	95
Reputation	0.20	85	90	90	85
Sustainability	0.10	90	80	85	90
Total scores					

Each performance category is scored on a scale from 0 (unsatisfactory) to 100 (excellent) and assigned a weight based on its relative importance. Suppliers are considered "preferred" if they score between 90 and 100. Preferred suppliers are those that Michelle Equipment will work with on new product development, approve for new business, and assist in maintaining a competitive position. An "acceptable" supplier rating is between 70 and 89. In this category, the supplier is required to provide a plan to Michelle Equipment on how to achieve preferred status. A score of 0–69 means that the supplier has a "developmental" supplier rating. What are the scores of the four suppliers and how would you evaluate each of them? Which supplier would you pick?

ESSAY/PROJECT QUESTIONS

1. Go to the Institute for Supply Management website (www.ism.ws) and find the listing for the latest ISM Annual International Supply Management Conference. Then find the conference proceedings and report on a paper that was presented regarding a topic covered in this chapter.

2. Find a company online that is using a development program to improve a supplier's performance and/or capabilities and report on its experiences.

3. Find a company online that has successfully implemented a supplier certification program and write an essay on this company and its experiences.

4. Pick a company online that is using SRM and report on its success and/or challenges with the software solution.

5. Many organizations find it necessary to recognize and celebrate the achievements of their best suppliers. Go online, and identify a company that has used a supplier recognition program and report on its experiences. What are some of the benefits the company derives from its suppliers?

6. Find a company online that is providing SRM software solutions. Provide examples of their success stories.

7. The Planning Perspectives, Inc., regularly surveys auto manufacturers on the level of supplier relations. Please select a major auto manufacturer and trace the progress made in supplier relations over time. What factors contributed to the rise or fall in the rankings?

8. Pick a recent supply chain scandal reported in the popular press or online. Describe what led to the scandal and the contributing factors. How could the company have avoided the pitfall?

CASES

1. Donnell Truong Ventures*

Donnell Truong is the chief operating office of a vast real-estate empire. His major holding is resort hotels. His resort properties are rated five-star hotels and are in over forty countries. The challenge of keeping such a high rating in an extremely competitive industry that relies so heavily on customer perception and expectations is enormous. All Donnell's hotels contain a casino. He expects each of his hotel/casino general managers to ensure the clientele are treated as special. More importantly, Donnell demands that the customer satisfaction ratings are always a 5, a rating of outstanding in the survey his hotels administer.

The hotel industry is an excellent example of an industry that depends extensively on suppliers. In addition to the services it provides within its confines, Donnell's hotels/casinos offer recommendations to five-star dining, connections to cruises, access to golf courses, membership to local spas, and much more. Consequently, although it docs have a supplier relationship management program for its direct suppliers such as food suppliers, liquor suppliers, etc., Donnell decided they must go beyond this "routine" approach and develop a supplier certification for the businesses they recommend to their guests. Donnell believes this is necessary because his five-star rating depends on his clientele's total experience, including his resorts' recommendation of a cruise, restaurant, etc. to rich clientele. Therefore, these indirect or complementary suppliers must be certified as well.

Donnell is confident that the businesses that "supply" the added amenities that influence the total experience for his clientele would be supportive of this initiative. Much of their business is dependent on his resorts' recommendation and goodwill. In theory, being part of his complementary supplier certification program is a win–win for everyone. The challenge is that these "complementary suppliers" provide services, not goods. What would be the key metrics?

Donnell and his executive team perused the research on strong supplier relationships. For their situation, they believed four intrinsic characteristics were paramount—trust, commitment, adaptation, and personal relationships. Donnell was big on quantitative performance metrics. The next action was to identify the specific metrics that would demonstrate the "complementary suppliers" adherence to the four intrinsic characteristics.

Discussion Questions

1. Are the four intrinsic characteristics the best ones to base the relationship performance measures for Donnell Truong Ventures? If not, what characteristics would be more suitable? In either case, justify your answer with specific examples.

2. Since Donnell Truong Ventures is developing a certification for "complementary suppliers," should they use the same metrics they use for direct suppliers? Explain why or why not.

3. List and defend any other metrics you think should be used for this certification.

©2019 Cengage Learning

*Written by Rick Bonsall, D. Mgt., McKendree University, Lebanon, IL. The people and institution are fictional and any resemblance to any person or any institution is coincidental. This case was prepared solely to provide material for class discussion. The author does not intend to illustrate either effective or ineffective handling of a managerial situation.

2. Jaeger Industrial Solutions*

Nora Forrester, director, supply chain management for Jaeger Industrial Solutions, is planning her budget requirements for the next fiscal year. Jaeger Industrial Solutions provides custom-control panels, specialized wiring harnesses, etc., for chemical-processing facilities, water treatment and cooling systems, and electrical power stations. This hardware is crucial to the productivity and safety of these facilities.

Her predecessor, Jerimiah Cosgrove, was a strong advocate for multiple sourcing. He had always believed that having multiple suppliers gave Jaeger's a financial edge. Jerimiah's approach was to pit the suppliers against each other. Using this method, he was able to squeeze out every extra cent from their bids. Cost was his primary and in many cases his only consideration. This approach led to a glut of suppliers.

Nora's philosophy was different. Although she was cost conscious, Nora believed that quality outweighed penny pinching. Furthermore, Nora believed that in today's competitive environment strong supplier relationships were worth the additional cost. Plus, with so many suppliers, the task of monitoring their performance added a level to her team's workload that didn't seem justifiable based on the benefit it actually provided. Consequently, Nora decided to trim the list of suppliers from 1,000 to 100. Obviously, this would be a challenging task.

Nora had her team analyze all 1,000 suppliers. Under Jerimiah they had basically focused only on cost; however, to some degree they had captured data on eight major performance categories—cost, quality, delivery, responsiveness, environment, technology, business metrics, and total cost of ownership. Since the data were limited, Nora determined that for this task they would initially concentrate on cost, quality, responsiveness, and business metrics. Nora decided to place an emphasis on a fundamental criterion that spanned these four categories. She chose C^3 behavior—collaboration, cooperation, and coordination.

Discussion Questions

1. Is Nora's choice of C^3 behavior the best way to measure suppliers moving forward? If so, explain the benefits of using C^3 behavior. If not, then provide another option and justify your choice.

2. Considering the C^3 behavior, identify two of the items listed under **business metrics** in Table 3.1 and explain why and how they fit this fundamental criterion.

3. Comment on Nora's strategy of trimming the number of suppliers—what would she hope to accomplish? Do you think it is a smart plan?

*Written by Rick Bonsall, D. Mgt., McKendree University, Lebanon, IL. The people and institution are fictional and any resemblance to any person or any institution is coincidental. This case was prepared solely to provide material for class discussion. The author does not intend to illustrate either effective or ineffective handling of a managerial situation.

3. Cyber Logic Systems—Supplier Relationships*

Cyber Logic Systems is a U.S. company that specializes in cyber security. It recently expanded its operations to Europe and South America. During this expansion, Rhonda Mendoza was promoted from director of operations to vice president of supply chain management. Although Cyber Logic Systems' primary product is software, often new hardware is required to support the robust software. Because the regulations and specifications for hardware differ in each market area, Rhonda instituted a supplier certification process. She felt this was crucial to ensure supplier compliance with the applicable regulations and specifications.

Because new cyber security systems must be in place as quickly as possible to avoid further damage to customers' databases from hackers, any new hardware must be ready for immediate use. Therefore, to guarantee suppliers can meet this requirement, a weighted criteria evaluation system is utilized as part of the supplier certification process. Rhonda's department collects performance data on all suppliers. A weight is assigned to each element of the performance criteria based on its criticality to the customer's needs (service specifications) and the emphasis placed on it in the applicable regulations. This information is monitored and the suppliers are graded based on their performance. Suppliers who fail to meet the standards set by Cyber Logic Systems are immediately replaced. The following Supplier Scorecard shows how suppliers A, B, C, and D are performing on the specific performance measures.

	SUPPLIER RATINGS					SUPPLIER FINAL VALUE			
PERFORMANCE MEASURE	SUPPLIER A	SUPPLIER B	SUPPLIER C	SUPPLIER D	WEIGHT	SUPPLIER A	SUPPLIER B	SUPPLIER C	SUPPLIER D
Cost	80	85	70	78	0.10				
Delivery	85	80	85	82	0.15				
Environmental	75	85	65	88	0.10				
Quality	95	93	90	89	0.20				
Responsiveness	80	90	95	84	0.25				
Technology	92	90	87	98	0.20				
Total scores									

Vendors are classified based on their overall performance.

- Unacceptable—less than 60—the supplier is dropped from further business

- Conditional—equal to 60 and less than 70—supplier needs development to improved performance and may be dropped if performance continues to lag

- Certified—equal to 70 and less than 90—the supplier meets intended purpose or performance

- Preferred—90 or higher—supplier will be considered for involvement in new product development and opportunities for more business

However, Rhonda realized that although suppliers must meet the standards of her supplier certification process, Cyber Logic Systems has a responsibility as well to the suppliers. To support quality-focused suppliers, Rhonda established a supplier development process to complement and enhance the supplier certification process. One very

*Written by Rick Bonsall, D. Mgt., McKendree University, Lebanon, IL. The people and institution are fictional and any resemblance to any person or any institution is coincidental. This case was prepared solely to provide material for class discussion. The author does not intend to illustrate either effective or ineffective handling of a managerial situation.

important aspect of the supplier development process was to create a cross-functional supplier development team. This team is composed of Cyber Logic Systems personnel and supplier personnel. The objective is to discuss strategic alignment, performance expectations, and measurement. The communication and relationship functions of the cross-functional team provide a win–win situation that helps improve the supplier's performance.

Rhonda believes in the carrot-and-the-stick approach to supplier relationships. In addition to the supplier evaluation and certification processes, she has also introduced a supplier recognition program. The suppliers are recognized annually for outstanding performance in several areas such as on-time delivery, quality, responsiveness, cost savings, and much more.

Administering supplier relationships is a huge task for any organization; therefore, to enhance Cyber Logic Systems ability to manage supplier relationships effectively and efficiently, Rhonda launched a supplier relationship management (SRM) system. She chose an analytic SRM that allows her to analyze her entire supplier base. Rhonda's focus as vice president of supply chain management is on long-term procurement strategies. Analytic SRM provides her the capability to assess the past state of supplier relations, the current state of supplier relations, and determine the best direction for Cyber Logic Systems to go in the future.

The SRM system provides Cyber Logic Systems the capability to integrate both internal users and external partners into the system; thus, providing everyone a view of the supply chain. Furthermore, it allows increased collaboration through information sharing. Since some information is sensitive and cannot or should not be shared with everyone, SRM systems can be customized by role, for example, suppliers and internal users. Rhonda explained to her team that the obvious benefit is information visibility. Internal users and external partners have access to information pertinent to their roles. Finally, for Rhonda, it allows optimization of decision-making.

Discussion Questions

1. Based on the supplier scorecard, what classification does each supplier fit into?

2. Are there any suppliers Rhonda should be concerned about, that is, replace, give additional business to, or place into her supplier development program? Why or why not?

3. Assuming Cyber Logic Systems recognizes suppliers at the annual awards banquet if they meet the preferred classification standard for any of the specific performance measures, would any of the four suppliers qualify for an award? If so, who and for which performance measures?

©2019 Cengage Learning

ENDNOTES

1. "Supplier Relationship Management: How Key Suppliers Drive Your Company's Competitive Advantage," PwC; https://www.pwc.no/no/publikasjoner/pwc-supplier-relationship-management.pdf

2. "FCA US Honors Outstanding Supplier Partners at Sixth Annual Awards Ceremony," PR Newswire, July 15, 2016; http://www.prnewswire.com/news-releases/fca-us-honors-outstanding-supplier-partners-at-sixth-annual-awards-ceremony-300299372.html

3. Corporate Partnering Institute; http://corporatepartnering.com/4-wisdom.htm

4. "Building Better Supplier Relationships at Ford," *Industry Week*, March 14, 2016; http://www.industryweek.com/manufacturing-leader-week/building-better-supplier-relationships-ford

5. "OEM-Supplier Relations Study Shows Strong Gains for Toyota and Honda, with Ford, Nissan, FCA and GM Falling Well Behind," Planning Perspectives, Inc., May 18, 2015; http://www.prnewswire.com/news-releases/oem-supplier-relations-study-shows-strong-gains-for-toyota-and-honda-with-ford-nissan-fca-and-gm-falling-well-behind-300084605.html

6. "Supplier Relations: GM Better, but Toyota, Honda Lead," May 16, 2016; http://www.freep.com/story/money/cars/general-motors/2016/05/16/supplier-relations-gm-better-but-toyota-honda-lead/84284124/

7. "ISM Glossary of Key Supply Management Terms: Supplier Partnership," Institute of Supply Management website.

8. "Our Supply Chain Strategy," Ford Sustainability Report 2015–16; http://corporate.ford.com/microsites/sustainability-report-2015-16/supply-strategy.html

9. "Our Supply Chain Strategy," Ford Sustainability Report 2015–16; http://corporate.ford.com/microsites/sustainability-report-2015-16/supply-strategy.html

10. "Ford to Share Environmental Stewardship Program for Its Suppliers at G7 Alliance Forum on Resource Efficiency," Ford, March 21, 2016; https://media.ford.com/content/fordmedia/fna/us/en/news/2016/03/21/ford-to-share-environmental-stewardship-program-for-its-supplier.html

11. "Our Supply Chain Strategy," Ford Sustainability Report 2015–16; http://corporate.ford.com/microsites/sustainability-report-2015-16/supply-strategy.html

12. Trebilcock, B., "How They Did It: Supplier Relationship at Raytheon," *Supply Chain Management Review*, March/April 2015; http://www.scmr.com/plus/SCMR1503_F_Raytheon.pdf

13. "Raytheon: Who We Are Website"; http://www.raytheon.com/ourcompany/

14. Trebilcock, B., "How They Did It: Supplier Relationship at Raytheon," *Supply Chain Management Review*, March/April 2015; http://www.scmr.com/plus/SCMR1503_F_Raytheon.pdf

15. Lewis, Jordan D., *Trusted Partners: How Companies Build Mutual Trust and Win Together.* New York: The Free Press, 1999: 7.

16. "Buyers Target Strategic Partners," *Purchasing*, April 5, 2001; www.manufacturing.net/pur/

17. "Supplier Selection & Management Report," March 2002, Institute of Management and Administration (IOMA).

18. Covey, S. R., "Covey Quotations," Stephen R. Covey Sayings; http://www.goodreads.com/author/quotes/1538.Stephen_R_Covey

19. MacDonald, M., "Managing Change: A Matter of Principle," *Supply Chain Management Review*, January/February 2002.

20. "Delivering Value through Strategic Supplier Relationships," October 2013; http://www.procurementandsupply.com/resource/2a.%20Delivering%20value%20through%20strategic%20supplier%20relationships%20-%20Debbie%20Johnstone.pdf

21. Drab, D., "Economic Espionage and Trade Secret Theft: Defending against the Pickpockets of the New Millennium," August 2003, Xerox Corporation; http://www.xerox.com/downloads/wpaper/x/xgs_business_insight_economic_espionage.pdf

22. Hannon, D., "Best Practices: Hackett Group Outlines the World-Class Procurement Organization," *Purchasing*, December 8, 2006.

23. "Supplier Scorecard Guidelines SG-0110," Northrup Grumman, June 23, 2016; http://www.northropgrumman.com/suppliers/OasisDocuments/Supplier_Scorecard_Guidelines.pdf

24. "ISM Glossary of Key Supply Management Terms: Total Cost of Ownership," Institute of Supply Management website.

25. Humphries, A. S., and L. McComie, "Managing and Measuring for Supply Chain Relationships Performance"; http://www.sccindex.com/Documents/Food Supply Chains CH2.pdf

26. Ibid.

27. Finstad, R., "Total Recall: A Flawed System of Trade," *Far Eastern Economic Review* 70(9), November 2007: 46–50.

28. Viswanatha, A., and C. Rogers, "VW Engineer Pleads Guilty in Emissions-Cheating Scandal," *Wall Street Journal*, September 9, 2016; http://www.wsj.com/articles/former-vw-engineer-to-plead-guilty-in-emissions-cheating-scandal-1473433341

29. Atiyeh, C., "Everything You Need to Know About the VW Diesel-Emissions Scandal," *Car and Driver*, November 15, 2016; http://blog.caranddriver.com/everything-you-need-to-know-about-the-vw-diesel-emissions-scandal/

30. Woodyard, C., and K. Johnson, "Reports: VW Emissions Probe Widens to Supplier Bosch," *USA Today*, September 16, 2016; http://www.usatoday.com/story/money/cars/2016/09/16/reports-vw-emissions-probe-widens-supplier-bosch/90523484/

31. Sorokanich, B., "Report: Bosch Warned VW About Diesel Emissions Cheating in 2007," *Car and Driver*, September 28, 2015; http://blog.caranddriver.com/report-bosch-warned-vw-about-diesel-emissions-cheating-in-2007/

32. McGee, P., "Bosch Product Under Scrutiny in VW Emissions Scandal," *Financial Times*, October 4, 2016; https://www.ft.com/content/6e0ec870-798e-11e6-97ae-647294649b28/

33. "Glossary of Key Supply Management Terms: Supplier Certification," Institute of Supply Management website.

34. See www.federalmogul.com/en-US/Suppliers/Pages/SupplyNet-Scorecard.aspx#.UuqR4bTDXlc

35. ISO 9000—Quality Management; http://www.iso.org/iso/home/standards/management-standards/iso_9000.htm

36. The ISO Survey of Management System Standard Certifications—2015; http://www
    .iso.org/iso/iso-survey

37. Jarvis, A., and C. MacNee, "Improved Customer Satisfaction—Key Result of ISO 9000
    User Survey," December 2, 2011; http://www.iso.org/iso/home/news_index/news_
    archive/news.htm?refid=Ref1543

38. "ISO 14000—Environmental Management—The ISO 14000 Family of International
    Standards"; http://www.iso.org/iso/theiso14000family_2009.pdf

39. "ISO 14001 Key Benefits"; http://www.iso.org/iso/iso_14001_-_key_benefits.pdf

40. "The ISO Survey of Management System Standard Certifications—2015"; http://www
    .iso.org/iso/iso-survey

41. Handfield, R. B., D. R. Krause, T. V. Scannell, and R. M. Monzka, "Avoid the Pitfalls in
    Supplier Development," *Sloan Management Review,* Winter 2000: 37–49.

42. Ibid.

43. "Supplier Continuous Quality Improvement (SCQI) Program"; https://supplier.intel
    .com/static/quality/scqi.htm

44. "Supplier Continuous Quality Improvement (SCQI) Program"; https://supplier.intel
    .com/static/quality/scqi.htm

45. Honeywell Six Sigma; https://www51.honeywell.com/hrsites/neo/howweworksixsigmaplus
    .html

46. "Boeing Honors 12 Suppliers for Outstanding Performance in 2015"; http://boeing
    .mediaroom.com/2016-04-28-Boeing-Honors-12-Suppliers-for-Outstanding-
    Performance-in-2015

47. Ibid.

48. "Intel Honors Eight Companies with Supplier Continuous Quality Improvement
    Award"; https://newsroom.intel.com/news-releases/intel-honors-eight-companies-
    with-supplier-continuous-quality-improvement-award-4/

49. "Intel Honors 26 Companies with the Preferred Quality Supplier and Achievement
    Awards," Intel; https://newsroom.intel.com/news-releases/intel-honors-27-companies-
    with-preferred-quality-supplier-and-achievement-awards/

50. Press Releases: "Hormel Foods Announces Recipients of Prestigious Supplier Award,"
    August 19, 2016; http://www.hormelfoods.com/Newsroom/Press-Releases
    /2016/08/20160819

51. "Hormel Foods Honors Suppliers with Spirit of Excellence Awards," April 18, 2013;
    http://www.hormelfoods.com/Newsroom/Press-Releases/2013/04/20130418

52. "Accenture Builds High Performance in Supplier Relationship Management with mySAP
    SRM Solutions"; https://www.accenture.com/jp-ja/~/media/Accenture/Conversion-
    Assets/DotCom/Documents/Local/ja-jp/PDF_1/Accenture-SRM-Building-High-
    Performace6.pdf

53. "SAP Supplier Relationship Management (SAP SRM)"; https://help.sap.com/srm

54. Barling, B., "The Five Tenets of SRM," *AMR Research,* June 10, 2002.

Chapter 4

ETHICAL AND SUSTAINABLE SOURCING

Through our products, we are continuously striving to make consumers' lives healthier, easier and richer. Through our actions, we are simultaneously working to source responsibly, to conserve the natural resources on which our products depend, and to strengthen the communities producing them.

— **Ken Powell, Chairman and CEO of General Mills[1]**

We're committed to continuously improving our products, processes, people and corporate citizenship. We aim to chart a new path in sustainable business practices. Our goal is to set the standard against which sustainability efforts in the spirits industry are measured.

— **Ed Shirley, President and CEO of Bacardi Limited[2]**

Learning Objectives

After completing this chapter, you should be able to

- Understand and appreciate the trends in ethical and sustainable sourcing.
- Define and describe the terms used in ethical and sustainable sourcing.
- Describe the differences between ethical and sustainable sourcing.
- Understand how ethical and sustainable strategies are developed and implemented.
- Understand the use of environmental supplier certifications.
- Discuss the benefits of strategic supplier alliances.
- Describe how and why sourcing practices are benchmarked.
- Discuss why firms would want to assess their sourcing capabilities.

Chapter Outline

Introduction

Ethical and Sustainable Sourcing Defined

Developing Ethical and Sustainable Sourcing Strategies

Ethical and Sustainable Sourcing Initiatives

Early Supplier Involvement

Strategic Alliance Development

Rewarding Supplier Performance

Benchmarking Successful Sourcing Practices

Assessing and Improving the Firm's Sourcing Function

Summary

SCM Profile | Mitsubishi Acquires Sustainable Food Capabilities

When the Mitsubishi Corporation acquired part of agricultural trader Olam, it was driven by a growing demand for food grown sustainably. Mitsubishi is hoping to access Singapore-based Olam's expertise with small farmers in remote regions of Asia and Africa. The Olam-Mitsubishi deal is evidence that sustainability is beginning to impact deals in agricultural supply chains.

Olam, for example, buys and sells commodities like coffee, cotton, and cocoa. They have become so successful that now, one in eight chocolate bars consumed in the world is made from beans handled by Olam. While the $1.1 billion Mitsubishi paid for Olam is not entirely about Olam's sustainability capabilities, the price confirms that there is indeed value to be found in sustainable practices. Mitsubishi believes demand for sustainable products is gathering momentum and it also knows it would take years to create a trading network similar to that of Olam from scratch.

Olam invests heavily in sustainability. In 2014, they provided $184 million in loans to farmers, spent $6 million on training and community development, and another $30 million on corporate responsibility and sustainability programs. Sunny Verghese, Olam's CEO, says companies acting in a sustainable manner have an edge over competitors since buyers of agricultural end products are seeking suppliers who can fulfill the increasing demands of investors, NGOs, and consumers for sustainability. "Sustainability absolutely brings competitive advantage," he says.

On the other hand, with commodity traders and food companies under increasing scrutiny from NGOs and pressure groups that are holding organizations to account, companies face a threat to their reputations if they fail to pursue sustainability.

As an initiation into the business, Olam's new traders spend time in remote rural farming areas where they can appreciate the importance of sustainability at the ground level. Company personnel acknowledge its importance when it actually leads to financial returns. Mr. Verghese says: "The real 'ah-ha' moment for securing buy-in for sustainability is when you can demonstrate the real financial value of initiatives either through added revenues or cost-savings."[3]

INTRODUCTION

As discussed in Chapters 2 and 3, purchasing, sourcing, or supply management departments are today seen as highly valued and strategic contributors to their organizations because of their ability to impact product design and quality, cost of goods sold, and manufacturing cycle time, all of which impact the firm's profitability. Several concerns that have emerged for purchasing departments over the past five to ten years are the use of ethical and sustainable sourcing practices. Global population growth, the increasing awareness of environmental issues, and consumers' desires for better corporate responsibility have combined to place unprecedented pressures on company personnel to effectively manage the firm and its supply chains. Additionally, as world economies expand and contract, this places pressure on managers to squeeze costs out of operations to survive over the long haul. Corporate concerns regarding cost, environmental, and ethical performances have allowed purchasing personnel to have a tremendous impact on their companies' and their supply chains' successes and reputations. These and other strategic purchasing topics are discussed in this chapter.

The influence of the purchasing department both within the organization and outside its boundaries is quite unique in that it interacts with customers and suppliers; internal design, production, finance, marketing, and accounting personnel; and also the firm's executive managers. As companies take a more proactive role in managing their supply chains, purchasing departments are then seen as one of the primary designers and facilitators of important inward- and outward-facing sourcing policies. These policies might include a number of ethical, sustainable, and cost-oriented practices such as those described in this chapter. Indeed, in a recent U.S. retailer survey conducted by Deloitte, 92 percent of respondents indicated their organizations were either currently enhancing their ethical sourcing capabilities or planning to do so in the future.[4]

World events that have impacted supply chains such as the global recession, the tsunami in Japan, and more recently the British vote to exit the European Union (EU) hastened many organizations' plans to institute better supply chain strategies. The goals of these strategies include reducing dependencies on foreign suppliers, reducing delivery cycle times and carbon footprints, and improving quality, customer service, and ethical reputations. Additionally, the increasing number of global competitors, demands by customers for companies to become more ethically and environmentally focused, and the high costs of fuel and materials place added pressures on firms to improve their supply chain management performance.

Today, these trends have become the drivers of strategic sourcing and supply chain management initiatives. Taking the notion of sourcing one step further, **strategic sourcing** can be thought of as managing the firm's external resources in ways that support the long-term goals of the firm. This includes the development of ethical and sustainable sourcing initiatives, managing and improving supplier relationships and capabilities, identification and selection of environmentally and socially conscious suppliers, and monitoring and rewarding supplier performance. Some of these topics have been introduced in earlier chapters and will only be lightly touched upon here, while others particularly related to ethical and sustainable sourcing will be covered in greater detail in this chapter.

Developing socially responsible and environmentally friendly sourcing strategies that also create a competitive advantage is no easy task. Creating and implementing these strategies might provide some benefits for the firms involved but can ultimately fail, because of misaligned strategies, lack of commitment, unrealized goals, and loss of trust in buyer–supplier relationships. Purchasing managers proactively managing their firms' supply chains must also come to understand that some sourcing strategies are better suited to some supply chains than to others. Indeed, firms may have dozens of supply chains associated with their most important inbound purchased items and outbound finished products. Some of these supply chains may be driven by a low-cost overall strategy, while others may have the environment, quality, or customer service as the overriding objective. Even different parts and components used in one product may have diverging supply chain strategies. In the following sections, the development of successful ethical and sustainable sourcing strategies is discussed.

ETHICAL AND SUSTAINABLE SOURCING DEFINED

Ethical Sourcing

To establish a common ground for further discussion, it is necessary to first define and describe the origins of the terms *ethical* and *sustainable* sourcing. To start with, **business ethics** is the application of ethical principles to business situations and has been very widely studied. A library search, for instance, would reveal over 250 books dedicated solely to the topic of business ethics. Generally speaking, there are two approaches to deciding whether or not an action is ethical. The first approach is known as **utilitarianism**. This would mean that an ethical act creates the greatest good for the greatest number of people. The second approach is known as **rights and duties** and states that some actions are right in themselves without regard for the consequences. This approach maintains that ethical actions recognize the rights of others and the duties those rights impose on the ones performing the actions.

The practice of business ethics is also referred to as **corporate social responsibility (CSR).** Much of the discussion to date of corporate social responsibility assumes that a corporation can act ethically just as an individual can. Many companies, for instance, have formal CSR initiatives that include ethical sourcing. The majority of S&P 500 companies have now committed to act as responsible corporations and do some type of CSR reporting. CSR initiatives and reporting are also growing globally. In 2014, the EU adopted annual corporate social responsibility reporting requirements. Under the amendment, companies exceeding an average of 500 employees on their balance sheet will be subject to mandatory reporting. This amounts to about 6,000 companies.[5] In another example, Konica Minolta is expanding the scope of its CSR activities to include its new "CSR Logistics" program. Through cooperation with its business partners, the company will improve aspects such as human rights, ethics, health and safety, and environmental considerations in the logistics stage. These joint efforts with business partners will contribute to solving social challenges and will enhance corporate values across Konica Minolta and its business partners.[6]

Extending from business ethics then, the term **ethical sourcing** can be defined as:

> *That which takes into account the public consequences of organizational buying, or bringing about positive social change through organizational buying behavior.*[7]

Ethical sourcing practices include promoting diversity by intentionally buying from small firms, ethnic minority businesses, and women-owned enterprises; discontinuing purchases from firms that use child labor or other unacceptable labor practices; or buying from firms in underdeveloped nations.

Purchasing managers and other corporate executives play a central role in promoting ethical sourcing by creating a supportive organizational culture, developing policies that outline the firm's desire to practice ethical sourcing, communicating these policies to supply chain trading partners, and then developing tactics that specifically describe how ethical sourcing will be implemented. Massachusetts-based athletic footwear retailer Reebok launched its ethical sourcing program in the early 1990s. It emphasizes the roles played by supplier factory managers in maintaining ethical workplace conditions. Reebok also tries to collaborate with its competitors in establishing common human rights guidelines, since they all may be buying merchandise from the same suppliers. In 2002, Reebok unveiled an Internet-based human rights compliance-monitoring software application, generating considerable interest from other firms about buying the application. In response, Reebok established a not-for-profit organization built around the technology and in 2004 launched the Fair Factories Clearinghouse with the backing of the National Retail Federation.[8] U.K.-based Lush Fresh Handmade Cosmetics sources its raw materials globally, and suppliers must sign a pledge confirming no animal testing has been done. The company supports Fair Trade and Community Trade initiatives. "At the heart of our brand is a commitment to look after people, animals and the planet," says Mark Wolverton, president and CEO, Lush North America.[9]

Purchasing goods from suppliers in developing countries can be risky in that if human rights, animal rights, safety, or environmental abuses become associated with the firm's suppliers or foreign manufacturing facilities, this could lead to negative publicity for the buyer, along with product boycotts, a tarnished company image, brand degradation, lower employee morale, and ultimately lower sales, profits, and stock prices. This very thing happened to running gear manufacturer Nike in the mid-1990s when it contracted with Pakistani suppliers to make footballs. Unfortunately, the work was subcontracted to local villagers, where children as young as ten were used in the production processes. Similar problems for Nike also cropped up in Cambodia and Malaysia at about the same time. In 1998, CEO Phil Knight acknowledged that, "Nike product has become synonymous with slave wages, forced overtime, and arbitrary abuse." Nike then pledged to reform this company image. In Malaysia, for example, Nike reimbursed workers, paid to relocate them, and then met with representatives of its thirty contract Malaysian factories about enforcing labor standards.[10]

As described above, companies seeking to reduce production costs through use of foreign facilities expose themselves to these types of risks. To minimize these risks, ethical sourcing policies should include:

- Determining where all purchased goods come from and how they are made;
- Knowing if suppliers promote basic workplace principles (such as the right to equal opportunity and to earn a decent wage; the prohibition of bonded, prison, or child labor; and the right to join a union);
- Use of ethical ratings for suppliers alongside the other standard performance criteria;
- Use of independent verification of supplier compliance;
- Reporting of supplier compliance performance to shareholders; and
- Providing detailed ethical sourcing expectations to suppliers.[11]

Use of ethical supply chain sourcing practices can be fraught with difficulties. Modern supply chains can encompass many countries, each with its own set of labor issues, wages, and working and living conditions. Many companies may not even be aware of their complete supply chains (beyond their immediate or first-tier suppliers and customers). For example, Nike's footwear is supplied by 150 contract footwear factories in fourteen countries and their apparel is supplied by 430 contract apparel factories operating in forty-one countries.[12] Consequently, the **Ethical Trading Initiative (ETI)** is an alliance of organizations seeking to take responsibility for improving working conditions and agreeing to implement the ETI Base Code, a standard for ethical practices for the firm and its suppliers. The ETI Base Code is shown in Table 4.1.

The purchase of **fair trade products** is an activity that is becoming increasingly popular as firms seek to demonstrate a more ethical approach to purchasing. A fair trade product refers to one that is manufactured or grown by a disadvantaged producer in a developing country that receives a fair price for its goods. Typically, the term refers to farming products such as coffee, cocoa, bananas, sugar, tea, and cotton, which are produced in developing countries and exported to large firms in developed countries. However, the term is increasingly applied to all sorts of products. For instance, MEC, the Canadian outdoor retailing cooperative, reported thirty new fair trade–certified clothing styles, a new fair trade factory partner, and expansion of its fair trade program into Thailand. Currently, all of MEC's factory partners in India are working under its fair trade program.[13]

Agencies such as the Fairtrade Foundation, Fairtrade International, and the World Fair Trade Organization seek out and certify products as being fair trade products.[14] Leading retailers offer items for sale that are designated as fair trade products. Fair Trade USA, the certifier of fair trade products in the United States, reports that consumers are increasing their commitment to fair trade faster than ever before. In the United States today, there are hundreds of companies offering fair trade products.[15] In 2011, over 1.2 million farmers and workers in more than sixty countries participated in fair trade. According to Fairtrade International, nearly six out of ten consumers have seen the Fairtrade mark and almost nine in ten of them trust it.[16]

Table 4.1	**The Ethical Trading Initiative's Base Code**
CLAUSES	**ABBREVIATED EXPLANATIONS**
1. Employment is freely chosen	No forced, bonded, or involuntary prison labor. Workers are not required to pay "deposits" to their employer and are free to leave after reasonable notice.
2. Freedom of association and the right to collective bargaining are respected	Workers have the right to join trade unions and to bargain collectively. Employers adopt an open attitude toward the activities of trade unions. Worker representatives are not discriminated against. Where the right to collective bargaining is restricted under law, employers facilitate the development of parallel means for bargaining.
3. Working conditions are safe and hygienic	A safe and hygienic work environment shall be provided. Adequate steps shall be taken to minimize the causes of hazards in the workplace. Workers shall receive regular health and safety training. Accommodations shall be clean, safe, and meet the basic needs of workers. The company shall assign responsibility for health and safety to a senior management representative.
4. Child labor shall not be used	There shall be no new recruitment of child labor. Persons under 18 shall not be employed at night or in hazardous conditions. Policies and procedures shall conform to the provisions of the relevant International Labor Organization standards.
5. Living wages are paid	Wages and benefits for a standard work week meet national legal or industry standards, whichever is higher. Wages should be enough to meet basic needs. All workers shall be provided with written and understandable information about their employment conditions before they enter employment and about the particulars of their wages each time that they are paid.
6. Working hours are not excessive	Working hours comply with national laws and benchmark industry standards, whichever affords greater protection. Workers shall not on a regular basis be required to work in excess of forty-eight hours per week and shall be provided with at least one day off for every seven-day period. Overtime shall be voluntary, shall not exceed twelve hours per week, and shall always be compensated at a premium rate.
7. No discrimination is practiced	There is no discrimination in hiring, compensation, access to training, promotion, termination, or retirement based on race, caste, national origin, religion, age, disability, gender, marital status, sexual orientation, union membership, or political affiliation.
8. Regular employment is provided	Work performed must be on the basis of recognized employment relationships established through national law and practice. Obligations to employees under labor or social security laws shall not be avoided through the use of labor-only contracting, subcontracting, or apprenticeship schemes.
9. No harsh or inhumane treatment is allowed	Physical abuse or discipline, the threat of physical abuse, sexual or other harassment, or other forms of intimidation shall be prohibited.

Source: Ethical Trading Initiative website: www.ethicaltrade.org

Sustainable Sourcing

While the concept of **sustainable sourcing** can vary quite substantially from company to company, in 2007, the U.K. Food Industry Sustainability Strategy Champions Group on Ethical Trade identified three key areas to focus on to establish sustainable sourcing:

- Respect human rights and reduce poverty by creating profitable trading;
- Work within the finite limits of the planet's resources; and
- Move toward a low carbon economy.

In other words, purchasing fairly, profitably, and environmentally were the organization's three priorities and these tend to be the common thread in most other sustainable sourcing concepts today. For Unilever, the multinational consumer goods company with over 400 product brands, sustainable agriculture sourcing means growing food in ways which sustain the soil, minimize water and fertilizer use, and protect biodiversity while enhancing farmers' livelihoods. It defines sustainable sourcing using eleven social, economic, and environmental indicators including soil health, soil loss, pest management, energy, water, the local economy, and animal welfare. Unilever's biggest brand Knorr now sources 92 percent of its top thirteen vegetable and herb ingredients from sustainable sources. Unilever's goal is to source 100 percent of its agricultural raw materials sustainably by 2020.[17]

The notion of protecting the earth's environment has been a topic of concern for many years, and it has recently become a popular topic of debate as politicians and voters have made global warming a political issue. Former U.S. vice president and longtime environmentalist Al Gore, for example, starred in the award-winning 2006 global warming documentary *An Inconvenient Truth* (he won the Nobel Peace Prize in 2007 for his environmental work). Additionally, awards such as the Goldman Environmental Prize have served as a support mechanism for environmental reform, providing global publicity for specific environmental problems.

The Goldman Prize began in 1990 and awards $175,000 to each prize recipient. Winners are announced every April to coincide with Earth Day. As of April 2016, there have been 175 prize winners, including the 1991 prize winner, Dr. Wangari Maathai from Kenya. In the 1970s, Maathai founded the Green Belt Movement, an environmental organization concentrating on the planting of trees, environmental conservation, and women's rights in Africa. In 2004, she also became the first African woman to receive the Nobel Peace Prize for "her contribution to sustainable development, democracy and peace."[18] Other people such as David Brower, the former executive director of the Sierra Club; Eileen O'Neill, head of Discovery Channel and proponent of their Planet Green multimedia initiative; Patrick Moore, director and cofounder of Greenpeace International; and many others have played major roles in championing the modern environmental movement.[19]

Growing out of this environmental awareness was the idea of **green purchasing**. Green purchasing is a practice aimed at ensuring that purchased products or materials meet environmental objectives of the organization such as waste reduction, hazardous material elimination, recycling, remanufacturing, and material reuse. According to the globally recognized Institute for Supply Management, green purchasing is defined as *making environmentally conscious decisions throughout the purchasing process, beginning with product and process design, and through product disposal.*[20] Companies such as California-based healthcare provider Kaiser Permanente and beer producer Anheuser-Busch have been recognized as corporate trailblazers in green purchasing. In 2001, Kaiser Permanente formed an environmental stewardship council focusing on green buildings, green purchasing, and environmentally sustainable operations. Anheuser-Busch, for example, worked with its suppliers to reduce the lid diameter of four types of cans, saving millions of pounds of aluminum each year as well as reducing the energy needed to produce and transport the cans.[21]

The term **sustainability** as applied to supply chains is a broad term that includes green purchasing as well as financial performance and some aspects of social responsibility. It can be defined as *the ability to meet the needs of current supply chain members without hindering the ability to meet the needs of future generations in terms of economic, environmental, and social challenges.* The idea of sustainability is certainly not new as evidenced by the way early Native Americans thought and lived and as Gifford Pinchot, the first chief forester of the U.S. Forest Service, wrote in an article in 1908:

> *Are we going to protect our springs of prosperity, our raw material of industry and commerce and employer of capital and labor combined; or are we going to dissipate them? According as we accept or ignore our responsibility as trustees of the nation's welfare, our children and our children's children for uncounted generations will call us blessed, or will lay their suffering at our doors.*[22]

For businesses and their trading partners, sustainability is seen today as doing the right things in ways that make economic sense. Some have begun referring to sustainability in terms of supporting the **three P's**, which refers to *people*, *planet*, and *profit*. The objectives then are not only to sustain the world we live in but to sustain employees and the firm's balance sheet as well. For years, Walmart's food sustainability initiative is gaining steam, as shown in the nearby SCM Profile.

Sustainable sourcing is one activity within the larger umbrella term of sustainability—it includes green purchasing, some form of financial benefit, as well as aspects of ethical sourcing. Very simply, it has been defined as

> *A process of purchasing goods and services that takes into account the long-term impact on people, profits, and the planet.*[24]

Leading companies practicing sustainable sourcing seek to:

- *Grow revenues* by introducing new and differentiated sustainable products and services;
- *Reduce costs* by increasing resource efficiencies, avoiding use of noncompliant suppliers, and rethinking transportation and distribution systems;

SCM Profile | Walmart's Food Sustainability Initiative

Walmart recently began a new food sustainability initiative, with the goals of lowering the cost of food, improving access to healthy food, and providing transparency on food origins and ingredients. "The future of food is absolutely critical for both our society and for our business, which means we have a huge opportunity to make a difference here," says Doug McMillon, president and CEO of Walmart. "We've learned on our sustainability journey that we're most successful when our initiatives create social and environmental value and business value at the same time. Food is our number one category worldwide, and we are going to do even more in our grocery business in the years ahead. Paving a sustainable future for food is necessary for society and our business."

Walmart's food sustainability efforts are contained within the following four "pillars":

- Affordable: Working collaboratively with suppliers, Walmart provides everyday low costs for customers and decreases the environmental impact of agricultural practices. The company is launching a Climate Smart Agriculture Platform, which will provide greater visibility on agricultural yields, greenhouse gas emissions, and water usage.

- Accessible: Since 2010, Walmart and Sam's Club facilities have donated more than 1.5 billion pounds of food, surpassing their initial goal of 1.1 billion pounds. In addition, Walmart and the Walmart Foundation will elevate their commitment to accessibility by aiming to provide 4 billion healthier meals to those who need them in the United States over the next five years.

- Healthier: Walmart is committed to ensuring that eating healthier is easy and affordable. The company has reduced sodium by 13 percent and sugar levels by 10 percent in its private label products, and launched its "Great for You" icon to empower consumers to identify healthier food options on store shelves.

- Safe and Transparent: Walmart is creating a transparent food chain to foster improved food safety, worker safety, and animal welfare. Additionally, Walmart is working to provide more information and transparency about the products on its shelves, so customers can see where items come from, how they are made, and what ingredients are in them.[23]

- *Manage risk* by managing brand and reputation, and developing approaches for meeting regulations and capturing sustainability-conscious customers; and

- *Build intangible assets* by further enhancing brand and reputation through social and environmental responsibility.[25]

To accomplish these goals, companies must develop collaborative relationships with their key suppliers and customers to make sustainable sourcing a beneficial reality.

The Hershey Co., for example, decided in 2012 that all of its chocolate will come from certified sustainable cocoa sources, thus joining the strategies of other big chocolate producers such as Mars and Nestlé. Kip Walk, director of cocoa for Blommer Chocolate Co., points out, "Up to now most of the focus for sustainable products has been in Europe, Australia and Canada. Hershey's announcement brings sustainability into focus for the United States." All the major chocolate brands are looking to have a 100 percent sustainable supply by 2020.[26]

Local and national governments are now getting involved to set some clear targets for organizations to achieve. China's approach to sustainability can be found in its goals for energy use per unit of GDP, water use per unit of value-added industrial output, and sulfur dioxide emissions. When a surge of manufacturing output in 2010 resulted in greenhouse gas emissions in excess of what China's five-year plan called for, the government cut off power to heavy industrial districts, forcing many plants to close temporarily. This dramatic move (unthinkable in most industrialized countries) demonstrated that, in China, sustainability goals are no less important than economic goals.[27] Today, sustainability is increasingly moving from voluntary to legally mandated initiatives, including sustainability reporting requirements. Almost three-quarters of U.S. companies on the S&P 500 issued some type of corporate sustainability report in 2014, according to research from the Governance & Accountability Institute. Despite growing pressure from green investor groups and organizations such as the Global Reporting Initiative, sustainability reporting in any meaningful way remains a largely voluntary effort on the part of American companies. In contrast, new EU requirements for sustainability reporting go into effect in 2017.[28]

From the supplier's perspective, there are methods used to help determine what buyers want, in terms of environmentally friendly goods. In their 2013 Consumer Recycling and Sustainability Survey, for example, tire maker Bridgestone Americas surveyed consumers in twenty cities and found that:

- Most consumers are holding companies accountable for the sustainability of their products;

- The top three ways companies can show they are environmentally responsible are (1) creating products that minimize energy and water use, (2) generating less waste, and (3) minimizing carbon emissions;

- More than 86 percent of respondents said they recycle, while 36 percent regarded themselves as serious recyclers.[29]

Companies and government agencies alike are coming to realize that every purchase has a global environmental impact, and with careful sourcing, money can be saved. Collection, transport, manufacturing, and scrapping of raw materials and finished goods require the use of fossil fuels; goods purchased from distant suppliers require greater amounts of fuel for transportation; goods transported via ship or rail use less fuel than trucks or airlines; plant-based goods generally have a smaller environmental impact than petroleum-based goods; factories powered by solar or wind energy have a smaller environmental impact than factories powered by oil or coal; and energy-efficient goods consume less energy.

DEVELOPING ETHICAL AND SUSTAINABLE SOURCING STRATEGIES

To achieve the objectives described thus far in this chapter, a number of sourcing strategies must be considered and implemented. Care must be taken, though, when developing these plans. Failure to align sourcing strategies with overall supply chain objectives, for example, may result in considerable resources being expended to design and manage a set of sourcing activities, only to find that the resulting impact on the firm and its supply chains is something other than what was ultimately desired.

In one of the more important papers written on this topic, Martin Fisher uses two types of supply chains as examples—those for **functional products** and those for **innovative products**.[30] Functional products are maintenance, repair, and operating (MRO) materials and other commonly purchased items and supplies. These items are characterized by low profit margins, relatively stable demands, and high levels of competition. Thus, companies purchasing functional products most likely concentrate on finding a dependable supplier selling at a low price. Equipment maintenance and office cleaning products, for example, fall into this category.

Examples of some well-known innovative consumer goods are the Amazon Kindle and Tesla's Model S automobile; in factory settings, innovative products might be new types of control mechanisms, new software applications, or new robotics systems. Innovative products are characterized by short product life cycles, volatile demand, high profit margins, and relatively less competition. Consequently, the sourcing criteria for these products may be more closely aligned with a supplier's quality reputation, delivery speed and flexibility, and communication capabilities.

The Edison Awards recognize and honor some of the most innovative goods and services each year. Originally established in 1987 by the American Marketing Association and now an independent organization, the Edison Awards is focused on fostering innovation and takes nominations from around the world for products which are then judged for their excellence in concept, value, delivery, and impact.[31] Winners are given the Edison Award winning seal and are allowed to publicize the honor. They can also participate in a customized marketing plan that includes product sampling, social media, product reviews, and national media outreach. Some of the past award winners include GM, Harvard Business School, Tesla, Lenovo, Apple, TED, MIT, and Black and Decker. Table 4.2 describes some of the winners for 2016.

Overlaying both of these types of purchases is whether or not to invoke an ethical or sustainable sourcing strategy. This adds yet another layer of complexity to the sourcing decision. Many of the commonly used sourcing strategies of thirty years ago do not work well today. For instance, "squeezing" or hard-bargaining suppliers to generate a lower annual **purchasing spend** (or purchasing expense) may ultimately prove harmful to buyer–supplier relationships, eventually leading to deteriorations in quality, ethical reputation, sustainability performance, and customer service as suppliers seek ways to cut corners in order to keep their profit margins at desired levels. If long-term sourcing plans are to be successful, they must support the firm's long-term strategies, and suppliers must also see some benefit from the initiatives implemented. A framework for ethical and sustainable sourcing strategy development is shown in Table 4.3.

In step 1 in Table 4.3, the firm formalizes its ethical and sustainable sourcing policies. Obviously, these policies will vary based on use of foreign suppliers, types of items purchased, and the firm's experiences with this type of sourcing. Ethical sourcing policies should include the importance placed on fair working conditions; use of minority,

Table 4.2	Some of the 2016 Edison Award Winners
Vegetable Factory™ by Spread Co., Ltd.	A fully-automated, large-scale agricultural innovation that can produce 30,000 heads of lettuce a day in a controlled indoor environment and can be built almost any-where. Their mission is to bring food security around the world in an eco-friendly way.
Abom Goggles by Abom, Inc.	Snow goggles with active antifog technology. A small lithium battery heats a transparent film that sits between the two-part lens and keeps fog away for up to six hours.
MasterClass by MasterClass	MasterClass creates online classes from the best in the world so anyone anywhere can get access to genius (e.g., Dustin Hoffman teaches acting; Serena Williams teaches tennis). Instead of webcams, classes are filmed by Academy and Emmy award winning directors and feature interactive tools.
Kuna Smart Home Security Light by Kuna Systems	A smart home security system built into an outdoor light for break-in prevention. Consists of a Wi-Fi camera, siren, and two-way intercom; Kuna detects people at your door and lets you see and interact with them through a live video feed on your smartphone.
Daisy Squeeze Sour Cream by Daisy Brand LLC	A squeezable inverted foil sour cream pouch; it supports multiple uses for sour cream (topping and ingredient), helps prevent contamination, and minimizes waste.
Cryogenic Carbon Capture™ by Sustainable Energy Solutions, LLC	Nearly eliminates all emissions from fossil-fueled power plants at half the cost of alternatives, while enabling greater adoption of solar and wind through built in, grid-scale energy storage.
LoanGifting™ by RKS	A web platform enabling students to crowdfund their educations by receiving gifts of student loan repayment. Donors are able to help rescue the $40 million individuals burdened with $1.3 trillion in student debt.

Source: Edison Awards: www.edisonawards.com

Table 4.3	Ethical and Sustainable Sourcing Strategy Framework	
STEPS	**DESCRIPTION**	
1. Establish corporate ethical and sustainable sourcing policies.	Establishes a vision and direction and enforces the importance of ethical and sustainable sourcing.	
2. Train purchasing staff; communicate policies to suppliers and customers.	Ensures that buyers are skilled in environmental and social considerations in sourcing and that suppliers and customers understand why and how purchasing decisions are made.	
3. Prioritize items based on ethical and sustainability opportunities and ease of implementation. Get started.	Allows buyers to "pick low hanging fruit" to provide evidence for successful strategy implementation.	
4. Develop a performance measurement system.	Measurement provides accountability and a way to improve over time. Should be reviewed periodically.	
5. Monitor progress, make improvements. Increase use of certified fair trade and green products and services.	Use performance measures to identify weaknesses. Step up efforts to develop better capabilities in the firm and its supply base.	
6. Expand focus to include other departments and customers. Increase brand value.	Use the purchasing department's success and influence to grow awareness in the firm and among customers. Communicate successes and programs to stakeholders.	

Source: Based in part on Newman, D., "Steps You Can Take to 'Green' Your Procurement," *Summit* 9(4), 2006: 10; "Buying a Better World," found at www.forumforthefuture.org

women-owned, and small businesses; guidelines on human rights and use of child labor; use of subcontracting; and supplier reporting and verification procedures. Sustainable sourcing policies should include supplier compliance issues in terms of waste reduction, energy conservation, use of renewable energy, hazardous material elimination, recycling, remanufacturing, and material reuse.

In step 2, training and communication of the policies occurs. It is all well and good to develop ethical and/or sustainable sourcing policies, but the firm must also do an adequate job of implementing these policies. In early 2000, for instance, iconic Canadian retailer Hudson's Bay had begun developing proactive sustainable sourcing plans, but in 2002, they were accused of using sweatshops for their outsourced manufacturing. As it turned out, they had not properly communicated the new vendor codes of conduct to their suppliers. Additionally, the shareholders and general public had no idea of their social compliance programs. This caused a number of actual and perceived problems for Hudson's Bay to overcome. Today, their social compliance programs are formalized and widely communicated, and they audit all supplier facilities for compliance to their codes of conduct.[32]

Step 3 is all about getting started. It is important to keep efforts simple early on, find successes quickly, and then build on these successes. If companies cannot show some financial benefit from ethical and sustainable sourcing policies, then ultimately these efforts will fail. Buyers might consider concentrating on products where the market for fair trade and green products is mature, as with office supplies, cleaning supplies, and some apparel. Fragrance Du Bois, a Paris-based perfume house, is doing this in a big way, as shown in the nearby SCM Profile.

Step 4 calls for the design of performance metrics to gauge the success of the firm's efforts. Measures can be qualitative or quantitative and in the general areas of cost, quality, time, flexibility, and innovativeness. In managed supply chains, performance indicators should be standardized across trading partners. Metrics for sustainability can be used in the areas of packaging, energy use, hazardous materials, and recycling. Metrics could include the number of fair trade–certified products purchased, the number of ethical standards adopted by suppliers, the number of suppliers adopting the ETI's Base Code, and the number of small and minority suppliers used. As products, suppliers, and markets change, these metrics should be revisited and potentially revised. More on performance measurement can be found in Chapters 13 and 14.

Step 5 is to monitor performance and outcomes, while adjusting the work plans, priorities, policies, and use of suppliers to more adequately meet the ethical and sustainability

SCM Profile: Fragrance Du Bois Protects Its Supply of Oud

Fragrance Du Bois has acquired its own source of one of the world's most sought after perfume ingredients–oud. Oud, or agarwood, comes from the Aquilaria tree, and today is in extremely high demand, particularly from high-end brands in the fragrance industry. Natural oud lends a fragrance a unique aroma, providing depth and longevity.

Supplies of oud are dwindling, since the Aquilaria tree has been harvested to near extinction. Demand for pure, natural oud continues to outstrip supply, with prices on a rising trend for more many years. Synthetic products have been created to meet the growing demand, but industry experts agree that there is nothing like the real thing. Fragrance Du Bois is growing Aquilaria trees to create a sustainable, renewable, and ethically sound supply of oud for their perfumes. As a result, Fragrance Du Bois is expanding its oud-based perfumes. The company is also opening new boutiques in Dubai, London, Paris, Luxembourg, and Geneva.

Fragrance Du Bois' investment in agarwood plantations is helping to save the Aquilaria tree from extinction. The company is also expanding the plants being grown to include patchouli, vetiver, tonka beans, bamboo, rose, pine, cypress, and lemongrass. Fragrance Du Bois is today safeguarding its supply of the highly valued oud and the near-extinct Aquilaria tree.[33]

goals of the firm. It may be that certain elements in the various programs or conduct codes need to be revised as the firm and its operating environments change. Over time as the firm and its suppliers adjust to these policies, improvements can be made, more fair trade products and green products will be identified, and further initiatives will be developed.

Finally, step 6 addresses the impact of ethical and sustainable sourcing on other facets of the organization, its trading partners, and ultimately the firm's brand. As successes are realized, it will become easier for the firm to operate more ethically and sustainably. Eventually, other divisions and trading partners will become interested. Consumers will start expecting it. Increasingly, companies are taking their ethical and sustainable factors and leveraging them for greater brand value. Even during the recent global recession, consumers preferred organizations that addressed various ethical and sustainable issues. In fact, in a 2014 Nielsen survey of Canadian consumers, about 55 percent said they preferred to work for a socially responsible company, and 40 percent said they were willing to pay extra for products and services from companies that are committed to making a positive social and environmental impact. That's up from 33 percent in 2011.[34]

As personnel in design, marketing, production, and other departments begin working with purchasing personnel to develop these and other sourcing strategies, a number of initiatives, some of which have already been introduced in earlier chapters, may be used separately or in some combination to support the organization's long-term goals. These proactive sourcing initiatives, when combined with internal operations and customer relationship initiatives, form the foundation for successful supply chain management and, ultimately, competitive advantage for the firm. The following section discusses a number of these ethical and sustainable sourcing initiatives.

ETHICAL AND SUSTAINABLE SOURCING INITIATIVES
Ethical and Sustainable Supplier Certification Programs

Seeking and then creating **strategic supplier alliances** have become important objectives of firms actively managing their supply chains. Strategic alliances are a more formalized type of collaborative relationship, involving commitments to long-term cooperation and trust, shared benefits and costs, joint problem solving, continuous improvement, and information sharing. Because of these relationships, suppliers invest more of their resources toward becoming specialized in areas required by the buyer, to establish production and/ or storage facilities close to the buyer's facilities, to purchase compatible communication and information systems, and to invest in better technologies that will ultimately improve supplier performance.

Ethical and sustainable supplier certifications are one way to identify strategic alliance candidates or to further develop existing alliances. In many cases, certification programs are simply based on internationally recognized certifications such as the Switzerland-based International Organization for Standardization's ISO 9000 family of quality certifications and the ISO 14000 family of environmental certifications.[35] For some organizations, these types of certification requirements are good, but may not be specific enough in areas of importance to the firm. In these cases, firms develop their own formal certification programs, which may include ISO certification as one element of the certification process. Other certification requirements might include, for example, the Forest Stewardship Council (FSC) certification for recycled paper, Energy Star certification for various environmental standards, or fair trade certifications for social and ethical performance.

The use of **ethical and environmental certifications** for suppliers is increasing. The New York–based nonprofit Rainforest Alliance and California-based nonprofit Fair Trade USA certify billions of dollars worth of coffee, bananas, and cocoa each year from suppliers in dozens of countries, and in exchange, suppliers work to preserve the environment and improve conditions for farm workers.[36] Massachusetts-based Integrity Interactive Corp. offers a web-based service that allows a firm to communicate a code of ethics to its supply chain members. The website delivers the company's code of ethics to suppliers, collects certifications, and reports results back to the initiating company. The certification website allows companies to identify rogue suppliers before they can cause problems or disruptions in their supply chains. Suppliers who fail to certify according to the ethical requirements can then face various consequences. World-class companies such as Ryder System and Kraft Heinz are busy using the system to certify their suppliers.[37]

Supply Base Rationalization Programs

As first mentioned in Chapter 2, firms in many cases seek to reduce purchases from marginal or poor-performing suppliers while increasing and concentrating purchases among their more desirable, top-performing suppliers. Firms doing this are practicing **supply base rationalization**, also referred to as **supply base reduction** or **supply base optimization**; this has been a common occurrence since the late 1980s. Indeed, activities aimed at fostering buyer–supplier partnerships and increasing the performance and value of suppliers are simply easier when fewer suppliers are involved. Thus, supply base rationalization programs have the benefits of reduced purchase prices due to quantity discounts, fewer supplier management problems, closer and more frequent collaborations between buyer and supplier, and greater overall levels of quality and delivery reliability (since only the best suppliers remain in the supply base).

Companies can design supply base rationalization initiatives based in part on ethical and sustainable performance requirements—in this way, firms will interact more frequently and closely with suppliers exhibiting preferred ethical and sustainable habits. Building relationships with suppliers that are leaders in these areas can bring many benefits to the firm, including those mentioned above, along with brand enhancement and better environmental and ethical performance. Two international standards by the World Resources Institute (WRI) and the World Business Council on Sustainable Development (WBCSD), known as the GHG Protocol standards, cover individual product carbon footprints and for the first time allow buyers to measure and question their suppliers' greenhouse gas emissions. In 2014, 86 percent of Fortune 500 companies responding to a carbon disclosure survey had used the GHG Protocol standards.[38]

Outsourcing Products and Services

Purchasing spend as a percentage of sales has been increasing over the years, in part because firms have opted to **outsource** the production of materials, parts, services, and assembled components to concentrate more resources and time on the firm's core business activities. As first described in Chapter 2, many organizations are outsourcing more, while making fewer of the parts that go into their finished goods. In managed supply chains where a higher level of trust permeates buyer–supplier relationships, the use of outsourcing is also growing. Firms are also outsourcing to suppliers with outstanding ethical and sustainable reputations, due in part to brand enhancement and the lower potential costs of sustainability. Georgia-based Metcam, for example, a sheet metal component manufacturer, is a supplier to a number of companies seeking to outsource for sustainability reasons. Metcam's ISO 14000 environmental certification has helped it get this type of business. Michigan-based furniture maker Steelcase, for example, outsourced to Metcam to help it reach its sustainability goals. Steelcase has its suppliers track information on recycled content, materials used, and transportation costs.[39]

Outsourcing solely based on low cost can be quite dangerous, as witnessed by the devastating loss of 1100 workers after the collapse of the Rena Plaza in Dhaka, Bangladesh, in April 2013. The facility housed a number of clothing manufacturers that were being used by several large clothing suppliers. The nonprofit Supplier Ethical Data Exchange (Sedex) focuses on responsible and ethical business practices and provides reports to industrial buyers to help avoid these and other outsourcing risks. Over 22 percent of independent audits, for example, revealed fire safety noncompliance in Bangladesh (the leading noncompliance country) followed by 18 percent in China and 17 percent in Pakistan. "Fire safety concerns are at the top of risk issues. If a building is vulnerable in any way, it provides big risks to suppliers, companies, and investors," says Mark Robertson, a spokesperson at Sedex. "Companies and their investors ignore these risks at their peril," he adds.[40]

Ron Kifer, CIO at California-based Applied Materials Inc., tries to ensure that the outsourcing his company does is aligned with the company's social and ethical objectives. "We just got into IT outsourcing within the past couple of years, and we're trying to apply the same ideas: giving back to community, supporting the economies in which we live and work, and green initiatives. We need to make sure that our suppliers are operating to the same high standards as the company," he says.[41] A number of other strategic sourcing initiatives are discussed in the following sections.

EARLY SUPPLIER INVOLVEMENT

As relationships with suppliers become more trusted, reliable, and long-term in nature, key suppliers often become more heavily involved in the internal operations of their industrial customers, including managing inventories of their own products at their customers' points of use and participating in their customers' new product and process design activities. Key supplier representatives might participate in making decisions on product part and assembly designs, new product materials usage, and even the design of the processes to be used in manufacturing new products. Thus, strategic suppliers play a greater role in their customers' decision-making processes as trading relationships mature, which in turn further strengthens the supply chain. California-based semiconductor company Novellus, a subsidiary of Lam Research, has a long history of getting suppliers involved in the product design process. It has allowed them to reduce production lead times and time to market while reducing costs and thus producing better profit margins. Before, Novellus experienced production delays and higher costs as a result of suppliers having problems manufacturing their parts. Now, since the suppliers are part of the design process from the start, these problems do not occur.[42]

While serving on a customer's new product development team, a supplier representative's input can help the firm to reduce material cost, improve product quality and innovation, and reduce product development time. Cost reductions occur with use of more standardized parts, fewer parts, and less expensive materials. Cost, quality, innovation, and delivery timing improvements can all occur when suppliers use the information gained through **early supplier involvement** to design parts at their own facilities to match a buyer's specifications. These parts can be timed to be in place and available when first needed by the buyer. Use of these **value engineering** techniques with help from the supplier allows firms to design better quality and cost savings into the products from the time a product first hits the shelves. Over the product's life, this can generate significant savings and revenues while reducing the need for cost-savings initiatives later on.

Early supplier involvement is perhaps one of the most effective supply chain integration techniques. Buyers and suppliers working together—sharing proprietary design and manufacturing information that their competitors would love to see—establishes a level of trust and cooperation that results in many future collaborative and potentially successful projects. Discussions of several other early supplier involvement activities follow.

Vendor Managed Inventories

Vendor managed inventory (VMI) services is perhaps one of the more value-enhancing activities performed by trusted suppliers. When past performance allows companies to develop trust in a supplier's ability to manage its own inventories at the buyer's site, then carrying costs can be reduced and stockouts avoided. From the buyer's perspective, allowing a supplier to track and manage purchased inventories, while determining delivery schedules and order quantities, saves time and money. From the supplier's perspective, it means avoiding ill-advised orders from buyers, deciding how and where inventories are to be placed, as well as when to ship and how to ship. Further, suppliers have the opportunity to educate their customers about other products. VMI programs have become very popular. According to data from a 2015 survey conducted by Gatepoint Research, almost 70 percent of the respondents were using VMI. Most of the respondents were senior managers at Fortune 1000 companies.[43]

Ideally, these valued suppliers manage their customers' inventories using real-time visibility of inventory movements in customers' storage areas or at the point of assembly or sale. This can be accomplished with barcode labels and scanners that instantly update computer counts of inventories as the items are used or sold, or through use of radio frequency identification systems (discussed in Chapter 7). This data can then be made available to suppliers using compatible inventory management systems or via a secured website. This allows a supplier to profile demand, determine an accurate forecast, and then ship an order quantity when the inventory levels become low enough.

Walmart is generally given credit for popularizing the use of VMI in the mid-1990s when it initiated an arrangement with Procter & Gamble to manage Walmart's diaper inventories. A similar arrangement with Rubbermaid soon followed.[44] Ohio-based Datalliance, the leading VMI service provider, sees the concept exploding. According to Carl Hall, Datalliance president, "More and more, retailers are looking to their product suppliers to help streamline their supply chains all the way to the individual store and shelf. Now a growing number of retailers are asking suppliers to also take on the job of store level replenishment planning in order to further improve product availability while at the same time reducing administrative costs. Done on a collaborative basis, direct store replenishment can increase sales and margins while reducing costs for both the retailer and the supplier. That's why we're putting even more emphasis on providing solutions for this growing practice."[45]

A shared form of VMI is termed **comanaged inventories**. In this case, the buyer and supplier reach an agreement regarding how information is shared, order quantities, when an order is generated, and the delivery timing and location. This type of controlled VMI may be preferable for very high-value, strategic item purchases, where the customer desires more input into the day-to-day supply activities, or perhaps when the customer is still assessing a supplier's ability to take full responsibility for the order fulfillment process.

STRATEGIC ALLIANCE DEVELOPMENT

As the growth of supply chain management continues, firms become more adept at managing their suppliers and more willing to assist them in improving their production and service capabilities. Simply put, **strategic alliance development**, an extension of supplier development (covered in Chapter 3), refers to increasing the firm's key or strategic suppliers' capabilities. As supply bases become smaller, more opportunities for creating collaborative relationships with these suppliers also occur. As a whole then, supply bases become more manageable. The more basic supplier management activities tend to become somewhat less time-consuming as strategic supplier alliances begin to constitute more and more of the supply base. Consequently, strategic alliance development starts to occupy more of the purchasing function's time and resources.

Many business owners and executives realize that strategic supplier alliances, if successful, can result in better market penetration, better service, and access to new technologies and knowledge, compared to companies with no such alliances. Memphis Light, Gas and Water Division, for example, has a strategic alliance with SPX for the supply of transformers. Both companies benefit from the alliance, as described in the nearby SCM Profile.

Supplier development activities become more vital to companies as they come to depend more and more on a smaller group of high-performance suppliers. Alliance development can even extend to a firm's second-tier suppliers, as the firm's key suppliers begin

SCM Profile | **MLGW's Strategic Alliance with SPX**

Memphis Light, Gas and Water Division (MLGW), located in Memphis, TN, is one of the largest power utilities in the United States. When MLGW needs a power transformer, the selection and approval process can take up to eight months, if the supplier has not already been approved. In times of high demand, a supplier alliance can allow procurement of equipment that might not be quickly available for other customers. During such times, it is essential to have an alliance in place particularly for long lead time parts and equipment. MLGW's current power transformer alliance partner is SPX Transformer Solutions.

Nationwide, it is not unusual to find utilities with forty-year-old power transformers. A majority of those transformers are coming to the end of their useful life. When demand trends up, lead times for transformers typically begin to rise unless there are existing alliances. Consequently, MLGW has entered into five-year purchasing alliances for power transformers, high-voltage circuit breakers, and substation switchgear. MLGW has seen huge benefits that include better delivery times and excellent equipment pricing. Having a strategic alliance also helps operations and maintenance crews. The crews do not have to learn a whole new piece of equipment each time a new transformer is ordered. Alliances reduce the inventory of spare parts since the same manufacturer's product is already in the system. Alliances also give access to the manufacturer's subject-matter experts in the event technical guidance on application is needed.

One of the biggest advantages of an alliance is reserving slots in the manufacturer's schedule. This advantage is huge when unexpected events occur. During one emergency, having an alliance in place allowed MLGW to receive a power transformer in just twelve weeks—from the time the purchase order was placed until the time the transformer was delivered. This was made possible by the cancellation of a production slot by another customer. Because of the alliance, MLGW was able to reap the benefit of last-minute changes in the manufacturer's production schedule.[46]

to form their own supplier alliance development activities. Alliance development among the firm and its key suppliers tends to be much more of a collaborative activity, requiring both sides to commit time, people, communication, and monetary resources to achieving goals that will benefit both parties. The company and its strategic suppliers jointly decide on improvement activities, resources required, and the means to measure progress. As the improvements take place, suppliers eventually become capable of passing these same capabilities on to their key suppliers, thus extending these capabilities up their supply chains.

Strategic alliance development requires companies to improve their relationships, learn from their mistakes and successes, and make investments to enable collaborative problem solving. Many firms are hiring strategic relationship managers, whose job is to build trust, commitment, and mutual value with alliance partners. These relationship managers work on negotiating win–win collaborations resulting in mutual benefits, such that alliances become the norm among the various business units in the organization. Raytheon, a U.S. government defense systems contractor, is going a step further by forming a Supplier Advisory Council as a way to communicate and improve relationships with its most strategic suppliers. In early May 2014, senior executives from Raytheon's Integrated Defense Systems met with senior executives from thirteen of their key suppliers. The suppliers came to help launch Raytheon's first Supplier Advisory Council (SAC). The ultimate goal was to earn and provide preferential treatment as the Customer-of-Choice, or the customer who receives the best terms, manufacturing capacity as needed, and supplier innovations that can win in the marketplace.[47] Strategic supplier alliances, like products, have their own life cycles, requiring ongoing management, development, and negotiating activities to monitor success, manage conflict, evaluate the current fit with partners, revisit the ground rules for working together, and make adjustments through mutual problem solving and information sharing. Organizing and managing a successful alliance program is thus very important to a firm's competitiveness. Table 4.4 describes the strategic alliance organization process.

To make strategic alliance programs successful, firms must determine how to organize a program that can cut across functional boundaries; disseminate program information quickly and effectively throughout the organization; acquire the necessary resources; create program acceptance by the line managers and their employees; achieve concrete, measurable success; and reward supplier performance. Some firms have chosen to organize around their key alliance partners by assigning alliance managers to each of these partners. Others have decided to create an alliance board to oversee alliances and coordinate

Table 4.4	Maintaining a Successful Strategic Alliance Program
STEPS	**DISCUSSION**
1. Determine the key strategic parameters to organize around.	Can be based on business units, geographic areas, industries, key alliance partners, or combinations of these.
2. Facilitate the dissemination of information.	Alliance management and development information should be centrally controlled and available through internal websites, pamphlets, and workshops.
3. Elevate the importance of the strategic alliance program.	Assign a director or vice president of alliance programs, reporting to top management. Establish consistent procedures for alliance programs throughout the organization.
4. Provide continuous evaluation of alliance performance, visibility, and support.	Management can increase the value and acceptance of alliance programs when successes are made visible to the firm's lower level managers and employees. Alliance management requires resources and ongoing reevaluation.
5. Reward suppliers as performance merits.	Rewards typically include increased business and other nonmonetary awards.

Source: Adapted from Dyer, J., P. Kale, and H. Singh, "How to Make Strategic Alliances Work," *Sloan Management Review* 42(4), 2001: 37–43.

alliance managers in various divisions within the organization or in different geographic regions of the world.

The supplier alliance management function can act as a clearinghouse for information regarding all types of alliance needs, from negotiation strategies to problem-solving assistance to outreach programs and workshops. To give the alliance management function credibility, the program director should report to the organization's top management. This facilitates the use of company resources as well as provides internal visibility to the function. Alliance strategies, goals, policies, and procedures can then be generated and communicated across the entire organization. Finally, since alliance goals change over time, they must be evaluated periodically. Performance evaluation metrics must be established; and, as alliances show signs of success, strategies can be shared across the various alliance boundaries. As briefly mentioned earlier, continued success depends on both the supplier and the buyer receiving value from the alliance. The topic of negotiations with strategic alliance partners follows.

Negotiating Win–Win Strategic Alliance Agreements

When negotiating with alliance partners, the most advantageous outcome occurs when both parties utilize **collaborative negotiations**. This is sometimes also referred to as **integrative** or **win–win negotiations**. In other words, both sides work together to maximize the joint outcome or to create a joint optimal result. The belief is that there is more to gain from collaborating rather than trying to seek an outcome that favors primarily one side's interests (referred to as **distributive negotiations**). For collaborative negotiations to succeed, members from both parties must trust each other, believe in the validity of each other's perspective, and be committed to working together. From the perspective of key supply chain trading partners, these requirements should already be present, so collaborative negotiations may be easier to achieve in actively managed supply chains.

Successful collaborative negotiations require open discussions and a free flow of information between parties, preferably in face-to-face meetings. Professor Kate Vitasek, an international authority on collaborative relationships, describes in her book, "Getting to We: Negotiating Agreements for Highly Collaborative Relationships," the process for moving from "what's in it for me" to "what's in it for we." Collaborative partners must abide by a set of principles—reciprocity, autonomy, honesty, equity, loyalty, and integrity, to drive collaborative behaviors and achieve mutually successful outcomes. Jaguar's successful deal with Unipart Logistics over the past twenty-five years illustrates this. Both companies were having problems. Jaguar buyers were waiting too long for replacement parts from Unipart, making both companies look bad. The CEO's of both companies decided to create a partnership with a shared vision and internal and external alignments. Ultimately, the luxury car manufacturer went from ninth to first in JD Power and Associates' survey of customer satisfaction. The result was that Jaguar sold more cars because of the increased service and Unipart Logistics earned more money. This was collaborative negotiating at its best.[48]

In contrast, distributive negotiations are adversarial (what's in it for me) and usually mean that some information will be withheld, distorted, delayed, or completely misrepresented. The likelihood that one or the other or some combination of these two negotiation methods occurs depends on the nature of the trading relationship, the strategic nature of the item(s) being negotiated, and potentially the balance of power in the relationship. In the automotive sector, particularly at Toyota, collaborative negotiations are described to be part of a *lean thinking* approach to supplier relationships, although automobile manufacturers typically enjoy high levels of buyer dominance that may tilt the negotiating scales somewhat in the buyer's favor.

Table 4.5	Developing a Collaborative Negotiation Infrastructure
STEPS	**DESCRIPTION**
1. Build a preparation process	Gain an understanding of both parties' interests; brainstorm value-maximizing solutions and terms; identify objective criteria wherein both sides evaluate fairness of an agreement.
2. Develop a negotiation database	Review previous negotiations to catalogue standards, practices, precedents, metrics, creative solutions used, and lessons learned.
3. Design a negotiation launch process	Create an environment allowing parties to first focus on how they will work together to create a shared vocabulary, build working relationships, and map out a shared decision-making process.
4. Institute a feedback mechanism	Create a debriefing process to provide feedback to negotiating teams and capture lessons learned.

Source: Adapted from Kliman, S., "Enabling Win-Win," *Executive Excellence* 17(4), 2000: 9–11.

To maximize the likelihood of achieving equitable collaborative negotiations, supply chain partners should first develop a collaborative negotiation infrastructure and then facilitate a negotiating approach that supports win–win outcomes. Table 4.5 describes the steps in developing a collaboration infrastructure. Over time, purchasing representatives will get better at collaborative negotiations as they become more familiar with their trading partners' interests, learn from previous negotiations, and determine how best to work with each trading partner. Managers or negotiating team leaders can also aid in this process by encouraging exchanges of information, dealing fairly with negotiating problems, and brainstorming options for achieving mutual gains.

REWARDING SUPPLIER PERFORMANCE

Rewarding suppliers for improving or maintaining high levels of performance accomplishes several objectives. For one thing, it provides an incentive to all suppliers to meet and surpass specific performance goals. It also can provide an incentive to marginal suppliers to achieve a level of performance that will allow their status to be upgraded, potentially resulting in continued business. Finally, it can give suppliers an incentive to create and share rewards, in turn, with *their* suppliers.

Rewards can be either monetary or nonmonetary. Sharing the benefits of good performance is one of the central foundations of building effective supply chains. As mentioned at the start of the chapter, both suppliers and buyers must be able to realize benefits from supply chain relationships. Without this incentive, suppliers may keep any improvements within their operations quiet, while also keeping the benefits. With time, this lack of information and benefit sharing stunts the growth of relationships within the supply chain and results in lower overall supply chain trust and performance. According to Ellen Malfliet, marketing and communications manager at PearlChain, a supply chain software provider in Belgium, "Everyone within the value chain is focused on the customer right now. Take automobile manufacturing, for example, where raw materials suppliers, manufacturers, distributors, and dealers must all work together in a collaborative environment in order to turn out a viable end product. In the end, the successful customer experience translates into success for all parties across the supply chain, not just those that are actually facing the customer. Everyone wins."[49]

More and more, companies are rewarding suppliers for their ethical and environmental performance. Companies like Nike, Unilever, and Nestlé understand the role suppliers can play in reducing carbon footprints and enhancing brands. Nike, at one time, was targeted by ethical activists but today is a leader in managing conditions within the factories making its products. It is one of a growing group of companies going beyond requirements for social audits of factories to look at how its practices can put pressure on other companies to act in a similar fashion.[50] In the past few years, Walmart has been working to redefine itself as a green company, and doing so has raised its bottom line. Due to its size and retail dominance, Walmart has tremendous influence on its suppliers and is rewarding them with more business based on carbon emission reductions, water conservation, and renewable energy performance.[51]

Performance motivation can come in several forms, including punishment and various reward mechanisms. Motivational tools can be used as an integral part of supplier management and supplier development programs. Punishment may take the form of a reduction or elimination of future business, a downgrade of the supplier's status from key to marginal, or a **billback penalty** equal to the costs resulting from a late delivery or poor material quality, for example. On the other hand, when performance meets or exceeds expectations, suppliers can be rewarded in some way.

Many formal strategic supplier agreements allow suppliers to benefit in the following ways:

- A share of the cost reductions resulting from supplier improvements;
- A share of the cost savings resulting from a supplier's suggestions made to the focal firm;
- More business and/or longer contracts for higher performance;
- Access to in-house training seminars and other resources; and
- Company and public recognition in the form of awards.

These benefits tend to stimulate further capital investment among suppliers to improve their operating capabilities, leading to even greater levels of quality, service, and environmental, ethical, or cost performance. The U.S. healthcare industry is a good case in point. Hospital costs in the United States continue to escalate rapidly, so hospitals offer incentives to suppliers to keep costs down. Ed Hardin, the system vice president of Supply Chain Management at Texas-based CHRISTUS Health, says "Frankly, it's an honorable and profitable thing to do business with CHRISTUS Health. Today, third-parties seek the privilege to work with an organization that is highly collaborative, keeps their word, and rewards high-performing suppliers with more business. Not only is it a privilege, but we also find a willingness from these third-parties to provide value-adds beyond our agreements. Violating our trust, doing the end-run around supply chain has consequences."[52]

BENCHMARKING SUCCESSFUL SOURCING PRACTICES

Benchmarking, the practice of copying what other businesses do best, is a very effective way to quickly improve sourcing practices and supply chain performance. Without benchmarking, firms must learn through their own experiences the methods and tools that work the best. Benchmarking allows firms to potentially leapfrog the experience-gaining stage by trying things that have worked well for other companies. Meaningful benchmarking data regarding sourcing practices can be obtained in any number of ways, both formal and informal—from using evaluation surveys distributed to a firm's customers and suppliers regarding *their* sourcing and supplier management practices, to discussing sourcing strategies with colleagues at business association meetings or conferences, to collecting published trade information on benchmarking studies.

A large number of resources are available for firms seeking to learn about and implement successful sourcing practices. The Center for Advanced Purchasing Studies (CAPS), an Arizona-based, nonprofit, independent research organization, helps firms achieve competitive advantage by providing leading-edge research information regarding strategic purchasing. For instance, CAPS provides research studies, benchmarking reports, and best practices case studies, along with organizing purchasing symposiums and roundtable discussions for purchasing professionals and academics.[53]

Another organization, the Supply Chain Council, a subsidiary of APICS, helps practitioners reduce their supply chain costs and improve customer service by providing their Supply Chain Operations Reference (SCORE) model as a framework for supply chain improvement. They also provide case studies and bring together practitioners to discuss best practices in periodic business conferences around the world.[54]

The Arizona-based Institute for Supply Management (ISM), established in 1915, provides a wide variety of resources to supply management professionals worldwide, including a monthly publication featuring the latest supply management trends and information and the globally recognized Certified Purchasing Manager (CPM), Certified Professional in Supply Management (CPSM), and Accredited Purchasing Practitioner (APP) programs. They also publish the globally recognized *Journal of Supply Chain Management*, organize several annual global supply management conferences, and support many seminars and web conferences for supply management professionals.[55]

The issue of best purchasing practices has been the subject of a number of research studies over the years, and these findings have proven very beneficial for firms seeking to benchmark best sourcing practices.[56] Some of the research has found a positive relationship between purchasing benchmarking and firm performance. A number of the successful sourcing practices found to be common among the companies studied were:

- use of a central database to access information on parts, suppliers, lead times, and other purchasing information;
- software applications for sharing information with suppliers;
- use of the Internet for supplier searches;
- alliances with key suppliers for specific components;
- supplier certification and the elimination of the need for incoming quality checks for key supplier deliveries;
- involving suppliers in the research and development processes of new products;
- reducing the firm's supply base;
- continuous measurement of supplier performance, and establishing supplier improvement targets; and most recently,
- creating an ethical and sustainable supply chain.

With specific regard to the best ethical purchasing practices, the U.K.-based Chartered Institute of Procurement & Supply (CIPS) has developed a code of ethics for procurement, which is summarized below:

- commit to eradicating unethical business practices including bribery, fraud, corruption, and human rights abuses, such as modern slavery and child labor;

- conduct all business relationships with respect, honesty, and integrity, and avoid causing harm to others as a result of business decisions;

- actively support and promote corporate social responsibility (CSR);

- avoid any business practices which might bring the procurement profession into disrepute;

- use procurement strategies to drive unethical practices from the supply chain;

- ensure procurement decisions minimize any negative impact on human rights and the environment while endeavoring to maximize value and service levels;

- put ethical policies and procedures in place, regularly monitored and updated, and ensure compliance;

- take steps to prevent, report, and remedy unethical practices; and

- provide a safe environment for the reporting of unethical practices.[57]

ASSESSING AND IMPROVING THE FIRM'S SOURCING FUNCTION

As stated throughout this textbook so far, the sourcing function is one of the most value-enhancing functions in an organization. Today, purchasing staff members are viewed as strategic members of the organization and are expected to generate cost savings and quality enhancements of goods and services. Consequently, it is preferable to periodically monitor the purchasing function's performance against set standards, goals, and/or industry benchmarks. Thus, as the firm strives to continuously improve its products and processes, purchasing can also gauge its success in improving its own value-enhancing contributions to the firm and its supply chains.

As stated earlier, criteria can be utilized to provide feedback to the purchasing department staff regarding their contributions to the strategic goals of the firm. Surveys or audits can be administered among purchasing personnel as part of the annual evaluation process; assessments can include feedback from internal customers of the sourcing function, such as engineering, sales, marketing, and finance personnel. Feedback may even be included from supplier representatives. Assessment criteria to evaluate the purchasing department's performance should include some or all of the following:

- participating in value engineering/value analysis efforts;

- finding and evaluating ethical and sustainable suppliers;

- optimizing the supply base;

- managing and developing local, regional, and global suppliers;

- creating early supplier involvement initiatives;

- creating strategic supplier alliances;

- furthering the integration and development of existing key suppliers;

- contributing to new product development efforts;

- initiating supplier cost reduction programs;

- contributing to the improvement of purchased product and service quality; and

- maintaining and improving internal cooperative relationships.

Since these criteria require both qualitative and quantitative assessments, the performance evaluation tool recommended here would be some form of weighted-factor rating method, as covered in Chapter 3. Because of the tremendous potential value of these activities, supply management staff members should be continuously auditing their capabilities and successes in these areas.

Thus, the skill set requirements of purchasing professionals have been changing as purchasing, sourcing, or supply management has evolved from the tactical, clerical function it was about thirty years ago to the highly demanding strategic function it is today. To achieve the type of world-class performance suggested by the preceding assessment criteria, sourcing personnel must today exhibit world-class skills. One recent survey of procurement professionals conducted by *Purchasing* magazine found that their top three responsibilities were negotiating contracts, selecting suppliers, and managing supplier relationships. Given the recent economic downturn, controlling costs is also seen as a very important activity of purchasing personnel. Important cost-controlling activities include reducing the supply base, negotiating global agreements with suppliers, and adopting new technologies suited to purchasing activities.[58]

SUMMARY

Managing supply chains successfully often starts with the sourcing activity. We hope we have provided, in this and previous chapters, evidence of the strategic role played by the sourcing function and the impact of sourcing on supply chain management. Firms that fail to recognize this importance will simply not experience the same level of success in the long run. Two relatively new sourcing topics, ethical and sustainable sourcing, are quickly gaining importance with regard to how firms are choosing to operate. Sourcing personnel are playing an important role today in helping the firm to achieve success in these two areas while maintaining cost, quality, and customer service priorities. The sourcing process is thus composed of a number of related activities that, when taken together, provide competitive advantage to the firm. Firms can maximize this advantage by developing effective supply chain strategies and then assessing and revising these strategies periodically as missions, markets, competitors, and technologies change. As we head into the internal operations segment of this text, we hope you will continue to consider the sourcing issues discussed and how they interact with other processes as materials, services, and information move down the supply chain to the firm's immediate customers and, eventually, to end users.

KEY TERMS

benchmarking, 131

billback penalty, 131

business ethics, 113

collaborative negotiations, 129

comanaged inventories, 126

corporate social responsibility, 114

distributive negotiations, 129

early supplier involvement, 125

ethical and environmental
   certifications, 124

ethical sourcing, 114

Ethical Trading Initiative, 115

fair trade products, 115

functional products, 120

green purchasing, 117

innovative products, 120

integrative, 129

outsource, 124

purchasing spend, 120

rewarding suppliers, 130

rights and duties, 114

strategic alliance
   development, 127

strategic sourcing, 113

strategic supplier alliances, 123

supply base optimization, 124

supply base rationalization, 124

supply base reduction, 124

sustainability, 117

sustainable sourcing, 118

three P's, 118

utilitarianism, 113

value engineering, 125

vendor managed inventory, 126

win–win negotiations, 129

DISCUSSION QUESTIONS

1. What is strategic sourcing?

2. What is the difference between purchasing and strategic sourcing?

3. What is ethical sourcing, and why would firms do it?

4. What do business ethics, utilitarianism, and rights and duties have to do with ethical sourcing?

5. What are some common practices or activities of ethical sourcing?

6. What are some of the risks of ethical sourcing? How about the potential advantages? Do you think ethical sourcing is a good practice? Why?

7. In what ways is corporate social responsibility different from business ethics?

8. How could purchasing goods from suppliers in developing countries be risky? How should firms reduce this risk?

9. What is a fair trade product? Could farmers in the United States make fair trade products?

10. What is sustainable sourcing, and how does it differ from ethical sourcing and from green purchasing?

11. What are the benefits of sustainable sourcing? Can firms actually make money from sustainable sourcing? Do you think it is a good practice? Why?

12. What are the three P's? What do they have to do with sustainability?

13. How could you apply sustainability to a supply chain?

14. Describe some sustainable and ethical things your university is doing.

15. How are ethical and sustainable sourcing policies designed in an organization?

16. How is the U.S. government getting involved in sustainability requirements?

17. What are innovative and functional products? Can firms buy functional products in an ethical way? A sustainable way? What about innovative products?

18. What are the benefits of obtaining ethical and sustainable certifications? Why would a buyer want its suppliers to have these certifications?

19. What advantages do company-designed supplier certification programs have over industry certifications like ISO 9000?

20. What is supply base rationalization, and what are its advantages and disadvantages?

21. What is outsourcing? How is it different from purchasing? Would a firm ever want to outsource a core product or process? Why or why not?

22. When would firms want to insource a product or process?

23. Do companies outsource for ethical or sustainable reasons? If so, provide some examples. How might this impact a firm's reputation?

24. What is sourcing's role in value engineering, and what benefits does this give to the firm?

25. Why is early supplier involvement a good way to integrate the supply chain?

26. Why would suppliers want to be involved on a buyer's new product development team?

27. Describe the differences between vendor-managed inventories and co-managed inventories, and when it might be advisable to do either of them.

28. What is the difference between supplier management and strategic alliance development?

29. If your firm had a large number of strategic supplier alliances, what would be the best way to manage them?

30. What makes supplier alliances fail? How can firms reduce the failure rate?

31. Describe the differences between integrative and distributive negotiations, and when each should be used.

32. Why might second- and even third-tier suppliers be important to the focal firm?

33. What is a common method for developing second-tier suppliers?

34. If your firm had 500 suppliers and they each had 100 suppliers, how many second-tier suppliers would your firm have? What if your firm reduced its supply base to twenty?

35. What are some typical supplier rewards and punishments that a buyer could use?

36. If you work for a company, describe how it rewards and punishes its suppliers. Do you think appropriate methods are being used? Why or why not?

37. What is benchmarking? What are some different ways you could use benchmarking to improve your performance at school?

38. Why would a firm want to monitor its own purchasing performance?

39. Describe several successful ethical sourcing practices.

40. How could a company use benchmarking and performance measurement to improve its ethical and sustainable purchasing practices?

ESSAY/PROJECT QUESTIONS

1. Go to the International Organization for Standardization website (www.iso.ch), and write a short description and history of the organization, including some of the various certifications that can be obtained.

2. Go to the CAPS website (www.capsresearch.org), and find the latest cross-industry benchmarking report; then determine the overall purchase dollars as a percentage of sales in the United States. What benchmarking research is CAPS doing now?

3. Go to the Fair Factories Clearinghouse website (www.fairfactories.org), and describe the organization, along with some of the current events underway.

4. Go to the Goldman Environmental Prize website (www.goldmanprize.org), and describe the most recent award winners.

5. What is an ASP? Find some on the Internet that are not listed in the chapter, and describe what they do.

6. Gather information on business ethics and ethical purchasing, and report on several of the most current news items and controversies.

CASES

1. Maryann Franklin Industries*

Connie Fox is chief executive officer of Maryann Franklin Industries (MFI). MFI is feeling the pressure of a declining economy. Connie knows they will weather this storm; however, she believes this is the time to institute better cost controls. MFI has grown very quickly over the last ten years and Connie realizes that with the growth came some cost issues that were ignored. She feels that the current situation provides an excellent opportunity to have her staff look into approaches to reduce expenses.

*Written by Rick Bonsall, D. Mgt., McKendree University, Lebanon, IL. The people and institution are fictional and any resemblance to any person or any institution is coincidental. This case was prepared solely to provide material for class discussion. The author does not intend to illustrate either effective or ineffective handling of a managerial situation.

Connie knows that every department had opportunities to reduce expenses; however, she believes the buggiest opportunity is in the supply chain management division. Leonard Butler is her vice president of supply chain management. Connie told Leonard that she needed him to find ways to reduce cost without reducing quality. Furthermore, if possible, she would be delighted if he could actually improve quality while still reducing cost.

Leonard brought his staff together to discuss the task. Johnathan Robert, director of supply chain management, suggested a three-pronged approach. The first prong would be to examine the number of suppliers and determine if there were ways to reduce the number. He believed that through supply base optimization, MFI could implement significant reductions in cost. Johnathan believed that a key tool in supply base optimization was to segment the suppliers, based on risk or value.

Johnathan's second idea was to review their current global contracts with their suppliers and determine which ones could be renegotiated. His thought was that if they explained to the suppliers that they were working on reducing their supply base, some would be amenable to negotiations. Leonard chimed in and said that was a good idea. He stated, "We must make sure we do not prose this as a threat. Instead, explain that we hope they see this as an opportunity to strengthen our relationship and to build a stronger strategic alliance."

The third prong was to engage outside sources to help MFI find best practices within the supply chain community. Benchmarking against what other companies are doing would be the most effective and efficient method for improvement.

Discussion Questions

1. Johnathan Robert suggested that segmenting their suppliers would enable supply base optimization. Utilize the Internet to research ways to segment suppliers. Find at least three categories of segmentation and explain how these support supply base optimization.

2. Although Leonard agreed with Johnathan's idea about renegotiating contracts with suppliers, he did have a major concern. Was Leonard proposing they engage in collaborative or distributive negotiations? Explain what attributes of the specific type of negotiations you picked. Support your choice and how they relate to Leonard's concern.

3. Go to APICS, http://www.apics.org/docs/default-source/scc-non-research/apicsscc_scor_quick_reference_guide.pdf and download the Quick Reference Guide. In the section titled SCOR Metrics, select one metric from three of the five categories (reliability, responsiveness, agility, cost, and assessment management efficiency) and explain in your view how the metrics can lead to benchmark improvements and indicate best practices.

©2019 Cengage Learning

2. Fitz-Simmons Consultants*

Fitz-Simmons Consultants is an international company that advises international corporations on ethical and sustainable sourcing. As the world matures in its view of how to treat people and the environment, more companies are focused on ethical and

*Written by Rick Bonsall, D. Mgt., McKendree University, Lebanon, IL. The people and institution are fictional and any resemblance to any person or any institution is coincidental. This case was prepared solely to provide material for class discussion. The author does not intend to illustrate either effective or ineffective handling of a managerial situation.

sustainable sourcing. It is evident in the international business community that this is an essential topic to address if one wants to be considered a world class organization.

Fitz-Simmons Consultants decided to develop guidelines for assessing a supplier's ethical and sustainable credentials. They determined that the best source to utilize as a benchmark was the United Nations Development Programme* (UNDP). The UNDP has established a set of goals for seventeen different areas, such as clear water and sanitation, climate actions, zero hunger, and others.

Reviewing its clientele list, Fitz-Simmons determined that they needed to divide their clientele's suppliers into several groups. For the first grouping, they focused on responsible consumption and waste reduction. They developed a supplier certification program based on the following areas: decreasing waste through prevention, reduction, recycling, and reuse. Furthermore, they ascertained that a supplier should not only adopt these practices but also incorporate them into their annual reporting metrics.

The challenge Fitz-Simmons discovered as they developed the guidelines for their clients was that many had good supplier relationships, however, not all of these suppliers currently met the requirements Fitz-Simmons proposed. Fitz-Simmons realized that the supplier certification program was the end goal. What they also needed was a method to get the suppliers from their current state through the certification process. Otherwise, Fitz-Simmons' clientele would see no value in the certification process if it upended their current supplier relationships.

Discussion Questions

1. Clearly, if Fitz-Simmons' clientele have good supplier relationships, they have worked at supplier development. If they want to maintain those relationships with their suppliers, what are some critical first steps that must be taken to ensure suppliers buy-in to the new program?

2. Once the new supplier certification program for ethical and sustainable sourcing is up and running, what would be the process to prune the number of suppliers? Recommend some criteria for enabling this step.

3. Outside of the obvious benefit of a company continuing to do business with its suppliers, how can a company add value to the suppliers adhering to the certification program? Provide specific examples of what the company can do.

©2019 Cengage Learning

3. Dean Vanwinkle Enterprises**

Dean Vanwinkle Enterprises is a multibillion dollar corporation that sources from around the globe. Dean Vanwinkle is the chairman and CEO of the corporation. He has always been a strong advocate for human rights. He believes his company has done a good job of sourcing from suppliers who hold similar values. However, Dean has recently become very uneasy with the way the world seems to be trending. He feels that because

*United Nations Development Programme, www.undp.org

**Written by Rick Bonsall, D. Mgt., McKendree University, Lebanon, IL. The people and institution are fictional and any resemblance to any person or any institution is coincidental. This case was prepared solely to provide material for class discussion. The author does not intend to illustrate either effective or ineffective handling of a managerial situation.

of the recent economic conditions throughout the world, its suppliers may be cutting corners. Dean decides to discuss this with his board of directors and his senior staff.

Dean expresses his concerns to the board and senior staff. He explains that Vanwinkle Enterprises has an enormous amount of clout because of its huge purchasing power. Dean wants to use that buyer power not only to make the best financial deals, but also to ensure they are only working with suppliers who are ethical in their dealing with their workforce and communities.

Dean tasks Antonia Bentley, senior vice president of human resources, to develop a set of criteria and a process to evaluate how suppliers are performing in this area. Antonia suggests that the best avenue to start this project is to look at corruption and its potential effects on suppliers and their workforce. Antonia begins her task by researching this through Transparency International.*

Antonia believes that corruption in government breeds corruption throughout society, including business. Consequently, she decides that if a specific country is rated as highly corrupt, then this is a starting point to identify the company's suppliers from those countries and examine their performance in relation to this topic.** Antonia has her staff develop a list of all their suppliers and their home countries. She directs them to input this data into the supplier relationship management (SRM) system. Further, her staff is to utilize the data from the Transparency International Corruption Perception Index and input the data for each country from 2012 through 2016. The current listing shows a ranking of one to 176. Some countries are ranked the same; for example, Denmark and New Zealand are ranked number one, meaning they are the least corrupt. Antonia is surprised to see that the United States is ranked 18; she assumed the United States would be closer to number one. Using the SRM database will enable Antonia to quickly identify suppliers whose home country is perceived as highly corrupt.

Antonia requested the information from 2012 to 2016 so that she could see the trend. As she reviewed the list of countries and suppliers, she believed it was necessary to ascertain if a country was declining (more corrupt) or rising (less corrupt) in the ratings. Suppliers in countries with declining ratings would be placed at the top of the list for immediate evaluation.

Antonia and her staff brainstormed the types of criteria they should use when examining the ethical values of the suppliers. Since Dean's emphasis was on human rights, they decided to use information from the ETI's Base Code.† There were nine major items within the code. They decided that although all were very important, the best strategy for the moment was to identify those areas where they could obtain concrete data from either a public source or the supplier itself. They chose the following criteria—right to collectively bargain, no child labor used, living wages are paid, and working hours are not excessive.

Antonia provided the following proposal to Dean. They would identify suppliers with potential ethical issues based on their home country's corruption perception index. Those in countries with a declining rating would be evaluated first. They would gather data on each of the four criterion and input that data into the SRM database. This would enable them to effectively analyze it. They would then contact the suppliers whom they were concerned about and explain their concerns.

*Transparency International: www.transparancy.org.
**Transparency International Corruption Perception Index: http://www.transparency.org/news/feature/corruption_perceptions_index_2016.
†Ethical Trading Initiative: www.ethicatrade.org.

Discussion Questions

1. Using Table 4.1, replace two of the four criteria Antonia and her staff decided on. Explain why your two choices are more suitable to use to evaluate the suppliers.

2. Go to http://www.transparency.org/news/feature/corruption_perceptions_index_2016 and review the Corruption Perception Index 2016. Antonia asked you to review the following countries—Djibouti, Laos, Morocco, and Sierra Leone. What is your evaluation of these countries, meaning besides their overall ranking, what concerns if any do you have? What recommendations would you give Antonia based on the data?

3. Is the process developed by Antonia fair? Explain your viewpoint.

©2019 Cengage Learning

ADDITIONAL RESOURCES

Anderson, M., and P. Katz., "Strategic Sourcing," *International Journal of Logistics Management* 9(1), 1998: 1–13.

Burt, D., D. Dobler, and S. Starling, *World Class Supply Management: The Key to Supply Chain Management.* 7th ed. New York: McGraw-Hill/Irwin, 2003.

Kaplan, N., and J. Hurd, "Realizing the Promise of Partnerships," *Journal of Business Strategy* 23(3), 2002: 38–42.

Lummus, R., R. Vokurka, and K. Alber, "Strategic Supply Chain Planning," *Production and Inventory Management Journal* 39(3), 1998: 49–58.

Simchi-Levi, D., P. Kaminsky, and E. Simchi-Levi, *Designing and Managing the Supply Chain: Concepts, Strategies, and Case Studies.* 2nd ed. New York: McGraw-Hill/Irwin, 2003.

Vonderembse, M., "The Impact of Supplier Selection Criteria and Supplier Involvement on Manufacturing," *Journal of Supply Chain Management* 35(3), 1999: 33–39.

END NOTES

1. Anonymous, "General Mills Releases Global Responsibility Report," *Food and Beverage Close-Up,* May 3, 2013: 1.

2. Anonymous, "Bacardi Limited; Bacardi Cuts Water Use in Half, Reduces Energy Consumption and Greenhouse Gases by One-Third," *Global Warming Focus,* April 8, 2013: 11.

3. Terazono, E., "Mitsubishi Seeks Olam's Sustainable Approach," *FT.com,* October 28, 2015: 1.

4. Burnson, P., "Private Label Sourcing at a Crossroads," *Logistics Management* 52(10), 2013: 24–25.

5. Branny, K., and J. Nwagbaraocha, "How Are You Treating Your Employees, Your Neighbors and Mother Earth? New EU Directive Clarifies the Scope of CSR Reporting," *EHS Today,* September 12, 2014: 1.

6. Anonymous, "Konica Minolta Launches 'CSR Logistics,' Joint Initiative with DHL Supply Chain," *News Bites – Electronics,* July 13, 2015:1.

7. Worthington, I., M. Ram, H. Boyal, and M. Shah, "Researching the Drivers of Socially Responsible Purchasing: A Cross-National Study of Supplier Diversity Initiatives," *Journal of Business Ethics* 79(3), 2008: 319–331.

8. Berthiaume, D., "Reebok's Sourcing Strategy Places Ethics First," *Chain Store Age,* January 2006: 32A.

9. Wilson, M., "Bigger Is Better for Lush," *Chain Store Age* 92(1), 2016: 12–13.

10. Boggan, S., "Nike Admits Mistakes over Child Labor," *Independent/UK*, October 20, 2001; www.independent.co.uk; Levenson, E., "Citizen Nike," *CNNMoney.com*, November 17, 2008; www.cnnmoney.com/2008

11. Coleman, F., "In Search of Ethical Sourcing," *Directorship* 33(2), 2007: 38–39; Cooper, B., "Perspectives on the Ethical Sourcing Debate in the Clothing Industry," *Just-Style*, November 2007: 21.

12. See http://marketrealist.com/2014/12/overview-nikes-supply-chain-manufacturing-strategies/

13. Anonymous, "MEC Introduces 30 New Fair Trade Styles," *Manufacturing Close-Up*, May 20, 2016: 1.

14. Murray, S., "Confusion Reigns over Labeling Fair Trade Products," *Financial Times*, June 13, 2006: 2. Also see: http://www.fairtrade.net, http://www.wfto.com

15. Anonymous, "Fair Trade USA—Mainstream Consumers Drive Fair Trade Certified Sales Up 24 Percent," *Economics Week*, March 25, 2011: 658.

16. See, for instance, http://www.fairtrade.net/

17. See https://www.unilever.com/sustainable-living/the-sustainable-living-plan/reducing-environmental-impact/sustainable-sourcing/

18. For more information, see the Goldman Environmental Prize web page: www.goldmanprize.org and also www.nobelprize.org

19. See, for example, Androich, A., "Get Your Green On," *RealScreen*, July/August 2007: 14; Watson, T., "Environmental Pioneer Dies," *USA Today*, November 7, 2000: 24A.

20. To visit the Institute for Supply Management website, go to www.ism.ws

21. Turner, M., and P. Houston., "Going Green? Start with Sourcing," *Supply Chain Management Review* 13(2), 2009: 14–20.

22. Pinchot, G., *The Conservation of Natural Resources.* Washington, DC: U.S. Department of Agriculture, 1908. (Farmers' Bulletin, 327) NAL Call no.: 1 Ag84F no.327; also see Beatley, T., "Sustainability 3.0 Building Tomorrow's Earth-Friendly Communities," *Planning* 75(5), 2009: 16–22.

23. Springer, J., "Walmart Launches Food Sustainability Initiative," *Supermarket News*, October 6, 2014: 1.

24. Mulani, N., "Sustainable Sourcing: Do Good While Doing Well," *Logistics Management* 47(7), 2008: 25–26.

25. Ibid.

26. Anonymous, "Brave New Chocolate," *Candy Industry* 178(1), 2013: 50–55.

27. Anonymous, "China Treats Sustainability and Economic Growth as Complementary, Not Conflicting, Goals," *Economics Week*, March 2, 2012: 585.

28. Grayson, E., and G. Kjelleren, "Environmental Sustainability: What Businesses and Their Lawyers Need to Know," *GPSolo* 33(3), 2016: 33–36.

29. Bridgestone Americas Media Center, "Bridgestone Releases Earth Day 2013 Consumer Recycling and Sustainability Survey Findings"; http://www.bridgestoneamericasmedia.com/2013-04-22-Bridgestone-Releases-Earth-Day-2013-Consumer-Recycling-and-Sustainability-Survey-Findings

30. Fisher, M., "What Is the Right Supply Chain for Your Product?" *Harvard Business Review* 75(2), 1997: 105–116.

31. See http://www.edisonawards.com

32. Reeve, T., and J. Steinhausen, "Sustainable Suppliers, Sustainable Markets," *CMA Management* 81(2), 2007: 30–33.

33. Anonymous, "Fragrance Du Bois Partners with Asia Plantation Capital to Source 100% Natural, CITES-Certified, Oud Oil," *PR Newswire,* September 17, 2015: 1.

34. Allison, C., "Doing Well by Doing Good," *Canadian Grocer* 128(6), 2014: 17.

35. The interested reader is invited to navigate the ISO website: www.iso.org

36. Alpert, B., "Do-Gooders Who Could Do Better," *Barron's* 87(46), 2007: 40–41.

37. Anonymous, "Integrity Interactive Corporation, New Integrity Interactive Service," *Business & Finance Week,* April 14, 2008: 195.

38. Jeffries, E., "Setting Standards on Carbon," *Supply Management* 17(3), 2012: 44–46; also see http://ghgprotocol.org/standards

39. Andel, T., "Sustainability's Chain Reaction," *Material Handling & Logistics,* April 15, 2013: 1.

40. Sulliovan, R., "The Devastating Cost of Cheap Outsourcing," *FT.com,* June 16, 2013: 1.

41. Pratt, M., "Ethical Outsourcing," *Computerworld* 42(17), 2008: 32–33.

42. Atkinson, W., "Novellus Realizes Benefits of Early Supplier Involvement," *Purchasing* 137(4), 2008: 15.

43. Anonymous, "Gatepoint Research Finds Legacy Systems Fail to Deliver on Vendor Managed Inventory," *Wireless News,* June 20, 2015: 1.

44. Shister, N., "Applying the Ideas of the Wal-Marts of the World to Smaller Companies," *World Trade* 19(3), 2006: 26–29.

45. Anonymous, "Computers, Software: Datalliance Expands Staff to Support Growth in VMI," *Marketing Weekly News,* May 19, 2012: 509.

46. Simon, J., "MLGW Eliminates Long Lead Times," *Transmission & Distribution World* 66(1), 2014: 54.

47. Trebilcock, B., and J. Sandor, "How They Did It: Supplier Relationship Management at RAYTHEON," *Supply Chain Management Review* 19(2), 2015: 18–23.

48. Vitasek, K., "Getting to We: Negotiating Agreements for Highly Collaborative Relationships," *Government Procurement* 24(3), 2016: 14; Nyden, J., and K. Vitasek, "The Fine Art of Negotiation," *Supply & Demand Chain Executive* 13(1), 2012: 8, 10, 12–14, 16.

49. McCrea, B., "The Evolution of Supply Chain Collaboration Software," *Logistics Management* 54(9), 2015: 62S–64S, 66S, 68S.

50. Murray, S., "Commercial Approach Can Help Fill the Gap," *FT.com,* June 19, 2012: 1.

51. Anonymous, "Social Sciences," *Library Journal* 136(7), 2011: 1.

52. Barlow, R., "CHRISTUS Supply Chain Targets Teamwork as No. 1 Aim," *Healthcare Purchasing News* 40(8), 2016: 10, 12–16.

53. See http://www.capsresearch.org for more information

54. See http://supply-chain.org for more information

55. See http://www.ism.ws for more information.

56. See, for instance, Andersen, B., T. Fagerhaug, S. Randmael, J. Schuldmaier, and J. Prenninger, "Benchmarking Supply Chain Management: Finding Best Practices," *Journal of Business and Industrial Marketing* 14(5/6), 1999: 378–389; Carr, A., and L. Smeltzer. "The Relationship among Purchasing Benchmarking, Strategic Purchasing, Firm Performance, and Firm Size," *Journal of Supply Chain Management* 35(4), 1999: 51–60; Ellram, L., G. Zsidisin, S. Siferd, and M. Stanly, "The Impact of Purchasing and Supply Management on Corporate Success," *Journal of Supply Chain Management* 38(1), 2002: 4–17; Krause, D., S. Vachon, and R. Klassen, "Special Topic Forum on Sustainable Supply Chain Management," *Journal of Supply Chain Management* 45(4), 2009: 18–25.

57. See https://www.cips.org/cips-for-business/supply-assurance/corporate-ethical-procurement-and-supply/corporate-code-of-ethics/

58. Avery, S., "Today's Travel Procurement Professional Knows How to Manage Supplier Relationships," *Purchasing* 138(2), 2009: 54.

Chapter 5
DEMAND FORECASTING

No software, no matter how powerful, and no analyst, no matter how talented, can guarantee perfect (or even highly accurate) forecasts. The objective should be to deliver forecasts as accurate as can reasonably be expected given the nature of what is being forecast.

> — *Michael Gilliland and Udo Sglavo, Analyticsmagazine.com*[1]

Accurate forecasting optimizes customer service, minimizes inventory overstocks and lays the groundwork for effective marketing at Nestlé.

> —*Nestlé*[2]

For retailers, making better business decisions depends heavily on the ability to forecast demand accurately. By predicting demand at the store and SKU level, retailers can optimize order quantities, stock levels and store shipment allocations. Most importantly, retailers are better able to compete for shoppers' attention and earn their loyalty.

> —*Tom O'Reilly, President and CEO, Aptaris*[3]

Learning Objectives

After completing this chapter, you should be able to

- Explain the role of demand forecasting in a supply chain.
- Identify the components of a forecast.
- Compare and contrast qualitative and quantitative forecasting techniques.
- Calculate and assess the accuracy of forecasts.
- Explain collaborative planning, forecasting, and replenishment.

Chapter Outline

Introduction

The Importance of Demand Forecasting

Forecasting Techniques

Forecast Accuracy

Collaborative Planning, Forecasting, and Replenishment

Useful Forecasting Websites

Forecasting Software

Summary

SCM Profile — The ISM Report on Business

The Institute of Supply Management (ISM), formerly known as the National Association of Purchasing Management (NAPM), surveys supply management professionals participating on the Business Survey Committee comprising more than 300 purchasing and supply executives, seeking information on "changes in production, new orders, new export orders, imports, employment, inventories, prices, lead times, and the timeliness of supplier deliveries in their companies, comparing the current month to the previous month." The *ISM Report on Business*, available the first business day of each month, is considered to be an accurate indicator of the overall direction of the economy and the health of the manufacturing and nonmanufacturing sectors. Three quotes regarding the value of the report follow:[4]

> *I find the surveys conducted by the purchasing and supply managers to be an excellent supplement to the data supplied by various departments and agencies of the government.*
>
> —Alan Greenspan, former Chairman of the Federal Reserve Board

> *The ISM Manufacturing Report on Business has one of the shortest reporting lags of any macro-economic series and gives an important early look at the economy. It also measures some concepts (such as lead times and delivery lags) that can be found nowhere else. It makes an important contribution to the American statistical system and to economic policy.*
>
> — Joseph E. Stiglitz, former Chairman of President Clinton's Council of Economic Advisors

> *The ISM Manufacturing Report on Business is extremely useful. The PMI, the Report's composite index, gives the earliest indication each month of the health of the manufacturing sector. It is an essential component for assessing the state of the economy.*
>
> —Michael J. Boskin, Hoover Institute Senior Fellow

The ISM report provides several indices for the manufacturing sector: New Orders, Production, Employment, Supplier Deliveries, Inventories, Customers' Inventories, Prices, Backlog of Orders, Exports, and Imports. The most important index is the Purchasing Managers Index (PMI) developed by Theodore Torda, Senior Economist of the U.S. Department of Commerce, and introduced in 1982. The PMI is a composite of five weighted seasonally adjusted indices (weights are shown in parentheses): New Orders (0.20), Production (0.20), Employment (0.20), Supplier Deliveries (0.20), and Inventories (0.20). A reading below 50 indicates contraction and a reading over 50 indicates growth or expansion in the manufacturing sector of the economy compared to the previous month. The purchasing surveys provide comprehensive information for tracking the economy and developing business forecasts. In January 2008, ISM started computing a composite index for the nonmanufacturing sector. The NMI (Nonmanufacturing Index) is based on four equally weighted indicators: Business Activity (seasonally adjusted), New Orders (seasonally adjusted), Employment (seasonally adjusted), and Inventories. An NMI index over 50 indicates growth or expansion in the nonmanufacturing sector of the economy compared to the previous month, and a reading under 50 indicates contraction.[5] Purchasing and supply executives use the report in a variety of ways. For example, the Customers' Inventories Index is a strong indicator of future new orders and production and is used to measure changes in supply chain activity.

INTRODUCTION

Much has been written about demand-driven supply chains. In today's competitive environment, organizations are moving to a more effective demand-driven supply chain to enable them to respond quickly to shifting demand. Consumers are now more demanding and discriminating. The market has evolved into a "pull" environment with customers dictating to suppliers what products they desire and when they need them delivered. If a retailer cannot get the product it wants at the right quantity, price, and time from one supplier, it will look for another company that can meet its demands. Any temporary stockout has a tremendous potential downside on sales, profitability, and customer relationships.

There are several ways to closely match supply and demand. One way is for a supplier to hold plenty of stock available for delivery at any time. While this approach maximizes sales revenues, it is also expensive because of the cost of carrying inventory and the possibility of write-downs at the end of the selling season. Use of flexible pricing is another approach. During heavy demand periods, prices can be raised to reduce peak demand. Price discounts can then be used to increase sales during periods with excess inventory or slow demand. This strategy can still result in lost sales, though, as well as stockouts, and thus cannot be considered an ideal or partnership-friendly approach to satisfying demand. In the short term, companies can also use overtime, subcontracting, or temporary workers to increase capacity to meet demand for their products and services. In the interim, however, firms will lose sales as they train workers, and quality may also tend to suffer.

Managing demand is challenging because of the difficulty in forecasting future consumer requirements accurately. In order for supply chain integration to be successful, suppliers must be able to accurately forecast demand so they can produce and deliver the right quantities demanded by their customers in a timely and cost-effective fashion. Thus, it is imperative that suppliers along the supply chain find ways to better match supply and demand to achieve optimal levels of cost, quality, and customer service to enable them to compete with other supply chains. Any problems that adversely affect the timely delivery of products demanded by consumers will have ramifications throughout the supply chain.

Zara Espana, S.A., a Spanish clothing and accessories retailer, is a giant player in the fashion industry with a major advantage over its competitors due to its fast response time. Zara commits to only 15–20 percent of the season's products six months in advance, but nearly 50 percent of its clothing lines are designed and manufactured during the current season.[6] Product life cycles in the fashion industry are short and so is the selling season. Their tight integration of design, planning, and production enables Zara to respond quickly to market needs. Since its lead time for new product introduction is only two weeks, Zara in effect has to forecast demand just two weeks in advance. The flow of current information among customers, store managers, market specialists, designers, and production staff also mitigates the bullwhip effect (which tends to result in higher safety stock levels). Zara is thus able to avoid the overproduction and heavy discounting so common in the fast fashion industry due to inaccurate forecasting.

THE IMPORTANCE OF DEMAND FORECASTING

Forecasting is an important element of demand management. It provides an estimate of future demand and the basis for planning and sound business decisions. Since all organizations deal with an unknown future, some error between a forecast and actual demand is to be expected. Thus, the goal of a good forecasting technique is to minimize the deviation between actual demand and the forecast. Since a forecast is a prediction of the future, factors that influence demand, the impact of these factors, and whether they will continue to influence future demand must be considered in developing an accurate forecast. In addition, buyers and sellers should share all relevant information to generate a single consensus forecast so that the correct decisions on supply and demand can be made. Improved forecasts benefit not only the focal company but also the trading partners in the supply chain. Having accurate demand forecasts allows the purchasing department to order the right amount of parts and materials, the operations department to produce the right quantity of products, and the logistics department to deliver a correctly sized order. Thus, timely and accurate demand information is a critical component of an effective supply chain. Inaccurate forecasts would lead to imbalances in supply and demand. In today's competitive business environment, collaboration (or cooperation and information sharing) between buyers and sellers is the rule rather than the exception. The benefits of better forecasts are lower inventories, reduced stockouts, smoother production plans, reduced costs, and improved customer service.

As discussed in the chapter-opening SCM Profile, the Institute of Supply Management (ISM) has been publishing monthly, the Manufacturing ISM *Report on Business* since 1931, except for a four-year interruption during World War II. The indices for the manufacturing sector include New Orders, Production, Manufacturing Employment, Supplier Deliveries, Inventories, Customers' Inventories, Prices, Backlog of Orders, Exports, and Imports. Many business executives use these indices to forecast the overall direction of the economy and the health of the manufacturing sector. For example, purchasing and supply managers utilize the Customers' Inventories Index to help forecast future new orders, make production decisions, and measure changes in supply chain activity. The *Wall Street Journal* publishes the *ISM Report on Business*, which includes both the manufacturing and non-manufacturing sectors.

Many have argued that demand forecasting is both an art and a science. Since there are no accurate crystal balls available, it is impossible to expect 100 percent forecast accuracy at all times. The impact of poor communication and inaccurate forecasts resonates all along the supply chain and results in the *bullwhip effect* (described in Chapter 1) causing stockouts, lost sales, high costs of inventory and obsolescence, material shortages, poor responsiveness to market dynamics, and poor profitability. Numerous examples exist showing the problems that companies faced when their sales forecasts did not match customer demands during new product introductions. For instance, in October 2016, Spin Master, a Toronto-based toymaker introduced Hatchimals, the season's hottest toy. The furry, robotic bird-like toy animals that hatch from an egg have been a big hit and available stock could not meet the heavy demand for the toys. Hatchimals sell for $69.99 in stores, but because of the severe shortage, the toys are listed on Craigslist, Kijiji, and Ebay for three to four times its original price.[7] This indicates the challenge faced by companies in forecasting sales, ramping up production to meet the demand for their products, and defending their market position.

FORECASTING TECHNIQUES

Understanding that a forecast is very often inaccurate does not mean that nothing can be done to improve the forecast. Both quantitative and qualitative forecasts can be improved by seeking inputs from trading partners. **Qualitative forecasting methods** are based on opinions and intuition, whereas **quantitative forecasting methods** use mathematical models and relevant historical data to generate forecasts. The quantitative methods can be divided into two groups: time series and associative models.

Qualitative Methods

Qualitative forecasting methods are based on intuition or judgmental evaluation and are generally used when data is limited, unavailable, or not currently relevant. This approach can vary widely in cost, and accuracies depend to a large extent on the skill and experience of the forecaster(s) and the amount of relevant information, time, and money available. Specifically, qualitative techniques are used to develop long-range projections when current data is no longer very reliable, and for new product introductions when current data simply does not exist. Discussions of four common qualitative forecasting models follow.

Jury of Executive Opinion

A group of the firm's senior management executives who are knowledgeable about their markets, their competitors, and the business environment collectively develop the forecast. This technique has the advantage of several individuals with considerable experience working together, but if one member's views dominate the discussion, then the value and reliability of the outcome can be diminished. This technique is applicable for long-range planning and new product introductions and is also commonly used for general demand forecasting. This type of forecasting is commonly used by commercial banks in the United States for medium-term forecasts.

Delphi Method

The Delphi method was first developed by Project RAND in the late 1950s and can be used for a wide range of applications, including forecasting. A group of internal and external experts are surveyed during several rounds in terms of future events and long-term forecasts of demand, in hopes of converging on a consensus forecast. Group members do not physically meet and thus avoid the scenario where one or a few experts could dominate a discussion. The answers from the experts are accumulated after each round of the survey and summarized. The summary of responses is then sent out to all the experts in the next round, wherein individual experts can modify their responses based on the group's response summary. This iterative process continues until a consensus is reached. The process can be both time-consuming and very expensive. This approach is applicable for high-risk technology forecasting; large, expensive projects; or major new product introductions. Ultimately, the value of a Delphi forecast is dependent upon the qualifications of the expert participants. With the Delphi technique, the number of experts can vary widely, depending on the circumstances, the available time, and the number of experts available.

Sales Force Composite

The sales force represents a good source of market information. This type of forecast is generated based on the sales force's knowledge of the market and estimates of customer needs. Due to the proximity of the sales personnel to the consumers, the forecast tends to be reliable, but individual biases could negatively impact the effectiveness of this approach. For example, if bonuses are paid when actual sales exceed the forecast, there is a tendency for the sales force to under-forecast.

Customer Surveys

A forecasting questionnaire can be developed that uses inputs from customers on important issues such as future purchasing needs, new product ideas, and opinions about existing or new products. The survey can be administered through telephone, mail, Internet, or personal interviews. The data collected from these surveys is then analyzed, and forecasts are developed from the results. For example, a 2015 Deloitte consumer study confirms that smartphones are indispensable for all demographics and locations. In a follow-up 2016 study on consumer attitudes around mobile, Deloitte finds consumers look at their smartphones 47 times a day and that number increases to 82 times for 18- to 24-year-olds.[8] Since Google's Android is the dominant smartphone operating system, it made strategic sense for Google to get into the fast-growing hardware market with the development of the Pixel smartphone. According to Rick Osterloh, head of Google's newly formed hardware unit, "Building hardware and software together lets us take full advantage of capabilities like the Google Assistant. It lets us harness years of expertise we've built up in machine learning and AI to deliver the simple, smart and fast experiences that our users expect from us."[9]

Quantitative Methods

Quantitative forecasting models use mathematical techniques that are based on historical data and can include causal variables to forecast demand. **Time series forecasting** is based on the assumption that the future is an extension of the past; thus, historical data can be used to predict future demand. **Cause-and-effect forecasting** assumes that one or more factors (independent variables) are related to demand and, therefore, can be used to predict future demand.

Since these forecasts rely solely on past demand data, all quantitative methods become less accurate as the forecast's time horizon increases. Thus, for long-time horizon forecasts, it is generally recommended to utilize a combination of both quantitative and qualitative techniques.

Components of a Time Series

A time series typically has four components: trend, cyclical, seasonal, and random variations.

- *Trend variations:* Trends represent either increasing or decreasing movements over many years and are due to factors such as population growth, population shifts, cultural changes, and income shifts. Common trend lines are linear, S-curve, exponential, or asymptotic.

- *Cyclical variations:* Cyclical variations are wavelike movements that are longer than a year and are influenced by macroeconomic and political factors. One example is the **business cycle** (recessions or expansions that tend to occur every eight or ten years). Recent business cycles in the United States have been affected by global events such as the 1991 Mexican financial crisis, the 1997 Asian economic crisis, and the 2008 U.S. financial crisis (considered the worst economic disaster since the U.S. Great Depression of 1929).

- *Seasonal variations*: Seasonal variations show peaks and valleys that repeat over a consistent interval such as hours, days, weeks, months, years, or seasons. Due to seasonality, many companies do well in certain months and not so well in other months. For example, snow blower sales tend to be higher in the fall and winter but taper off in the spring and summer. A fast-food restaurant will see higher sales during the day around breakfast, lunch, and dinner. U.S. hotels experience large crowds during traditional holidays such as July 4, Labor Day, Thanksgiving, Christmas, and New Year.

- *Random variations:* Random variations are due to unexpected or unpredictable events such as natural disasters (hurricanes, tornadoes, fire), strikes, and wars. Examples included the recent eruption at Iceland's Eyjafjallajökull volcano, which caused ash clouds to reach mainland Europe. Numerous flights to England and Europe were shut down, which led to the highest air travel disruption since the World War II.[10] Another natural disaster is the earthquake of magnitude 7.0 that hit Haiti in 2010. The Haitian government reported that 250,000 residences and 30,000 commercial buildings were badly damaged; 230,000 people died, 300,000 were injured, and 1,000,000 were made homeless as a result of the earthquake.[11] In 2016, Matthew Hurricane wreaked havoc on property and people across the Western Atlantic, Haiti, Cuba, Dominican Republic and Lucayan Archipelago, southeastern United States, and the Canadian Maritimes. The cost of damages exceeded $10.5 billion.[12]

Time Series Forecasting Models

As discussed earlier, time series forecasts are dependent on the availability of historical data. Forecasts are estimated by extrapolating the past data into the future. Due to the availability of historical data, time series models are more widely used. For time series models, the more commonly used models are averages, simple trend, and exponential smoothing. In general, demand forecasts are used in planning for procurement, supply, replenishment, and corporate revenue.

Several common time series approaches, such as naïve, simple moving average, weighted moving average, and exponential smoothing forecasts, are discussed next.

Naïve Forecast

Using the **naïve forecast**, the estimate for the next period is equal to the actual demand for the immediate past period. The formula is:

$$F_{t+1} = A_t$$

where F_{t+1} = forecast for period $t + 1$

A_t = actual demand for period t

For example, if the current period's actual demand is 100 units, then the next period's forecast is 100 units. This method is inexpensive to understand, develop, store data for, and operate. However, there is no consideration of causal relationships, and the method may not generate accurate forecasts. Many economic and business series are considered good candidates for using the naïve forecast because the series behave like random walks.

Simple Moving Average Forecast

The **simple moving average forecast** uses historical data to generate a forecast and works well when the demand is fairly stable over time. The formula for the n-period moving average forecast is shown below:

$$F_{t+1} = \frac{\sum_{i=t-n+1}^{t} A_i}{n}$$

where F_{t+1} = forecast for period $t + 1$

n = number of periods used to calculate moving average

A_i = actual demand in period i

When n equals 1, the simple moving average forecast becomes the naïve forecast. The average tends to be more responsive if fewer data points are used to compute the average. However, random events can also impact the average adversely. Thus, the decision maker must balance the cost of responding slowly to changes versus the cost of responding to random variations. The advantage of this technique is that it is simple to use and easy to understand. A weakness of the simple moving average method is its inability to respond to trend changes quickly. Example 5.1 illustrates the simple moving average forecast.

Example 5.1   Simple Moving Average Forecasting

PERIOD	ACTUAL DEMAND
1	1,600
2	2,200
3	2,000
4	1,600
5	2,500
6	3,500
7	3,300
8	3,200
9	3,900
10	4,700
11	4,300
12	4,400

Using the data provided, calculate the forecast for period 5 using a four-period simple moving average.

SOLUTION

$$F_5 = \text{forecast for period 5} = \frac{1,600 + 2,200 + 2,000 + 1,600}{4} = 1,850$$

An Excel spreadsheet solution is shown in Figure 5.1.

Figure 5.1   Moving Average Forecasting Using an Excel Spreadsheet

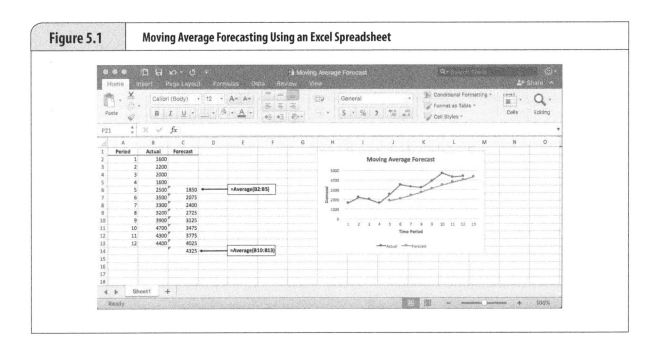

Weighted Moving Average Forecast

The simple moving average forecast places equal weights $(1/n)$ on each of the n-period observations. Under some circumstances, a forecaster may decide that equal weighting is undesirable. An n-period weighted moving average forecast is the weighted average of the n-period observations, using unequal weights. The only restriction is that the weights should be nonnegative and sum to 1. The formula for the n-period weighted moving average forecast is shown below:

$$F_{t+1} = \sum_{i=t-n+1}^{t} w_i A_i$$

where F_{t+1} = forecast for period $t+1$

n = number of periods used in determining the moving average

A_i = actual demand in period i

w_i = weight assigned to period i; $\Sigma w_i = 1$

For example, the three-period weighted moving average forecast with weights $(0.5, 0.3, 0.2)$ is:

$$F_t = 0.5\,A_{t-1} + 0.3\,A_{t-2} + 0.2\,A_{t-3}.$$

Note that generally a greater emphasis (and thus the highest weight) is placed on the most recent observation and, hence, the forecast would react more rapidly than the three-period simple moving average forecast. However, the forecaster may instead wish to apply the smallest weight to the most recent data such that the forecast would be less affected by abrupt changes in recent data. The weights used thus tend to be based on the experience of the forecaster, and this is one of the advantages of this forecasting method. Although the forecast is more responsive to underlying changes in demand, it still lags demand because of the averaging effect. As such, the weighted moving average method does not do a good job of tracking trend changes in the data. Example 5.2 illustrates the weighted moving average forecast.

Exponential Smoothing Forecast

Exponential smoothing is a sophisticated weighted moving average forecasting technique in which the forecast for the next period's demand is the current period's forecast adjusted by a fraction of the difference between the current period's actual demand and forecast. This approach requires less data than the weighted moving average method because only two data points are needed. Due to its simplicity and minimal data requirement, exponential smoothing is one of the most widely used forecasting techniques. This model, like other time series models, is suitable for data that shows little trend or seasonal patterns. Other higher-order exponential smoothing models (which are not covered here)

Example 5.2   Weighted Moving Average Forecasting

Based on data provided in Example 5.1, calculate the forecast for period 5 using a four-period weighted moving average. The weights of 0.4, 0.3, 0.2, and 0.1 are assigned to the most recent, second most recent, third most recent, and fourth most recent periods, respectively.

SOLUTION

$$F_5 = 0.1(1{,}600) + 0.2(2{,}200) + 0.3(2{,}000) + 0.4(1{,}600) = 1{,}840$$

An Excel spreadsheet solution is shown in Figure 5.2.

Figure 5.2	Weighted Moving Average Forecasting Using an Excel Spreadsheet

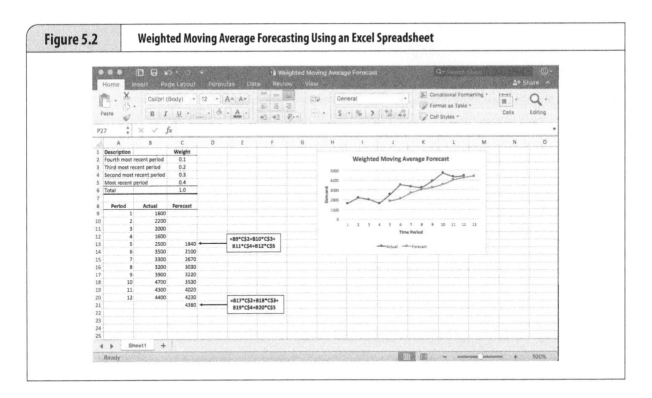

can be used for data exhibiting trend and seasonality. The exponential smoothing forecasting formula is:

$$F_{t+1} = F_t + \alpha(A_t - F_t)$$

or

$$F_{t+1} = \alpha A_t + (1 - \alpha)F_t$$

where F_{t+1} = forecast for period $t + 1$

F_t = forecast for period t

A_t = actual demand for period t

α = smoothing constant ($0 \leq \alpha \leq 1$)

The exponential smoothing forecast is equivalent to the naïve forecast when α is equal to 1. With an α value closer to 1, there is a greater emphasis on recent data, resulting in a major adjustment of the error in the last period's forecast. Thus with a high α value, the model is more responsive to changes in the recent demand. When α has a low value, more weight is placed on past demand (which is contained in the previous forecast), and the model responds slower to changes in demand. The impact of using a small or large value of α is similar to the effect of using a large or small number of observations in calculating the moving average. In general, the forecast will lag any trend in the actual data because only partial adjustment to the most recent forecast error can be made. The initial forecast can be estimated using the naïve method, that is, the forecast for next period is the actual demand for the current period. Example 5.3 illustrates the exponential smoothing forecast.

Example 5.3   Exponential Smoothing Forecasting

Based on data provided in Example 5.1, calculate the forecast for period 3 using the exponential smoothing method. Assume the forecast for period 2 is 1,600. Use a smoothing constant (α) value of 0.3.

SOLUTION

Given: $F_2 = 1,600, \alpha - 0.3$

$$F_{t+1} = F_t + \alpha(A_t - F_t)$$
$$F_3 = F_2 + \alpha(A_2 - F_2) = 1,600 + 0.3(2,200 - 1,600) = 1,780$$

Thus, the forecast for week 3 is 1,780.

An Excel spreadsheet solution is shown in Figure 5.3.

Figure 5.3   Exponential Smoothing Forecasting Using an Excel Spreadsheet

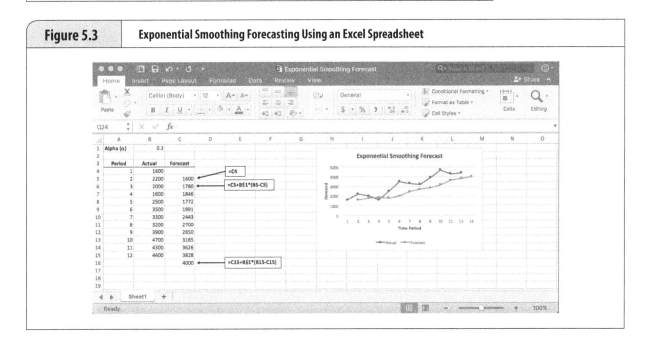

Linear Trend Forecast

A **linear trend forecast** can be estimated using simple linear regression to fit a line to a series of data occurring over time. This model is also referred to as the simple trend model. The trend line is determined using the least squares method, which minimizes the sum of the squared deviations to determine the characteristics of the linear equation. The trend line equation is expressed as:

$$\hat{Y} = b_0 + b_1 x$$

where $\hat{Y}$ = forecast or dependent variable

x = time variable

b_0 = intercept of the vertical axis

b_1 = slope of the trend line

The coefficients b_0 and b_1 are calculated as follows:

$$b_1 = \frac{n\sum(xy) - \sum x \sum y}{n\sum x^2 - (\sum x)^2}$$

$$b_0 = \frac{\sum y - b_1 \sum x}{n}$$

where $x =$ independent variable values

$y =$ dependent variable values

$n =$ number of observations

Example 5.4 illustrates the linear trend forecast.

Example 5.4   Linear Trend Forecast

The demand for toys produced by the Miki Manufacturing Company is shown below.

PERIOD	DEMAND	PERIOD	DEMAND	PERIOD	DEMAND
1	1,600	5	2,500	9	3,900
2	2,200	6	3,500	10	4,700
3	2,000	7	3,300	11	4,300
4	1,600	8	3,200	12	4,400

The company desires to know the trend line and the forecast for period 13.

SOLUTION

PERIOD (x)	DEMAND (y)	x^2	xy
1	1,600	1	1,600
2	2,200	4	4,400
3	2,000	9	6,000
4	1,600	16	6,400
5	2,500	25	12,500
6	3,500	36	21,000
7	3,300	49	23,100
8	3,200	64	25,600
9	3,900	81	35,100
10	4,700	100	47,000
11	4,300	121	47,300
12	4,400	144	52,800
$\sum x = 78$	$\sum y = 37{,}200$	$\sum x^2 = 650$	$\sum xy = 282{,}800$

$$b_1 = \frac{n\sum(xy) - \sum x \sum y}{n\sum x^2 - (\sum x)^2} = \frac{12(282{,}800) - 78(37{,}200)}{12(650) - 78^2} = 286.71$$

$$b_0 = \frac{\sum y - b_1 \sum x}{n} = \frac{37{,}200 - 286.71(78)}{12} = 1{,}236.4$$

The trend line is then $\hat{Y} = 1{,}236.4 + 286.7x$

To forecast the demand for period 13, we substitute $x = 13$ into the trend equation above.

The linear trend forecast for period 13 $= 1{,}236.4 + 286.7(13) = 4{,}963.5 = 4{,}964$ toys.

An Excel spreadsheet solution is shown in Figure 5.4.

Cause-and-Effect Models

The cause-and-effect models have a cause (independent variable or variables) and an effect (dependent variable). One of the most common models used is regression analysis. In demand forecasting, the external variables that are related to demand are first identified.

Figure 5.4	Forecasting Using Simple Linear Regression Using an Excel Spreadsheet

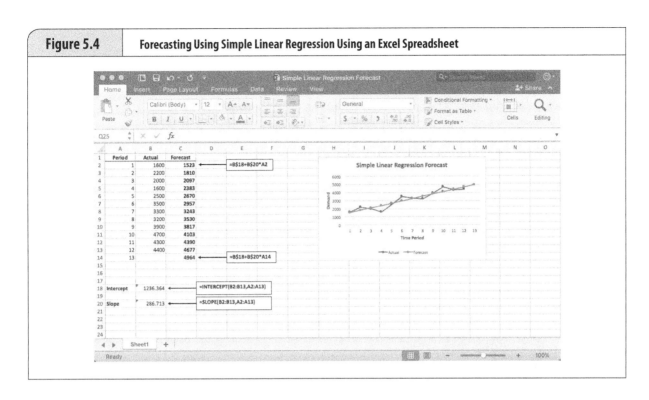

Once the relationship between the external variable and demand is determined, it can be used as a forecasting tool. Let's review several cause-and-effect models.

Simple Linear Regression Forecast

When there is only one explanatory variable, we have a simple regression model equivalent to the linear trend model described earlier. The difference is that the x variable is no longer time, but instead, an explanatory variable of demand. For example, demand could be dependent on the size of the advertising budget. The regression equation is expressed as:

$$\hat{Y} = b_0 + b_1 x$$

where $\hat{Y}$ = forecast or dependent variable

x = explanatory or independent variable

b_0 = intercept of the vertical axis

b_1 = slope of the regression line

Example 5.5 illustrates the simple linear regression forecast.

Multiple Regression Forecast

When several explanatory variables are used to predict the dependent variable, a **multiple regression forecast** is applicable. Multiple regression analysis works well when the relationships between demand (dependent variable) and several other factors (independent or explanatory variables) impacting demand are strong and stable over time. The multiple regression equation is expressed as:

Example 5.5   Simple Linear Regression Forecasting

Data on sales and advertising dollars for the past six months are shown below.

$ SALES (y)	$ ADVERTISING (x)
100,000	2,000
150,000	3,000
125,000	2,500
50,000	1,000
170,000	3,500
135,000	2,750

Determine the linear relationship between sales and advertising dollars.

SOLUTION

$ SALES (y)	$ ADVERTISING (x)	x^2	xy
100,000	2,000	4,000,000	200,000,000
150,000	3,000	9,000,000	450,000,000
125,000	2,500	6,250,000	312,500,000
50,000	1,000	1,000,000	50,000,000
170,000	3,500	12,250,000	595,000,000
135,000	2,750	7,562,500	371,250,000
$\Sigma y = 730{,}000$	$\Sigma x = 14{,}750$	$\Sigma x^2 = 40{,}062{,}500$	$\Sigma xy = 1{,}978{,}750{,}000$

$\hat{Y} = b_0 + b_1 x$

$$b_1 = \frac{n\sum(xy) - \sum x \sum y}{n\sum x^2 - (\sum x)^2} = \frac{6(1{,}978{,}750{,}000) - 14{,}750(730{,}000)}{6(40{,}062{,}500) - 14{,}750^2} = 48.43836$$

$$b_0 = \frac{\sum y - b_1 \sum x}{n} = \frac{730{,}000 - 48.43836(14{,}750)}{6} = 2{,}589.041$$

$b_0 = 2{,}589.041$

$\hat{Y} = 2{,}589.04 + 48.44X$

The linear regression results indicate that a one-dollar increase in advertising will increase sales by $48.44. Further, a planned monthly advertising expenditure of $4,000 would yield a sales forecast of $196,349.

$$\hat{Y} = b_0 + b_1 x_1 + b_2 x_2 + \ldots + b_k x_k$$

where $\hat{Y}$ = forecast or dependent variable

x_k = kth explanatory or independent variable

b_0 = constant

b_k = regression coefficient of the independent variable x_k

Although the mathematics involved in determining the parameters of the equation is complex, numerous software programs such as Excel, SAS, and SPSS statistical packages can be used to solve the equation. Any statistics textbook should provide the formula for calculating the regression coefficient values and discussion of the assumptions and challenges of using multiple regression techniques. Multiple regression forecasting requires much more data than any of the other techniques discussed earlier, and the additional cost must be balanced against possible improvement in the level of forecast accuracy.

FORECAST ACCURACY

The ultimate goal of any forecasting endeavor is to have an accurate and unbiased forecast. The cost associated with prediction error can be substantial and include the costs of lost sales, safety stock, unsatisfied customers, and loss of goodwill. Companies must strive to do a good job of tracking forecast error and taking the necessary steps to improve their forecasting techniques. Typically, forecast error at the disaggregated (stock keeping unit) level is higher than at the aggregated (company as a whole) level. **Forecast error** is the difference between the actual quantity and the forecast. Forecast error can be expressed as:

$$e_t = A_t - F_t$$

where e_t = forecast error for period t
A_t = actual demand for period t
F_t = forecast for period t

Several measures of forecasting accuracy are shown below:

Mean absolute deviation (MAD) $= \dfrac{\sum\limits_{t=1}^{n} |e_t|}{n}$

Mean absolute percentage error (MAPE) $= \dfrac{100}{n} \sum\limits_{t=1}^{n} \left| \dfrac{e_t}{A_t} \right|$

Mean square error (MSE) $= \dfrac{\sum\limits_{t=1}^{n} e_t^2}{n}$

Running sum of forecast errors (RSFE) $= \sum\limits_{t=1}^{n} e_t$

where e_t = forecast error for period t

A_t = actual demand for period t

n = number of periods of evaluation

The RSFE is an indicator of bias in the forecasts. **Forecast bias** measures the tendency of a forecast to be consistently higher or lower than the actual demand, over time. A positive RSFE indicates that the forecasts are generally lower than actual demand, which can lead to stockouts. A negative RSFE shows that the forecasts are generally higher than actual demand, which can result in excess inventory carrying costs.

The **tracking signal** is used to determine if the forecast bias is within the acceptable control limits. It is expressed as:

$$\text{Tracking signal} = \frac{\text{RSFE}}{\text{MAD}}$$

If the tracking signal falls outside preset control limits, there is a bias problem with the forecasting method, and an evaluation of the way forecasts are generated is warranted. A biased forecast will lead to excessive inventories or stockouts. Some inventory experts suggest using a tracking signal of ± 4 for high-volume items and ± 8 for lower-volume items. Over time when the quality of forecasts improved, it is recommended that the control limits be reduced to ± 3. As tighter limits are instituted, there is a greater probability of finding exceptions that actually require no action, but it also means catching changes in demand earlier, which could lead to further improvement in forecasts. Example 5.6 illustrates the use of these forecast accuracy measures.

In one study, researchers found that bias in the forecast could be intentional, driven by organizational issues such as motivation of staff and satisfaction of customer demands, influencing the generation of forecasts.[13] For example, sales personnel tend to favor under-forecasting so they can meet or exceed sales quotas, and production people tend to over-forecast because having too much inventory presents less of a problem than the alternative.

Example 5.6   Forecast Accuracy Measures

The demand and forecast information for the XYZ Company over a twelve-month period is shown in the table below.

PERIOD	DEMAND	FORECAST	PERIOD	DEMAND	FORECAST
1	1,600	1,523	7	3,300	3,243
2	2,200	1,810	8	3,200	3,530
3	2,000	2,097	9	3,900	3,817
4	1,600	2,383	10	4,700	4,103
5	2,500	2,670	11	4,300	4,390
6	3,500	2,957	12	4,400	4,677

Calculate the 12 period MAD, MSE, MAPE, RSFE, and tracking signal. Assume that the control limit for the tracking signal is ± 3. What can be concluded about the quality of the forecasts?

SOLUTION

PERIOD	DEMAND	FORECAST	ERROR (e)	ABSOLUTE ERROR	e^2	ABSOLUTE % ERROR
1	1,600	1,523	77	77	5,929	4.8
2	2,200	1,810	390	390	152,100	17.7
3	2,000	2,097	−97	97	9,409	4.9
4	1,600	2,383	−783	783	613,089	48.9
5	2,500	2,670	−170	170	28,900	6.8
6	3,500	2,957	543	543	294,849	15.5
7	3,300	3,243	57	57	3,249	1.7
8	3,200	3,530	−330	330	108,900	10.3
9	3,900	3,817	83	83	6,889	2.1
10	4,700	4,103	597	597	356,409	12.7
11	4,300	4,390	−90	90	8,100	2.1
12	4,400	4,677	−277	277	76,729	6.3
Total			0	3,494	1,664,552	133.9
Average				291.17	138,712.7	11.16
			RSFE	MAD	MSE	MAPE

MAD = 291.2

MSE = 138,712.7

MAPE = 11.2%

RSFE = 0

$\text{Tracking signal} = \dfrac{\text{RSFE}}{\text{MAD}} = 0$

The results indicate no bias in the forecasts, and that the tracking signal is well within the control limits of ± 3. However, the forecasts are on average 291 units or 11.2 percent off from actual demand. This situation might require attention to determine the underlying causes of the variation or to find a more accurate forecasting technique.

SCM Profile | Terra Technology 2015 Forecasting Benchmark Study[14]

Terra Technology, a Connecticut-based business planning advisor, is in its fifth year of a study of demand planning performance. The 2015 study encompasses 500 distribution centers, 450,000 item locations, nearly 5 billion physical cases, and more than $130 billion in combined company annual sales. Overall, the study finds that the new product introductions tripled over a five-year period. However, due to the unpredictability of new introductions and the absence of historical data, it is more difficult to predict demand. Weekly forecast error at the item level has remained essentially flat since 2010. Bias for the group has been improved to 5 percent, its lowest level in five years. Sales increases relied more on promotions and new products introductions, but caused forecasting to be more challenging, with increased errors and bias four times higher than regular sales.

The following are key findings from the study:

- Network complexity continues to outpace sales. Since 2010, the number of items grew by 32 percent compared to a 4 percent increase in sales. As a result, average sales per item dropped by 22 percent.

- The rate of new product introductions is considerably higher, with the number of distinct items for sale nearly tripling in the last five years, up 187 percent; 82 percent of these have since been discontinued.

- The long tail continues to grow longer and now accounts for 81 percent of items. A different view of the data shows that the top 10 percent of items generate 75 percent of sales, whereas the bottom 50 percent contribute only 1 percent.

- Existing demand planning technology and processes have reached their limits, with forecast value-added and accuracy remaining essentially flat, varying by no more than ±2 percent since 2010. This is a tribute to planners who have managed to maintain the status quo despite rapid proliferation but is not sustainable.

- Demand sensing provides a step-change in performance that management seeks by automating the use of market data, more than doubling forecast value-added and cutting average forecast error by 37 percent.

The key to generating accurate forecasts is collaborative forecasting with different partners inside and outside the company working together to eliminate forecasting error. A collaborative planning, forecasting, and replenishment system, discussed later in the chapter, provides for free exchange of forecasting data, point-of-sale data, promotions, and other relevant information between trading partners; this collaborative effort, rather than more sophisticated and expensive forecasting algorithms, can account for significant improvements in forecasting accuracy.

COLLABORATIVE PLANNING, FORECASTING, AND REPLENISHMENT

Collaborative planning, forecasting, and replenishment (CPFR) is a concept first developed by the Voluntary Interindustry Commerce Solutions (VICS) Association, which merged with GS1 US in 2012. According to the Council of Supply Chain Management Professionals, CPFR is:

> *A concept that aims to enhance supply chain integration by supporting and assisting joint practices. CPFR seeks cooperative management of inventory through joint visibility and replenishment of products throughout the supply chain. Information shared between suppliers and retailers aids in planning and satisfying customer demands through a supportive system of shared information. This allows for continuous updating of inventory and upcoming requirements, essentially making the end-to-end supply chain process more efficient. Efficiency is also created through the decrease expenditures for merchandising, inventory, logistics, and transportation across all trading partners.*[15]

The objective of CPFR is to optimize the supply chain by improving demand forecast accuracy, delivering the right product at the right time to the right location, reducing inventories across the supply chain, avoiding stockouts, and improving customer service. This can be achieved only if the trading partners are working closely together and are willing to share information and risk through a common set of processes. The real value of CPFR comes from an exchange of forecasting information rather than from more sophisticated forecasting algorithms to improve forecasting accuracy. The fact is that forecasts developed solely by the firm tend to be inaccurate. When both the buyer and seller collaborate to develop a single forecast, incorporating knowledge of base sales, promotions, store openings or closings, and new product introductions, it is possible to synchronize buyer needs with supplier production plans, thus ensuring efficient replenishment. The jointly managed forecasts can be adjusted in the event that demand or promotions have changed, thus avoiding costly corrections after the fact.

On the surface, when decisions are made with incomplete, one-sided information, it may appear that companies have optimized their internal processes when, in reality, inventory has merely shifted along the supply chain. Without supply chain trading partners collaborating and exchanging information, the supply chain will always be suboptimal and contain excess inventories, resulting in less-than-maximum supply chain profits.

CPFR is an approach that addresses the requirements for good demand management. The benefits of CPFR include the following:

- Strengthens partner relationships
- Provides analysis of sales and order forecasts
- Uses point-of-sale data, seasonal activity, promotions, new product introductions, and store openings or closings to improve forecast accuracy
- Manages the demand chain and proactively eliminates problems before they appear
- Allows collaboration on future requirements and plans
- Uses joint planning and promotions management
- Integrates planning, forecasting, and logistics activities
- Provides efficient category management and understanding of consumer purchasing patterns
- Provides analysis of key performance metrics (e.g., forecast accuracy, forecast exceptions, product lead times, inventory turnover, percentage stockouts) to

reduce supply chain inefficiencies, improve customer service, and increase revenues and profitability.

California boating supply retailer West Marine, an early adopter of CPFR, benefited greatly from its implementation. Within a few years of the start of its CPFR program, West Marine had developed relationships with 200 suppliers and achieved 85 percent forecast accuracy, 80 percent on-time shipments, and 96 percent in-stock deliveries during its peak season. West Marine had to address both business processes and cultural issues. The company worked with its suppliers to match supply and demand. While collaboration with external constituents is critical for CPFR success, it is equally important that effective collaboration within the company is emphasized. For example, logistics, planning, and replenishment associates must work closely together. West Marine identified the following ten performance improvement steps in its successful implementation of CPFR[16]:

1. Seek long-term, holistic solutions, not quick or myopic fixes.

2. Reconcile conflicting goals and metrics.

3. Pursue inclusive problem solving; do not depend upon "experts" who don't have accountability for the business.

4. Instill collaborative processes that encourage idea creation, shared problem solving, and high adoption rates across organizational boundaries.

5. Use a disciplined and iterative set of methodologies such as CPFR, SCOR, or Six Sigma to help teams define issues, root causes, and solutions.

6. Develop a culture of continuous improvement, particularly at the customer-facing associate level, because those employees are most likely to know what is needed.

7. Create clear accountabilities and assign authority with a focus on core business processes rather than on traditional organizational "silos" or loyalties.

8. Commit to technology enablement for execution, communication, exception management, and root-cause analysis.

9. Reduce decision cycle times.

10. Implement rapidly.

As part of their CPFR initiative, the company worked closely with suppliers to match supply and demand. The CPFR program has been extended to West Marine's supplier network. Other early adopters of CPFR are Procter & Gamble and Walmart.

The top three challenges for CPFR implementation are the difficulty of making internal changes, cost, and trust. As with any major implementation, internal resistance to change must be addressed by top management. Change is always difficult; however, if top management is committed to the project, then the project is much more likely to succeed. Companies will need to educate their employees on the benefits of the process changes and the disadvantages of maintaining the status quo. There is also the question of reducing the scale of CPFR and, therefore, the cost of implementation for smaller trading partners. While cost is an important factor, companies with no plans for adopting CPFR should determine if they are at a competitive disadvantage. Trust, a major cultural issue, is considered a big hurdle to widespread implementation of CPFR because many retailers are reluctant to share the type of proprietary information required by CPFR. While the suppliers of Walmart such as Procter & Gamble, for instance, may be willing to share sensitive data with Walmart, they do not want other suppliers to obtain this information. However, other experts do not believe that trust is the stumbling block for mass adoption of CPFR. Jim

Uchneat of Benchmarking Partners, Inc., said, "Trust may be a catch-all phrase that covers a host of other problems, but I have never found trust between people to be the issue. CPFR won't shift the power dynamics in a retailer/buyer relationship. If people are hoping that this is the case and refer to this as 'trust,' then they are fooling themselves. Lack of trust is more often related to the unreliable data in systems and the lack of integration internal to retailers and manufacturers."[17]

In another example, Demand Solutions is a provider of CPFR software solutions.[18] With the Demand Solutions Collaboration software, companies are able to synchronize customer demand with supplier capabilities for optimized inventory and production. In addition, supply chain collaboration can provide companies with lasting competitive advantages. According to Demand Solutions, their software can result in increased supply chain visibility, optimized inventories, reduced stockouts, lower costs, satisfied customers, and increased revenue.

USEFUL FORECASTING WEBSITES

Several forecasting websites that provide a wealth of information on the subject are shown below:

1. Institute for Business Forecasting & Planning (https://ibf.org/)

   The Institute of Business Forecasting & Planning (IBF), established in 1982, is a membership organization recognized worldwide for fostering the growth of demand planning, forecasting, and sales and operations planning (S&OP), as its mission.

   The IBF provides education, benchmarking research, training, certification, conferences, and advisory services on a global scale. IBF is instrumental in helping businesses increase cash flow, market share, and growth by improving forecasting and planning performance. Learning, sharing, and advancing are the foundational cycle that IBF members and their companies experience. No other organization has as much depth and experience in providing educational content for demand planning and forecasting as IBF.[19] The institute publishes the *Journal of Business Forecasting*.

2. International Institute of Forecasters (www.forecasters.org/)

   The International Institute of Forecasters (IIF), a nonprofit organization founded in 1982, is dedicated to developing and furthering the generation, distribution, and use of knowledge on forecasting through the following objectives[20]:

   - Develop and unify forecasting as a multidisciplinary field of research drawing on management, behavioral sciences, social sciences, engineering, and other fields.
   - Contribute to the professional development of analysts, managers, and policy makers with responsibilities for making and using forecasts in business and government.
   - Bridge the gap between theory and practice, with practice helping to set the research agenda and research providing useful results.
   - Bring together decision makers, forecasters, and researchers from all nations to improve the quality and usefulness of forecasting.

   The Institute also publishes the *International Journal of Forecasting*, *Foresight: The International Journal of Applied Forecasting*, and *The Oracle*.

3. Forecasting Principles: Evidence-based Forecasting (www.forecastingprinciples.com/)

   The Forecasting Principles site summarizes all useful knowledge about forecasting so that it can be used by researchers, practitioners, and educators. (Those who might want to challenge this are invited to submit missing information.) This knowledge is provided as principles (guidelines, prescriptions, rules, conditions, action statements, or advice about what to do in given situations). This site describes all evidenced-based principles on forecasting and provides sources to support the principles. The primary source is *Principles of Forecasting*, a comprehensive summary of forecasting knowledge which involved 40 authors and 123 reviewers.[21]

4. Several forecasting blogs:

(i) Business Forecasting (www.businessforcastingblog.com)

Clive Jones, the person responsible for starting this business forecasting blog had this to say on his website: "This blog is about my fascination with forecasting and predictive analytics. I have worked professionally in forecasting and data analytics for enterprise IT (Microsoft, Hewlett Packard, Agilent Technologies) since 1995, and, earlier, for public utilities and government agencies. Started Spring 2012, *businessforecastblog* was relaunched in 2014. My intention is to create greater understanding of the range of techniques—both basic and leading edge—that are crashing like a wave against traditional marketing and forecasting. I think there is a place for writing which ranges from computational and analytical detail to videos and interviews relating to economic forecasts and forecasters."[22]

(ii) No Hesitations: A Blog by Francis Diebold (http://fxdiebold.blogspot.com.au)

Francis Diebold is a professor of economics at the University of Pennsylvania. His blog "contains news and views, comments and criticisms, rants and raves, focusing mostly, but not exclusively, on dynamic predictive modeling in economics and finance."[23]

FORECASTING SOFTWARE

Forecasts are seldom calculated manually. If a forecaster uses a quantitative method, then a software solution can be used to simplify the process and save the time required to generate a forecast. Several leading forecasting software providers and their products are shown below.

1. *Business Forecast Systems, Inc.* (www.forecastpro.com/)

Founded in 1986, Business Forecast Systems, Inc. (BFS), is the maker of Forecast Pro, the leading software solution for business forecasting, and is a premier provider of forecasting education. With more than 35,000 users worldwide, Forecast Pro helps thousands of companies improve planning, cut inventory costs, and decrease stockouts by improving the accuracy of their forecasts. Headquartered in Belmont, Massachusetts, BFS was cofounded by Dr. Robert (Bob) Goodrich and Eric Stellwagen and is privately held.[24]

The company offers three editions of Forecast Pro to address the different needs of its customers: Forecast Pro Unlimited, Forecast Pro TRAC, and Forecast Pro XE. Several of the forecasting approaches discussed in this chapter, such as moving average, trend, and exponential smoothing models, are included in the software. Honeywell Safety Products is an example of one of the company's customers that has benefited greatly from use of Forecast Pro software. Their experience with Forecast Pro is discussed in the nearby SCM Profile on Honeywell.

2. *John Galt* (www.johngalt.com/)

Founded in 1996, Chicago-based John Galt Solutions has a proven track record of providing "affordable and automated solutions for consumer-driven supply chains" and delivering "custom solutions that match individual needs, no matter how big the business is, or what challenges are faced."[25] With its ForecastX Wizard

SCM Profile | Honeywell Improves Customer Service with Better Forecasting

Honeywell Safety Products (HSP) is a leading supplier of personal protective equipment for the electrical safety and general industrial worker industry. Their products include a wide variety of safety helmets, respirators, and first aid kits. HSP has more than $800 million in yearly sales. Their major challenges are lumpy, inconsistent demand and proliferation of SKUs. HSP forecasts on a monthly basis more than 32,000 data series for its U.S. and Canadian market. These challenges led them to Forecast Pro TRAC. During the implementation period, the management team reviewed forecasts generated from Forecast Pro TRAC in parallel with forecasts from their existing software. HSP also compared how the forecasts would change over a twelve-month period using Forecast Pro TRAC and their current system. After going live with Forecast Pro TRAC, HSP decided that tracking accuracy be at the item/class level. The results show an improving trend for the first three quarters using MAPE (mean absolute percentage error) from Q1 (24.4%) to Q2 (13.6%) to Q3 (12.9%). According to Lisa Gardner, demand manager, "The analysis showed that since implementing Forecast Pro TRAC, without question, there has been a definite improvement in forecast accuracy across almost every product line." In addition, John Romano, director, SIOP & Materials Planning, Honeywell Safety Products said, "Forecast Pro has allowed us to have deeper discussions with better information. By coupling the quantitative framework provided by Forecast Pro TRAC with the qualitative input from sales and marketing, we are able to create true consensus. The end result is not only buy-in from different parts of the organization, but a crisper view of the market and its needs."[26]

and Atlas Planning Suite, it provides a wide range of affordable, easy-to-implement supply chain planning solutions for mid-market companies.

The company's basic forecasting software, ForecastX Wizard, combines a statistical forecasting engine with Microsoft Excel, giving forecasters a blend of accuracy, ease of use, and flexibility. The ForecastX Wizard Premium has more interactive features, enhanced inventory planning, closed-loop collaboration, and streamlined reporting. More than 5,000 customers today use solutions from John Galt to increase forecast accuracy, optimize inventory levels, and maximize supply chain performance.

3. *JustEnough* (www.justenough.com/)

JustEnough solves complex demand problems without overcomplicating things.[27] While other companies might focus on the science side of demand management with solutions using complex metrics, JustEnough software allows planning decisions to be executed based on the company's expertise.

The Strandbags Group, one of Australia's largest specialty retailers, has more than 350 stores in Australia, New Zealand, the Middle East, and South Africa. Using JustEnough's Sales Forecasting and Inventory Planning Solutions, the company was able to "send stock to stores where it is most likely to sell, optimized sales potential for each product based on actual sales history, and improved promotions, using forecasts that ensure inventory always meets customer expectations." According to Nathan Toussaint, business analyst at Strandbags, "At the store level, it was nearly impossible for us to know what needs to be in a SKU combination. But JustEnough has a unique way of forecasting and replenishing Strandbags' stocks accurately at the store/SKU level. This would be very labor-intensive otherwise."[28]

Another JustEnough customer is Ackermans, one of the oldest consumer retailers in South Africa selling baby ware, baby furniture, consumer goods, apparel, and financial services products. The company has more than 450 stores located across Southern Africa. "We needed something that wasn't too complicated or so overly sophisticated that it was going to make users run for the hills," said Bouwer Strydom, Ackermans' planning manager. "It also couldn't be too complex or expensive for us to maintain. It had to fit in with our ongoing business processes without us having to re-engineer anything to fit replenishment. We determined that the demand forecasting solution from JustEnough would be able to grow with us, as opposed to us having to grow into it."[29]

4. *Avercast, LLC* (http://www.avercast.com/)

Avercast, with over 40 years of experience in demand management, has "developed cutting edge software to satisfy the most demanding requirements. Avercast's industry leading 204 forecasting algorithms power the fastest and most efficient enterprise level demand management software suite in the industry."[30]

S. Bacher, one of South Africa's oldest distributors and wholesalers, uses Avercast Business Forecasting software. According to Justin Seef, S. Bacher's procurement director, "This is the perfect solution for the medium-sized business . . . After using Avercast for six months our inventory was reduced by 23 percent. We can easily drill down to the item level using Avercast. It is very simple, does what it needs to do and does it effectively."[31]

5. *SAS* (https://www.sas.com/en_us/home.html)

The SAS Forecast Server "generates large quantities of forecasts quickly and automatically without the need for human intervention unless so desired. This enables organizations to plan more efficiently and effectively for the future. The automation and scalability of SAS Forecast Server enable even the largest enterprise to operate more efficiently by producing forecasts for a broad range of planning challenges as well as allowing forecasters to focus their efforts on the most important forecasts. It is designed for any organization that needs large-scale forecasting and/or requires automation because of the large number of forecasts or a lack of skilled forecasters. This can range from analysts responsible for the actual creation of the forecasts to the managers and directors responsible for overseeing the forecasting and planning processes."[32]

Nestlé is an example of a global company that has managed its forecasting function well with SAS Forecast Server and SAS Inventory Optimization solutions (see the nearby SCM profile on the company).

Cloud-Based Forecasting

Instead of investing in the software described above, many companies are choosing to use cloud services to track and forecast demand. **Cloud-based forecasting** can be described as using supplier-hosted or software-as-a-service (SaaS) advanced forecasting applications that are provided to companies on a subscription basis. Today, cloud-based forecasting is accomplished with state-of-the-art time series forecasting algorithms using seasonal and cyclical adjusting models. Some also utilize artificial intelligence-based expert systems to select the forecasting method best suited for a customer's environment.

SCM Profile | **Accurate Forecasting at Nestlé Improves Customer Service**

Nestlé is the world's biggest food company with more than 330,000 employees in 469 locations in 86 countries. Every day, more than one billion units of product are manufactured, showing the sheer size of the company's market. Nestlé must ensure that the right products are delivered to the shelves at the right time. To achieve that, Nestlé needs good forecasts. No marketing promotion, no matter how well conceived, could succeed without having the products available on the shelves for customers to purchase. Nestlé has more than 10,000 products which makes planning more complicated on a global scale. When you throw in product categories, diverse sales regions, and departments, there are many activities to manage. Other factors such as seasonal influences, weather affecting a good harvest, demand swings, and perishability of food products further complicate production planning and logistics.

According to Baumgartner, head of global demand planning performance and statistical forecasting, "To have the right quantity of the right products at the right place and time, we rely heavily on being able to predict the orders our customers will place as precisely as possible. The critical factor in this complex environment is being able to assess the reliability of forecasts. Two elements have attracted the most attention within this context: dealing with volatility, and SAS. Predictability of demand for a certain product is highly dependent on that product's demand volatility. Especially for products that display wide fluctuations in demand, the choice and combination of methods is very important. SAS Forecast Server simplifies this task tremendously." Nestlé's ability to predict the orders customers will place as accurately as possible will enable the company to deliver the right quantity of the right products at the right place and time.

At Nestlé, there is an important focus on "mad bulls," a term used to describe high volume products with high volatility. An example of a mad bull is Nescafé, which has normal sales on a fairly regular basis throughout the year, but marketing/trade promotions often cause a surge in demand for the product. Nestlé realizes that the SAS Forecast Server cannot totally replace professional demand planners. Product planners now have more time available to make better production decisions for highly volatile products.[33]

With cloud-based forecasting, organizations can easily detour around outdated in-house applications, instantly increase data storage and data analysis capabilities as needed, and provide workers with new capabilities without devoting time and resources to software, hardware, and extensive training. Users need only a browser and can be up and running in one day. Firms can reduce their IT costs significantly, improve employee productivity, and improve forecast accuracy, which also reduces stockout costs and inventory carrying costs. Many of these applications are provided as part of larger cloud-based enterprise management applications such as transportation management, customer relationship management, and sales force management systems. A few examples are provided here.

Arizona-based AFS Technologies provides on-demand trade promotion management and other software solutions to the consumer packaged goods industry.[34] Its easy-to-use tools allow users to get a clear-cut picture of sales, from warehouse to customer, and perform sales forecasting along with a number of other applications. Canada-based Angoss Software offers KnowledgeSCORE on-demand predictive sales analytics as part of firms' CRM strategies.[35] Their cloud-based data analysis capabilities combine best-of-breed predictive analytics technologies for big data needs and can improve field sales productivity and sales forecasting. Mailplus, an Australian mail courier service, began using a cloud-based integrated business management system from NetSuite because its in-house system could no longer handle Mailplus's rapid growth. "The more franchises we added to our system, the greater the system stress—to point that it was crashing almost daily and costing us thousands of dollars a month to maintain and service," says Chris Burgess, Mailplus CEO. It uses the NetSuite SuiteCloud system for a wide range of applications including sales and financial forecasting.[36] Halo, a leading provider of data integration and analytics software for supply chain planning, has developed the Halo SkuBrain application to assist beverage suppliers and distributors to combine sales and production forecasting and inventory replenishment planning in a single cloud-based application. According to Keith Peterson, CEO and president, "Many of Halo's beverage customers worldwide have needs for a robust demand supply planning solution at an affordable investment level. The planning needs in the beverage industry are unique—lots of SKU's, heavy seasonality, and rapid introduction of new flavors and packaging make this a challenging area to plan. SkuBrain for Beverage fits a major gap in the market for a powerful solution that fits between spreadsheets and expensive planning systems—offering analytics specific to beverage. With the rapid growth in craft beverages, fast rising players require a clear plan to ensure customer service levels are met. And, with so many SKU's launched seasonally, SkuBrain offers capabilities to support forecasts for new product introductions."[37]

SUMMARY

Forecasting is an integral part of demand management since it provides an estimate of future demand and the basis for planning and making sound business decisions. A mismatch in supply and demand could result in excessive inventories and stockouts and loss of profits and goodwill. Proper demand forecasting enables better planning and utilization of resources for businesses to be competitive. Both qualitative and quantitative methods are available to help companies forecast demand better. The qualitative methods are based on judgment and intuition, whereas the quantitative methods use mathematical techniques and historical data to predict future demand. The quantitative forecasting methods can be divided into time series and cause-and-effect models. Since forecasts are seldom completely accurate, management must monitor forecast errors and make the necessary improvements to the forecasting process.

Forecasts made in isolation tend to be inaccurate. Collaborative planning, forecasting, and replenishment (CPFR) is an approach in which companies work together to develop mutually agreeable plans while taking responsibility for their actions. The objective of CPFR is to optimize the supply chain by generating a consensus demand forecast, delivering the right product at the right time to the right location, reducing inventories, avoiding stockouts, and improving customer service. Major corporations such as Walmart, West Marine, and Procter & Gamble are early adopters of CPFR.

The computation involved in generating a forecast is seldom done manually. Forecasting software solutions such as Forecast Pro, SAS, and Microsoft Excel are readily available. More recently, cloud-based forecasting solutions have made it possible to have forecasting and other supply chain software on-demand on the Internet.

KEY TERMS

business cycle, 150

cause-and-effect forecasting, 150

cloud-based forecasting, 167

collaborative planning, forecasting, and replenishment, 161

forecast bias, 159

forecast error, 159

linear trend forecast, 155

multiple regression forecast, 157

naïve forecast, 151

qualitative forecasting methods, 148

quantitative forecasting methods, 148

simple moving average forecast, 151

time series forecasting, 150

tracking signal, 159

DISCUSSION QUESTIONS

1. Explain demand management.

2. What is demand forecasting? Why is demand forecasting important for effective supply chain management?

3. Explain the impact of a mismatch in supply and demand. What strategies can companies adopt to influence demand?

4. What are qualitative forecasting techniques? When are these methods more suitable?

5. What are the components of a time series? Explain the difference between a time series model and an associative model. Under what conditions would one model be preferred to the other?

6. Explain the impact of the smoothing constant in the simple exponential smoothing forecast.

7. Explain the impact of forecasting horizon on forecast accuracy.

8. Compare and contrast the jury of executive opinion and the Delphi techniques.

9. What are the key differences between the weighted moving average and the simple exponential smoothing forecasting methods?

10. Name three measures of forecasting accuracy.

11. How could the MAD be used to generate a better smoothing constant for an exponential smoothing forecast?

12. What is a tracking signal? Explain how the tracking signal can help managers improve the quality of forecasts.

13. Explain the key features of CPFR. Why would a company consider adopting CPFR?

14. West Marine identified ten performance improvement steps in its successful implementation of CPFR. Is West Marine's approach unique, or can its experience be duplicated at another company? What are the key challenges that other companies will face in implementing CPFR?

15. Why is widespread adoption of CPFR below expectations?

16. What is cloud-based forecasting, and why do companies use this in solving their supply chain forecasting problems? Will cloud services replace the Microsoft desktop?

PROBLEMS

1. Ms. Winnie Lin's company sells computers. The monthly sales for a six-month period are as follows:

MONTH	SALES
Jan	18,000
Feb	22,000
Mar	16,000
Apr	18,000
May	20,000
Jun	24,000

a. Plot the monthly data on a sheet of graph paper.

b. Compute the sales forecast for July using the following approaches: (1) a three-month moving average; (2) a weighted three-month moving average using 0.50 for June, 0.30 for May, and 0.20 for April; (3) a linear trend equation; and (4) exponential smoothing with α (smoothing constant) equal to 0.40, assuming a February forecast of 18,000.

c. Which method do you think is the least appropriate? Why?

d. Calculate the MAD for each of the four techniques in part b. Which is the best? Why?

2. The U.S. monthly inflation rate for 2016 is shown below:

MONTH	INFLATION	MONTH	INFLATION
January	1.4	July	0.8
February	1.0	August	1.1
March	0.9	September	1.5
April	1.1	October	1.6
May	1.0	November	1.7
June	1.0	December	2.1

a. Compute the inflation rate for January 2017 using the exponential smoothing forecast with $\alpha = 0.3$ and 0.5. Assume that the forecast for February 2016 is 1.4.

b. What is the MAD for each of the forecasts generated using the exponential smoothing method? Which method is better?

3. The owner of the Chocolate Outlet Store wants to forecast chocolate demand. Demand for the preceding four years is shown in the following table:

YEAR	DEMAND (POUNDS)
1	68,800
2	71,000
3	75,500
4	71,200

Forecast demand for year 5 using the following approaches: (1) a three-year moving average; (2) a three-year weighted moving average using 0.40 for year 4, 0.20 for year 3, and 0.40 for year 2; and (3) exponential smoothing with $\alpha = 0.30$, and assuming the forecast for period 1 = 68,000.

4. Monthly demand for Accugolf's top-rated golf balls in dozens for the last twelve months are shown below:

MONTH	INFLATION	MONTH	INFLATION
January	5,500	July	7,500
February	5,700	August	7,200
March	6,000	September	6,800
April	5,800	October	6,300
May	6,300	November	6,000
June	7,000	December	5,800

a. Develop a simple regression model for sales of golf balls.

b. What is the forecast for sales of golf balls in January of the upcoming year?

5. The forecasts generated by three forecasting methods and actual demand for the Torrance Company are as follows:

MONTH	DEMAND	FORECAST 1	FORECAST 2	FORECAST 3
1	269	275	268	280
2	289	266	287	295
3	294	290	292	290
4	278	284	298	280
5	268	270	274	270
6	269	268	270	260

Compute the MSE and MAD for each forecasting method. Which forecasting method is the best? Would your decision on which forecasting method performs better depend on which forecasting accuracy measure (MAD or MSE) is selected?

6. The Toro Cutlery Company has collected the below monthly sales information:

MONTH	SALES	MONTH	SALES	MONTH	SALES
January	20,000	May	92,000	September	30,000
February	16,000	June	30,000	October	90,000
March	42,000	July	90,000	November	80,000
April	100,000	August	50,000	December	90,000

The company is examining two forecasting methods, moving average and exponential smoothing for forecasting sales.

a. What will the forecast be for January the following year using a three-, four-, and five-month moving average?

b. What will the forecast be for January the following year using exponential smoothing with an α value of 0.5? Assume forecast for February is 20,000.

7. The Sun Devils Corporation is deciding which of two forecasting models to use. The forecasts for the two models and actual demand are provided below:

MONTH	SALES	MODEL 1 FORECAST	MODEL 2 FORECAST
1	170	175	172
2	190	165	185
3	195	190	190
4	180	185	195
5	170	170	175
6	170	165	170
7	160	160	165
8	175	170	175
9	180	185	180
10	175	170	175

Compute the MAPE and RSFE for the two forecasting methods. Is RSFE a good forecasting accuracy measure?

8. The Dominguez Hills Company has the following forecasts generated by two forecasting methods. Actual sales for the same time periods are shown below:

YEAR	SALES	FORECAST 1	FORECAST 2
1	880	875	850
2	895	866	890
3	890	890	895
4	880	885	890
5	860	875	875
6	870	870	880
7	860	860	860
8	875	870	875

Compute the tracking signal for each forecasting method. Why is tracking signal important in assessing the performance of a forecasting model?

ESSAY/PROJECT QUESTIONS

1. Find a software company online providing forecasting solutions, and provide a description of the experience of one of its customers' use of the product.

2. Find a company online that is using collaborative planning, forecasting, and replenishment, and report on its experiences.

3. Find a software company online providing forecasting solutions, and list the different forecasting techniques that are included in its software.

4. Write a report comparing Apple's demand forecasts of their iPhones and actual sales for each generation of iPhone models since the phone was first introduced in 2007.

5. Go to one of the forecasting blogs such as Business Forecasting (www.businessforcast-ingblog.com) and No Hesitations, a blog by Francis Diebold (http://fxdiebold.blogspot.com.au), and describe the latest topic of discussion.

CASES

1. Quincy Snodgrass Enterprises—Forecasting*

Quincy Snodgrass is an entrepreneur and a lover of the outdoors. He has worked for various companies since he graduated college with his business administration degree in management. Over the years, he has saved every extra penny and now has the starting capital he needs; consequently, he plans to open his own business. Quincy plans to open a landscaping business. The primary services he'll offer are grass cutting, edging, and bush trimming. Obviously, this will only provide income in the spring, summer, and early fall. Therefore, he plans to offer snow removal in the winter. His goal is to continue to provide those baseline services and expand into actual landscaping work.

Quincy's initial challenge is to develop a forecast of how many customers he'll have each month. This is essential to determine if he needs to hire any additional labor throughout the season. Unfortunately, none of the jobs Quincy has had involved forecasting. Quincy is digging deep into his memory to recall his supply chain management course and the chapter on forecasting. He knows he has two methods to choose from, qualitative and quantitative.

Quincy is a numbers guy and is partial to using a quantitative method if possible, but he doesn't rule out the option of using one of the qualitative methods. He had worked many summers for other yardwork companies. Knowing he wanted to own his own business someday, Quincy took notes on how things went. Since his customer base would be in a series of small towns, Quincy knows he cannot charge as much as the companies that served larger communities. Consequently, volume is necessary to earn the revenue he will need.

Quincy focused on three small towns, Smithburg with a population of 700, Emeryville with 1,800, and Golf Creek with 2,500. He believes he can get 10 percent of the homes in each town to hire him. Quincy used information from the county files to estimate

*Written by Rick Bonsall, D. Mgt., McKendree University, Lebanon, IL. The people and institution are fictional and any resemblance to any person or any institution is coincidental. This case was prepared solely to provide material for class discussion. The author does not intend to illustrate either effective or ineffective handling of a managerial situation.

that on average, the number of homes is equal to about 25 percent of the population, meaning in Smithburg (700) the potential number of homes is about 175. Quincy believes his calculations are reasonable and could be the foundation for using a qualitative method to kick off his forecasting.

Discussion Questions

1. Since Quincy doesn't have any historical data (only an estimate of the number of customers he'll serve each month), which specific type of qualitative method is he using? What would be the total number of customers based on his assumptions? Is this a realistic number to allow the business to survive? He estimates his average fee will be $25.

2. Because of the type of communities, overtime Smithburg will provide 20 percent of the homes as customers, Emeryville still 10 percent, and Golf Creek only 7 percent. Assuming he was charging $25 per home, what effect does this change in monthly forecast have on his monthly revenue? Should he change his price either up or down? Explain.

3. Quincy has been gathering data for over five years now. He has a record of how many customers he had each month. He also has information on the weather, for example, which month has the most rain. Quincy wants to use these data to improve his forecasting. He has a choice of cause-and-effect models. Based on what data he has and what he wants to do, what would be the best method from the choices he has? Explain the elements of the forecasting equation.

©2019 Cengage Learning

2. Alvin Ortega's Social Media Dream*

Alvin Ortega is an avid social media fan. One of his favorite means of communication is Twitter. In addition to being a social media fanatic, Alvin is also a bit of a programming genius. To build his programming skills, Alvin is pursuing a degree in computer science. Although his programming skills are at a much higher level than any of his classmates, Alvin is sticking to his degree program because he plans to create his own social media platform. He is filling all his elective courses with business courses. Not only does he want to understand the ins and outs of managing a company, he believes the credentials will enhance his chance of getting investors for his business.

Alvin is working on a social media platform similar to Twitter; however, his has some unique features that he believes will enable it to compete with Twitter. As he begins working on his business plan, he decides he needs some real data to illustrate the potential of his creation. Unfortunately, since he hasn't launched his company yet, he has no data of his own. He searches the Internet and discovers data on statista, a website that provides statistical information on various industries. He searches for information on Twitter and finds data on the number of users per quarter from 2010 through 2016. He is elated! Alvin decides to use the data from 2010 to 2011 to illustrate the potential he believes his social media platform could have. Although the

*Written by Rick Bonsall, D. Mgt., McKendree University, Lebanon, IL. The people and institution are fictional and any resemblance to any person or any institution is coincidental. This case was prepared solely to provide material for class discussion. The author does not intend to illustrate either effective or ineffective handling of a managerial situation.

Sources: Statista, https://www.statista.com; Twitter, www.twitter.com

numbers are Twitter users, he plans to explain that he used their historical user data as a baseline for forecasting his potential user base.

Alvin decides to test four different forecasting methods—two-quarter moving average, three-quarter moving average, exponential smoothing with a smoothing constant of 0.2, and exponential smoothing with a smoothing constant of 0.9. Using the Twitter data as his baseline, Alvin wants to see which forecasting method is the most accurate. Alvin creates the table shown below and prepares to calculate the forecasts using each of the four aforementioned methods.

QUARTER/YEAR	ACTUAL NUMBER OF USERS IN MILLIONS	FORECASTED DEMAND—2-QUARTER MOVING AVERAGE	ABSOLUTE FORECAST ERROR	FORECASTED DEMAND—3-QUARTER MOVING AVERAGE	ABSOLUTE FORECAST ERROR	EXPONENTIAL SMOOTHING WITH SMOOTHING CONSTANT OF 0.2	ABSOLUTE FORECAST ERROR	EXPONENTIAL SMOOTHING WITH SMOOTHING CONSTANT OF 0.9	ABSOLUTE FORECAST ERROR
Q1/2010	30								
Q2/2010	40								
Q3/2010	49								
Q4/2010	54								
Q1/2011	68								
Q2/2011	85								
Q3/2011	101								
Q4/2011	117								
Q1/2012									

Discussion Questions

1. Forecast demand using the two-quarter moving average and the three-quarter moving average.

2. Forecast demand using exponential smoothing, one with the smoothing constant of 0.2 and the other with a smoothing constant of 0.9. *Note:* Set the forecast for Q1/2010 equal to the demand level for Q1/2010.

3. Calculate the mean absolute deviation (MAD) of each forecasting method. Which forecasting method would you recommend Alvin Ortega use? Explain why.

©2019 Cengage Learning

3. Hammerstein University—Enrollment*

Hammerstein University president Blake Sherman was worried about the survival of his university. The state of Illinois had been having financial troubles for years. For the past two years it was at an impasse in passing a budget. One consequence was that students were not getting the state tuition funds they had received in past years. This issue had multiple results. (1) Less students were enrolling because of the lack of state funds. (2) Those students who did enroll were tentative about remaining in school and this generated a high dropout rate. (3) To support the students, Hammerstein University increased its own tuition assistance program. All three results were affecting Hammerstein University's financial well-being.

*Written by Rick Bonsall, D. Mgt., McKendree University, Lebanon, IL. The people and institution are fictional and any resemblance to any person or any institution is coincidental. This case was prepared solely to provide material for class discussion. The author does not intend to illustrate either effective or ineffective handling of a managerial situation.

The key to survival was simple. Enrollment has to be maintained at a level to support the current level of degree programs, staff, and faculty. In addition, there still are the basic expenses of running Hammerstein University such as building repairs, grounds upkeep, and travel costs for sporting events. If the enrollment could not be maintained at the required level, Blake knew he would have to make some significant cuts. Degree programs that were not paying for themselves may need to be cut. This obviously would affect faculty. Cosmetic repairs for building or the grounds may need to be deferred to later. The potential financial crisis may make it necessary to temporarily shut down some sports. Blake feared that while these types of actions would ease the financial crisis in the short term, the same actions could further reduce enrollment and result in a slow downward spiral.

Blake had his admissions staff provide the enrollment for the past six semesters. The following table provides the data.

SEMESTER	ENROLLMENT
2017 fall	
2017 spring	3,120
2016 fall	3,249
2016 spring	3,716
2015 fall	3,520
2015 spring	3,170
2014 fall	3,094

Blake has the vice president of finance, Leroy Hardy, to calculate how many students represented a breakeven point under the current financial situation. He then asked Leroy to calculate what the enrollment breakeven point would be if the state began to provide tuition assistance again to their students. Leroy said for the enrollment breakeven point for no-state tuition was 3,265. The enrollment breakeven point for state tuition being paid was 3,000.

Blake had not yet been told the forecast for fall 2017. However, as he looked over the past enrollments, he was not optimistic. Both spring 2017 and fall 2016 enrollments were below the breakeven point for no-state tuition. Although he would have to wait for the figures from admissions staffs, he believed he needs to begin looking at options if the state didn't pass a budget that included tuition assistance.

Discussion Questions

1. Calculate the potential enrollment for fall 2017 using a three-semester weighted moving average, with weights 0.1, 0.3, and 0.6, with 0.06 for the most recent semester. Start your forecast for the spring 2016 semester and continue to fall 2017.

2. Calculate the potential enrollment for fall 2017 using exponential smoothing with a forecast for fall 2014 of 3,094 and a smoothing constant of 0.2. Which forecast do you think is the best? Why?

3. Which forecast or forecasts match or exceed the enrollment breakeven point if the state continues to not pay tuition assistance? Which match or exceed the enrollment breakeven point if the state pays tuition assistance? What is the next task Blake should have his staff do, based on these forecasts?

END NOTES

1. "Focus on Forecasting: Worst Practices in Business Forecasting," Analyticsmagazine.com; http://analytics-magazine.org/focus-on-forecasting-worst-practices-in-business -forecasting/

2. "How to Keep Fresh Products on the Shelves," SAS; http://www.sas.com/en_us/customers/forecasting-supply-chain-nestle.html#

3. O'Reilly, T., "Demand Forecasting Success Stories," *Aptaris Insights*, November 2016; https://goaptaris.com/demand-forecasting-success-stories/

4. The Institute for Supply Management's ISM Report On Business® is available at https://www.instituteforsupplymanagement.org/ISMReport/index.cfm?SSO=1

5. "ISM Report On Business® Frequently Asked Questions"; http://www.ism.ws/ISMReport/content.cfm?ItemNumber=10706&navItemNumber=12957

6. Hiiemaa, K., "In the Success Stories of H&M, Zara, Ikea and Walmart, Luck Is Not a Key Factor," *ERPLY*, March 18, 2016; https://erply.com/in-the-success-stories-of-hm-zara-ikea-and-walmart-luck-is-not-a-key-factor/

7. Nyugen, L., "Hatchimals Craze Causes Frustration as Demand Outstrips Supply," *Canadian Press*, November 25, 2016; http://globalnews.ca/news/3088222/hatchimals-craze-causes-frustration-as-demand-outstrips-supply/

8. "2016 Global Mobile Consumer Survey: US Edition," Deloitte; https://www2.deloitte.com/us/en/pages/technology-media-and-telecommunications/articles/global-mobile-consumer-survey-us-edition.html

9. "Technology: Why Google's Pixel Is More about Strategy than Smartphones," Knowledge@Wharton, November 15, 2016; http://knowledge.wharton.upenn.edu/article/googles-pixel-strategy-smartphones/

10. "2010 Eruptions of Eyjafjallajökull"; http://en.wikipedia.org/wiki/2010_eruptions_of_Eyjafjallajökull

11. "2010 Haitian Earthquake"; http://en.wikipedia.org/wiki/2010_Haiti_earthquake

12. "Hurricane Matthew"; https://en.wikipedia.org/wiki/Hurricane_Matthew

13. Lawrence, M., M. O'Conner, and B. Edmundson, "A Field Study of Forecasting Accuracy and Processes," *European Journal of Operational Research* 22(1), April 1, 2000: 151–160.

14. "2015 Forecasting Benchmark Study Highlights," Terra Technology; http://beetfusion.com/sites/default/files/Terra%20Technology%202015%20Forecasting%20Benchmark%20Study%20Highlights.pdf

15. "Supply Chain Management Terms and Glossary," Council of Supply Chain Management Professionals; http://cscmp.org/sites/default/files/user_uploads/resources/downloads/glossary-2013.pdf

16. Smith, L., "West Marine: A CPFR Success Story"; http://www.lomag-man.org/cpfr_industrie_achat_distribution/documentation_cpfr/WestMarineA_CPFRSuccStory-SupChManReManNet_an.pdf

17. J. Uchneat, "CPFR's Woes Not Related to Trust," *Computerworld*, July 22, 2002; www
    .computerworld.com/news/2002/story/0,11280,72834,00.html

18. "Supply Chain Collaboration," Demand Solutions; http://www.demandsolutions.com/
    collaborative-planning-cpfr-supply-chain-collaboration-software.html

19. "What Is the IBF? The Institute of Business Forecasting & Planning," Institute of Busi-
    ness Forecasting & Planning; https://ibf.org/index.cfm?fuseaction=showObjects&obje
    ctTypeID=4

20. "About the IIF," International Institute of Forecasting; http://forecasters.org/about/

21. "About ForPrin," *Forecasting Principles*; http://www.forecastingprinciples.com/index
    .php?option=com_content&view=article&id=34&Itemid=234#Objectives

22. Business Forecasting Blog; http://businessforecastblog.com/about/

23. No Hesitation: A Blog by Francis X. Diebold; http://fxdiebold.blogspot.com.au

24. Forecasting Pro: About Us; http://www.forecastpro.com/company/about/index.htm

25. John Galt the Forecast Xperts; http://www.forecastpro.com/company/about/index.htm

26. "Honeywell Safety Products Protects Customer Service with Better Forecasting," Fore-
    cast Pro; http://www.forecastpro.com/customers/success/honeywell.htm

27. "JustEnough: Company Overviews," JustEnough; http://www.justenough.com/
    about-us/

28. "JustEnough Restocks Strandbags' Stores with Fast-Moving Products, Reactively
    Replenishes Slower Items," JustEnough; http://www.justenough.com/resources/
    case-studies/strandbags/

29. "Ackermans: JustEnough Provides Visibility Into Premier Retailer's Stock Mix," JustEn-
    ough; http://www.justenough.com/resources/case-studies/ackermans/

30. Avercast Supply Chain Software; http://www.avercast.com/

31. Avercast Customer Reviews; http://www.avercast.com/Reviews2.php

32. SAS Forecast Server Fact Sheet; https://www.sas.com/content/dam/SAS/en_us/doc/
    factsheet/sas-forecast-server-102236.pdf

33. "How to Keep Fresh Products on the Shelves," SAS; http://www.sas.com/en_us/custom-
    ers/forecasting-supply-chain-nestle.html#

34. See afsi.com for more information.

35. Anonymous, "Angoss Software Corporation," *Marketing Weekly News*, July 14, 2012: 149.

36. Anonymous, "Computer Software—NetSuite Cloud Helps Accelerate Mailplus'
    Growth by 24 Percent," *Marketing Weekly News*, December 1, 2012: 208.

37. "Halo Releases Cloud-based Forecasting and Inventory Solution for Beverage Sup-
    pliers and Distributors," Halo Business Intelligence; https://halobi.com/2016/04/
    halo-releases-cloud-based-forecasting-and-inventory-solution-for-beverage-suppliers-
    and-distributors/

PART 3

Operations Issues in Supply Chain Management

Chapter 6   Resource Planning Systems

Chapter 7   Inventory Management

Chapter 8   Process Management—Lean and Six Sigma in the Supply Chain

Chapter 6

RESOURCE PLANNING SYSTEMS

Leaders must never forget the people on the line getting it done. Do everything you can to give them a sense of purpose and a clear understanding of the mission you're trying to accomplish, ensure they share your beliefs and ascertain that they have what they need to get the job done.

—**General Colin L. Powell, chairman of the Joint Chiefs of Staff, 1989–93**[1]

One of the worst mistakes I have seen is actually coding bad practices into a new system through customization. Look for efficiency improvements in systems and processes based on best industry practices before choosing to pursue changes to the implementation products.

—**Patrick Pate, city manager, Manassas, Virginia**[2]

Perhaps the most important driver of our success is culture. We fundamentally believe that we need a culture founded in a growth mindset. It starts with a belief that everyone can grow and develop; that potential is nurtured, not predetermined; and that anyone can change their mindset.

—**Satya Nadella, chief executive officer, Microsoft**[3]

Learning Objectives

After completing this chapter, you should be able to

- Describe the chase, level, and mixed aggregate production strategies.
- Describe the hierarchical operations planning process in terms of materials planning (APP, MPS, MRP) and capacity planning (RRP, RCCP, CRP).
- Compute available-to-promise quantities, MRP explosion, and DRP implosion.
- Describe the limitations of legacy MRP systems, and why organizations are migrating to integrated ERP systems.
- Describe an ERP system, and understand its advantages and disadvantages.
- Describe best-of-breed versus single integrator ERP implementations.

Chapter Outline

Introduction

Operations Planning

The Aggregate Production Plan

The Master Production Schedule

The Bill of Materials

The Material Requirements Plan

Capacity Planning

The Distribution Requirements Plan

The Legacy Material Requirements Planning Systems

The Development of Enterprise Resource Planning Systems

Implementing Enterprise Resource Planning Systems

Enterprise Resource Planning Software Applications

Summary

SCM Profile

ERP Software Paves Road to Victory

Joe Gibbs Racing (JGR) was founded by the former Washington Redskins coach, Joe Gibbs, in 1991. JGR first competed in the NASCAR in 1992 and is one of the most famous and successful professional stock car racing teams in the United States. JGR features thirteen racing teams, four cars in the NASCAR's Spring Cup Series, and three cars in the NASCAR's Xfinity Series.

JGR employs about 560 employees who reside in a 400,000-square-foot race shop to design and manufacture proprietary parts for its stock race cars. The company operates thirty computer-numerical-control machines running two shifts a day. JGR uses a job-based ERP system called JobBOSS to manage its business processes. JobBOSS is a comprehensive ERP business management system that includes accounting, forecasting, scheduling, sequencing, material and inventory management, and time tracking. It also includes add-on solutions like quality and customer relationship management.

JGR acknowledges that the production efficiencies of JobBOSS play an important role in its continued success in the stock car racing community. For example, JobBOSS creates operational efficiencies by allowing JGR to predict, in real time, the availability of parts and supplies, manage inventory and capacities, schedule production, and control overall shop floor productivity. Moreover, JobBOSS provides the necessary visual of the shop floor production to easily accommodate emergency jobs. The JobBOSS system has also helped JGR increase manufacturing innovations while reducing costs by allowing engineers to track manufacturing costs for comparison to alternatives in the future. Tools in the JobBOSS system allow JGR engineers to quickly determine manufacturing lead time to meet delivery due date. Part shortage in this time-sensitive racing industry is very unforgiving because race cars cannot compete in the race without the proper parts.

JGR attributes much of its continued success in winning races to the efficiency of the job-based ERP system which allows the company to produce quality automobile parts, transport the vehicles to the track, and successfully compete in races without interruption. Since JobBOSS is designed to be job-based, JGR engineers can invent prototypes, design new parts, or modify existing work orders easily. The ERP system not only helped to streamline JGR's operations from the front office to the shop floor but also helped to manage delivery of race cars to the track.

Recently, JGR implemented an add-on module called KnowledgeSync event manager to provide real-time visibility into key activities, information, and milestones. This add-on can proactively send reports to designated users at specified intervals automatically. For example, a quality management personnel may receive a notification email that a certain machine just scrapped five critical parts. Notifications can also be sent externally such as to alert key suppliers of overdue shipments as well. Instead of wasting valuable time to extract exception reports, alerts on stock shortages, missed opportunities, and changes to a job's status can be programmed to be sent to the relevant personnel automatically. By utilizing the capabilities of JobBOSS and the add-on module, JGR facilitates its rapid growth and continue to manufacture and race cars at an increasing level of excellence.[4]

INTRODUCTION

Resource planning is the process of determining the production capacity required to meet demand. In the context of resource planning, *capacity* refers to the maximum workload that an organization can complete in a fixed period. A discrepancy between an organization's capacity and demand results in inefficiencies, either in underutilized resources or unfulfilled orders. The goal of resource planning is to minimize this discrepancy.

One of the most critical activities of an organization is to balance the production plan with capacity; this directly impacts how effectively the organization deploys its resources in producing goods and services. Developing feasible operations schedules and capacity plans to meet delivery due dates and minimize waste in manufacturing or service organizations is a complex problem. The need for better operations scheduling continues to challenge operations managers, especially in today's intensely competitive global marketplace. In an environment fostering collaborative buyer–supplier relationships, the challenge of scheduling operations to meet delivery due dates and eliminate waste is becoming more complex. The problem is compounded in an integrated supply chain, where a missed due date or stockout cascades downstream, magnifying the **bullwhip effect** and adversely affecting the entire supply chain.

Operations managers are continuously involved in resource and operations planning to balance capacity and output. Capacity may be stated in terms of labor, materials, or equipment. With too much excess capacity, unit production cost is high due to idle workers and machinery. However, if workers and machinery are stressed due to too little capacity, quality levels are likely to deteriorate. Firms generally run their operations at about 85 percent of capacity to allow time for scheduled repairs and maintenance and to meet unexpected surges in demand.

This chapter describes the hierarchical operations planning process in terms of materials and capacity planning. A hypothetical industrial example is used to demonstrate the hierarchical planning process. This chapter also discusses the evolution of the manufacturing planning and control system from the material requirements planning to the enterprise resource planning system. The chapter-opening SCM Profile describes how an enterprise resource planning system helps a race car company to compete in the stock car racing arena successfully.

OPERATIONS PLANNING

Operations planning is usually hierarchical and can be divided into three broad categories: (1) **long-range**, (2) **intermediate** or **medium-range**, and (3) **short-range planning horizons**. While the distinctions among the three can be vague, long-range plans usually cover a year or more, tend to be more general, and specify resources and outputs in terms of aggregate hours and units. Medium-range plans normally span six to eighteen months, whereas short-range plans usually cover a few days to a few weeks depending on the type and size of the firm. Long-range plans are established first and are then used to guide the medium-range plans, which are subsequently used to guide the short-range plans. Long-range plans usually involve major, strategic decisions in capacity, such as the construction of new facilities and purchase of capital equipment, whereas medium-range plans involve minor changes in capacity such as changes in employment levels. Short-range plans are the most detailed and specify the exact end items and quantities to make on a weekly, daily, or hourly basis.

Figure 6.1 shows the planning horizons and how a business plan cascades into the various hierarchical materials and capacity plans. The **aggregate production plan** (APP) is a long-range materials plan. Since capacity expansion involves the construction of a new

| Figure 6.1 | Manufacturing Planning and Control System |

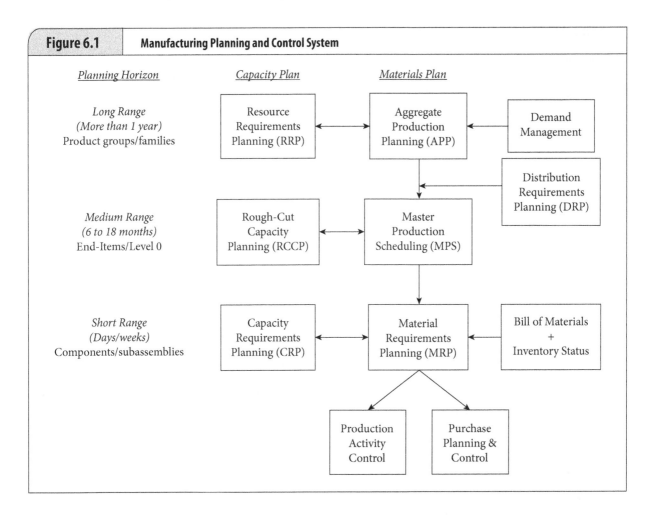

facility and major equipment purchases, the aggregate production plan's capacity is usually considered fixed during the planning horizon. The aggregate production plan sets the aggregate output rate, workforce size, utilization and inventory, and/or backlog levels for an entire facility. The **master production schedule** (MPS) is a medium-range plan and is more detailed than the aggregate production plan. It shows the quantity and timing of the end items that will be produced. The **material requirements plan** (MRP) is a short-range materials plan. MRP is the detailed planning process for the required component parts to support the master production schedule. It is a system of converting the end items from the master production schedule into a set of time-phased component part requirements.

Material requirements planning was first developed in the 1960s. As it gained popularity among manufacturers in the 1980s and as computing technologies emerged, MRP grew in scope into **manufacturing resource planning** (MRP-II). MRP-II combined MRP with master production scheduling, rough-cut capacity planning, capacity requirement planning, and other operations planning software modules. Eventually, the MRP-II system evolved into **enterprise resource planning** (ERP) in the 1990s.

Distribution requirements planning (DRP) describes the time-phased net requirements from central supply warehouses and distribution centers. It links production with distribution planning by providing aggregate time-phased net requirements information to the master production schedule.

THE AGGREGATE PRODUCTION PLAN

Aggregate production planning is a hierarchical planning process that translates annual business plans and demand forecasts into a production plan for all products. As shown in Figure 6.1, *demand management* includes determining the aggregate demand based on forecasts of future demand, customer orders, special promotions, and safety stock requirements. This forecast of demand then sets the aggregate utilization, production rate, workforce levels, and inventory balances or backlogs. Aggregate production plans are typically stated in terms of product families or groups. A **product family** consists of different products that share similar characteristics, components, or manufacturing processes. For example, an all-terrain vehicle (ATV) manufacturer who produces both automatic and manual drive options may group the two different types of ATVs together, since the only difference between them is the drive option. Production processes and material requirements for the two ATVs are likely to be very similar and, thus, can be grouped into a family.

The planning horizon covered by the APP is normally at least one year and is usually extended or rolled forward by three months every quarter. This allows the firm to see its capacity requirements at least one year ahead on a continuous basis. The APP *disaggregates* the demand forecast information it receives and links the long-range business plan to the medium-range master production schedule. The objective is to provide sufficient finished goods in each period to meet the sales plan while meeting financial and production constraints.

Costs relevant to the aggregate planning decision include inventory cost, setup cost, machine operating cost, hiring cost, firing cost, training cost, overtime cost, and costs incurred for hiring part-time and temporary workers to meet peak demand. There are three basic production strategies that firms use for completing the aggregate plan: (1) the *chase strategy*, (2) the *level strategy*, and (3) the *mixed strategy*. Example 6.1 provides an illustration of an APP.

The Chase Production Strategy

The **chase production strategy** adjusts capacity to match the demand pattern. Using this strategy, the firm will hire and lay off workers to match its production rate to demand. The workforce fluctuates from month to month, but finished goods inventory remains constant. Using Example 6.1, the ATV Corporation will use six workers to make 120 units in January, and then lay off a worker in February to produce 100 units, as shown in

---

Example 6.1   An Aggregate Production Plan for the ATV Corporation

The ATV Corporation makes three models of all-terrain vehicles: Model A, Model B, and Model C. Model A uses a 0.4-liter engine, Model B uses a 0.5-liter engine, and Model C uses a 0.6-liter engine. The aggregate production plan is the twelve-month plan that combines all three models together in total monthly production. The planning horizon is twelve months. The APP determines the size of the workforce, which is the constrained resource. Table 6.1 shows the annual aggregate production plan from January to December, assuming the beginning inventory for January is 100 units (30 units each of Model A and Model B, and 40 units of Model C), and the firm desires to have an ending inventory of 140 units at the end of the year. On average, 1 unit of ATV requires eight labor hours to produce, and a worker contributes 160 hours (8 hours × 5 days × 4 weeks) per month. Note that the 1,120 labor hours needed in December as shown in Table 6.1 excludes the labor hours (8 hours × 40 units = 320 hours) required to produce the additional 40 units, which is the difference between the January beginning inventory of 100 units and the desired December ending inventory of 140 units. The final column in Table 6.1 (planned capacity) refers to a typical manufacturing workforce situation wherein the firm desires to maintain a minimum core workforce of ten workers while relying on overtime and subcontracting to handle the forecasted high seasonal demands.

Table 6.1	ATV Corporation's Aggregate Production Plan		
		CAPACITY (LABOR HOURS)	
PERIOD	**FORECAST DEMAND**	**NEEDED**	**PLANNED**
January	120 units	960 hrs	10 workers
February	100 units	800 hrs	10 workers
March	300 units	2,400 hrs	12 workers + overtime
April	460 units	3,680 hrs	18 workers + overtime
May	600 units	4,800 hrs	25 workers + overtime
June	700 units	5,600 hrs	25 workers + overtime + subcontracting
July	760 units	6,080 hrs	25 workers + overtime + subcontracting
August	640 units	5,120 hrs	25 workers + overtime
September	580 units	4,640 hrs	25 workers + overtime
October	400 units	3,200 hrs	20 workers
November	200 units	1,600 hrs	10 workers
December	140 units	1,120 hrs	10 workers
	5,000 units	40,000 hrs	

Table 6.2	An Example of the Chase Production Strategy				
			CAPACITY NEEDED (LABOR)		**ENDING**
PERIOD	**FORECAST DEMAND (UNITS)**	**PRODUCTION (UNITS)**	**HOURS**	**WORKERS**	**INVENTORY (UNITS)**
January	120	120	960	6	100
February	100	100	800	5	100
March	300	300	2,400	15	100
April	460	460	3,680	23	100
May	600	600	4,800	30	100
June	700	700	5,600	35	100
July	760	760	6,080	38	100
August	640	640	5,120	32	100
September	580	580	4,640	29	100
October	400	400	3,200	20	100
November	200	200	1,600	10	100
December	140 + 40	180	1,120 + 320	9	140
	5,040	5,040	40,320	252	

Table 6.2. In March, the firm must hire ten additional workers so that it has enough labor to produce 300 units. An additional eight workers must be hired in April. The firm continues its hiring and lay-off policy to ensure its workforce and production capacity matches demand. In December, 180 units will be produced (although the demand is 140) because of the firm's desire to increase its ending inventory by 40 units in December.

The chase strategy obviously has a negative motivational impact on the workers, and it assumes that workers can be hired and trained easily to perform the job. In this strategy, the finished goods inventories always remain constant but the workforce fluctuates in response to the demand pattern. Figure 6.2 shows that the chase production curve perfectly overlaps on the demand curve. The inventory level remains constant at 100 units until December, when it increases by 40 units. Hiring, training, and termination costs are significant cost components in the chase production strategy.

This strategy works well for **make-to-order** manufacturing firms since they cannot rely on finished goods inventory to satisfy the fluctuating demand pattern. Make-to-order firms generally produce one-of-a-kind, specialty products based on customer specifications. Make-to-order firms cannot build ahead of orders since they do not know the actual specifications of the finished goods. However, make-to-order products generally require highly skilled labor, capable of producing unique products using general-purpose equipment. Although a chase production strategy works well when unskilled labor is required, the strategy can be problematic when highly skilled workers are needed, especially in a tight labor market.

The Level Production Strategy

A **level production strategy** relies on a constant output rate and capacity while varying inventory and backlog levels to handle the fluctuating demand pattern. Using this strategy, the firm keeps its workforce levels constant and relies on fluctuating finished goods inventories and backlogs to meet demand. Since the level production strategy keeps a constant output rate and capacity, it is more suited for firms that require highly skilled labor. The workforce is likely to be more effective and their morale is higher when compared to the chase strategy. Using the Example 6.1 forecast information, a level production strategy calls for a monthly production rate of 420 units ([5,000 units annual demand + 40 units additional ending inventory] ÷ 12 months). Thus, this strategy requires a constant workforce of twenty-one workers, as shown in Table 6.3.

The firm allows finished goods inventories to accrue while cumulative demand remains less than cumulative production, and then relies on a series of backlogs to handle the

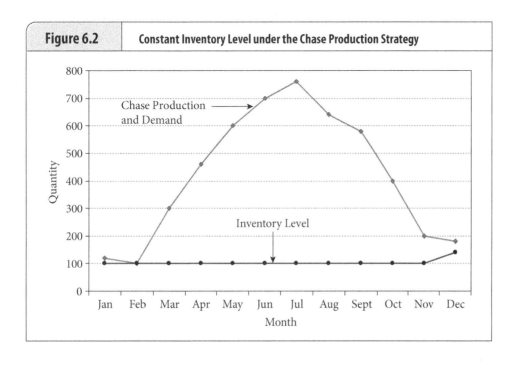

| **Figure 6.2** | **Constant Inventory Level under the Chase Production Strategy** |

Table 6.3	An Example of Level Production Strategy				
			CAPACITY NEEDED (LABOR)		ENDING INV/
PERIOD	FORECAST DEMAND (UNITS)	PRODUCTION (UNITS)	HOURS	WORKERS	(BACKLOG) (UNITS)
January	120	420	3,360	21	400
February	100	420	3,360	21	720
March	300	420	3,360	21	840
April	460	420	3,360	21	800
May	600	420	3,360	21	620
June	700	420	3,360	21	340
July	760	420	3,360	21	0
August	640	420	3,360	21	(220)
September	580	420	3,360	21	(380)
October	400	420	3,360	21	(360)
November	200	420	3,360	21	(140)
December	140 + 40	420	3,360	21	140
	5,040	5,040	40,320	252	

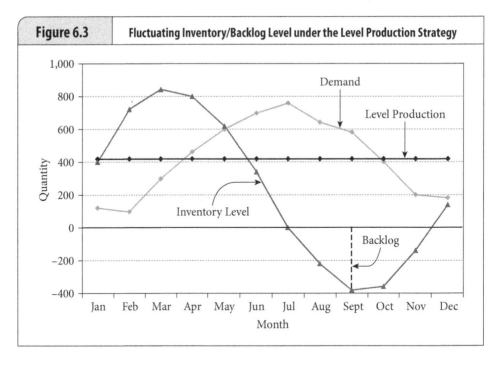

Figure 6.3   Fluctuating Inventory/Backlog Level under the Level Production Strategy

demand from August through November. Figure 6.3 shows that level production is characterized by the fluctuating inventory/backlog level while the workforce and production capacity remain constant. Inventory carrying and stockout costs are major cost concerns in the level production strategy. This strategy works well for **make-to-stock** manufacturing firms, which typically emphasize immediate delivery of off-the-shelf, standard goods at relatively low prices. Firms whose trading partners seek the lowest prices of stock items might select the level production strategy. Additionally, this strategy works well in a situation where highly skilled workers are needed in a tight labor market.

The Mixed Production Strategy

Instead of using either the chase or level production strategy, many firms use a **mixed production strategy** that strives to maintain a stable core workforce while using other short-term means such as overtime, an additional shift, subcontracting, or the hiring of part-time and temporary workers to manage short-term high demand. Usually, these firms will then schedule preventive maintenance, produce complementary products that require similar resources but different demand cycles, or continue to produce the end items, holding these as finished goods inventory during the off-peak demand periods.

For example, ATV manufacturers can produce snowmobiles to smooth out the seasonal effect of the two products. Table 6.1 shows the mixed strategy (referred to earlier, using the planned capacity column) in which the firm strives to maintain a minimum core workforce of ten workers while avoiding hiring above 25 workers during the peak or high demand season. Hiring above 25 workers may strain other capacities, such as machine capacity and the availability of component parts. Instead, the mixed strategy uses overtime and subcontracting to cope with the high demand periods. If labor is the only constrained capacity, it may hire enough workers to run an additional shift to cope with the high demand. We can see here that firms with multiple products and with customers seeking both low-cost and make-to-order items may opt for this type of production strategy to minimize stockouts and cycle time.

THE MASTER PRODUCTION SCHEDULE

The master production schedule is a time-phased, detailed disaggregation of the aggregate production plan, listing the exact end items to be produced. It is more detailed than the aggregate production plan. The MPS planning horizon is shorter than the aggregate production plan's, but must be longer than a firm's production lead time to ensure the end item can be completed within the planning horizon.

For example, disaggregating ATV Corporation's January and February aggregate production plans may yield the master production schedule shown in Table 6.4. The plan results in time-phased production requirements of the specific model of ATV to produce for every week in January and February. The sum of the weekly MPS matches the quantity of the APP for that same month. For example, the MPS quantities for January and February

Table 6.4	ATV's Master Production Schedule for January and February			
		MPS QUANTITY		
PERIOD	**APP QUANTITY**	**MODEL A**	**MODEL B**	**MODEL C**
January—week 1	120 units	10	10	10
January—week 2		10	10	10
January—week 3		20	0	10
January—week 4		0	20	10
February—week 1	100 units	20	0	0
February—week 2		0	20	0
February—week 3		0	0	20
February—week 4		20	20	0
Total	220 units	80	80	60

in Table 6.4 (80, 80, and 60 units for the three models) equal the monthly APP quantities of 120 and 100 units, respectively. The master production schedule provides more detail by breaking down the aggregate production plan into specific weekly demand for Model A, Model B, and Model C.

For the service industry, the master production schedule may just be the appointment book or scheduling software, which is created to ensure that capacity in the form of skilled labor matches demand. Master production schedules in the form of appointments are not overbooked to ensure capacity is not strained. The firm continues to revise and add appointments to the MPS until it obtains the best possible schedule. An example is to schedule patients' appointments in a hospital by means of a medical appointment scheduling software application.

Master Production Schedule Time Fence

The master production schedule is the production quantity required to meet demand from all sources and is the basis for computing the requirements of all time-phased end items. The material requirements plan uses the MPS to compute component part and subassembly requirements. Frequent changes to the MPS can be costly and may create system nervousness.

System nervousness can be defined as a situation wherein a small change in the upper-level production plan causes a major change in the lower-level production plan. For example, in the case of the clinic booking new appointments, it is very difficult for the clinic to book additional appointments for the current period because it is very likely that the appointment book is already fully booked. If a patient insists that she must see the doctor immediately, it is likely that another patient's appointment may have to be delayed or the clinic would need to work overtime to see an additional patient. However, it is much easier for the clinic to book new appointments farther into the future.

System nervousness can create serious problems for manufacturing firms. For example, if the January production plan for the ATV Corporation is suddenly doubled during the second week of January, the firm would be forced to quickly revise purchase orders, component assembly orders, and end-item production orders, causing a ripple effect of change within the firm and up its supply chain to its suppliers. The change would also likely cause missed delivery due dates. The firm needs sufficient lead time to purchase items and manufacture the end items, especially if manufacturing lead times and lot sizes are large.

Many firms use a **time fence system** to deal with this problem. The time fence system separates the planning horizon into two segments: a *firmed* and a *tentative segment*. A firmed segment is also known as a **demand time fence**, and it usually stretches from the current period to a period several weeks into the future. A firmed segment stipulates that the production plan or MPS cannot be altered except with the authorization of senior management. The tentative segment is also known as the **planning time fence**, and it typically stretches from the end of the firmed segment to several weeks farther into the future. It usually covers a longer period than the firmed segment, and the master scheduler can change production to meet changing conditions. Beyond the planning time fence, the computer can schedule the MPS quantities automatically, based on existing ordering and scheduling policies.

Available-to-Promise Quantities

In addition to providing time-phased production quantities of specific end items, the MPS also provides vital information on whether additional orders can be accepted for delivery in specific periods. This information is particularly important when customers are relying on the firm to deliver the right quantity of products purchased on the desired delivery date. This information is the **available-to-promise (ATP) quantity**, or the uncommitted portion of the firm's planned production (or scheduled MPS). It is the difference between confirmed customer orders and the quantity the firm planned to produce, based on the MPS. The available-to-promise quantity provides a mechanism to allow the master scheduler or sales personnel to quickly negotiate new orders and delivery due dates with customers or to quickly respond to customers' changing demands. The three basic methods of calculating the available-to-promise quantities are (1) *discrete available-to-promise*, (2) *cumulative available-to-promise without look ahead*, and (3) *cumulative available-to-promise with look ahead*. The discrete available-to-promise (ATP:D) computation is discussed next. Readers who are interested in the other two methods are referred to Fogarty, Blackstone, and Hoffmann (1991).[5]

The ATV Corporation's January and February master production schedule for Model A, Model B, and Model C is used in Table 6.5 to demonstrate the ATP:D method for computing the ATP quantities. Let us assume there are four weeks each in January and February, which are shown in the first row and are labeled Week 1 to Week 8. The MPS row indicates the time-phased production quantities derived from the master production schedule in Table 6.4. These are the quantities to be produced by manufacturing as planned. The number labeled "BI" is the beginning inventory heading into the first week of January. Committed customer orders are orders that have already been booked for specific customers. Finally, the ATP:D quantities are the remaining unbooked or unpromised units.

Calculating Discrete Available-to-Promise Quantities

The ATP:D is computed as follows:

1. The ATP for the first period is the sum of the beginning inventory and the MPS, minus the sum of all the committed customer orders (CCOs) from period 1 up to but not including the period of the next scheduled MPS.

2. For all subsequent periods, there are two possibilities:

   a. If no MPS has been scheduled for the period, the ATP is zero.

   b. If an MPS has been scheduled for the period, the ATP is the MPS quantity minus the sum of all CCOs from that period up to but not including the period of the next scheduled MPS.

3. If an ATP for any period is negative, the deficit must be subtracted from the most recent positive ATP, and the quantities must be revised to reflect these changes.

As a check, the sum of the BI and MPS quantities for all periods must equal the sum of all CCOs and ATPs. Using these guidelines, the ATP:D quantities in Table 6.5 are computed as follows:

Model A

1. $\text{ATP}_1 = \text{BI} + \text{MPS}_1 - \text{CCO}_1 = 30 + 10 - 10 = 30$
2. $\text{ATP}_2 = \text{MPS}_2 - \text{CCO}_2 = 10 - 0 = 10$
3. $\text{ATP}_3 = \text{MPS}_3 - \text{CCO}_3 - \text{CCO}_4 = 20 - 28 - 0 = -8$ (need to use 8 units from ATP_2)

   Revising: $\text{ATP}_2 = 10 - 8 = 2$ and $\text{ATP}_3 = -8 + 8 = 0$
4. $\text{ATP}_4 = 0$ (no scheduled MPS)

Table 6.5	Discrete ATP Calculation for January and February									
WEEK		1	2	3	4	5	6	7	8
Model A—0.4 Liter Engine									
MPS	BI = 30	10	10	20	0	20	0	0	20
Committed Customer Orders		10	0	28	0	0	20	0	10
ATP:D		30	2	0	0	0	0	0	10
Model B—0.5 Liter Engine									
MPS	BI = 30	10	10	0	20	0	20	0	20
Committed Customer Orders		20	10	7	0	0	20	18	0
ATP:D		13	0	0	2	0	0	0	20
Model C—0.6 Liter Engine									
MPS	BI = 40	10	10	10	10	0	0	20	0
Committed Customer Orders		20	10	0	0	0	10	0	15
ATP:D		30	0	10	0	0	0	5	0

5. $ATP_5 = MPS_5 - CCO_5 - CCO_6 - CCO_7 = 20 - 0 - 20 - 0 = 0$

6. $ATP_6 = 0$ (no scheduled MPS)

7. $ATP_7 = 0$ (no scheduled MPS)

8. $ATP_8 = MPS_8 - CCO_8 = 20 - 10 = 10$

Checking the calculations, the sum of the BI and MPS quantities for the eight periods equals 110 units, which is also the sum of the CCOs and the ATPs for the same periods. Further, the calculation shows that 30 units of the Model A ATV can be promised for delivery in the first week of January or later, 2 units can be promised in the second week or later, and another 10 units can be promised for delivery in the eighth week or later. The eight-period total ATP of 42 units is the difference between the sum of the beginning inventory and MPS (110 units), and the sum of the committed customer orders (68 units) for the eight weeks. Also note that although no MPS has been scheduled for the sixth week, the committed customer orders of 20 units are still possible, since the units can come from the uncommitted MPS of the previous weeks.

Model B

1. $ATP_1 = BI + MPS_1 - CCO_1 = 30 + 10 - 20 = 20$

2. $ATP_2 = MPS_2 - CCO_2 - CCO_3 = 10 - 10 - 7 = -7$ (need to use 7 units from ATP_1)

   Revising: $ATP_1 = 20 - 7 = 13$ and $ATP_2 = -7 + 7 = 0$

3. $ATP_3 = 0$ (no scheduled MPS)

4. $ATP_4 = MPS_4 - CCO_4 - CCO_5 = 20 - 0 - 0 = 20$

5. $ATP_5 = 0$ (no scheduled MPS)

6. $ATP_6 = MPS_6 - CCO_6 - CCO_7 = 20 - 20 - 18 = -18$ (need to use 18 units from ATP_4 since $ATP_5 = 0$)

   Revising: $ATP_4 = 20 - 18 = 2$ and $ATP_6 = -18 + 18 = 0$

7. $ATP_7 = 0$ (no scheduled MPS)

8. $ATP_8 = MPS_8 - CCO_8 = 20 - 0 = 20$

Checking, the BI plus the eight MPS weekly quantities equals 110 units and the CCOs plus the ATPs for the eight periods also equals 110 units. The calculation shows that 13 units of the Model B ATV can be promised for delivery in the first week or later, 2 units can be promised for delivery in the fourth week or later, and another 20 units can be promised for delivery in the eighth week or later. The eight-period total ATP of 35 units is the difference between the sum of the beginning inventory and MPS (110 units), and the sum of the committed customer orders (75 units) for the eight-week period. Note that although no MPS has been scheduled for the seventh week, the CCO of 18 units came from the uncommitted MPS quantities of the previous weeks.

Model C

1. $ATP_1 = BI + MPS_1 - CCO_1 = 40 + 10 - 20 = 30$
2. $ATP_2 = MPS_2 - CCO_2 = 10 - 10 = 0$
3. $ATP_3 = MPS_3 - CCO_3 = 10 - 0 = 10$
4. $ATP_4 = MPS_4 - CCO_4 - CCO_5 - CCO_6 = 10 - 0 - 0 - 10 = 0$
5. $ATP_5 = 0$ (no scheduled MPS)
6. $ATP_6 = 0$ (no scheduled MPS)
7. $ATP_7 = MPS_7 - CCO_7 - CCO_8 = 20 - 0 - 15 = 5$
8. $ATP_8 = 0$ (no scheduled MPS)

Checking, the total BI and eight-period MPS is 100 units and the total CCOs and ATPs for the eight periods is also 100 units. The calculation shows that 30 units of Model C ATV can be promised for delivery in the first week of January or later, 10 units can be promised in the third week or later, and another 5 units can be promised in the seventh week or later. The total of eight-period ATP of 45 units is the difference between the sum of the BI and MPS (100 units), and the sum of the committed customer orders (55 units) for the eight-week period.

Note that while the total uncommitted production quantity can easily be computed by subtracting all CCOs from the scheduled MPS, it lacks time-phased information. For this reason, the ATP quantities must be determined as shown. This enables the master scheduler or salesperson to quickly book or confirm new sales to be delivered on specific due dates. Reacting quickly to demand changes and delivering orders on time are necessities in high-performing supply chains, and the tools discussed here enable firms to effectively meet customer needs. In supply chain relationships, using the MPS and ATP information effectively is essential to maintaining speed and flexibility (which impacts customer service) throughout the supply chain as products make their way to end users.

THE BILL OF MATERIALS

The **bill of materials (BOM)** is an engineering document that shows an inclusive listing of all component parts and subassemblies making up the end item. Figure 6.4 is an example of a *multilevel bill of materials* for the ATV Corporation's all-terrain vehicles. It shows the parent–component relationships and the exact quantity of each component, known as the **planning factor**, required for making a higher-level part or assembly. For example, "engine assembly" is the immediate *parent* of "engine block," and conversely "engine block" is an immediate *component* of "engine assembly." The "24-inch solid steel bar" is a *common component part*, because it is a component of the "6-inch steel bar" and the "12-inch steel bar." The *planning factor* of "connecting rods" shows that four connecting rods are needed

| Figure 6.4 | Bill of Materials for the ATV |

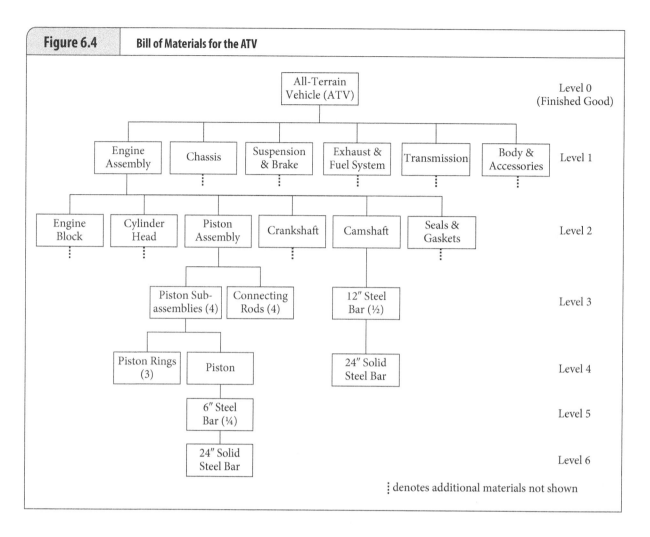

to make one "piston assembly." Note that twelve "piston rings" (3 × 4) are needed to assemble one ATV since there are three "piston rings" in each "piston subassembly," and there are four "piston subassemblies" in each "piston assembly."

The BOM is shown in various levels, starting from Level 0. The level numbers increase as one moves down on the BOM. Level 0 is the final product, which is the **independent demand** item. In this case, it is the ATV. It has a demand pattern that is subject to trends and seasonal variations, and to general market conditions. Gross requirements of Level 0 items come from the master production schedule (i.e., Table 6.4 in the ATV Corporation example). The next level in the BOM is Level 1, which consists of all components and subassemblies required for the final assembly of 1 unit of an ATV. The gross requirements of Level 1 components and subassemblies are computed based on the demand for ATVs as specified in Level 0. Therefore, the requirements for all the items in Level 1 and below are called **dependent demand** items. For example, the engine assembly, chassis, suspension and brake, and transmission used to assemble the ATV are dependent demand items. However, if the components or subassemblies are sold as *service parts* to customers for repairing their ATVs, then they are independent demand items.

Correspondingly, the multilevel bill of materials can also be presented as an **indented bill of materials** as shown in Table 6.6. At each level of indentation, the level number

Table 6.6	Indented Bill of Materials—All-Terrain Vehicles	
PART DESCRIPTION	**LEVEL**	**PLANNING FACTOR**
Engine Assembly	1	1
Engine Block (components not shown)	2	1
Cylinder Head (components not shown)	2	1
Piston Assembly	2	1
Piston Subassembly	3	4
Piston Rings	4	3
Pistons	4	1
6" Steel Bar	5	¼
24" Solid Steel Bar	6	1
Connecting Rods	3	4
Crankshaft (components not shown)	2	1
Camshaft	2	1
12" Steel Bar	3	½
24" Solid Steel Bar	4	1
Seals & Gaskets (components not shown)	2	1
Chassis (components not shown)	1	1
Suspension & Brake (components not shown)	1	1
Exhaust & Fuel System (components not shown)	1	1
Transmission (components not shown)	1	1
Body & Accessories (components not shown)	1	1

increases by one. The indented bill of materials in Table 6.6 can be seen as an illustration of the multilevel bill of materials (Figure 6.4) rotated 90 degrees counterclockwise.

Another type of bill of materials is the **super bill of materials**, which is useful for planning purposes. It is also referred to as a *planning bill of materials, pseudo bill of materials, phantom bill of materials*, or *family bill of materials*. Using the ATV Corporation's BOM in Figure 6.4 as an example, a simplified product structure diagram can be created for the family of ATVs that consists of different engine sizes (i.e., models) and transmission options. Instead of stating the planning factor, the percentage of each option is used. Figure 6.5 shows that 33⅓ percent of the ATVs are Model A, Model B, and Model C, respectively. Similarly, 75 percent of the ATVs use automatic transmissions and the remaining 25 percent use manual transmissions. Therefore, the ATV Corporation's January planned production (120 units) consists of 40 units each of Model A, Model B, and Model C (see Table 6.4. Similarly, 90 (75 percent × 120) units of the ATVs will be manufactured with automatic transmissions, and the remaining 30 (25 percent × 120) units will be manufactured with manual transmissions.

The super bill of materials enables the firm to forecast the total demand of ATVs and then break down the forecast into different models and transmission options using the correct percentage, instead of forecasting the demand for each option individually. It provides quick information on the quantity of components for each option needed for the scheduled production. In addition, it also reduces the number of master production schedules. For the ATV Corporation example, the number of master production schedules was reduced from six (3 models × 2 transmission options) to one.

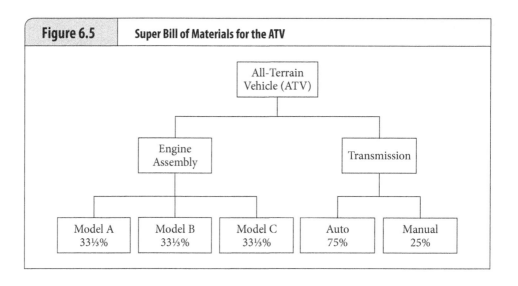

Figure 6.5 — **Super Bill of Materials for the ATV**

When the exact proportion of each option is uncertain, the percentage can be increased slightly to cover the uncertainty. For example, the ATV Corporation may increase its automatic transmission option to 78 percent and manual option to 27 percent, for a total of 105 percent. The firm raises its total planned production by 5 percent to cover uncertainty. This is known as **option overplanning**.

THE MATERIAL REQUIREMENTS PLAN

As illustrated in the ATV bill of materials in Figure 6.4, **dependent demand** is a term used to describe the internal demand for parts based on the **independent demand** of the final product, for which the parts are used. Subassemblies, components, and raw materials are examples of dependent demand items. Dependent demand may have a pattern of abrupt and dramatic changes because of its dependency on the demand of the final product, especially if the final product is produced in large lot sizes. Once the independent demand of the final product is known or forecasted, the dependent demand item requirements can be exactly calculated using material requirements planning (MRP) software, along with when the items should be assembled or purchased.

For example, the ATV Corporation's MPS (Table 6.4) shows that 120 ATVs will be produced in January. The firm thus knows that 120 handlebars and 480 wheel rims will be needed. The demand for handlebars, wheel rims, and all of the other dependent demand items can be calculated using the MRP, based on the BOM and the demand of the final product as stated on the MPS.

Material requirements planning is a software-based production planning and inventory control system that has been used widely by manufacturing firms for computing dependent demand and timing requirements. With the advent of computer and information technologies, the span of MRP evolved to include aggregate production planning, master production scheduling, and capacity requirements planning to become **closed-loop MRP**. It further evolved into manufacturing resource planning (MRP-II) by including other aspects of materials and resource planning. A complete MRP-II system consists of many modules that enable the firm to book orders, schedule production, control inventory, manage distribution, and perform accounting and financial analyses.

While there are vendors still supporting their original MRP systems, most application providers have expanded their systems to enable the users to perform more sophisticated analyses and integrate organization-wide activities, including operations and facilities that are located in different countries from the head office. The current generation of MRP system is known as the ERP system.

Material requirements planning is used to calculate the exact quantities, need dates, and planned order releases for components and subassemblies needed to manufacture the final products listed on the MPS. MRP begins the computation process by first obtaining the requirements of the final product (the Level 0 item on the BOM) from the MPS to calculate the requirements of Level 1 components and then working its way down to the lowest level components, taking into account existing inventories and the time required for each processing step. While these manufacturing and delivery lead times are disregarded in the MPS, they are considered in the MRP computation process. For example, if a parent item requires an immediate component with a three-week lead time, the component must be ordered three weeks ahead of the need date.

For MRP, a dependent demand management system, to work effectively, it requires (1) the independent demand information (the demand for the final product or service part) from the MPS; (2) parent–component relationships from the bill of materials, including the planning factor and lead-time information; and (3) the inventory status of the final product and all of its components. The MRP takes this information to compute the *net requirements* of the final product and components, and then offsets the net requirements with appropriate lead times to ensure orders are released on time for fabricating the higher level components or purchasing the lower level components. This information, called **planned order releases**, is the most important output of the MRP. For items manufactured in-house, planned order releases are transmitted to the shop floor, but for purchased items, planned order releases are transmitted to suppliers directly or via the purchasing department.

A key benefit of MRP is that production information—such as scheduled receipts, on-hand inventories, net requirements, and planned order releases—is available for the entire planning horizon; thus, it provides *visibility* for schedulers to plan ahead. However, the need for offsetting net requirements by the lead time to obtain planned order releases causes a *loss of visibility* in the planning horizon of components. This problem is especially acute for products with a deep bill of materials. Another drawback of the MRP is that it ignores capacity and shop floor conditions.

Terms Used in Material Requirements Planning

Prior to exploring the MRP logic, let us look at some terms as they apply to the MRP:

- *Parent*: The item generating the demand for lower level components. Level 0 is the final product. It is the parent of all Level 1 components. Similarly, each Level 1 item becomes the parent of the Level 2 components used to make that item. For example, Figure 6.4 shows that "piston assembly" is a parent of "piston subassemblies" and "connecting rods."

- *Components*: The parts demanded by a parent. For example, Figure 6.4 shows that "piston assembly" is a component of "engine assembly."

- *Gross requirement*: A time-phased requirement prior to considering on-hand inventory and lead time to obtain the item. It is satisfied from inventory and production.

- *Net requirement*: The unsatisfied item requirement for a specific time period. It equals the gross requirement for that period minus the current on-hand inventory and any scheduled receipts. Net requirement must be met from future production or purchase.

- *Scheduled receipt*: A committed order awaiting delivery for a specific period. It is an order released in a past period and due to be received in a specific later period. This information is updated automatically by the MRP software logic system once an order has been placed. For example, an item with a two-week lead time ordered on the first week of the month becomes a scheduled receipt on the third week.

- *Projected on-hand inventory*: The projected inventory at the end of the period. It equals the beginning inventory minus the gross requirement, plus the scheduled receipt and any planned receipt from an earlier planned order release.

- *Planned order receipt*: A projected receipt based on the generation of a planned order release. It is used as a placeholder for the planned order release, prior to offsetting the production and/or delivery lead time.

- *Planned order release*: A specific order to be released to the shop (if the component is made in-house) or to the supplier (if the component is purchased) to ensure that it is available on the need date. A key consideration here is that the *planned order releases of the parent determine the gross requirements of the components*.

- *Time bucket*: The time period used on the MRP. It is usually expressed in days or weeks. The current period is the *action time bucket*.

- *Explosion*: The common term used to describe the process of converting a parent item's planned order releases into component gross requirements.

- *Planning factor*: The number of components needed to make a unit of the parent item. For example, Figure 6.4 shows that three "piston rings" are needed to make a "piston subassembly."

- *Firmed planned order*: A planned order that the MRP software logic system cannot automatically change when conditions change. The primary purpose of a firmed planned order is to prevent *system nervousness*, similar to the time fence system explained earlier in the master production schedule discussion.

- *Pegging*: Relates gross requirements for a component to the planned order releases that created the requirements.

- *Low-level coding*: Assigns the lowest level on the bill of materials to all common components to avoid duplicate MRP computations. For example, Figure 6.4 shows that "24-inch solid steel bar" is a common component in Level 4 and Level 6. Instead of computing its planned order releases at Level 4 and Level 6 separately, a low-level code of 6 is assigned to the item. Its net requirements at Level 4 are added to those at Level 6, and the MRP explosion logic is performed at Level 6 only.

- *Lot size*: The order size for MRP logic. Lot size may be determined by various lot-sizing techniques, such as the EOQ (a fixed order quantity) or lot-for-lot (LFL) (order whatever amount is needed each period). A lot size of 50 calls for orders to be placed in multiples of 50. With a net requirement of 85 units, using LFL order sizing will result in an order of 85 units; however, an order of 100 units would be placed when using a fixed order quantity of 50 (order sizes are multiples of 50).

- *Safety stock*: Protects against uncertainties in demand, supply, quality, and lead time. Its implication in MRP logic is that the minimum projected on-hand inventory should not fall below the safety stock level.

An Example of MRP Computation without Net Requirements and Planned Order Receipts

An MRP computation is provided in Example 6.2. (This example and all the answer keys in this chapter do not use net requirements or planned order receipts in the MRP computation.)

Example 6.2   An MRP Example at the ATV Corporation

Model A's production schedule for the ATV Corporation is used to illustrate the MRP logic. Its gross requirements are first obtained from the master production schedule in Table 6.4, and the inventory status shows that 30 units of Model A are available at the start of the year. The parent–component relationships and planning factors are available from the BOM in Figure 6.4. Assuming the following lot sizes (Q), lead times (LT), and safety stocks (SS) are used, the MRP computations of the Model A ATV and some of its components are as follows:

MODEL A ATV—LEVEL 0		1	2	3	4	5	6	7	8
Gross Requirements		10	10	20	0	20	0	0	20
Scheduled Receipts			10						
Projected On-hand Inventory	30	20	20	20	20	20	20	20	20
Planned Order Releases		20		20			20		

Q = 10; LT = 2; SS = 15

×1   ×1   ×1

ENGINE ASSEMBLY—LEVEL 1		1	2	3	4	5	6	7	8
Gross Requirements		20		20		20			
Scheduled Receipts		20							
Projected On-hand Inventory	2	2	2	0	0	0	0	0	0
Planned Order Releases		18			20				

Q = LFL; LT = 2; SS = 0

×1   ×1

PISTON ASSEMBLY—LEVEL 2		1	2	3	4	5	6	7	8
Gross Requirements		18			20				
Scheduled Receipts		20							
Projected On-hand Inventory	10	12	12	12	22	22	22	22	22
Planned Order Releases				30					

Q = 30; LT = 1; SS = 10

×4

CONNECTING RODS—LEVEL 3		1	2	3	4	5	6	7	8
Gross Requirements				120					
Scheduled Receipts									
Projected On-hand Inventory	22	22	22	52	52	52	52	52	52
Planned Order Releases			150						

Q = 50; LT = 1; SS = 20

Level 0 MRP Computation—Model A ATV

The first row is the planning horizon for the eight weeks in January and February. The gross requirements are derived directly from the MPS. The scheduled receipt of 10 units in Week 2 is due to an order placed last week, or earlier but scheduled to be delivered on Week 2. The order size for the Model A ATV is in multiples of 10 units, the lead time is two weeks, and the desired safety stock is 15 units. The projected on-hand inventory of 20 units for the first week is computed by taking the beginning inventory of 30 units and subtracting the gross requirement of 10 units in that week. The projected on-hand inventory of 20 units in Week 2 is computed by taking the previous balance of 20 units, adding the scheduled receipt of 10 units, and subtracting the gross requirement of 10 units.

During the third week, additional Model A ATVs must be completed to ensure the on-hand balance is above the safety stock level of 15 units. Since the opening inventory of 20 units is entirely consumed to meet the week three gross requirement, the net requirement here is 15 units (the safety stock). Given that orders must be in multiples of ten, 20 units must be ordered in the first week to satisfy both the lead time and the safety stock requirements. Simply stated, if 20 units are needed in the third week, the two-week lead time requires the order to be placed two weeks earlier, which explains why there is a planned order release of 20 units in the first week. The on-hand inventory balance of 20 units at the end of the third week is computed by taking the previous balance of 20 units, adding the planned order receipt of 20 units (due to the planned order release in the first week), and subtracting the gross requirement of 20 units.

Similarly, the gross requirements of 20 units each in the fifth and eighth week consumed the beginning inventory, triggering a net requirement of 15 units for those periods and a planned order release of 20 units each during the third and sixth week, respectively.

Level 1 MRP Computation—Engine Assembly

The BOM in Figure 6.4 indicates that the gross requirements for the engine assembly are derived from the planned order releases of the Model A ATV. Since the planning factor is 1 unit, the Model A ATV's planned order releases translate directly into gross requirements for engine assembly in the first, third, and sixth week (as indicated by the arrows in Example 6.2). The scheduled receipt of 20 units in the first week is due to a committed order placed previously. The gross requirements of 20 units each for the third and sixth week triggered net requirements of 18 and 20 units, which turn into planned order releases for the first and fourth week, respectively (note here that no safety stock is required and the lot size is LFL, thus order sizes vary according to whatever quantities are needed to have end-of-period inventories of zero).

Level 2 MRP Computation—Piston Assembly

The gross requirements for the piston assembly are derived directly from the planned order releases of engine assembly (recall that based on the BOM in Figure 6.4, the engine assembly is the immediate parent of the piston assembly and the planning factor is one). Therefore, the gross requirements of piston assembly are 18 and 20 units, respectively, for the first and fourth weeks. Computations of its projected on-hand balances and planned order releases are similar to earlier examples (note here that inventories must not drop below the safety stock requirement of ten and order quantities must be made in multiples of 30).

Level 3 MRP Computation—Connecting Rods

The BOM in Figure 6.4 indicates that four connecting rods are required for each piston assembly. Thus, the gross requirement for connecting rods in the third week is obtained by multiplying the planned order releases for piston assemblies by four. Due to the requirement to offset the lead times in each MRP computation, the planned order release for connecting rods can be determined only up to the second period, although the gross requirements of the Model A ATV are known for the first eight weeks. This is known as *loss of visibility*, as discussed earlier.

Since there are no lower-level components shown for the connecting rods, we can assume that the ATV Corporation purchases this component. Thus, the planned order releases would be used by the purchasing department (as shown by the purchase planning and control function in Figure 6.1) to communicate order quantities and delivery requirements to its connecting rod supplier. Production activity control involves all aspects of shop floor scheduling, dispatching, routing, and other control activities. In supply chain settings, manufacturing firms share their planned order release information with their strategic suppliers through electronic data interchange (EDI), their ERP system, or other forms of communication. Since the firm manufactures its own piston assemblies, the planned order release for this part is communicated to shop floor operators and used to trigger production in that week. We can see, then, that planned order releases for purchased items eventually become the independent demand gross requirements for the firm's suppliers. Communicating this information accurately and quickly to strategic suppliers is a necessary element in an effective supply chain information system.

An Example of MRP Computation with Net Requirements and Planned Order Receipts

Example 6.3 shows the use of net requirements and planned order receipts in the MRP computation. Note that the computation of projected on-hand inventory differs slightly from Example 6.2. It is now possible to show negative projected on-hand inventory.

A general sequence to compute the MRP for an item is to (1) fill in the gross requirements for all time periods using its planning factor and parent's planned order releases, (2) compute the projected on-hand inventory, net requirement, and planned order receipt for the period, (3) if there is a planned order receipt, use the lead time to offset planned order release for the period, and (4) repeat steps 2, 3, and 4 until all the periods have been evaluated.

Level 0 MRP Computation—Model A ATV

The projected on-hand inventory of 20 units for the first and second weeks is computed as in Example 6.2. During the third week, the projected on-hand inventory is the beginning inventory of 20 units minus the gross requirement of 20 units, which equals to zero. However, additional Model A ATVs must be assembled to ensure the on-hand balance is above the safety stock level of 15 units. Thus, the net requirement is 15 units. Given that orders must be in multiples of ten, the planned order receipt is 20 units. To ensure that the 20 units of Model A ATV are received on week 3, the firm must place the order in the first week to meet the two-week lead time requirement.

Similarly, the gross requirements of 20 units each in the fifth and eighth week consumed the beginning of period inventory, triggering a net requirement of 15 units and planned order receipt of 20 units for those periods. Therefore, planned order releases of 20 units each must be placed during the third and sixth week to ensure the items are received on the fifth and eighth week, respectively.

Level 1 MRP Computation—Engine Assembly

Like Example 6.2, the gross requirements for the engine assembly came from the planned order releases of the Model A ATV. Since the planning factor is 1 unit, the planned order releases of Model A ATV translated to gross requirements for engine assembly of

Example 6.3   An MRP Example at the ATV Corporation with Net Requirements and Planned Order Receipts

The same master production schedule in Table 6.4, BOM in Figure 6.4, order lot sizes, and delivery lead times for the ATV Corporation are used to demonstrate net requirements and planned order receipts in the MRP computation.

MODEL A ATV—LEVEL 0		1	2	3	4	5	6	7	8
Gross Requirements		10	10	20	0	20	0	0	20
Scheduled Receipts			10						
Projected On-hand Inventory	30	20	20	0 (20)	20	0 (20)	20	20	0 (20)
Net Requirements				15		15			15
Planned Order Receipts				20		20			20
Planned Order Releases		20		20			20		

Q = 10; LT = 2; SS = 15

×1   ×1   ×1

ENGINE ASSEMBLY—LEVEL 1		1	2	3	4	5	6	7	8
Gross Requirements		20		20			20		
Scheduled Receipts		20							
Projected On-hand Inventory	2	2	2	−18 (0)	0	0	−20 (0)	0	0
Net Requirements				18			20		
Planned Order Receipts				18			20		
Planned Order Releases		18		20					

Q = LFL; LT = 2; SS = 0

×1   ×1

PISTON ASSEMBLY—LEVEL 2		1	2	3	4	5	6	7	8
Gross Requirements		18			20				
Scheduled Receipts		20							
Projected On-hand Inventory	10	12	12	12	−8 (22)	22	22	22	22
Net Requirements					18				
Planned Order Receipts					30				
Planned Order Releases				30					

Q = 30; LT = 1; SS = 10

×4

CONNECTING RODS—LEVEL 3		1	2	3	4	5	6	7	8
Gross Requirements				120					
Scheduled Receipts									
Projected On-hand Inventory	22	22	22	−98 (52)	52	52	52	52	52
Net Requirements				118					
Planned Order Receipts				150					
Planned Order Releases			150						

Q = 50; LT = 1; SS = 20

20 units each in the first, third, and sixth week. Again, the scheduled receipt of 20 units in the first week is due to a committed order placed previously. The gross requirements of 20 units each for the third and sixth week resulted in negative 18 and negative 20 units projected on-hand inventory for week 3 and 6, respectively. Therefore, the net requirements for week 3 and 6 are 18 and 20 units, respectively. Since the order lot size is lot-for-lot and there is no safety stock requirement, the planned order receipts are identical to the net requirements. As the lead time is two weeks, the planned order receipts turn into planned order releases of 18 and 20 units for the first and fourth week, respectively.

Level 2 MRP Computation—Piston Assembly

The gross requirements for the piston assembly came from the planned order releases of engine assembly. Therefore, the gross requirements of piston assembly are 18 and 20 units, respectively, for the first and fourth weeks. In week 4, the projected on-hand inventory is negative 8 units (beginning inventory of 12 units minus gross requirement of 20 units). Therefore, the net requirement is 18 units to cover the shortage of 8 units in projected on-hand inventory and safety stock requirement of 10 units. Since the order lot size is 30 units and lead time is one week, the planned order receipt and planned order release are 30 units in week 4 and 3, respectively.

Level 3 MRP Computation—Connecting Rods

Since the BOM in Figure 6.4 shows that four connecting rods are required for each piston assembly, the gross requirement for connecting rods in the third week is 120 units ($30 \times 4 = 120$). In week 3, the projected on-hand inventory is the beginning inventory of 22 units minus the gross requirement of 120 units, which equals to negative 98 units. Since the safety stock is 20 units, the net requirement is 118 units ($98 + 20 = 118$). Since the order lot size is 50 units and lead time is one week, the planned order receipt and planned order release are 150 units in weeks 3 and 2, respectively.

CAPACITY PLANNING

The material plans (the aggregate production plan, the master production schedule, and the material requirements plan) discussed so far have focused exclusively on production and materials management, but organizations must also address capacity constraints. Excess capacity wastes valuable resources such as idle labor, equipment, and facilities, while insufficient capacity adversely affects quality levels and customer service. Thus, a set of capacity plans is used in conjunction with the materials plan to ensure capacity is not over- or underutilized.

In the context of capacity planning, **capacity** refers to a firm's labor and machine resources. It is the maximum amount of output that an organization is capable of completing in a given period of time. Capacity planning follows the basic hierarchy of the materials planning system as shown in Figure 6.1. At the aggregate level, **resource requirements planning** (RRP), a long-range capacity planning module, is used to check whether aggregate resources are capable of satisfying the aggregate production plan. Typical resources considered at this stage include gross labor hours and machine hours. Generally, capacity expansion decisions at this level involve a long-range commitment, such as new machines or facilities. If existing resources are unable to meet the aggregate production plan, then the plan must be revised. The revised APP is reevaluated using the resource requirements plan until a feasible production plan is obtained.

Once the aggregate production plan is determined to be feasible, the aggregate production information is disaggregated into a more detailed medium-range production plan, the master production schedule. Although RRP has already determined that aggregate capacity is sufficient to satisfy the APP, medium-range capacity may not be able to satisfy the MPS. For example, the master production schedule may call for normal production quantities when much of the workforce typically takes vacation. Therefore, the medium-range capacity plan, or **rough-cut capacity plan** (RCCP), is used to check the feasibility of the master production schedule.

The RCCP takes the master production schedule and converts it from production to capacity required, then compares it to capacity available during each production period. If the medium-range capacity and production schedule are feasible, the master production schedule is firmed up. Otherwise, it is revised, or the capacity is adjusted accordingly. Options for increasing medium-range capacity include overtime, subcontracting, adding resources, and an alternate routing of the production sequence.

Capacity requirements planning (CRP) is a short-range capacity planning technique that is used to check the feasibility of the material requirements plan. The time-phased material requirements plan is used to compute the detailed capacity requirements for each workstation during specific periods to manufacture the items specified in the MRP. Although the RCCP may show that sufficient capacity exists to execute the master production schedule, the CRP may indicate that production capacity is inadequate during specific periods.

Capacity Strategies

Capacity expansion or contraction is an integral part of an organization's manufacturing strategy. Effectively balancing capacity with demand is an intricate management decision as it directly affects a firm's competitiveness. Short- to medium-term capacity can be increased through the use of overtime, additional shifts, and subcontracting, whereas long-term capacity can be increased by introducing new manufacturing techniques, hiring additional workers, and adding new machines and facilities. Conversely, capacity contraction can be attained by reducing the workforce, and disposing idle machines and facilities.

The three commonly recognized capacity strategies are lead, lag, and match capacity strategies. A **lead capacity strategy** is a proactive approach that adds or subtracts capacity in anticipation of future market conditions and demand, whereas a **lag capacity strategy** is a reactive approach that adjusts its capacity in response to demand. In favorable market conditions, the lag strategy generally does not add capacity until the firm is operating at full capacity. The lag capacity strategy is a conservative approach that may result in a lost opportunity when demand increases rapidly, whereas the lead strategy is more aggressive and can often result in excess inventory and idle capacity. Leaders in the electronics industry usually favor the lead capacity strategy because of the short product life cycles. A **match** or **tracking capacity strategy** is a moderate strategy that adjusts capacity in small amounts in response to demand and changing market conditions.

THE DISTRIBUTION REQUIREMENTS PLAN

The **distribution requirements plan** (DRP) is a time-phased finished-goods inventory replenishment plan in a distribution network. Distribution requirements planning is a logical extension of the MRP system, and its logic is analogous to MRP. Distribution requirements planning ties the physical distribution system to the manufacturing planning and control system by determining the aggregate time-phased net requirements of the finished goods, and provides demand information for adjusting the MPS. A major difference between MRP and DRP is that while MRP is driven by the production schedule specified in the MPS to compute the time-phased requirements of components, the DRP is driven by customer demand for the finished goods. Hence, the MRP operates in a dependent demand situation, whereas the DRP operates in an independent demand setting. The result of MRP execution is the production of finished-goods inventory at the manufacturing site, whereas DRP time-phases the movements of finished goods inventory from the manufacturing site to the central supply warehouse and distribution centers.

A clear benefit of the DRP system is that it extends manufacturing planning and control visibility into the distribution system to allow the firm to adjust its production plans and to avoid stocking excessive finished goods inventory. By now it should be clear that excessive inventory is a major cause of the bullwhip effect. Distribution requirements planning provides time-phased demand information needed for the manufacturing and distribution systems to effectively allocate finished goods inventory and production capacity to improve customer service and inventory investment. A distribution requirements planning example is provided in Example 6.4.

Example 6.4   A DRP Example at the ATV Corporation

The ATV Corporation's January and February distribution schedule for its Model A ATV is used to illustrate the DRP replenishment schedules from the firm's central supply warehouse to its two distribution centers. The time buckets used in the DRP are the same weekly time buckets used in the MRP system. DRP uses the order quantity, delivery lead time, on-hand balance, and safety stock information to determine the planned order releases necessary to meet anticipated market demand.

Gross requirements from the two distribution centers in Las Vegas and East Lansing are first obtained from the demand management system. The same MRP logic is used to compute the planned order releases of the two distribution centers. The gross requirements of the central supply warehouse reflect the cascading demand of Las Vegas and East Lansing distribution centers. The gross requirements of 14 units in the first week for the central supply warehouse are the sum of the planned order releases of the two distribution centers. The planned order releases of the central supply warehouse are passed on to the manufacturing facility, where they are absorbed into the MPS. This process is commonly referred to as **implosion**, where demand information is gathered from a number of field distribution centers and aggregated in the central warehouse, and eventually passed onto the manufacturing facility. While both the processes are similar, the *implosion* DRP logic is different from the *explosion* notion in MRP, where a Level 0 finished good is broken into its component requirements.

Scheduled Receipts and Projected On-hand Inventory

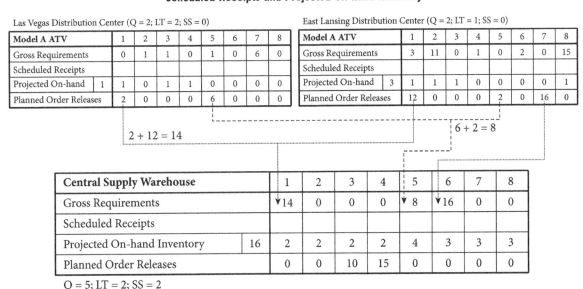

Las Vegas Distribution Center (Q = 2; LT = 2; SS = 0)

Model A ATV		1	2	3	4	5	6	7	8
Gross Requirements		0	1	1	0	1	0	6	0
Scheduled Receipts									
Projected On-hand	1	1	0	1	1	0	0	0	0
Planned Order Releases		2	0	0	0	6	0	0	0

East Lansing Distribution Center (Q = 2; LT = 1; SS = 0)

Model A ATV		1	2	3	4	5	6	7	8
Gross Requirements		3	11	0	1	0	2	0	15
Scheduled Receipts									
Projected On-hand	3	1	1	1	0	0	0	0	1
Planned Order Releases		12	0	0	0	2	0	16	0

2 + 12 = 14

6 + 2 = 8

Central Supply Warehouse		1	2	3	4	5	6	7	8
Gross Requirements		▼14	0	0	0	▼ 8	▼16	0	0
Scheduled Receipts									
Projected On-hand Inventory	16	2	2	2	2	4	3	3	3
Planned Order Releases		0	0	10	15	0	0	0	0

Q = 5; LT = 2; SS = 2

THE LEGACY MATERIAL REQUIREMENTS PLANNING SYSTEMS

For over five decades, an MRP system was the first choice among manufacturing firms in the United States for planning and managing their purchasing, production, and inventories. To improve the efficiency and effectiveness of the manufacturing planning and control system, many manufacturers have utilized **electronic data interchange** (EDI) to relay planned order releases to their suppliers. This information system has worked well for coordinating internal production, as well as purchasing.

By the end of the twentieth century, however, the global business environment has changed. Many savvy manufacturers and service providers were building multiplant international sites, either to take advantage of cheaper raw materials and labor or to expand their markets. Business executives found themselves spending more time dealing with international subcontractors using different currencies and languages among varying political environments. The need to access real-time information on customers' requirements, production levels and available capacities, company-wide inventory levels, and plants capable of meeting current order requirements increased. The existing MRP systems simply could not handle these added tasks.

To fully coordinate the information requirements for purchasing, planning, scheduling, and distribution of an organization operating in a complex multiunit global environment, an enterprise-wide information system was needed. Thus, ERP systems that operated from a single, centralized database were engineered to replace the legacy MRP systems.

The term **legacy MRP system** is a broad label used to describe an older information system that usually works at an operational level to schedule production within an organization. Many legacy systems were implemented in the 1960s, 1970s, and 1980s and subjected to extensive modifications as requirements changed over the years. Today, these systems have lasted beyond their originally intended life spans. The continuous modifications of these systems made them complex and cumbersome to work with, especially when considering they were not designed to be user-friendly in the first place. Legacy systems were designed to perform a very specific operational function and were programmed as independent entities with little regard for meeting requirements or coordinating with other functional areas. Communication between legacy systems is often limited, and visibility across functional areas is severely restricted. Legacy systems were implemented to gather data for transactional purposes and, thus, lacked any of the analytical capabilities required for today's complex global environment.

Manufacturing Resource Planning

The development of the legacy system can be traced back to the evolution of the MRP system, the closed-loop MRP system, and the **manufacturing resource planning** (MRP-II) system. The development of closed-loop MRP was a natural extension of the MRP system. It was an attempt to further develop the MRP into a formal and explicit manufacturing planning and control system by adding capacity requirements planning and feedback to describe the progress of orders being manufactured. The originally developed MRP is a part of the closed-loop MRP system.

Manufacturing resource planning was an outgrowth of the closed-loop MRP system. Business and sales plans were incorporated, and a financial function was added to link financial management to operations, marketing, and other functional areas. The concept of manufacturing resource planning was that the information system should link internal operations to the financial function to provide management with current data, including sales, purchasing, production, inventory, and cash flow. It should also be able to perform "what-if" analyses as internal and external conditions change. For example, MRP-II enables the firm to determine the impact on profit and cash flow if the firm is only able to fill 85 percent of its orders due to late deliveries of raw materials. MRP-II is an explicit and formal manufacturing information system that integrates the internal functions of an organization, enabling it to coordinate manufacturing plans with sales, while providing management with essential accounting and financial information.

Manufacturing resource planning has further evolved to include other functional areas of the organization. Although it synchronizes an organization's information systems and provides insight into the implications of aggregate production plans, master production schedules, capacities, materials plans and sales, it primarily focuses on one unit's internal operations. It lacks the capability to link the many operations of an organization's foreign branches with its headquarters. It also lacks the capability to directly interface with external supply chain members. For this reason, enterprise-wide information systems began to be developed.

THE DEVELOPMENT OF ENTERPRISE RESOURCE PLANNING SYSTEMS

While legacy MRP systems continue to be used and modified to include other functional areas of an organization, the growth of supply chain management, e-commerce, and global operations has created the need to exchange information directly with suppliers, customers, and foreign branches of organizations. The concept of the manufacturing information system thus evolved to directly connect all functional areas and operations of an organization and, in some cases, its suppliers and customers via a common software infrastructure and database. This type of information system is referred to as an ERP system.

The typical ERP system is an umbrella system that ties together a variety of specialized systems, such as manufacturing resource planning, logistics and warehousing, accounting and finance, human resource management, customer relationship management and supply chain management using a common, shared, centralized database. However, exactly what is tied together varies on a case-by-case basis, based on the ERP system capabilities and the needs of the organization. Figure 6.6 illustrates a generic ERP system, where a centralized database and software application infrastructure are used to drive a firm's information systems and to link the operations of its branches, suppliers, and customers with the firm's headquarters.

Enterprise resource planning is a broadly used industrial term to describe the multi-module application software for managing an enterprise's internal functional activities, as well as its suppliers and customers. Initially, ERP software focused on integrating the internal business activities of a multifacility organization, or enterprise, to ensure that it was operating under the same information system. With the onset of supply chain management, ERP vendors today are designing their products to include modules for managing suppliers and customers. For example, ERP enables an organization to deal directly with key suppliers to assess the availability of their resources, as if they are an extended unit of the firm. Similarly, ERP also allows key customers to directly access the firm's inventory information and manufacturing and delivery schedules.

ERP utilizes the idea of a centralized and shared database system to tie the entire organization together, as opposed to the legacy MRP system that uses multiple databases and interfaces that frequently result in duplicate and inconsistent information across different

Figure 6.6	A Generic ERP System

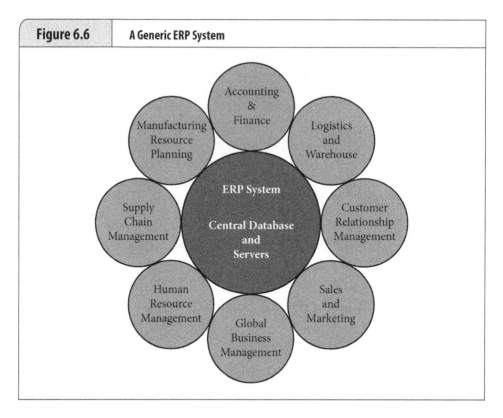

branches or even departments within an organization. With ERP, information is entered once at the source and made available to all users. It eliminates the inconsistency and incompatibility created when different functional areas use different systems with overlapping data.

The legacy MRP system typically utilizes multiple software packages and databases for different functional areas. Usually, each functional area implements its own information system based on its unique needs, with very little input or coordination from the other functional areas. The different packages within an organization often are incompatible with each other and prevent transactions from taking place directly between systems. The multiple databases also cause the same information to be stored in multiple locations; thus, multiple entries of the same data are required. This need to enter the same data repeatedly is a major cause of inconsistency in database management. For example, a customer, ATV Inc., may be entered as ATV Inc. in one database and ATV Incorporated in another database. From an information system's perspective, ATV Inc. and ATV Incorporated are two distinct customers.

With a shared, centralized database system, ERP is capable of automating business processes rapidly and accurately. For example, when taking a sales order, a sales agent has all the necessary information of the customer (e.g., the credit history, rating, and limit from the finance and accounting module), the company's production and inventory levels (from the operations module), and the delivery schedule (from the sales and marketing module) to complete the sale. After the sale is confirmed and entered into the centralized database, other supply chain partners affected by the transaction can directly utilize the same information system to take appropriate proactive actions. For example, suppliers can find out the production schedules planned by upstream supply chain members so that raw materials and components can be produced accordingly to support sales. Similarly, downstream companies can also utilize the same information system and database to access delivery schedules of raw materials and components ordered from their upstream supply chain members.

Thus, ERP integrates the internal operations of an enterprise with a common software platform and centralized database system. It also ties together supply chain member processes using the same information system. ERP provides the mechanism for supply chain members to share information so that scarce resources can be fully utilized to meet demand, while minimizing the bullwhip effect and supply chain inventories. Production changes and other modifications can also be executed quickly and efficiently to minimize delivery lead times. Example 6.5 illustrates a typical ERP transaction.

The Rapid Growth of Enterprise Resource Planning Systems

The use of ERP systems has rapidly spread from manufacturing to the service sector and has become widely used in many university classrooms. Many universities in the United States, for instance, have cooperated with major ERP software providers to integrate ERP training into their business curricula. Many universities have also migrated their student information systems like course registrations and transcripts to the ERP platform. There are many reasons, some of which are discussed in the following paragraph, for the rapid growth of ERP since the early 1990s.

At the turn of the twenty-first century, many firms were uncertain as to how the Year 2000 Millennium Bug or Y2K bug (conversion of the year from 1999 to 2000) would affect their information systems. Most information systems installed were programmed to use the last two digits of the year (e.g., the year 1998 would be shown as 98). Using the same logic,

---

Example 6.5   A Hypothetical ERP Transaction

The following example demonstrates a hypothetical ERP transaction for the ATV Corporation. The ATV Corporation makes three models of all-terrain vehicles: Model A, Model B, and Model C. The corporation is headquartered in the United States with manufacturing facilities in the United States and Mexico. ATV sells its products in the United States, Canada, and Mexico. Its sales representatives make quarterly visits to customers to take sales orders and provide necessary customer services. The following steps describe a sales transaction by a sales representative during a typical visit to a retail customer in Canada.

We assume here that a dealer ordered 100 units of Model A and 150 units of Model B, to be delivered within 30 days.

1. *Ordering*   The field sales representative takes the order of 100 units of Model A and 150 units of Model B. Using the Internet, the sales rep accesses the sales and marketing module of the ERP system at the ATV Corporation headquarters in the United States to check the price and other related information, such as quantity discounts, guarantees, and rebates. The sales rep also accesses the customer's credit history and rating from the finance and accounting module.

2. *Availability*   Simultaneously, the ERP system checks the inventory status and the available-to-promise quantities of its manufacturing facilities in the United States and Mexico and notifies the sales rep whether the order can be filled on time. The sales rep finds that the Mexico factory has sufficient inventory to fill the Model A order immediately, while the Model B order can be manufactured in ten days from the U.S. factory. Logistics information shows that shipping from Mexico to Canada takes two weeks, and delivery from the U.S. factory takes one week. Thus, the order is accepted, and the factory in Mexico receives instructions to ship 100 units of Model A to Canada immediately. The inventory status is updated accordingly. An invoice will be printed, and the finance and accounting module will be updated to reflect the partial delivery upon shipment of the goods from Mexico.

3. *Manufacturing*   The operations module immediately schedules the production of 150 units of Model B at the U.S. factory. All dependent demand items and labor necessary to produce 150 units of Model B are scheduled to meet the due date. For components manufactured in-house, planned order releases are transmitted to the shop floor. For purchased items, the information is sent to the suppliers.

   The human resource module checks to ensure that there are sufficient workers in the U.S. factory to complete the order. If not, the personnel manager will be notified and additional workers may be employed.

4. *Order Tracking*   An advance shipping notice (ASN) that provides delivery information to the dealer's receiving operations is transmitted. The customer relationship management module allows the customer to track the status of its order.

the year 2000 would be recorded as 00, which might also be interpreted as the year 1900, or 98 years prior to 1998. This could adversely affect time-sensitive programming logic (e.g., interest calculations). In addition, the legacy MRP systems had been modified so extensively over the years that the many layers of program codes made it too complex and redundant to correctly assess the true impact of Y2K. The extensive modifications to the legacy systems had also made them too expensive to maintain. Thus, many savvy business managers took a proactive approach to set aside sufficient budgetary funds to replace their legacy MRP systems with the more efficient ERP systems to reduce costs and deal with the Y2K problem as well.

The rapid development of computer and information technology over the last three decades has also contributed positively to the growth of ERP. Enterprise resource planning is the key building block of global business management information systems. As the global business environment continues to change, ERP has evolved to become more flexible to adapt to mergers and acquisitions and to provide more real-time monitoring and response. Tasks that were previously limited to mainframe computers are now easily implemented on servers and desktop computers that cost only a fraction of the capital investment previously needed. Information systems that were previously off-limits are now accessible to many smaller organizations.

A recent development in ERP is **cloud computing.** Software vendors such as Oracle Cloud and Microsoft Azure have begun to offer cloud-based services where end users can simply log on to remote servers without installing any software or storing data on local hard drives. The cloud is a metaphor for the Internet. In its simplest terms, cloud computing means accessing programs or storing data over the Internet (on some other company's server) instead of the user's local hard drive. With a high-speed online connection, cloud computing can be done anywhere and anytime. The popular Microsoft Office product, Microsoft 365, for example, is now available in the cloud.

Cloud computing can also be done by accessing the application software from a local computer and storing the data in the cloud. The data in the cloud can be synchronized on one or more local hard drives. This allows data to be accessed offline via the local hard drive when Internet connection is unavailable. However, the downside is that the user must ensure the latest data are synchronized in the cloud and local hard drive before accessing it. Also, storing, accessing, and synchronizing data in the cloud causes a noticeable delay in the storage and retrieval process compared to using a local hard drive. Despite these minor drawbacks, it is hard to imagine any technologically savvy business or student not utilizing the cloud to store, retrieve, and share data in this digital age. The following SCM Profile describes a new policy imposed by the U.S. Food and Drug Administration in the pharmaceutical industry may boost the adoption of cloud-based ERP solutions among small and medium-sized enterprises (SMEs).

SCM Profile | **The Changing Face of Pharmaceutical Distribution Traceability**

On November 27, 2013, President Obama signed the Drug Quality and Security Act (DQSA) into law. Title II of the DQSA, the Drug Supply Chain Security Act (DSCSA), outlines critical steps to build an electronic, interoperable system to identify and trace certain prescription drugs as they are distributed in the United States.

The DSCSA specifies that by January 2015, pharmaceutical companies must only purchase products from authorized trading partners and exchange transactional data on a lot batch level. Moreover, trading partners shall have a process in place to investigate and quarantine suspected products, and notify the U.S. Food and Drug Administration (FDA) and immediate trading partners. By November 2017, pharmaceutical manufacturers must add a product identifier to each individual package and homogeneous case of product. The product identifier contains the product's standardized numerical identifier, lot number, and expiration data in both human and machine-readable format. By November 2023, the DSCSA will turn into an electronic, serialized records retention system. Item level products will be serialized and associated with its parent shipper case and pallet, thus making it possible to trace an individual drug in the supply chain.

Because of DSCSA, many pharmaceutical companies are now seeking out pharmaceutical-specific enterprise resource planning (ERP) solutions to support their operations. The traceability requirement put a huge burden on small and medium-sized enterprises (SMEs). Most ERP systems do not currently track down to the individual item level and it is very expensive to modify an ERP system to identify a product's serial number. However, the penalty for noncompliance is much more severe because the company's license may be revoked by the Drug Enforcement Agency (DEA).

To stay compliant, pharmaceutical companies must (1) preserve the licensing information of their customers at both the federal and state levels, (2) be able to use a common coding scheme to report the sales of pharmaceutical products, (3) be able to trace the products in the supply chain, and (4) be able to report the movement of DEA controlled substances from the point of manufacture to the point of sale.

Pharmaceutical companies must streamline their processes to ensure traceability and understand what are required under DSCSA. The cloud platform ERP solutions are a viable option because it is highly regulated and flexible. It is possible to implement the same solution on premise or in the cloud to cater to SMEs or large organizations. Based on the current DSCSA, it is getting more and more detailed as we get closer to 2023. The ability to trace individual drug allows regulators to clean up the pharmaceutical supply chain and reduce the number of counterfeit drugs on the market.[6]

IMPLEMENTING ENTERPRISE RESOURCE PLANNING SYSTEMS

ERP systems have continued to evolve, and integration of e-commerce, customer relationship management, and supply chain management applications are now considered ERP requirements by most organizations. While many firms believe a well-designed and implemented ERP system can translate into a substantial competitive advantage, research analysts and industrial practitioners are still debating the usefulness of ERP, and the advantages and disadvantages of using a **best-of-breed solution** versus a **single integrator solution**. It is important to understand that ERP is not a panacea for poor business decisions, but in the right hands it can be a valuable tool to enhance competitiveness.

The *best-of-breed* solution picks the best application or module for each individual function required for the supply chain (thus, best of breed). Although best-of-breed vendors fill a void in the ERP market with specialized applications that mainstream ERP vendors may not provide, the resulting system can include several different applications that must be integrated to work as a single coordinated system to achieve the global scope required of the ERP. A major criticism of the best-of-breed solution is that multiple software infrastructures and databases may have to be used to link the multiple applications obtained from different vendors. This may severely affect the ability of the system to update the databases rapidly and efficiently—a similar problem of the legacy MRP systems.

The *single integrator* approach picks all the desired applications from a single vendor for the ERP system. The obvious advantages are that all of the applications should work well together, and getting the system up and running should be easier. As companies become more global, and as firms desire to expand their systems with other compatible modules later on, the notion of using a single integrator solution becomes more attractive. On the other hand, as information technology continues to evolve and as competition increases in the ERP software market, ERP vendors are designing their products to be more compatible with each other.

Choosing whether to utilize a single integrator ERP solution or combine niche software is a challenge facing many companies today. If the firm's IT department has its way, the company will choose a single integrator solution for their ERP implementation; if people overseeing other business processes have their way, a company is likely to choose the best-of-breed solution.[7]

The emergence of the single integrator ERP solution over the last decade does not signal the extinction of best-of-breed software vendors. While it is rare now, to find major companies using best-of-breed ERP packages, best-of-breed vendors will continue to fill the niches left by the large ERP vendors. Some businesses such as small and medium-sized enterprises require unique best-of-breed software to do advanced or big data analytical decision-making. Businesses are often interested in tasks that extend beyond core ERP functions, into areas like sales and operations planning or analyses using ERP data. Many best-of-breed ERP vendors have thrived by creating early software innovations around the "edges of ERP," exploiting gaps left by ERP product suites. Many of these surviving vendors, for example, are in inventory management systems.[8] Finally, businesses often turn to best-of-breed system vendors when the cost savings expected from their ERP implementations fail to materialize. In general, best-of-breeds are better suited to more intricate workplaces, while single integrator ERP solutions fit the less complex business environments.[9] The following SCM Profile describes how the preference between single integrator and best-of-breed implementation has blurred over the years.

Implementing an ERP system has proven to be a real challenge for many companies. Most ERP systems are written based on the best practices of selected firms. Thus, a condition required for implementation of the system is that the user's business processes must conform to the approaches used in the software logic. These processes can be significantly different from those currently used within the company. Having to adapt a company's business processes to conform to a software program is a radical departure from the conventional business practice of requiring the software to be designed around the business processes.

Two primary requirements of successful implementation of ERP are computer support and accurate, realistic inputs. Instead of implementing the entire system at once, some organizations choose to implement only those applications or modules that are absolutely critical to operations at that time. New modules are then added in later phases. This ensures that the system can be implemented as quickly as possible while minimizing interruption of the existing system. However, many implementations have failed due to a variety of reasons, as follows:

- *Lack of top management commitment*: While management may be willing to set aside sufficient funds to implement a new ERP system, it may not take an active role in the implementation process. Often, this leads users to revert to the old processes or systems because of their lack of interest in learning the capabilities of the new ERP system.
- *Lack of adequate resources*: Implementing a new ERP system is a long-term commitment requiring substantial capital investment. Although the cost has become more affordable due to the rapid advent of computer technology, full

implementation may still be out of reach for many small organizations. In addition, small firms may not have the necessary workforce and expertise to implement the complex system.

- *Lack of proper training*: Many employees may already be familiar with their legacy MRP systems. Thus, when a new ERP system is implemented, top management may assume that users are already adequately prepared and underestimate the training required to get the new system up and running. Lack of financial resources can also reduce the amount of training available for its workforce.

SCM Profile | 2016 State of ERP: Gaining Speed

Supply chain management (SCM) application is the software modules used in sourcing, purchase order processing, supplier management, inventory management, good receipt, warehouse management, and customer requirement processing. Though SCM application is growing faster than the broader enterprise resource planning (ERP) software market, the preference between choosing the large ERP providers and best-of-breed SCM application has blurred over the years. The large ERP providers such as SAP, Oracle, Info, and Microsoft are now moving to create all-inclusive, end-to-end solutions that encompass multiple trading partners along the supply chain.

The traditional large ERP providers are gaining ground in the SCM application arena over the last several years. In a recent study by Gartner, it was reported that 63 percent of survey respondents are committed to the large ERP providers, whereas only 18 percent of the respondents are committed to using best-of-breed solutions. The study concluded that companies have a strong preference for large ERP providers, especially SAP. The study also noted that 57 percent of the companies would rather purchase their SCM application from a large ERP provider in the future.

There are several reasons that large ERP providers are steadily marching into the SCM application arena. For example, companies that have already implemented an ERP solution are likely to work with their existing ERP providers to gain additional SCM capabilities. Moreover, most ERP solutions are already playing a key role in supporting supply chain processes, from planning to procurement and to logistics. The large ERP providers are exploiting the opportunity to expand into the SCM functionality front by aggressively acquiring smaller SCM solution providers or by developing new SCM solutions in-house. Today's ERP applications offer functionally-rich SCM solutions that integrate cloud-based options that are even more advanced than the specialized best-of-breed SCM solutions. These cloud-based solutions do not require any customization and can be easily integrated into an existing large ERP application, thus making the single integrator implementation approach more attractive.

Traditional large ERP providers such as SAP and Oracle have improved their SCM capabilities to include transportation management, warehouse management, planning, and procurement offerings to the point that best-of-breed solutions no longer make sense. The single integrator approach of using SCM solutions from the existing ERP provider results in better total cost of ownership, standardization of processes and technology, and data consistency across the extended supply chain.

However, as the large ERP providers are adding SCM functions in their ERP solutions, smaller best-of-breed SCM developers are expanding supply chain visibility and developing targeted solutions in their offerings. Creativity and innovations in the business process management software arena will determine whether the single integrator approach by large ERP providers will displace the best-of-breed SCM developers.[10]

- *Lack of communication*: Lack of communication within an organization, or between the firm and its ERP vendor can be a barrier for successful implementation. Lack of communication usually results in the wrong specifications and requirements being implemented.
- *Incompatible system environment*: In certain cases, the firm's environment does not give ERP a distinct advantage over other systems. For example, there is no advantage for a small, family-owned used-car dealer in a small town to implement an expensive new ERP system.

Advantages and Disadvantages of Enterprise Resource Planning Systems

When properly installed and operating, an ERP system can provide a firm and its supply chain partners with a significant competitive advantage, which can fully justify the investments of time and money in ERP. A fully functional ERP system can enhance the firm's capability to fully utilize capacity, accurately schedule production, reduce inventory, meet delivery due dates, and improve the efficiency and effectiveness of the supply chain. Let us look at some specific advantages and disadvantages.

Enterprise Resource Planning System Advantages

As mentioned earlier, the primary advantage of ERP over the legacy MRP systems is that ERP uses a single database and a common software infrastructure to provide a broader scope and up-to-date information, enabling management to make better decisions swiftly. ERP is also robust in providing real-time information and, thus, can communicate information about operational changes to supply chain members quickly. ERP systems are also designed to take advantage of Internet technology. Thus, users can access the system via the Internet.

ERP helps organizations reduce supply chain inventories due to the added visibility throughout the entire supply chain. It enables the supply, manufacturing, and logistics processes to flow smoothly by providing visibility of the order fulfillment process throughout the supply chain. Supply chain visibility leads to reductions of the bullwhip effect and helps supply chain members to better plan production and end-product deliveries to customers.

ERP systems also help organizations to standardize manufacturing processes. Manufacturing firms often find that multiple business units across the company make the same product using different processes and information systems. ERP systems enable the firm to automate some of the steps of a manufacturing process. Process standardization eliminates redundant resources and increases productivity.

ERP enables an organization, especially a multibusiness-unit enterprise, to efficiently track employees' time and performance and to communicate with them via a standardized method. Performance can be monitored across the entire organization using the same measurements and standards. The use of a single software platform and database also allows the ERP system to integrate financial, production, supply, and customer order information. By having this information in one software system rather than scattered among many different systems that cannot communicate with one another, companies can keep track of materials, orders, and financial status efficiently and coordinate manufacturing, inventory, and shipping among many different locations and business units at the same time.

Enterprise Resource Planning System Disadvantages

While the benefits of ERP systems can be impressive, ERP is not without shortcomings. For example, a substantial capital investment is needed to purchase and implement the system. Considerable time and money must be set aside to evaluate the available ERP applications, to purchase the necessary hardware and software, and then to train employees to operate the new system. Total cost of ERP ownership includes hardware, software, professional, and software customization services, training, and other internal staff costs. ERP systems are very complex and have proven difficult to implement, particularly in large multibusiness unit organizations.

However, the primary criticism of ERP is that the software is designed around a specific business model based on specific business processes. Although business processes are usually adopted based on best practices in the industry, the adopting firm must change its business model and associated processes to fit the built-in business model designed into the ERP system. Thus as mentioned earlier, the adopting firm must restructure its processes to be compatible with the new ERP system. This has resulted in a very unusual situation where a software system determines the business practices and processes a firm should implement, instead of designing the software to support existing business practices and processes.

Despite the widespread adoption of costly ERP systems by large firms since the Y2K scramble, many implementation challenges remain unsolved, and scores of ERP systems today are grossly underutilized.[11,12] Intricate business process reengineering challenges arise when business processes are adapted to the software. Consequently, firms struggle to justify their investment and find ways to better utilize their ERP systems. This raises the question of whether large firms can effectively manage their operations and supply chain activities without sophisticated information technology.

ENTERPRISE RESOURCE PLANNING SOFTWARE APPLICATIONS

ERP systems typically consist of many modules that are linked together to access and share a common database. Each module performs distinct functions within the organization and is designed so that it can be installed on its own or with a combination of other modules. Most ERP software providers design their products to be compatible with their competitors' products, so that modules from different providers can be combined. Integration of customer relationship management, supply chain management, and e-procurement modules into the ERP system is now becoming relatively commonplace.

Today, there are scores of ERP software providers, each targeting a specific market segment and industry type. In terms of market share, SAP and Oracle are the two prominent ERP providers, followed by Microsoft and Infor. Though each software company configures its products differently from its competitors, some common modules of ERP systems are described here:

- *Accounting and finance*: This module assists an organization in maintaining financial control and accountability. It tracks accounting and financial information such as revenues, costs, assets, liabilities, and other accounting and financial information of the company. It is also capable of generating routine and advanced accounting and financial reports, product costing, budgeting, and analyses.

- *Customer relationship management*: This module manages customer relationships. It enables collaboration between the organization and its customers by providing relevant, personalized, and up-to-date information. It also enables customers to track sales orders. The customer relationship management module allows the user to communicate with existing customers and acquire new customers through sales automation and partner relationship management. This module allows the firm to segment customers and track their purchase activities, and then design customized promotions appealing to each customer segment.

- *Human resource management*: It helps an organization plan, develop, manage, and control its human resources. It allows the firm to deploy the right people to support its overall strategic goals and to plan the optimal workforce levels based on production levels.

- *Manufacturing resource planning*: It schedules materials and tracks production, capacity, and the flow of goods through the manufacturing process. It may even include the capability for quality planning, inspection, and certifications. This is probably the most important module for manufacturing companies.

- *Supply chain management*: This module handles the planning, execution, and control of activities involved in a supply chain. It helps to strengthen a firm's supply chain networks to improve delivery performance. Major functions of this module include sourcing, purchase order processing, good receipt, supplier management, and customer requirement processing. It may also include various logistics functions like transportation, warehousing, and inventory management. The supply chain management module creates value by allowing the user to optimize its internal and external supply chains.

ERP systems have continued to evolve in the twenty-first century. The industry has differentiated between very large enterprise and SME sectors. New best-of-breed vendors continued to emerge rapidly in the SME sector. Another development in the ERP industry is the advent of cloud computing solutions which require lower startup cost and total cost of ownership. SMEs are now able to experiment with cloud-based ERP solutions. As information technology continues to become more sophisticated, ERP software providers will continue to add new functions and capabilities to their systems.

SUMMARY

While both manufacturing and service organizations rely on effective production and capacity planning to balance demand and capacity, manufacturers have the added advantage of being able to build up inventory as stored capacity. Service firms are unable to inventory their services, so they rely upon backlogs or reservations, cross-training, or queues to match supply with demand. However, excess capacity results in underutilized equipment and workforce and eventually leads to unnecessary cost, adversely impacting all firms along the supply chain.

This chapter covers materials planning, capacity planning, and enterprise resource planning, which are all widely used for balancing demand with supply. An example was used to demonstrate how the aggregate production plan, master production schedule, material requirements plan, and distribution requirements plan are related to each other. This chapter also briefly discusses how the various materials plans are related to the capacity plans. A central piece of the materials plan is the material requirements plan, which takes information from the master production schedule, the bill of materials, and inventory status to compute planned order releases. For items that are produced in-house, planned order releases are released to the shop floor to trigger production. For purchased items, planned order releases are released to suppliers.

Finally, this chapter discusses the enterprise resource planning system, including its relationships with the traditional MRP and MRP-II systems, its advantages and disadvantages, implementation issues, and ERP modules. The goal of ERP development was to build a single software application that runs off a common shared database to serve the needs of an entire organization, regardless of its units' geographical locations and the currency used. Despite its complexity and considerable costs, ERP provides a way to integrate different business functions of different businesses, on different continents. The integrated approach can have a tremendous payback if companies select the right applications and implement the software correctly. Unfortunately, many companies that have installed these systems have failed to realize the benefits expected.

Implementing ERP should be viewed as a long-term, ongoing project. No matter what resources a firm has initially committed to replacing legacy systems, selecting and implementing ERP applications and training users, ERP requires ongoing management commitment and resources. As needs and technologies change and new applications are designed, new functionality and business processes will need to be continuously revisited and improved.

KEY TERMS

aggregate production plan, 185

available-to-promise (ATP) quantity, 193

best-of-breed solution, 213

bill of materials (BOM), 195

bullwhip effect, 185

capacity, 205

capacity requirements planning, 206

chase production strategy, 187

closed-loop MRP, 198

cloud computing, 212

demand time fence, 192

dependent demand, 196

distribution requirements plan, 206

distribution requirements planning, 186

electronic data interchange, 208

enterprise resource planning, 186

implosion, 207

indented bill of materials, 196

independent demand, 196

intermediate, 185

lag capacity strategy, 206

lead capacity strategy, 206

legacy MRP system, 208

level production strategy, 189

long-range, 185

make-to-order, 189

make-to-stock, 190

manufacturing resource planning, 186

master production schedule, 186

match, 206

material requirements plan, 186

material requirements planning, 198

medium-range, 185

option overplanning, 198

planned order releases, 199

planning factor, 195

planning time fence, 192

product family, 187

mixed production strategy, 191

resource requirements planning, 205

rough-cut capacity plan, 206

short-range planning horizons, 185

single integrator solution, 213

super bill of materials, 197

system nervousness, 192

time fence system, 192

tracking capacity strategy, 206

DISCUSSION QUESTIONS

1. Why is it important to balance production capacity with market demand?

2. Describe long-range, medium-range, and short-range planning in the context of materials plan and capacity plan. How are they related?

3. Describe aggregate production planning, master production planning, material requirements planning, and distribution requirements planning. How are these plans related?

4. Describe how MRP evolved into closed-loop MRP, MRP-II, and eventually into ERP.

5. Compare and contrast chase versus level production strategies. Which is more appropriate for an industry where highly skilled laborers are needed? Why?

6. Is a level production strategy suitable for a pure service industry, such as professional accounting and tax services or law firms? Can these firms inventory their outputs?

7. What is the purpose of low-level coding?

8. What is the purpose of available-to-promise quantity, and how is it different from on-hand inventory?

9. What is system nervousness? Discuss how it can be minimized or avoided.

10. What are the crucial inputs for material requirements planning?

11. What is a BOM, and how is it different from the super BOM?

12. Are manufacturing or purchasing lead times considered in the MPS and the MRP?

13. What is the difference between scheduled receipts and planned order releases?

14. In MRP computation, do the gross requirements of level 3 items come from the gross requirements or planned order releases of the level 2 items? Explain how this works.

15. What is the difference between an MRP explosion and a DRP implosion?

16. Briefly describe resource requirements planning, rough-cut capacity planning, and capacity requirements planning. How are these plans related?

17. How are the various capacity plans (RRP, RCCP, CRP) related to the material plans (APP, MPS, MRP)?

18. Why are production planning and capacity planning important to SCM?

19. Why have so many firms rushed to implement ERP systems over the past ten years?

20. Describe the limitations of a legacy MRP system.

21. Why is it important to learn the fundamentals of the traditional MRP system, even if it is considered an outdated, legacy system?

22. What are the advantages of an ERP system over the legacy MRP system?

23. Explain best-of-breed and single integrator ERP implementations. What are the advantages and disadvantages of the best-of-breed implementation?

24. Explain why many ERP implementations have failed to yield the expected benefits over the last ten years.

25. Describe how a cloud-based ERP system works. When might a firm use a cloud-based ERP?

ESSAY/PROJECT QUESTIONS

1. It is inevitable that cloud computing will significantly affect how businesses and students use information technology in the next few years. If you have not done so, search on the Internet to sign up for free cloud storage on OneDrive, Google Drive, and/or Dropbox. Do not forget to sync your files to your local hard drives.

2. Visit the websites of SAP, Oracle, and Microsoft, and use the information to write a brief report of each company and its ERP software. Do their products offer the same configurations or functionalities?

3. Use the Internet to search for relevant information to prepare a brief report on how SAP and Oracle expanded their product lines. Which of the two firms is known for its aggressive strategy of acquiring smaller best-of-breed providers?

4. Use the Internet to search for information to write a report on whether the trend is toward a single integrator or best-of-breed ERP implementation.

5. Use resources available on the Internet to prepare a report on the current and projected ERP market total revenue and the rate of growth over the next five years.

6. Use resources available on the Internet to prepare a story about a firm that has successfully implemented an ERP system.

7. Use resources available on the Internet to prepare a report that describes a failed ERP implementation. What can be learned from this company?

8. Explore the websites of SAP and Oracle, and use the information to write a report to discuss their (a) supply chain management, (b) supplier relationship management, and (c) customer relationship management software applications.

9. Use resources on the Internet to write a report describing Microsoft's strategy and competitive position in the ERP market.

10. Use resources on the Internet to write a report on the current stage of ERP implementation in the United States, Europe, and China.

SPREADSHEET PROBLEMS

1. Given the following production plan, use a (a) chase production strategy and (b) level production strategy to compute the monthly production, ending inventory/(backlog), and workforce levels. A worker can produce 100 units per month. Assume the

beginning inventory as of January is 0, and the firm desires to have zero inventory at the end of June.

MONTH	JAN	FEB	MAR	APR	MAY	JUN
Demand	2,000	3,000	5,000	6,000	6,000	2,000
Production						
Ending Inventory						
Workforce						

2. Given the following production plan, use a (a) chase production strategy and (b) level production strategy to compute the monthly production, ending inventory/(backlog), and workforce levels. A worker can produce 50 units per month. Assume that the beginning inventory in January is 500 units, and the firm desires to have 200 units of inventory at the end of June.

MONTH	JAN	FEB	MAR	APR	MAY	JUN
Demand	2,000	3,000	5,000	6,000	6,000	2,000
Production						
Ending Inventory						
Workforce						

3. Given the following production schedule, compute the available-to-promise quantities.

WEEK	1	2	3	4	5	6	7	8
Model A								
MPS BI = 60	20	30	20	20	20	50	0	20
Committed Customer Orders	50	10	30	10	20	20	10	0
ATP:D								

4. Given the following production schedule, compute the available-to-promise quantities.

WEEK	1	2	3	4	5	6	7	8
Model B								
MPS BI = 20	20	0	20	20	0	20	20	20
Committed Customer Orders	10	10	10	10	10	0	0	10
ATP:D								

5. The bill of materials for product A with the associated component parts and planning factors (in parenthesis) are showed below. How many units of the following components are required to make one unit of the product A?

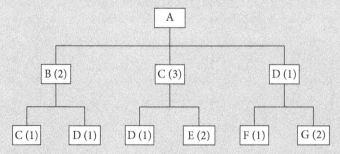

a. Component B
b. Component C
c. Component D

    d. Component E

    e. Component F

    f. Component G

6. Given the following information, complete the planned order releases and projected on-hand balances for component part X.

PART X		WEEK 1	WEEK 2	WEEK 3	WEEK 4	WEEK 5
Gross Requirements		80	0	90	0	90
Scheduled Receipts		60				
Projected Balance	120					
Planned Order Releases						

Q = 60; LT = 3 weeks; Safety Stock = 5

7. Given the following information, complete the planned order releases and projected on-hand balances for component part Y.

PART Y		WEEK 1	WEEK 2	WEEK 3	WEEK 4	WEEK 5
Gross Requirements		80	50	90	0	80
Scheduled Receipts		160				
Projected Balance	120					
Planned Order Releases						

Q = 20, LT = 2 weeks, Safety Stock = 10

8. The bills of materials for two finished products (D and E), inventory status, and other relevant information are given below. Compute the planned order releases and projected on-hand balances for parts D, E, and F.

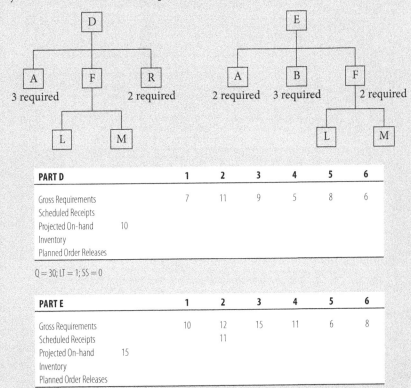

PART D		1	2	3	4	5	6
Gross Requirements		7	11	9	5	8	6
Scheduled Receipts							
Projected On-hand Inventory	10						
Planned Order Releases							

Q = 30; LT = 1; SS = 0

PART E		1	2	3	4	5	6
Gross Requirements		10	12	15	11	6	8
Scheduled Receipts			11				
Projected On-hand Inventory	15						
Planned Order Releases							

Q = LFL; LT = 2; SS = 3

PART F	1	2	3	4	5	6
Gross Requirements						
Scheduled Receipts	60					
Projected On-hand 20						
Inventory						
Planned Order Releases						

Q = 60; LT = 1; SS = 0

9. The bill of materials for a finished product E, inventory status, and other relevant information are given below. Compute the planned order releases and projected on-hand balances for parts E, F, and M.

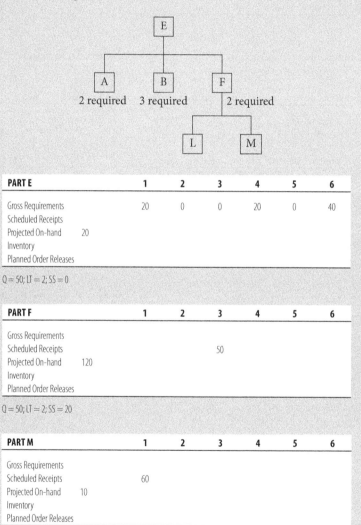

PART E	1	2	3	4	5	6
Gross Requirements	20	0	0	20	0	40
Scheduled Receipts						
Projected On-hand 20						
Inventory						
Planned Order Releases						

Q = 50; LT = 2; SS = 0

PART F	1	2	3	4	5	6
Gross Requirements						
Scheduled Receipts			50			
Projected On-hand 120						
Inventory						
Planned Order Releases						

Q = 50; LT = 2; SS = 20

PART M	1	2	3	4	5	6
Gross Requirements						
Scheduled Receipts	60					
Projected On-hand 10						
Inventory						
Planned Order Releases						

Q = 60; LT = 1; SS = 30

10. Crop-Quick Inc. replenishes its three distribution centers in Boston, Denver, and Houston from its Las Vegas central supply warehouse. The distribution schedule for one of its products for the next six weeks is shown below. Use proper distribution requirements planning logic to complete the replenishment schedules of the three distribution centers and the central supply warehouse.

BOSTON DISTRIBUTION CENTER	1	2	3	4	5	6
Gross Requirements	0	20	0	55	0	0
Scheduled Receipts						
Projected On-hand 10						
Inventory						
Planned Order Releases						

Q = 30; LT = 1; SS = 5

DENVER DISTRIBUTION CENTER	1	2	3	4	5	6
Gross Requirements	0	20	10	0	0	20
Scheduled Receipts		11				
Projected On-hand 15						
Inventory						
Planned Order Releases						

Q = LFL; LT = 2; SS = 2

HOUSTON DISTRIBUTION CENTER	1	2	3	4	5	6
Gross Requirements	50	0	0	45	0	0
Scheduled Receipts						
Projected On-hand 20						
Inventory						
Planned Order Releases						

Q = 60; LT = 1; SS = 0

LAS VEGAS CENTRAL WAREHOUSE	1	2	3	4	5	6
Gross Requirements						
Scheduled Receipts						
Projected On-hand 50						
Inventory						
Planned Order Releases						

Q = 20; LT = 1; SS = 0

CASES

1. Teen's Scene*

Myrtle Mendez is an entrepreneur. She started a clothing manufacturing business and established a store a few years ago that focused on teens. Her brand and store are called Teen's Scene. Initially, Myrtle worried about just getting the business running and keeping the financials above water. As her success grew, Myrtle realized that she needed to think more about the big picture. What was the direction she wanted her company to go? Did she want her business to stay as a single store? Did she want to get her brand sold in other clothing stores? Did she want to expand locally, that is, just within the city of Chicago? Or, was there another avenue of growth she should pursue?

* Written by Rick Bonsall, D. Mgt., McKendree University, Lebanon, IL. The people and institution are fictional and any resemblance to any person or any institution is coincidental. This case was prepared solely to provide material for class discussion. The author does not intend to illustrate either effective or ineffective handling of a managerial situation.

Although her company was relatively small, Myrtle had a senior staff, a director of operations (DO), a director of finance (DF), and a director of supply chain management (DS). Myrtle was a very hands-on owner and president of her company. Myrtle knew that each of her senior staff were experts in their areas; therefore, she decided the best course of action was to engage them in the planning of her company's future.

Myrtle and her staff spent many weeks discussing the situation. Rolando Curry (DF) was concerned about the financial effect expansion. Rolando supported expansion; however, he emphasized that the specific strategy selected should be based on its financial impact. For example, how would it affect labor costs? What about inventory costs?

Essie Floyd (DO) agreed with Rolando that the selection of a specific strategy was a crucial first step. Essie explained that the type of production strategy the company chose to utilize would be one that they would be "stuck" with for at least a year, maybe more. The production strategy would dictate such things as capacity, scheduling, and training. Therefore, while she understood Rolando's concerns, she disagreed that the financials were the primary consideration. Essie believed that they should instead look at it primarily from the perspective of production. What strategy would enable them to run the production smoothly? Essie preferred a strategy where she would have a stable workforce she could count on.

Andy Allen (DS) said that in theory both Essie and Rolando were correct. However, as director of supply chain management, Andy's perspective was different. If they planned to sell their clothing line to other stores, they must focus on ensuring that the availability of the product was constant and consistent. If they didn't have the inventory to provide to local stores, then those stores may eventually drop them as a supplier. Andy's argument to Rolando was that if they were too cautious about the financials, they may be putting the company in a position where they would fall short of meeting customer expectations.

Myrtle listened to their views and realized that each one had valid points. Selecting the wrong strategy could result in her company failing financially in the long term. Furthermore, technically, her store was her manufacturing company's customer, although the teens were the ultimate end users. If she added other intermediate suppliers between her manufacturing company and the teens, that is, other clothing stores, they would be her manufacturing company's critical customers. Obviously, as her own customer she knew about any problems that would cause a disruption in supply; however, other stores wouldn't care about the reasons. Consequently, a disruption in supply would be a major cause of customer dissatisfaction. Finally, she understood Essie's point of view very clearly. A stable trained workforce was essential to the quality of their product. A strategy that may seem more attractive from a financial perspective, that is, keeping labor costs low, could affect their ability to maintain the level of quality they currently had.

Myrtle met again with her senior staff. She shared that she had thought a lot about their individual views. While the discussions had provided a lot of food for thought, Myrtle said she needed each director to formally present their case in writing. Once she had those documents, they would meet and discuss the merits of each case. The desired outcome of that meeting would be to make a decision on an approach that minimized the negative effects each of them had identified and maximized the Teen's Scene's opportunity for success.

Discussion Questions

1. If Myrtle and her staff decided to expand the business by selling the Teen's Scene brand to other clothing stores, which production strategy would be the best? Explain why your choice would be the best by addressing how the concerns of each director are resolved or at least minimized.

2. One of the options that Myrtle is considering is the lead capacity strategy. Based on the case and the issues all three directors voiced, do you agree that this is the best capacity strategy? Explain why or why not. If you don't agree, describe what would be a better capacity strategy.

3. Essie Floyd (DO) and Andy Allen (DS) have different concerns. What system or systems can Teen's Scene procure and implement that would provide a resolution for both directors? Identify the system or systems and explain why they would alleviate the specific concerns of each director. Be specific.

©2019 Cengage Learning

2. Fox's Furniture Division*

Beulah Burton is the vice president of Fox's Furniture Division. Fox is a corporation with businesses in many different industries. The furniture division has always been profitable; however, many years have passed since any overhaul of systems, equipment, or processes has been done. Jo Simon, chief executive officer of Fox Industries, believed the time was right to give the furniture division a face lift. That was one reason she hired Beulah. Beulah has a reputation within the furniture industry of modernizing furniture companies.

As Beulah reviewed the current systems, equipment, and processes, she was shocked at how outdated things were. Fox Furniture Division was at least two decades behind the rest of the industry. Beulah was further amazed that it was a profitable division. Beulah wondered how much waste was going unnoticed because of antiquated systems. She was convinced that a lot of data were missing and this made any analysis ineffective.

Beulah met with Jo and explained that Fox needed an enterprise resource planning system. She believed that the furniture division had continued to make a profit only because most of the workers had been there for years. However, as they retired, she was convinced that their knowledge could not be easily replaced by new employees. Fox needed better data collection and data management. Clearly, this would be a huge undertaking.

Once the ERP system was installed and operational the first reports began to flow. Beulah realized that there was a lot of excess inventory. It was more than just too many of a certain part, for example, wood spindles. It was a case of having inventory that was not used for any of their current product line. They had tens of thousands of dollars of obsolete inventory sitting in their warehouses.

Discussion Questions

1. You work for Beulah Burton. She directs you to determine what specific actions the furniture division needs to take in order to clean up the inventory system and to have the new system implemented effectively. What will you report?

2. You are part of a team tasked by Beulah to anticipate what problems may occur in the planning and implementation of an ERP system. Think about the scenario presented in the case. What specific problems may they encounter? What common problems, (i.e., ones happening in many companies) may they encounter? What solutions or contingencies do you recommend?

* Written by Rick Bonsall, D. Mgt., McKendree University, Lebanon, IL. The people and institution are fictional and any resemblance to any person or any institution is coincidental. This case was prepared solely to provide material for class discussion. The author does not intend to illustrate either effective or ineffective handling of a managerial situation.

3. Do you agree with Beulah's plan to jump all the way in, concerning an ERP system? Why? Shouldn't Jo have slowed things down and said they would implement it more piecemeal? Explain your thoughts.

3. Owen Poole CPA*

The first quarter of the year is Owen's favorite time. Owen Poole is a certified public accountant (CPA) and he loves the tax season. Although he understands that tax reform would be best for everyone if it simplified the process, he is glad that the idea of reform has been just talk. Owen enjoys the challenge of figuring out what deductions clients can take and how to maximize his clients' tax refunds. Owen sees it as a battle between himself and the internal revenue service. The only thing Owen likes more than the challenge itself is winning!

When Owen was earning his degree in accounting he took several electives in other business topics. One of his favorite ones was supply chain management. Owen enjoyed the big picture perspective this course emphasized. Understanding business from a broad perspective is crucial to Owen's own business because many of his clients are businesses, not individuals. As part of his services, Owen gives advice to his business clients on how to improve their bottom line. He explains to them that he will search out every penny possible in deductions to enhance their bottom line. However, he explains that they can help themselves by implementing more effective and efficient processes within their business. Although Owen isn't an expert in many of these processes, he understands enough to point his clients in the right direction. Since a significant portion of Owen's clients are small businesses, often just a few years old, his advice is helpful and very welcomed.

Today Owen is meeting with Van Ward. Van's business has been growing very rapidly. As Owen reviews Van's financial statements he notices that Van's profit has been decreasing slightly despite his company's growth. Van's financial statements tell Owen a lot. He knows that there has not been much invested in resource planning systems. Consequently, as Van's business has grown, so have the inefficiencies. Owen decided that will be the topic for today—to help Van understand the need for investment in this area.

Discussion Questions

1. Put yourself in Owen's position. What questions would you ask Van to better understand his needs concerning resource planning?

2. Enterprise resource planning software is expensive. As Owen, you know that Van cannot afford to buy and implement a complete ERP system. In your opinion, what two common modules of an ERP system do you believe are the most crucial to any business? Provide a recommendation to Van, justifying your choice of the two modules for his business. How does the investment potentially benefit him?

3. Currently, Van is using a chase production strategy. Owen believes that this is an inefficient strategy. Do you agree with Owen? If so, what option would you recommend to Van? If you disagree with Owen, explain why Van is on the right track with his strategy.

* Written by Rick Bonsall, D. Mgt., McKendree University, Lebanon, IL. The people and institution are fictional and any resemblance to any person or any institution is coincidental. This case was prepared solely to provide material for class discussion. The author does not intend to illustrate either effective or ineffective handling of a managerial situation.

ADDITIONAL RESOURCES

Chopra, S., and P. Meindl. *Supply Chain Management: Strategy, Planning, and Operation.* 6th ed. Essex, England: Pearson, 2016.

Fogarty, D. W., J. H. Blackstone, and T. R. Hoffmann. *Production and Inventory Management.* 2nd ed. Cincinnati: South-Western Publishing, 1991.

Hopp, W. J., and M. L. Spearman, "To Pull or Not to Pull: What Is the Question?" *Manufacturing & Service Operations Management* 6(2), 2004: 133–148.

Jacobs, F. R., and R. B. Chase. *Operations and Supply Chain Management.* 15th ed. Boston: McGraw-Hill, 2018.

Orlicky, J. *Material Requirements Planning: The New Way of Life in Production and Inventory Management.* New York: McGraw-Hill, 1975.

Simchi-Levi, D., P. Kaminsky, and E. Simchi-Levi. *Designing and Managing the Supply Chain.* 3rd ed. Boston: McGraw-Hill Irwin, 2008.

Vollmann, T. E., W. L. Berry, D. C. Whybark, and F. R. Jacobs. *Manufacturing Planning and Control for Supply Chain Management.* 6th ed. Boston: McGraw-Hill Irwin, 2011.

Monk, E. F., and Wagner, B. J., *Concepts in Enterprise Resource Planning.* 4th ed. Boston: Cengage Learning, 2013.

END NOTES

1. Doerfler, S., "Spotlight On: General Colin L. Powell," *Inside Supply Management Magazine* 28(2), March 2017: 21.

2. Pate, P., "Managing Technology Implementations," *Public Management* 99(2), March 2017: 24–25.

3. Nadella, S., Microsoft 2015 Citizenship Report, 2015, p. 21.

4. Felix, C., "ERP Software Paves Road to Victory," *Production Machining* 16(12), December 2016: 36–39.

5. Fogarty, D. W., J. H. Blackstone, and T. R. Hoffmann. *Production & Inventory Management.* 2nd ed. Cincinnati: South-Western, 1991.

6. Snyder, M., "The Changing Face of Pharmaceutical Distribution Traceability," *Pharmaceutical Processing* 31(1), January/February 2016: 22–25.

7. Field, A. M., "Stretching the Limits of ERP," *The Journal of Commerce* 8, January 2007: 76–78.

8. Roberto, M., "ERP Enters Age of Infrastructure," *Manufacturing Business Technology* 25(7), July 2007: 24–25.

9. Curt, B., "The ERP Edge," *Multichannel Merchant* 3(7), July 2007: 50–54.

10. McCrea, B., "2016 State of ERP: Gaining Speed," *Modern Materials Handling* 71(8), August 2016: 70–76.

11. Jutras, C., "The ERP in Manufacturing Benchmark Report," *Aberdeen Group, Inc.* August 2006: 1–31.

12. Maas, J.-B., P. C. Fenema, and J. Soeters, "ERP System Usage: The Role of Control and Empowerment," *New Technology, Work, and Employment* 29(1), March 2014: 88–103.

Chapter 7

INVENTORY MANAGEMENT

If you're in a partnership, you're only as good as your weakest partners.

— **Robert Kraft, chairman and CEO, Kraft Group**[1]

What has made us successful over the last 10 years is not going to make us successful over the next 10 years.

— **Bob Weidner, president and CEO, Metals Service Center Institute**[2]

Whether for one store or 1,000, good inventory management can keep customers happy and retailers profitable. Many convenience stores are using technical advances to take the guesswork out of buying to keep the turns coming.

— **Gail Fleenor, contributing editor, Convenience Store Decisions**[3]

Cost reduction is a universal and global issue that transcends industries, locations, and business units. To best achieve it, experts say, supply managers should review their current business and manufacturing processes. They need to look beyond cost of materials to find other areas—including inventory reduction, workflow reorganization, equipment optimization, waste minimization, and supplier negotiation—in which cost reduction can be attained.

— **Stan J. Woszczynski, chief manufacturing officer, Cummins**[4]

Learning Objectives

After completing this chapter, you should be able to

- Distinguish dependent from independent demand inventories.
- Describe the four basic types of inventories and their functions.
- Describe the costs of inventory and inventory turnovers.
- Describe ABC classification, the ABC inventory matrix, and cycle counting.
- Describe RFID and how it can be used in inventory management.
- Describe the EOQ model and its underlying assumptions.
- Describe the quantity discount and the EMQ models and their relationships with the basic EOQ model.
- Describe the various statistical ROP models.
- Describe the continuous review and periodic review systems.

Chapter Outline

Introduction

Dependent Demand and Independent Demand

Concepts and Tools of Inventory Management

Inventory Models

Summary

SCM Profile   Does Inventory Management Matter?

Inventory management is one of the most critical tasks of an organization. Inventory managers can exploit some of the typical tools in ERP systems to help manage inventory. For example, an ERP system provides ABC classifications and inventory turnovers to help managers focus on the high value items. Also, managers can use replenishment reports and forecasts that include safety stocks, lead times, review cycles, reorder points, and economic order quantities to maintain the right mix and amount of inventory.[5]

The Institute for Supply Management's Report on Business shows the overall U.S. economy continued to grow for the 94th consecutive month in April 2017.[6] A growing economy means there are more inventories in the supply chain. Although there are many factors that affect inventory management, inventory experts recommend a number of lean inventory practices. First, inventory managers should pay close attention to demand planning. Although ERP systems can generate sales forecasts readily, the key to better inventory management is to disseminate that information to the supply chain team to ensure expectations are clear and consistent throughout all supply chains. Second, top management commitment on inventory policies is necessary to lower inventory costs while raising customer service levels. Third, it is necessary to employ a centralized inventory management application to manage the information, as well as to execute and monitor the process to ensure customer orders are fulfilled accurately and efficiently across the supply chains. Fourth, managers should utilize accurate, real-time data capture technology to ensure inventory accuracy. Fifth, managers should exploit advanced shipping notices, radio frequency identification, and other digital technologies to smooth out the receiving process. Finally, proper employee training is vital to effective inventory management. Although it is top management who sets the firm's strategy, with middle management responsible for running the processes, it is the floor associates who are executing the transactions. Employee training is necessary at all levels of management.[7]

If the economy slows down rapidly, the ERP system may not react fast enough to reflect declining sales. Hence, manual adjustments may be needed. For example, use of the economic order quantity and reorder point to calculate order quantities and frequencies may result in excessive inventory because the historical annual usage becomes overstated due to the declining sales. Similarly, sales forecasts and safety stocks based on historical data in the ERP system are now overstated. Items for which the on-hand quantity stayed above its safety stock over the last twelve months may indicate excessive inventory. Thus, manual adjustments of the stock levels may be necessary.[8]

Much of the success with inventory management is about establishing and maintaining operational discipline. When inventory is poorly managed, one of two outcomes is inevitable—being saddled with devastating stockouts or costly overstocks. Stockouts occur when a business lacks the correct mix and quantity of inventory to meet customer demand. This results in lost sales and customer dissatisfaction. Conversely, allowing slow moving stock to pile up in storage raises inventory costs and constricts the flow of working capital. This chapter discusses the concepts and tools of inventory management.

INTRODUCTION

Inventory can be one of the most expensive assets of an organization. It may account for more than 10 percent of total revenue or total assets for some organizations. Although companies in the manufacturing sector usually carry more inventory than service firms, effective inventory management is nonetheless important to both manufacturers and service organizations. Table 7.1 shows the amount of inventory, and the ratio of inventory to total revenue and total assets, of a few large globally recognized manufacturing and service firms. While the inventory to total assets ratio for service organizations (such as the first two casino hotel companies shown in Table 7.1) is relatively low compared to most manufacturers, inventory management for service firms poses a different challenge. Casino hotels, for example, carry a wide range of perishable food items to stock the diverse restaurants operating within their properties. Managing perishable inventory presents a unique challenge to operations managers.

Inventory management policy affects how efficiently a firm deploys its assets in producing goods and services. Developing effective inventory control systems to reduce waste and stockouts in manufacturing or service organizations is a complex problem. The right amount of inventory supports manufacturing, logistics, and other functions, but excessive inventory is a sign of poor inventory management that creates an unnecessary waste of scarce resources. In addition, excessive inventory adversely affects financial performance. The need for better inventory management systems continues to challenge operations managers.

This chapter first explains the difference between dependent demand and independent demand items. Then it focuses on the independent demand items to describe the basic concepts and tools of inventory management, including the ABC inventory control system, inventory costs, and radio frequency identification. The chapter also discusses the three fundamental deterministic inventory models and the two major types of stochastic inventory models.

Table 7.1	Inventory Investment Compared to Total Revenue and Total Assets					
COMPANY	FINANCIAL YEAR END	TOTAL REVENUE ($)	TOTAL ASSETS ($)	YEAR END INVENTORY ($)	INVENTORY/ TOTAL REVENUE (%)	INVENTORY/ TOTAL ASSETS (%)
Las Vegas Sands Corp.	Dec 31, 16	11,410	20,469	46	0.40	0.22
MGM Mirage	Dec 31, 16	6,455	28,173	98	1.52	0.35
Microsoft Corp.	Jun 30, 16	85,320	193,694	2,251	2.64	1.16
Ford Motor Co.	Dec 31, 16	151,800	237,951	8,898	5.86	3.74
General Motors Company	Dec 31, 16	166,380	221,690	13,788	8.29	6.22
Toyota Motor Corp.	Mar 31, 16	252,708	421,972	11,863	4.69	2.81
Walmart Stores, Inc.	Jan 31, 17	485,873	198,825	43,046	8.86	21.65
Target Corp.	Jan 28, 17	69,495	37,431	8,309	11.96	22.20
Pfizer, Inc.	Dec 31, 16	52,824	171,615	3,050	5.77	1.78
Intel Corp.	Dec 31, 16	59,387	113,327	5,553	9.35	4.90
Advanced Micro Devices, Inc.	Dec 31, 16	4,272	3,321	204	4.78	6.14

Source: Annual Reports on Form 10-K. All numbers in millions, except ratios.

DEPENDENT DEMAND AND INDEPENDENT DEMAND

Inventory management models are generally separated by the nature and types of the inventory being considered and can be classified as dependent demand and independent demand models.

Dependent demand is the internal demand for parts based on the demand of the final product in which the parts are used. Subassemblies, components, and raw materials are examples of dependent demand items. Dependent demand may have a pattern of abrupt and dramatic change because of its dependency on the demand of the final product, particularly if the final product is produced in large lot sizes. Dependent demand can be calculated once the demand of the final product is known. Hence, material requirements planning (MRP) software is often used to compute exact material requirements.

The dependent demand inventory system was discussed in Chapter 6. For example, the ATV Corporation's master production schedule discussed in Table 6.4 in Chapter 6 shows that 120 all-terrain vehicles will be produced in January. The firm thus knows that 120 handlebars and 480 wheel rims will be needed. The demand for handlebars, wheel rims, and other dependent demand items can be calculated based on the bill of materials and the demand of the final product as stated on the master production schedule.

Independent demand is the demand for a firm's end products and has a demand pattern affected by trends, seasonal patterns, and general market conditions. For example, the customer demand for all-terrain vehicles is independent demand. Batteries, headlights, seals, and gaskets originally used in assembling the all-terrain vehicles are dependent demands; however, the replacement batteries, headlights, seals, and gaskets sold as *service parts* to the repair shops or end users are independent demand items. Similarly, the original battery used in assembling your new car is a dependent demand item for the automobile manufacturer, but the new battery that you bought to replace the original battery is an independent demand item. Independent demand items cannot be derived using the material requirements planning logic from the demand for other items and, thus, must be forecasted based on market conditions.

CONCEPTS AND TOOLS OF INVENTORY MANAGEMENT

Savvy operations managers are concerned with controlling inventories not only within their organizations but also throughout their many supply chains. An effective independent demand inventory system ensures smooth operations and allows manufacturing firms to store up production capacity in the form of work-in-process (WIP) and finished goods inventories. While some service firms are unable to inventory their output, such organizations may rely on appointment backlogs, labor scheduling, and cross-training to balance supply and demand.

All manufacturing and service organizations are concerned with effective inventory planning and control. Inventory requires capital investment, handling, and storage space, and it is also subject to deterioration and shrinkage. Although a firm's operating costs and financial performance can be improved by reducing inventory, the risk of stockouts can be devastating to customer service. Therefore, companies must strike a delicate balance between inventory investment and customer service. This section discusses some important concepts and tools of inventory management. Vendor-managed inventory and co managed inventory, discussed in Chapter 4, will not be explored here.

The Functions and Basic Types of Inventory

Inventory includes all the materials and goods that are purchased, partially completed materials and component parts, and the finished goods produced. The primary functions of inventory are to *buffer* uncertainty in the marketplace and to *decouple*, or break the dependencies between stages in the supply chain. For example, an appropriate amount of inventory, known as *safety stock* or *buffer stock*, can be used to cushion uncertainties due to fluctuations in supply, demand, and/or delivery lead time. Similarly, the right amount of inventory enables a work center to operate without interruption when other work centers in the same production process are off-line for maintenance or repair. Keeping the correct amount of inventory at each work center also allows a faster work center to operate smoothly when it is constrained by slower upstream work centers.

In the increasingly global business environment, it is not unusual that organizations use the concept of *geographical specialization* to manufacture their products in developing countries. In this scenario, the developing countries specialize in cheap labor and abundant raw materials, whereas the manufacturing firms provide the technology and capital to produce the goods. The ability to geographically separate the consumption of the finished goods from production is a key function of inventory. For manufacturers, inventory also acts as *stored capacity*. For instance, snowmobile manufacturers can build up inventory by producing snowmobiles year-round in anticipation of peak demand during the busy winter season.

There are four broad categories of inventories: raw materials; work-in-process; finished goods; and maintenance, repair, and operating (MRO) supplies.

- *Raw materials* are unprocessed purchased inputs or materials for manufacturing the finished goods. Raw materials become part of finished goods after the manufacturing process is completed. There are many reasons for keeping raw material inventories, including volume purchases to create transportation economies or take advantage of quantity discounts; stockpiling in anticipation of future price increases or to avoid a potential short supply; or keeping safety stock to guard against supplier delivery or quality problems.

- *Work-in-process* describes materials that are partially processed but not yet ready for sales. One reason to keep WIP inventories is to decouple processing stages or to break the dependencies between work centers.

- *Finished goods* are completed products ready for shipment. Finished goods inventories are often kept to buffer against unexpected demand changes and in anticipation of production process downtime; to ensure production economies when the setup cost is very high; or to stabilize production rates, especially for seasonal products.

- *Maintenance, repair, and operating supplies* are materials and supplies used when producing the products but are not parts of the products. Solvents, cutting tools, and lubricants for machines are examples of MRO supplies. The two main reasons for storing MRO supplies are to gain purchase economies and to avoid material shortages that may shut down production.

Inventory Costs

The bottom line of effective inventory management is to control inventory costs and minimize stockouts. Inventory costs can be categorized in many ways: as direct and indirect costs, fixed and variable costs, and order (or setup) and holding (or carrying) costs.

Direct costs are those that are directly traceable to the unit produced, such as the amount of materials and labor used to produce a unit of the finished good. **Indirect costs** are those that cannot be traced directly to the unit produced, and they are synonymous with manufacturing overhead. Maintenance, repair, and operating supplies; heating; lighting; buildings; equipment; and plant security are examples of indirect costs. **Fixed costs** are independent of the output quantity, but **variable costs** change as a function of the output level. Buildings, equipment, plant security, heating, and lighting are examples of fixed costs, whereas direct materials and labor costs are variable costs. A key focus of inventory management is to control variable costs since fixed costs are generally considered *sunk costs*. Sunk costs are costs that have already been incurred and cannot be recovered or reversed.

Order costs are the direct variable costs associated with placing an order with the supplier, whereas **holding** or **carrying costs** are the costs incurred for holding inventory in storage. Order costs include managerial and clerical costs for preparing the purchase, as well as other incidental expenses that can be traced directly to the purchase. Examples of holding costs include handling charges, warehousing expenses, insurance, pilferage, shrinkage, taxes, and the cost of capital. In a manufacturing context, **setup costs** are used in place of order costs to describe the costs associated with setting up machines and equipment to produce a batch of product. However, in inventory management discussions, *order costs* and *setup costs* are often used interchangeably.

Inventory Investment

Inventory serves many important functions for manufacturing and service firms; however, excessive inventory is detrimental to a firm's financial health and competitive edge. Whether inventory is an asset that contributes to organizational objectives or a liability depends on its management.

Inventory is expensive and it ties up a firm's working capital. Moreover, inventory requires storage space and incurs other carrying costs. Some products such as perishable food items and hazardous materials require special handling and storage that add to the cost of holding inventory. Inventory can also deteriorate quickly while it is in storage. In addition, inventory can become obsolete very quickly as new materials and technologies are introduced. Most importantly, large piles of inventory delay a firm's ability to respond swiftly to production problems and changes in technologies and market conditions.

Inventory investment can be measured in several ways. The typical annual physical stock counts to determine the total dollars invested in inventory provide an absolute measure of inventory investment. The inventory value is then reported in a firm's balance sheet. This value can be compared to the budget and past inventory investments. However, the absolute dollars invested in inventory do not provide sufficient evidence about whether the company is using its inventory wisely. A widely used measure to determine how efficiently a firm is using its inventory to generate revenue is the **inventory turnover ratio** or **inventory turnovers**. This ratio shows how many times a company turns over its inventory in an accounting period. Higher turnovers are generally viewed as a positive trend because it indicates the company generates more revenue per dollar in inventory investment. Moreover, higher turnovers allow the company to increase cash flow and reduce warehousing and carrying costs. Conversely, a low inventory turnover may point to overstocking or deficiencies in the product line or marketing effort. Table 7.2 shows recent inventory turnover ratios for the same eleven firms shown in Table 7.1.

Table 7.2	Inventory Turnover Ratios				
COMPANY	FINANCIAL YEAR END	TOTAL REVENUE ($)	COST OF REVENUE ($)	YEAR END INVENTORY ($)	INVENTORY TURNOVER RATIO
Las Vegas Sands Corp.	Dec 31, 16	11,410	5,837	46	126.89
MGM Mirage	Dec 31, 16	6,455	5,496	98	56.08
Microsoft Corp.	Jun 30, 16	85,320	32,780	2,251	14.56
Ford Motor Co.	Dec 31, 16	151,800	135,488	8,898	15.23
General Motors Company	Dec 31, 16	166,380	145,125	13,788	10.53
Toyota Motor Corp.	Mar 31, 16	252,708	201,125	11,863	16.95
Walmart Stores, Inc.	Jan 31, 17	485,873	361,256	43,046	8.39
Target Corp.	Jan 28, 17	69,495	48,872	8,309	5.88
Pfizer, Inc.	Dec 31, 16	52,824	12,329	3,050	4.04
Intel Corp.	Dec 31, 16	59,387	23,196	5,553	4.18
Advanced Micro Devices, Inc.	Dec 31, 16	4,272	3,274	204	16.05

Source: Annual Reports on Form 10-K. All numbers in millions, except ratios.

The formula for the inventory turnover ratio can be stated as:

$$\text{Inventory turnover ratio} = \frac{\text{Cost of revenue}}{\text{Average inventory}}.$$

Inventory turnover ratio can be computed for any accounting period—monthly, quarterly, or annually. Cost of revenue is also the cost of goods sold, which is readily available from a firm's income statement. The average inventory is the mean of the beginning and ending inventory for a period. However, a firm's inventory may fluctuate widely in a financial year; thus, the average of the beginning and ending inventory may be a poor indicator of the firm's actual average inventory for the year. In this case, the average of the twelve monthly ending inventories can be used as the average inventory when computing the annual inventory turnover ratio. In Table 7.2, since the average of the monthly inventories was not available in the *annual reports*, the financial year-end closing inventory was used to compute the ratio.

In 2016, for instance, Las Vegas Sands Corp. (LVS) turned over its inventory a staggering 127 times. However, the nature of LVS's business may suggest that a major portion of its revenue came from hotel room and gaming sales, with the inventory consisting mostly of goods for the restaurants. Thus, the revenue generated by hotel room and gaming sales could be excluded from the calculation of the turnover ratio. Firms put a significant emphasis on improving their turnovers. It is not uncommon for firms, especially manufacturers and retailers to run promotions and clearance sales to reduce year-end inventory.

The ABC Inventory Control System

A common problem with many inventory management systems is the challenge to maintain accurate inventory records. Many organizations use **cycle counting** to reconcile discrepancies between their physical inventory and inventory record on a monthly or quarterly basis. Cycle counting, or physically counting inventory on a periodic basis, also helps to identify obsolete stocks and inventory problems so that remedial action can be taken in a reasonable amount of time. However, cycle counting can be costly and time-consuming and can disrupt operations. The following SCM profile demonstrates the importance and applications of annual physical inventory count and cycle counting in businesses.

SCM Profile   **Keeping Accurate Physical Inventory**

In the United States, the generally accepted accounting principles (GAAP) and IRS rules require businesses to either conduct an annual physical inventory count or implement a perpetual counting system. The former requires a business to physically count its entire inventory, whereas the latter is a perpetual counting system where a subset of inventory in a specified location is counted on a stipulated day. In cycle counting, the process is repeated in such a way that all the items in inventory are counted at least once in an accounting period. The physical inventory count is a much more invasive process that can put the entire business operations on hold. Cycle counting reduces disruption in business operations, and is popular among organizations with large inventory, especially among firms that cannot be closed for an extended period for annual physical inventory count.

In addition to compliance with rules and regulations, performing physical inventory count or cycle count is critical to the success of any business because the process reconciles inventory errors by checking actual stock against inventory records. Moreover, the process provides information of where all the stock is, allows the firm to write off inventory losses to lessen the tax burden, and identifies shrinkage problems due to damage and theft. Usually, the business manager of the unit is responsible to ensure the inventory count is properly performed, and inventory records reflect actual quantities on hand.

For example, a convenience store marketer with more than forty years of experience stresses that poor inventory management is a common problem that plagues many convenience stores. He highlights a list of suggestions to achieve an effective inventory control system. For instance, the storekeeper must be absolutely dedicated to details, and the store must be clean, neat, and inventory-ready because neither customers nor the inventory crew are comfortable touching dirty merchandise. Space-constrained, low-visibility areas are generally high-theft targets. It is also difficult to count inventory that are stored in cramped areas. Since tobacco products and packaging are small, he also recommends that incoming and outgoing employees must conduct a complete pack count of tobacco products at every shift change.[9]

In the October 2016 issue of the *Editor & Publisher* trade journal, a general manager in the publishing industry agrees that conducting inventory counts is not a glamorous job but accurate inventory is just as important to the overall health of the organization as are other essential production functions. The general manager also emphasizes that physical inventory counts must be conducted by a detail-oriented individual who has good knowledge of the inventories. Paper stock tends to be the most significant inventory and expense of a publishing firm. In this industry, the two options to discharge paper stock as production cost are (1) discharge the entire ream of paper stock as production cost once it is opened or (2) discharge actual quantity of paper used. The latter is preferred by smaller operations because it counts unused paper stock on partial rolls as inventory. The downside is that the process takes more effort to do physical inventory.[10]

The **ABC inventory control system** is a useful tool to determine which inventories should be counted more frequently and managed more closely and which others should not. ABC analysis is often combined with the **80/20 rule** or **Pareto analysis**. The 80/20 rule suggests that 80 percent of the objective can be achieved by doing 20 percent of the tasks, but the remaining 20 percent of the objective will take up 80 percent of the tasks. The Pareto analysis recommends that tasks falling into the first category be assigned the highest priority and managed closely.

The ABC inventory control system prioritizes inventory items into groups A, B, and C. However, it is not uncommon that some firms choose to use more than three categories.

Table 7.3	ABC Inventory Classification	
CLASSIFICATIONS	PERCENT OF TOTAL ANNUAL DOLLAR USAGE	PERCENT OF TOTAL INVENTORY ITEMS
A Items	80	20
B Items	15	40
C Items	5	40

The *A items* are given the highest priority, while *C items* have the lowest priority and are typically the most numerous (the *B items* fall somewhere in between). Greater attention, safety stocks, and resources are devoted to the high-priority or *A items*. The priority is most often determined by annual dollar usage. However, priority may also be determined by product shelf life, sales volume, whether the materials are critical components, or some other criteria. A summary of the classification is provided in Table 7.3.

When prioritizing inventories by annual dollar usage, the ABC system suggests that approximately 20 percent of the items make up about 80 percent of the total annual dollar usage, and these items are classified as the *A items*. The *B items* make up roughly 40 percent of the items and account for about 15 percent of the total annual dollar usage, while the *C items* are the remaining 40 percent of the items, making up about 5 percent of the total annual dollar usage of inventory. Since the *A items* are the highest annual dollar usage items, they should be monitored more frequently and may have higher safety stock levels to guard against stockouts, particularly if these items are used in products sold to supply chain trading partners. The *C items* would then be counted less frequently, and stockouts may be allowed to save inventory space and carrying costs. For example, St. Onge, a Pennsylvania-based engineering and logistics firm, migrated to an ABC inventory classification system to allow them to allocate more resources to their more profitable A items.[11]

ABC inventory classification can be done monthly, quarterly, annually, or any fixed period. For the fast-moving consumer market, an *A item* may become a *C item* within months or even weeks. For these cases, the ABC inventory classification based on annual dollar usage might not be useful to management. An illustration of an ABC inventory classification using annual dollar usage is shown in Example 7.1.

Example 7.1   ABC Inventory Classification Based on Annual Dollar Usage

Note that in this example, the *A items* only account for about 67 percent of the total annual dollar volume, while the *B items* account for about 28 percent. This illustrates that judgment must also be applied when using the ABC classification method, and the 80/20 rule should only be used as a general guideline.

INVENTORY ITEM NUMBER	ITEM COST ($)	ANNUAL USAGE (UNITS)	ANNUAL USAGE ($)	PERCENT OF TOTAL ANNUAL DOLLAR USAGE	CLASSIFICATION BY ANNUAL DOLLAR USAGE
A246	1.00	22,000	22,000	35.2	A
N376	0.50	40,000	20,000	32.0	A
C024	4.25	1,468	6,239	10.0	B
R221	12.00	410	4,920	7.8	B
P112	2.25	1,600	3,600	5.8	B
R116	0.12	25,000	3,000	4.8	B
T049	8.50	124	1,054	1.7	C
B615	0.25	3,500	875	1.4	C
L227	1.25	440	550	0.9	C
T519	26.00	10	260	0.4	C
Total Annual Dollar Usage:			**$62,498**	**100%**	

The ABC Inventory Matrix

The ABC inventory analysis can be expanded to assist in identifying obsolete stocks and to analyze whether a company is stocking the correct inventory by comparing two ABC analyses. First, an ABC analysis is done based on annual inventory dollar usage (as shown in Example 7.1) to classify inventories into A, B, and C groups. Next, a second ABC analysis is done based on current or on-hand inventory dollar value (as shown in Example 7.2) to classify inventories again into A, B, and C groups. Finally, the two ABC analyses are combined to form an **ABC inventory matrix** as shown in Figure 7.1. The *A items* based on current inventory value should match the *A items* based on annual inventory dollar usage, falling within the unshaded diagonal region of the figure. Similarly, the B and C items should match when comparing the two ABC analyses. Otherwise, the company is stocking the wrong items. The ABC inventory matrix also suggests that some overlaps are expected between two borderline classifications (as indicated by the wide diagonal region). For instance, some marginal *B items* based on annual inventory dollar usage might appear as *C items* based on the current inventory value classification and vice versa.

Referring to Figure 7.1, plots in the upper-left shaded triangle of the ABC inventory matrix indicate that some *A items* based on annual inventory dollar usage are showing up as *B* or *C items* based on the current inventory value classification and that some *B items* have similarly been classified as *C items*. This suggests that the company has current inventories for its *A* and *B items* that are too low, and is risking stockouts of their higher dollar usage items. Conversely, plots in the lower-right shaded triangle show that some *C items* based on annual inventory dollar usage are showing up as *A* and *B items* based on current inventory value, and some *B items* are similarly showing up as *A items*; thus indicating that the company has current inventories for its *B* and *C items* that are too high, and is incurring excess inventory carrying costs. This may also point to the presence of excessive *obsolete stock* if the inventory turnover ratios are very low. Obsolete stocks should be disposed of so that valuable inventory investment and warehouse space can be used for productive

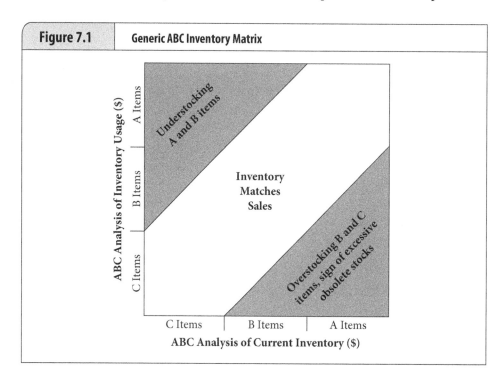

Figure 7.1   **Generic ABC Inventory Matrix**

inventory. When used in conjunction with inventory turnovers, the ABC inventory matrix is a powerful tool for managing inventory investment. Example 7.2 shows the classifications based on current inventory value for the same ten items shown in Example 7.1, and it also shows the annual dollar usage classifications.

The two ABC analyses from Examples 7.1 and 7.2 are combined and plotted on the ABC inventory matrix shown in Figure 7.2. Each inventory item is plotted on the matrix using the "percent of total current inventory" on the horizontal axis and the "percent of total annual dollar usage" on the vertical axis. For instance, the coordinate of the item "T519"

Example 7.2   ABC Inventory Classification Based on Current Inventory Value

| | | | | | CLASSIFICATION BY | |
INVENTORY ITEM NUMBER	ITEM COST ($)	CURRENT INVENTORY (UNITS)	CURRENT INVENTORY VALUE ($)	PERCENT OF TOTAL CURRENT INVENTORY	CURRENT INVENTORY VALUE	ANNUAL DOLLAR USAGE
T519	26.00	300	7,800	40.5	A	C
A246	1.00	5,600	5,600	29.1	A	A
L227	1.25	1,200	1,500	7.8	B	C
C024	4.25	348	1,479	7.7	B	B
R221	12.00	80	960	5.0	B	B
P112	2.25	352	792	4.1	B	B
T049	8.50	50	425	2.2	C	C
N376	0.50	800	400	2.1	C	A
R116	0.12	2,100	252	1.3	C	B
B615	0.25	120	30	0.2	C	C
Total Physical Inventory ($):			$19,238	100%		

Figure 7.2   ABC Inventory Matrix for Example 7.2

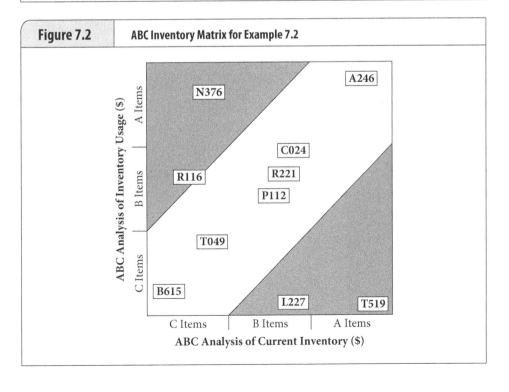

would be (40.5, 0.4). The vertical axis ranges from 0.4 to 35.2 percent, and the horizontal axis ranges from 0.2 to 40.5 percent, thus "T519" falls on the extreme lower-right corner of the matrix. The plots in Figure 7.2 show that six of the inventory items fell along the diagonal, suggesting the appropriate stocking levels. The company has probably overstocked items "T519" and "L227" and understocked "N376" and possibly "R116." It is important however, that the inventory turnover ratios for each item be used in conjunction with the ABC inventory matrix to get a sense of how fast or slow inventories are turning over.

Radio Frequency Identification

The barcode has been used to identify the manufacturer and content of a package or container for decades. However, it cannot store enough information to distinguish goods at the item level. Direct line of sight is required to read a barcode, and the information stored on it is static and not updatable. **Radio frequency identification (RFID)** has been used as an eventual successor to the barcode for tracking an individual unit of goods. RFID tags do not require direct line of sight to be read, and information on the tag is updatable. RFID technology is used in libraries, for passport identification, animal tracking, medical disciplines, toll payments, and in many other fields. There is a related technology called **near field communication (NFC)** that was designed as a secure form of data exchange between an NFC tag or Android-powered device with another Android-powered device. NFC is a

SCM Profile | **RFID and Inventory Management**

RFID technology has today evolved into an integral part of inventory management. Several large retailers, such as Levi's, American Apparel, and the U.K.-based hypermarket chain Marks & Spencer, are experimenting with blanket RFID coverage by installing fixed position readers in the stores and distribution centers. They are also using robots with built-in RFID readers to scan RFID-tagged items in the store at night. Retailers believe they can enhance the customer experience by putting RFID tags at the item level. Moreover, item-level tagging not only reduces inventory costs associated with manpower, but also increases the speed and accuracy of physical inventory counts.

Using item-level RFID, Macy's implemented a new order fulfillment program called "Pick to the Last Unit" (P2LU) with its women's dresses. Macy's realized that it could exploit its brick-and-mortar stores to function as warehouses to allow customers to shop over the Internet, and fulfill the orders by shipping from the stores. In addition to cutting $1 billion of inventory from its stores, P2LU ensures that the last unit of an item in any store is available for sale and is easily located for order fulfillment.[12]

A research conducted by BCC Research estimated that the global market for RFID technologies will grow from $16.2 billion in 2016 to $38.0 billion in 2021. The technology is making major inroads into new applications in inventory management, including fraud prevention in the retail industry. Luxury goods and expensive retail merchandise have not only been targets of theft but also fakes and counterfeits. To prevent cheap counterfeit wine, for example, from being repackaged into the bottle of an expensive wine with all the packaging and labeling intact, an RFID capsule can be fitted over the capped or corked wine bottle. The capsule contains unique RFID information to authenticate the bottle of wine and to certify that it has not been tempered with.[13]

specialized subset of RFID technology. The following SCM profile shows some applications of RFID in inventory management.

There are two major RFID standards: the **electronic product code (EPC)** standard, managed by the EPCglobal, Inc.,[14] a subsidiary of GS1 that created the UPC barcode; and the 18000 standard of the International Standards Organization (ISO). Walmart Stores, Inc., and the Department of Defense were among the two largest adopters of RFID.[15] Walmart adopted the EPC standard, whereas the Department of Defense chose the EPC standard for general purpose applications and the ISO standard for air interface communications between the readers and the tags. The EPC standard is more widely adopted, especially in the commercial sector.

Like barcode technology, a reader is used to read the information stored in RFID tags. However, the reader does not have to be placed directly in line of sight of the tag to read the radio signal—a significant advantage of RFID over barcode. The original RFID tag classes were first developed by the MIT Auto-ID Center. The oldest class 0 and 1 later passed onto EPCglobal as a basis to create the newer EPC Gen 2 standard. The EPC standards call for six classes of tags as shown in Table 7.4. Class 0 tags are read only tags, but class 1 tags can be programmed once to update the information stored on the tags. Like a rewritable CD, class 2 tags are enhanced Generation 2 class 1 tags that can be rewritten multiple times. Classes 0, 1, and 2 are **passive RFID tags** that do not store power on the tags, and classes 3 and 4 are **active RFID tags** that contain a power source to boost their range. Class 5 tags can communicate with other class 5 tags and other devices.

The current EPC standard is the 96-bit ultra-high-frequency (UHF) class 1, Gen 2 write-once-read-many (WORM) tag. The management board of GS1, which oversees EPCglobal standards, ratified the new EPC Gen2v2.0.1 in 2015.[16] Gen2v2, a fully backward-compatible EPC standard operating in the 860 to 960 MHz UHF range, is a major update since 2008. This generation of tags is expected to pave the way to the class 2 high-memory full read/write tags. A 256-bit version of the tag is being created, but full details

Table 7.4	EPCglobal's Tag Classes	
CLASS TYPE	**FEATURES**	**TAG TYPE**
Class 0	Read only	Passive (64 bits only) Generation 1, factory preprogramed read-only passive tag
Class 1*	Write once, read many	Passive (minimum 96 bits) Generation 1 and 2, read-only passive tag like class 0 and has one-time filed programmability
Class 2	Read/write	Passive (minimum 96 bits) Passive tag with read-wrote capability
Class 3	Read/write with battery power to enhance range	Semi-active tag with read-write memory, onboard sensor, and an incorporated battery to provide increased coverage
Class 4	Read/write active transmitter	Read-write active tag with integrated transmitter for communication using the battery onboard
Class 5	Read/write active transmitter	Active tag that can communicate with other class 5 tags

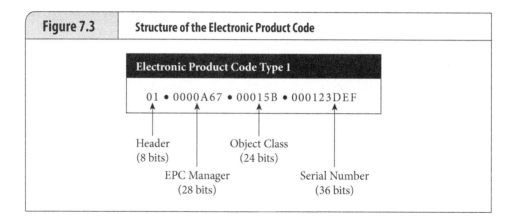

Figure 7.3   **Structure of the Electronic Product Code**

are not yet available. Class 3 tags have not yet been fully defined whereas class 4 and 5 tags are in the early definition stage.

The current 96-bit EPC is a number made up of a header and three sets of data as shown in Figure 7.3. The 8-bit *header* identifies the version of the EPC being used; the 28-bit *EPC manager* identifies the manufacturer (and even plant) of the product; the 24-bit *object class* identifies the unique product family; and the 36-bit *serial number* uniquely identifies the individual physical item being read. The 8-bit header can identify 256 (2^8) versions of EPC; the 28-bit EPC manager can classify 268,435,456 (2^{28}) companies; the 24-bit object class can identify 16,777,216 (2^{24}) product families per company; and the 36-bit serial number can differentiate 68,719,476,736 (2^{36}) specific items per product family. Using this mammoth combination (which is unmatched by the barcode), it is not difficult to envisage that RFID can revolutionize inventory management in the supply chain.

Components of a Radio Frequency Identification System

An RFID system consists of four parts: the tag, reader, communication network, and RFID software. The tag consists of a computer chip and an antenna for wireless communication with the handheld or fixed-position RFID reader, and the communication network connects the readers to transmit inventory information to the enterprise information system. The RFID software manages the collection, synchronization, and communication of the data with warehouse management, ERP, and supply chain planning systems, and stores the information in a database. Figure 7.4 shows a generic RFID system.

Though RFID was designed for use at the item level to identify individual items, current implementation focuses at the aggregate level where tags are placed on cases, crates, pallets, or containers due to the high cost of the tags. A passive 96-bit RFID tag costs approximately 7 to 15 cents today compared to $2 in 1999,[17,18] but it is still not financially feasible to tag individual low-ticket items. Thus, the existing focus is at the aggregate level focusing on cases or pallets of items, although some retailers have started to place RFID tags on individual high-ticket items like cameras and electronic products to deter theft and closely manage the expensive inventory.

How Radio Frequency Identification Automates the Supply Chain

RFID is a valuable technology for tracking inventory in the supply chain. It can synchronize information and physical flow of goods across the supply chain from manufacturers to retail outlets and to the consumers at the right place at the right time. Likewise, RFID can track returned goods through the supply chain and prevent counterfeiting. It also helps

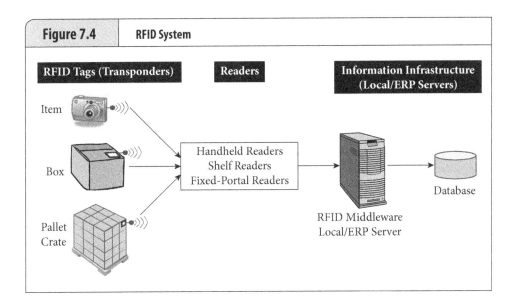

| Figure 7.4 | RFID System |

to reduce out-of-stock items. There is no doubt that RFID is an invaluable tool for improving inventory management and supply chain efficiencies. The steps by which the RFID can automate the supply chain follow.

1. *Materials Management*: As a supply vehicle enters the warehouse, the fixed-portal RFID reader positioned at the entrance reads the tags on the pallets or individual items to provide handling, routing, and storage information of the incoming goods. Inventory status can be updated automatically.

2. *Manufacturing*: An RFID tag can be placed on the unit being produced so that specific customer configurations can be incorporated automatically during the production process. This is invaluable in a make-to-order environment.

3. *Distribution Center*: As the logistics vehicle arrives at the loading dock, the fixed-portal RFID reader communicates with the tag on the vehicle to confirm that it is approved to pick up goods. When the loaded vehicle leaves the dock and crosses the portal, the reader picks up the signals from the tags to alert the RFID software and ERP system to update the inventory automatically and initiate an advance shipping notice (ASN), proof of pickup, and invoices.

4. *Retail Store*: As the delivery vehicle enters the unloading dock, the fixed-portal reader picks up the signals from the tags, and the RFID software application processes the signals to provide specific handling instructions and initiate automatic routing of the goods. The RFID reader can also be placed on the store shelf to trigger automatic replenishments when an item reaches its reorder point. Moreover, inventory status can be updated in real time automatically at any stage of the supply chain, and handheld readers can be used to assist in cycle counting. Item-level tagging can be used to recommend complementary products. For instance, a computer screen and a reader can be placed in the changing room, so when a consumer tests a tagged suit in the changing room, the reader picks up the signal to suggest matching shirts and shoes on an LCD screen. When RFID is fully implemented at the item level, it is not difficult to envisage that instead of waiting for a cashier, a consumer could simply walk out the door of a store with the purchase. A reader built into the door would be able to recognize the items in the consumer's cart and charge the consumer's pre-approved credit card automatically.

Global RFID Implementation and Challenges[19,20,21]

Radio frequency identification is one of the latest developments in inventory management. RFID technology has also been adopted by major retailers worldwide, including Marks & Spencer and Tesco in the United Kingdom and Metro Group in Germany. In the United States, Walmart mandated its suppliers to tag all shipments to its warehouses with RFID. Likewise, the U.S. Department of Defense has also required that pallets delivered to its warehouses from its largest suppliers be tagged with RFID.

Tagging strategies differ considerably by region. In the United States, the focus is on case- or pallet-level tagging, whereas European retailers focus on item-level tagging. U.S. retailers focus on case- and pallet-level tagging for inventory management to help reduce inventory and stockouts while simultaneously improving customer service. Consumer-privacy issues and high implementation costs for hardware and tags deter American retailers from moving into item-level tagging. In Europe, the cultural climate has made it easier to deploy RFID, and retailers are using the technology at the item level for category management and garment sorting and are looking at RFID for smart shelves such as automatic replenishment. While most retailers in Asia expect to gain from integrating RFID technology along their supply chains, China is skeptical about sharing potentially confidential information with foreign businesses and lags behind other nations in RFID technology use. In Japan, the RFID market focuses on government applications, logistics usage, and asset tagging.

However, rapid industry adoption has proved more challenging than initially believed and, as in the case of Walmart, has had mixed success. Tag and RFID system costs are among the major impediments to a faster adoption of the technology. RFID tags can cost ten to twenty times more than simple barcodes. Globally, the RFID industry still does not have its own UHF spectrum allocation though the new Gen2v2.0.1 standard uses 860 to 960 MHz. Differences between radio frequencies in various parts of the world are another major hurdle to broader adoption. While the United States favors the 915 MHz UHF, the Europeans prefer the 868 MHz UHF. The Chinese use frequencies from 840.25–844.75 to 920.25–924.75 MHz, while in Japan, 125–134 kHz, 13.56 MHz, 2.4–2.5 GHz, and 5.8 GHz are used, with the 950–956 MHz UHF allocated for unlicensed, low-power use. Another challenge of RFID is that UHF signals are reflected by metal and absorbed by water. Finally, with limited benefit information from a few RFID pilot projects, it is difficult for a company to calculate returns.

While considerable progress has been made on code standardization over the last few years, much work remains to be done. The United States and Europe have jointly worked on a common standard based on the modified EPCglobal UHF Gen-2 standard, but China and Japan have decided to develop their own. China supports its own EPC classification system for domestic product labeling, whereas Japan uses its Ubiquitous ID standard. Using competing RFID standards is likely to eventually lead to the need for costly multi-protocol readers that can handle tags that comply with the different standards. Despite all the challenges, RFID continues to replace barcode technology in inventory management.

Big Data Decision-Making

Another recent development that may change inventory management and combine with RFID to enable better business decision-making is big data. **Big data** broadly refers to collections of data sets that are too large and complex to be processed by traditional database management tools or data processing software applications. Instead, massive parallel software running on hundreds or even thousands of servers simultaneously is often required to store and process the data. RFID generates a huge amount of data as inventory moves through the supply chain. Big data technology helps to process the data in real time to take advantage of the information captured by RFID.

An example of how big data can enhance competitive advantage is Google's search engine. Google's core business is targeted marketing and advertising. To excel in this business, Google captures and exploits two types of big data—a comprehensive index and library of all the contents on the web and the behavior of Google users worldwide as they interact with its products and services. Google stores and indexes all the information on the web. On a big data perspective, Google processes about 12 billion searches each month. The company estimated that the web consists of 60 trillion pages that are stored in an index that exceeds 100 million gigabytes. Having a comprehensive index of the web and consumer behavior in real time allow Google to serve highly relevant searches and ads that closely mirror the user's intent.[22]

INVENTORY MODELS

A variety of inventory models for independent demand items are reviewed in this section by classifying the models into two broad categories. First, the deterministic inventory models are discussed that assume demand, delivery lead time, and other parameters are deterministic. These models use fixed parameters to derive the optimum *order quantity* to minimize *total inventory costs*. Thus, these models are also known as the **fixed order quantity models**. The economic order quantity, quantity discount, and economic manufacturing quantity models are the three most widely used fixed order quantity models. Following this, the statistical reorder point is discussed, where demand and/or lead time are not constant but can be estimated by means of a normal distribution. Finally, the continuous review and periodic review systems are discussed.

The Economic Order Quantity Model

The **economic order quantity (EOQ) model** is a classic independent demand inventory system that provides many useful ordering decisions. The basic order decision is to determine the optimal order size that minimizes total annual inventory costs—that is, the sum of the annual order cost and the annual inventory holding cost. The issue revolves around the trade-off between annual inventory holding cost and annual order cost: When the order size for an item is small, orders have to be placed on a frequent basis, causing high annual order costs; however, the firm then has a low average inventory level for this item, resulting in low annual inventory holding costs. When the order size for an item is large, orders are placed less frequently, causing lower annual order costs, but high average inventory levels for this item, resulting in higher annual expenses to hold the inventory. The EOQ model thus seeks to find an optimal order size that minimizes the sum of the two annual costs. In EOQ computations, the term *carrying cost* is often used in place of holding cost and *setup cost* is used in place of order cost.

Assumptions of the Economic Order Quantity Model

Users must carefully consider the following assumptions when determining the economic order quantity:

1. *The demand is known and constant.* For example, if there are 365 days per year and the annual demand is known to be 730 units, then daily usage must be exactly two units throughout the entire year.

2. *Order lead time is known and constant.* For example, if the delivery lead time is known to be ten days, every delivery will arrive exactly ten days after the order is placed.

3. *Replenishment is instantaneous.* The entire order is delivered at one time and partial shipments are not allowed.

4. *Price is constant.* Quantity or price discounts are not allowed.

5. *The holding cost is known and constant.* The cost or rate to hold inventory must be known and constant.

6. *Order cost is known and constant.* The cost of placing an order must be known and remains constant for all orders.

7. *Stockouts are not allowed.* Inventory must be available at all times.

Deriving the Economic Order Quantity

The EOQ can be derived easily from the total annual inventory cost formula using basic calculus. The total annual inventory cost is the sum of the annual purchase cost, the annual holding cost, and the annual order cost. The formula can be shown as:

$$\text{TAIC} = \text{Annual purchase cost} + \text{annual holding cost} + \text{annual order cost}$$
$$\text{TAIC} = \text{APC} + \text{AHC} + \text{AOC} = (R \times C) + (Q/2 \times k \times C) + (R/Q \times S)$$

where

TAIC = total annual inventory cost
APC = annual purchase cost
AHC = annual holding cost
AOC = annual order cost
R = annual requirement or demand
C = purchase cost per unit
S = cost of placing one order
k = holding rate, where annual holding cost per unit = $k \times C$
Q = order quantity

Since R, C, k, and S are deterministic (i.e., assumed to be constant terms), Q is the only unknown variable in the TAIC equation. The optimum Q (the EOQ) can be obtained by taking the first derivative of TAIC with respect to Q and then setting it equal to zero. A second derivative of TAIC can also be taken with respect to Q to prove that the TAIC is a concave function, and thus $\frac{d\text{TAIC}}{dQ} = 0$ is at the lowest point (i.e., minimum) of the total annual inventory cost curve. Thus,

$$\frac{d\text{TAIC}}{dQ} = 0 + (\tfrac{1}{2} \times k \times C) + (-1 \times R \times S \times 1/Q^2)$$
$$= \frac{kC}{2} - \frac{RS}{Q^2}$$

then setting $\frac{d\text{TAIC}}{dQ}$ equal to zero,

$$\frac{kC}{2} - \frac{RS}{Q^2} = 0$$
$$\Rightarrow \frac{kC}{2} = \frac{RS}{Q^2}$$
$$\Rightarrow Q^2 = \frac{2RS}{kC}$$
$$\Rightarrow \text{EOQ} = \sqrt{\frac{2RS}{kC}}$$

The second derivative of TAIC is

$$\frac{d^2\text{TAIC}}{dQ^2} = 0 - \left(-2 \times \frac{RS}{Q^3}\right) = \left(\frac{2RS}{Q^3}\right) \geq 0,$$

implying that the TAIC is at its minimum when $\frac{d\text{TAIC}}{dQ} = 0$.

The annual purchase cost drops off after the first derivative is taken. The managerial implication here is that purchase cost does not affect the order decision if there is no quantity discount (the annual purchase cost remains constant regardless of the order size, as long as the same annual quantity is purchased). Thus, the annual purchase cost is ignored in the classic EOQ model. Example 7.3 provides an illustration of calculating the EOQ. It should be noted that all demand must be converted to the annual requirement, and holding cost is the product of holding rate and unit cost of the item. For example, if the annual holding rate, k, is 12 percent and the item cost, C, is \$10 per unit, the holding cost, kC, is \$1.20 per unit per year.

Figure 7.5 shows the relationships between annual holding cost, annual order cost, and total annual holding plus order cost. Using the data in Example 7.3, at the EOQ (600 units), annual holding cost (\$1,200) equals annual order cost (\$1,200). At or close to the EOQ, the annual total cost curve is rather flat, indicating that it is not very sensitive to small variations in the economic order quantity. Therefore, the classic EOQ model is said to be very *robust* to minor errors in estimating cost parameters, such as holding rate, order cost, or annual usage. Table 7.5, for example, compares the annual total cost at an EOQ of 600 units and at 10 percent below and above the EOQ. The analysis shows that the cost variations range from only 0.01 to 0.56 percent above the minimum total cost.

Figure 7.5 and Table 7.5 show that if the order size is smaller than the EOQ, the annual holding cost is slightly lower, whereas the annual order cost is slightly higher. The net

---

Example 7.3   Calculating the EOQ at the Las Vegas Corporation

The Las Vegas Corporation purchases a critical component from one of its key suppliers. The operations manager, Dr. Suhaiza Zailani, wants to determine the economic order quantity, along with when to reorder, to ensure the annual inventory cost is minimized. The following information was obtained from historical data:

$$
\begin{aligned}
\text{Annual requirements } (R) &= 7{,}200 \text{ units} \\
\text{Setup cost } (S) &= \$100 \text{ per order} \\
\text{Holding rate } (k) &= 20\% \\
\text{Unit cost } (C) &= \$20 \text{ per unit} \\
\text{Order lead time } (LT) &= 6 \text{ days} \\
\text{Number of days per year} &= 360 \text{ days}
\end{aligned}
$$

Thus,

$$\text{EOQ} = \sqrt{\frac{2RS}{kC}} = \sqrt{\frac{2 \times 7{,}200 \text{ units} \times \$100}{0.20 \times \$20}} = 600 \text{ units}$$

Also:

1. The annual purchase cost $= R \times C = 7{,}200$ units $\times$ \$20 $=$ \$144,000.
2. The annual holding cost $= Q/2 \times k \times C = (600/2) \times 0.20 \times \$20 =$ \$1,200.
3. The annual order cost $= R/Q \times S = (7{,}200/600) \times \$100 =$ \$1,200.
   (Note that when using the EOQ, the annual holding cost equals the annual order cost.)
4. The total annual inventory cost $=$ \$144,000 $+$ \$1,200 $+$ \$1,200 $=$ \$146,400.
5. For an order lead time of six days, the reorder point (ROP) would be:
   ROP $= (7{,}200/360) \times 6 = 120$ units
   Thus, the purchasing manager should reorder the part from the supplier whenever the physical stock is down to 120 units, and 600 units should be ordered each time. The order cycle can also be computed as follows:
6. Number of orders placed per year $= 7{,}200/600 = 12$ orders.
7. Time between orders $= 360/12 = 30$ days.

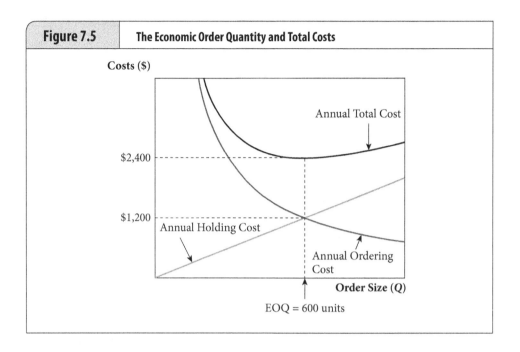

Figure 7.5   **The Economic Order Quantity and Total Costs**

Costs ($)

Annual Total Cost

$2,400

$1,200

Annual Holding Cost

Annual Ordering Cost

Order Size (Q)

EOQ = 600 units

Table 7.5   **Percent Variation in Total Annual Cost**

Q (UNITS)	AHC ($)	AOC ($)	ATC ($)	VARIATION (%)
540	1,080.00	1,333.33	2,413.33	0.56
550	1,100.00	1,309.09	2,409.09	0.38
560	1,120.00	1,285.71	2,405.71	0.24
570	1,140.00	1,263.16	2,403.16	0.13
580	1,160.00	1,241.38	2,401.38	0.06
590	1,180.00	1,220.34	2,400.34	0.01
EOQ = 600	1,200.00	1,200.00	2,400.00*	0.00
610	1,220.00	1,180.33	2,400.33	0.01
620	1,240.00	1,161.29	2,401.29	0.05
630	1,260.00	1,142.86	2,402.86	0.12
640	1,280.00	1,125.00	2,405.00	0.21
650	1,300.00	1,107.69	2,407.69	0.32
660	1,320.00	1,090.91	2,410.91	0.45

* indicates minimum total cost at the EOQ.

effect is a slightly higher annual total cost. Similarly, if the order quantity is slightly larger than the EOQ, the annual holding cost is slightly higher, whereas the annual order cost is slightly lower. The net effect is again a slightly higher annual total cost.

Figure 7.6 shows the movement of physical inventory and the relationships of the EOQ, average inventory, lead time, reorder point, and order cycle. Continuing with the use of the data in Example 7.3, at time 0, the firm is assumed to start with a complete order of 600 units. The inventory is consumed at a steady rate of 20 units per day. On the 24th day,

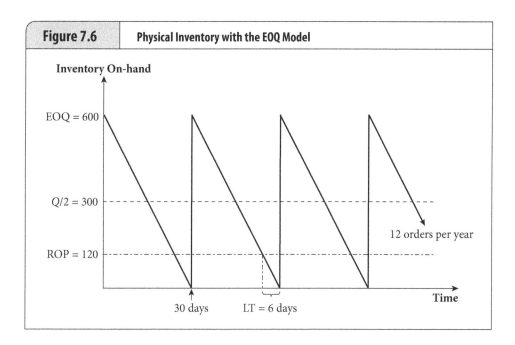

Figure 7.6 | **Physical Inventory with the EOQ Model**

Inventory On-hand

EOQ = 600

Q/2 = 300

12 orders per year

ROP = 120

Time

30 days   LT = 6 days

the ROP of 120 is reached and the firm places its first order of 600 units. It arrives six days later (on the 30th day). The 120 units of inventory are totally consumed immediately prior to the arrival of the first order. The vertical line on the 30th day shows that all 600 units are received (this is the instantaneous replenishment assumption of the EOQ model). A total of twelve orders (including the initial 600 units) will be placed during the year to satisfy the annual requirement of 7,200 units.

The Quantity Discount Model

The **quantity discount model** or **price-break model** is one variation of the classic EOQ model. It relaxes the constant unit price assumption by allowing purchase quantity discounts. In this case, the unit price of an item is allowed to vary with the order size. For example, a supplier may offer a price of $5 per unit for orders up to 200 units, $4.50 per unit for orders between 201 and 500 units, and $4 per unit for orders of more than 500 units. This creates an incentive for the buyer to purchase in larger quantities to take advantage of the quantity discount, provided the savings is greater than the extra cost of holding larger inventory levels. Unlike the EOQ model, the annual purchase cost now becomes an important factor in determining the optimal order size and the corresponding total annual inventory cost. The quantity discount model must consider the trade-off between purchasing in larger quantities to take advantage of the price discount (while also reducing the number of orders required per year) and the higher costs of holding inventory. With the quantity discount model, there are thus two variables in the TAIC equation (the purchase price C and the order quantity Q). Hence, a new approach is needed to find the optimal order quantity.

The purchase price per unit, C, is no longer fixed, as assumed in the classical EOQ model derivations. Consequently, the total annual inventory cost must now include the annual purchase cost, which varies depending on the order quantity. The new total annual inventory cost formula can now be stated as:

$$\text{Total annual inventory cost} = \text{annual purchase cost} + \text{annual holding cost} + \text{annual order cost,}$$

or

$$\text{TAIC} = \text{APC} + \text{AHC} + \text{AOC} = (R \times C) + [(Q/2) \times (k \times C)] + [(R/Q) \times S]$$

The quantity discount model yields a total annual inventory cost curve for each price level; hence, no single curve is relevant to all purchase quantities. The relevant total annual inventory cost curve is a combination of the cost curves for each price level, starting with the top curve where the price is the highest, and dropping down curve by curve at the price break point. A **price break point** is the minimum quantity required to get a price discount. There is an EOQ associated with each price level, however the EOQ may not be *feasible* at that particular price level because the order quantity may not lie in the given quantity range for that unit price. Due to the stepwise shape of the total inventory cost curve, the optimal order quantity lies at either a *feasible EOQ* or at a *price break point*.

A fairly straightforward two-step procedure can be used to solve the quantity discount problem. Briefly, the two steps can be stated as follows:

1. Starting with the lowest purchase price, compute the EOQ for each price level until a feasible EOQ is found. If the feasible EOQ found is for the lowest purchase price, this is the optimal order quantity. The reason is that the EOQ for the lowest price level is the lowest point on the total annual inventory cost curve (see Figure 7.7). If the feasible EOQ is not associated with the lowest price level, proceed to step 2.

2. Compute the total annual inventory cost for the feasible EOQ found in step 1, and for all the price break points at each *lower* price level. Price break points *above* the feasible EOQ will result in higher total annual inventory cost, thus need not be evaluated. The order quantity that yields the lowest total annual inventory cost is the optimal order quantity.

Examples 7.4 and 7.5 illustrate the quantity discount model.

The Economic Manufacturing Quantity Model

The **economic manufacturing quantity (EMQ)** or **production order quantity (POQ) model** is another variation of the classic EOQ model. It relaxes the *instantaneous replenishment* assumption by allowing usage or partial delivery during production. The EMQ model is especially appropriate for a manufacturing environment where items are being manufactured and consumed simultaneously; hence, the name economic manufacturing quantity. Inventory builds up gradually during the production period rather than at once as in the EOQ model.

For instance, let us assume that the production lot size for a manufactured product is 600 units, the manufacturer's production rate is 100 units per day, and its demand is 40 units per day. The manufacturer thus needs six days (600/100) to produce a batch of 600 units. While being produced, the items are also consumed simultaneously; hence, inventory builds up at the rate of 60 units (100−40) per day for six days. The maximum inventory is 360 units (60 × 6 days), which is less than the lot size of 600 units as would have been in the case of the classic EOQ model. The lower inventory level implies that the holding cost of the EMQ model is less than

Example 7.4   Finding the Optimal Order Quantity with Quantity Discounts at the Kuantan Corporation

The Kuantan Corporation purchases a component from a supplier who offers quantity discounts to encourage larger order quantities. The supply chain manager of the company, Dr. Hadiyan Wijaya Ibrahim, wants to determine the optimal order quantity to ensure the total annual inventory cost is minimized. The company's annual demand forecast for the item is 7,290 units, the order cost is $20 per order, and the annual holding rate is 25 percent. The price schedule for the item is:

ORDER QUANTITY	PRICE PER UNIT
1–200	$5.00
201–500	$4.50
501 and above	$4.00

The two questions of interest here are: (1) What is the optimal order quantity that will minimize the total annual inventory cost for this component and (2) what is the minimum total annual inventory cost?

SOLUTION:

Step 1: Find the first feasible EOQ starting with the lowest price level:

$$EOQ_{C=\$4.00} = \sqrt{\frac{2 \times 7{,}290 \text{ units} \times \$20}{0.25 \times \$4}} = 540 \text{ units}$$

This is a *feasible* EOQ because order size of 540 units falls within the order quantity range for the price level of $4.00 per unit. Thus, 540 units is the optimal order quantity. In this case, the optimal order size falls on a feasible EOQ.

Step 2: The minimum total annual inventory cost is then:

$$\begin{aligned} TAIC &= APC + AHC + AOC = (R \times C) + (Q/2 \times k \times C) + (R/Q \times S) \\ &= (7{,}290 \times \$4) + (540/2 \times 0.25 \times \$4) + (7{,}290/540 \times \$20) \\ &= \$29{,}160 + \$270 + \$270 = \$29{,}700 \end{aligned}$$

The annual holding cost equals the annual order cost because the optimal order quantity falls on an EOQ.

Cost curves A, B, and C in Figure 7.7 are the annual inventory costs at price levels of $5, $4.50, and $4, respectively. Since each cost curve is only applicable for its price range, the relevant total annual inventory cost is the combination of these three cost curves where the total cost drops vertically at each price break point, curve by curve, to the next lower cost curve. Figure 7.7 shows that the feasible EOQ for the lowest price level is the lowest point on the total annual inventory cost curve; thus, it is the optimal order quantity. The two infeasible EOQs for the price levels of $4.50 and $5 are also shown in Figure 7.7 to reiterate that if an EOQ falls outside of its price range, it is irrelevant to the total annual inventory cost.

Figure 7.7	Total Annual Inventory Cost Where the EOQ at the Lowest Price Level Is the Optimal Order Quantity

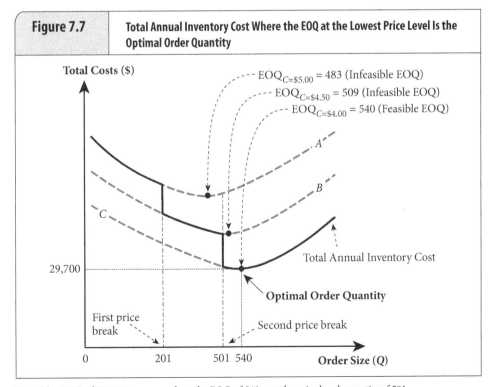

Note: The TAIC of $29,700 corresponds to the EOQ of 540, not the price break quantity of 501.

Example 7.5 Finding the Optimal Order Quantity with Quantity Discounts at the Soon Corporation

The Soon Corporation is a multinational company that purchases one of its crucial components from a supplier who offers quantity discounts to encourage larger order quantities. The supply chain manager of the company, Dr. Mohd Rizaimy Shaharudin, wants to determine the optimal order quantity to minimize the total annual inventory cost. The company's annual demand forecast for the item is 1,000 units, its order cost is $20 per order, and its annual holding rate is 25 percent. The price schedule is:

ORDER QUANTITY	PRICE PER UNIT
1–200	$5.00
201–500	$4.50
501 and above	$4.00

The first price break point is 201 units and the second is 501 units. What is the optimal order quantity that will minimize the total annual inventory cost for this component and what is the total annual inventory cost?

SOLUTION:

Step 1: Find the first feasible EOQ starting with the lowest price level of $4.00:

A. $EOQ_{C=\$4.00} = \sqrt{\dfrac{2 \times 1,000 \text{ units} \times \$20}{0.25 \times \$4}} = 200$ units

B. This quantity is *infeasible* because an order quantity of 200 units does not fall within the required order quantity range to qualify for the $4 price level (the unit price for an order quantity of 200 units is $5). Next, we evaluate the EOQ at the next higher price level of $4.50:

C. $EOQ_{C=\$4.50} = \sqrt{\dfrac{2 \times 1,000 \text{ units} \times \$20}{0.25 \times \$4.50}} = 189$ units

D. This quantity is also *infeasible* because it fails to qualify for the $4.50 price level. Moving on to the next higher price level of $5:

E. $EOQ_{C=\$5.00} = \sqrt{\dfrac{2 \times 1,000 \text{ units} \times \$20}{0.25 \times \$5}} = 179$ units

This order quantity is the *first feasible EOQ* because a 179-unit order quantity corresponds to the correct price level of $5 per unit.

Step 2: Find the total annual inventory costs for the first feasible EOQ found in step 1 and for the price break points at each lower price level (201 units at $4.50 and 501 units at $4).

$$TAIC = APC + AHC + AOC = (R \times C) + (Q/2 \times k \times C) + (R/Q \times S)$$

A. $TAIC_{EOQ=179,\ C=\$5} = (1,000 \times \$5) = (179/2 \times 0.25 \times \$5) + (1,000/179 \times \$20)$
$= \$5,000 + \$111.88 + \$111.73 = \$5,223.61$

B. $TAIC_{Q=201,\ C=\$4.50} = (1,000 \times \$4.50) + (201/2 \times 0.25 \times \$4.50) + (1,000/201 \times \$20)$
$= \$41,500 + \$113.06 + \$99.50 = \$4,712.56$

C. $TAIC_{Q=501,\ C=\$4} = (1,000 \times \$4) + (501/2 \times 0.25 \times \$4) + (1,000/501 \times \$20)$
$= \$4,000 + \$250.50 + \$39.92 = \$4,290.42$

Comparing the total annual inventory costs in A, B, and C, the optimal order quantity is 501 units, which qualifies for the deepest discount. In this case, the optimal order size falls on a *price break point;* hence, the annual holding cost ($250.50) does not equal the annual order cost ($39.92). When the quantity discount is large compared to the holding cost, it makes sense to purchase in large quantities and hold more inventory. However, this ignores the fact that excessive inventory hides production problems and can become obsolete very quickly. In the attempt to find the optimal order quantity to minimize inventory cost, a manager should also consider the impact of excessive inventory on firm performance. Figure 7.8 demonstrates the characteristics of the cost curves for this example. Cost curves A, B, and C are the annual inventory costs at price levels of $5, $4.50, and $4, respectively. The relevant total annual inventory cost is derived from these three cost curves by joining the relevant portion of each cost curve vertically at the price break points.

the EOQ model given the same cost parameters. It is also clear that the production rate must be greater than the demand rate; otherwise, there would not be any inventory buildups. On the seventh day, the production of the first batch stops and the inventory starts to deplete at the demand rate of 40 units for the next 9 days (360/40). The first production lot and the subsequent usage of the inventory take 15 days (6 + 9) to complete, and then the second cycle repeats.

Figure 7.9 depicts the inventory versus time for the EMQ model. The item is produced in lot size of Q, at the production rate of P, and consumed at the demand rate of D. Hence, inventory builds up at the rate of $(P - D)$ during the production period, T_p. At the end of the production period (T_p), inventory begins to deplete at the demand rate of D until it is exhausted at the end of the inventory cycle, T_C.

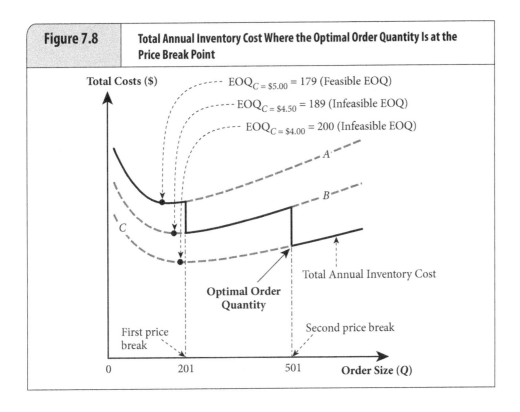

Figure 7.8 — Total Annual Inventory Cost Where the Optimal Order Quantity Is at the Price Break Point

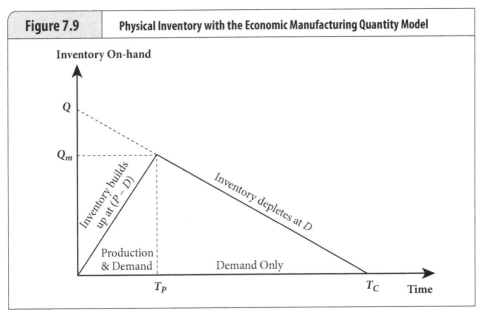

Figure 7.9 — Physical Inventory with the Economic Manufacturing Quantity Model

The production rate, P, which can be expressed as Q/T_p, is the production lot size divided by the time required to produce the lot. The maximum inventory, Q_M, can be obtained by multiplying the inventory build-up rate with the production period, and can be expressed as $(P - D) \times T_p$. These relationships can be stated as:

$$P = \frac{Q}{T_p} \quad \text{and} \quad Q_M = (P - D) \times T_p$$

Therefore, $T_P = \frac{Q}{P}$ and substituting $\frac{Q}{P}$ for T_P in Q_M gives,

$$Q_M = (P - D) \times \frac{Q}{P}$$
$$= \frac{PQ}{P} - \frac{DQ}{P}$$
$$= Q\left(1 - \frac{D}{P}\right)$$

Hence, the average inventory, $\dfrac{Q_M}{2} = \dfrac{Q}{2}\left(1 - \dfrac{D}{P}\right)$.

The total annual inventory cost can be stated as:

Total annual inventory cost = Annual product cost + annual holding cost + annual setup cost,

or

$$\text{TAIC} = \text{APC} + \text{AHC} + \text{ASC} = [R \times C] + \left[\left(\frac{Q}{2}\left(1 - \frac{D}{P}\right)\right) \times k \times C\right] + [R/Q \times S]$$

where

    TAIC = total annual inventory cost
    APC = annual product cost
    AHC = annual holding cost
    ASC = annual setup cost
    R = annual requirement or demand
    C = total cost of one unit of the finished product
    S = cost of setting up the equipment to process one batch of the product
    k = holding rate, where annual holding cost per unit = $k \times C$
    Q = order quantity.

Like the EOQ model where Q is the only unknown variable in the TAIC equation, the optimum Q (the EMQ) can be obtained by taking the first derivative of TAIC with respect to Q and then setting it equal to zero. A second derivative of TAIC can also be taken with respect to Q to prove that the TAIC is a concave function, and thus $\frac{d\text{TAIC}}{dQ} = 0$ is at the lowest point of the cost curve. Thus,

$$\frac{d\text{TAIC}}{dQ} = 0 + \left[½\left(1 - \frac{D}{P}\right) \times k \times C\right] + \left[-1 \times R \times S \times 1/Q^2\right]$$
$$= \left[\frac{kC}{2}\left(1 - \frac{D}{P}\right)\right] - \frac{RS}{Q^2}$$

Then setting $\frac{d\text{TAIC}}{dQ}$ equal to zero and solving for the EMQ,

$$\left[\frac{kC}{2}\left(1 - \frac{D}{P}\right)\right] - \frac{RS}{Q^2} = 0$$
$$\Rightarrow \left[\frac{kC}{2}\left(1 - \frac{D}{P}\right)\right] = \frac{RS}{Q^2}$$
$$\Rightarrow Q^2 = \frac{2RS}{kC\left(1 - \dfrac{D}{P}\right)} = \frac{2RS}{kC\left(\dfrac{P-D}{P}\right)} = \frac{2RS}{kC}\left(\frac{P}{P-D}\right)$$

And the EMQ $= \sqrt{\left(\dfrac{2RS}{kC}\right)\left(\dfrac{P}{P-D}\right)}$

The second derivative of the *TAIC* is

$$\frac{d^2\text{TAIC}}{dQ^2} = 0 - \left(-2 \times \frac{RS}{Q^3}\right) = \left(\frac{2RS}{Q^3}\right) \geq 0,$$

implying that the TAIC is at its minimum when $\frac{d\text{TAIC}}{dQ} = 0$.

Similar to the EOQ model, the annual product cost drops off after the first derivative is taken, indicating that product cost does not affect the order decision if the unit cost of each product produced is constant; thus, the annual product cost is also ignored in the EMQ model. Example 7.6 provides an illustration of calculating the EMQ for a manufacturing company.

The Statistical Reorder Point

The two major inventory management decisions are to determine (1) the right order quantity or lot size and (2) when to release an order. Three basic independent demand lot-sizing techniques have been discussed, but as of yet, the question of when to order has not been fully discussed. The **reorder point (ROP)** is the lowest inventory level at which a new order must be placed to avoid a stockout. In a deterministic setting where both the demand

---

Example 7.6   Calculating the EMQ at the Lone Wild Boar Corporation

The Lone Wild Boar Corporation manufactures a crucial component internally using the most advanced technology. The operations manager wants to determine the economic manufacturing quantity to ensure that the total annual inventory cost is minimized. The daily production rate (P) for the component is 200 units, annual demand (R) is 18,000 units, setup cost (S) is $100 per setup, and the annual holding rate (k) is 25 percent. The manager estimates that the total cost (C) of a finished component is $120. It is assumed that the plant operates year-round and there are 360 days per year.

SOLUTION:

1. The daily demand rate, $D = 18{,}000/360 = 50$ units per day.

2. $\text{EMQ} = \sqrt{\left(\dfrac{2RS}{kC}\right)\left(\dfrac{P}{P-D}\right)} = \sqrt{\left(\dfrac{2 \times 18{,}000 \times 100}{0.25 \times 120}\right)\left(\dfrac{200}{200-50}\right)} = 400$ units.

3. The highest inventory level, $Q_M = Q\left(1 - \dfrac{D}{P}\right) = 400\left(1 - \dfrac{50}{200}\right) = 300$ units.

4. The annual product cost $= R \times C = 18{,}000$ units $\times \$120 = \$2{,}160{,}000$.

5. The annual holding cost $\dfrac{Q_M}{2} \times k \times C = \dfrac{300}{2} \times 0.25 \times \$120 = \$4{,}500$.

6. The annual setup cost $= R/Q \times S = (18{,}000/400) \times \$100 = \$4{,}500$.
   (Note that at the EMQ, the annual holding cost equals the annual setup cost.)

7. The TAIC $= \$2{,}160{,}000 + \$4{,}500 + \$4{,}500 = \$2{,}169{,}000$.

8. The length of a production period, $T_p = \dfrac{\text{EMQ}}{P} = 400/200 = 2$ days.

9. The length of each inventory cycle, $T_C = \dfrac{\text{EMQ}}{D} = 400/50 = 8$ days.

10. The rate of inventory buildup during production, $(P-D) = 200 - 50 = 150$ units per day.

11. The number of inventory cycles per year $= 360$ days/8 days $= 45$ cycles.

Figure 7.10 illustrates the EMQ model for the Lone Wild Boar Corporation. A unique observation regarding the classic EOQ, quantity discount, and the EMQ models is that when ordering at the EOQ or EMQ, the annual order or setup cost equals the annual holding cost, except in the quantity discount model when the optimal order quantity falls on a price break point.

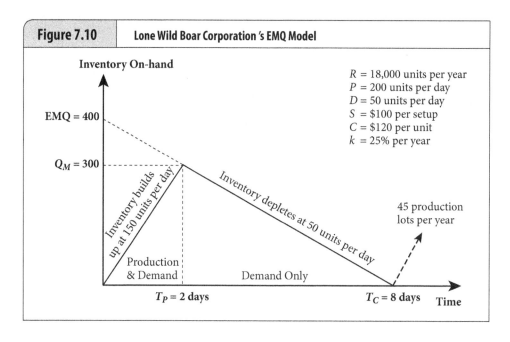

Figure 7.10 | **Lone Wild Boar Corporation 's EMQ Model**

and delivery lead time are known and constant, Example 7.3 showed that the reorder point was equal to the demand during the order's delivery lead time. In reality, the demand and delivery lead time tend to vary. Uncertain demand or lead time raises the possibility of stock-outs, thus requiring *safety stock* to be held to safeguard against variations in demand or lead time. Next, we discuss how the probabilistic demand pattern and lead time affect the ROP.

The Statistical Reorder Point with Probabilistic Demand and Constant Lead Time

This model assumes the lead time of a product is constant while the demand during the delivery lead time is unknown but can be specified using a normal distribution. Since the statistical reorder point is to determine the lowest inventory level at which a new order should be placed, demand prior to a purchase order does not directly affect the ROP. Figure 7.11 illustrates the relationship between safety stock and the probability of a stockout. If the average demand during the lead time is represented by μ, and the ROP is represented by x, then the safety stock is $(x - \mu)$, which can be derived from the standard deviation formula $\left(Z = \frac{x-\mu}{\sigma}\right)$. Then, if the probability of stockout is represented by α, the probability that inventory is sufficient to cover demand or the *in-stock probability* is $(1 - \alpha)$. The in-stock probability is commonly referred to as the **service level** (actually, the calculation of the true service level requires use of a loss function for a stockout, which is beyond the

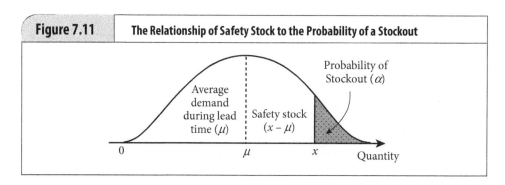

Figure 7.11 | **The Relationship of Safety Stock to the Probability of a Stockout**

scope of this text). Next, the Z-value can be determined from the standardized normal curve and a desire to achieve a specific service level (see the Z-table in the Appendix). For example, a 97.5 percent service level ($\alpha = 2.5\%$) corresponds to the Z-value of 1.96. Note that at the middle of the normal curve, where the reorder point equals the average demand, the required safety stock is zero and the probability of stockout would be 50 percent.

The statistical reorder point (x) can be calculated as the average demand during the order's delivery lead time plus the desired safety stock, or

$$\text{ROP} = \bar{d}_{LT} + Z\sigma_{dLT}$$

The safety stock, $Z\sigma_{dLT}$ or ($x - \mu$), can be derived from the standard deviation formula of the normal curve as shown earlier, and σ_{dLT} is the standard deviation of demand during the delivery lead time. Example 7.7 illustrates the calculation of the ROP with probabilistic demand and constant delivery lead time.

The safety stock computation as shown in Example 7.7 needs to be modified if the standard deviation is available for daily demand and not lead time demand. In this situation, if the delivery lead time is greater than one day, the standard deviation of daily demand (σ_d) must be converted to the standard deviation of lead time demand (σ_{dLT}). If the daily demand is identically distributed, we can use the statistical premise that the variance of a series of independent occurrences is equal to the sum of the variances. That is, the variance of demand during the lead time equals the sum of the variances of all the identical daily demand that covers the lead time period. This can be expressed as:

$$\sigma^2_{dLT} = \sigma^2_d + \sigma^2_d + \sigma^2_d + \cdots = \sigma^2_d(LT)$$

where

σ^2_{dLT} = variance of demand during the lead time
σ^2_d = variance of the identically and independently distributed daily demand
LT = lead time in days

Thus, the standard deviation of demand during the lead time is $\sigma_{dLT} = \sigma_d\sqrt{LT}$. Hence, the safety stock and the statistical reorder point can be stated as:

$$\text{Safety stock} = Z\sigma_d\sqrt{LT}$$
$$\text{and ROP} = \bar{d}_{LT} + Z\sigma_d\sqrt{LT}.$$

Example 7.8 illustrates this calculation.

Example 7.7   Calculating the Statistical Reorder Point Using Probabilistic Demand and Constant Delivery Lead Times at London, Inc.

London, Inc., stocks a crucial part that has a normally distributed demand pattern during the reorder period. Past demand shows that the average demand during lead time (μ) for the part is 550 units, and the standard deviation of demand during lead time (σ_{dLT}) is 40 units. The supply chain manager wants to determine the safety stock and statistical reorder point that result in 5 percent stockouts or a service level of 95 percent. Alternately, the manager wants to know the additional safety stock required to attain a 99 percent service level.

SOLUTION:
The normal distribution Z-table in Appendix 1 shows that a 95 percent service level (5 percent stockouts allowed) corresponds to a Z-value of 1.65 standard deviations above the Average.
The required safety stock is

$$(x - \mu) = Z\sigma_{dLT} = 1.65 \times 40 = 66 \text{ units.}$$

The ROP $= \bar{d}_{LT} + Z\sigma_{dLT} = 550 + 66 \text{ units} = 616 \text{ units.}$ This means the manager must reorder the part from their supplier when their current stock level reaches 616 units.

Alternately, the required safety stock at a 99 percent service level $= Z\sigma_{dLT} = 2.33 \times 40 = 93$ units. The additional safety stock compared to the 95 percent service level is 27 units.

Example 7.8   Calculating the Statistical Reorder Point at Brussels, Inc., Using the Standard Deviation of Daily Demand and Constant Delivery Lead Times

Brussels, Inc., is a local liquor retailer specializing in selling beer at big discounts. Historical data show that the demand for beer has a normal distribution. The average daily demand for beer at Brussels is 150 cases, and its standard deviation for daily demand is 30 cases. Brussels' supplier maintains a very reliable and constant lead time of six days. The manager desires to determine the standard deviation of demand during lead time, the safety stock and statistical reorder point that results in a 97.5 percent service level, and the safety stock reduction if the manager decides to attain a 90 percent service level.

SOLUTION:
Average daily demand, $\bar{d} = 150$ cases

Standard deviation of daily demand, $\sigma_d = 30$ cases

Lead time, LT = 6 days

$$\text{The standard deviation of demand during lead time, } \sigma_{dLT} = \sigma_d \sqrt{LT}$$
$$= 30\sqrt{6} \text{ cases} = 73.5 \text{ cases}$$

The Z-table shows that a 97.5 percent service level (2.5 percent stockouts allowed) corresponds to the Z-value of 1.96 standard deviations above the mean.

The corresponding safety stock, $Z\sigma_d \sqrt{LT} = 1.96 \times 30\sqrt{6} = 144$ cases.

The ROP $= \bar{d}_{LT} + Z\sigma_d \sqrt{LT} = (150 \times 6) + 144 = 1,044$ cases. Thus, ordering more beer when they have a current inventory of 1,044 cases will result in a 97.5 percent service level.

For the lower service level of 90 percent, safety stock $= Z\sigma_d \sqrt{LT} = 1.28 \times 30\sqrt{6} = 94$ cases. The safety stock reduction would be 50 cases.

The Statistical Reorder Point with Constant Demand and Probabilistic Lead Time

When the demand of a product is constant and the lead time is unknown but can be specified by means of a normal distribution, the safety stock is used to buffer against variations in the lead time instead of demand. The safety stock is then (daily demand $\times Z\sigma_{LT}$), and the reorder point is:

$$\text{ROP} = (\text{daily demand} \times \text{average lead time in days}) + (\text{daily demand} \times Z\sigma_{LT})$$

where

σ_{LT} = the standard deviation of lead time in days

The calculation is demonstrated in Example 7.9.

Example 7.9   Calculating the Statistical Reorder Point at the Harpert Store Using Constant Demand and Probabilistic Lead Time

The Harpert Store has an exclusive contract with Brussums Electronics to sell their most popular mp4 player. The demand of this mp4 player is very stable at 120 units per day. However, the delivery lead times vary and can be specified by a normal distribution with a mean lead time of eight days and a standard deviation of two days. The supply chain manager at Brussums desires to calculate the safety stock and reorder point for a 95 percent service level (in-stock probability).

SOLUTION:
Daily demand $(d) = 120$ units.

Average lead time $(\overline{LT}) = 8$ days.

Standard deviation of lead time $(\sigma_{LT}) = 2$ days.

A service level of 95 percent yields a $Z = 1.65$ from the Z-table.

$$\text{Required safety stock} = d \times Z\sigma_{LT} = 120 \text{ units} \times 1.65 \times 2 = 396 \text{ units.}$$
$$\text{ROP} = (d \times \overline{LT}) + (d \times Z\sigma_{LT}) = (120 \times 8) + 396 = 1,356 \text{ units.}$$

Brussums must order more mp3 players from Harpert when its current inventory reaches 1,356 units.

The Statistical Reorder Point with Probabilistic Demand and Lead Time

When both the demand and lead time of a product are unknown but can be specified by means of a normal distribution, safety stock must be held to cover the variations in both demand and lead time, resulting in higher safety stocks when compared to variations in the demand or lead time only. The reorder point can be computed as follows:[23]

$$\text{ROP} = (\overline{d} \times \overline{\text{LT}}) + Z\sigma_{\text{dLT}}$$

where

σ_{dLT} = Standard deviation of demand during the lead time

$$= \sqrt{\sigma_{\text{LT}}^2(\overline{d})^2 + \sigma_{\text{d}}^2(\overline{\text{LT}})}$$

where

σ_{LT} = Standard deviation of lead time days

σ_{d} = Standard deviation of daily demand

Note that this standard deviation formula (σ_{dLT}) can be applied to all the previous reorder point examples by observing the following fact: "constant" or "no variation" means zero standard deviation. Therefore:

1. When the lead time and demand are constant, then σ_{LT} and σ_{d} are zero, and the average daily demand and average lead time would be the deterministic demand and lead time. Thus, the reorder point is the demand during lead time period.

2. When the daily demand is probabilistic and lead time is constant, then σ_{LT} is zero and the average lead time would be the deterministic lead time. Using this guideline, the reorder point in Example 7.8 can also be computed as:

$$\text{ROP} = (150 \times 6) + 1.96\sqrt{0^2(150)^2 + 30^2(6)} = 900 + 1.96 \times 30\sqrt{6} = 1{,}044$$
cases.

3. When the daily demand is constant and the lead time is probabilistic, then σ_{d} is zero and the average daily demand would be the deterministic daily demand. Using this guideline, the reorder point in Example 7.9 can also be computed as:

$$\text{ROP} = (120 \times 8) + 1.65\sqrt{2^2(120)^2 + 0^2(8)} = 960 + 1.65 \times 2(120) = 1{,}356 \text{ units.}$$

Example 7.10 demonstrates the safety stock and reorder point computation when both the daily demand and lead time are probabilistic.

The Continuous Review and the Periodic Review Inventory Systems

The order quantity and reorder point inventory models discussed thus far assume that the physical inventory levels are precisely known at every point in time. This implies that stock movements must be updated in real time and that there are no discrepancies between physical inventory and the stock record. In other words, a *continuous review* of the physical inventory is required to make sure that orders are initiated when physical inventories reach their reorder points. In practice, a **continuous review system** can be difficult to achieve and very expensive to implement. Inventory review costs can be lowered by using a **periodic review system** instead, where physical inventory is reviewed at regular intervals, such as weekly or monthly. However, more safety stock would be

> ### Example 7.10   Calculating the Statistical Reorder Point at the Dosseldorf Store Using Probabilistic Demand and Delivery Lead Time
>
> The Dosseldorf Store is the sole distributor of a popular cell phone. The demand for this cell phone is normally distributed with an average daily demand of 120 units and a standard deviation of 18 units per day. The cell phones are ordered and shipped directly from the manufacturer. Past delivery records for the manufacturer show that delivery lead times are normally distributed with an average of eight days and a standard deviation of two days. The supply chain manager at Dosseldorf desires to determine the safety stock required and the reorder point for a 95 percent service level.
>
> **SOLUTION:**
> Average daily demand, $\bar{d} = 120$ units.
> Standard deviation of daily demand, $\sigma_d = 18$ units.
> Average lead time, $\overline{LT} = 8$ days.
> Standard deviation of lead time, $\sigma_{LT} = 2$ days.
> A desired service level of 95 percent yields $Z = 1.65$ from the Z-table.
> The required safety stock $= Z\sigma_{dLT}$
> $$= 1.65 \times \sqrt{\sigma_{LT}^2(\bar{d})^2 + \sigma_d^2(\overline{LT})}$$
> $$= 1.65 \times \sqrt{2^2(120)^2 + 18^2(8)} = 1.65 \times 245.34 = 405 \text{ units.}$$
> The ROP $= (\bar{d} \times \overline{LT}) + Z\sigma_{dLT} = (120 \times 8) + 405 = 1,365$ units.
>
> Dosseldorf must order more cell phones from its supplier when its current stock reaches 1,365 units to achieve a 95 percent service level.

required for the periodic review system to buffer the added variation due to the longer review period.

When analyzing the continuous review and the periodic review systems, the following symbols are used:

> s = order point
> S = maximum inventory level
> Q = order quantity
> R = periodic review
> $n = 1, 2, 3 \ldots$

The Continuous Review System

The continuous review system implies that physical inventory is known at all times, so it is more expensive to administer. However, the only uncertainty is the magnitude of demand during the delivery lead time; thus, the only safety stock required is for potential stockouts during this time period. There are two continuous review systems, described below.

1. *(s, Q) continuous review policy*: This policy orders the same quantity, *Q*, when physical inventory reaches the reorder point, *s*. The quantity, *Q*, can be determined by one of the fixed order quantity methods (such as the EOQ). This policy works properly only if the quantity demanded is 1 unit at a time. Otherwise, the inventory level may fall below the reorder point, *s*.

2. *(s, S) continuous review policy*: When current inventory reaches or falls below the reorder point, *s*, sufficient units are ordered to bring the inventory up to a predetermined level, *S*. If the quantity demanded is 1 unit at a time, this system is similar to the (s, Q) policy. However, if the quantity demand is larger than 1 unit and when physical inventory falls below the reorder point, then the order size is larger than

Q. For instance, suppose $s = 10$, $S = 120$, and current inventory is 11 units. If the next demand is 3 units, then on-hand inventory will be reduced to 8 units. Consequently, an order size of 112 units would be released.

The Periodic Review System

The periodic review system reviews physical inventory at specific intervals of time. Although this system is cheaper to administer, a higher level of safety stock is needed to buffer against uncertainty in demand over a longer planning horizon. There are three periodic review systems, described below.

1. *(nQ, s, R) periodic review policy*: If at the time of inventory review, the physical inventory is equal to or less than the reorder point, s, the quantity, nQ, is ordered to bring the inventory up to the level between s and $(s + Q)$. Recall that $n = 1, 2, 3, \ldots$, and the order size is then some multiple of Q. No order is placed if the current inventory is higher than the reorder point. For example, let $s = 100$ and $Q = 50$. If the current inventory is 20 units at the time of the review, then $2Q$ quantities $(2 \times 50 = 100)$ are ordered to bring the inventory level up to 120 units.

2. *(S, R) periodic review policy*: At each review time, a sufficient quantity is ordered to bring the inventory up to a predetermined maximum inventory level, S. This policy places a variable-sized order as long as the physical inventory is less than the maximum inventory level, S. If order cost is high, this is obviously not a preferred system. However, it may work well if a large variety of items are ordered from the same supplier.

3. *(s, S, R) policy*: If at the time of inventory review, the physical inventory is equal to or less than the reorder point, s, a sufficient quantity is ordered to bring the inventory level up to the maximum inventory level, S. However, if the physical inventory is higher than the reorder point s, no order is placed. This policy addresses the major deficiency of the (S, R) policy.

SUMMARY

Organizations rely on inventory to balance supply and demand and to buffer uncertainties in the supply chain. However, inventory can be one of the most expensive assets of an organization; hence, it must be managed closely. The right amount of inventory supports business operations, but too little of it can adversely affect customer service. Conversely, excess inventory not only leads to unnecessary inventory carrying cost but hides production problems and other flaws in a company.

This chapter covered the crucial roles of inventory and various inventory management techniques that are widely used for balancing demand with supply. The classic ABC inventory classification was discussed along with the ABC inventory matrix as a means to monitor if a firm is stocking the right inventories. Ample examples were used to demonstrate the order size and order period inventory models. This chapter also covered two of the latest developments in inventory management—RFID and big data. Radio frequency identification certainly has the potential to drastically change the way inventories are managed in the future, and big data analysis allows firms to gain a competitive advantage through better decision-making.

KEY TERMS

80/20 rule, 238

ABC inventory control system, 238

ABC inventory matrix, 240

active RFID tags, 243

big data, 246

carrying costs, 236

continuous review system, 261

cycle counting, 237

dependent demand, 234

direct costs, 236

economic manufacturing quantity (EMQ), 252

economic order quantity (EOQ) model, 247

electronic product code (EPC), 243

fixed costs, 236

fixed order quantity models, 247

holding, 236

independent demand, 234

indirect costs, 236

inventory turnover ratio, 236

inventory turnovers, 236

near field communication (NFC), 242

order costs, 236

Pareto analysis, 238

passive RFID tags, 243

periodic review system, 261

price break point, 252

price-break model, 251

production order quantity (POQ) model, 252

quantity discount model, 251

radio frequency identification (RFID), 242

reorder point (ROP), 257

service level, 258

setup costs, 236

variable costs, 236

DISCUSSION QUESTIONS

1. Describe and provide examples of dependent and independent demand.

2. Describe the four basic types of inventory.

3. What is the ABC inventory system and how is it used to manage inventory?

4. What is the ABC inventory matrix and how is it used to manage inventory?

5. Describe inventory turnover and how it can be used to manage inventory.

6. Why is it important to conduct cycle counting?

7. What is the electronic product code (EPC)?

8. Briefly describe how RFID can be used to manage inventory.

9. Explain why item-level tagging is more expensive than case-level tagging in RFID.

10. What is big data?

11. How can firms use big data to make better decisions?

12. What is the purpose of the EOQ and the ROP? How can they be used together?

13. What are the assumptions of the EOQ model?

14. What are the two major costs considered in the EOQ model? Why is the total purchase price not a factor affecting the order quantity?

15. How is the quantity discount model related to the EOQ model?

16. How is the EMQ model related to the EOQ model?

17. Discuss whether the EOQ model is still useful if a small error was made while estimating one of the cost parameters used in the EOQ computation.

18. Assume that you used the EOQ model to compute the order quantity for an item, and the answer was 20 units. Unfortunately, the minimum lot size for the item is 24 units. Discuss how this is going to impact your annual holding cost, annual order cost, and annual total inventory cost.

19. Explain whether the continuous review or periodic review inventory system is likely to result in higher safety stock. Which is likely to require more time and effort to administer? Why?

20. Use the inventory turnover ratios in Table 7.2 to comment on which firm is the most efficient in deploying its inventory to generate sales.

21. What is the order quantity when the annual order or setup cost equals the annual holding cost in the (a) EOQ model, (b) quantity discount model, and (c) EMQ model?

22. Why is inventory management important to SCM?

23. Describe the difference between annual physical inventory count and cycle counting.

24. Describe near field communication (NFC), its relationship with RFID, and its applications.

ESSAY/PROJECT QUESTIONS

1. Visit the website of EPCglobal, Inc., and use the information to write a brief report on RFID technology and the state of RFID implementation.

2. Use the Internet to search for relevant information to prepare a brief report on the state of RFID implementation in North America, Europe, and Asia.

3. Use resources available on the Internet to prepare a report on the RFID implementation at Walmart Stores, Inc.

4. Use resources available on the Internet to prepare a brief report on big data and business analytics.

5. Use resources available on the Internet (e.g., https://finance.yahoo.com/ or http://www.cnbc.com/) to access the annual reports (financial statements and balance sheets) of three of your favorite listed companies to (a) extract their latest total revenue, cost of revenue, total assets, and year-end or average inventory, and use these numbers to (b) prepare their inventory/total revenue ratio, inventory/total assets ratio, and the inventory turnover ratio. Comment on how they performed based on these ratios. (Hint: See Tables 7.1 and 7.2.)

SPREADSHEET PROBLEMS

1. The revenue for a firm is $2,500,000. Its cost of revenue is $850,000, and its average inventory for the year is $62,000. What is the inventory turnover?

2. Given the following information, what is the annual inventory turnover ratio?

Revenue	$22,000,000
Cost of Revenue	$1,250,000
Quarter 1 Ending Inventory	$85,000
Quarter 2 Ending Inventory	$98,000
Quarter 3 Ending Inventory	$125,000
Quarter 4 Ending Inventory	$68,000

3. Given the following information, compute the economic order quantity, annual holding cost, annual order cost, and annual total inventory cost.

Annual requirements (R)	= 50,000 units
Order cost (S)	= $150 per order
Holding rate (k)	= 15%
Unit cost (C)	= $100 per unit

4. The annual requirement of a part is 360,000 units. The order cost is $120 per order, the holding rate is 12 percent, and the part cost is $2,500 per unit. What are the (a) EOQ, (b) annual holding cost, (c) annual order cost, and (d) annual total inventory cost?

5. The weekly requirement of a part is 950 units. The order cost is $85 per order, the holding cost is $5 per unit per year, and the part cost is $250 per unit. The firm operates fifty-two weeks per year. Compute the (a) EOQ, (b) annual holding cost, (c) annual order cost, and (d) annual total inventory cost.

6. The monthly demand for a part is 1,500 units. The order cost is $285 per order, the holding cost is $56 per unit per year, and the part cost is $850 per unit. The firm operates twelve months per year. Compute the (a) EOQ, (b) annual holding cost, (c) annual order cost, and (d) annual total inventory cost.

7. Icy Snowmobile, Inc., has an annual demand for 1,200 snowmobiles. Their purchase cost for each snowmobile is $2,500. It costs about $250 to place an order, and the holding rate is 35 percent of the unit cost. Compute the (a) EOQ, (b) annual holding cost, (c) annual order cost, and (d) total annual inventory cost.

8. Steamy Speedboats has an annual demand for 1,500 speedboats. Its supplier offers quantity discounts to promote larger order quantities. The cost to place an order is $300, and the holding rate is 32 percent of the purchase cost. The purchase cost for each speedboat is based on the price schedule given below. Compute the (a) optimal order quantity, (b) annual purchase cost, (c) annual holding cost, (d) annual order cost, and (e) total annual inventory cost.

ORDER QUANTITY	PRICE PER UNIT
1–50	$18,500
51–100	$18,000
101–150	$17,400
151 and above	$16,800

9. Using the Steamy Speedboats problem above, assume that the order cost has dropped from $300 to $50. What are the (a) optimal order quantity, (b) annual purchase cost, (c) annual holding cost, (d) annual order cost, and (e) total annual inventory cost?

10. Using the Steamy Speedboats problem above, assume that the holding rate has dropped from 32 to 15 percent. What are the (a) optimal order quantity, (b) annual purchase cost, (c) annual holding cost, (d) annual order cost, and (e) total annual inventory cost?

11. Frankfurt Electronics produces a component internally using a state-of-the-art technology. The operations manager wants to determine the optimal lot size to ensure that the total annual inventory cost is minimized. The daily production rate for the component is 500 units, annual demand is 36,000 units, setup cost is $150 per setup, and the annual holding rate is 30 percent. The manager estimates that the total cost of a finished component is $80. If we assume that the plant operates year-round, and there are 360 days per year, what are the (a) daily demand, (b) optimal lot size, (c) highest inventory, (d) annual product cost, (e) annual holding cost, (f) annual setup cost, (g) total annual inventory cost, (h) length of a production period, (i) length of each inventory cycle, (j) rate of inventory buildup during the production cycle, and (k) the number of inventory cycles per year? Plot the movement of the inventory during one production cycle using time on the horizontal axis and on-hand inventory on the vertical axis (see Figure 7.10).

12. Paris Store stocks a part that has a normal distribution demand pattern during the reorder period. Its average demand during lead time is 650 units and the standard deviation of demand during lead time is 60 units. What are the safety stock and statistical reorder point that result in a 97.5 percent service level?

13. Lindner Congress Bookstore sells a unique calculator to college students. The demand for this calculator has a normal distribution with an average daily demand of 15 units and a standard deviation of 4 units per day. The lead time for this calculator is very stable at five days. Compute the standard deviation of demand during lead time, and determine the safety stock and statistical reorder point that result in 5 percent stockouts.

14. The daily demand of a product is very stable at 250 units per day. However, its delivery lead time varies and can be specified by a normal distribution with a mean lead time of twelve days and standard deviation of three days. What are the safety stock and reorder point for a 97.5 percent service level?

15. The daily demand of a product can be specified by a normal distribution. Its average daily demand is 250 units with a standard deviation of 40 units. The delivery lead time of this product is also normally distributed with an average of ten days and a standard deviation of three days. What are the safety stock and reorder point for a 95 percent service level?

16. Given the following inventory information, perform an ABC analysis.

ITEM NUMBER	UNIT COST ($)	ANNUAL USAGE
B8867	6.00	100
J1252	5.25	6,500
K9667	0.25	4,000
L2425	1.00	1,500
M4554	5.50	2,000
T6334	70.00	500
W9856	0.75	800
X2215	1.50	8,000
Y3214	32.00	1,000
Y6339	4.00	3,500

17. Given the following inventory information, construct an (a) ABC analysis by annual dollar usage, (b) ABC analysis by current inventory value, and (c) an ABC inventory matrix. Is the firm stocking the correct inventories?

ITEM NUMBER	UNIT COST ($)	ANNUAL USAGE (UNITS)	CURRENT INVENTORY (UNITS)
B8867	6.00	100	8,000
J1252	5.25	6,500	120
K9667	0.25	4,000	1,000
L2425	1.00	1,500	375
M4554	5.50	2,000	500
T6334	70.00	500	800
W9856	0.75	800	20,000
X2215	1.50	8,000	2,000
Y3214	32.00	1,000	500
Y6339	4.00	3,500	125

18. Given the following inventory information, construct an (a) ABC analysis by annual dollar usage, (b) ABC analysis by current inventory value, and (c) ABC inventory matrix. Is the firm stocking the correct inventories?

ITEM NUMBER	UNIT COST ($)	ANNUAL USAGE (UNITS)	CURRENT INVENTORY (UNITS)
A967	32.00	1	4,500
B886	6.00	100	8,000
C314	5.25	32	115
D879	12.50	54	254
E536	0.05	125	120
F876	0.07	423	500
G112	0.12	500	1,008
H098	1.22	235	750
J125	5.25	6,500	120
K966	0.25	4,000	1,000
L242	1.00	1,500	375
M455	5.50	2,000	500
N007	7.21	54	525
P231	5.25	32	300
Q954	3.25	25	240
T633	70.00	500	800
W985	0.75	800	20,000
X221	1.50	8,000	2,000
Y321	32.00	1,000	500
Z633	4.00	3,500	125

19. Given the following information for an important purchased part, compute the (a) EOQ, (b) total purchase cost, (c) annual holding cost, (d) annual order cost, (e) annual total cost, (f) reorder point, (g) number of orders placed per year, and (h) time between orders. Use Microsoft Excel to plot the cost curves (annual holding cost, annual order cost, and annual total cost) on the vertical axis, and the order quantity on the horizontal axis.

Annual requirements (R)	= 5,000 units
Order cost (S)	= $100 per order
Holding rate (k)	= 20%
Unit cost (C)	= $20 per unit
Lead time (LT)	= 6 days
Number of days per year	= 360 days

20. Given the following information for a purchased part, compute the (a) EOQ, (b) total purchase cost, (c) annual holding cost, (d) annual order cost, (e) annual total cost, (f) reorder point, (g) number of orders placed per year, and (h) time between orders. Use Microsoft Excel to plot the cost curves (annual holding cost, annual order cost, and annual total cost) on the vertical axis and the order quantity on the horizontal axis.

Monthly demand	= 3,500 units
Order cost (S)	= $250 per order
Holding cost (kC)	= $8.65 per unit per year
Unit cost (C)	= $85 per unit
Lead time (LT)	= 12 days
Number of days per year	= 365 days

21. Kopi Luwak produces the world's most expensive coffee by using coffee beans that have been digested by wild civet cat. The coffee beans, widely known as "cat poop coffee" can be packaged in one pound bags at a daily production rate of 700 bags. The coffees are shipped to retailers at a constant rate of 120 bags every day of the year. Due to the scarcity of partly digested coffee beans from civet cat feces, the senior operations manager, Dr. Hadiyan Wijaya Ibrahim, uses economic manufacturing quantity (EMQ) to produce the coffee. The setup cost is $250 per setup and the annual holding rate is 25 percent. The manager estimates that the total cost of a bag of coffee is $85. If we assume that there are 360 days per year, what are the (a) annual demand, (b) EMQ, (c) highest inventory, (d) annual product cost, (e) annual holding cost, (f) annual setup cost, (g) total annual inventory cost, (h) length of a production period, (i) length of each inventory cycle, (j) rate of inventory buildup during the production cycle, and (k) the number of inventory cycles per year? Plot the movement of the inventory during one production cycle using time on the horizontal axis and on-hand inventory on the vertical axis (see Figure 7.10).

22. Given the following information for a part manufactured in-house, can you compute the economic manufacturing quantity? Provide a brief explanation to support your answer.

Annual demand	= 500,000 units
Daily production rate	= 1,000 units
Setup cost	= $250 per order
Holding rate	= 40 percent per year
Value of finished part	= $120 per unit
Number of days per year	= 360 days

CASES

1. Sharp's Sandwich Shop—Inventory Management*

Dawn Sharp is the owner of Sharp's Sandwich Shop. Her shop is open 24/7 and serves many different types of sandwiches, from classic breakfast sandwiches to more exotic burgers and other sandwiches usually consumed at lunch and dinner. Not all of the menu items are available all day. Dawn has divided her menu into four timeframes—breakfast, lunch, dinner, and after hours. Breakfast runs from 5 a.m. to 11 a.m. Lunch begins at 11 a.m. and ends at 3 p.m. Dinner begins early, at 3 p.m., and continues until 9 p.m. Between 9 p.m. and 5 a.m., customers can select sandwiches from the after-hour's section of the menu.

*Written by Rick Bonsall, D. Mgt., McKendree University, Lebanon, IL. The people and institution are fictional and any resemblance to any person or any institution is coincidental. This case was prepared solely to provide material for class discussion. The author does not intend to illustrate either effective or ineffective handling of a managerial situation.

Sharp's Sandwich Shop is in the heart of downtown New York City. Some periods are more brisk than others; however overall, because it is the city that never sleeps, business is reasonably steady most days. New Yorkers are fast moving and always in a rush. Consequently, no one wants to wait very long for their sandwich, no matter how unique or complicated it may be. Because of this, Dawn has set up a system where the kitchen produces specific sandwiches in bulk. For example, a basic ham and cheese on rye bread can be made in advance, wrapped, and placed in the ready bin. This way, when a customer orders a ham and cheese on rye, they get it quickly.

One challenge to this system is warm sandwiches. Depending on the complexity, that is, is it a plain cheese burger, or one with specific toppings selected by the customer, a premade warm sandwich can be made and placed in the warmer.

Another challenge to this system is that Sharp's sandwiches are very popular because of the quality of the sandwiches. Part of the quality is their freshness. Therefore, whether it is a cold sandwich or a warm sandwich, neither can stay in the premade bins too long. After a set period of time, if a sandwich is still in the bin it is removed and placed in the charity bin. The charity bin contains food that is still edible; however, won't be sold to Sharp's customers. The food in the charity bin is donated to a local homeless shelter twice a day.

Dawn strongly believes in giving back to the community. Her company sponsors runs for several causes throughout the year. Therefore, although it would be easier to throw out the food whose freshness life has reached its limit according to her standard of quality, giving it to the homeless shelter is an important outreach program for her. However, obviously, Dawn's business model is based on selling the food, not giving it away. She realizes she cannot completely prevent items from sitting in the bins past her standard-of-freshness quality time. However, as she reviews her monthly financial statements, Dawn sees a trend of increasing waste, that is, more going into the charity bin.

As Dawn examines her financials, she notices that her sandwich shop is going through certain inventory items faster than usual. From the ingredients listed, Dawn suspects that more of the high-end sandwiches are reaching her freshness quality time limit. Furthermore, as she compares the point-of-sale data to her inventory expense data, she concludes that there are spikes in the day where more sandwiches are reaching the charity bin.

Dawn speculates on what could be the issue. She reflects back on her class in supply chain management, specifically the inventory management chapter. She realizes that her primary focus had been on freshness, a key quality metric. She also recognized that timely service was another key quality metric that enabled her to get high customer satisfaction ratings. In hindsight, Dawn grasps that she had ignored basic inventory requirements while focusing on quality. Because of the freshness issue, more and more, her staff was making two sandwiches and only charging for one. Dawn firmly believes she cannot compromise on the quality; however, she needs to improve her inventory management in order to eliminate the growing waste.

Discussion Questions

1. Dawn understands her customers very well. She knows that they want two things: (1) speed in getting the sandwich, no matter what type and (2) the sandwich must taste fresh. As Dawn works out how to improve her inventory management process, how can she utilize the ABC inventory classification system as part of the remedy for this situation?

   - Think outside the box. Consider which type of inventory she really needs to classify using the ABC classification system.

2. As we examine this case, we know that the basic issue is low inventory turnover. Consequently, the bins are overstocked during specific times and items must be discarded because they exceed the freshness quality time limit. As she considers this point, Dawn is debating if she needs to use the EOQ model or the EMQ model. Provide a recommendation to Dawn on which model would be the most effective for her situation. Explain why your choice is better than the one you did not select.

3. Considering Sharp's Sandwich Shop's inventory issue, justify to Dawn what type of inventory review system she should establish. Go one step further, explain how this supports your previous answers to the above questions.

©2019 Cengage Learning

2. Lamb's Automotive Supplies*

Molly Lamb has been a car aficionado since she was a teenager. This passion led her to open an automotive supply store. Her primary customers are small car repair shops. Many of these shops service a variety of makes and models. The other customer base is car buffs such as herself. These customers are car hobbyists and they own "classic" cars. They often buy an older clunker and rebuild it. They prefer to rebuild it as much as they can to the original specifications. Consequently, finding parts for these older makes/models is a challenge and building an inventory is even more difficult.

Because Molly is such an old car enthusiast, she has often scoured the Internet, junk yards, and other places for usable old car parts. Molly has a section of her warehouse set aside for "classic" car parts, from starters, to hub caps, to door handles, etc. There is no real competitor in this segment of her business. While a few places may have the odd part or two for older models, Molly has a significant inventory for most makes and models going back to the 1940s. Because of the generation of the customers she is serving, the newest make/model is from the early 1970s.

The remainder of Lamb's Automotive Supplies' inventory is for more recent makes and models, those built within the last ten years. This section of the inventory is much larger than the one for the "classic" cars; however, despite its size, its dollar value isn't much higher. One challenge Molly has is warehouse space. Inventory capacity is basically directly related to space. Therefore, in order to serve both customer segments as best she can, Molly must maximize her warehouse space.

Although Molly is aware of what inventory she has on hand, she has never actually used a specific inventory system. Now that her warehouse is reaching capacity, Molly realizes she must have a better inventory management process. Adding more warehouse space isn't an option. She must use the space she has more efficiently. Molly begins to ponder how she can do this without creating a potential inventory shortage for either customer segment.

Discussion Questions

1. Since the parts for the "classic" cars are difficult to obtain, Molly has decided that she must set aside a certain percentage of the warehouse for these parts. When she locates a specific part for this customer segment, Molly has to buy it and place it in her inventory because once the opportunity passes, it may never return. How does this affect the inventory management of the parts for newer cars? What systems or

*Written by Rick Bonsall, D. Mgt., McKendree University, Lebanon, IL. The people and institution are fictional and any resemblance to any person or any institution is coincidental. This case was prepared solely to provide material for class discussion. The author does not intend to illustrate either effective or ineffective handling of a managerial situation.

processes do you recommend to Molly to ensure she does not develop shortages for the parts for the car repair shops? Explain how your recommendation helps Molly.

2. Considering Molly's situation and her two distinct customer bases, do you think the ABC classification system would benefit her? If so or if not, explain why.

3. Explain whether the EOQ or statistical reorder point methods can enable Molly to better manage her "classic" car parts inventory.

©2019 Cengage Learning

3. Crabtree Electronics*

Sylvester Bush owns Crabtree Electronics. His business has been going very well since he opened a few years ago. Most of his customers are other small businesses that need electronic parts such as circuit boards, transistors, resistors, capacitors, etc. A small percentage of his customers are hobbyists who enjoy building their own home sound systems and other items.

As with many businesses today, Crabtree Electronics is feeling a bit of a pinch because the overall economy isn't doing well. Sylvester is confident that business will eventually pick up; however, until then he needs to tighten his belt a bit. One area that he hasn't monitored as closely as he should is inventory. Sylvester knows that excess inventory is just money sitting on the shelf. In the past, he has used his gut as the driver of what and how much he should purchase. His understanding of his customers and their needs has been sufficient so far.

Sylvester wants to do more than just save some money now during the lean times. He wants to establish an inventory system that enables him to capture continuous savings through effective inventory control. His inventory doesn't contain many high-priced items. Most of the items his customers require are relatively low-cost items such as transistors, resisters, integrated circuit boards, wire, etc. If they need some item that is high priced, Sylvester orders it for them. Since he can get these items within two days, often within one, this process works well for the expensive parts. Sometimes customers cannot wait even one day; in those cases, Sylvester directs them to another source. This seldom happens so neither Sylvester nor his customers have any concern about him not carrying those very expensive parts. Also, since the requests for such parts are rare, Sylvester doesn't want to have them sitting in his inventory gathering dust. Sylvester wants to ensure his inventory turns over frequently. Sylvester begins to consider all his options.

Discussion Questions

1. Sylvester Bush is a good businessman; however, he isn't familiar with inventory control systems. Develop a chart for Sylvester with pros on one side and cons on the other. Help him make the choice between the ABC classification system and the EOQ. Based on the inventory he carries and his general process, which approach is best for him? Or, should he employ both, why?

2. Crabtree Electronics deals in relatively low cost parts. However, they also deal in large volumes of those parts. Some of the businesses he supplies often get large contracts that require them to buy electronic parts in bulk. Is there a way for Sylvester to turn this into an advantage for his business? What would you recommend he do and why? How would your recommendation benefit him and his customers?

*Written by Rick Bonsall, D. Mgt., McKendree University, Lebanon, IL. The people and institution are fictional and any resemblance to any person or any institution is coincidental. This case was prepared solely to provide material for class discussion. The author does not intend to illustrate either effective or ineffective handling of a managerial situation.

3. Many electronic parts are physically small. Sylvester's warehouse is brimming with rows upon rows of bins with hundreds and sometimes thousands of parts in them. Although some of the inventory models assume that the physical inventory levels are precise at any point in time, in reality they are not. Consider Sylvester's situation. Sell Sylvester on a specific inventory review system. Explain why it is the best for his situation and what benefit he will receive by using the system you suggest.

©2019 Cengage Learning

ADDITIONAL RESOURCES

EPCglobal, "EPC Radio-Frequency Identity Protocols Generatio-2 UHF RFID," EPCglobal Inc., 2013.

EPCglobal, "EPC/RFID UHF Air Interface Protocol 2.0.1," EPCglobal Inc., April 2015.

Fogarty, D. W., J. H. Blackstone, and T. R. Hoffmann, *Production & Inventory Management*, 2nd ed. Cincinnati: South-Western, 1991.

Hax, A., and D. Candea, *Production and Inventory Management*. Englewood Cliffs, NJ: Prentice-Hall, 1984.

Jacobs, F. R., and R. B. Chase, *Operations and Supply Chain Management*, 15th ed. Boston: McGraw-Hill/Irwin, 2018.

Jacobs, F. R., W. L. Berry, D. C. Whybark, and T. E. Vollmann, *Manufacturing Planning and Control for Supply Chain Management*, 6th ed. Boston: McGraw-Hill/Irwin, 2011.

Krajewski, L. J., M. J. Malhorta, and L. P. Ritzman, *Operations Management: Processes and Supply Chains*, 11th ed. Reading, MA: Prentice-Hall, 2016.

END NOTES

1. Doerfler, S., "Improving the Process," *Inside Supply Management Magazine* 28(1), January/February 2017: 27.

2. Anonymous, "Continuing to Use Technology Is Called Vital Key to Ongoing Success for Metals Distributor Sectors," *American Metal Market*, February 24, 2016, http://ezproxy.library.unlv.edu/login?url=http://search.proquest.com0/docview/1776015698?accountid=3611, accessed May 18, 2017.

3. Fleenor, G., "Turning to Inventory Management," *Convenience Store Decisions* 27(5), May 2016: 60–61.

4. Murphy, M., "Debrief: Robert Kraft on Buying the Patriots, Drafting Tom Brady, and Being Pals with Trump," *Bloomberg Businessweek*, May 15–21, 2017: 54–59.

5. Anonymous, "ERP Aids Inventory Analysis," *Metal Center News*, Summer 2016: 2–3.

6. Holcomb, B. J., "ISM Report on Business: Manufacturing," *Inside Supply Management* 28(3), April 2017: 12.

7. Michel, R., "Best Practices for Better Inventory Management," *Logistics Management* 55(2), February 2016: 44–48.

8. Friedman, D., "TechTips: Inventory Management Tips," *Supply House Times* 59(9), November 2016: 114–115.

9. Callahan, J., "Convenience Store Solutions: Achieving Inventory Control," *Convenience Store Decisions* 27(2), December 2016: 16.

10. Simpkins, J., "Production: Keeping Count," *Editor & Publisher* 149(10), October 2016: 28–30.

11. Napolitano, M., "Top 8 Guidelines to Improve Inventory Management," *Logistics Management* 57(3), March 2013: 40–43.

12. Berthiaume, D., "RFID Update," *Chain Store Age* 92(2), February/March 2016: 22.

13. Romeo, J., "RFID: A Fast Track for Improved Security," *Security* 54(2), February 2017: 36–38.

14. http://www.gs1.org/epcglobal, accessed May 25, 2017.

15 Anonymous, "Wal-Mart, DOD Start Massive RFID Rollout; Is Everybody Ready?" *Inventory Management Report* 5(1), January 2005: 1, 10–12.

16. GS1, "EPC/RFID UHF Air Interface Protocol 2.0.1," EPCglobal, April 2015, http://www.gs1.org/sites/default/files/docs/epc/Gen2_Protocol_Standard.pdf, accessed May 19, 2017.

17. Songini, M. L., "Procter & Gamble: Wal-Mart RFID Effort Effective," *ComputerWorld* 41(9), February 26, 2007: 14.

18. "RFID Frequently Asked Question," *RFID Journal*, https://www.rfidjournal.com/faq/show?85, accessed May 25, 2017.

19. Fish, L. A., and W. C. Forrest, "A Worldwide Look at RFID," Supply *Chain Management Review* 11(3), April 1, 2007: 48–55.

20. Hoffman, W., "Wave of the Future: Changes in Technology, Industry Consolidation, Global Standards Begin to Raise RFID's Profile," *Journal of Commerce* 9(35), September 8, 2008: 44.

21. Wu, N., H. H. Tsai, Y. S. Chang, and H. C. Yu, "The Radio Frequency Identification Industry Development Strategies of Asian Countries," *Technology Analysis & Strategic Management* 22(4), May 2010: 417–431.

22. Dearborn, J., "BIG Data: A Quick-Start Guide for Learning Practitioners," *T+D* 68(5), May 2014: 52–57.

23. Narsimhan, S., D. W. McLeavey, and P. Billington, *Production Planning and Inventory Control,* 2nd ed. Saddle River, NJ: Prentice Hall, 1995.

Chapter 8

PROCESS MANAGEMENT—LEAN AND SIX SIGMA IN THE SUPPLY CHAIN

We unified all of these individual stores into a team, and our goal is to consistently grow with an operating environment that is scalable and sustainable. We are working hard using lean practices and lean thinking to gain that scalable and sustainable performance.

— **Robert Benjamin, COO of Pacific Elite Collision Centers**[1]

We've continued to focus on what we can control—cost management and operational execution. We continue on a lean manufacturing journey and are focused on improving safety, quality, efficiency and inventory turns.

— **Doug Oberhelman, chairman and CEO of Caterpillar**[2]

There is a perception that workers in manufacturing don't need skills because the machinery does all the work, but nothing could be further from the truth. It is critical for workers to bring critical thinking and teamwork to the table to ensure that the machinery continues to produce high-quality products in the most cost-efficient manner possible.

— **Greg Higdon, president and CEO of the Kentucky Association of Manufacturers**[3]

Learning Objectives

After completing this chapter, you should be able to

- Discuss and compare the major elements of lean and Six Sigma.
- Describe why lean and Six Sigma are integral parts of SCM.
- Discuss the Toyota Production System and its association with lean production.
- Discuss the linkage between lean programs and environmental protection.
- Describe the historical developments of lean and Six Sigma.
- Describe and use the various tools of Six Sigma.
- Understand the importance of statistical process control for improving quality.

Chapter Outline

Introduction

Lean Production and the Toyota Production System

Lean Thinking and Supply Chain Management

The Elements of Lean

Lean Systems and the Environment

The Origins of Six Sigma Quality

Comparing Six Sigma and Lean

Six Sigma and Supply Chain Management

The Elements of Six Sigma

The Statistical Tools of Six Sigma

SCM Profile   Victaulic Finds Big Advantages with Lean

Pennsylvania-based Victaulic Co., a manufacturer of pipe-joining systems, recognized a few years ago that a lean implementation was needed. The company, which employs about 4,000 people worldwide, began implementing lean in stages, beginning with their manufacturing area.

Lean training at Victaulic helped employees become familiar with the company's plans for lean, using a hands-on workshop, which included the lean philosophy and how workers could use tools to continue the lean evolution in manufacturing. Lean leaders worked with employees to turn their ideas into actions. At Victaulic, the leaders were in sales, quality, operations, customer care, supply chain, finance, and other areas.

Victaulic's lean goals were increased safety and improved delivery, productivity, and inventory turns. Data were collected for metrics in each goal area and these told the company where it could make changes to have the biggest impact on each goal. New data then tracked the results of any changes made.

Victaulic's injury rate, for instance, has dropped nearly 87 percent over the latest seven-year period. Their new hazard identification program identified and removed hazards, and injuries have been reduced across all Victaulic facilities. Another lean initiative dealt with customer delivery rates. Before lean was implemented, only 64.7 percent of stock items and 32.4 percent of nonstock items were delivered by the promised due dates. Using lean initiatives, today's on-time delivery rates top 97 percent for both stock and nonstock items.

Prior to lean, Victaulic factories used poor forecasting methods, made product in large batches, and transferred them between various locations to keep supply levels balanced. This led to double handling, wasted capacity, and excess labor. With their new kanban system, every time a container quantity is emptied, it triggers demand. This has allowed for more frequent and smaller quantities to be produced. This pull system, along with the new product delivery system, cut delivery time from thirty-plus days to less than eight days. As a result, Victaulic became more of a problem-solver, making it a much more valuable supply chain partner.

At one Victaulic facility, the manufacturing floor was reconfigured to cut down on wasted movement and to increase employee safety by eliminating repetitive stress. This move reduced incidents and injuries. Reorganizing entire facilities resulted in the operation of fewer vehicles, thus reducing equipment and fuel costs. Simple things like arranging equipment in U-shaped layouts based on the order machines are used, along with putting components at their points of use, greatly reduced the need for fork trucks. The lean team also used employee input to manufacture ergonomically enhanced workstations and incorporated the paint line so castings could be inspected and hung directly for painting. The results included a productivity improvement of 35 percent, along with less fatigue and fewer mistakes. The company now feels it has reached the point where lean is part of the culture that drives its success.[4]

INTRODUCTION

As discussed in earlier chapters, supply chain management goals are concerned with achieving process integration, low cost, and high levels of quality and responsiveness throughout the supply chain. Customer expectations make it necessary for firms to adopt strategic initiatives emphasizing speed, innovation, cooperation, quality, and efficiency. Lean thinking and Six Sigma quality, two important operating philosophies that are central to the success of supply chain management, seek to achieve these strategic initiatives, while at the same time resolve the trade-offs that can exist when simultaneously pursuing the goals of high quality, fast response, and low cost.

In the 1990s, supply chain management emerged as a strategy combining several practices already in use—**quick response (QR)**, **efficient consumer response (ECR)**, Just-in-Time (JIT), and Japanese **keiretsu relationships**. The first two are concerned with speed and flexibility, while keiretsu involves partnership arrangements. The QR program was developed by the U.S. textile industry in the mid-1980s as an offshoot of JIT and was based on merchandisers and suppliers working together to cope with the demand for large numbers of SKUs with short product life cycles and high seasonalities. QR allowed garment manufacturers to respond more quickly to consumer needs by sharing information, resulting in better customer service and less inventory and waste.[5] In the early 1990s, ECR was developed by a U.S. grocery industry task force charged with making grocery supply chains more competitive. Point-of-sale transactions at grocery stores were forwarded via computer to upstream distributors and manufacturers, allowing the grocery stores to keep stocks replenished while minimizing the need for safety stock inventories.[6] Keiretsu networks are cooperative memberships between Japanese manufacturing firms and their suppliers. The stronger suppliers are prevented from doing too well while the weaker suppliers are prevented from failing, due to a web of constraints that keiretsu networks place on their member firms. Group members pay an insurance premium for the safety net that insulates each of them.[7]

Supply chain management is thus closely associated with all of these concepts. While many argue that Henry Ford and his company invented JIT practices (although not called JIT at the time), the term **Just-in-Time** was originally associated with Toyota managers like Mr. Taiichi Ohno along with his kanban system, encompassing continuous problem-solving in order to eliminate waste. Use of the term *lean* has today largely replaced use of the term JIT and is associated with the Toyota Production System. Lean thinking is broader, although closely related to JIT, and describes a philosophy incorporating tools that seek to economically optimize time, human resources, assets, and productivity, while improving product and service quality. In the early 1980s, these practices started making their way to the Western world, first as JIT and then today, as **lean production**, **lean manufacturing**, or simply **lean thinking**. Lean thinking has evolved into a way of doing business for many organizations.

Quality assessment and improvement is a necessary element of lean production. First, as the process of waste elimination begins to shrink inventories (primarily safety stocks and lot sizes), problems with human resource requirements, queuing, lead times, quality, and delivery timing are typically uncovered both in the production process and with inbound and outbound materials. Eventually, these problems are remedied, resulting in higher levels of quality and customer service (consider that quality must improve since safety stocks are reduced and items are produced more quickly since lot sizes are reduced). Second, as the drive to continuously reduce throughput times and inventories continues, the need for a continuing emphasis on improving quality throughout the productive system results in the need for an overall quality improvement or Six Sigma program. **Six Sigma** stresses a commitment by the firm's top management to help the firm identify customer expectations and excel in meeting and exceeding those expectations. Since global economic changes (such as the most recent global recession) along with changes in technology and competition cause customer expectations to change, firms must then commit to a program of continual reassessment and improvement; this, too, is an integral part of Six Sigma. Thus, to achieve the primary objectives of low cost, high quality, and fast response, supply chain management requires the use of lean and Six Sigma thinking throughout the supply chain. These topics are discussed in this chapter.

LEAN PRODUCTION AND THE TOYOTA PRODUCTION SYSTEM

The term lean production essentially refers to the **Toyota Production System** in its entirety, which was created and refined by several of Toyota's key executives over a number of decades. In 2010, Toyota came under fire for a number of recalls involving over 8 million vehicles worldwide for several quality and safety problems. While these problems were indeed serious, they do not diminish the value of lean production or the Toyota Production System. In fact, in 2010, Toyota promised a return to their "customer first" principles.[8] In 2015, Toyota once again earned the title of the most valuable automotive brand in the world, according to Interbrand's 2015 "Best Global Brands" annual report. Interbrand estimated Toyota's 2015 brand value at $49 billion. "Making guests our top priority, Toyota has done a better job than ever this year of delivering exciting new, ever-better products with exceptional styling, performance and value," said Jack Hollis, group vice president of Toyota Division Marketing at Toyota Motor Sales, USA.[9] Several of the important events in the creation of the Toyota Production System are described next.

Mr. Sakichi Toyoda invented the power loom in 1902 and in 1926 founded the Toyoda Automatic Loom Works. In 1937, he sold his loom patents to finance an automobile manufacturing plant to compete with Ford and General Motors, both of which accounted for over 90 percent of the vehicles sold in Japan at the time. Sakichi's son Kiichiro Toyoda was named managing director of the new facility.[10]

Kiichiro spent a year in Detroit studying Ford's manufacturing system and others, and then returned to Japan, where he adapted what he learned to the production of small quantities of automobiles, using smaller, more frequently delivered batches of materials. This later was referred to as the Just-in-Time system within Toyoda. At Ford, its system was designed such that parts were fabricated, delivered directly to the assembly line, and then assembled onto a vehicle within just a few minutes. Henry Ford had called this *flow production*, the precursor to JIT.[11]

Mr. Eiji Toyoda, nephew of Sakichi, began working at Toyoda in 1936 and was named managing director of the renamed and reorganized Toyoda Automotive Works in 1950. Eiji too, traveled to Detroit to study Ford's automobile manufacturing system and was particularly impressed with their quality improvement activities, most notably their employee suggestion system. He was also impressed with Ford's daily automobile output of 7,000 cars, compared to Toyoda's comparatively miniscule *thirteen year total output* of just 2,700 cars. Back in Japan, he implemented the concepts he had seen in the United States and this became the foundation of what was later referred to as the Toyota Production System.

In 1957, the company was again renamed and became the Toyota Company. They introduced their first U.S. car that year—the Toyopet Crown. While popular in Japan, the car's quality, speed, and styling problems resulted in sales of only 288 units in fourteen months in the United States. Consequently, Toyota withdrew from the U.S. market to further analyze U.S. consumers and their demands for reliability. "No detail was unimportant, and they paid very close attention to customers," says Dave Cole, chairman of Michigan-based Centre for Automotive Research. In 1965, the Corona was introduced in the United States and by 1972 U.S. sales had reached 1 million units.[12] In 1982, Eiji established Toyota Motor Sales USA, and finally in 1983, Eiji renamed the firm the Toyota Motor Corporation.

Taiichi Ohno began his career at the Toyoda Automatic Loom Works in 1932. He eventually expanded on the concepts established by Kiichiro and Eiji, by developing and refining methods to produce items only as they were needed for assembly. He visited Detroit several times to observe auto manufacturing techniques. After World War II, the Toyoda production facilities were rebuilt, with Taiichi playing a major role in establishing the low-batch production principles he developed earlier. These principles proved very valuable at the time, since postwar Japan was experiencing severe materials shortages. What Taiichi and Eiji had both realized during their trips to the United States was the tremendous waste everywhere (referred to as **muda** in Japan). These wastes of labor, inventories, space, time, and processing were certainly things Toyoda could not afford. From this realization came the idea that parts should be produced only as needed by the next step in an entire production process. When a type of signal or card (called a **kanban**) was used, the system became much more effective. This began to be called the kanban or JIT system within Toyoda.

Refinements to the JIT concepts continued under Taiichi's tutelage, and he later attributed the system to two things—Henry Ford's autobiography wherein he explained the Ford manufacturing system and U.S. supermarket operations characterized by daily supply deliveries, which Ohno observed during a visit to the United States in 1956. The final two notable people in the development of the Toyota Production System were Shigeo Shingo, a quality consultant hired by Toyota, and W. Edwards Deming who happened to be in Japan after the war, helping to conduct the census. Deming became known to Ohno and others at Toyota when he began attending professional manufacturing meetings in Japan to discuss statistical quality control techniques. By the 1950s in Japan, Deming had created and was discussing his fourteen-point quality management guideline and his ideas for continuous improvement with many Japanese manufacturing engineers and managers.

Shingo developed the concept of **poka-yoke** in 1961, when he was employed at Toyota. Poka-yoke means error- or mistake-proofing. The idea is to design processes such that mistakes or defects are prevented from occurring in the first place, and if they do occur, further errors are also prevented. These fail-safe mechanisms can be electrical, mechanical, visual, procedural, or any other method that prevents problems, errors, or defects, and they can be implemented anywhere in the organization. Poka-yoke thus leads to higher levels of quality and customer service.[13]

In the latter part of the 1950s as mentioned earlier, Toyota was experiencing quality problems that were impacting potential sales in the United States. To remedy this, Toyota implemented what they referred to as total quality control (TQC) in concert with their JIT system. This then became the final piece of the Toyota Production System and was later refined and renamed total quality management (TQM). Interestingly, in the first quarter of 2007, Toyota sold more vehicles worldwide than General Motors (GM), ending GM's 76-year reign as the world's largest auto maker.[14] (For the years 2014 through 2016, the top three automobile makers were Volkswagen (VW), Toyota, and GM, with VW holding the top spot in 2016.[15])

Actually, the term *lean production* did not originate at Toyota. It was first used in a benchmarking study conducted by the International Motor Vehicle Program (IMVP) at the Massachusetts Institute of Technology. The IMVP conducted a global automobile quality and productivity benchmarking study which eventually culminated in the book, *The Machine that Changed the World*, wherein the elements of lean production and the benchmarking results were presented.[16] The word "lean" was suggested because the Japanese facilities in the benchmarking study, when compared to their U.S. counterparts, used half the manufacturing labor, half the space, and half the engineering hours to produce a new automobile model in half the time. They also used much less than half the average inventory levels to produce the same number of vehicles, and had far fewer defects. The term "lean" seemed appropriate, and as they say, the term went viral.

The use of lean thinking has spread rapidly over the years among many manufacturers, services, and small businesses in numerous industries. For example, what can an oil company do when oil prices drop rapidly, as was seen in 2014 to 2015? Turn to lean production. The New York-based Hess Corp. cut about $400,000 from the cost of drilling each North Dakota well over the first half of 2015, along with sharply reducing the time it took to drill a well. Company officials said that applying lean manufacturing principles kept its 1,200 Bakken field oil wells profitable. "This stuff really does work when you have a culture that is behind it," Hess President Greg Hill said. "We haven't even scratched the surface."[17] Major tire manufacturer Goodyear, once considered a stodgy bureaucratic company, has even implemented lean thinking in its product development process, throughout its global operations. The company has reduced lead time by more than half and increased their success rate in introducing new profitable products to near perfection.[18] The nearby SCM Profile describes use of lean thinking at an auto repair company.

SCM Profile | Using Lean at Elite

Elite Collision Centers began in 1998 as a single-shop operation in Fullerton, CA. By 2014, the rebranded company had become Pacific Elite Collision Centers, a fourteen-store company in the Los Angeles, Orange County, and the Inland Empire region. In 2015, the company named Robert Benjamin its new COO. He had nearly twenty years of experience in lean manufacturing principles.

Benjamin leveraged his background in implementing lean principles to help further improve operations at Elite. The company's general managers meet once a month for a training and development day, to develop ways to solve any problems they've encountered, and to share best practices. "We've seen a very good turn in productivity and throughput, as well as quality and service, because of our focus on lean value and the ability to come together monthly and develop those store leadership teams," Benjamin says. Regional managers also have weekly problem-solving meetings. "They are focused on fixing problems, and keeping those problems from coming back," Benjamin says.

The company's vision for implementing lean is focused on growing the company through outstanding service and process development. "We want to have good, quality product every time, but we do that through process development," Benjamin says. "We've developed our people, taught them about customer value and how to eliminate waste, as well as fix problems. We ruthlessly pursue the elimination of waste."

The company can level its workloads fairly easily because of the close geographic clustering of the stores, and its call center has also helped keep the workload balanced. "We aren't just load leveling between stores, but also leveling the daily workload," Benjamin says. "We've been able to avoid that trap of having 90 percent of the work come in on Monday and go out on Friday. By leveling the load throughout the week, we can give great customer service and meet more customer demand."[19]

LEAN THINKING AND SUPPLY CHAIN MANAGEMENT

Simply put, the objective of supply chain management is to balance the flow or supply of materials with downstream customer requirements throughout the supply chain, such that costs, quality, and customer service are at optimal levels. Lean production emphasizes reduction of waste, continuous improvement, and the synchronization of material flows from within the organization and eventually including the organization's first-tier suppliers and customers. In many respects, then, supply chain management seeks to incorporate lean thinking across entire supply chains. Supply chain management encourages cross-training, satisfying internal customer demand, moving products or people through the production system quickly, and communicating end-customer demand forecasts and production schedules up the supply chains. In addition, it seeks to optimize inventory levels across entire supply chains. Thus, when implemented within the focal firm and its trading partners, the realized benefits of lean are much more significant.

Firms are increasingly implementing and sharing lean strategies along their supply chains. As a matter of fact, one of the newest terms in the lean lexicon is **yokoten**. Yokoten is a Japanese term meaning "across everywhere". In lean terminology, it is used to mean the sharing of best practices. Lean firms are using yokoten to reach out to closely linked suppliers and customers to make their supply chains leaner. For manufacturers, most of their products' final costs derive from supply chains. Consequently, supply chains represent the best opportunities for results from lean implementations. When *Logistics Management* magazine conducted a lean survey among hundreds of their subscribers, they found that use of lean improvements to supply chains had grown significantly—from just 30 percent in 2007 to 46 percent in 2011, a growth of over 50 percent.[20] That trend continues today.

Many firms successfully implement a few lean activities at a time, based on resources, product characteristics, customer needs, and supplier capabilities. Coffeehouse giant Starbucks has a vice president of lean thinking who travels from region to region with his lean team, looking for ways to reduce the wasted movements of its baristas. This in turn gives baristas more time to interact with customers and improve the Starbucks experience. The results are streamlined operations, happier customers, and a better bottom line.[21] Noted lecturer and author of many books on lean and associated topics, Norman Bodek suggests that maybe half of U.S. manufacturing companies are into some aspect of lean.[22] The following section is a discussion of the lean elements.

THE ELEMENTS OF LEAN

Table 8.1 presents the major lean elements that are discussed in this section of the chapter, along with a short description of each element. As noted above, lean programs can vary significantly, based on a company's resource capabilities, product and process orientation, and past failures or successes with other improvement projects. Firms with a mature lean program will most likely be practicing a significant number of these elements.

Waste Elimination

One of the primary and long-term goals of all lean endeavors is **waste elimination**. The desired outcome is value enhancement. Firms reduce costs and add value to their products and services by eliminating waste from their productive systems. Scott Sedam, president of TrueNorth Development, a global provider of lean methods to the construction industry, sums up the importance of waste reduction in construction: "In the end, what our industry

Table 8.1	The Elements of Lean
ELEMENTS	**DESCRIPTIONS**
1. Waste elimination	Eliminating waste is the primary concern of lean thinking. This includes reducing excess inventories, material movements, production steps, scrap losses, rejects, and rework.
2. Lean supply chain relationships	Firms work with suppliers and customers with the mutual goal of eliminating waste, improving speed, and improving quality. Key suppliers and customers are considered partners.
3. Lean layouts	Work-in-progress (WIP) inventories are positioned close to each process, and lay-outs are designed to reduce movements of people and materials. Processes are positioned to allow smooth and level flows of work through the facility.
4. Inventory and setup time reduction	Inventories are reduced by reducing production batch sizes, setup times, and safety stocks. This tends to create or uncover processing problems which are then controlled.
5. Small batch production scheduling	Firms produce frequent small batches of product, with frequent product changes to enable a level production schedule. Smaller, more frequent purchase orders are communicated to suppliers, and more frequent deliveries are offered to customers. Kanbans are used to pull WIP through the system.
6. Continuous improvement	As queues and lead times are reduced, problems surface more quickly, causing the need for continual attention to problem-solving and process improvement. With lower safety stocks, quality levels must be high to avoid process shutdowns. Attention to supplier, WIP, and finished goods quality levels are high.
7. Workforce empowerment	Employees are cross-trained to add processing flexibility and to increase the workforce's ability to solve problems. Employees are trained to provide quality inspections as parts enter a process area. Employee roles are expanded and they are given top management support and resources to identify and fix problems.

Source: Lamming, R., *Beyond Partnership: Strategies for Innovation and Lean Supply*. London: Prentice Hall, 1993; Ohno, T., *The Toyota Production System: Beyond Large-Scale Production*, Portland, OR: Productivity Press, 1988; Schonberger, R. J., *Japanese Manufacturing Techniques*. New York, NY: The Free Press, 1982; Womack, J., and D. Jones, *Lean Thinking: Banish Waste and Create Wealth for Your Corporation*. New York, NY: Simon and Schuster, 1996.

needs is a culture change, a 'hair on fire' attitude that every penny counts and every associate, whether manager, direct employee, supplier or trade, feels responsible. That's the challenge, and that's the goal. Getting there is not easy, but it has been done in many other industries. Now it's home building's turn at the plate, and not a moment too soon".[23]

Waste is a catch-all term encompassing things such as excess wait times and inventories, wasted or unneeded material and people movements, too many processing steps, variabilities in processing, and *any other nonvalue-adding activity*. Taiichi Ohno of Toyota, described what he termed the **seven wastes**, which have since been applied across many industries around the world, to identify and reduce waste. The seven wastes are shown and described in Table 8.2. The common term across the seven wastes is *excess*. Obviously, firms require some level of inventories, material and worker movements, and processing times, but the idea is to determine the *right* levels of these things and then decide how best to achieve them.

Unfortunately, many companies and their trading partners view waste as simply a cost of doing business. To identify and eliminate waste, workers and managers must be continually assessing processes, methods, and materials for their value contributions to the firm's salable products and services. This is accomplished through worker–management interactions and commitment to the continued elimination of waste, and frequent solicitation of feedback from customers. Significant waste reduction results in a number of positive outcomes including lower costs, shorter lead times, better quality, and greater competitiveness. During the economic downturn beginning in 2009, eliminating waste enabled firms

Table 8.2	The Seven Wastes
WASTES	**DESCRIPTION**
Overproducing	Production of unnecessary items to maintain high utilization.
Waiting	Excess idle machine and operator time; materials experiencing excess wait time for processing.
Transportation	Excess movement of materials between processing steps; transporting items long distances using multiple handling steps.
Overprocessing	Nonvalue-adding manufacturing, handling, packaging, or inspection activities.
Excess inventory	Storage of excess raw materials, work-in-process, and finished goods.
Excess movement	Unnecessary movements of employees to complete a task.
Scrap and rework	Scrap materials and product rework activities due to poor-quality materials or processing.

Source: Ohno, T., *Toyota Production System.* Portland, OR: Productivity Press, 1988.

to stay profitable while sales levels were declining. The use of lean programs increased in popularity during those years.

Using the Five-Ss to Reduce Waste

Another technique for waste reduction has been termed the **Five-Ss**. The original Five-Ss came from Toyota and were Japanese words related to industrial housekeeping. The idea is that by implementing the Five-Ss, the workplace will be cleaner, more organized and safer, thereby reducing processing waste and injury accidents, and improving productivity. A Five-S system is not only a housekeeping program but also a problem identification and prevention system. When something is found to be missing or out of place, the problem solution should be to repeatedly ask "why?" until the root (or most basic) cause is found and corrected. Toyota's Taiichi Ohno said that until why is asked five times, the root cause has probably not been identified. This is called the **Five-Why** (or 5Y) root cause process.[24] Table 8.3 lists and describes each of these terms and presents the equivalent S-terms used in the English version of the Five-S system.

The goals of the first two (sorting and setting in order) are to eliminate searching for parts and tools, avoid unnecessary movements, and avoid using the wrong tools or parts. Work area tools and materials are evaluated for their appropriateness, and approved items are arranged and stored near their place of use. Seiso/sweep refers to proper workplace cleaning and maintenance, while Seiketsu/standardize seeks to reduce processing variabilities by eliminating nonstandard activities and resources. Shitsuke/self-discipline or sustain means using effective work habits through use of the first four terms.

Table 8.3	The Five-Ss	
JAPANESE S-TERM	**ENGLISH TRANSLATION**	**ENGLISH S-TERM IN USE**
1. Seiri	Organization	Sort
2. Seiton	Tidiness	Set in order
3. Seiso	Purity	Sweep or shine
4. Seiketsu	Cleanliness	Standardize
5. Shitsuke	Discipline	Self-discipline or sustain

Source: Becker, J., "Implementing 5S: To Promote Safety & Housekeeping," *Professional Safety* 46(8), 2001: 29–31; Rooney, S., and J. Rooney, "Lean Glossary," *Quality Progress* 38(9i6), 2005: 41–47.

The Five-S system can be employed in any service or manufacturing environment. Many lean efforts begin with implementation of the Five-Ss. Firms can conduct a "waste hunt" using the Five-Ss, then follow up with a "red-tag event" to remove or further evaluate all nonessential, red-tagged items. Some companies have also added their own "sixth-S"—for surprises or safety—for assessing the safety of work conditions.[25]

Lean Supply Chain Relationships

Quite commonly, firms hold safety stocks of purchased goods because their suppliers' delivery times are inconsistent or the quality of the goods do not always meet specifications. Internally, extra WIP inventories are stored as a way to deal with temperamental processing equipment or other variabilities causing processing problems. On the distribution side, firms hold stocks of finished goods in warehouses prior to shipment to customers, in some cases for months at a time, to avoid stockouts and maintain high customer service levels. Holding high levels of these inbound, internal, and outbound inventories costs the firm money while not adding much, if any value to the products or the firm; thus, they are considered wastes.

When the focal firm, its suppliers, and its customers begin to work together to identify customer requirements, remove wastes and reduce costs, while improving quality and customer service, it marks the beginning of lean supply chain relationships. Companies like Kansas-based Cox Machine, an aerospace component manufacturer, have been doing this successfully for years. Cox uses mutually beneficial shipping methods, advance shipping notices, and barcoding to help their customers reduce their lead times and inventories. Cox shares their forecasts with their suppliers so they can deliver just when the materials are needed. When materials arrive, they are delivered directly to the machine cell, which reduces inventories.[26]

Using lean thinking with suppliers includes having them deliver smaller quantities, more frequently, to the point of use at the focal firm. While this reduces average inventory levels, it also means higher inbound transportation costs—to reduce these costs, suppliers might consider locating warehouses or production facilities close to the buyer. To entice suppliers to make these investments, buyers use fewer suppliers in order to give them a greater share of their total purchasing needs.

Making small, frequent purchases from just a few suppliers puts the focal firm in a position of greater dependence on these suppliers. It is therefore extremely important that deliveries always be on time, delivered to the right location, in the right quantities, and be of high quality, since existing inventories will be lower. In the automobile industry, Honda and Toyota have been the top two auto companies with regard to building supplier relationships since 2002, according to the Automotive Supplier Working Relations Index (WRI) published annually by Planning Perspectives. According to the study, Ford, General Motors, Nissan, and Fiat Chrysler would have earned between $144 and $285 more profit per vehicle if they matched the supplier relationships of the leaders Toyota and Honda.[27]

Firms can also use lean thinking with their key customers. As these relationships develop, the focal firm reserves more of its capacity for these large, steady customers. They locate production or warehousing facilities close to these customers and make frequent small deliveries of finished products to their customers' points of use, thus reducing transportation times and average inventory levels. Lean thinking with customers means determining how to give them exactly what they want and when they want it, while minimizing waste as much as possible. New York-based printed circuit board manufacturer IEC Electronics uses a new product introduction ambassador to hand-deliver prototypes to customers and answer any questions they might have, to build better customer relationships.[28]

It can be seen, then, that mutual dependencies and mutual benefits occur among all of these **lean supply chain relationships**, resulting in increased product value and competitiveness for all of the trading partners.

Lean Layouts

The primary design objective with **lean layouts** is to reduce wasted movements of workers, customers, and/or WIP inventories, while achieving smooth product (or customer) flow through the facility. Moving inventory and people around a facility does not add value. Lean layouts allow people and materials to move only when and where they are needed, as quickly as possible. Thus, whenever possible, processing centers, offices, or departments that frequently transfer parts, customers, or workers between them should be located close together, to minimize the times for these movements. In this way, layouts can add value, by reducing processing times. The nearby SCM Profile of Warner Electric provides a good discussion of lean layouts.

Lean layouts are very visual, meaning that lines of visibility are unobstructed, making it easy for operators at one processing center to monitor work occurring at other centers. In

SCM Profile	Warner Electric's World-Class Lean Production Plant

Illinois-based Warner Electric recently completed a 96,000-square-foot plant near Columbia City, IN. The world-class facility allowed Warner Electric to consolidate production activities from three different locations. The consolidation gave Warner Electric the opportunity to develop a state-of-the-art operation using lean principles.

The new plant provided an opportunity for a "blank sheet" layout. Several kaizen events were held to establish the optimal equipment layout and material flow. The goal was to eliminate the wasted movements, wait times, and inventory throughout the entire production process. "Teams of up to 15 members each were formed, representing all levels of employees, from production associates, material handlers and engineers to corporate executives," says Stan Owens, Warner Electric's general manager.

Each team began by mapping the current production processes of all products. Cardboard cutouts of machines were used to experiment with plant layouts. Each proposed layout was evaluated using lean techniques. "We also had a separate team evaluate raw material, finished goods inventory and material flow," says Owens.

Optimized productivity begins immediately when raw materials are delivered to the plant receiving dock. All material receipts are initiated by an order to the supplier triggered by a kanban card from an empty container. Receiving and quality personnel, along with material handlers, all own and drive the process. Lean accounting techniques require inventory be at the lowest possible level. This is achieved through a very responsive supply chain that provides smaller, more frequent deliveries tracked electronically with minimal intervention.

All raw material and finished goods at the plant are delivered and retrieved utilizing a unique system that cycles through the plant every two hours. Material handling associates are devoted to keeping production lines supplied with components. In order to reduce travel times, most materials are stored at the point-of-use, rather than a central location. "One of the most significant measures of our success can be found in our production 'up-time' and 'productivity,' both of which are up over 15 percent year over year," says Owens.[29]

manufacturing facilities, all purchased and WIP inventories are located on the production floor at their points of use, and the good visibility makes it easy to spot inventory build-ups and potential bottlenecks. When these and other production problems occur, they are spotted and rectified quickly. The relative closeness of the processing centers facilitates teamwork and joint problem-solving and requires less floor space than conventional production layouts.

Lean layouts allow problems to be tracked to their source more quickly as well. As processed items flow from one processing center to the next, a quality problem, when found, can generally be traced to the previous work center, provided inspections are performed at each processing stage. These layout advantages are also discussed in the chapter-opening SCM Profile of Victaulic.

Manufacturing Cells

Manufacturing cells or **work cells** are designed to process any parts, components, or jobs requiring the same or similar processing steps, saving duplication of equipment and labor. These similarly processed parts are termed **part families**. In many cases, these manufacturing cells are U-shaped to facilitate easier operator and material movements within the cell, as shown in Figure 8.1. In assembly line facilities, manufacturing cells are positioned close to the line, feeding finished components directly to the line instead of delivering them to a stock area where they would be brought back out when needed. Manufacturing cells are themselves actually small assembly lines and are designed to be flexible, allowing machine configurations to change as processing requirements dictate.

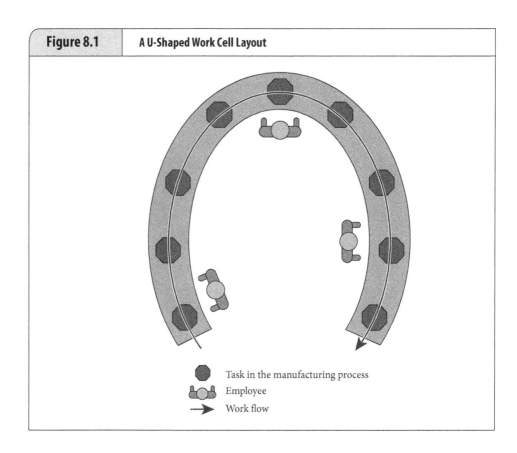

Figure 8.1	A U-Shaped Work Cell Layout

⬟ Task in the manufacturing process

Employee

→ Work flow

Inventory and Setup Time Reduction

In lean thinking, excess inventories are considered a waste, since they can hide a number of purchasing, production, and distribution problems within the organization. Just as water in a lake hides boat-damaging rocks beneath its surface, so excess inventories hide value-damaging problems along a supply chain. And, just as reducing the water levels causes rocks to become detectable, so too the reduction of inventory levels causes problems to surface in the organization and among its trading partners. Once these problems are detected, they can be solved, allowing the system to run more effectively with lower inventory investment. For example, reducing safety stocks of purchased materials will cause stockouts and potential manufacturing disruptions when late supplier deliveries occur. Firms must then either find a way to resolve the supplier's delivery problem or find a more reliable supplier. Either way, the end result is a smoother running supply chain with less inventory investment. The same story can be applied to production machinery. Properly maintained equipment breaks down less often, so less safety stock is needed to keep down-stream processing areas supplied with parts to be further processed.

Another way to reduce inventory levels is to reduce purchase order quantities and production lot sizes. Figure 8.2 illustrates this point. When order quantities and lot sizes are cut in half, average inventories are also cut in half, assuming usage remains constant. Unfortunately, this means that the firm must make more purchase orders (potentially increasing annual order costs). Suppliers must also make more deliveries, potentially increasing delivery costs or purchase costs. Thus, ordering costs and delivery costs must be reduced. This can be accomplished by automating or simplifying the purchasing process, and by giving the supplier more of the firm's business to gain negotiating leverage.

Reducing manufacturing lot sizes also means increasing the number of **equipment setups**. Since setting up production equipment for the next production run takes valuable time, increasing the number of setups means the firm must find ways to reduce these setup times. Setup times can be reduced in a number of ways including doing setup preparation work while the previous production lot is still being processed, moving machine

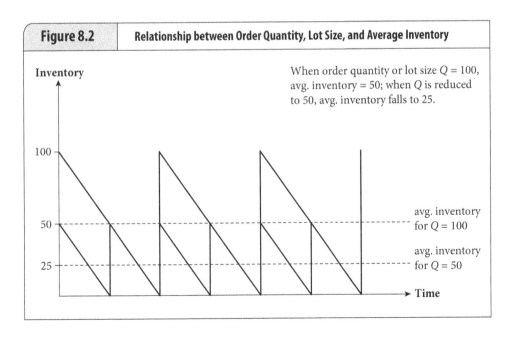

Figure 8.2	Relationship between Order Quantity, Lot Size, and Average Inventory

When order quantity or lot size $Q = 100$, avg. inventory = 50; when Q is reduced to 50, avg. inventory falls to 25.

avg. inventory for $Q = 100$

avg. inventory for $Q = 50$

tools closer to the machines, improving tooling or die couplings, standardizing setup procedures, practicing various methods to reduce setup times, and purchasing automated machines that require less setup time.

Finally, once inventories have been reduced and the flow problems detected and solved, the firm can reduce inventories still further, uncovering yet another set of problems to be solved. With each inventory reduction iteration, the firm runs leaner, cheaper, faster, and with higher levels of product quality.

Small Batch Production Scheduling

Continuing with the elements of lean, saying that a manufacturer should purchase small quantities more frequently, and produce items using small lot sizes with more setups is one thing, but actually accomplishing this feat is something else. Many firms have tried and failed, eventually returning to carrying high levels of inventory and producing with large lot sizes, rather than dealing with the many problems accompanying lean production. Use of level production schedules of small batches though, communicated throughout the production processes and to outside suppliers, is a primary strategy of lean production.

Small batch scheduling drives down costs by reducing purchased, WIP, and finished goods inventories, and it also makes the firm more flexible to meet varying customer demand. Figure 8.3 illustrates this point. In the same period of time, the firm with small lot sizes and short setup times can change products nine times, while the firm with large lot sizes and long setup times can only change products three times (and has yet to produce product D). Maintaining a set, level, small batch production schedule will also allow suppliers to anticipate and schedule deliveries resulting in fewer late deliveries. Wisconsin-based Woller Precision, for example, produces small batch quantities of aluminum interior commercial aircraft components such as seats, divans, and tables. It also makes parts for the medical and defense industries. Woller Precision's investment in automated machining has reduced setup times and changed the way the company looks at workflow. Customers continue to want lower prices, and one way to reduce part costs is to shrink lot sizes and inventory. Gone are the days of amortizing setup costs by producing large lot sizes that tie up finances in inventory until the customer places their final order. Now parts can be completed quickly in the automated machining cell, letting Woller Precision reduce both

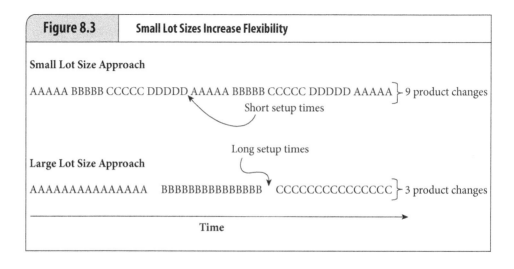

Figure 8.3	Small Lot Sizes Increase Flexibility

Small Lot Size Approach

AAAAA BBBBB CCCCC DDDDD AAAAA BBBBB CCCCC DDDDD AAAAA } 9 product changes

Short setup times

Long setup times

Large Lot Size Approach

AAAAAAAAAAAAAAAA   BBBBBBBBBBBBBBBB   CCCCCCCCCCCCCCCC } 3 product changes

Time

the finished goods inventory and work in process. "Five years ago, companies didn't have a problem putting a couple months of inventory on shelves. Now customers demand short lead times and require new levels of speed, quality and cost-saving for their projects. Our automated horizontal machining system delivers this, resulting in a 50% decrease in work in process. The cell can produce parts quickly, so we no longer have money tied up in raw materials, extra parts or outside services," says Aaron Woller, president of Woller Precision.[30]

Moving small production batches through a lean production facility is often accomplished with the use of **kanbans**. The Japanese word "kanban" has several meanings in Japan—it can refer to a billboard, as in "The Donut Shoppe," or more historically, to a uniform worn by servants of the samurai to indicate they acted on the authority of their clan or lord. Mr. Chihiro Nakao, a former Toyota manager who worked directly with Taiichi Ohno recalls a story about the origins of the word kanban at Toyota—Mr. Ohno supposedly caught a worker trying to pull materials too early from an upstream work center and he yelled, "Who are you and where did you come from?! What makes you think you have any right to this material?! Show me your kanban!"[31] Thus, the origin of the more modern "permission slip" or "authority" definition of the word kanban. In most lean facilities it simply refers to a signal.

When manufacturing cells need parts or materials, they use a kanban to signal their need for the items from the upstream manufacturing cell, processing unit, or external supplier providing the needed material. In this way, nothing is provided until a downstream demand occurs. That is why a lean system is also known as a **pull system**. Ideally, parts are placed in standardized containers, and kanbans exist for each container. Figure 8.4 illustrates how a kanban pull system works. When finished components are moved from Work cell B to the final assembly line, the following things occur:

1. The container holding finished parts in work cell B's output area is emptied and a **production kanban** (a light, flag, or sign) is used to tell work cell B to begin processing more components to restock the empty container in its output area.

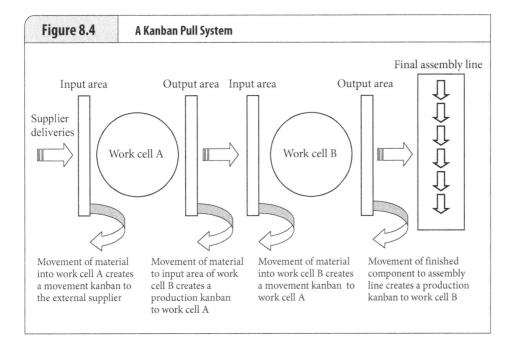

| Figure 8.4 | A Kanban Pull System |

Final assembly line

Input area   Output area   Input area   Output area

Supplier deliveries

Work cell A   Work cell B

Movement of material into work cell A creates a movement kanban to the external supplier

Movement of material to input area of work cell B creates a production kanban to work cell A

Movement of material into work cell B creates a movement kanban to work cell A

Movement of finished component to assembly line creates a production kanban to work cell B

2. During this stage, when parts are moved from work cell B's input area to its processing area, the container holding these parts is emptied and a withdrawal kanban (a light, flag, or sign) is used to indicate to work cell A that more parts are needed. This authorizes a full container of parts to move from work cell A's output area to work cell B's input area, and the empty container is moved to work cell A's output area.

3. As this movement occurs, a production kanban is used to authorize work cell A to begin processing parts to restock its empty container in the output area.

4. Finally, as full containers of parts are emptied and used in work cell A's processing area, the emptied containers in work cell A's input area create a withdrawal kanban seen by the external supplier who then restocks work cell A's empty containers in the input area.

Thus, it can be seen that kanbans are used to control the flow of inventory through the facility. Inventories are not allowed to accumulate beyond the size of each container and the number of containers in the system. When containers are full, production stops until an output area container is emptied, which generates another production kanban.

A simple relationship can be used to determine the number of containers or kanban card sets for a lean production system:

$$\text{No. of containers} = \frac{DT(1+S)}{C}$$

where

D = the demand rate of the assembly line

T = the time for a container to make an entire circuit through the system, from being filled, moved, being emptied, and returned to be filled again

C = the container size, in number of parts

S = the safety stock factor, from 0 to 100 percent

Example 8.1 illustrates the container calculation.

Example 8.1   Calculating the Number of Containers in a Kanban System

Mejza Manufacturing has an assembly line with a demand of twenty part 1's per hour at work cell B. The container used for this part holds five part 1's. If it takes two hours for a container to make a circuit from work cell B to the next assembly area and back again, and if it is desired to carry 10 percent excess of part 1 in the system, then the number of containers needed in the system is:

$$\text{No. of containers} = \frac{DT(1+S)}{C} = \frac{20\frac{\text{parts}}{\text{hr}}(2\,\text{hr})(1+0.1)}{5\,\text{parts}} = 8.8 \rightarrow 9$$

The maximum part 1 inventory for this system would then be the total number of containers times the container size, or $9 \times 5 = 45$ units.

Referring to Example 8.1, reducing inventory in the system (one of the objectives of lean production) occurs when the number of containers used is reduced. When this happens, the circuit time for each container would also have to be reduced to enable the demand to be met. This can be done by reducing setup time, processing time, wait time, move time, or some combination of these.

Continuous Improvement

As alluded to already, lean systems are never-ending works in progress. Compact layouts are designed to allow work to flow sequentially and quickly through the facility. Inventory is moved from supplier delivery vehicles to the shop floor and placed in containers in designated work cell storage areas.

Purchase orders and production batches are small. In this system, problems often will surface, at least initially, as suppliers struggle to deliver the right parts frequently and on time, and as workers strive to maintain output levels while spending more time during the day setting up machines for small production runs. To make the lean system work better, employees continuously seek ways to reduce supplier delivery and quality problems, and in the production area they solve movement problems, visibility problems, machine breakdown problems, machine setup problems, and internal quality problems. In Japanese manufacturing facilities, this is known as **kaizen**. A literal translation of kaizen is "good change." Some firms embrace what is known as a **kaizen blitz**, which is a rapid improvement event or workshop, aimed at finding big improvements quickly. Most kaizen improvements though, are small individual events, emphasizing creativity.

Quality improvement is certainly part of the ongoing continuous improvement effort in lean systems. For example, receiving a batch of goods from an external supplier or an internal work cell that does not meet design requirements is like not getting a batch at all. Because of low safety stock levels, processing areas needing these supplies will very quickly be out of stock and unable to operate. High quality levels are then necessary throughout the production system to meet demand. Further discussions of quality and continuous improvement can be found in later segments of this chapter.

Workforce Commitment

Since lean systems depend so much on waste reduction and continuous improvement for their success, employees must play a significant role in this process. Managers show strong support for lean production efforts by providing subordinates with the skills, tools, time, and other necessary resources to identify process problems and implement solutions. Managers can also create a culture in which workers are encouraged to speak out when problems are found. Georgia-based UTC invests heavily in employee education. The company will pay for any worker to obtain an associate's, bachelor's, or master's degree. "The goal for UTC is to have the most highly educated workforce in the world," explains Emily Michelbach, human resources manager at the Athens plant. At the corporate level, UTC has spent over $1 billion on the program to date.[32]

In lean manufacturing systems, employees are cross-trained on many of the various production processes to enable capacities to be adjusted as needed when machines break down or when workers are absent. Employees are given time during their day to work on reducing machine setup times, as well as to solve other production problems when they occur. They are also expected to perform a number of quality checks on processed items coming into their work cells. When quality problems are found, workers are empowered to shut down the production process until the source of the problem can be found and corrected. Most employees who work for lean companies enjoy their jobs; they are given a number of responsibilities and are considered one of the most important parts of a successful lean organization.

LEAN SYSTEMS AND THE ENVIRONMENT

In Chapter 4, the topics of ethical and sustainable procurement were introduced and their importance to supply chain management was discussed. Since lean systems are ultimately concerned with waste reduction throughout the firm and its supply chains, the linkage between lean and environmental sustainability should seem clear.

Many organizations have realized the positive impact lean systems can have on the environment—adopting lean practices reduces waste and the costs of environmental management, which in turn leads to improved environmental performance. Further, lean systems increase the possibility that firms will adopt more advanced environmental management systems, leading to yet further performance improvements. Professors King and Lennox analyzed thousands of companies in the early 1990s and found ample evidence of this linkage between the concept of lean and environmental sustainability. They found that firms minimizing inventories and adopting quality standards were more likely to practice pollution prevention.[33]

Other examples abound. A number of LEED-certified buildings (Leadership in Energy and Environmental Design, which is a rating system to evaluate the environmental performance of a building) are using lean methods during the building's design phase. These include the first LEED Healthcare-certified project, Group Health Cooperative's Puyallup, Washington Medical Center, and a Veterans Administration Healthcare Center in Kernersville, NC, which incorporates daylighting, high-efficiency HVAC, and a green roof. Iowa-based Rockwell Collins decided to use their successful lean program to reduce its carbon footprint, starting in 2009. Their goal was to achieve a 15 percent reduction by 2014. They eventually exceeded this goal by 3 percent.[34]

As discussed in this first portion of the chapter, creating lean processes is a necessary element in successful supply chain management. A second, equally necessary element is the practice of continuous quality improvement—one of the best examples of this is Six Sigma quality. A discussion of Six Sigma quality and its relationship to lean thinking and supply chain management follows.

THE ORIGINS OF SIX SIGMA QUALITY

Six Sigma quality, many times simply referred to as Six Sigma, was pioneered by global communications leader Motorola in 1987, and is a statistics-based decision-making framework designed to make significant quality improvements in value-adding processes. Six Sigma (with capital Ss) is a registered trademark of Motorola. In the 1980s, a senior staff engineer at Motorola named Mikel Harry formed a team of engineers to experiment with problem-solving using statistical analyses, and this became the foundation for Six Sigma. Richard Schroeder, vice president of customer service at Motorola, heard about Harry's work, and applied the methodology to his job at Motorola. Soon, both groups were announcing large reductions in errors and related costs. Ultimately, both men left Motorola and formed the Six Sigma Academy, concentrating on training. Today, the firm has been renamed SSA & Company and is a management consultancy based in New York City.[35]

Since Six Sigma is all about pleasing the customer, a very straightforward customer-oriented definition of quality can be employed—*the ability to satisfy customer expectations.* This definition is echoed by the American Society for Quality when it states: "Quality is defined by the customer through his/her satisfaction." In this sense, both a fast-food hamburger and a steakhouse chopped sirloin sandwich can be considered to possess equally high quality, if they meet or exceed the expectations of their customers.

Quality perfection is represented by the term Six Sigma, which refers to the statistical likelihood that 99.99966 percent of the time, a process sample average will fall below a control limit placed 4.5 standard deviations (or sigmas) above the true process mean, assuming the process is in control. This represents the goal of having a defect occur in a process only 0.00034 percent of the time, or 3.4 times out of every million measurement opportunities—very close to perfection. Interestingly, this description makes it sound like the methodology should be called 4½ sigma. The 1½ sigma difference is the subject of much debate, explained by a somewhat confusing term called **sigma drift**.[36] Sigma drift refers to the idea that process variations will grow over time, as process measurements drift off target. In truth, any process exhibiting a change in process variation of 1.5 standard deviations would be detected using quality control charts, instigating an improvement effort to get the process back on target. Table 8.4 shows the **defects per million opportunities (DPMO)** to be expected for various sigmas, using the Six Sigma methodology.

The Six Sigma concept though, is not just concerned with statistics. It is a broad improvement strategy that includes the concepts and tools of **total quality management**, a focus on the customer, performance measurement, and formal training in quality control methods. Six Sigma embodies an organizational culture wherein everyone from CEO, to production worker, to frontline service employee is involved in quality assessment and improvement. Six Sigma is proactive in nature and seeks to permanently fix the root causes of problems, instead of repeatedly spending time and money tinkering with and patching-up processes as problems occur in the business. In Six Sigma, sources of process variation are sought out and remedied prior to the time these variations can cause production and customer satisfaction problems.

Today, many organizations practice Six Sigma, including early adopters Honeywell, General Electric, and Dow Chemical. In 1999, Ford Motor Company became the first U.S. automaker to adopt a Six Sigma strategy. Automobile manufacturing provides a great example of the need for Six Sigma. Since automobiles have roughly 20,000 **opportunities for a defect to occur** (OFD), and assuming an automobile manufacturer operates at an impressive 5½ sigma level (32 DPMO from Table 8.4), this would equate to about one defect for every two cars produced. Improving to the Six Sigma level would mean about one defect for every fifteen automobiles produced. Calculating the DPMO can be accomplished using the following formula:

$$\text{DPMO} = \frac{\text{number of defects}}{(\text{OFD per unit}) (\text{number of units})} \times 1{,}000{,}000$$

Table 8.4	Six Sigma DPMO Metrics	
NO. STANDARD DEVIATIONS ABOVE THE MEAN	**PERCENT OF DEFECT-FREE OUTPUT**	**DEFECTS PER MILLION OPPORTUNITIES (DPMO)**
2	69.15	308,537
2.5	84.13	158,686
3	93.32	66,807
3.5	97.73	22,750
4	99.38	6,210
4.5	99.865	1,350
5	99.977	233
5.5	99.9968	32
6	99.99966	3.4

Note: Standard deviations include a 1.5-sigma "drift."

Example 8.2 illustrates the calculation of DPMO and the use of Table 8.4.

Example 8.2   Calculating the DPMO for Blakester's Speedy Pizza

Blake Roberts, owner of Blakester's Speedy Pizza, keeps track of customer complaints. For each pizza delivery, there are three possible causes of complaints: a late delivery, a cold pizza, or an incorrect pizza. Each week, Blake tracks the delivery "defects" for pizza deliveries, and then uses this information to determine his company's Six Sigma quality level. During the past week, his company delivered 620 pizzas. His drivers received sixteen late delivery complaints, nineteen cold pizza complaints, and five incorrect pizza complaints. Blake's defects per million opportunities is:

$$\text{DPMO} = \frac{\text{number of defects}}{(\text{OFD per unit}) (\text{number of units})} \times 1{,}000{,}000$$

$$= \frac{40}{(3)(620)} \times 1{,}000{,}000 = 21{,}505 \text{ defective pizza deliveries per million.}$$

From Table 8.4, it can be concluded that Blakester's is operating at slightly better than 3.5 Sigma.

Increasingly, companies are using Six Sigma programs to generate cost savings or increased sales through process improvements. In fact, Motorola reported savings of $16 billion from 1986 to 2001, GE saved $4.4 billion from 1996 to 1999, and Honeywell saved $1.8 billion from 1998 to 2000. More recently, Indiana-based truck trailer manufacturer Wabash National used Six Sigma to help it achieve an operating income of $202.5 million in 2016, an increase of 12 percent over the prior year, and a record performance for the fifth consecutive year.[37] These types of outcomes are possible as firms identify customer requirements, uncover all of the opportunities for errors or defects to occur, review performance against Six Sigma performance standards, and then take the actions necessary to achieve those standards. The most successful projects meet strategic business objectives, reduce product and service variations to optimal levels, and produce a product or service that satisfies the customer.

In countries such as China and India, where competitive advantage has largely been due to the low cost of labor, many Chinese and Indian companies are today looking to quality management as a way to help them better compete in global markets. The China National Institute for Standards, for example, the national standardization body for China, developed standards for Six Sigma practices in 2012.[38] Additionally, a survey conducted in 2012 of manufacturing companies in Germany, France, Scandinavia, the United States, Canada, India, and China found that 47 percent had launched Six Sigma programs, 43 percent had started zero-defect programs, and 83 percent had implemented continuous improvement programs. A majority in each case were either satisfied or very satisfied with the results.[39] One remarkable story in India deserves a note here—the work of the dabbawalas in Mumbai (dabbawala means "one who carries a box"). Dabbawalas collect freshly cooked meals in boxes from the homes of Mumbai residents and deliver them to their offices for a small monthly fee. Five thousand dabbawalas deliver 200,000 boxes per day using only bicycles, buses, and trains. Forbes Magazine awarded a Six Sigma certification in 2001 to the dabbawalas based on a 99.999999 percent delivery accuracy rate (an amazingly low rate of 1 error for every 16 million transactions). Further, the dabbawalas have no knowledge of Six Sigma.[40]

Like any other improvement strategy or program, however, Six Sigma cannot guarantee continued or even initial business success. Poor management decisions and investments, or a company culture not conducive to change, can undermine even the best Six Sigma program. Ironically, Six Sigma originator Motorola struggled financially for a number of years; in 2009, after losing billions over a three-year period, Motorola was split into two independent companies—Motorola Mobility and Motorola Solutions. In 2012, Google acquired Motorola Mobility.[41] Camera and filmmaker Polaroid, another early user of Six Sigma, filed for Chapter 11 bankruptcy protection in 2001, and the following year, they sold their name and all of their assets to a subsidiary of Illinois-based Bank One Corp.[42]

COMPARING SIX SIGMA AND LEAN

Six Sigma and lean actually have many similarities. For lean practices to be successful, purchased parts and assemblies, work-in-process, and finished goods must all meet or exceed quality requirements. Also, recall that one of the elements of lean is continuous improvement, and these are the areas where the practice of Six Sigma can be put to good use in a lean system. Evidence points to the growing use of both of these initiatives simultaneously.

Successful manufacturing companies over the long term must ultimately offer high-quality goods at reasonable prices, while providing a high level of customer service. Rearranging factory floor layouts and reducing batch sizes and setup times will reduce manufacturing lead times and inventory levels, providing better delivery performance and lower cost. These are lean production activities. Reducing waste uncovers process problems. Solving these process problems requires performance monitoring, use of statistical quality control techniques, and creating long-term relationships with high-quality suppliers; these activities are part of Six Sigma. This short explanation describes how the two concepts can work together to achieve better overall firm performance. Lean production is all about reducing waste, while Six Sigma is all about solving problems and improving quality. The melding of these methods is called lean Six Sigma, discussed next.

Lean Six Sigma

A term is now being used to describe the combining of lean thinking and Six Sigma quality practices—**lean Six Sigma**, or simply **lean Six**. Since 2007, the U.S. Defense Department's Lean Six Sigma office has completed more than 330 projects and trained more than 1,000 officials on the techniques of lean Six, allowing them to take on new projects themselves. Further, more than 30,000 department employees have been trained in lean Six. Ireland-based Abbott Diagnostics Longford, a healthcare manufacturing facility, applied numerous lean Six Sigma techniques to enhance its processes, and linked its core competencies to principles of operational excellence. As a result, the facility dramatically cut costs, lead times, nonconformance rates, inventory, energy costs, and waste, while improving output and employee development and morale. In 2015, Longford earned the Shingo Prize for its accomplishments.[44] The nearby SCM Profile describes the city of Houston's lean Six Sigma efforts.

SIX SIGMA AND SUPPLY CHAIN MANAGEMENT

By now, the supply chain management objectives of better customer service, lower costs, and higher quality should be starting to sound familiar. To sustain and improve competitiveness, firms must perform better in these areas than their competitors. Through better process integration and communication, trading partners along the supply chain realize how poor-quality products and services can cause negative reactions to occur, such as greater levels of safety stock throughout the supply chain, lost time and productivity due to product and component repairs, the increased costs of customer returns and warranty repairs, and, finally, loss of customers and damage to reputations.

SCM Profile   Houston's Lean Six Sigma Journey

In 2011, at the mayor's request, the city of Houston's employees began embracing lean Six Sigma. The city's finance director formed a lean Six Sigma team. Myja Lark, who also coordinates lean Six Sigma programs for the city, said the change in operating culture was significant. "We have a lot of tenured employees—they've been here for 20 or 30 years," she said. "And they've created a situation where they almost feel like their job is a possession rather than a process. So [we're] training people not only in the methodology but to think differently about their jobs."

One of the lean Six Sigma team's first projects was in the city's fleet management department. The department was supposed to use their ERP software to confirm service and submit payment whenever an invoice was received for work done to a vehicle. That process was taking an average of 111 days, not including payment. Suppliers were cutting off service and calling the mayor's office to complain. Using process mapping, reengineering, and waste removal efforts, the processing time was eventually reduced to 2.5 days, and the department's staff was reduced from six people to one.

Since 2011, the lean Six Sigma team has completed more than two dozen projects using visual controls, kanban systems, and other tools. "We estimate $25 million in either incremental revenue or savings. A large part of that came from the accounts receivable and collection process. We've got about $3 million to $4 million in lean Six Sigma projects. As a direct result of not hiring folks, we've had about $1 million in cost avoidance," says Jesse Bounds, deputy assistant director of the finance department.

Since the city's lean Six Sigma initiative began, fifty-two employees have been trained as green belts, and most are working toward full certification. Just more than 1,000 yellow belts have been trained citywide, some in every operational department. "We play a mentoring role, but they receive the training and it's on them to succeed. And they definitely have the support of their management to take the time they need to do it," says Bounds.[43]

The impact of poor quality on the supply chain and potential damage to a firm's reputation can be illustrated by the problems toy-maker Mattel had to deal with regarding the Chinese-made toys it was selling in many of its global markets in 2007. Mattel announced it was pulling 9 million Chinese-made Barbies, Polly Pockets, and other toys off store shelves, due to quality and safety problems. Some of the toys had high levels of lead paint and while others had tiny magnets that could come off and be swallowed. Some of the magnets were in fact swallowed, causing physical harm to the children involved. Obviously, the cost to Mattel and its suppliers, the toy retailers, and the children who played with these toys was very high.[45] Thus, the impacts of poor quality can be felt throughout the supply chain and ultimately by end customers.

Six Sigma is an enterprise-wide philosophy, encompassing an organization's suppliers, employees, and customers. It emphasizes a commitment by the organization to strive toward excellence in the production of goods and services that customers want. Firms implementing a Six Sigma program have made a decision to understand, meet, and then strive to exceed customer expectations, and this spills over to their trading partners as well. Connecticut-based Pratt & Whitney, a manufacturer of aircraft engines, has been ramping up production of jet engines since 2014, with the goal of tripling output by 2020.

The company relies on suppliers to produce roughly 80 percent of the components and parts. As part of this initiative, the company has invested more than $10 billion in long-term agreements with ninety key suppliers. To aid this endeavor, Pratt & Whitney recently opened an operations command center, which focuses on lean and continuous improvement between the company and its 400 suppliers worldwide. "Our goal is to identify supply chain issues early and collaborate with the suppliers early before a potential constraint or impediment occurs," explains Rita Peralta, general manager of the Command Center.[46]

Many successful companies use Six Sigma methods to assure that their suppliers are performing well and that their customers' needs are being met. Ultimately, this translates into end consumers getting what they want, when they want it, for a price they are willing to pay. While Six Sigma programs tend to vary somewhat in the details from one organization to another, all tend to employ a mix of qualitative and quantitative elements aimed at achieving customer satisfaction. The most common elements addressed in most Six Sigma programs are discussed in the following section.

THE ELEMENTS OF SIX SIGMA

The philosophy and tools of Six Sigma are borrowed from a number of resources including quality professionals such as W. Edwards Deming, Philip Crosby, and Joseph Juran; the Malcolm Baldrige National Quality Award and the International Organization for Standardization's ISO 9000 and 14000 families of standards; the Motorola and General Electric practices relating to Six Sigma; and statistical process control techniques originally developed by Walter Shewhart. From these resources, a number of commonly used elements emerge that are collectively known today as Six Sigma. A few of the quality resources are discussed next, followed by a brief look at the qualitative and quantitative elements of Six Sigma.

Deming's Contributions

W. Edwards Deming's theory of management is explained in his book *Out of the Crisis* and essentially states that since managers are responsible for creating the systems that make organizations work, they must also be held responsible for the organization's problems (not the workers). Thus, only management can fix problems, through application of the right tools, resources, encouragement, commitment, and cultural change. Deming's theory of management was the centerpiece of his teachings around the world (Deming died in 1993) and includes his fourteen points for management, shown in Table 8.5.[47]

Deming's fourteen points are all related to Six Sigma principles, covering the qualitative as well as quantitative aspects of quality management. He was convinced that high quality was the outcome of a philosophy geared toward personal and organizational growth. He argued that growth occurred through top management vision, support, and value placed on all employees and suppliers. Value is demonstrated through investments in training, equipment, continuing education, support for finding and fixing problems, and teamwork both within the firm and with suppliers. Use of statistical methods, elimination of inspected-in quality, and elimination of quotas are also required to improve quality. Today, Deming's work lives on through the Deming Institute, a nonprofit organization he founded to foster a greater understanding of Deming's principles and vision. The institute provides conferences, seminars, and training materials to managers seeking to make use of the Deming operating philosophy.[48]

The Malcolm Baldrige National Quality Award

The **U.S. Baldrige Quality Award** was signed into law on August 20, 1987, and is named in honor of then U.S. President Reagan's Secretary of Commerce, who helped draft an early version of the award, and who was tragically killed in a rodeo accident shortly before the award was enacted. The objectives of the award, which by the way is given only to U.S. firms, are:

- to stimulate U.S. firms to improve quality and productivity,
- to recognize firms for their quality achievements,
- to establish criteria and guidelines so that organizations can independently evaluate their own quality improvement efforts, and
- to provide examples and guidance to those companies wanting to learn how to manage and improve quality and productivity.

The Baldrige Award is managed by the Baldrige Performance Excellence Program, and administered by the National Institute of Standards and Technology (NIST). Up to eighteen awards are given annually and are typically presented by the President of the United States to organizations across six sectors: small business, service, manufacturing, education, healthcare, and nonprofit/government. The applicants are evaluated in seven areas: leadership; strategic planning; customer focus; measurement, analysis, and knowledge management; workforce focus; operations focus; and results.[51] A number of companies have even sprung up to help companies apply for, and hopefully win an award. Table 8.8 shows the 109 Baldrige Award winners from 1988 through 2016.

Table 8.8	Malcolm Baldrige National Quality Award Recipients (1988–2016)[52]					
YEAR	SMALL BUSINESS	MANUFACTURING	SERVICE	EDUCATION	HEALTHCARE	NONPROFIT/GOV'T.
1988	Globe Metallurgical	Motorola; Westinghouse Comm. Nuclear Fuel Div.				
1989		Xerox Bus. Products and Sys; Milliken & Co.				
1990	Wallace Co.	Cadillac Motor Car Co.; IBM Rochester	FedEx Corp.			
1991	Marlow Industries	Solectron Corp.; Zytec Corp.				
1992	Granite Rock Co.	AT&T Network Sys. Group; Texas Instr. Def. Sys. & Electronics Grp.	AT&T Universal Card Svcs.; The Ritz-Carlton Hotel Co.			
1993	Ames Rubber Corp.	Eastman Chemical Co.				
1994	Wainwright Indus.		AT&T Consumer Comm Svcs.; GTE Directories			
1995		Armstrong World Ind. Bldg. Prod. Ops.; Corning Telecomm. Prod. Div.				
1996	Custom Research; Trident Precision Mfg.	ADAC Laboratories	Dana Comm. Credit			
1997		3M Dental Prod. Div.; Solectron	Merrill Lynch Credit; Xerox Business Svcs.			

Table 8.8	Malcolm Baldrige National Quality Award Recipients (1988–2016)[53] (continued)					
1998	Texas Nameplate	Boeing Airlift and Tanker Programs; Solar Turbines				
1999	Sunny Fresh Foods	STMicroelectronics—Region Americas	BI; The Ritz-Carlton Hotel Co.			
2000	Los Alamos Nat'l. Bank	Dana Corp.—Spicer Drvshft Div.; KARLEE	Operations Mgt. Int'l.			
2001	Pal's Sudden Svc.	Clarke American Checks		Chugach Sch. Dist.; Pearl River Sch. Dist.; Univ. of Wisc.-Stout		
2002	Branch-Smith Printing Div.	Motorola Comm., Gov't., and Indus. Sol. Sector			SSM Health Care	
2003	Stoner	MEDRAD	Boeing Aerospace Support; Caterpillar Financial Svcs. Corp.	Community Consol. Sch. Dist. 15	Baptist Hosp.; St. Luke's Hosp. of Kan. City	
2004	Texas Nameplate	The Bama Companies		K. W. Monfort Coll. of Bus.	R. W. Johnson Univ. Hosp.	
2005	Park Place Lexus	Sunny Fresh Foods	DynMcDermott Petroleum Opns.	Jenks Public Schools; Richland College	Bronson Meth. Hosp.	
2006	MESA Products		Premier		N. Mississippi Medical Center	
2007	PRO-TEC Coating				Mercy Health Sys.; Sharp HealthCare	City of Coral Springs; US Army ARDEC
2008		Cargill Corn Milling		Iredell-Statesville Schools	Poudre Valley Health System	
2009	MidwayUSA	Honeywell Federal Mfg. & Technologies			Heartland Health	VA Cooperative Studies Program
2010	Studer Grp.; Freese and Nichols; K&N Mgt.	MEDRAD; Nestle Purina PetCare		Montgomery Cty. Pub. Sch.	Advocate Good Sam. Hosp.	
2011					Henry Ford Health Sys.; Schneck Med. Ctr.; Southcentral Fndn.	Concordia Publishing House
2012	MESA	Lockheed Missiles and Fire Cont.			N. Miss. Health Svcs.	City of Irving, TX
2013				Pewaukee School District	Sutter Davis Hospital	
2014			PwC-Public Sector		Hill Country Memorial; St. David's HealthCare	Elevations Credit Union
2015	MidwayUSA			Charter School of San Diego	Charleston Area Medical Center Health System	Mid-America Transplant
2016	Momentum Group; Don Chalmers Ford				Memorial Hermann Sugar Land Hospital; Kindred Nursing and Rehab. Center-Mountain Valley	

All Malcolm Baldrige Award applications receive from 300 to 1,000 hours of review by quality professional volunteers and are scored in the seven areas listed above. Finalists are visited wherein performance is reassessed and final scores tabulated, with the winners selected from this group. Over 1,600 organizations have applied for the Baldrige Award and seven have won it twice (the most recent double winner was Missouri-based retailer MidwayUSA in 2015). Companies may obtain a copy of the Baldrige Award criteria and perform self-assessments using the form and its point scoring guidelines. Completing a self-assessment using the Baldrige Award criteria identifies the firm's strengths and weaknesses and can aid in implementing various quality and productivity improvement initiatives. To date, thousands of firms have requested copies of the official application.

The ISO 9000 and 14000 Families of Management Standards

In 1946, delegates from twenty-five countries met in London and decided to create a new international organization, with the objective "to facilitate the international coordination and unification of industrial standards." The new organization, called the International Organization for Standardization or ISO, officially began operations on February 23, 1947. ISO is the world's largest developer of voluntary international standards (there are currently over 19,000 ISO standards). Now located in Geneva, Switzerland, ISO today has 162 member countries (note that individuals and companies cannot become members).[54]

ISO standards are voluntary, are developed in response to market demand, and are based on consensus among the member countries. This ensures widespread applicability of the standards. ISO considers evolving technology and member interests by requiring a review of its standards at least every five years to decide whether they should be maintained, updated, or withdrawn. In this way, ISO standards retain their position as state of the art.

ISO standards are technical agreements that provide the framework for compatible technology worldwide. Developing consensus on this international scale is a major operation. In all, there are some 3,000 ISO technical groups with approximately 50,000 experts participating annually to develop ISO standards. Examples include standards for agriculture and construction, mechanical engineering, medical devices, and information technology developments such as the digital coding of audio–visual signals for multimedia applications.

In 1987, ISO adopted the ISO 9000 family of international quality standards, and revises them every five years. ISO 9001:2008 sets out the criteria for a quality management system and is the only standard in the family with a certification for organizations. It can be used by any organization, large or small, regardless of its field of activity. As of 2015, over 1 million organizations in over 170 countries possess this certification.[55] The standards have been adopted in the United States by the American National Standards Institute (ANSI) and the American Society for Quality (ASQ). In many cases worldwide, companies will not buy from suppliers who do not possess an ISO 9000 certification.

After the rapid acceptance of ISO 9000 and the increase of environmental standards around the world, ISO assessed the need for international environmental management standards. They formed an advisory group for the environment in 1991, which eventually led to the adoption of the ISO 14000 family of international environmental management standards in 1997. ISO 14001:2004 sets out the criteria for an environmental management system and offers organizations this certification. Some of the more recently adopted 14000 standards are the ISO 14006 standard for the management of ecodesign, ISO 14031, which provides guidance on the design and use of environmental performance evaluation, and the ISO 14064 standard for greenhouse gas accounting and verification.

Together, the ISO 9000 and 14000 families of certifications are the most widely used standards of ISO, with more than 1.3 million organizations in 175 countries holding one or both types of certifications. For both types of standards, European and Asian companies vastly exceed other companies in getting certified. The standards that have earned the ISO 9000 and ISO 14000 families a worldwide reputation are known as "generic management system standards," meaning that the same standards can be applied to any type of organization.

The DMAIC Improvement Cycle

Figure 8.5 shows the five-step DMAIC improvement cycle, an important element of Six Sigma, listing the sequence of steps necessary to drive process improvement. The cycle can be applied to any process or project, both in services and manufacturing firms. The improvement cycle begins with customer requirements and then seeks to analyze and modify processes or projects so they meet those requirements.

Each of the steps is described below:

1. *Define*: Identify customers and their service or product requirements critical to achieving customer satisfaction (also known as **critical-to-quality (CTQ) characteristics**). Identify any gaps between the CTQ characteristics and process outputs. Where gaps exist, create Six Sigma projects to alleviate the gaps.

2. *Measure*: Prepare a data-collection plan to quantify process performance. Determine what to measure for each process gap and how to measure it. Use check sheets to organize measurements.

3. *Analyze*: Perform a process analysis using the performance data collected. Use Pareto charts and fishbone diagrams to identify the root causes of the process variations or defects.

4. *Improve*: Design an improvement plan, then remove the causes of process variation by implementing the improvement plan. This will require modifying, redesigning, or reengineering the process. Document the improvement and confirm that process gaps have been significantly reduced or eliminated.

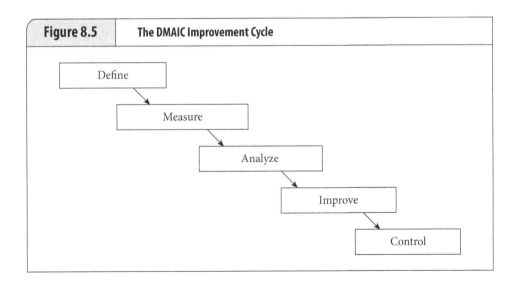

| **Figure 8.5** | **The DMAIC Improvement Cycle** |

5. *Control*: Monitor the process to assure that performance levels are maintained. Design and use statistical process control charts to continuously monitor and control the process. When performance gaps are once again identified, repeat steps 1–5.

Using the DMAIC improvement cycle allows the firm to continuously monitor and improve processes that are keys to customer satisfaction. By concentrating on these key processes and the CTQ characteristics, firms can make large and radical improvements in processes, products, and customer satisfaction. Deaconess Health System, a six hospital system in Indiana, has used the DMAIC cycle since 2011 to improve contractual reimbursements from their managed care plans. After five months, their dollars collected per day had increased by over $3,800, and this had been sustained for seven months when the article was published. The simple DMAIC cycle allowed them to organize their efforts.[56]

Six Sigma Training Levels

In order to develop and successfully complete Six Sigma improvement projects, specific training in quality improvement methods is available. A number of organizations offer courses and certifications in Six Sigma methods, and the somewhat standardized training levels are summarized in Table 8.9. Global manufacturing giant GE began using Six Sigma in the 1980s, and today, all GE employees are receiving training in the strategy, statistical tools, and techniques of Six Sigma. Eventually, all employees earn their Six Sigma Green Belt designations. Training courses are offered at various levels including basic Six Sigma awareness seminars, team training, Master Black Belt, Black Belt, and Green Belt training.[57] Several of the statistical tools of Six Sigma are discussed next.

Table 8.9	The Six Sigma Training Levels[58]
TRAINING LEVELS	**DESCRIPTION**
Yellow Belt	Basic understanding of the Six Sigma methodology and the tools within the DMAIC problem-solving process, including process mapping, cause-and-effect tools, simple data analysis, and process improvement and control methods. Role is to be an effective team member on process improvement project teams.
Green Belt	A specially trained team member allowed to work on small, carefully defined Six Sigma projects, requiring less than a Black Belt's full-time commitment. Has enhanced problem-solving skills, and can gather data and execute experiments in support of a Black Belt project. They spend approximately 25 percent of their time on Six Sigma projects of their own or in support of Black Belt projects.
Black Belt	Has a thorough knowledge of Six Sigma principles. Exhibits leadership, understands team dynamics, and assigns team members with roles and responsibilities. Has a complete understanding of the DMAIC model, a basic knowledge of lean concepts, and can quickly identify "nonvalue-added" activities. Coaches project teams and provides group assessments. Identifies projects, selects project team members, acts as an internal consultant, mentors Green Belts, and provides feedback to management.
Master Black Belt	A proven mastery of process variability reduction and waste reduction. Can effectively provide training at all levels. Challenges conventional wisdom through the demonstration of the application of Six Sigma principles and provides guidance and knowledge to lead and change organizations. Directs Black and Green Belts on the performance of their Six Sigma projects and also provides guidance and direction to management teams regarding the selection of projects and the overall health of a Six Sigma program.

THE STATISTICAL TOOLS OF SIX SIGMA

Flow Diagrams

Also called **process diagrams** or **process maps**, this tool is the necessary first step to evaluating any manufacturing or service process. **Flow diagrams** use annotated boxes representing process action elements and ovals representing wait periods, connected by arrows to show the flow of products or customers through a process. Once a process or series of processes is mapped out, potential problem areas can be identified and further analyzed for excess inventories, wait times, or capacity problems. A simple example of a customer flow diagram for a restaurant is shown in Figure 8.6. Using the diagram, restaurant managers can then observe each process activity and wait period element, looking for potential problems requiring further analysis.

Check Sheets

Check sheets allow users to determine the frequencies of specific problems. For the restaurant example shown in Figure 8.6, managers can make a list of potential problems based on experience and observation, and then direct employees to keep counts of each problem on check sheets for a given period of time (long enough to allow for true problem level determinations). At the end of the data-collection period, problem areas can be reviewed and compared. Figure 8.7 shows a typical check sheet that might be used in a restaurant.

Pareto Charts

Pareto charts, useful for many applications, are based at least initially, on the work of Vilfredo Pareto, a nineteenth-century Italian economist. In 1906, Pareto described the unequal distribution of wealth in his country, observing that 20 percent of the people

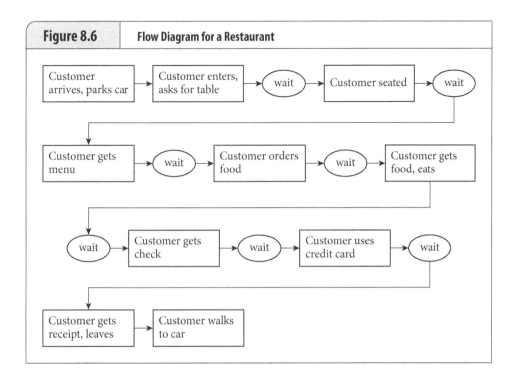

Figure 8.6   **Flow Diagram for a Restaurant**

Figure 8.7	Check Sheet for Problems at a Restaurant

Problem	Mon.	Tues.	Wed.	Thurs.	Fri.	Sat.	Sun.	Totals	% of Total
long wait	//////	/////	////////	///////	/////////	//////////	////	48	26.5
cold food		//	/	/	///	//		9	5.0
bad food	//	/	///		/	////		11	6.1
wrong food	//////	//	/	//	/////	///	/	19	10.5
bad server	//////	///	/////	/	//////	//	/	24	13.3
bad table		/	//		/	///	/	8	4.4
room temp.			//	///	/////	/////		15	8.3
too expensive	/	//	/	/	///	///		11	6.1
no parking			//		/////	////////		14	7.7
wrong change	///////	/	////		////	///		18	9.9
other		/	//			/		4	2.2
Totals	26	18	31	14	42	43	7	181	100

owned about 80 percent of the wealth. Decades later, Joseph Juran described what he called the **Pareto Principle** referring to the observation that 20 percent of something is typically responsible for 80 percent of the results. Eventually this became widely known as the Pareto Principle or 80/20 Rule.[59] Applied to quality improvement, this refers to the common observation that a few of a firm's problems account for most of the problem occurrences. In other words, firms should fix the few biggest problems first.

The Pareto chart shown in Figure 8.8 is useful for presenting data in an organized fashion, indicating process problems from most to least severe. The top two restaurant problems in Figure 8.7 account for about 40 percent of the instances where problems were observed. Two Pareto charts are shown in Figure 8.8. Note that we could look at the total problem events either from a problem-type or day-of-the-week perspective and see that *long wait* and *bad server* are the two largest problems, while Saturdays and Fridays are the days when most of the problem events occur. Finding the root causes and implementing solutions for these two problems would significantly decrease the number of problem events at the restaurant.

Cause-and-Effect Diagrams

Once a problem has been identified, **cause-and-effect diagrams** (also called **fishbone diagrams** or **Ishikawa diagrams**) can be used to aid in brainstorming and isolating the causes of a problem. Figure 8.9 illustrates a cause-and-effect diagram for the most troublesome *long wait* problem of Figure 8.8. The problem is shown at the front end of the diagram. Each of the four diagonals or fishbones of the diagram represents potential groups of causes. The four groups of causes shown—material, machine, methods, and manpower—commonly referred to as **the 4 M's**, are the standard classifications of problem causes and represent a very thorough list for problem–cause analyses. In almost all cases, problem causes will be in one or more of these four areas.

Typically, Six Sigma team members will gather and brainstorm the potential causes for a problem in these four areas. Each branch on the four diagonals represents one potential cause. Subcauses are also part of the brainstorming process and are shown as smaller

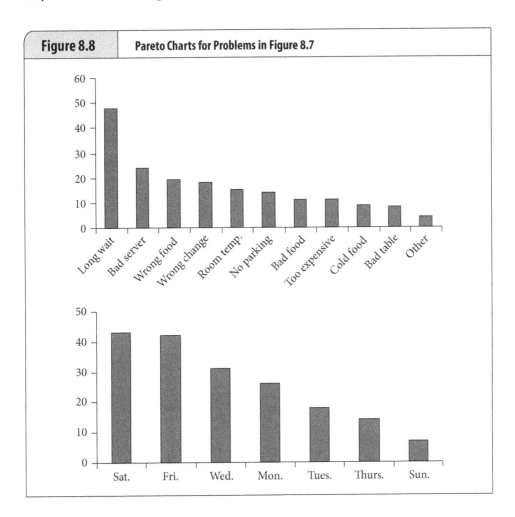

Figure 8.8 **Pareto Charts for Problems in Figure 8.7**

branches attached to each of the primary causes. Breaking a problem down like this into its causes and subcauses allows workers to then go back to the process and determine the relative significance of each cause and subcause using more specific checklists and Pareto charts once again. Eventually, the firm begins working to eliminate the causes of the problem, starting with the most significant **root causes** and subcauses until most of the problem's impact disappears.

A properly thought-out cause-and-effect diagram can be a very powerful tool for use in Six Sigma efforts. Without its use, workers and management risk trying to eliminate causes that have little to do with the problem at hand, or working on problems that are quite minor compared to other, more significant problems. Once most of a problem's causes are identified and eliminated, the associated process should be back under control and meeting customer requirements. At this point, firms can design and begin using statistical process control charts, discussed next.

Statistical Process Control

An important part of Six Sigma and any quality improvement effort, **statistical process control** (SPC) allows firms to visually monitor process performance, compare the performance to desired levels or standards, and take corrective steps quickly before process variabilities get out of control and damage products, services, and customer relationships.

Figure 8.9	Cause-and-Effect Diagram for the Long Wait Problem

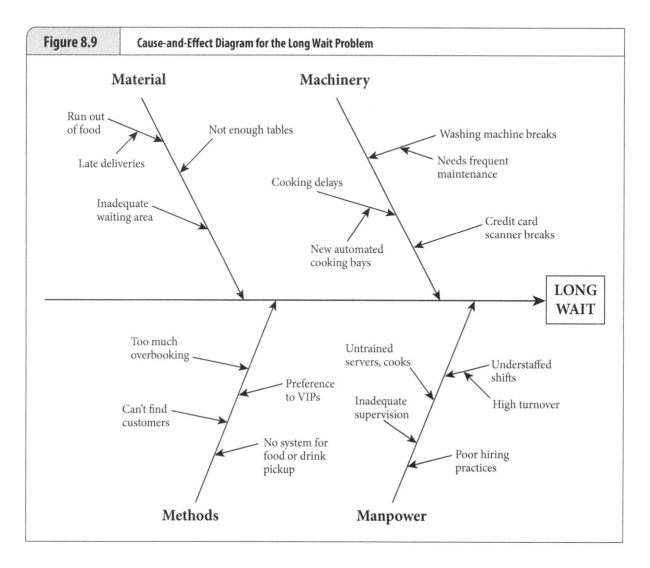

Once a process is working correctly, firms gather process performance data, create **control charts** to monitor process variabilities, and then collect and plot sample measurements of the process over time. The means of these sample measures are plotted on the control charts. If the sample means fall within the acceptable control limits and appear *normally distributed* around the desired measurement, the process is in *statistical control* and the process is permitted to continue; sample measurements and control chart plots also continue. When a sample plot falls out of the acceptable limits or when the plots no longer appear normally distributed around the desired measurement, the process is deemed to be *out of control.* The process is then stopped, problems and their causes are identified, and the causes are eliminated as described earlier. Control chart plots can then resume once the process is back in control.

Control charts are graphic representations of process performance over time, showing the desired measurement (the center line of the control chart) and the process' upper and lower control limits. This visual aid makes it very easy for operators or other workers to plot data and compare performance over time.

Variations

Variations in process measurements can be either **natural variations** or **assignable variations**. All processes are affected by these variations, and environmental noise or natural variations are to be expected. When only natural variations are present, the process is in statistical control. Assignable variations are those that can be traced to a specific cause (such as the causes shown in Figure 8.9). These assignable variations are created by causes that can be identified and eliminated and thus become the objective of statistical process control efforts.

Samples

Because of the likelihood of small variations in process measures, samples of data are collected and the sample means are then plotted onto control charts. Sample measures can be either **variable data** or **attribute data**, and each requires a different type of control chart. Variable data are continuous, such as weight, time, and length (as in the weight of a box of cereal, the time to serve a customer, or the length of a steel rod). Attribute data indicate the presence of some attribute such as color, satisfaction, workability, or beauty (for instance, determining whether or not a car was painted the right color, if a customer liked the meal, if the light bulb worked, or if the dress was pretty).

Variable data samples are shown as the mean of the sample's measures (for instance, an average of 12.04 ounces in a sample of five boxes of cereal), whereas attribute data are shown as the percent defectives within a sample (for instance, 10 percent or 0.10 of the light bulbs in a sample that did not work). The two types of control charts follow.

Variable Data Control Charts

When measuring and plotting variable process data, two types of control charts are needed: the $\bar{x}$ **chart** (or x-bar chart) and the **R chart**. The $\bar{x}$ chart is used to track the central tendency of the sample means, while the R chart is used to track sample ranges, or the variation of the measurements within each sample. A perfect process would have sample means equal to the desired measure and sample ranges equal to zero. It is necessary to view *both of these charts* in unison, since a sample's mean might look fine, even though several of the measures might be far from the desirable measure, making the sample range very high. It could also be the case that the sample's range looks fine (all measures are quite close to one another), even though all of the measures are far from the desired measure, making the sample's mean look bad. For variable data then, *both* the $\bar{x}$ chart and the R chart must show that the samples are in control before the process itself is considered in control.

Constructing the $\bar{x}$ Chart and the R Chart

The first step in constructing any control chart is to gather data (provided the process is already in control and working well). Typically about twenty-five or thirty samples of size five to ten are collected, spaced out over a period of time. Then for each sample, the mean ($\bar{x}$) and the range (R) are calculated. Next, the *overall mean* ($\bar{\bar{x}}$) and the *average range* ($\bar{R}$) of all the samples are calculated. The $\bar{\bar{x}}$ and $\bar{R}$ measures become the center lines (the desired measures) of their respective control charts. Example 8.3 provides the data used to calculate the center lines of the $\bar{x}$ chart and the R chart. The formulas used to calculate the center lines, $\bar{\bar{x}}$ and $\bar{R}$, are:

$$\bar{\bar{x}} = \frac{\sum_{i=1}^{k} \bar{x}_i}{k} \quad \text{and} \quad \bar{R} = \frac{\sum_{i=1}^{k} R_i}{k}$$

where k indicates the number of samples and i indicates the specific sample.

For the data shown in Example 8.3 we see that $\bar{\bar{x}} = 11.96$ and $\bar{R} = 0.39$. If these measures are seen as acceptable by the Hayley Girl Soup Co., then they can use these to construct their control charts. These means are also used to calculate the upper and lower control limits for the two control charts. The formulas are:

$$\text{UCL}_{\bar{x}} = \bar{\bar{x}} + A_2 \bar{R} \quad \text{and} \quad \text{LCL}_{\bar{x}} = \bar{\bar{x}} - A_2 \bar{R}$$
$$\text{UCL}_R = D_4 \bar{R} \quad \text{and} \quad \text{LCL}_R = D_3 \bar{R}$$

where A_2, D_3, and D_4 are constants based on the size of each sample (n) and are shown in Table 8.10 (the constants used are based on an assumption that the sampling distribution is normal and that the control limits are ±3.0 standard deviations from the population mean, which contains 99.73 percent of the sampling distribution). The constants for various sample sizes are shown in Table 8.10.

Example 8.3   Variable Data Samples of Soup Cans at Hayley Girl Soup Co.

The Hayley Girl Soup Co., a soup manufacturer, has collected process data in order to construct control charts to use in their canning facility. They collected twenty-four samples of four cans each hour over a twenty-four-hour period, and the data are shown below for each sample:

HOUR	1	2	3	4	$\bar{x}$	R
1	12	12.2	11.7	11.6	11.88	0.6
2	11.5	11.7	11.6	12.3	11.78	0.8
3	11.9	12.2	12.1	12	12.05	0.3
4	12.1	11.8	12.1	11.7	11.93	0.4
5	12.2	12.3	11.7	11.9	12.03	0.6
6	12.1	11.9	12.3	12.2	12.13	0.4
7	12	11.7	11.6	12.1	11.85	0.5
8	12	12.1	12.2	12.3	12.15	0.3
9	11.8	11.9	12	12	11.93	0.2
10	12.1	11.9	11.8	11.7	11.88	0.3
11	12.1	12	12.1	11.9	12.03	0.2
12	11.9	11.9	11.7	11.8	11.83	0.2
13	12	12	11.8	12.1	11.98	0.3
14	12.1	11.9	12	11.7	11.93	0.4
15	12	12	11.7	11.2	11.73	0.8
16	12.1	12	12	11.9	12.00	0.2
17	12.1	12.2	12	11.9	12.05	0.3
18	12.2	12	11.7	11.8	11.93	0.5
19	12	12.1	12.3	12	12.10	0.3
20	12	12.2	11.9	12	12.03	0.3
21	11.9	11.8	12.1	12	11.95	0.3
22	12.1	11.8	11.9	12	11.95	0.3
23	12.1	12	11.9	11.9	11.98	0.2
24	12	12.3	11.7	12	12.00	0.6
MEANS					**11.96**	**0.39**

Table 8.10	Constants for Computing Control Chart Limits ($\pm 3\sigma$)[60]		
SAMPLE SIZE, n	MEAN FACTOR, A_2	UCL, D_4	LCL, D_3
2	1.88	3.268	0
3	1.023	2.574	0
4	0.729	2.282	0
5	0.577	2.115	0
6	0.483	2.004	0
7	0.419	1.924	0.076
8	0.373	1.864	0.136
9	0.337	1.816	0.184
10	0.308	1.777	0.223

Using the variable data in Example 8.3 along with Table 8.10 for a sample size of four, the upper and lower control limits for both the $\bar{x}$ chart and the R chart for the Hayley Girl Soup Co. can be determined:

$$\text{UCL}_{\bar{x}} = \bar{\bar{x}} + A_2 \bar{R} = 11.96 + 0.729(0.39) = 12.24$$
$$\text{LCL}_{\bar{x}} = \bar{\bar{x}} - A_2 \bar{R} = 11.96 - 0.729(0.39) = 11.68$$

and

$$\text{UCL}_R = D_4 \bar{R} = 2.282(0.39) = 0.89$$
$$\text{LCL}_R = D_3 \bar{R} = 0(0.39) = 0$$

Next, the means and control limits can be used to construct the two control charts. In Figure 8.10, the data sample means and ranges are plotted on the two control charts, showing the center lines and control limits. From these plots, it appears that the process is indeed in statistical control, and the Hayley Girl Soup Co. can begin using these charts to monitor the canning process. If the process appears out of control on either chart, the control charts would not be useful and should be discarded until problem causes are identified and eliminated and the process is in statistical control.

Once a good set of control charts have been created and samples from the process are being statistically monitored, the following steps should be followed:

1. Collect samples of size 4–5 periodically (depending on the type of process and ease of data collection).

2. Plot the sample means on both control charts, monitoring whether or not the process getting out of control.

3. When the process begins to appear out of control, use check sheets, Pareto charts, and fishbone diagrams to investigate causes and eliminate process variations.

4. Repeat steps 1–3.

Attribute Data Control Charts

When collecting attribute data regarding whether or not a process is producing good or bad (nondefective or defective) output, use of $\bar{x}$ and R charts no longer apply. In these cases, either **P charts**, which monitor the *percent defective* in each sample, or **C charts**, which count the *number of defects* per unit of output, are used. Each of these is discussed next.

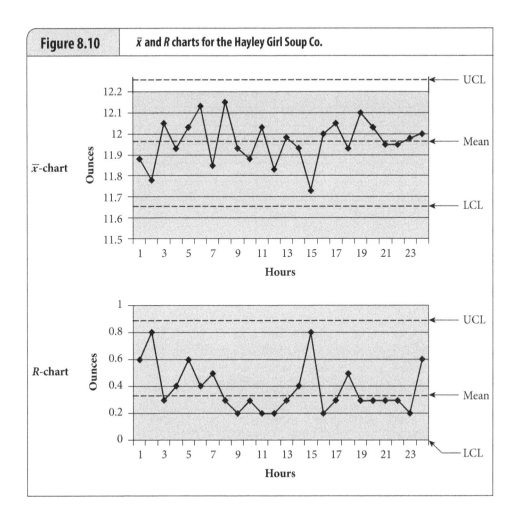

| Figure 8.10 | $\bar{x}$ and R charts for the Hayley Girl Soup Co. |

Using and Constructing P Charts

This is the most commonly used attribute control chart. If large sample sizes are used when collecting data, they are assumed to be normally distributed and the following formulas can be used to calculate the center line ($\bar{P}$) and the upper and lower control limits for the P chart:

$$\bar{P} = \frac{\sum_{i=1}^{k} P_i}{k}$$

where $\bar{P}$ is the mean fraction defective for all samples collected, k represents the number of samples, P is the fraction defective in one sample, and i represents the specific sample, and

$$UCL_p = \bar{P} + z\sigma_p$$
$$LCL_p = \bar{P} - z\sigma_p$$

where z is the number of standard deviations from the mean (recall when $z = 3$, the control limits will contain 99.73 percent of all the sample data plots) and σ_p is the standard deviation of the sampling distribution. The sample standard deviation is calculated using:

$$\sigma_P = \sqrt{\frac{(\bar{P})(1 - \bar{P})}{n}}$$

where n is the size of each sample. Example 8.4 provides the data used to determine $\bar{P}$, σ_P, and the control limits for the P chart.

As shown in Example 8.4, $\bar{P} = 0.014$. Calculating σ_P:

$$\sigma_P = \sqrt{\frac{(0.014)(0.986)}{100}} = 0.012$$

Now the control limits can be calculated (assuming the limits contain 99.73 percent of the data points, or $z = 3$):

$$UCL_P = 0.014 + 3(0.012) = 0.05$$

and

$$LCL_P = 0.014 - 3(0.012) = 0$$

Note that the lower control limit is truncated at zero, as is the case in most P charts. Figure 8.11 shows the P chart for the CeeJay Lightbulb Co. with the fraction defectives from Example 8.4. Viewing the chart, the process appears to be in control, since the data points are randomly dispersed around the centerline and about half the data points are on

---

Example 8.4   Attribute Data for the CeeJay Lightbulb Co.

The CeeJay Lightbulb Co. makes 40-watt light bulbs, and they have decided to begin monitoring their quality using a P chart. So, over the past thirty days, they have collected and tested 100 bulbs each day. The chart below shows the fraction defectives for each sample and the overall average fraction defective, or $\bar{P}$.

DAY	FRACTION DEFECTIVE	DAY	FRACTION DEFECTIVE
1	0.01	16	0.04
2	0.02	17	0
3	0	18	0
4	0.03	19	0.01
5	0	20	0.03
6	0.01	21	0.02
7	0.04	22	0
8	0	23	0.01
9	0	24	0.02
10	0.02	25	0.01
11	0.02	26	0.03
12	0.03	27	0
13	0	28	0.02
14	0.04	29	0.01
15	0.01	30	0
			$\bar{P} = \mathbf{0.014}$

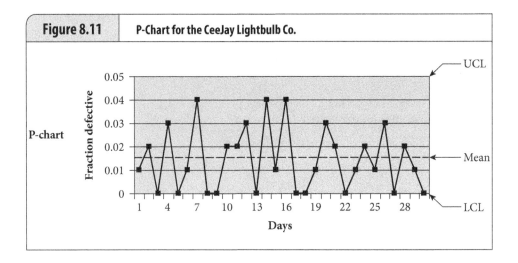

Figure 8.11   P-Chart for the CeeJay Lightbulb Co.

each side of the centerline. Thus, the CeeJay Lightbulb Co. can begin using this control chart to monitor their lightbulb quality.

Using C Charts

When multiple errors can occur in a process resulting in a defective unit, then we can use C charts to control the *number* of defects per unit of output. C charts are useful when a number of mistakes or errors can occur per unit of output, but they occur infrequently. Examples can include a hotel stay, a newspaper, or a construction project. The control limits for C charts are based on the assumption of a Poisson probability distribution of the item of interest (commonly used when defects are infrequent). In this case, the distribution variance is equal to its mean. For C charts then,

$$\bar{c} = \text{mean errors per unit of measure (and also the sample variance)},$$

$$\sqrt{\bar{c}} = \text{sample standard deviation, and}$$

$$\bar{c} \pm 3\sqrt{\bar{c}} = \text{upper and lower control limits.}$$

Example 8.5 can be used to illustrate the calculation of the C chart's control limits. In the example, the units of measure are days, thus the average daily defects are 29.1 (the centerline and also the variance). The upper and lower control limits are 45.3 and 12.9, respectively. The Casey Publishing Co. can use the C chart centerline and control limits based on the thirty-day error data to monitor their daily editorial error rate.

Example 8.5   Monitoring Editorial Defects at Casey Publishing, Inc.

Eight editorial assistants are monitored for defects in the firm's printed work on a monthly basis. Over the past thirty days, a total number of 872 editorial mistakes were found. Computing the centerline and control limits, we find:

$$\bar{c} = \frac{872}{30} = 29.1 \text{ mistakes per day, and}$$

$$\text{UCL}_c = 29.1 + 3\sqrt{29.1} = 45.3 \text{ and } \text{LCL}_c = 29.1 - 3\sqrt{29.1} = 12.9.$$

Acceptance Sampling

When shipments of a product are received from suppliers, or before they are shipped to customers, samples can be taken from the shipment and measured against some quality acceptance standard. The quality of the sample is then assumed to represent the quality of the entire shipment (particularly when shipments contain many units of product, sampling is far less time consuming than testing every unit to determine the overall quality of an incoming or outgoing shipment). Ideally, if strategic alliance members within a supply chain are using Six Sigma quality improvement tools to build quality into the products they sell, then acceptance sampling can be eliminated and used only when new or untested suppliers furnish products or materials to the firm. In these situations, **acceptance sampling** can be used to determine whether or not a shipment will be accepted, returned to the supplier, or used for billback purposes when defects are fixed or units are eliminated by the buyer.

One topic that arises is how big to make the test sample. One way to assure that the quality of the sample represents the quality of the entire shipment is to make the sample size equal to the size of the shipment (in other words, examine every unit). Since this is usually impractical, firms must assume the risk of incorrectly judging the quality of the shipment based on the size of the sample—the smaller the sample size, the greater the risk of incorrectly judging a shipment's quality.

There is a cost to both the supplier and buyer when incorrect quality assessments are made. When a buyer rejects a shipment of *high-quality* units because the sample quality level *did not* meet the acceptance standard, this is termed **producer's risk**. When this happens, it is called a **type-I error**. Conversely, when a buyer accepts a shipment of *low-quality* units because the sample *did* meet the acceptance standard, this is termed **consumer's risk** and is the result of a **type-II error**. Obviously, trading partners wish to avoid or minimize the occurrence of both these types of errors. To minimize type-I and type-II errors, buyers and sellers must derive an acceptable sampling plan by agreeing on unacceptable defect levels and a sample size big enough to result in minimal numbers of type-I and type-II errors.

Statistical Process Control and Supply Chain Management

Ideally, long-standing strategic supply chain partners would not need to monitor their inbound and outbound product quality—quality would already be extremely high and employees can spend their time on more productive pursuits. However, most processes and suppliers are not yet perfect, and the level of competition is so fierce in most industries that firms find they must continually be assessing and reassessing process and product quality levels. Managers should identify processes that are critical to achieving the firm's objectives, decide how to monitor process performance, gather data and create the appropriate control charts, and create policies for collecting process samples and monitoring process and product quality over time. Managers must also work to create a culture where quality improvements are encouraged and employees are empowered to make the changes that will result in improved product and service quality.

SUMMARY

Supply chain management, lean thinking, and Six Sigma quality make up a hierarchy for breakthrough competitive advantage. In order for supply chain management to reach its full potential and provide benefits to its members, trading partners must adopt a lean-operating philosophy. Similarly, the primary ingredient in the success of a lean program is the use of Six Sigma quality improvement tools. There are a number of practices mentioned within each of these topics that overlap or are very similar such as top management support, workforce involvement, and continuous improvement. This is not surprising given the close ties between supply chain management, lean, and Six Sigma. Considerable time has been spent here, covering lean and Six Sigma because of their critical importance in achieving successful supply chain management and it is hoped that you have gained an appreciation for the topics presented here.

KEY TERMS

acceptance sampling, 315

assignable variations, 309

attribute data, 309

C charts, 311

cause-and-effect diagrams, 306

x̄ chart, 309

check sheets, 305

consumer's risk, 315

control charts, 308

critical-to-quality (CTQ) characteristics, 303

defects per million opportunities, 293

efficient consumer response (ECR), 277

equipment setups, 287

fishbone diagrams, 306

Five-Ss, 283

Five-Why, 283

flow diagrams, 305

Ishikawa diagrams, 306

Just-In-Time, 277

kaizen, 291

kaizen blitz, 291

kanban, 279

kanbans, 289

keiretsu relationships, 277

lean layouts, 285

lean manufacturing, 277

lean production, 277

lean Six, 295

lean Six Sigma, 295

lean supply chain relationships, 285

lean thinking, 277

manufacturing cells, 286

muda, 279

natural variations, 309

opportunities for a defect to occur, 293

P charts, 311

Pareto charts, 305

Pareto Principle, 306

part families, 286

poka-yoke, 279

process diagrams, 305

process maps, 305

producer's risk, 315

production kanban, 289

pull system, 289

quick response (QR), 277

R chart, 309

root causes, 307

seven wastes, 282

sigma drift, 293

Six Sigma, 277

statistical process control, 307

the 4 M's, 306

total quality management, 293

Toyota Production System, 278

type-I error, 315

type-II error, 315

U.S. Baldrige Quality Award, 300

variable data, 309

waste elimination, 281

work cells, 286

yokoten, 281

DISCUSSION QUESTIONS

1. Explain why lean thinking and Six Sigma are so important to successful supply chain management.

2. Briefly explain the primary concerns and objectives of lean production.

3. How is lean production associated with JIT?

4. What does the Toyota Production System have to do with JIT and lean production?

5. What person or people at Toyota is (are) most responsible for the development of the JIT concept?

6. Why was Toyota's first U.S. car such a failure? What did it learn from this experience?

7. Who was responsible for first using the term "lean" as it related to the auto industry?

8. How is lean thinking associated with supply chain management?

9. Use an example to show how you could use lean thinking with a supplier and a customer.

10. What is yokoten and what does it have to do with lean thinking?

11. Which do you think is the most important element of lean thinking?

12. What are the seven wastes and can you discuss these in terms of a business you are familiar with?

13. What are the five Ss? Apply these to improve how you can complete your daily homework or study assignments.

14. What are the advantages of close supplier and customer relationships when practicing lean?

15. What are the advantages and disadvantages of making small, frequent purchases from just a few suppliers? How do we overcome the disadvantages?

16. Why should lean layouts be "visual"?

17. What are manufacturing cells and why are they important in lean production?

18. Reducing lot sizes and increasing setups are common practices in most lean production settings. Why?

19. What is the origin of the term *kanbans* and why are they used in lean systems?

20. Why are lean systems also known as pull systems?

21. What is kaizen, and why is it so important for successful lean production? What is a kaizen blitz?

22. Discuss the linkage between lean systems and environmental sustainability.

23. Describe Six Sigma's origins and the main parties involved. Why is the concept called "Six Sigma"?

24. How is Six Sigma different from TQM?

25. Describe the lean Six Sigma approach.

26. Describe three ways by which your university can improve quality using elements of Six Sigma.

27. Describe Deming's theory of management and how it can be used to improve quality.

28. Which of Deming's fourteen points might be the most important? Why?

29. Which do you like better—Deming's, Crosby's, or Juran's approach to quality?

30. Why do you think the Baldrige Award is available only to U.S. companies?

31. In viewing the Baldrige Award's seven performance categories, how would your firm stack up in these areas (use the university or your most recent employer if you are not currently employed).

32. What are the two most widely used ISO standards and why are they so popular? If you are working, is your firm ISO certified? Is McDonald's?

33. What are critical-to-quality characteristics and how are they used in Six Sigma?

34. What is the DMAIC improvement cycle and how can you use it to improve your college study habits?

35. Construct a flow diagram of the ticket purchase/football game attendance process at your university. What areas would you investigate further to identify problems?

36. Construct a cause-and-effect diagram for the following problem: The university course registration and payment process takes too long. Brainstorm some potential causes.

37. What are the two types of process variation and which one does statistical process control seek to eliminate? What can be done with the other one?

38. Define "variable data" and explain why two control charts are needed to assure that these types of processes are under control.

39. Can a process exhibit sample measurements that are all inside the control limits and still be considered out of control? Explain.

40. What are some variable data and attribute data that can be collected to track the quality of education at your university?

41. How can P charts be used in a manufacturing facility?

42. Explain the difference between a C chart and a P chart.

43. Can a process be considered in control but *incapable* of meeting design requirements? Explain.

44. If one goal of a supplier partnership is to eliminate acceptance sampling, then when would it get done?

ESSAY/PROJECT QUESTIONS

1. Go to the Baldrige Award website (https://www.nist.gov/baldrige) and find out what organizations have won the award since 2016. Report on any new developments with respect to the Baldrige Award and its recipients—have any declared bankruptcy or are any in financial trouble?

2. Write a report on Volkswagen and its recall and ethical problems in 2015.

3. Search the Internet and article databases at your university for the terms *sustainability* and *supply chain management* and write a report on the importance of sustainability in the practice of supply chain management using company examples.

4. Discuss the implementation of lean and Six Sigma among Chinese and Vietnamese companies.

5. Search the Internet and article databases at your university for the term *lean Six* and write a report on the latest uses of this method using company examples.

PROBLEMS

1. Heavey Compressors uses a lean production assembly line to make its compressors. In one assembly area, the demand is 100 parts per eight-hour day. It uses a container that holds eight parts. It typically takes about six hours to round-trip a container from one work center to the next and back again. Heavey also desires to hold 15 percent safety stock of this part in the system.

   a. How many containers should Heavey Compressors be using?
   b. Calculate the maximum system inventory for this part.
   c. If the safety stock percentage is reduced to zero, how would this impact the number of containers, all else being equal?

2. Using the information from problem 1, if Heavey desires to reduce their number of containers to eight, how does this impact the system? What has to change, if it assumed that demand, container size, and safety stock percentage don't change, and what is that change?

3. Eakins Enterprises makes model boats and it is switching to a lean manufacturing process. At one assembly area, Eakins is using one part container that holds 250 parts and it wants the output to be approximately 100 finished parts per hour; they also desire a 10 percent safety stock for this part. How fast will the container have to make it through the system to accomplish this?

4. A lean system has twenty-two containers, each of which can hold fifteen parts. The lead time required to round-trip one container through the system is four hours. The required safety stock is 10 percent.

   a. What is the maximum demand rate this system can accommodate?
   b. The company wants to accommodate double the maximum demand rate found in (a). What are all the ways the system could be changed to accomplish this?

5. Jim Corner, owner of Corner Bike Rentals, wants to start analyzing his company's quality. For each bike rental, there are four types of customer complaints: (1) bike not working properly, (2) bike wrong size, (3) bike uncomfortable, and (4) bike broken during operation. During the past week, his company rented 280 bikes. He received twenty-six total complaints.

   a. What is his company's DPMO for the past week?
   b. What is their Six Sigma operating level?
   c. If Jim wanted to operate at the five-sigma level, what would his errors have needed to be over the past week?

6. Julie works at Gentry Flower Shoppe, which operates at the four-sigma level, with about 6,000 DPMO, which was determined recently. At that time, Gentry was found to have 1,500 total defects. They want to improve to the five-sigma level or about 500 DPMO. Assuming nothing else changes, what would its new total defect level have to be?

7. The following sample information was obtained by taking four doughnuts per hour for twelve hours from Fawcett Bakery's doughnut process and weighing them:

HOUR	WEIGHTS (GRAMS)	HOUR	WEIGHT (GRAMS)
1	110, 105, 98, 100	7	89, 102, 101, 99
2	79, 102, 100, 104	8	100, 101, 98, 96
3	100, 102, 100, 96	9	98, 95, 101, 100
4	94, 98, 99, 101	10	99, 100, 97, 102
5	98, 104, 97, 100	11	102, 97, 100, 101
6	104, 97, 99, 100	12	98, 100, 100, 97

For the data shown above,

  a. Find the $\bar{x}$ and R for each sample.
  b. Find the $\bar{\bar{x}}$ and $\bar{R}$ for the twelve samples.
  c. Find the three-sigma UCL and LCL for the mean and range charts.
  d. Plot the data. Does the process look to be in statistical control? Why/why not?

8. Through process measuring a number of pizza delivery times, Mary Jane's Pizzeria finds the mean of all samples to be 27.4 minutes, with an average sample range of 5.2 minutes. It tracked four deliveries per hour for eighteen hours to obtain its samples.

  a. Is this an example of variable or attribute sampling data?
  b. Find the UCL and LCL for both the $\bar{x}$ and R charts.

9. A company produces 8-pound bags of rice. As shown below, it gathered five samples with six bags in each sample for quality-control purposes. The weights of each of the bags are listed below.

	BAGS IN EACH SAMPLE					
SAMPLE	1	2	3	4	5	6
1	7.98	8.34	8.02	7.94	8.44	7.68
2	8.33	8.22	8.08	8.51	8.41	8.28
3	7.89	7.77	7.91	8.04	8	7.89
4	8.24	8.18	7.83	8.05	7.9	8.16
5	7.87	8.13	7.92	7.99	8.1	7.81

  a. Find the $\bar{x}$ and R for each of the five samples.
  b. Find the $\bar{\bar{x}}$ and $\bar{R}$.
  c. Find the three-sigma UCL and LCL for the mean and range charts.
  d. Plot the data. Does the process look to be in statistical control? Why/why not?

10. Ten customers per hour were asked by the cashier at Stanley's Deli if they liked their meal, and the fraction that said "no" are shown below, for a twelve-hour period.

HOUR	FRACTION DEFECTIVE	HOUR	FRACTION DEFECTIVE
1	0	7	0.1
2	0.2	8	0
3	0.4	9	0
4	0.1	10	0.2
5	0.1	11	0
6	0.2	12	0.1

For the data shown above, find

  a. $\bar{P}$
  b. σ_p
  c. The 3-sigma UCL and LCL
  d. Plot the data. Does customer satisfaction at Stanley's appear to be in statistical control? How can we improve the analysis?

11. A company collects 20 samples with 100 eggs in each sample. They want to construct a P chart to track the proportion of broken eggs in each sample. The table below shows the number of defective eggs per sample.

SAMPLE	EGGS	SAMPLE	EGGS	SAMPLE	EGGS
1	3	8	6	15	5
2	5	9	4	16	0
3	3	10	9	17	2
4	4	11	2	18	6
5	2	12	6	19	2
6	4	13	5	20	1
7	2	14	1	TOTAL	72

a. Determine $\bar{P}$.

b. Determine σ_P.

c. Determine the 3-sigma UCL and LCL.

d. Plot the data. Does the egg process appear to be in statistical control?

12. Roberto's Steakhouse tracks customer complaints every day and then follows up with their customers to resolve problems. For the past thirty days, they received a total of twenty-two complaints from unhappy customers. Using this information, calculate

a. $\bar{c}$

b. The 3-sigma control limits

CASES

1. Sharp's Sandwich Shop—Quality Control*

Dawn Sharp is the owner of Sharp's Sandwich Shop. Her shop is open 24/7 and serves many different types of sandwiches, from classic breakfast sandwiches to more exotic burgers and other sandwiches usually consumed at lunch and dinner.

Recently, Dawn addressed inventory management as one of her major production issues. Dawn's goal is to give her customers quick service and a quality product. To accomplish this goal, Dawn divided her menu into four timeframes: breakfast, lunch, dinner, and after hours. Breakfast runs from 5 a.m. to 11 a.m.; lunch begins at 11 a.m. and ends at 3 p.m.; dinner begins early, at 3 p.m., and continues until 9 p.m. Between 9 p.m. and 5 a.m. you can select your sandwich from the after-hour's section of the menu.

Sharp's Sandwich Shop is in the heart of downtown New York and New Yorkers are fast moving and always in a rush. Consequently, customers do not want to wait very long for the sandwich, no matter how unique or complicated it may be. To remedy this, Dawn set up a system where the kitchen produces specific sandwiches in bulk. For example, a basic ham and cheese on rye bread can be made in advance, wrapped, and placed in the ready bin. This way, when a customer orders a ham and cheese on rye, they get it quickly. One of the challenges to this system is that Sharp's sandwiches are very popular because of the quality of the sandwiches. Part of the quality is their freshness. Therefore, whether it is a cold

*Written by Rick Bonsall, D. Mgt., McKendree University, Lebanon, IL. The people and institution are fictional and any resemblance to any person or any institution is coincidental. This case was prepared solely to provide material for class discussion. The author does not intend to illustrate either effective or ineffective handling of a managerial situation.

sandwich or a warm sandwich, neither can stay in the premade bins too long. After a set period of time, if a sandwich is still in the bin it is removed and placed in the charity bin. The charity bin contains food that is still edible; however, won't be sold to Sharp's customers. The food in the charity bin is donated to a local homeless shelter twice per day.

As Dawn evaluated her inventory problem that was related to the premade sandwich system, she discovered a parallel issue—quality. As part of her revised inventory system, all sandwiches placed in the charity bin are recorded in a waste log. This process enables Dawn to reconcile the "waste" sent to the charity bin to actual waste, that is, items that are thrown in the trash. Previously, Dawn had assumed that a significant quantity of her overall waste (95 percent) were items placed in the charity bin. However, as she compared her numbers, Dawn discovered that more was going into the trash than she thought.

This revelation was very disturbing to Dawn. Quality was the primary driver in her business. The waste created by her focus on freshness was something Dawn could control and her new inventory system concerning premade sandwiches has improved that situation. However, the total waste numbers indicated that sandwiches of unacceptable quality were reaching the customer and they were returning the food. This was alarming because New Yorkers were quick to complain and spread the word about poor quality to their friends. Unlike the inventory issue, which was an issue of expense control, this quality issue was one of customer satisfaction and ultimate survival of her business in a city with an abundance of competition.

Once again, Dawn reflects back on her class in supply chain management, specifically the process management chapter on lean and Six Sigma. Dawn recognized that, in a way, she had taken her eye off of quality. Sharp's Sandwich Shop neither had a clear process to collect data on quality, nor did it utilize any of the quality tools to analyze defects or root causes. Dawn knew that it was crucial to her business to begin data collection and analysis immediately. Bad customer experiences would spread throughout her customer base in a New York minute. However, her kitchen and eating area were a very fast paced environment. Dawn needed data collection processes that didn't demand a lot of the food preparers' or the servers' time. Plus, with all the responsibilities of running the business, Dawn's available time for analysis was limited as well. Finally, Dawn instinctively knew that Sharp's Sandwich Shop had to go beyond data collection and analysis. She needed processes that enabled her to address multiple issues such as inventory management and quality.

Discussion Questions

1. Sharp's Sandwich Shop has two conflicting quality issues—speed and freshness. The premade sandwich system enhances speed; however, it has the potential of affecting freshness. What type of system can Dawn implement that will enable her to keep the process of premade sandwiches, yet guarantee that freshness will be unaffected? Explain how the system would work and why it can effectively enable her to accomplish both goals without any concern that one or the other must suffer.

2. Currently, Dawn is evaluating the quality of the food by the waste, meaning as the cost of waste increases she senses that the quality of the product is decreasing. Recommend to Dawn a better method to evaluate quality than just cost.

3. Dawn decides that she alone cannot implement a good quality program. Clearly, her staff must be involved. Although she has excellent employees, Dawn knows they do not understand the tools of quality. Furthermore, she understands that if things appear too complicated then she won't get their buy-in. Dawn contacts you and requests that you explain to her staff some basic quality tools that will enable them to improve quality, yet are not complex, and will not demand a lot of their time.

2. Downey College*

Tuition is the life blood of any four-year college and Downey College is no exception. Each year the Student Affairs Office initiates a campaign to get students to fill out their Free Application for Federal Student Aid (FAFSA) application. As with any tuition aid program, there is a timeframe when you must apply. If you miss the application deadline, then you must wait until the following period.

Downey College has lost several students during the enrollment process because the students did not complete their FAFSA application on time. Without the help of federal aid, the students were unable to take the courses they registered for. Hannah Hunt, vice president of Student Affairs, was eager to improve this process. Competing for student enrollment was a significant challenge and losing students because of FAFSA application errors was frustrating. Hunt decided to review the data from last year to determine how she could tackle the issue this year.

Last year Hannah had her staff develop a check sheet on common errors concerning FAFSA applications. There were five major areas and an "other" area. She had them collect data by student status, that is, freshman, sophomore, junior, and senior. The information is listed below.

ERROR	FRESHMAN 520 applications	SOPHOMORE 500 applications	JUNIOR 580 applications	SENIOR 530 applications	Total Errors	% of Total
Not filing by deadline	/////	////	boxed//////	///		
Wrong FSA ID	//	/	//	////		
Wrong SSN	////	///	/			
Did not sign FAFSA	/////	/////	//	///		
Understating income	///////	////	//	/////		
Filing wrong year's FAFSA	//	//	/////	///		
Other	/////	////	//	////		

Discussion Questions

1. Hannah Hunt's staff is very small; thus, she has limited resources available to tackle these issues. She can focus on either a specific error or on a specific class, for example, freshman. What do you recommend she do and why? Explain the benefit of your recommendation.

2. What is the sigma level of their FAFSA application program? Does the sigma level per class, for example, senior, change your recommendation on whether to focus on a specific error or a specific class? Is there any advantage in this perspective of the data? Explain your opinion to Hannah Hunt.

3. Hannah Hunt believes that filling out and submitting the FAFSA application is a no brainer. She believes that a Six Sigma level should be easy to obtain. Do you agree? Is this a realistic expectation? Explain your viewpoint.

*Written by Rick Bonsall, D. Mgt., McKendree University, Lebanon, IL. The people and institution are fictional and any resemblance to any person or any institution is coincidental. This case was prepared solely to provide material for class discussion. The author does not intend to illustrate either effective or ineffective handling of a managerial situation.

3. Automotive Repair Shop War*

Johnny Cruz is the best mechanic in a 50-mile radius. He lives in the small town of Oxbow, Texas. In fact, all the towns within 50 miles of Oxbow are small, with approximately 1,500 residents each. Most businesses survive in this region because competition is scarce. Not all the towns have every convenience. There may be a theater within a cluster of three towns within 30 miles of each other or a major grocery store in one town while the others have small convenience stores. No one is sure how this process developed; however, it has ensured a respectable living for those in the county.

Johnny Cruz' automotive repair shop benefitted from this type of arrangement. His business has been steady for several years with a strong customer base from four towns in the area. However, Rosie Lamb opened an automotive repair shop six months ago in Knuckle Falls, Texas, and is competing for the same customer base. At first Johnny wasn't worried. He had a solid reputation as a good mechanic and he never gouged anyone. However, as the months slowly passed, Johnny noticed that some of his regular customers stopped coming in for routine maintenance such as oil changes and brake jobs. Some others with major repair needs were going to Rosie as well.

Johnny was a good businessman and knew he needed to stem this flow of customer defections quickly. He went to the local community college and talked with a business professor about the situation. One thing Johnny understood was that he needed data so he could analyze the problem, develop solutions, and make effective decisions. Johnny had read about programs such as Six Sigma. Although he wasn't familiar with it, he did realize that it meant to identify a problem, collect data, analyze the data, and develop alternative solutions. Then, he could select what appeared to be the best solution, implement it, and then circle back around and see how effective it was.

Discussion Questions

1. Is Johnny Cruz approaching this situation sensibly? Do you think Six Sigma is the best approach or is it overkill? Do you agree with Johnny? If so, explain how Six Sigma can help Johnny. If you don't agree with Johnny, what alternatives does he have?

2. Six Sigma has a lot of tools Johnny can use. Be the community college professor in Oxbow, Texas, and explain which tool or tools you would use and in what order. What would each tool enable Johnny to do?

3. Using the problem of defecting customers, develop a fictional cause-and-effect diagram. Develop the four main categories and add the bones of possible causes or issues. Explain, based on your hypothetical scenario, what you see as Johnny's possible major causes.

©2019 Cengage Learning

*Written by Rick Bonsall, D. Mgt., McKendree University, Lebanon, IL. The people and company are fictional and any resemblance to any person or company is coincidental. This case was prepared solely to provide material for class discussion. The author does not intend to illustrate either effective or ineffective handling of a managerial situation.

ADDITIONAL RESOURCES

Burt, D. N., D. W. Dobler, and S. L. Starling, *World Class Supply Management: The Key to Supply Chain Management,* 7th ed. New York: McGraw-Hill, 2003.

Crosby, P. B., *Quality Is Free.* New York: McGraw-Hill, 1979.

Crosby, P. B., *Quality without Tears.* New York: McGraw-Hill, 1984.

Deming, W. E., *Out of the Crisis.* Cambridge, MA: MIT Center for Advanced Engineering Study, 1986.

Evans, J. R., and W. M. Lindsay, *The Management and Control of Quality,* 4th ed. Cincinnati, OH: South-Western, 1999.

Heizer, J., and B. Render, *Principles of Operations Management,* 4th ed. Upper Saddle River, NJ: Prentice-Hall, 2000.

Jacobs, F., and R. Chase, *Operations and Supply Management: The Core.* New York: McGraw-Hill/Irwin, 2008.

Juran, J., and A. Godfrey, *Juran's Quality Handbook.* New York: McGraw-Hill, 2000.

Krajewski, L., L. Ritzman, and M. Malhotra, *Operations Management: Processes and Value Chains,* 8th ed. Upper Saddle River, NJ: Pearson/Prentice-Hall, 2007.

Lucier, G., and S. Seshadri, "GE Takes Six Sigma Beyond the Bottom Line." *Strategic Finance* 82(11), 2001: 40–46.

Smith, G., *Statistical Process Control and Quality Improvement.* New York: Macmillan, 1991.

Vokurka, R. J., and R. R. Lummus, "The Role of Just-in-Time in Supply Chain Management." *International Journal of Logistics Management* 11(1), 2000: 89–98.

END NOTES

1. Albright, B., "New Identity, New Growth," *Automotive Body Repair Network* July 2016: 33–34, 36.

2. Anonymous, "Future Equipment Concerns Weigh Heavily on Industry," *American Metal Market* March 1, 2015: 1.

3. Shepherd, J., "Manufacturers Help Colleges Improve Tech Training Curriculum," *The Lane Report* 30(6), 2015: 26.

4. Manoway, D., "Rallying Behind Lean," *Industrial Engineer* 47(7), 2015: 44–48.

5. Lowson, R., "Retail Operational Strategies in Complex Supply Chains," *International Journal of Logistics Management,* 12(1), 2001: 97–111.

6. Harris, J., P. Swatman, and S. Kurnia, "Efficient Consumer Response (ECR): A Survey of the Australian Grocery Industry," *Supply Chain Management,* 4(1), 1999: 35.

7. Mukherji, A., "The Economic and Sociological Dimensions of Business Networks: Examining Differences between Japanese and U.S. Structures," *Advances in Competitiveness Research* 9(1), 2001: 72–86.

8. Reed, J., and B. Simon, "Toyota's Long Climb Comes to an Abrupt Halt," *Financial Times* February 6, 2010: 9.

9. Anonymous, "Toyota Remains Most Valuable Global Automotive Brand According to Interbrand," *Journal of Transportation* October 24, 2015: 59.

10. For histories of lean and the Toyota Production System see, for instance, Becker, R., "Learning to Think Lean: Lean Manufacturing and the Toyota Production System,"

Automotive Manufacturing & Production 113(6), 2001: 64–65; Dahlgaard, J., and S. Dahlgaard-Park, "Lean Production, Six Sigma Quality, TQM and Company Culture," *TQM Magazine* 18(3), 2006: 263–277.

11. Information on the Ford manufacturing system was found at www.lean.org

12. Arndorfer, J., C. Atkinson, J. Bloom, and M. Cardona, "The Biggest Moments in the Last 75 Years of Advertising History," *Advertising Age* 76(13), 2005: 12–15; and Reed and Simon, ref. 4.

13. Manivannan, S., "Error-Proofing Enhances Quality," *Manufacturing Engineering* 137(5), 2006: 99–105.

14. Nakamoto, M., and J. Reed, "Toyota Claims Global Top Spot from GM," *FT.com* April 24, 2007: 1.

15. See, for example, Schmitt, B., "Nice Try VW: Toyota Again World's Largest Automaker," *Forbes.com* January 27, 2016; and Anonymous, "Leading Motor Vehicle Manufacturers Worldwide in 2016, Based on Global Sales (in Million Units)," *Statista*, https://www.statista.com/statistics/275520/ranking-of-car-manufacturers-based-on-global-sales

16. Womack, J., D. Jones, and D. Roos, *The Machine that Changed the World.* New York, NY: Maxwell MacMillan International, 1990.

17. Manoway, D., "Rallying Behind Lean," *Industrial Engineer* 47(7), 2015: 44–48.

18. Morgan, B., "Manufacturers Seek Aggressive Growth," *Industry Week* July 8, 2016: 1.

19. Albright, B., "New Identity, New Growth," Automotive Body Repair Network July 2016: 33–34, 36.

20. Napolitano, M., "Still Doing More with Less," *Logistics Management* 50(11), 2011: 44–52.

21. Jargon, J., "Latest Starbucks Buzzword: 'Lean' Japanese Techniques," *Wall Street Journal* August 4, 2009: A1.

22. Jusko, J., "Lean Confusion," *Industry Week* 259(9), 2010: 32.

23. Sedam, S., "Building Lean—Beyond Value Engineering," *Professional Builder* September 2010: 1.

24. Simonis, R., "5S without 5Y is Just Housekeeping," *Industry Week* April 14, 2015: 1.

25. Anonymous, "Tool for Productivity, Quality, Throughput, Safety," *Management Services* 50(3), 2006: 16–18; Becker, J., "Implementing 5S: To Promote Safety & Housekeeping," *Professional Safety* 46(8), 2001: 29–31.

26. Beason, M., "Lean Machining—Integrating the Supply Chain," *Manufacturing Engineering* 151(2), 2013: 75–79.

27. Anonymous, "Poor Supplier Relationships Cost US Automakers $2bn," *Supply Management* 20(6), 2015: 8.

28. Katz, J., "Going Lean Revives Circuit Board Manufacturer," *Material Handling & Logistics* January 17, 2012: 1.

29. Anonymous, "Plant Practices: Optimized For Efficiency and Value," *Industrial Maintenance & Plant Operation* September 22, 2015: 1.

30. Waurzyniak, P., "Automating for Maximum Efficiency," *Manufacturing Engineering* 152(5), 2014: 109–113.

31. Harriman, F., "Origins of the Term 'KANBAN' from Conversations with Chihiro Nakao," www.fredharriman.com/resources/OriginsofKanban (February 22, 2010).

32. Blanchard, D., "Lean Culture Helps Carrier Transicold Keep Its Cool," *Material Handling & Logistics* April 7, 2016: 1.

33. King, A., and M. Lenox, "Lean and Green? An Empirical Examination of the Relationship between Lean Production and Environmental Performance," *Production and Operations Management* 10(3), 2001: 244–256.

34. Higginbotham, J., "LEED For Healthcare Offers New Paths to Green," *Building Design & Construction* November 2014: 1; and Hurley, B., C. McArtor, and C. Land, "Continuously Improving Sustainability," *Industrial Engineer* 46(9), 2014: 36–40.

35. Phillips, E., "Six Sigma: The Breakthrough Management Strategy Revolutionizing the World's Top Corporations," *Consulting to Management* 13(4), 2002: 57–59. Also see the SSA & Co. website: www.ssaandco.com

36. Information about Six Sigma and sigma drift can be found at multiple locations, for example, www.isixsigma.com, or www.wikipedia.org/Six_Sigma

37. Pulakanam, V., "Costs and Savings of Six Sigma Programs: An Empirical Study," *The Quality Management Journal* 19(4), 2012: 39–54; Anonymous, "Wabash National Reaches Record Operating Income in 2016," *Trailer/Body Builders* February 1, 2017: 1.

38. Boulanger, M., "Six Sigma Standard: Panacea or Albatross?" *ASQ Six Sigma Forum Magazine* 12(1), 2012: 28–29.

39. Spindelndrier, D., F. Lesmeister, and R. Schmitt, "People Matter Most," *Industrial Management* 54(6), 2012: 12–17.

40. Moore, K., "The Emergent Way: How to Achieve Meaningful Growth in an Era of Flat Growth," *Ivey Business Journal Online* November/December 2011: 1.

41. See, for example, *CRN* June 4, 2007: 12; Ante, S., "Motorola Is Split into Two," *The Wall Street Journal* January 5, 2011: 1; and *Google Official Blog: "We've Acquired Motorola Mobility,"* Google (retrieved May 22, 2012).

42. "Business Brief—Primary PDC Inc.: Joint Bankruptcy Plan Filed to Dissolve Former Polaroid," *Wall Street Journal* January 17, 2003: B-3.

43. Kelly, S., "Creating a Culture of Continuous Improvement and Sustainable Management Systems at Abbott Diagnostics Longford," *Global Business and Organizational Excellence* 36(1), 2016: 6.

44. Brandt, D., "Messing with Process," *Industrial Engineer* 47(2), 2015: 5.

45. Gilbert, J., and J. Wisner, "Mattel, Lead Paint, and Magnets: Ethics and Supply Chain Management," *Ethics & Behavior* 20(1), 2010: 33–46.

46. Blanchard, D., "Leaning into the Supply Chain," *Industry Week* September 5, 2014: 1.

47. Deming, W. E., *Out of the Crisis*. MIT Press, 1986.

48. See www.deming.org for more information.

49. *Quality Is Free* is out of print; Crosby, P. B., *Quality without Tears*, McGraw Hill, 1984.

50. Butman, J., and J. Roessner, "Na Immigrant's Gift: The Life of Quality Pioneer Joseph M. Juran," PBS Documentary Video, produced by Howland Blackiston, copyright WoodsEnd, Inc.

51. See, for example, http://www.whatissixsigma.net/jurans-quality-trilogy/

52. Baldrige information was obtained from www.nist.gov/baldrige

53. See http://patapsco.nist.gov/Award_Recipients/index.cfm

54. ISO information was obtained from the organization's website, www.iso.org

55. See https://www.iso.org/the-iso-survey.html

56. Cash, B., "Getting It All," *ASQ Six Sigma Forum Magazine* 12(2), 2013: 9–14.

57. Information found in www.ge.com/sixsigma

58. Descriptions found in www.isixsigma.com, www.asq.org, and www.xlp.com

59. Found at http://management.about.com/cs/generalmanagement/a/Pareto081202

60. Adapted from Table 27 of the ASTM STP 15D ASTM *Manual on Presentation of Data and Control Chart Analysis*, © 1976 American Society for Testing and Materials, Philadelphia, PA.

PART 4

Distribution Issues in Supply Chain Management

Chapter 9   Domestic U.S. and Global Logistics

Chapter 10   Customer Relationship Management

Chapter 11   Global Location Decisions

Chapter 12   Service Response Logistics

Chapter 9

DOMESTIC U.S. AND GLOBAL LOGISTICS

Intermodalism is set to grow even faster, as more business is conducted in cross-border. The North American Free Trade Agreement [NAFTA] is becoming far more cohesive—one only has to look at what's happening in the automotive sector to see that.

—**Tony Hatch, rail analyst and principal of ABH Consulting**[1]

While the U.S. economy continues to move forward, logistics managers need to brace themselves for a volatile period of rate fluctuation due to global unease. Just on the oil front alone, we need to remember that the U.S. still relies on OPEC production to balance supply.

—**Patrick Burnson, executive editor of Logistics Management**[2]

Learning Objectives

After completing this chapter, you should be able to

- Understand the strategic importance of logistics.
- Identify the various modes of transportation.
- Understand how U.S. regulation and deregulation have impacted transportation.
- Discuss the global aspects of logistics.
- Describe how logistics affects supply chain management.
- Examine and understand the interrelatedness of transportation, warehousing, and material handling.
- Identify a number of third-party logistics service providers.
- Describe the various reverse logistics activities.

Chapter Outline

Introduction

Transportation Fundamentals

Warehousing and Distribution

The Impacts of Logistics on Supply Chain Management

Environmental Sustainability in Logistics

Logistics Management Software Applications

Global Logistics

Reverse Logistics

Summary

SCM Profile | Bigger, Longer, Faster

In transportation, bigger, longer, and faster usually means better. Since economies of scale in transportation can mean fewer trips, less fuel consumed, better equipment utilization, and lower labor costs, logistics providers have occasionally utilized enormous capacities to gain the benefits of transportation-scale economies. And, with the continuing demand for greater shipping speed, some companies are designing ever-faster systems to satisfy demand. Several examples are provided here.

MOTOR CARRIERS

In Australia, large tractor units pull three, four, and even more trailers along long stretches of open road between cities in unpopulated areas with no rail service. These long tractor/trailer combinations are known as road trains. In Australia, road trains can legally be up to 180 feet in length, barreling along at speeds of up to 65 mph. In 2006, the record was set for road train length in Clifton, Queensland, Australia, when a Mack Titan tractor pulled 112 trailers for 328 feet. The road train was 4,836 feet long and weighed 2,900,000 pounds.[3]

RAIL CARRIERS

As of 2016, the fastest regularly scheduled train service is the Shanghai Maglev in China. Charging only about $8 per person, the Maglev runs 19 miles from Shanghai's Pudong International Airport to the Longyang metro station on the outskirts of Shanghai. The train takes just over seven minutes to complete the trip using magnetic levitation technology and reaches a top speed of 267 miles per hour.[4] Currently, the fastest train though, is Japan Railways' maglev bullet train. The bullet train travelled at 603 kph (374 mph), in a test run in 2016 (that's a mile in ten seconds!).[5]

AIR CARRIERS

The new Airbus A380 jetliner and the old Spruce Goose may be big, but they are nowhere near the biggest—that title belongs to the Antonov An-225 commercial jet freighter. It was built in 1988 for the Soviet space program to airlift rocket boosters and their space shuttle. At 275 feet in length with a 290-foot wingspan and a maximum takeoff weight of 640 tons, it dwarfs 787's. When the Soviet Union collapsed in 1990, the aircraft was temporarily mothballed, and then eventually refurbished and put back into service in 2001 for Antonov Airlines. It has transported things once thought impossible by air, such as locomotives and 150-ton generators. It also has allowed vast quantities of relief supplies to be quickly transported to disaster areas, such as quake-stricken Haiti in February 2010.[6]

WATER CARRIERS

The largest supertanker ever built was the *Seawise Giant*, built by Sumitomo Heavy Industries in 1979. The ship was 1,504 feet long with 340,000 square feet of deck, and was too big to pass through the English Channel, the Suez Canal, or the Panama Canal. Fully loaded, the ship weighed 646,000 tons and standing on end, it would be taller than the Empire State Building. The ship was by far the largest ship ever built and had a number of owners and names over the years, but was simply too big; it was scrapped in 2010. The largest containership is currently the CSCL Globe which was built in 2014. It has an overall length of 1,312 feet and can carry up to 19,100 20-foot containers.[7]

PIPELINE CARRIERS

In the North Sea, the world's longest underwater pipeline, finished in 2007 by Norsk Hydro ASA, delivers natural gas from Norway's offshore gas fields to processing plants 746 miles away in the United Kingdom. The sections of pipe were assembled and welded together using the world's largest pipeline-laying ships and then laid continuously on the seafloor, in depths up to 3,000 feet. The world's longest on-land pipeline was completed in December 2012, built by the China National Petroleum Corporation and stretching 5,400 miles from the central part of China to Shanghai in the east and Guangzhou and Hong Kong in the south. The pipeline cost $22.5 billion to build and helps bring natural gas to 500 million people.[8]

INTRODUCTION

Logistics is necessary for moving purchased materials from suppliers to buyers, moving work-in-process materials within a firm, moving finished goods to customers, returning or recycling goods, and also storing these items along the way in supply chains. Effective logistics systems are needed for commerce to exist in any industrialized society. Products have little value to customers until they are moved to customers' usage areas at a point in time when they are needed. Logistics thus provides what are termed **time utility** and **place utility**. Time utility is created when customers get products delivered at precisely the right time, not earlier and not later. The logistics function creates time utility by determining how deliveries can be made in a timely manner and where items should be held prior to delivery. Place utility is created when customers get things delivered to their desired locations.

The official definition of **logistics** from the globally recognized council of supply chain management professionals is:

> *The process of planning, implementing, and controlling procedures for the efficient and effective transportation and storage of goods including services and related information from the point of origin to the point of consumption for the purpose of conforming to customer requirements.*[9]

So it can be seen that transportation, warehousing, information systems, and customer service play very significant roles in the logistics function. For supply chains in particular, logistics is what creates the flow of goods between supply chain partners, such that costs, service requirements, competitive advantage, and profits can be optimized.

When moving around within a city, between cities, or between countries, it is impossible to ignore the business of logistics, whether it be large trucks ambling along the roadways; trains pulling boxcars, cattle cars, and tanker cars next to highways; warehouses storing goods in cities' industrial sections; airplanes taking off at airports; container ships unloading cargo; or barges floating slowly down rivers. In the United States and other highly industrialized nations, the movement of goods is ever-pervasive. Without it, we as consumers would never have opportunities to find what we want, when we want it, at the many retail outlets we routinely visit each day.

The U.S. freight transportation system moved 49.5 million tons of goods valued at more than $52.7 billion each day in 2015—about 56 tons of freight per year for every

Table 9.1	For-Hire Logistics Services Contributions to U.S. GDP[10]							
	1980	**1985**	**1990**	**1995**	**2000**	**2005**	**2010**	**2014**
Total U.S. GDP	2,788	4,218	5,801	7,415	9,952	12,623	14,783	15,961
For-Hire Logistics Services GDP (% U.S. GDP)	102.6 (3.7)	137.1 (3.3)	172.8 (3.0)	231.7 (3.1)	301.4 (3.0)	369.5 (2.9)	421 (2.8)	441 (2.8)

man, woman, and child in the United States. As of 2014 in the United States, there were 4.2 million miles of public roads, 140,000 miles of rail track, 2.2 million miles of gas distribution pipelines, 25,000 miles of navigable waterways, 19,000 general and certificated airports, and 183 shipping ports.[11] Using the latest available statistics from the U.S. Department of Transportation, at the end of 2014 the total annual U.S. for-hire logistics services contribution to the U.S. gross domestic product (GDP) was approximately 2.8 percent or $441 billion. Table 9.1 shows the growth of for-hire logistics expenditures in the United States, which has more than quadrupled in thirty-one years.

In this chapter, the many logistics activities are discussed, along with logistics nomenclature and related events affecting businesses each day. Included are discussions of the modes of transportation, transportation regulation and deregulation, warehousing and distribution, a number of logistics decisions firms must make, the impact of logistics on supply chain management, the global issues affecting logistics, the impact of e-commerce on logistics activities, and the management of product returns, also called reverse logistics. Some of the transportation basics are reviewed next.

TRANSPORTATION FUNDAMENTALS

This section reviews a number of important transportation elements within the logistics function, including the objective of transportation, legal forms of transportation, the modes of transportation, intermodal transportation, transportation pricing, transportation security, and transportation regulation and deregulation in the United States. This provides a good foundation for discussing the remaining topics in the chapter, as well as an appreciation for the complex nature of transportation issues in logistics.

The Objective of Transportation

Although one might think the overriding objective of transportation is obvious—that is, moving people and things from one place to another—for-hire transportation services can go broke doing this inefficiently. For example, over the past twenty years, a number of U.S. passenger airlines have sought bankruptcy protection and asked for concessions from labor unions to keep operating. Some of these airlines include American, Ryan International, United, Continental, America West, US Airways, Delta, Northwest, Hawaiian, Frontier, Aloha, Mesa, and Southern Air. The steep economic downturn from 2009 to 2011, combined with steadily rising fuel prices, only made things more troublesome for transportation companies. As a matter of fact, by 2014, fuel costs accounted for 35 percent of U.S. airline operating costs (this was triple the percent of cost compared to 2000). During this same period, over 8,500 U.S. trucking companies went bankrupt, taking about 325,000 trucks off the road. Since 2011, decreasing fuel costs have reversed this trend. Jet fuel prices, for example, fell from $2.92 per gallon in 2011 to $1.25 per gallon in 2016. Today, truckload volumes are increasing about 2 percent per year and there are about 3.6 million trucks on the road.[12]

Logistics managers seek to maximize value for their employers by correctly communicating the firm's service needs to for-hire transportation providers. Additionally, services and prices are negotiated such that the transportation provider's delivery costs are covered while allowing them an acceptable profit contribution. Finally, logistics managers must ensure the desired services are performed effectively. In the transportation industry, competitive prices may not be high enough to cover firms' fixed and variable costs and this has created a tremendous problem for a number of airlines and trucking companies as mentioned above, when fuel prices rise over a period of time. In the most general terms, transportation objectives should then be to *satisfy customer requirements while minimizing costs and making a reasonable profit*. For logistics or perhaps supply chain managers, this also means deciding which forms of transportation, material handling, and storage, along with the most appropriate vehicle scheduling and routing, to use.

Legal Forms of Transportation

For-hire transportation service companies are classified legally as common, contract, exempt, or private carriers. The distinguishing characteristics of each of these classifications are discussed below.

Common Carriers

Common carriers offer transportation services to all shippers at published rates between designated locations. Common carriers must offer their transportation services to the general public without discrimination, meaning they must charge the same rates for the same service to all customers. In the United States, a common carrier is legally bound to carry all passengers or freight as long as there is enough space, the fee is paid, and no reasonable grounds to refuse exist. Because common carriers serve the general public, they are the most heavily regulated of all carrier classifications. Some U.S. examples of common carriers are Southwest Air, Amtrak, UPS, Greyhound, and Carnival Cruise Lines.

Contract Carriers

Contract carriers might also be common carriers; however, as such, they are not bound to serve the general public. Instead, contract carriers serve specific customers under contractual agreements. Typical contracts are for movement of a specified cargo for a negotiated and agreed-upon price. Some contract carriers have specific capabilities that allow them to offer lower prices than common carriers might charge for the same service. For instance, Southwest Air might enter into a contractual agreement with the Dallas Cowboys football team to provide transportation for the team's out-of-town games. Shippers and carriers are free to negotiate contractual agreements for price, the commodity carried, liability, delivery timing, and types of service.

Exempt Carriers

Exempt carriers are also for-hire carriers, but they are exempt from regulation of services and rates. Carriers are classified as exempt if they transport certain exempt products such as produce, livestock, coal, garbage, or newspapers. School buses, taxis, and ambulances are also examples of exempt carriers. The exempt status was originally established to allow farmers to transport agricultural products on public roads, but today the status has been broadened to include a number of commodities. Rail carriers hauling coal between specific locations are exempt from economic regulation, for instance. All carriers can also act as exempt carriers for these specific commodities and routes.

Private Carrier

A **private carrier** is not subject to economic regulation and typically transports goods for the company owning the carrier. Firms transporting their own products typically own and operate fleets of trucks and/or airplanes, large enough to make the cost of transportation less than what it would be if the firm hired a transportation provider. Flexibility and control of product movements also play major roles in the ownership of a private carrier. Walmart, for instance, with its private fleet of trucks, was able to respond even quicker than U.S. government relief workers after Hurricane Katrina struck the Louisiana Gulf Coast in the summer of 2005. Immediately after the disaster, Walmart began hauling food, water, and other relief supplies with its private fleet of trucks to community members and other organizations in the affected areas. In three weeks, it hauled 2,500 truckloads of supplies to these areas; additionally, it was able to reopen its stores quickly in the hardest hit areas. Shortly after the hurricane, New Orleans Sheriff Harry Lee was quoted as saying, "If [the] American government would have responded like Walmart has responded, we wouldn't be in this crisis."[13]

The Modes of Transportation

There are five modes of transportation: motor (truck), rail, air, water, and pipeline carriers. Each of these modes offers distinct advantages to customers, and their selection depends on a number of factors including the goods to be transported, how quickly the goods are needed, the price shippers are willing to pay, and the locations of shippers and customers. Discussion of each of the modes follows.

Motor Carriers

Motor carriers (or trucks) are the most flexible mode of transportation and account for 70 percent of all the freight tonnage moved in the United States (about 10.5 billion tons in 2015) which is by far the largest of the five modes. Motor carriers offer door-to-door service, local pickup and delivery, and small as well as large shipment hauling. It has very low fixed and variable costs, can compete favorably with rail and air carriers for short-to-medium hauls (distances shorter than 1,000 miles), and is still competitive with other forms of transportation for long cross-country shipments, particularly if there are multiple delivery locations. Motor carriers can also offer a variety of specialized services from refrigerated, to livestock, to automobile hauling.

The primary disadvantages for motor carriers are weather and traffic problems. The tragic collapse of the eight-lane Minneapolis, Minnesota, I-35 West Bridge, over the Mississippi River in August 2007 killed thirteen people and provided a painful reminder of the importance of a nation's transportation infrastructure. Per day, more than 140,000 vehicles, including approximately 5,700 commercial vehicles, used Minnesota's busiest bridge. (In 2005, the bridge was inspected and received a low rating, indicating that it should have been either repaired or replaced.[14] The replacement bridge opened to traffic on September 18, 2008.[15]) Incidentally, every four years, the American Society of Civil Engineers' Report Card for America's Infrastructure depicts the condition and performance of American transportation infrastructure in the familiar form of a school report card—assigning letter grades based on the physical condition and needed investments for improvement. Aviation, inland waterways, and roads received grades of "D," while ports and bridges received grades of "C+," and rail tracks received a grade of "B."[16]

Motor carriers are most often classified as **less-than-truckload (LTL) carriers** or **truckload (TL) carriers**. LTL carriers move small packages or shipments that take up less than one truckload, and the shipping fees are higher per hundred weight (cwt) than TL fees, since the carrier must consolidate many small shipments into one truckload and then break the truckload back down into individual shipments at the destinations for individual deliveries. For many shippers, using LTL carriers is a much less expensive alternative than using a TL carrier. The LTL industry amounts to only about 5 percent of total trucking revenues and, in the United States, is comprised of a few very large, national LTL carriers along with a sizeable number of small regional carriers. As of the end of 2015, the five largest LTL carriers in the United States in terms of revenue were FedEx Freight ($5.7 billion), EXPO Logistics ($3.5 billion), YRC Freight ($3.0 billion), Old Dominion Freight ($2.9 billion), and UPS Freight ($2.5 billion). Most of the regional LTL carriers are small, privately owned companies that specialize in overnight and second-day deliveries. Today, the top five carriers represent about 50 percent of the total U.S. LTL market.[17]

TL carriers, on the other hand, have trailers dedicated to a single shipper's cargo. A customer loads a trailer full and then the TL company transports the shipment to a final destination where it is received and unloaded. At the end of 2015, the top five TL carriers in terms of revenues were Swift ($3.5 billion), Schneider ($2.4 billion), J.B. Hunt ($1.8 billion), Landstar ($1.7 billion), and Werner ($1.6 billion). The industry is quite fragmented—about 70 percent of the companies operate fewer than five trucks. In contrast to the LTL market, the top five TL carriers represent only about 8 percent of the market.[18]

Motor carriers can also be classified based on the types of goods they haul. **General freight carriers** carry the majority of goods shipped in the United States and include common carriers, whereas **specialized carriers** transport liquid petroleum, household goods, agricultural commodities, building materials, and other specialized items. In Australia, extra-long truck and trailer combinations (referred to as **road trains**) transport goods between geographically dispersed communities not served by rail (see the chapter-opening SCM Profile for discussions of this and other unique transportation services).

Rail Carriers

Rail carriers compete most favorably when the distance is long and the shipments are heavy or bulky. At one time in the United States, rail carriers transported the majority of goods shipped; however, since World War II, their share of the transportation market has steadily fallen. The $60 billion industry consists of 140,000 rail miles operated by 7 Class I or large railroads, 21 regional railroads, and 510 local railroads. Not only does the 140,000-mile system move more freight than any other freight rail system worldwide, but also it provides 221,000 jobs. Today in the United States, rail carriers account for about 1.8 billion tons of freight hauled each year.[19]

Rail service is relatively slow and inflexible; however, rail carriers are less expensive than air and motor carriers and can compete fairly well on long hauls. To better compete, railroads have purchased trucking companies and can thus offer point-to-point pickup and delivery service using motor carrier trailers and rail flatcars that carry the trailers (known as **trailer-on-flatcar service** or TOFC service). Railroads are also at somewhat of a disadvantage compared with motor carriers with respect to shipment damages, equipment availability, and service frequency.

Because of their abundance, rail companies use each other's rail cars; however, keeping track of the rail cars and getting them where they are needed can be problematic. With advances in railroad routing and scheduling software and rail car identification systems, this has become less of a problem for rail carriers. **Real-time location systems** (RTLSs) on rail cars use active, Wi-Fi-enabled radio frequency identification (RFID) tags to allow tracking of rail cars (and their assets) in real time. The tag is programmed to broadcast a signal identifying its location at regular time intervals. Sensors can also be added to the RTLS tags to monitor the temperature inside refrigerated cars, for example, and transmit a signal if the temperature goes out of a preset range.[20]

In the United States, railroad infrastructure and aging equipment have also been problems for the railroads; however, there has been a spending resurgence since the mid-1980s to replace worn track segments and rail cars, to upgrade terminals, and to consolidate through mergers and acquisitions. Unfortunately, train derailments have begun occurring more frequently, which is forcing the issue of replacing old rail track. In Bridgeport, Connecticut, an eastbound commuter train, for instance, derailed in March 2012, coming to rest in the path of a westbound train that sideswiped it, injuring seventy people and tearing up significant amounts of track. As a result, the Connecticut Department of Transportation is spending over $100 million to upgrade 56 miles of track along its New York commuter rail corridor.[21]

One of the trends in rail transportation is the use of **high-speed trains**. Today, they are operated in the United States by Amtrak along the northeast corridor (Boston–New York—Washington D.C.). Bombardier Inc., a Montreal-based transportation and aerospace company, designed and manufactured Amtrak's Acela Express, an electric high-speed train. These trains can make the Washington D.C. to Boston trip in about 5.5 hours, averaging approximately 85 miles per hour, although top speeds can reach 120 miles per hour (other slower trains and lack of straight-line track have tended to reduce the average speeds).[22] Eventually, with further improvements, speeds are expected to reach 160 mph.[23]

SCM Profile | Hyperloop's Wild Ride

Elon Musk, CEO of Tesla Motors and SpaceX, stirred a wave of interest in 2013 with a technology known as hyperloop—a vacuum tube with pods carrying people or freight, moving at 750 miles per hour. The idea was floated as a potential alternative to California's plans for a high-speed rail line between San Francisco and Los Angeles. Coming from this visionary entrepreneur, it attracted enough attention to trigger a race among start-ups trying to prove the technology is in fact practical.

Now, Hyperloop One is building a 500-meter section of exposed track near Las Vegas, Nevada, which will be tested in 2017. It plans to have a full-scale, 3-kilometer trial operating in a tube before the end of 2017. "When we demonstrate the prototype, everyone will realize we can solve problems of urban congestion—we can free up land, redefine cities. It's a big deal," says Rob Lloyd, CEO of Hyperloop One. Supporters of the hyperloop concept maintain that the technologies needed to make it work have all been proven and that the real challenges that need to be overcome involve the business model and financing.

Hyperloop One is aiming to initially carry freight rather than passengers to get around the regulatory concerns about safety, but says it will begin moving people once the technology is proven. The plan for the proposed LA to San Francisco route is for capsules carrying six to eight people departing every 30 seconds, with tickets costing around $20 each way. Cruising at top speed, the 350-mile trip would take about 30 minutes. The estimated cost of building a line from LA to San Francisco is $16 billion.[24]

While the Acela Express is the only high-speed railroad operating in the United States, other states such as California and Florida are moving ahead with planning for high-speed trains. In 2009, President Obama launched an ambitious high-speed rail program in the United States, for which Congress appropriated $10.5 billion. With these funds, California committed to building a $68 billion high-speed line that will run from San Francisco to Los Angeles at speeds reaching 200 mph with stops at twenty-four stations. Construction is slated to be finished prior to 2029. In Florida, since the state declined government assistance, a privately funded "higher-speed" rail project will soon link Miami and Orlando. Called All Aboard Florida, the $3 billion train will travel at average speeds of 81 mph (true high-speed rail is typically more than 155 mph). When it opens, the rail will be the first time a privately owned company has developed and opened a train line in the United States in more than 100 years.[25]

China today operates the longest high-speed rail network (about 16,000 km), with a ridership of about 250 million per year. In 2015, China signed contracts for 351 more high-speed trains.[26] Other countries such as France and Japan also have extensive high-speed rail lines operating. The inaugural high-speed French rail service between Paris and Lyon was in 1981 and has since expanded to connect cities across France and in neighboring countries. The Japanese Shinkansen high-speed rail began operations in 1964 between Tokyo and Osaka. A number of other European countries also use high-speed rail. Malaysia and Singapore recently announced their plans to build a high-speed line connecting Kuala Lumpur and Singapore. It is due for completion in 2020. Hyperloop, the brainchild of Tesla CEO Elon Musk, is a new vacuum tube form of high-speed rail and is discussed in the nearby SCM Profile. This and other high-speed rail capabilities can provide an attractive alternative to air and other forms of ground transportation, depending on the cost and location of terminals.[27]

Air Carriers

Transporting goods (and people) by air is very expensive relative to other modes but also very fast, particularly for long distances. The world's airlines carry over 3 billion passengers each year. In 2015, the total cargo hauled was about 58 million tons of freight creating revenues of $50.8 billion. Providing these services generates 9.9 million direct jobs. Comparing contributions to GDP, the global air transport industry is larger than the automotive industry. In fact, if air transport were a country, its GDP would rank it twenty-first in the world, similar to that of Switzerland or Sweden.[28]

Air carriers account for only a small portion of total freight hauled, since aircraft cannot carry extremely heavy or bulky cargo (an exception is the world's largest commercial cargo airliner, the Ukrainian-built Antonov An-225, described in the chapter-opening SCM Profile). For light, high-value goods that need to travel long distances quickly, air transportation is the best of the modal alternatives. For movements over water, the only other modal alternative is water carriage, where the transportation decision is based on timing, cost, and shipment weight. Though the incidence of shipment damage is quite low and schedule frequency is good, air transportation is limited in terms of geographic coverage. Most small cities in the United States, for example, do not have airports or regularly scheduled air service; therefore, air transportation service must be combined with motor carrier service for these locations.

Today, about half of the goods transported by air are carried by freight-only airlines like FedEx, the world's largest air cargo airline (number two is Emirates SkyCargo, followed by UPS).[29] This represents a significant change since the late 1960s when most air cargo was hauled by passenger airlines. Today, most passenger air carriers are opting to use smaller, more fuel-efficient aircraft, which has reduced their ability to haul cargo. Economic growth in markets such as China has continued to fuel increases in international air cargo. Today, most of the air cargo demand is in the Asia-Pacific region, followed by Europe and then North America.[30]

Water Carriers

Shipping goods by **water carrier** is very inexpensive but also very slow and inflexible. There are several types of water transportation: inland waterway, lake, coastal and inter-coastal ocean, and global deep-sea carriers. Inland waterway carriers (mainly barges) are used to haul heavy, bulky, low-value materials such as coal, grain, and sand, and compete primarily with rail and pipeline carriers. Inland water transport is obviously limited to areas accessible by water (the Mississippi and Columbia Rivers are examples in the United States), and hence growth in this area of transportation is also limited. Like rail and air transportation, water carriers are typically paired with motor carriers to enable door-to-door pick-up and delivery service.

Inland waterway barge transportation in the United States is expected to benefit from the higher demand for oil and petrochemical shipments over the period 2017–2022. The use of marine transportation by the petroleum and petrochemical industry is one of the major reasons for establishing refineries and petrochemical facilities along navigable inland waterways. Texas and Louisiana account for approximately 80 percent of the U.S. production of petrochemicals. To carry these shipments, new high-capacity tank barges are being built, and a number of new vendors have started to provide shipping services for transportation of liquid-bulk cargo.[31]

There have also been developments in **deep-sea transportation** that have made water transportation cheaper and more desirable, even with the slow transportation times. The development and use of supertankers and containerships have added a new dimension to water transportation. Many of today's oil supertankers are more than 1,200 feet long (that's four U.S. football fields) and carry over 2 million barrels of oil. The largest oil supertanker was the *Seawise Giant* (as described in the chapter-opening SCM Profile). Oil-producing nations can now cheaply ship large quantities of oil anywhere around the globe where demand exists. Additionally, small shippers can ship items overseas cheaply, because of the ability to consolidate small shipments in containers that are placed on board containerships.

Shipping containers allow almost any packaged product to be shipped overseas, and they add an element of protection to the cargo. Containerships carry the majority of the world's water-transported manufactured goods, and they can carry more than 10,000 stan-dard 20-foot containers (these are normally 20 feet in length, 8.5 feet in height, and 8 feet wide but can vary), holding up to 52,000 pounds each, with a total containership value sometimes as high as $300 million. At any given time, there are approximately 5 to 6 mil-lion containers being shipped around the globe.[32]

Pipeline Carriers

Pipeline carriers are very specialized with respect to the products they can carry; how-ever, once the initial investment of the pipeline is recovered, there is very little additional maintenance cost, so long-term pipeline transportation tends to be very inexpensive. Pipelines can haul materials that are only in a liquid or gaseous state and so the growth potential for pipelines is quite limited. One of the items pipelines haul is coal, and they do this by first pulverizing coal into small particles and then suspending it in water to form **coal slurry**. When the coal slurry reaches its destination, the coal and water are separated. Other items transported include water, oil, gasoline, and natural gas. The continuous nature of pipeline flow is what makes it unique. Once the product reaches its destination, it is continuously available. Pipelines are today being constructed to haul large quantities of natural gas and oil from desolate areas to existing processing facilities hundreds and even thousands of miles away (see the chapter-opening SCM Profile for more discussion of pipelines). So long as the world remains dependent on energy products such as coal, oil, and natural gas, there will be a need for pipeline transportation.

One of the more controversial pipelines is the proposed Keystone XL pipeline, which would transport 830,000 barrels per day of crude oil from the oil sands region of Alberta, Canada, to Steele City, Nebraska, where it would join an existing pipeline going to the U.S. gulf coast. Several state governments along with a number of U.S. government politicians are touting the benefits (lower gas prices and more jobs) as well as the costs to the environment (oil spills and native habitat destruction). President Donald Trump issued the permits within days of taking office in 2017, stipulating that American steel be used in the pipeline work. To date though, the decision to begin has not been reached on the project.[33]

Intermodal Transportation

Intermodal transportation, or the use of combinations of the various transportation modes, is a very popular transportation arrangement and can make the movement of goods cheaper, quicker, and more secure. Intermodal transportation dates at least to the early 1800s, when wooden containers were used to transport coal on the Bridgewater Canal in England. Horse-drawn vehicles were used to transfer the coal to and from the canal barges. During World War II, pallets were used to transfer U.S. military equipment quickly between warehouses, trucks, trains, ships, and airplanes. The reduced freight handling meant fewer personnel and faster shipping times. The use of standardized containers grew quickly in the United States when the Interstate Commerce Commission ruled in 1954 that railroads could carry truck trailers and containers on rail flatcars. In the 1970s, third-party shipping agents began moving shippers' goods in trailers and then using railroads for part of the transportation. The early success of these agents spawned hundreds of similar companies, driving the growth of intermodal traffic. Finally, deregulation of the transportation industry spurred intermodal growth to the levels of today.[34]

Most large intermodal transportation companies today such as U.S. companies CLX Logistics, J.B. Hunt, Con-way, and RJW Transport offer one-stop, door-to-door shipping capabilities—they transport shippers' goods for a price and then determine the best intermodal transportation and warehousing arrangements to *meet customer requirements as cheaply as possible*. Here is a fictitious shipping example using a number of intermodal combinations:

> *A manufacturing company packs a standard 8-foot container for shipment to an overseas customer. The container is sealed and connected to a motor carrier trailer for transport to a nearby rail terminal. The container is then loaded onto a flatcar and double-stacked with another container, where it is then transported to a seaport on the U.S. West Coast. Upon arrival, the container is placed aboard a container ship and transported to Japan. In Japan, the container is off-loaded and moves through customs, where it is then loaded onto another motor carrier trailer for transport to its final destination, where it finally is unsealed, inspected, and unpacked. In this example, goods were packed, securely sealed, unsealed and unpacked one time. The container was used in three modes of transportation and was unsealed when customs authorities examined and accepted the goods.*

The above example highlights a number of intermodal transportation combinations. The most common combinations are truck **trailer-on-flatcar (TOFC)** and **container-on-flatcar (COFC)**, also called **piggyback service**. The same containers can be placed onboard containerships and freight airliners. These combinations attempt to combine the flexibility of motor carriers with the economy of rail and/or water carriers. The BNSF Railway, headquartered in Texas, operates one of the largest railroad networks in North America and is one of seven North American Class I railroads. It has over 32,500 track miles covering twenty-eight states and three Canadian provinces and has twenty-five intermodal facilities. BNSF moved 1.8 million coal shipments and moved enough grain to supply 90 million people with a year's supply of bread. As of 2016, BNSF had 41,000 employees, 8,000 locomotives, and more than 190,000 freight cars.[35]

Another example of intermodal transportation are **ROROs**, or roll-on-roll-off, vessels. These allow truck trailers, automobiles, heavy equipment, and specialty cargo to be directly driven on and off the ship, into secured below-deck garages without use of cranes. The New Jersey-based Atlantic Container Line operates the largest and most versatile combination RORO/containerships in the world, capable of carrying a wide variety of cargo. They have recently begun receiving their new G-4 combination RORO/containerships with a capacity of 3,800 standard 20-foot containers above deck and 1,300 vehicles below deck.[36]

Transportation Pricing

The two basic pricing strategies used by logistics service providers are **cost-of-service pricing** and **value-of-service pricing**. Further, when the shipments are large enough, carriers and shippers enter into **negotiated pricing**. Obviously, shippers want low prices and carriers want high profits, and these desires are often at odds with one another. Not too many years ago, logistics companies like UPS simply distributed their costs evenly and charged a uniform rate to all customers. As computer pricing models improved, companies were able to more closely identify their costs for various types of customers and differential pricing became more the norm, with small shippers and infrequent users seeing significant price increases. In the recent recession, poor economic conditions caused excess capacity due to lower shipping demand, which allowed shippers to negotiate better terms. Now, shippers have lost that leverage.[37] These and other pricing topics are discussed below.

Cost-of-Service Pricing

Cost-of-service pricing is used when carriers establish prices based on their fixed and variable costs of transportation. To do this, carriers must be able to identify the relevant costs and then accurately allocate these to each shipment. Cost-of-service pricing varies based on volume and distance. As shipping volume increases, the portion of fixed costs that are allocated to each shipment goes down, allowing the carrier to reduce its prices. Large-volume shipments also allow carriers to charge carload or truckload rates instead of less-than-carload or less-than-truckload rates. Cost-of-service pricing represents the base, or lowest, shipping price for carriers, and in a highly competitive market, carriers will price just above these levels to maintain some minimal level of profitability. As occurred during the recent global recession, many carriers were unable to maintain prices at even these lowest levels, resulting in a number of bankruptcies.

Value-of-Service Pricing

In this case, transportation providers price their services at the highest levels the market will bear. Prices are thus based on the level of competition and the current demand for each service. This is a profit-maximizing pricing approach. If a carrier has a service that is in high demand with little competition, prices will consequently be quite high. As other logistics companies notice the high-profit potential of this service, competition will eventually increase, causing prices to fall. As the level of competition increases, carriers will seek ways to reduce their costs to maintain profitability. Today, demand for some transportation services exceeds supply, and this has caused value-of-service pricing to predominate. In the airline industry, online booking capabilities combined with revenue management software to control prices as demand fluctuates have allowed airlines to use value-of-service pricing to maximize revenues.

Negotiated Pricing

Since the deregulation of transportation in the United States, negotiating transportation prices has become much more common among business shippers and logistics providers. In addition, shippers today are inclined to develop alliances with logistics companies because of the key role they play in allowing firms and their supply chains to be more responsive to changing demand. This has also tended to increase the use of negotiated prices. Shippers want carriers to use cost-of-service pricing, while carriers want to use value-of-service pricing. To maintain an equitable partnership, prices are negotiated such that they fall somewhere between these two levels, allowing carriers to cover their fixed and variable costs and make a reasonable profit, and allowing shippers to get the logistics services they want at reasonable prices.

Terms of Sale

In many cases, suppliers' terms of sale affect transportation costs. When goods are purchased from a supplier, it may quote a price that includes transportation to the buyer's location. This is known as **FOB destination pricing**, or "free-on-board" to the shipment's destination. This also means that the *supplier will be the legal owner of the product until it safely reaches its destination.* For high-value shipments, small shipments, or when the buyer has little transportation expertise, FOB destination pricing is typically preferred. Otherwise, the buyer may decide to purchase goods and supply its own transportation to the shipping destination; in this case, the supplier quotes the lower **FOB origin pricing**. The goods then become the *legal responsibility of the buyer at the supplier's finished goods pickup location.*

Rate Categories

Carrier prices or rates can be classified in a number of different ways. **Line haul rates** are the charges for moving goods to a nonlocal destination (e.g., between cities), and these can be further classified as *class rates, exception rates, commodity rates*, and *miscellaneous rates*. In the United States, **class rates** are published annually by the National Motor Freight Traffic Association (NMFTA), a nonprofit group of motor carrier companies. The class rate standards, called the National Motor Freight Classification (NMFC), are based on an evaluation of four transportation characteristics: density, stowability, handling, and liability. Together, these characteristics establish a shipment's "transportability." There are eighteen classes numbered from 50 to 500—the higher the class rating, the higher the price.[38] **Exception rates** are rates that are lower than the NMFC class rates for specific origin-destination locations or volumes and generally are established on an account-by-account basis. **Commodity rates** apply to minimum quantities of products that are shipped between two specified locations. **Miscellaneous rates** apply to contract rates that are negotiated between two parties and to shipments containing a variety of products (in this case, the rate is based on the overall weight of the shipment). Today, many of the rates carriers charge are classified as miscellaneous, since negotiated rates tend to be used primarily for large shipments.

Transportation Security

Transportation security in the United States, particularly **airline security**, has become a very important issue since September 11, 2001. Congress passed the Aviation and Transportation Security Act in November 2001, creating a large organization (the Transportation Security Administration, or TSA) to oversee transportation security. Today, the TSA's over 42,000 (full-time equivalent) transportation security officers screen more than 1.9 million passengers every day at more than 430 airports nationwide and conduct all of the cargo screening on domestic and international-outbound passenger aircraft.[39] In addition to the TSA, Congress passed the Homeland Security Act in November 2002, creating the Department of Homeland Security (DHS) to further coordinate and unify national homeland security efforts. It includes the TSA along with twenty-one other federal departments and agencies and has 230,000 employees with an annual budget of about $41 billion to provide overall U.S. security leadership.[40]

A number of problems and actions have resulted from this heightened emphasis on transportation security in the United States. The TSA has had numerous agency chiefs since 9/11 and has spent more than $12 billion to improve security on airplanes and in airports. One of the latest TSA initiatives began in 2016—automated security screening lanes and computed tomography (CT) scanners, at select hubs nationwide. The automated screening lanes incorporate technology and screening station modifications that enhance security effectiveness while decreasing the time travelers spend in security screening by approximately 30 percent. In December 2013, TSA launched its Pre ✓ application program, which is a shift toward a risk-based and intelligence-driven approach to security. Through this program, U.S. citizens and lawful permanent residents can apply directly to participate in Pre ✓ and undergo a background check in order to become eligible for a period of five years. So far, about 2 million people are using it.[41] Air cargo transported on passenger aircraft is also subjected to high levels of security checks in the United States. Today, 100 percent of air cargo must be prescreened, as mandated by the Improving America's Security Act of 2007.

With respect to the other modes of transportation, the TSA has been working with railroads to reduce the number of hours that toxic chemicals can spend in transit, resulting in a 54 percent reduction since 2006 in the overall risk of rail tanker explosions or spills. The TSA also has a pipeline security division, which essentially mandates all pipeline operators to implement a pipeline security program. For many truckers and other transportation workers such as U.S. deepwater port workers, one of the latest transportation security initiatives is the use of the **Transportation Worker Identification Credential (TWIC)**, which was mandated by the Maritime Transportation Security Act of 2002 and the Safe Port Act of 2006. The TWIC became mandatory for all port workers in 2009.[42]

Another type of security initiative is the use of PrePass, offered by the nonprofit organization HELP, which allows prequalified U.S. motor carriers to bypass state inspection and weigh stations at highway speeds, using automated vehicle identification technology. Today, over 500,000 prequalified commercial vehicles can bypass more than 300 inspection facilities using PrePass, allowing inspection personnel to spend more of their time inspecting other vehicles. Additionally, PrePass saves drivers five to eight minutes and a half gallon of fuel per bypass.[43]

Transportation Regulation and Deregulation in the United States

The transportation industry in the United States has gone through periods of both government regulation and deregulation. On the one hand, **transportation regulation** is argued by many to be good in that it tends to ensure adequate transportation service throughout the country while protecting consumers in terms of monopoly pricing, safety, and liability. On the other hand, **transportation deregulation** is argued to be good because it encourages competition and allows prices to adjust as supply, demand, and negotiations dictate. In addition, antitrust, safety, and security laws already in place tend to protect transportation consumers. This debate was the subject of a study in 1994 to determine the impact deregulation had on the U.S. motor carrier industry. The study concluded that transportation deregulation has resulted in greater use of cost-of-service pricing, rising freight rates for LTL shipments, and more safety problems, as operators tended to let fleets age and reduce maintenance levels.[44] Today, the U.S. transportation industry remains essentially deregulated; however, a number of regulations (primarily safety and security regulations) still exist and continue to be revised. Over the past few years, when bankruptcies and consolidations occurred, particularly in the airline industry, new calls for entire industry re-regulation have also emerged. Some of the history of transportation regulation and deregulation in the United States is reviewed next.

Transportation Regulation

Table 9.2 summarizes the major transportation regulations in the United States, starting with the Granger Laws of the 1870s, which led to the Interstate Commerce Act of 1887. Before this time, the railroads in the United States were charging high rates and discriminating against small shippers. So a number of Midwestern states passed laws to broadly regulate the railroads to establish maximum rates, prohibit local discrimination, forbid rail mergers (to encourage competition), and prohibit free passes to public officials. Though the U.S. Supreme Court later struck down these laws, the Granger movement made Congress realize the impacts of railroad monopolies. This led to the passage of the Interstate Commerce Act of 1887.

The 1887 act created the Interstate Commerce Commission (ICC), which required rail carriers to charge and publish reasonable rates, file them with the ICC, and make them available to the public, and which prohibited discriminatory practices (charging some shippers less than others for the same service). The act also prohibited agreements between railroads to pool traffic or revenues. Between 1887 and 1910, a number of amendments made to the 1887 act increased the ICC's control and enforcement power. These amendments restricted railroads from providing rates and services that were not in the public's best interest, created penalties for failure to follow published rates or for offering and accepting rebates, set maximum rates, and prevented railroads from owning pipelines or water carriers, unless approved by the ICC.

By 1917, increased competition combined with the rate restrictions had created a rail system unable to offer the efficient service the U.S. government needed in its war efforts, and thus the federal government seized the railroads. Railroad companies were guaranteed a profit while the government poured large sums of money into upgrading the rail system. By the end of World War I, Congress had come to realize that all of the negative controls placed on railroads were unhealthy for the industry. They wanted to return the railroads to private ownership. This brought about the first of a number of regulations aimed at positive control, namely, the **Transportation Act of 1920**.

Table 9.2	U.S. Transportation Regulation	
DATE	**REGULATION**	**SUMMARY**
1870s	Granger Laws	Midwestern states passed laws to establish maximum rates, prohibit discrimination, and forbid mergers for railroads (RRs).
1887	Interstate Commerce Act	States cannot regulate transportation; established Interstate Commerce Commission (ICC); regulated and published rates, outlawed discriminatory pricing, prohibited pooling agreements.
1920	Transportation Act	Instructed the ICC to establish rates that allowed RRs to earn a fair return; established minimum rates; allowed ICC to set intrastate rates; allowed pooling agreements if they were in the public's best interest.
1935	Motor Carrier Act	Extended the ICA of 1887 to include motor carriers and brought them under ICC control; established five classes of operators: common, contract, private, exempt, and broker; mergers must be OK'd by ICC.
1938	Civil Aeronautics Act	Established the Civil Aeronautics Board (CAB) to regulate air carriers; new entrants had to get CAB approval; CAB controlled rates; Civil Aeronautics Administration controlled air safety.
1940	Transportation Act	Extended the ICA of 1887 to include ICC control over domestic water transportation; ICC controlled entry, rates, and services.
1942	Freight Forwarders Act	Extended the ICA of 1887 to include ICC control over freight forwarders; ICC controlled entry, rates, and services.
1948	Reed-Bulwinkle Act	Amendment to the ICA of 1887 legalizing rate bureaus or conferences.
1958	Transportation Act	Amended the rule of rate making by stating that rates couldn't be held up to protect the traffic of any other mode.
1958	Federal Aviation Act	Created the Federal Aviation Agency to assume the mission of the CAA; FAA empowered to manage and develop U.S. airspace and plan the U.S. airport system.
1966	Dept. of Transportation Act	Assumed mission of FAA and a number of other agencies for research, promotion, safety, and administration of transportation; organized into nine operating and six administrative divisions; also established the National Transportation Safety Board.
1970	Railway Passenger Service Act	Created the National Railroad Passenger Corp. to preserve and upgrade intercity rail passenger service; resulted in the creation of Amtrak.
1975	Hazardous Materials Transportation Act	Strengthened laws to fight illegal dumping. Created a cradle-to-grave responsibility for hazardous materials. Established minimum standards for transport by all modes. Regulated by DOT.

The 1920 act instructed the ICC to ensure that rates were high enough to provide a fair return for the railroads each year (Congress initially set this at 6 percent return per year). When companies made more than the prescribed 6 percent, half of the excess was taken and used to fund low-interest loans to the weaker operators for updating their systems and increasing efficiency. The act also allowed the ICC to set minimum rates, allowed joint use of terminal facilities, and allowed rail company acquisitions and consolidations. Finally, to keep the railroads from becoming overcapitalized, the act prohibited railroads from issuing securities without ICC approval. The rail system thus became a regulated monopoly.

From 1935 to 1942, regulations were passed that applied to other modes of transportation and these were similar in nature to the 1920 act. A great deal of money was spent during the 1920s and during the Depression building the U.S. highway system. The time became ripe, then, for the emergence of for-hire motor carriers. The number of small trucking companies grew tremendously during this period, creating competition for the railroads, as shippers opted to use the cheaper for-hire motor carriers. The **Motor Carrier Act of 1935** brought motor carriers under ICC control, thus controlling entry into the market, establishing motor carrier classes of operation, setting reasonable rates, mandating ICC approval for any mergers or acquisitions, and controlling the issuance of securities.

In 1938, the federal government enacted another extension of the Interstate Commerce Act by including regulation of air carriers in the **Civil Aeronautics Act of 1938**. This act promoted the development of the air transportation system and the air safety and airline efficiency by establishing the Civil Aeronautics Board to oversee market entry, establish routes with appropriate levels of competition, develop regional feeder airlines, and set reasonable rates. The Civil Aeronautics Administration was also established to regulate air safety.

The **Transportation Act of 1940** further extended the Interstate Commerce Act of 1887 by establishing ICC control over domestic water transportation. The provisions for domestic water carriers were similar to those imposed on rail and motor carriers. In 1942, the 1887 act was once again extended to cover freight forwarders, with the usual entry, rate, and service controls of the ICC. Freight forwarders were also prohibited from owning any carriers.

A number of other congressional enactments occurred up through 1970, further strengthening and refining the control of the transportation market. In 1948, the **Reed-Bulwinkle Act** gave groups of carriers the ability to form rate bureaus or conferences wherein they could propose rate changes to the ICC. The **Transportation Act of 1958** established temporary loan guarantees to railroads, liberalized control over intrastate rail rates, amended the rule of rate-making to ensure more intermodal competition, and clarified the differences between private and for-hire motor carriers. The **Federal Aviation Act of 1958** replaced the Civil Aeronautics Administration with the Federal Aviation Administration (FAA) and gave the FAA authority to prescribe air traffic rules, make safety regulations, and plan the national airport system. In 1966, the **Department of Transportation Act** created the Department of Transportation (DOT) to coordinate the executive functions of all government entities dealing with transportation-related matters. It was hoped that centralized coordination of all the transportation agencies would lead to more effective transportation promotion and planning. Finally, to preserve and improve the rail system's ability to service passengers, the **Railway Passenger Service Act** was passed in 1970, creating Amtrak.

As discussed earlier, there have been a number of transportation regulations dealing with safety and security, and only the 1975 Hazardous Materials Transportation Act is shown in Table 9.2. Prior to this time, many landfills began refusing to accept hazardous waste, which created a rash of midnight dumping activities along roadways and in vacant lots. Poor coordination and lack of personnel created poor enforcement of existing laws. This law established minimum standards of regulation for transportation of hazardous materials, administered by the DOT. All hazardous waste transporters were forced to register with the proper state and federal agencies, track all pick-ups and deliveries, and clean up any spills during transports.

Transportation Deregulation

Beginning in 1976, Congress enacted a number of laws to reduce and eliminate many transportation regulations. These are summarized in Table 9.3. This began the movement toward less economic regulation by allowing market forces to determine prices, entry, and services. At this point in U.S. transportation history, consumers and politicians had the opinion that transportation economic regulations were administered more for the benefit of the carriers than the public. In addition, with the bankruptcy filings of a number of railroads in the mid-1970s combined with the Arab oil embargo of the same time period, regulation was receiving much of the blame for an inefficient transportation system.

Table 9.3	U.S. Transportation Deregulation	
DATE	**DEREGULATION**	**SUMMARY**
1976	Railroad Revitalization and Regulatory Reform Act	The "4-R Act." Railroads were allowed to change rates without ICC approval, within limits; ICC procedures were sped up.
1977	Air Cargo Deregulation Act	Freed all air cargo carriers from CAB regulations.
1978	Air Passenger Deregulation Act	Airlines freed to expand routes, change fares within limits; small community routes were subsidized; CAB ceases to exist in 1985.
1980	Motor Carrier Act	Fewer restrictions on entry, routes, rates, and private carriers.
1980	Staggers Rail Act	Freed railroads to further establish rates within limits; legalized contract rates; shortened ICC procedure turnaround.
1982	Bus Regulatory Reform Act	Amended the 1980 MCA to include buses.
1984	Shipping Act	Partial deregulation of ocean transportation.
1994	Trucking Industry Regulatory Reform Act	Motor carriers freed from filing rates with the ICC.
1994	FAA Authorization Act	Freed intermodal air carriers from economic regulation by the states.
1995	ICC Termination Act	Eliminated the ICC and moved regulatory duties to Dept. of Transportation.
1998	Ocean Shipping Reform Act	Deregulated ocean liner shipping; allowed contract shipping; rate filing not required.

The **Railroad Revitalization and Regulatory Reform Act**, commonly known as the 4-R Act, was passed in 1976 and made several regulatory changes to help the railroads. First, railroads were allowed to change rates without ICC approval, limited by *threshold costs* on one end and *market dominance* on the other. Threshold costs were defined as the firm's variable costs and the ICC determined whether the firm was in a market-dominant position (absence of market competition). A number of ICC procedures were also sped up to aid transportation manager decision-making. These same ideas appeared again in later deregulation efforts.

Air freight was deregulated in 1977. No longer were there any barriers to entry provided the firms were deemed fit by the Civil Aeronautics Board. Size restrictions were also lifted and carriers were free to charge any rate provided there was no discrimination. Finally, carriers did not have to file freight rates with the CAB. This was followed soon after by deregulation of air passenger service in 1978. The targeted beneficiary of passenger airline deregulation was the traveler. In introducing the bill to the Senate floor, Senator Ted Kennedy, one of the bill's principal sponsors, proclaimed, "This bill, while preserving the government's authority to regulate health and safety, frees airlines to do what business is supposed to do—serve consumers better for less." This was a phased-in approach, wherein carriers could slowly add routes to their systems while protecting other routes from competition. Fares could be adjusted within limits without CAB approval. To protect small communities from losing service, all cities with service in 1977 were guaranteed service for ten additional years. In 1981, all route restrictions were to be released, allowing any carrier to operate any route. Airline rates and mergers were to be released from regulation in 1983. Finally, the CAB was to shut down in 1985.

The impacts of deregulation on the U.S. airline industry were enormous—there were thirty-four air passenger carriers in 1977, and only five years later the number had increased to ninety. Some fares dropped substantially, while other fares went up, and routes to low-demand areas decreased substantially. By 1981, among the major U.S. airlines, only American, Delta, and TWA were making a profit. A number of notable airline failures also occurred in the years following deregulation. Braniff, for instance, after deregulation expanded rapidly in the United States and abroad, purchased a large number of planes, loaded up on debt, and then declared bankruptcy in 1982. They emerged from bankruptcy as a smaller airline; then seven years later declared bankruptcy again, after failing to obtain financing. A short time later, Braniff ceased operations completely. People Express, a new low-fare, no-frills airline that began right after deregulation, followed the Braniff large-expansion-high-debt model, and similarly had trouble operating by 1986, eventually selling out to rival Texas Air, which itself filed for bankruptcy in 1990. In all, some 150 airlines came and went during this period.[45] Fast-forward twenty-five years—by 2017, due to industry consolidation and further bankruptcies, the four largest U.S. airlines, American, Delta, Southwest, and United, controlled approximately 70 percent of the domestic U.S. market. Today there is enough monopoly power to charge for checked bags, charge up to $200 for a ticket change, eliminate food, reduce leg room, abandon routes to smaller cities, and, of course, raise airfares.

Motor carriers were deregulated in 1980. The objectives of this act were to promote competitive as well as safe and efficient motor transportation. Entry regulations were relaxed to make it easier to enter the market—firms had only to show a "useful public purpose" would be served. Route restrictions were removed and restrictions deemed to be wasteful of fuel, inefficient, or contrary to public interest were also removed. And, as with air passenger deregulation, a large number of new motor carriers began service. By 1981, more than 2,400 new motor carrier companies had started up in the United States. Unfortunately, by 1990, 11,490 of these companies had declared bankruptcy. This was more than the number of motor carrier bankruptcies in the forty-five years leading up to deregulation in 1980.[46]

Railroads were further deregulated with the **Staggers Rail Act of 1980**. The financial condition of railroads was worsening and this act was aimed at improving finances for the rail industry. With this act, rail carriers were free to change rates within a zone of rate freedom, but the ceiling or market dominance rate was established more definitively as 160 percent of variable costs and varied up to 180 percent depending on ICC cost formulas. After 1984, rate increases were to be tied to the rate of inflation. Contract rates were also allowed between railroads and shippers.

The **Shipping Act of 1984** marked the end of the initial push by Congress to deregulate the entire U.S. transportation industry. This act allowed ocean carriers to pool or share shipments, assign ports, publish rates, and enter into contracts with shippers. More recently, with the passage of the **ICC Termination Act of 1995** and the **Ocean Shipping Reform Act of 1998**, the Interstate Commerce Commission was eliminated and the requirement for ocean carriers to file rates with the Federal Maritime Commission also came to an end.

Thus, a number of changes in the U.S. transportation industry over the past century have occurred. Economic regulation of transportation occurred for several reasons. Initial transportation regulations were instituted to *establish the ground rules* as new forms of transportation developed and to *control prices, services*, and *routes* when monopoly power existed in the industry. Later, deregulation was used to *encourage competition* and *increase efficiency and safety*. Arguments remain as to the success and need for both transportation regulation and deregulation. In the future, as economic conditions change and as technology, political, and social changes occur, transportation regulations will also continue to change.

WAREHOUSING AND DISTRIBUTION

Warehouses provide very strategic supply chain services—they enable firms to store their purchases, work-in-progress, and finished goods, as well as perform breakbulk and assembly activities. Further, warehouses allow faster and more frequent deliveries of finished products to customers, which in turn can result in better customer service. Today, companies view warehouses as a competitive resource. Amazon.com, for example, has dramatically expanded its warehouse network over the years to compete better and to offer same-day service in some areas.

As disposable income increases, consumers buy more goods that must move through various distribution systems. In fast-growing economies like India and China, this means the demand for warehouses is growing rapidly. In the United States as well, the number of warehouses is growing and they are becoming larger too. From 2000 to 2012, over 3 billion square feet of warehousing space was added in the United States. In 2015, the average U.S. commercial warehouse size was approximately 215,000 square feet.[47] Today, 400,000-square-foot warehouses are becoming more prevalent (i.e., almost five soccer fields), and many are much larger. Target is a good example—it has a 1.5-million-square-foot import warehouse in Rialto, California, which was completed in 2011. As of 2017, Target's forty-one distribution centers in North America average about 1.3 million square feet.[48]

In many cases today, warehouses are not used to store things, but rather to receive bulk shipments, break them down, repackage various items into outgoing orders, and then distribute these orders to a manufacturing location or retail center. These activities are collectively referred to as **crossdocking**. In this case, the warehouse is more accurately described as a **distribution center**. In other cases, firms are moving warehouses closer to suppliers, closer to customers, or to more centralized locations, depending on the storage objectives and customer service requirements. So, warehouses are still very much in use—some just to store things and others to provide efficient throughput of goods. This section discusses a number of warehousing issues including their importance and the types of warehouses, risk pooling and warehouse location, and lean warehousing.

The Importance and Types of Warehouses

Firms hold inventories for a number of reasons as explained in Chapter 6—warehouses are used to support purchasing, production, and distribution activities. Firms order raw materials, parts, and assemblies, which are typically shipped to a warehouse location close to or inside the buyer's location, and then eventually transferred to the buyer's various operations as needed. In a retail setting, a warehouse might be regionally located, with the retailer receiving bulk shipments at the warehouse from many suppliers, then breaking these down and reassembling outgoing orders for delivery to each retail location, while using its private fleet of trucks, or for-hire transportation providers to move the orders to the retail locations. Similar distribution centers are used when manufacturers deliver bulk shipments to regional market areas and then break these down and ship LTL order quantities to customers.

Firms might operate **consolidation warehouses** to collect large numbers of LTL shipments from nearby regional sources of supply, and then consolidate and transport in TL or CL quantities to a manufacturing or user facility located at some distance from the consolidation warehouse. The use of consolidation warehouses and distribution centers allows firms to realize both purchase economies and transportation economies. Firms can buy goods in bulk at lower unit costs and then ship these goods at TL or CL rates either to a distribution center or directly to a manufacturing center or retailer. They can also purchase and move small quantity purchases at LTL rates to nearby consolidation warehouses.

Private Warehouses

Just as with the private forms of transportation, **private warehouses** refer to warehouses that are privately owned and used by an organization. For firms with large volumes of goods to store or transfer, private warehouses represent an opportunity to reduce the costs of warehousing as well as control the levels of service provided to customers. Currently, one of the largest e-commerce companies, the Alibaba Group, is expanding its number of private warehouses in China to streamline deliveries across the nation. Its logistics arm, Cainiao, has increased its warehouse space to about 54 million square feet as of 2016. Founded in 2013, Cainiao seeks to give Alibaba a driving role in China's fragmented package delivery industry. In partnership with delivery businesses, it crunches reams of data on everything from order trends to delivery routes and weather patterns to increase efficiency. "People may think that an Internet company shouldn't have property but Cainiao cannot just be a pure data company," says Cainiao president Judy Tong, referring to Alibaba's ownership of warehouses. "An app can't solve the problems of logistics."[49]

With private warehousing, firms are free to decide what to store, what to process, what types of security to provide, and the types of equipment to use, among other operational aspects. Private warehousing can also enable the firm to better utilize its workforce and expertise in terms of transportation, warehousing, and distribution center activities. As supply chains become more global to take advantage of cheaper sources of supply or labor, the use of private warehouses tends to increase. Finally, private warehouses can generate income and tax advantages through leasing of excess capacity and/or asset depreciation. For these reasons, private warehousing accounts for the vast majority of overall warehouse space in the United States.[50]

Private warehouses can be truly massive, as described earlier with Target's distribution centers. In fact, one of the largest private warehouses in the world is Target's import warehouse in Lacey, Washington. This gargantuan 2,000,000-square-foot facility (about the size of forty U.S. football fields) was built to distribute imported products to regional Target warehouses. Constellation Europe, a liquor wholesaler, has a private warehouse in Bristol, England, totaling just under 1,000,000 square feet. It can house up to 57 million bottles of wine at one time.[51]

Owning warehouses, though, can also represent a significant financial risk and loss of flexibility to the firm. The costs to build, equip, and then operate a warehouse can be very high and most small- to moderate-sized firms simply cannot afford private warehouses. Private warehouses also restrict firms to locations that may not prove optimal as time passes. Warehouse size or capacity is also somewhat inflexible, at least in the short term. Another problem can be insurance. Insurance companies, in many cases, do not like insuring goods in private warehouses, simply because security levels can be meager or nonexistent, creating a significant concern regarding fires or thefts of goods.

Public Warehouses

As the name implies, **public warehouses** are for-profit organizations that contract out or lease a wide range of light manufacturing, warehousing, and distribution services to other companies. Public warehouses provide a number of specialized services that firms can use to create customized shipments and goods. These services include the following:

- *Breakbulk*—Large-quantity shipments are broken down so that items can be combined into specific customer orders and then shipped out.

- *Repackaging*—After breakbulk, items are repackaged for specific customer orders. Warehouses can also do individual product packaging and labeling.

- *Assembly*—Some public warehouses provide final assembly operations to satisfy customer requests and to create customized final products.

- *Quality inspections*—Warehouse personnel can perform incoming and outgoing quality inspections.
- *Material handling, equipment maintenance, and documentation services.*
- *Short- and long-term storage.*

Besides the services shown here, public warehouses provide the short-term flexibility and investment cost savings that private warehouses cannot offer. If a firm's demand changes or its products change, the short-term commitments required at public warehouses allow the firm to quickly change warehouse locations. Public warehouses allow firms to test various market areas and withdraw quickly if demand does not materialize as expected. The cost for firms to use a public warehouse can also be very small if their capacity requirements are minimal.

More recently, pharmaceutical companies are using public warehouses in conjunction with third-party **cold chains** to ensure their product reaches buyers in good shape. Pharmaceutical cold chains refer to temperature-controlled (2–8°C) transportation, transfers, and warehousing. Currently, about half of the best-selling drugs require cold chains.[52] The demand for these and for food cold chains is growing dramatically. "We're seeing more focus on food quality and food safety," says Peter Mehring, CEO of British research firm Companies and Markets. "The level of interest from grocers and quick service restaurants has surged in the past year. There also are a number of studies attributing 30 to 50 percent of waste of harvest produce, seafood and meat throughout the supply chain," Mehring says. "Every hour produce spends at ambient temperature reduces approximately one day of shelf life. To extend shelf life, produce should be immediately cooled, but often it isn't done early enough, or properly. In the United States, growers have moved cooling to the field, but in other nations produce may take four hours to reach a pack house for cooling."[53]

One of the main disadvantages associated with public warehouses is the lack of control provided to the goods owners. Other problems include lack of communication with warehouse personnel, lack of specialized services or capacity at the desired locations, and the lack of care and security that might be given to products.

Firms might find it advantageous to use public warehouses in some locations and private warehouses in others. For large, established markets and relatively mature products, large firms may decide that owning and operating a warehouse makes the most sense, whereas the same firm may lease space and pay for services at public warehouses in developing markets and low-demand areas.

Risk Pooling and Warehouse Location

One of the more important decisions regarding private warehouses is where to locate them. The location decision affects the number of warehouses needed, the required capacities, the system inventory levels and customer service levels, and finally, the warehousing system costs. For a given market area, as the number of warehouses used increases, the warehousing system becomes more *decentralized*. In a **decentralized warehousing system**, responsiveness and delivery service levels will increase since goods will be closer to customers and can be delivered more quickly; however, warehousing system operating and inventory costs will also increase. Other costs that come into play here are outgoing transportation costs to customers and the transportation costs associated with the incoming deliveries of goods to each warehouse. Thus, the trade-off between costs and customer service must be carefully considered as the firm makes its warehouse location decisions. In a **centralized warehousing system**, fewer warehouses means that outbound transportation costs will be higher and service levels will be lower, but system costs will also be lower. This brings up the very important topic of **risk pooling**, which is discussed below.

Risk Pooling

Risk pooling describes the relationship between the number of warehouses, system inventories, and customer service, and it can be explained as follows:

> *When market demand is random, it is very likely that higher-than-average demand from some customers will be offset by lower-than-average demand from other customers. As the number of customers served by a single warehouse increases, these demand variabilities will tend to offset each other more often, thus reducing overall demand variance and the likelihood of stockouts. Consequently, the amount of safety stock in a warehouse system required to guard against stockouts decreases. Thus, the more* centralized *a warehousing system is, the* lower the safety stock *required to achieve a given system-wide customer service level (recall that in inventory parlance the customer service level is inversely proportional to the number of stockouts per period).*

As mentioned above, risk pooling assumes that demand at the markets served by a warehouse system is negatively correlated (higher-than-average demand in one market area tends to be offset by lower-than-average demand in another market area). In smaller market areas served by warehouses, this may not hold true and warehouses would then require higher levels of safety stock. This is why a smaller number of centralized warehouses serving large market areas require lower overall system inventories, compared to a larger number of decentralized warehouses serving the same markets.

A good illustration of this principle occurred in Europe after the formation of the European Union in 1993. Prior to that time, European logistics systems were formed along national lines. In other words, each country's distribution systems operated independently of the others, with warehouses located in each country. With the arrival of a single European market in 1993, these distribution systems no longer made economic sense. For example, Becton Dickinson, an American manufacturer of diagnostics equipment, was burdened in Europe in the early 1990s with just this type of country-specific and costly distribution system. After the formation of the European Union, the company closed its distribution centers in Sweden, France, Germany, and Belgium and shifted all of its distribution operations to a single automated center in Belgium. In less than a year, average stock levels were down 45 percent, write-offs fell by 65 percent, and stockouts were reduced by 75 percent. Other companies in Europe had similar results.[54]

The effect of risk pooling can be estimated numerically by the **square root rule**, which suggests that the system average inventory (as impacted by changing the number of warehouses in the system) is equal to the original system inventory times the ratio of the square root of the new number of warehouses to the square root of the original number of warehouses.[55] A simple illustration of risk pooling is shown in Example 9.1. In the example, reducing the number of warehouses from two to one causes a reduction in average inventory of approximately 29 percent, due to the risk pooling effect.

The differences between centralized and decentralized warehousing systems can be summarized as follows:

- *Safety stock and average system inventory*—As the firm moves toward fewer warehouses and a more centralized warehousing system, safety stocks and thus

---

Example 9.1   Risk Pooling at Thompson's Boot Barn

Thompson's Boot Barn currently owns two warehouses in Phoenix and Los Angeles to store its boots prior to shipping them out to retailers and other customers throughout the south-western United States. Bill Thompson, the owner, is considering a change to a more centralized system with just one warehouse in Las Vegas. He is curious to know the impact this will have on his system inventories. The Boot Barn's current inventories are approximately 6,000 boots in each warehouse, and its current stockout performance is about 1 percent. Using the square root rule, Bill calculates the new average inventory level needed to maintain the same stockout performance:

$$S_2 = \frac{\sqrt{N_2}}{\sqrt{N_1}}(S_1) = \frac{\sqrt{1}}{\sqrt{2}}(12,000) = \frac{1}{1.414}(12,000) = 8,486 \text{ boots}$$

where

S_1 = total system stock of boots for the N_1 warehouses
S_2 = total system stock of boots for the N_2 warehouses
N_1 = number of warehouses in the original system
N_2 = number of warehouses in the new system

Thompson's new system inventory would be reduced from 12,000 to 8,486 boots, or:

$$\% \text{ reduction} = \frac{(12,000 - 8,486)}{12,000} = 0.293 = 29.3\%$$

---

average inventory levels across the system are decreased. The magnitude of the reduction depends on the demand correlations in the various market areas.

- *Responsiveness*—As warehouse centralization increases, delivery lead times increase, increasing the risk of late deliveries to customers and reducing the ability of the organization to respond quickly to changes in demand. Customer service levels may thus be impacted because of issues such as traffic problems and weather delays.

- *Customer service to the warehouse*—As centralization increases, customer service levels provided by the warehouses' suppliers are likely to increase, reducing the likelihood of stockouts for a given level of average system warehouse inventory.

- *Transportation costs*—As centralization increases, outbound transportation costs increase, as LTL shipments must travel farther to reach customers. Inbound transportation costs decrease, since manufacturers and other suppliers are able to ship larger quantities at TL rates to fewer warehouse locations. The overall impact on transportation costs thus depends on the specific warehouse locations, the goods stored, the locations of suppliers, and the modes of transportation used.

- *Warehouse system capital and operating costs*—As centralization increases, warehouse capital and operating costs decrease because there are fewer warehouses, fewer employees, less equipment, and less maintenance costs.

Warehouse Location

A number of location models and theories have been proposed over the years to optimally locate factories, services, and warehouses. In Chapter 11, a number of location analysis tools are discussed, and these can certainly be useful for locating warehouses. Early in the development of modern transportation and warehousing networks, several well-known economists posited theories regarding warehouse locations that are discussed in this section.

German economist Johann Heinrich von Thünen, who is often regarded as the "father of location theory," argued in the 1820s that transportation costs alone should be minimized when considering facility locations.[56] His model assumed that market prices and manufacturing costs would be identical regardless of the location of the warehouse, so the optimum location would be the one that resulted in the minimum transportation costs. Another German economist a century later, Alfred Weber, proposed an industrial location theory very similar to von Thünen's; he argued that the optimum location would be found when the sum of the inbound and outbound transportation costs was minimized.[57]

In the 1940s, Edgar Hoover recommended three types of location strategies: the market positioned, product positioned, and intermediately positioned strategies.[58] The **market positioned strategy** locates warehouses close to customers to maximize customer service levels. This strategy might be recommended when there are high levels of competition and distribution flexibility. The **product positioned strategy** locates warehouses close to the sources of supply to enable the firm to collect various goods while minimizing inbound transportation costs. This strategy works well when there are large quantities of goods purchased from many sources of supply and assortments of goods ordered by customers. The **intermediately positioned strategy** places warehouses midway between the sources of supply and the customers. This strategy is recommended when distribution service requirements are relatively high and customers order product assortments purchased from many suppliers. In the 1950s, Melvin Greenhut's location theory was based on profit instead of transportation costs.[59] He argued that the optimum location would be the one that maximized profits, which may not coincide with the minimum cost location, because demand and prices can potentially vary based on location. None of the methods described here specifically deal with international site selection and today, this remains a complex problem.

Several location heuristics have been developed based on transportation costs, one of which is the center-of-gravity approach, discussed in Chapter 11. The weakness of this approach, as well as some discussed here, is that they fail to consider a number of other factors such as labor availability, labor rates, land cost, building codes, tax structure, construction costs, utility costs, and the local environment. Additionally, if a firm is using a public warehouse, the location selection criteria would need to include warehouse services, lease costs, communication capabilities, reporting frequency, and the operator's reputation. These factors may best be addressed using a weighted factor location analysis, also discussed in Chapter 11.

Lean Warehousing

As firms develop their supply chain management capabilities, items will be moving more quickly through inbound and outbound warehouses and distribution centers. These warehouses and distribution centers will thus have to develop leaner capabilities. Some examples of these capabilities include the following:

- *Greater emphasis on crossdocking*—Warehouse employees receive shipments, break them down, and mix units of product into outgoing shipments. Far fewer goods will be stored for any appreciable time and average warehouse inventory levels will decrease, while the number of stock-keeping units will increase.

- *Reduced lot sizes and shipping quantities*—Inbound and/or outbound shipping quantities are likely to be smaller and more frequent, containing mixed quantities of goods and thus requiring more handling.

- *A commitment to customers and service quality*—Warehouse employees perform warehouse activities so as to meet the requirements of their inbound and outbound suppliers and customers.
- *Increased automation*—To improve handling speed and reliability, more warehouse activities will become automated, from scanner/barcode computer tracking systems, to warehouse management software applications, to automated storage and retrieval systems.
- *Increased assembly operations*—As more firms implement lean systems and mass customization, warehouses will be called upon to perform final assembly operations to meet specific customer requirements. This will change the skill requirements of warehouse employees, along with equipment requirements.
- *A tendency to be green*—Since lean operations by their nature tend to produce less waste, a natural byproduct of lean warehousing is green warehousing.

Most distribution centers are adopting **lean warehousing** concepts. DHL Supply Chain, part of the Deutsche Post DHL Group, is combining wearable "smartglass" devices with warehouse management software at two U.S. warehouses. The company stated the technology replaced handheld scanners and paper job orders in tests at a Dutch warehouse, reducing the time needed to pick an item and pack it for shipping by 25 percent.[60] Pennsylvania-based manufacturer Crown Holdings changed its layout to eliminate the need to transport items between facilities, saving over 20,000 transportation miles, 27 tons of greenhouse gases, and many hours of labor time annually.[61] Alpha Comm Enterprises uses Netsuite's cloud warehousing application to obtain real-time warehouse and inventory management data as well as sales order information to allow the company to better respond to customers and to improve internal planning. It's vital for Alpha Comm to be able to run lean warehouses given the fast-paced market it serves where products reach obsolescence rapidly. All of Alpha Comm's lean warehousing efforts have paid off handsomely with company revenue dramatically increasing from $5 million to $55 million over a six-year period.[62] In fact, if a warehouse operation today is not implementing lean, it is falling behind its competition.

THE IMPACTS OF LOGISTICS ON SUPPLY CHAIN MANAGEMENT

As mentioned in this chapter's Introduction, logistics refers to the movement and storage of products from point of origin to point of consumption within the firm and throughout the supply chain and is thus responsible for creating time and place utility. In a managed supply chain setting, these logistics elements are extremely important in that products must be routinely delivered to each supply chain customer on time, to the correct location, at the desired level of quality, and at a reasonable cost. As mistakes occur in deliveries along the supply chain, more safety stocks must be held, adversely impacting both customer service levels and costs. To make up for lost time, overnight deliveries might also have to be used, adding yet more costs to the transportation bill.

For global supply chains, the logistics function is even more critical. Providing adequate transportation and storage, getting items through customs, delivering to foreign locations in a timely fashion, and logistics pricing can all impact the ability of a supply chain to serve a foreign market competitively. In many cases, firms are forced to use outside agents or **third-party logistics services** (3PLs) to move items into foreign locations effectively.

Purchases from foreign suppliers are also similarly affected by logistics considerations. When firms begin evaluating and using foreign suppliers, logistics costs and timing become critical factors in the sourcing decision. For instance, Chinese suppliers delivering goods to buyers along the U.S. East Coast are in many cases favoring an all-water route through the Panama Canal, rather than dealing with port and traffic congestion on the U.S. West Coast, followed by trucking and rail transportation within the United States. Buyers get cheaper freight rates and can plan on shipments arriving at a specific time when using an all-water route, whereas the chances of domestic U.S. shipments being held up because of port and traffic congestion and missed rail connections can be significant. All-water shipments have risen significantly since the early 1990s.[63] Because of this, Panama completed a $5 billion widening of the Panama Canal in 2016 to accommodate larger ships, and now Nicaragua is seeking Chinese investment to build a 170-mile, $80 billion canal to compete with the Panama Canal.[64] Containerized cargo numbers are up in every eastern U.S. port. Primarily, the growth has been the result of increased growth in global trade in general and an increase specifically in Asia-Pacific trade.

Thus, the value created for supply chains by logistics can readily be seen. It is what effectively links each supply chain partner. Poor logistics management can literally bring a supply chain to its knees, regardless of the production cost or quality of the products. Alternatively, good logistics management can be one of the elements creating a competitive advantage for supply chains. A number of these topics are explored further in this section.

Third-Party Logistics (3PL) Services

Most logistics companies offer both transportation and warehousing services, allowing firms to make better use of distribution alternatives such as transportation mode, storage location, and customs clearance. Some 3PLs provide complete end-to-end supply chain management services, including network optimization, light manufacturing, and other value-added services. In the United States, two recent trends impacting 3PLs are the near-shoring of manufacturing and the development of oil and gas production in the North Dakota Bakken Formation. Companies with the flexibility to offer logistics services in these areas are taking advantage of the increased service demand. Large 3PLs such as BNSF Logistics have developed significant Mexico–U.S. cross-border capabilities in recent years to deal with the near-shoring trend and are working with producers in North Dakota to offer the logistics services needed there.[65]

For small firms with no internal logistics expertise and large firms with many sizeable and varied logistics needs, outsourcing logistics requirements to 3PLs can help firms get the services they require at reasonable prices. Many firms outsource some or all of their logistics needs to allow more attention to be placed on their core competencies. In tough economic times, firms used 3PLs to help reduce costs while maintaining customer service levels. In 2009, a challenging time for most companies, 80 percent of U.S. companies used a 3PL for at least one area of their supply chains. In Europe, about 66 percent of every logistics euro spent was on outsourcing.[66] Today, use of 3PLs continues to grow, although at a slower rate, and industry consolidation is occurring. Shippers and 3PLs still agree on the benefits of 3PL usage: in a 2016 survey of 3PL usage undertaken by Korn Ferry International, 70 percent of shippers and 85 percent of 3PL services said the use of 3PLs contributed to lower logistics costs. Further, 83 percent of shippers and 94 percent of 3PL services said the use of 3PLs contributed to improved customer service.[67]

Outsourcing End-to-End Supply Chain Management Activities

In some cases, firms may opt to partner with a 3PL for the provision of most or all supply chain management activities. For small firms, it may be due to a lack of expertise. The sheer scale of supply chain activities and cost may also attract very large firms that prefer to free up valuable resources for other activities. For example, Kawasaki Motors Corp. U.S.A. had global motorcycle sales of about $1.8 billion in 2015. The U.S. operation also markets and distributes all-terrain vehicles, jet skis, and side-by-side utility vehicles, all manufactured at its plant in Lincoln, Nebraska. One recent change includes outsourcing all inbound logistics to United Parcel Service. "Instead of focusing so much of our efforts on maintaining logistics and distribution, we now depend on UPS for that, and we can focus on unit delivery from the factory to the dealers and marketing our products in the right way," says Kevin Allen, manager of public relations and brand experience.[68]

3PL Supply Base Reduction

As discussed in Chapter 4 of this text, reducing the supply base can provide a number of advantages for the organization. With 3PL service suppliers, the discussion is very similar—using fewer 3PLs enables the firm to select and use only the best-performing 3PLs as well as to give these 3PLs a bigger share of the firm's logistics needs. This, in turn, results in better levels of service and potentially lower prices. The larger share of business given to each 3PL can be used as leverage when negotiating prices, shipping schedules, and associated services. By the end of 2005, for instance, Hewlett-Packard had halved the number of 3PLs it was using and continued to reduce this number even further. Other companies are similarly seeking to achieve an "irreducible minimum" number of 3PL suppliers. As a matter of fact, a third-party logistics study by Penn State University in 2013 indicated that an average of 58 percent of the users of 3PL services are reducing the number of 3PLs they use or consolidating logistics outsourcing with fewer 3PLs.[69] Thus, 3PL supply base reduction should become an integral part of an effective logistics management strategy particularly in markets characterized by numerous 3PL choices.

Mode and 3PL Selection

To minimize logistics costs while meeting customer service requirements, firms identify the most desirable transportation modes and 3PL services available for the various markets they serve as well as for their inbound purchased materials. Other costs will also be affected by this decision, including inventory-in-transit carrying costs, packaging costs, warehousing costs, and shipment damage costs. Part 2 of this text discussed the topic of evaluating and selecting suppliers, and again, the topic here is very similar. Firms use a mix of quantitative and qualitative factors to evaluate and select 3PLs, and there are a number of comparative methods available to aid in the decision process, the most common of which is again, the weighted factor analysis. In a number of surveys conducted, important selection factors were found to be transit-time reliability, transportation rates, total transit time, willingness to negotiate rates and services, damage-free delivery frequency, financial stability, use of electronic data interchange, and willingness to expedite deliveries.[70]

Creating Strategic Logistics Alliances

Building an effective supply chain very often includes the creation of strategic alliances with providers of logistics services. In fact, in several surveys of various businesses and industries, transportation and warehousing companies were included as supply chain partners in more than 50 percent of the respondents that were actively managing supply chains.[71] In today's intensely competitive business climate, partnering with a 3PL makes even more sense. These partnerships underscore the importance and role played by logistics in supply chain management. A few examples are given here.

Florida-based S-One Holdings, a wholesale distributor, has streamlined its supply chain thanks to a seamless information exchange with its 3PL partner, UPS Global. BMG, an S-One subsidiary, fulfills as many as 5,500 orders a month and handles drop-shipping from manufacturers to 16 UPS warehouses in North America, Europe, and Asia Pacific. BMG and UPS worked together to integrate feeds from UPS' systems directly into NetSuite's cloud, allowing them to power bi-directional data exchange on sales orders, purchase orders, advance ship notices, return authorizations and more, via web services and an FTP server. The seamless integration now allows S-One to be directly integrated with UPS global and supports a $150 million business. Arizona-based Redcat Racing, a distributor of high-end radio-controlled cars, also has close relationship with its 3PL partner. Its biggest expense is shipping and holding inventory. Because it's running a cloud-based ERP and inventory management system, Redcat is able to extend the information to its 3PL partner to better balance inventory. Redcat can see at a glance how many orders they ship same day versus next day or two days; the days of the month that orders start increasing; which types of orders they are; and how to adjust. Ariens also partnered with a 3PL to create a more effective logistics system, and this discussion appears in the nearby SCM Profile.

SCM Profile | Ariens Finds the Right 3PL Partner

On a mission to find a third-party logistics (3PL) provider that could not only manage its transportation needs, but also provide it with state-of-the-art supply chain technology, Wisconsin-based lawnmower and snow blower manufacturer Ariens was looking for a better fit than its previous 3PL provider. A key issue was that Ariens was a small customer working with a very large 3PL.

A majority of Ariens' products are sold through individual dealers, with the remainder being sold through big box stores like Lowe's and Home Depot. In most cases, Ariens uses less-than-truckload (LTL) to ship products to dealers. "LTL'ing product from Wisconsin to all corners of the country and Canada isn't very cost effective," says James Merwin, vice president of supply chain, "so we push our products out in full truckloads to our regional DCs in order to get the goods closer to our end markets."

To make sure Ariens' transportation network is always optimized and efficient, the company partnered with a 3PL, Redwood Logistics, which provides a transportation management system (TMS), full transport capabilities, and a warehouse management system. Most importantly, Redwood was willing to customize, personalize, and adapt its systems to meet Ariens' specific needs. "From day one, they came in and walked us through their middleware, systems development, and ability to mold and shape the platform around our needs," says Merwin, "instead of trying to wedge us into an existing box." Ariens also based its selection on the new 3PL's analytics and reporting capabilities. "They're continually looking at our daily shipping activity, providing recommendations, and analyzing possible solutions," says Merwin.

Ariens is already seeing real results from its choice to switch to a new provider. The manufacturer is on pace to save about 2 percent of its total sales in freight costs compared to a few years ago. "When you take 2 percent in sales out of a business' expense budget, that goes right to the bottom line," says Merwin. "That's a huge savings for us."[72]

Other Transportation Intermediaries

In some cases, companies utilize **transportation intermediaries**, which may not own any significant logistics capital assets, to find the most appropriate transportation mode or 3PL service. For many small companies with limited logistics expertise, and in some cases for large companies, where the scale of logistics needs are great, use of these transportation services can make good economic sense. A few of these intermediaries are discussed next.

Freight Forwarders

Freight forwarders consolidate large numbers of small shipments to fill entire truck trailers or rail cars to achieve truckload or carload transportation rates. They can also provide air transportation consolidation services. These companies pass some of the savings on to the small shippers and then keep the rest as fees. Thus, freight forwarders provide valuable services to both the shipper (lower shipping costs) and the carrier (extra business and higher equipment utilization). Freight forwarders typically specialize in either domestic or global shipments, as well as air or ground shipments. These companies also provide documentation services, special freight handling, and customs clearance.

Lately, the freight forwarding business has been booming as shippers look for ways to further reduce costs. DHL Global Forwarding, for example, one of the highest rated firms in both ocean and air freight forwarding, is also the world's largest 3PL. DHL Global Forwarding also provides warehousing, distribution, and supply chain solutions. It offers shipping, tracking, export/international delivery, import/inbound delivery, domestic/local delivery, road and rail transportation, contract logistics, international mail, and other services. The parent organization, the DHL Group, is one of the largest private employers worldwide, with a presence in more than 220 countries.[73]

Logistics Brokers

Also referred to as **freight brokers** and **transportation brokers**, **logistics brokers** bring shippers and carriers together. The logistics broker is legally authorized to act on either the shipper's or carrier's behalf, and typically these companies are hired because of their knowledge of the many transportation alternatives available or the many shippers needing transportation. Besides helping goods move efficiently, brokers also handle cargo claims, obtain specialized equipment, use dependable carriers, and track deliveries in real time. Unfortunately, bad logistics brokers can expose shippers and carriers to significant liability, risk the double payment of freight charges, reduce on-time delivery rates, and harm reputations. Accordingly, shippers and carriers must carefully screen and select their logistics brokers.

Typical arrangements might find small businesses using a broker to handle many of their shipping needs, or trucking companies using brokers to find a back-haul job after a delivery is completed. A number of logistics broker directories exist, enabling shippers and carriers to find one meeting their needs. ThomasNet.com and FreightQuote.com are just two examples. FreightQuote.com allows shippers to obtain and compare quotes from hundreds of logistics companies.

Shippers' Associations

The American Institute for Shippers' Associations (AISA) defines **shippers' associations** as "nonprofit transportation membership cooperatives which arrange for the domestic or international shipment of members' cargo. Associations will contract for the physical movement of the cargo with motor carriers, railroads, ocean carriers, air carriers, and others. The ability to aggregate cargo and ship the collective membership cargo at favorable volume rates is the key to the existence of the modern day Shippers' Association."[74]

Shippers' associations allow multiple shippers to pool their volumes in order to increase shipment volumes. With a larger shipment volume, the shippers' association may be able to negotiate volume discounts or service contracts with ocean carriers on behalf of its members. These associations also benefit the carriers, in that they help to better utilize their equipment. Because shippers' associations do not identify themselves as 3PLs, brokers, or transportation providers, they are not required to publish or adhere to a number of U.S. transportation regulations and can keep service contracts confidential. Some of the disadvantages of membership include required minimum shipment volumes to receive the benefits of reduced rates. Additionally, some carriers refuse to do business with shippers' associations.

A number of these cooperatives exist for different industries. For example, the Midwest Shippers Association is a cooperative trade association working to advance the high-quality, value-added grain and oilseed industry in the Midwest United States. Its web portal connects food and feed ingredient buyers with suppliers of some of the highest quality grains, soybeans, oilseed, and raw grain ingredients. MSA connects farmer producers with markets, and exporters and importers with experienced shipping and logistics providers. The International Shippers Association members are international shippers and forwarders of commercial, military, and government household goods; unaccompanied baggage; and general commodities. Its mission is to provide its members with the lowest rates and best service for the transport of household goods, accomplished by establishing volume-induced discounts. These discounts are realized through contracts with preferred vendors.[75]

Intermodal Marketing Companies

Intermodal marketing companies (IMCs) are companies that act as intermediaries between intermodal railroad companies and shippers. They typically purchase large blocks of flatcars for piggyback service and then find shippers to fill containers, or motor carriers with truckloads, to load the flatcars. Essentially, these are transportation brokers for the rail industry. They get volume discounts from the railroads and pass some of this on to the shippers. These companies facilitate intermodal shipping and have become an important service to railroads. Shifting 25 percent of truckload freight to the railways by 2025 would result in 2.8 billion fewer hours spent in commuter traffic, 16 billion gallons of fuel saved, and 800,000 fewer tons of air pollution. Rail shipments are about three times more fuel-efficient than trucks—one ton of freight can be moved over 400 miles on a *single gallon* of diesel fuel.[76]

ENVIRONMENTAL SUSTAINABILITY IN LOGISTICS

Today, firms are facing growing pressure to improve environmental performance from customers as well as local, state, and federal governing bodies. Further, an enormous portion of the world's oil reserves are consumed to move goods around the globe (in 2015, the total global cost of logistics exceeded $4 trillion, with $1.4 trillion in the United States).[77] Today, company managers understand the negative impacts of transportation on carbon footprints, total costs, and overall oil consumption, and are doing something about it. Shifting motor carrier freight to railroads, as described above, is one strategy that reduces carbon emissions. Governments are also taking note of voter sentiment and beginning to enact more stringent environmental protection laws regarding transportation. Some examples are provided here.

In logistics, one of the big energy wastes comes from trucks returning from their deliveries empty (referred to as **empty miles**). To deal with this problem, some companies are turning to **horizontal collaboration**—the process of two or more companies cooperating at the same level on a certain market activity to realize benefits they could not achieve independently. While horizontal collaboration (HC) can encompass a number of supply chain processes, freight transportation is one activity that offers vast potential for a profitable partnership. Minnesota-based food company Land O' Lakes used to move a number of empty trucks along the eastern seaboard. Working with Nistevo.com, an online logistics matchmaker, it was able to partner with General Mills on one specific route. General Mills was sending its products from point A to point B on a similar schedule as Land O' Lakes was sending its products from point B to point A. Both were moving empty trucks back to their origination points. The two companies were able to synchronize loads and reduce empty miles. Through partnerships like this one, Land O' Lakes was able to save over $2 million a year.[78]

A number of nonprofit organizations have been formed to help logistics companies with their sustainability efforts. Freight activity since 1990 has grown by over 50 percent and is projected to nearly double again by 2040, producing more greenhouse gases and air pollution. Experts project that by 2050, global freight transport CO_2 emissions will surpass emissions from passenger vehicles. In the United States, the Environmental Protection Agency launched SmartWay in 2004, a certification program that reduces transportation emissions and improves supply chain efficiency. SmartWay helps companies improve supply chain sustainability by measuring, benchmarking, and improving freight transportation efficiency. The SmartWay website allows users to locate alternative fuel station locations, identify greener vehicles to purchase, and select certified SmartWay transportation companies. It also guides other countries seeking to develop freight sustainability programs.[79] The Coalition for Responsible Transportation (CRT), which began in 2007, includes importers, exporters, trucking companies, clean truck manufacturers, and ocean carriers. Through its Clean Truck Initiative, members of CRT work in partnership with U.S. ports to implement clean truck programs that are both environmentally and economically sustainable. CRT members invest millions of dollars in new clean equipment in partnership with federal and state governments, and local ports around the country. By partnering together, ports and their customers can improve the environmental quality of port communities.[80]

Europe's 3PLs and ports have been leading the way toward sustainability by introducing a number of green management initiatives. Damco, the logistics arm of Denmark's AP Moller-Maersk Group, launched a carbon footprint tracker in 2009 called the Supply Chain Carbon Dashboard that allows users to track their supply chain carbon footprint. "It immediately allows you to identify carbon hotspots in your supply chain," says Erling Nielsen, head of Maersk's supply chain development team. German logistics company DB Schenker's EcoTransIT World application allows customers to compare the energy consumption, CO_2 and pollutant emissions of all modes of transportation available, given the origination, destination, shipment volume, and freight being transported. Shippers can then select the best route and obtain all the emissions and energy data. Finally, EcoPorts, managed by the European Sea Ports Organization, is a nonprofit association with a current membership of ninety-two European ports and acts as a network platform to create effective collaborations addressing sustainability issues in European ports and supply chains. The "Eco-Port" status is obtained by any European port upon completion of a self-diagnosis method (SDM) checklist. Additional credit is provided to ports that are certified with PERS, the only port-sector-specific environmental management standard, and ISO 14001.[81]

LOGISTICS MANAGEMENT SOFTWARE APPLICATIONS

As mentioned briefly in Chapter 6, logistics management software applications can be added to ERP software suites of applications, as the firm's needs and the users' level of experience dictates. Some of the more popular logistics management applications (aside from the more specific environmental applications discussed above) include **transportation management systems**, **warehouse management systems**, and **global trade management**

systems. Companies typically find significant benefits with these logistics execution systems. Many shippers have been opting to use fee-based Internet logistics management portals instead of outright purchases of logistics software to further manage cost outlays. Still, the use of some form of logistics software remains significant. According to an industry survey conducted in 2015, about 60 percent of respondents were using a warehouse management system, and approximately half planned to buy new WMS software.[82] Some of these systems are briefly discussed next.

Transportation Management Systems

Transportation costs are a significant portion of total logistics costs for many organizations. To help reduce these costs while optimizing service levels, transportation management system (TMS) applications allow firms to find carriers, select the best mix of transportation services and pricing to determine the best use of containers or truck trailers, better manage transportation contracts, rank transportation options, clear customs, track fuel usage and product movements, and track carrier performance. Additionally, regulatory bodies, shippers, and customers want to know the locations of goods in-transit; thus, real-time information about a shipment's location while it is being transported to a final destination is required. Consequently, information may need to be provided by the manufacturer, 3PLs, agents, freight forwarders, and others as products move through global supply chains. Technologies employed to provide this visibility include barcode scanners, RFID tags, the Internet, and GPS devices. Assisting in the management of all this transportation-related information is the job of a TMS.

A great example of how a TMS is used is the Missouri-based manufacturer American Railcar Industries. It was having difficulty tracking its inbound shipments from suppliers. "We had visibility when the product was ready at suppliers, but then it went into a black hole once it left our vendors' docks until it arrived at our location," says American Railcar purchasing agent Brent Roever. So in 2009, it incorporated a Web-based TMS solution into its purchasing and logistics processes. Afterward, all of its purchase orders flowed from its ERP system into the TMS, where a preselected list of suppliers could view the orders. Suppliers responded to the orders and indicated how and when the order would be shipped. The system then notified the purchasing team at American Railcar when the shipment was picked up and when it was expected at the specified location based on established delivery times.[83]

The desire to secure national borders against unwanted shipments is causing a number of governments to more closely regulate the flow of goods across their countries' borders. This has potentially added transportation delay problems to shipments as companies deal with an added layer of bureaucracy and reporting at various border entry sites. To help mitigate delay problems, many TMS software applications now have capabilities for customs declaration; calculation and payment of tariffs, duties, and duty drawbacks; and advanced filing of shipment manifests.

Warehouse Management Systems

Many firms are purchasing ERP systems that include a TMS coupled with a warehouse management system (WMS) to further enhance their supply chain management effectiveness. For example, a company might use its TMS to forecast shipping volumes based on data provided by its WMS and then recommend the most efficient modes of shipping. The WMS could then pick items and schedule warehouse usage based on TMS shipping information. Warehouse management systems track and control the flow of goods from the receiving dock of a warehouse or distribution center until the item is loaded for outbound shipment to the customer. RFID tags placed on products and pallets within the distribution center are used to control the flow of goods. The goals of a WMS include reducing distribution center labor costs, streamlining the flow of goods, reducing the time products spend in the distribution center, managing distribution center capacity, reducing paperwork, and managing the crossdocking process. A WMS can improve warehouse productivity by repositioning products to reduce the distance that products and pickers must travel. Reducing these travel times can improve warehouse productivity by 10 to 20 percent.

Cold food distributor NFT recently was awarded a contract by Yoplait UK, an affiliate of General Mills UK. NFT will manage Yoplait's entire UK cold supply chain, including distribution of up about 500,000 cases per week. NFT's temperature-controlled site at the port of Tilbury in Essex is the largest chilled and fresh warehouse facility in Europe. With Yoplait products coming into the United Kingdom from France, it was essential to provide a strategic inbound location. The NFT facility is equipped with the Red Prairie warehouse management system, which provides web-enabled traceability for Yoplait's range of products.[85]

Use of TMSs and WMSs has also increased the use of RFID tags and technologies. As seen in the nearby SCM Profile, RFID systems in a distribution center can reduce labor intensity as well as improve order and inventory accuracy.

SCM Profile — Kimble Chase Manages Orders with RFID

Tennessee-based Kimble Chase Life Science, a manufacturer and distributor of glassware for pharmaceutical testing, is a good example of effective use of radio frequency identification (RFID) in a warehouse management system (WMS). The company uses an RFID system called iTRAK to manage the movement of goods and shipments in its Rockwood, TN manufacturing plant and distribution center.

Before implementing iTRAK, Kimble Chase used paper-based processes in the warehouse with order data coming from an enterprise resource planning (ERP) system. It was taking up to two days to get finished goods into the warehouse so they could be allocated and picked for customer orders. While the old process was supported by bar code scanning to verify outbound shipments, it was a tedious, labor-intensive process.

Now, cases now have a passive RFID tag affixed to them in the plant, making the receipt of finished goods into the warehouse an almost instant process as finished goods pass through a RFID reader station. In the shipping area, pallets that have been picked and are ready to ship are moved to a reader station, where all the case-level data is automatically captured and cross-referenced against the order data in iTRAK.

Products are shipped in cases and smaller "inner packs," which also need to be tracked. Some orders might have hundreds of cases and inner packs on each pallet. The previous method of verifying outbound orders was to hand scan and repack each case and inner pack on outbound pallets, which made the process both time consuming and error prone. With RFID, the picked pallet is simply moved to an RFID reader, where data is captured for the cases and inner packs within seconds, cross referencing it against the order data in iTRAK. As a result, the RFID-enabled WMS has dramatically improved labor efficiency and the accuracy of both outbound orders and finished goods in the warehouse.[84]

Global Trade Management Systems

As the desire to better manage complex global supply chains becomes more common, the need to comply with foreign and domestic security regulations also increases. This, combined with the continued search for cheaper supplies and reduced logistics expenditures, has brought about the need for global trade management (GTM) systems. Additionally, in 2017, when U.S. President Trump pulled the United States out of the Trans-Pacific Partnership (TPP) and stated a desire to renegotiate the North American Free Trade Agreement (NAFTA), it created more confusion among global trading partners. This has pushed more companies to explore and adopt GTM software. "Right now, there's a lot of confusion over how the U.S. presidential election will make an impact on trade agreements," says Will McNeill, principal research analyst with Gartner. For GTM software vendors, this has presented new opportunities to grow, expand, add capabilities, and help shippers manage their regional and global trade agreements. "GTM can be a good risk mediator," says McNeill. "You can use the intelligence built into the systems to really figure out what the global opportunities are. This is a chance for the software market to take advantage of this uncertainty."[86]

For many firms, the U.S. Customs and Border Protection (CBP) security filing requirement (shippers and carriers must submit cargo information to the CBP 24 hours prior to ocean freight being loaded onto a vessel bound for the United States) has added to the import documentation headaches. Illinois-based fastener importer, XL Screw Corp., with 100 to 300 import filings per month, decided it needed an in-house GTM system. The system proved to be a simple answer to CBP requirements. The biggest benefit for XL Screw is the ability to enter data for a specific shipment, store it in the system, and then use it to complete forms for other shipments.[87]

GLOBAL LOGISTICS

For global goods movements, logistics managers must be aware of a number of issues not impacting domestic movements such as regulatory requirements, import/export limitations, port and warehousing issues, and the modes of transportation available. In the United States, freight movement to Europe or Asia involves either air or water transportation and then most likely motor and/or rail transportation to the final destination. Between most contiguous countries, rail and motor carrier shipments tend to be the most common modes of transportation. There are also many logistics problems and infrastructure differences found as goods are moved from one country to another. In Europe, rail transportation tends to be much more prevalent and reliable than rail transportation in the United States because European track, facilities, and equipment are newer and better maintained. Water carriers may be the dominant mode of transportation in countries with a great deal of coastline and developed inland waterways. In under- and undeveloped countries, ports may be very poorly maintained and equipped and a paved highway system may be almost nonexistent. A number of these and other global logistics topics are discussed next.

Global Freight Security

While a number of logistics security topics have already been discussed, one issue needing further discussion is motor freight security at U.S. border crossings. In the past few years, the trucking industry has worked with U.S. Customs and Border Protection to develop the **Customs-Trade Partnership against Terrorism program (C-TPAT)** and its security program called the **Free and Secure Trade program (FAST)**. C-TPAT is a voluntary supply chain security program focused on improving the security of private companies' supply chains (international trucking in particular) with respect to terrorism. To participate in FAST, motor carriers must become C-TPAT certified, and their commercial drivers must complete an application and undergo a background check. FAST enrollment is open to truck drivers from the United States, Canada, and Mexico. The majority of dedicated FAST lanes are located in northern border ports in Michigan, New York, and Washington and at southern border ports from California to Texas. Participation in FAST requires that every link in the supply chain, from manufacturer to carrier to driver to importer, is C-TPAT certified. All FAST participants receive expedited cargo clearance and access to dedicated FAST lanes at border crossings. Today, over 11,000 companies worldwide have become C-TPAT certified, including U.S. importers/exporters, U.S./Canada highway carriers, U.S./Mexico highway carriers, rail and sea carriers, licensed U.S. customs brokers, U.S. marine port authority/terminal operators, U.S. freight consolidators, ocean transportation intermediaries and non-operating common carriers, Mexican and Canadian manufacturers, and Mexican long-haul carriers.[88]

Global Logistics Intermediaries

Global logistics intermediaries provide global shipping, consolidation, and import/export services for firms and offer expertise that can prove very useful for most organizations involved in global commerce. A number of these intermediaries that have not already been discussed are briefly discussed here.

Customs Brokers

Customs brokers move global shipments through customs for companies as well as handle the necessary documentation required to accompany the shipments. These specialists are often used by companies requiring expertise in exporting goods to foreign countries. Their knowledge of the many import requirements of various countries can significantly reduce the time required to move goods internationally and clear them through customs.

International or Foreign Freight Forwarders

These services move goods for companies from domestic production facilities to foreign destinations (or vice versa) using surface and air transportation and warehousing. They consolidate small shipments into larger TL or CL shipments, decide what transportation modes and methods to use, handle all of the documentation requirements, and then disperse the shipments at their destination. They also determine the best routing to use; oversee storage, breakbulk, and repackaging requirements; and provide for any other logistics requirements of the seller. Use of **foreign freight forwarders** can reduce logistics costs, increase customer service, and allow shippers to focus resources on other activities. Many companies exporting or importing goods use the services of foreign freight forwarders because of their expertise and presence in foreign markets.

Until recently, many shippers were importing and shipping high-quality, low-cost goods from "far-shore" operations (e.g., U.S. buyers purchasing goods from Chinese manufacturers). Today, some buyers are utilizing a strategy called **right-shoring**. Right-shoring combines near-shore, far-shore, and domestic opportunities into a single, flexible, and cost-driven approach to purchasing and logistics. As crude oil prices fluctuate, for example, buyers find they must be much more flexible regarding where crude oil is purchased. This has created an even greater need for globally connected freight forwarders.[89]

Trading Companies

Trading companies put buyers and sellers from different countries together and handle all of the export/import arrangements, documentation, and transportation for both goods and services. Most trading companies are involved in exporting and they usually take title to the goods until sold to foreign buyers. They enjoy economies of scale when exporting goods as they ship large quantities of consolidated shipments, using established transportation and warehousing services. In the United States, the Export Trading Company Act was signed into law in 1982 to promote U.S. exports and to help U.S. exporters improve their competitiveness. Within the U.S. Department of Commerce, the Export Trading Company Affairs (ETCA) office helps promote the development of joint ventures between U.S. and foreign companies and the use of export trade intermediaries. The ETCA office was created by the Export Trading Company Act of 1982.[90]

Non-Vessel Operating Common Carriers

Also referred to as NVOCCs or simply NVOs, **non-vessel operating common carriers** operate very similar to foreign freight forwarders but normally use only scheduled ocean liners. They consolidate small international shipments from a number of shippers into full container loads and then handle all of the documentation and transportation arrangements from the shippers' dock area. NVOCCs assume responsibility for cargo from point of origin to final destination; however, they do not own any vessels. They enter into contracts with ocean liners, which may then subcontract with rail or motor carriers for land travel.

Foreign-Trade Zones

Foreign-trade zones (FTZs) are secure sites within the United States under the supervision of the U.S. Customs and Border Protection. These sites are authorized by the Foreign-Trade Zones Board, chaired by the U.S. Secretary of Commerce, and are comparable to *free trade zones* that exist in many other countries today. FTZs, while located near ports or international airports in the United States, are considered to be outside U.S. Customs territory, where foreign or domestic merchandise can enter without formal customs entry or payment of duties or excise taxes. Companies operating in FTZs bring goods and materials into the designated U.S. site and might use storage, assembly, testing, packaging, repairing, and export services. No retail activities are allowed, however. If the final product is exported out of the United States, no domestic duties or excise taxes are levied. If the final product is imported into the United States from the FTZ, duties and taxes are paid at the time the goods leave the FTZ.

Congress established the Foreign-Trade Zones Board in 1934 to encourage U.S. firms to participate in global trade. As of 2017, there were over 250 general purpose FTZs in the United States located in all fifty states, bringing in about 12 percent of all imported goods (75 percent of which was crude oil). The FTZs are used by about 3,200 companies and directly support over 420,000 U.S. workers with more than $650 billion in merchandise moving through these areas each year. In addition to petroleum, pharmaceutical, automotive, and electronics companies are the largest users of U.S. FTZs.[91]

The North American Free Trade Agreement

The **North American Free Trade Agreement** (NAFTA), a trading accord between the United States and its two largest trading partners, Canada and Mexico, was initially agreed upon in December 1992, with the U.S. Congress passing it in November 1993, and put into effect on January 1, 1994. By 2008, all duties and quantitative restrictions within the three countries were removed. The objectives of NAFTA are to facilitate cross-border trade among the three countries, increase investment opportunities, and promote fair trade. Today, U.S. exports to Canada and Mexico support more than 3 million American jobs and 140,000 U.S. businesses. Canada and Mexico buy more Made-in-America goods and services than any other countries in the world. Regional trade has increased sharply over NAFTA's first two decades, from roughly $290 billion in 1993 to more than $1.1 trillion in 2016. Cross-border investment has also surged, with U.S. foreign direct investment in Mexico increasing from $15 billion to more than $100 billion. Due to the success of NAFTA, the United States today has free trade agreements with 20 countries.

NAFTA has not been without its detractors. Critics of the deal argue that it is to blame for job losses and wage stagnation in the United States, driven by low-wage competition, companies moving production to Mexico to lower costs, and a widening trade deficit. The U.S.-Mexico trade balance swung from a $1.7 billion U.S. surplus in 1993 to a $54 billion deficit by 2014. Economists like the Center for Economic and Policy Research's Dean Baker argue that this surge of imports caused the loss of up to 600,000 U.S. jobs over two decades, though he admits that some of this import growth would likely have happened even without NAFTA. U.S. environmental groups have been concerned that pollution and food safety laws have become more difficult to enforce. Others argue that because of subsidized agricultural exports to Mexico, the small Mexican farmer is being run out of business. Some in the United States saw NAFTA as a way to grow the Mexican economy and curb illegal immigration into the United States. However, migration into the United States, both legal and illegal, has increased since NAFTA began, mainly due to the Mexican peso crisis, enduring poverty in southern Mexico, and the most recent global economic recession. In response to these and other concerns, supplementary agreements continue to be added to NAFTA.[92]

REVERSE LOGISTICS

Reverse logistics (sometimes also known as **returns management**) refers to the backward flow of goods *from* customers in the supply chain occurring when goods are returned, either by the end-product consumer or by a business customer within the supply chain. In other words, reverse logistics refers to the movement, storage, and processing of returned goods. Returns are increasing in part, today because of the growth of online shopping, direct-to-store shipments, and direct-to-home shipments. Occasionally, the use of cheap and untested foreign suppliers causes a number of product recalls. On August 1, 2007, for example, California-based Mattel, the world's biggest toymaker, recalled almost 1 million Chinese-made toys because they were covered with paint containing high levels of lead. Mattel's primary Chinese supplier had subcontracted the work to a small Chinese toy manufacturer. The very next week, Mattel again was forced to announce a large recall for Chinese-manufactured toys containing small magnets that posed a choking hazard. In fact, eight of Mattel's nine toy recalls from 2004 to 2007 were for Chinese-made products.[93]

Traditional retail customer returns can account for 6 to 10 percent of sales, while returns to retail websites are 20 to 30 percent of sales. According to the Reverse Logistics

Association, the sheer volume of returns in the United States alone is $150 to $200 billion per year *at cost*. Additionally, the logistical costs to process these returns can also be very high—now running approximately $100 billion each year in the United States for transportation, handling, refurbishment, repackaging, remarketing, disposal, and lost sales. Besides the significant impact on costs, returns also can have a direct negative impact on the environment, customer service, the firm's reputation, and profitability if not managed properly. "Reverse logistics is all about damage control and making the process as customer-friendly as possible," says Lou Cerny, vice president of Sedlak Management Consultants. "You've already disappointed the customer once, now you have to close the loop as soon as possible."[94]

Some companies view returns as *zombie inventory* (inventory that just won't die). It sits unsold in storerooms, takes up space on store shelves, or creates bottlenecks in distribution centers, as workers try to determine what should be recycled, repaired, or discarded. However, other companies take a hidden-profit view of returns. "Reverse logistics enables the extension of the life of a product, so that its return is not a 100 percent loss," says Jim Gerard, a segment manager at UPS. "It's a process of receiving goods back for the purpose of preparing them for resale or to recapture the valuable part of the unit for reuse or resale in an entirely different area of the after-market," he adds.[95]

Many firms hire a 3PL company specializing in reverse logistics to ensure these items are managed correctly. Processing more than 600 million returned items annually, Pennsylvania-based Genco, for example, a division of FedEx, provides triage, test and repair, remarketing, and product liquidation solutions for companies. With $1.6 billion in annual revenue and more than 11,000 employees in over 130 operations, Genco offers various product lifecycle or reverse logistics services to companies in the technology, consumer, industrial, retail, and healthcare markets.[96]

The Impact of Reverse Logistics on the Supply Chain

Returns can represent significant challenges to a supply chain. In many cases, reverse logistics is viewed as an unwanted activity of supply chain management. In these cases, reverse logistics is seen simply as a cost of doing business or a regulatory compliance issue. Problems include the inability of information systems to handle returns or monitor reverse product flow, lack of worker training in reverse logistics procedures, little or no identification on returned packages, the need for adequate inspection and testing of returns, and the placing of potentially damaged returned products into sales stocks. A poor reverse logistics system can affect the entire supply chain financially and can have a large impact on how a consumer views a product brand, potentially impacting future sales. Some recent studies indicate the real costs of returns take up roughly 3 to 5 percent of total revenue. "Surprisingly, for the traditional bricks-and-mortar retail operations, returns are three to four times more expensive than forward-outbound-shipments. In some industries such as book publishing, catalog retailing, and greeting cards, over 20 percent of all products sold are eventually returned to the vendor," says Adam Robinson, who oversees the marketing strategy for Cerasis, a third-party logistics provider.[97]

From a marketing perspective, an effective returns process can create goodwill and enhance customers' perceptions of product quality and purchase risk. From a quality perspective, product failure and returns information can be used by quality personnel in root cause analyses and by design personnel to reduce future design errors (the number one reason for a product return is a defective or damaged item). From a logistics perspective, returned products can still create value as original products, refurbished products, or repair parts. This also tends to reduce disposal costs. Thus, while 46 percent of companies report losing money on product returns, about 8 percent actually report making money. Online shoe merchant Zappos has a very high return rate (about 35 percent) but views this as a competitive advantage—they provide free returns with no questions asked, but also boast very high repurchase rates.[98]

Reverse Logistics and the Environment

Reverse logistics can have a positive impact on the environment through activities such as recycling, reusing materials and products, or refurbishing used products. **Green reverse logistics programs** include reducing the environmental impact of certain modes of transportation used for returns, reducing the amount of disposed packaging and product materials by redesigning products and processes, and making use of reusable totes and pallets. "Sustainability is playing an important role in reverse logistics," says Paul Vassallo, marketing director for UPS. "More and more companies are looking to reduce their impact on the environment and search for carbon-neutral ways to dispose of product."[99]

SUMMARY

This chapter has discussed the important role logistics plays in general and to supply chains in particular. Though this is a very broad topic, we have attempted to review the elements within U.S. domestic and global logistics to give the reader an adequate understanding of the entire field of logistics and its relationship to supply chain management. These elements include the basics of transportation, third-party transportation providers, warehousing, sustainability in logistics, global logistics, and reverse logistics. It is hoped that readers have gained an understanding of the many elements within the broad topic of logistics and why these are so important to the successful management of supply chains.

KEY TERMS

air carriers, 339

airline security, 344

centralized warehousing system, 352

Civil Aeronautics Act of 1938, 347

class rates, 343

coal slurry, 341

cold chains, 352

commodity rates, 343

common carriers, 335

consolidation warehouses, 350

container-on-flatcar (COFC), 342

contract carriers, 335

cost-of-service pricing, 342

crossdocking, 350

customs brokers, 366

Customs-Trade Partnership against Terrorism program (C-TPAT), 365

decentralized warehousing system, 352

deep-sea transportation, 340

Department of Transportation Act, 347

distribution center, 350

empty miles, 361

exception rates, 343

exempt carriers, 335

Federal Aviation Act of 1958, 347

FOB destination pricing, 343

FOB origin pricing, 343

foreign freight forwarders, 366

foreign-trade zones, 367

Free and Secure Trade program (FAST), 365

freight brokers, 360

general freight carriers, 337

global trade management systems, 362

Green reverse logistics programs, 370

high-speed trains, 338

horizontal collaboration, 361

ICC Termination Act of 1995, 349

intermediately positioned strategy, 355

intermodal marketing companies, 361

intermodal transportation, 341

lean warehousing, 356

less-than-truckload (LTL) carriers, 336

line haul rates, 343

logistics, 333

logistics brokers, 360

market positioned strategy, 355

miscellaneous rates, 343

Motor Carrier Act of 1935, 346

motor carriers, 336

negotiated pricing, 342

non-vessel operating common carriers, 367

North American Free Trade Agreement, 368

Ocean Shipping Reform Act of 1998, 349

piggyback service, 342

pipeline carriers, 340

place utility, 333

private carrier, 336

private warehouses, 350

product positioned strategy, 355

public warehouses, 351

rail carriers, 337

Railroad Revitalization and Regulatory Reform Act, 348

Railway Passenger Service Act, 347

real-time location systems, 337

Reed-Bulwinkle Act, 347

returns management, 368

reverse logistics, 368

right-shoring, 366

risk pooling, 353

road trains, 337

ROROs, 342

shippers' associations, 360

Shipping Act of 1984, 349

specialized carriers, 337

square root rule, 353

Staggers Rail Act of 1980, 349

third-party logistics services, 356

time utility, 333

trading companies, 367

trailer-on-flatcar (TOFC), 342

trailer-on-flatcar service, 337

Transportation Act of 1920, 345

Transportation Act of 1940, 347

Transportation Act of 1958, 347

transportation brokers, 360

transportation deregulation, 345

transportation intermediaries, 360

transportation management systems, 362

transportation regulation, 345

transportation security, 344

Transportation Worker Identification Credential (TWIC), 344

truckload (TL) carriers, 336

value-of-service pricing, 342

warehouse management systems, 362

water carrier, 340

DISCUSSION QUESTIONS

1. What is logistics and how does it provide time and place utility?

2. Why are logistics issues important to business success?

3. What are the important activities or elements in logistics?

4. What is the objective of transportation, for a business?

5. Why do you think that for-hire logistics expenditures have quadrupled over the past thirty years in the United States?

6. List the legal forms and modes of transportation. Which mode is the least expensive? Which mode carries the most freight? Which mode is growing the fastest? Shrinking the fastest?

7. What are some intermodal transportation alternatives?

8. What is the difference between TL and LTL shipments? Why are LTL shipping fees higher per cwt than TL shipping fees?

9. What is a road train? If you had to classify them, would you say they are general freight carriers or specialized carriers?

10. Why do you think the fastest trains are found outside the United States? Where is the fastest train operating today?

11. When would you want to use value-of-service pricing instead of cost-of-service pricing? When would you want to use negotiated pricing?

12. What is FOB destination pricing and when would you want to use it?

13. What does transportation security refer to and which mode of transportation is most affected by security concerns?

14. What is PrePass and what are its advantages?

15. Is government regulation of transportation good or bad? Why?

16. Is transportation in the United States regulated today or deregulated? Why?

17. Describe three different types of warehouses and the advantages of each.

18. If storing goods in a warehouse is bad, since it increases inventory carrying costs, why are the number and size of warehouses increasing in the United States?

19. What is the difference between a distribution center and a warehouse?

20. What are cold chains and what type of warehouse is used for these?

21. Define risk pooling and the advantages and disadvantages of centralized warehousing. What assumption does risk pooling make?

22. For which situation (centralization or decentralization) does risk pooling result in less safety stock? Why?

23. What type of warehouse location strategy do you think Amazon uses? Why?

24. What is a lean warehouse? When are they used?

25. Why is logistics so important for successful supply chain management?

26. What are 3PLs and why are they used? What types of companies use them? Why is their use growing so rapidly?

27. Can 3PLs be effective supply chain partners? Why?

28. Are transportation intermediaries also a form of 3PL? Explain.

29. Describe several kinds of transportation intermediary.

30. What are the impacts of logistics on environmental sustainability? How can these impacts be minimized?

31. What are empty miles and how can carriers reduce them?

32. What are the most common logistics management software applications and why are they beneficial to users?

33. Could you have a TMS without an ERP system? Or without a WMS?

34. Describe what C-TPAT and FAST are. Which transportation modes use these?

35. What do you think the most pressing global logistics problem is today? Why?

36. Describe several global logistics intermediaries. Could they also be considered 3PLs?

37. What are foreign-trade zones? How are they different from free-trade zones? What benefits do they provide?

38. How has NAFTA affected trade among the United States, Canada, and Mexico? Is NAFTA good for domestic U.S., Mexican, and Canadian producers?

39. What is reverse logistics? How does it impact supply chain management?

40. How can reverse logistics have a positive impact on the environment? On profits? On customer service? On repeat purchases?

ESSAY/PROJECT QUESTIONS

1. Go to the BNSF website (www.bnsf.com) and describe the types of intermodal services offered.

2. Search on the term "green logistics" or "sustainable logistics" and write a report on logistics strategies used to reduce carbon emissions.

3. Write a report on Amazon's warehousing system in the United States.

4. Write a report on the global deregulation of the airline industry.

5. Search on the term "port security software" and describe how these software applications help to assure port security and global cargo security.

PROBLEMS

1. A current warehouse system has six warehouses with 3,000 units at each warehouse. If the company desires to change the number of warehouses to become more centralized and keep the same customer service level, determine the average warehouse inventory levels, using the number of warehouses below and the square root rule.

    a. Three warehouses

    b. One warehouse

    c. What is the percentage reduction in system inventory for the two systems above, compared to the original system?

2. A current warehouse system has six warehouses with 3,000 units at each warehouse. If the company desires to change the number of warehouses to become more decentralized and keep the same customer service level, determine the average warehouse inventory levels, using the number of warehouses below and the square root rule.

    a. Nine warehouses

    b. Twelve warehouses

    c. What is the percentage increase in system inventory for the two systems above, compared to the original system?

CASES

1. Whipple Logistics Company's Transportation Challenge*

Ruby Shelton is part of the executive development training program. As part of her executive development plan, Ruby has temporarily been assigned to the transportation division of Whipple Logistics Company. The objective is to expose her to different parts of the company as a method of grooming her for a senior position someday.

Ruby is excited about the opportunity. Her background is in operations management, therefore, she is familiar with transportation requirements, although not an expert. Doreen Delgado is Ruby's mentor in the program. Doreen is a senior vice president and participated in the program when she was a junior executive. She understands the value of such a learning experience.

Whipple Logistics Company has several new clients who want a briefing on the best mode of transportation for their businesses. Doreen assigned Ruby to this project. Doreen believes this is the perfect instrument to help Ruby develop a deep appreciation of the importance of selecting the best mode of transportation for specific products. Ruby is to prepare the briefing for the new clients.

Ruby understands that this is a great opportunity to learn more about Whipple's clients' needs. Her research illustrates that the best mode of transportation often depends on the industry using it. Industries that deal in bulk products such as corn, soybeans,

---

*Written by Rick Bonsall, D. Mgt., McKendree University, Lebanon, IL. The people and institution are fictional and any resemblance to any person or any institution is coincidental. This case was prepared solely to provide material for class discussion. The author does not intend to illustrate either effective or ineffective handling of a managerial situation.

wheat, cement, crude oil, and coal must decide which mode of transportation is best. That decision is often based on the distance over which the shipment must be moved. Trucks have a cost advantage for short distances up to 500 miles; consequently, they function primarily as the short haul option. As the distance increases, rail has a cost advantage over trucks; however, barges have the greatest cost advantage if a waterway connects the point of origin and the destination.

Although Whipple Logistics Company provides shipping services to all industries, the new clients were primarily shipping large bulk items. For bulk shipments barges are the least expensive mode of transportation. However, waterways do not go everywhere; consequently, the critical factors are the shipment origin and its proximity to navigable waterways.

Ruby began to investigate what besides cost could be a driving factor. She discovered that seldom were single barges alone used to haul cargo. Generally, barges are cabled together in what is called a 15-barge tow, giving it a capacity of 22,500 tons.[†] Ruby wondered how this compared to the capacity of rail and trucks. She knew that rail cars are also connected together to increase capacity. The standard is a 100-car train whose hauling capacity is 11,200 tons;[†] thus, it takes two 100-car trains to match a 15-barge tow. A third option is semitrucks or "18-wheelers." A single semitruck can haul 26 tons.[†] Unfortunately, the drawback of semitrucks is they are a single shipping system, unlike barges or rail cars that are combined to create a larger shipping system. Approximately 870 semitrucks[†] would be required to equal the cargo capacity of either a 15-barge tow or two 100-car trains.

Ruby decided that barges are the best bulk transportation option, if the origin and destination can be accessed by water. She appreciated that it was more complex that just cost though. One needs to factor in possible delays due to weather and the hauling capacity of a specific mode of transportation.

Discussion Questions

1. How should Ruby approach this briefing? Should she explain each type or should she discuss only the concept of intermodal transportation? Explain your recommendation; why do you think one approach is better than another, that is, what is the benefit to those being briefed?

2. In your opinion, which mode of transportation has the most potential for problems? Explain why you say that.

3. Identify the mode of transportation that is the most flexible and the one that is the least flexible. Explain why you consider them as the most and least flexible.

[†]Iowa Department of Transportation (2014). http://www.envisionfreight.com/value/?id=illustration

©2019 Cengage Learning

2. Treadwell Distribution Centers*

Treadwell Distribution Centers is a full service fulfillment company. Its clients contract with Treadwell to warehouse and distribute their goods. Treadwell also processes any returned items for its clients. Recently, the challenges associated with reverse logistics are growing.

*Written by Rick Bonsall, D. Mgt., McKendree University, Lebanon, IL. The people and institution are fictional and any resemblance to any person or any institution is coincidental. This case was prepared solely to provide material for class discussion. The author does not intend to illustrate either effective or ineffective handling of a managerial situation.

The volume of returns has grown significantly. In order to enhance their competitive advantage, Treadwell's clients are offering a free return policy. There is no charge for shipping items back to the warehouse. The companies provide their customers with a prepaid shipping label. In addition, there is no restocking fee. This policy, used by most of Treadwell's clients, has driven this increase in returned items.

Up to this point, Treadwell had a computerized-based management system, but not one that was specifically designed for warehouse management. Its system was sort of home grown and its capability was expanded as the business expanded. However, with the reverse logistics issues, the system is no longer viable.

In addition, government regulations and pressure from local environmental groups are creating another issue for Treadwell Distribution Centers—environmental sustainability. The environmental sustainability issue has two components that are contributing to the sustainability concerns—transportation and reverse logistics. From a transportation perspective Treadwell's trucks are racking up an increasing number of empty miles. More often than not, the trucks are returning empty.

Reverse logistics is another matter. Treadwell is getting pressure from its clients to collect data on the returns. In the past all Treadwell did was accept the return, follow a predetermined process to see if the return was salvageable and either dispose of it or send it back to the original manufacturer. However, the data the clients want are much more detailed, for example, can it be repaired or refurbished? Since Treadwell's competitors are offering enhanced data collection, so must Treadwell.

Discussion Questions

1. What is your recommendation to Treadwell concerning their issues of sustainability and reverse logistics? What actions can they take to remedy their management of these concerns? Explain the benefits of taking such actions.

2. Treadwell Distribution Centers is in a very competitive industry. Are there any options concerning reverse logistics that can enable Treadwell to turn it from a liability to an asset? Explain why you believe yes, or believe no.

3. Is there anyone Treadwell can turn to who can help them with the empty miles issue? If so, explain how. If not, explain why not.

©Cengage Learning

3. Honeycutt Warehouse and Shipping Corporation*

Honeycutt Warehouse and Shipping Corporation is a global company that specializes in shipping and warehousing of goods. It owns and operates its own transportation fleet consisting of barges, rail cars, and semitrucks. Ms. Minnie Harmon, chief operating officer, is looking to expand operations into several emerging markets. Minnie is looking at either acquiring other companies or building from scratch. Minnie is concerned about Honeycutt's carbon footprint. She is a strong believer in protecting the environment; thus, wants to improve their sustainability results.

*Written by Rick Bonsall, D. Mgt., McKendree University, Lebanon, IL. The people and institution are fictional and any resemblance to any person or any institution is coincidental. This case was prepared solely to provide material for class discussion. The author does not intend to illustrate either effective or ineffective handling of a managerial situation.

Since their warehouse and shipping facilities will be at the selected locations for many years, Minnie believes that warehouse location selection is one of the most critical decisions to be made. Therefore, she called her senior staff together to develop a proposal on how to address location selection and sustainability.

Minnie's staff discussed the usual factors that must be studied, and whether the location was domestic or worldwide. Key factors to consider were labor, land availability and cost, proximity to markets, proximity to suppliers, taxes, and incentives. Since the company is looking to expand into emerging markets, currency exchange, stability, and national competitiveness must also be examined.

As mentioned earlier, Minnie was concerned about the environment and wanted to ensure sustainability was addressed too. Therefore, one key to sustainability was reducing energy consumption. The company moves hundreds of thousands of tons of cargo each year. Honeycutt's fleet energy consumption is enormous; consequently, pollution is also a worry. Minnie's staff discussed how to address these sustainability issues. One method was to employ state-of-the-art technology such as more fuel-efficient engines, however, that could not be accomplished for the entire fleet at once because the cost would be prohibitive.

Minnie's staff realized that expanded warehouse location selection factors would enable them to minimize these sustainability concerns. Instead of focusing on either proximity to markets or suppliers, a more balance assessment could significantly reduce energy consumption and pollution. Thinking long term and analyzing the transportation needs from that viewpoint, they could ascertain a more efficient use of the transportation options. The Council of Logistics defines logistics as "the process of planning … the efficient, effective flow of goods … from point of origin to point of consumption." Consequently, Minnie and her staff knew they must utilize all the tools of logistics management to address not only the best cost per shipment, but also all the concerns associated with freight transportation, such as energy consumption and pollution. Therefore, although it had not been an element of their warehouse location selection process in the past, it must now include sustainability as a major factor.

Discussion Questions

1. Instead of focusing only on one modal alternative for their shipping, companies can use a combination of modes. Explain that approach and would this be an option for Honeycutt Warehouse and Shipping Corporation? Why?

2. What are some examples of tools, programs, or partnerships that Honeycutt Warehouse and Shipping Corporation can use to improve logistics sustainability? Explain how they can help.

3. What are some issues with barge, rail, and truck transportation systems that affect sustainability?

ADDITIONAL RESOURCES

Bloomberg, D. J., S. LeMay, and J. B. Hanna, *Logistics*. Upper Saddle River, NJ: Prentice Hall, 2002.

Coyle, J. J., E. J. Bardi, and C. J. Langley, *The Management of Business Logistics*. St. Paul, MN: West Publishing, 1996.

Lambert, D. M., J. R. Stock, and L. M. Ellram, *Fundamentals of Logistics Management*. New York: McGraw-Hill, 1998.

Sampson, R. J., M. T. Farris, and D. L. Shrock, *Domestic Transportation: Practice, Theory, and Policy.* 5th ed. Boston: Houghton Mifflin, 1985.

Stock, J. R., and D. M. Lambert, *Strategic Logistics Management.* 4th ed. New York: McGraw-Hill, 2001.

END NOTES

1. Burnson, P., "2016 Logistics Rate Outlook: A Global Ripple Effect," *Supplychain247.com* January 11, 2016: 1.

2. Levans, M., "Global Logistics: Prepare or Perish," *Logistics Management* 55(2), 2016: 9.

3. Material for road trains came from www.outback-australia-travel-secrets.com/australian-road-trains.html, www.truckersnews.com/riding-the-down-under-express, and www.ourterritory.com/katherine_region/road_trains.htm

4. See www.cntraveler.com/stories/2016-05-18/the-10-fastest-trains-in-the-world

5. See https://www.slashgear.com/japans-new-maglev-bullet-train-is-now-the-fastest-in-the-world-22380159/

6. Material for the Antonov An-225 came from Spaeth, A., "When Size Matters," *Air International* December 2009: 29; www.theaviationzone.com/factsheets/an225.asp; www.airbususa380.tripod.com/id6.html; and www.antonov.com/products/air/transport.html

7. See http://www.ship-technology.com/projects/cscl-globe-container-ship/

8. Material for the largest pipelines came from Anonymous, "China Begins Using World's Longest Gas Pipeline," www.pennenergy.com/articles/pennenergy/2012/12/china-begins-using-worlds-longest-gas-pipeline.html; Wise, J., "World's Longest Underwater Pipeline Will Tap the Sea," *Popular Mechanics* June 2007, www.popularmechanics.com/science/extreme_machines

9. Council of Supply Chain Management Professionals, www.cscmp.org/aboutcscmp/definitions

10. See https://www.rita.dot.gov/bts/sites/rita.dot.gov.bts/files/publications/national_transportation_statistics/index.html

11. See https://search.usa.gov/search?query=for-hiretruck+gdp+2016&op=Search&affiliate=dot-bts

12. "Number of Trucking Companies Declaring Bankruptcy Significantly Declines Last Quarter," http://www.roadscholar.com/blog/number-of-trucking-companies-declaring-bankruptcy-significantly-declines-last-quarter/; Hasbrouck, E., "FAQ About Airline Bankruptcies," *The Practical Nomad*, www.hasbrouck.org/articles/bankruptcy.html; Keeton, A., "Corporate News: Air Industry Faces Grim Year Ahead," *Wall Street Journal* September 16, 2009: B3; https://www.eia.gov/todayinenergy/detail.php?id=30012; http://www.trucking.org/article/ATA-Releases-2016-Edition-of-American-Trucking-Trends

13. Horowitz, S., "Wal-Mart to the Rescue: Private Enterprise's Response to Hurricane Katrina," *The Independent Review* 13(4), 2009: 511–528.

14. "Swift Currents, Debris Slow Recovery Effort," www.npr.org, August 13, 2007.

15. See http://www.dot.state.mn.us/i35wbridge/traffic_changes.html

16. See http://www.infrastructurereportcard.org/

17. See http://www.joc.com/sites/default/files/u48801/truck-tables_1_0.jpg

18. See http://www.joc.com/trucking-logistics/ltl-shipping/largest-us-ltl-truckload-carriers-raise-combined-revenue-86-percent-60-billion-sj-consulting-reports

19. See https://www.aar.org/data-center/rail-traffic-data; https://www.fra.dot.gov/Page/P0362

20. Trebilcock, B., "RTLS: Find a Needle in a Haystack," *Modern Materials Handling* 61(7), 2006: 42.

21. Mann, T., "Rail Corridor Hit with Major Outage," *Wall Street Journal* May 20, 2013: A3.

22. "Acela Express, USA," www.railway-technology.com/projects/amtrak/

23. Mitchell, J., "Amtrak Seeking Florida's Rail Funds," *Wall Street Journal* April 28, 2011: A9.

24. http://www.dailymail.co.uk/sciencetech/article-4290138/Hyperloop-prototype-revealed-Las-Vegas.html#ixzz4bFJXSP2G

25. Parrish, M., "Why Is There Still No High-Speed Rail Network in America?" *Manufacturing.net* March 18, 2016: 1

26. Anonymous, "China Issues Tender for 351 High-Speed Trains," *International Railway Journal* 55(8), 2015: 14.

27. Macklem, K., "Is There a Fast Train Coming?" *MacLean's* 116(8), 2003: 24–25; Yong Chia, W., "KL-SG High-Speed Rail Proposal—Drawing Closer for Mutual Benefit?" *Shares Investment: Facts & Figures*, September 21, 2013: 1; Spegele, B., and B. Davis, "High-Speed Train Links Beijing, Shanghai—Cornerstone of China's Rail Expansion Illustrates Megaprojects' Speed Bumps," *Wall Street Journal* June 29, 2011: A11.

28. See http://aviationbenefits.org/economic-growth/value-to-the-economy and http://www.joc.com/air-cargo/air-cargo-market-stay-subdued-2016-iata-says_20151210.html

29. https://www.google.com/#q=the+world%E2%80%99s+largest+air+cargo+airline

30. See www.boeing.com/resources/boeingdotcom/commercial/about.../cargo.../wacf.pdf

31. Anonymous, "Research and Markets – Barge Transportation Market in the US 2017-2021 with ACBL, Ingram Marine & Kirby Dominating," *PR Newswire Europe* December 16, 2016: 1.

32. Information found at en.wikipedia.org/wiki/Container_ship

33. Harper, D., and S. Nykolaishen, "A Canadian Perspective on the Keystone XL Pipeline," *Trends: ABA Section of Environment, Energy, and Resources Newsletter* 44(6), 2013: 2–5; http://www.bbc.com/news/world-us-canada-30103078

34. Martin, J., "Intermodal Transportation: Evolving Toward the 21st Century," *Transportation & Distribution* 37(2), 1996: 1–9.

35. BNSF website: www.bnsf.com

36. Atlantic Container Line website: www.aclcargo.com and http://gcaptain.com/acls-new-conro-atlantic-star

37. Richardson, H., "Pricing/Costing Series Part III—Pricing: Carriers Calculate Their Risks," *Transportation & Distribution* 35(3), 1994: 29–31.

38. See www.nmfta.org

39. See www.tsa.gov

40. See www.dhs.gov

41. https://www.tsa.gov/news/releases/2016/07/05/
tsa-american-airlines-jointly-testing-innovative-airport-security

42. See the following: Edmonson, R., "TWICs Technology Challenge," *Journal of Commerce* February 22, 2010: 1; Staff, "Risk of Train Terror Attack Reduced: DHS IG," *Journal of Commerce* March 2, 2009: 1.

43. http://prepass.com/about-us/

44. Jerman, R., and R. Anderson, "Regulatory Issues: Shipper Versus Motor Carrier," *Transportation Journal* 33(3), 1994: 15–23.

45. See, for instance, Dempsey, P., "The Disaster of Airline Deregulation," *Wall Street Journal* May 9, 1991: A15; Leonard, W., "Airline Deregulation: Grand Design or Gross Debacle?" *Journal of Economic Issues* 17(2), 1983: 453–465; O'Brian, B., and C. Solomon, "Braniff Files for Protection from Creditors," *Wall Street Journal* September 29, 1989: 1; Staff, "Texas Air Provides $10 Million in Aid to People Express," *Wall Street Journal* October 16, 1986: 1; and Staff, "Business Brief—Texas Air Corp," *Wall Street Journal* June 7, 1990: A1.

46. Barlett, D., and J. Steele, "The High Cost of Deregulation: Joblessness, Bankruptcy, Debt," *The Inquirer* October 24, 1991; www.philly.com/philly/news

47. http://www.3plogistics.com/pick-it-the-business-of-warehousing-in-north-america-2015-market-size-major-3pls-benchmarking-costs-prices-and-practices-report-is-released-by-armstrong-associates-inc/

48. http://www.mwpvl.com/html/target.html

49. Ruwitch, J., "Alibaba's Logistics Arm to Expand Warehouse Space," *Reuters Market News* May 28, 2015: 1.

50. Feare, T., "Jazzing up the Warehouse," *Modern Material Handling* 56(7), 2001: 71–72.

51. Found at: www.universal-storage.co.za/largest-warehouses.asp

52. Burnson, P., "Conquering the Cold Chain," *Logistics Management* 52(4), 2013: 36–38.

53. Dutton, G., "A Curve Ball for Cold Chain," *World Trade* 27(1), 2014: 36–38.

54. Brown, M., "The Slow Boat to Europe," *Management Today* June 1997: 83–86.

55. Maister, D. H., "Centralization of Inventories and the 'Square Root Law,'" *International Journal of Physical Distribution and Materials Management* 6(3), 1976: 124–134.

56. Warnenburg, C. M., trans., and P. Hall, ed., *Von Thunen's Isolated State*. Oxford, UK: Pergamon Press, 1966.

57. Friedrich, C. J., trans., *Alfred Weber's Theory of the Location of Industries*. Chicago: University of Chicago Press, 1929.

58. Hoover, E. M., *The Location of Economic Activity*. New York: McGraw-Hill, 1948.

59. Greenhut, M. L., *Plant Location in Theory and in Practice*. Chapel Hill: University of North Carolina Press, 1956.

60. Dittmann, P., "11 Ways To Optimize Your Warehouse," *Industrial Engineer* 48(2), 2016: 44–49.

61. Trunick, P., "The 3 W's of Green Warehouses," *World Trade* 26(4), 2013: 40–43.

62. Geddam, S., "How Cloud Enables and Supports the Lean Warehouse," *Manufacturing Business Technology* April 15, 2015: 1.

63. Fabey, M., "Changing Trade Winds," *Traffic World* 263(8), 2000: 41–42.

64. See Daley, S., "Lost in Nicaragua, a Chinese Tycoon's Canal Project," *New York Times online* April 3, 2016: 1; and Zamorano, J., and K. Martinez, "Panama Canal Opens $5B Locks, Bullish Despite Shipping Woes," *AP online* June 6, 2016: 1.

65. Burnson, P., "Top 50 3PLs: Seeing Into the Future," *Logistics Management* 52(6), 2013: 56S.

66. Blanchard, D., "When You'd Rather Not Do It Yourself," *Material Handling Management* October 2009: 48.

67. See https://www.kornferry.com/media/sidebar_downloads/2016_3PL_Study.pdf

68. DiMartino, M., "Kawasaki Thinks Small," *Orange County Business Journal* 39(11), 2016: 1, 17.

69. Kerr, J., "What's the Right Role for Global 3PLs?" *Logistics Management* 45(2), 2006: 51–54; and Trunick, P., "3PL Mergers: Wiifm?," *World Trade* 26(1), 2013: 30–32, 34.

70. See, for example, Abshire, R., and S. Premeaux, "Motor Carrier Selection Criteria: Perceptual Differences between Shippers and Carriers," *Transportation Journal* 31(1), 1991: 31–35; Bardi, E., P. Bagchi, and T. Raghunathan, "Motor Carrier Selection in a Deregulated Environment," *Transportation Journal* 29(1), 1989: 4–11; Foster, J., and S. Strasser, "Carrier/Modal Selection Factors: The Shipper/Carrier Paradox," *Transportation Research Forum* 31(1), 1990: 206–212; and Murphy, P., J. Daley, and P. Hall, "Carrier Selection: Do Shippers and Carriers Agree, or Not?" *Transportation Research* 33E(1), 1997: 67–72.

71. Mejza, M. C., and J. D. Wisner, "The Scope and Span of Supply Chain Management," *The International Journal of Logistics Management* 12(2), 2001: 37–56; and Tan, K. C., and J. D. Wisner, "A Comparison of the Supply Chain Management Approaches of U.S. Regional and Global Businesses," *Supply Chain Forum* 2(2), 2001: 20–28.

72. McCrea, B., "Ariens Finds Just the Right Fit," *Logistics Management* 55(11), 2016: 28–31.

73. http://www.dhl-usa.com/en/contact_center/contact_global_forwarding.html

74. See https://www.export.gov/article?id=What-is-a-Shippers-Association

75. Information obtained from www.midwestshippers.com and www.iamovers.org/AffiliateGroups/ISA.aspx?navItemNumber=671

76. See http://trinity-logistics-site.trinity-logistics.trinity-logistics.d3corp.com/services/intermodal/

77. See http://cerasis.com/2015/04/22/logistics-infographic/ and http://www.logisticsmgmt.com/article/state_of_logistics_2016_us_business_logistics_costs_slow_considerably_with

78. Saenz, M., Gupta, R., and Makowski, C., "Finding Profit in Horizontal Collaboration," *Supply Chain Management Review* 21(1), 2017: 16–22.

79. See www.epa.gov/smartway

80. See www.responsibletrans.org

81. See www.godiswilson.com, www.dcvelocity.com, www.dbschenkerusa.com, and www.ecoports.com

82. Bond, J., "2015 Software Usage Survey: The Pursuit of Supply Chain Compatibility," *Logistics Management Online* July 24, 2015: 1.

83. Hannon, D., "American Railcar Uses TMS to Shine Light on Inbound Supply Chain," *Purchasing* 139(3), 2010: 13.

84. Michel, R., "Is RFID Ready for a Reinvention?" *Logistics Management* 54(10), 2015: 42–44.

85. Anonymous, "Distributor NFT Gains Yoplait Contract in Britain," *Dairy Industries International* 82(3), 2017: 7.

86. McCrea, B., "5 GTM Trends to Watch in 2017," *Logistics Management* 56(2), 2017: 38–40.

87. McCrea, B., "GTM Has Arrived," *Logistics Management* 49(1), 2010: 34.

88. See https://www.cbp.gov/border-security/ports-entry/cargo-security/c-tpat-customs-trade-partnership-against-terrorism and Quinn, F., "Supply Chain Security in a High-Risk World," *Logistics Management* 50(1), 2011: 54–58.

89. Anonymous, "Freight Forwarders Best Foreign Performance," *Logistics Management* 48(8), 2009: 44.

90. U.S. Department of Commerce website: www.ita.doc.gov/td/oetca/staff.html

91. See https://www.cbp.gov/border-security/ports-entry/cargo-security/cargo-control/foreign-trade-zones/about#; http://enforcement.trade.gov/ftzpage/info/summary.html; Anonymous, "National Association of Foreign-Trade Zones Promotes Benefits of FTZs," *Economics Week* September 25, 2009: 29; the U.S. Department of Commerce Foreign-Trade Zones Board website: http://ia.ita.doc.gov/ftzpage/index; and Bolle, M., and B. Williams, "U.S. Foreign-Trade Zones: Background and Issues for Congress," September 5, 2012, http://www.fas.org/sgp/crs/misc/R42686.pdf

92. See: http://www.cfr.org/trade/naftas-economic-impact/p15790; Bedell, D., "Can NAFTA Fill the Gap?" *Global Finance* 24(3), 2010: 30–32; Schot, J., "North American Free Trade Agreement (NAFTA)," *The Princeton Encyclopedia of the World Economy* 2, 2009: 851–855; www.ustr.gov/trade-agreements; and www.europa.eu

93. Lawrence, D., "China Issues Food, Toy Recall Rules to Tighten Safety," *Bloomberg.com News* August 31, 2007, www.bloomberg.com/apps/news?pid=20601080&sid=asUaOAct_vrc&refer=asia

94. Rogers, L., "Going in Reverse to Move Forward," *Modern Materials Handling* 64(9), 2009: 28; Rogers, D., R. Lembke, and J. Benardino, "Reverse Logistics: A New Core Competency," *Supply Chain Management Review* 17(3), 2013: 40–47.

95. McCue, D., "Dealing with Zombie Inventory," *World Trade* 26(3), 2013: 39–42.

96. http://supplychain.fedex.com/

97. Burnson, P., "Time to Embrace Reverse Logistics," *Logistics Management* 55(3), 2016: 36–38.

98. Martinez, R., "Best Practices in Returns Management," *Multichannel Merchant* 26(12), 2010: 29.

99. Rogers, L., "Going in Reverse to Move Forward."

Chapter 10

CUSTOMER RELATIONSHIP MANAGEMENT

Customer independence and buying power coupled with new tools for communication are putting consumers and the organizations with whom they do business on equal footing. Technology prowess and transparent and responsive customer handling will be the new market differentiation in a commoditized world.

—*Mary Wardley, vice president, CRM and Enterprise Applications, at IDC*[1]

The CRM market is accelerating rapidly worldwide and the outlook has never been stronger.

—*Larry Augustin, CEO of SugarCRM*[2]

CRM solutions manage customer data, but have never once managed a customer relationship.

—*Loren Padelford, executive vice president at Skura*[3]

Learning Objectives

After completing this chapter, you should be able to

- Discuss the strategic importance of CRM.
- Describe the components of a CRM initiative.
- Calculate customer lifetime value.
- Discuss the implementation procedures for CRM programs.
- Describe how information is used to create customer satisfaction and greater profits for the firm.
- Describe how firms integrate existing CRM applications.
- Describe the emerging trends in CRM.

Chapter Outline

Introduction

Customer Relationship Management Defined

Key Tools and Components of CRM

Designing and Implementing a Successful CRM Program

Trends in CRM

Summary

| SCM Profile | NAMU Finds a Better CRM Application |

Richard Bexon, COO of Costa Rica-based NAMU Travel Group, described his organization's previous CRM system with one word—monster. Over the eight years the system was used, too many people customized the system and no manual was created to allow later users to make much use of the CRM. So, in 2015, NAMU got rid of their existing system and began using Bpm'online, a cloud-based CRM application. The results were amazing—271 percent ROI with a four-month payback and an average benefit of almost $300,000.

When NAMU began in 1999, it was a small vacation travel company, focusing principally on Costa Rica. "We needed a system to manage all that logistical information and put it all together," said Bexon. They started with Salesforce's free CRM software and began customizing it to fit their needs. As the company grew, the system eventually mutated beyond their control. Keeping the system running started looking like a science project. "Well, if you pickle this part and move this part it might work," Bexon said, regarding how they held things together.

Bpm'online ended up winning NAMU's business because of its size, ingenuity, and attention to NAMU's needs. Bpm'online representatives flew down to Costa Rica to make a sales presentation, while no other company would. Additionally, NAMU liked that it offered a web-based app, it was easy to use, and offered marketing, sales, and customer service capabilities. Bpm'online also "held our hand through this," said Bexon. Bpm'online helped with implementation and stayed on site for ten days to train staff on how to use it.

The new CRM system reduced costs by avoiding software and personnel expenses that were previously needed for the old system. It also improved productivity—managers saved approximately two hours per week per person, which allowed greater focus on sales. Eventually, NAMU realized a 10 percent improvement in sales and marketing productivity. Regarding the old system, Bexon explained, "This system had been touched by so many people and built in so many ways that we didn't really have any dashboards to look at, and pulling data was difficult. Once we could start pulling this data, we could really start making decisions."[4]

INTRODUCTION

Customer relationship management becomes necessary as soon as a company finds a market and some customers for its products and services. To keep customers satisfied, coming back and telling others, firms must continually develop new products and services while discovering ways to add more value to existing products and services. This is particularly true in today's tough, crowded economic climate, which has made customers smarter and more willing to switch company allegiances. The often-told story that "finding a new customer costs five times as much as keeping an old customer" is one of the motivations behind customer relationship management. Over time, value can be demonstrated to customers through reliable on-time delivery, high-quality products and services, competitive pricing, innovative new products and services, attention to varying customer needs, and the flexibility to respond to those needs adequately. Managing and improving customer relationships start with building core competencies that focus on customer requirements, and then continuing with delivering products and services in a manner resulting in high levels of customer satisfaction.

Customer relationship management, or simply CRM, has come to be associated with automated transaction and communication applications—a suite of software modules or a portion of the larger enterprise resource planning system as described in Chapter 7. The global market for CRM applications is growing rapidly—it was approximately $26 billion in 2015, up from $18 billion just three years earlier. CRM includes applications for sales force automation, marketing automation, and customer service and support management. Social media management, customer experience management, and activity and participant management are among some of the newly available CRM applications. Most large firms have made sizeable investments in CRM applications along with company websites that capture data in an effort to automate the customer relationship process, and in some respects these have provided significant benefits to the companies and their customers. Additionally, software-as-a-service (SaaS) or cloud-based applications dominate the CRM market and sales of these applications are growing twice as fast as other applications.[5]

The growth of CRM is expected to continue. In a Gartner business survey, approximately 49 percent of the firms responding stated they planned to increase their CRM investments in 2017, and the largest expenditures were going to be on help desk and customer service software. Salesforce has the largest share of the global CRM market, followed by SAP, Oracle, and Microsoft.[6]

Customers today like the convenience of communicating or transacting over the Internet; however, individualized contact between a company and its customers is also needed to ultimately keep customers satisfied and coming back. Two of the most recent trends in CRM are use of social networks and cloud computing and both of these will be discussed in this chapter. Companies are using both as a means to build better customer relationships. Some applications allow a company, for instance, to extract information automatically about people from a social network like LinkedIn and load it directly into one of its CRM systems. Other applications include the use of a service provider's eMarketing cloud to send e-mail "blasts" to thousands of customers.

Businesses are rediscovering the need to provide personalized services to their customers. Today we see that a firm's Internet presence and software applications, though desirable for many types of information or product transactions, are not sufficient to satisfy most customers in a wide range of industries. Touching products and talking face-to-face with company representatives remain integral parts of the customer experience. Thus, CRM must still include talking to customers, understanding their behavior and their requirements, and then building a system to satisfy those requirements. CRM must be more than just software.

With the rapid pace of technological change, comes many new and exciting ways to obtain and utilize customer information, and many of these will be highlighted throughout this chapter. While company–customer interactions are becoming more automated and as more e-services are created, organizations will still find they must continue to identify and develop new ways to add value to customer relationships in order to maintain a competitive advantage. Cultivating the human element in customer relationships will always remain a necessary factor in creating that value. Ultimately CRM, if used effectively, allows both sides to win—customers get what they want from businesses, while businesses continue to find new customers and satisfy old ones.

CUSTOMER RELATIONSHIP MANAGEMENT DEFINED

Simply put, **customer relationship management** refers to *building and maintaining profitable long-term customer relationships.* The elements comprising CRM vary based on the industry, the size of the company, and familiarity with CRM software applications. In the final analysis though, all forms of CRM seek to keep the firm's customers satisfied, which creates profits and other benefits for the firm. A few specific definitions of CRM are provided here:

- "The infrastructure that enables the delineation of, and increase in customer value, and the correct means by which to motivate valuable customers to remain loyal—indeed to buy again."[7]

- "… managing the relationships among people within an organization and between customers and the company's customer service representatives in order to improve the bottom line."[8]

- "… a core business strategy for managing and optimizing all customer interactions across an organization's traditional and electronic interfaces."[9]

Because of the intense competition in most markets today, CRM has become one of the leading business strategies—and potentially one of the most costly. Most executives, who haven't already implemented CRM applications, are planning on investing in them soon. And while investments in CRM are in the tens of billions of dollars each year as previously stated, it appears that some of this investment is not fundamentally improving customer relationships, making customers more loyal, or resulting in positive returns for the companies implementing CRM. While well-implemented and properly used CRM program can return about $5 for every $1 spent on CRM, a large percentage of programs, possibly 25–60 percent (depending on the survey) fail to meet expectations.[10]

So why are many CRM programs failing? Several researchers who have studied this problem refer to the "seven deadly sins of CRM failure." These are: viewing CRM primarily from a technology perspective, a lack of customer-centric vision, not understanding the concept of a customer's lifetime value, insufficient top management support, not reengineering business processes, underestimating the challenges in integrating various sources of data, and underestimating the challenge in effecting change.[11] Thus, it is the people aspect of CRM that is often lacking. "If people are not using the system consistently, referrals and follow-ups will fall through the cracks," explains Floyd Salamino, VP/consulting for Texas-based Marquis Software. "Staff involvement is crucial, so seek their participation early in the process to create ownership and buy-in." Because employee resistance can contribute to CRM failure, Salamino advises recognizing the individuals who tend to resist change and working with them to strengthen buy-in. "Think broadly. Who are you going to impact when implementing CRM?" asks Brett Wooden, chief retail officer for Oregon-based Providence Federal Credit Union. "If you implement CRM without collaboration, you begin to work in silos, and you can lose the transfer of knowledge, especially if departments are not used to having conversations or their workflow dependent on one another." Finally, Wooden adds, "Poor planning, a lack of communication, and overwhelming your staff can create negative thinking. Instead, ask employees a lot of questions right at the start. Find out their needs and look for potential roadblocks. Every organization is different, but your goals can be common."[12]

While corporations may collect customers' purchase, credit, and personal information, place it on a database, and use it to initiate some type of direct marketing activity, in too many cases no substantive efforts are put forth to engender a customer's trust and loyalty—*to build customer relationships*. If building and maintaining relationships were truly what companies were seeking, they would, for instance, return phone messages, make it easy to return or service products, and make it easy for customers to get accurate information and contact the right people inside the organization. Consider this—as a customer, how often, in your dealings with organizations, have you been made to feel valued?

Too often, companies today have delegated customer relationship management, certainly one of the most important activities of the firm, to third-party CRM services, software developers, and internal IT departments whose goal is to collect data, design databases, and use models to predict consumer buying patterns, for instance. Though it is a potentially valuable support element in CRM programs, data mining alone does not build the customer relationship. A number of years ago, Ms. Jessica Keyes, a well-known information system author and consultant stated in an interview in the magazine *Infotrends*, "Technology does not beget a competitive advantage, any more than paint and canvas beget a Van Gogh."[13] These kinds of activities should be used in tandem with individual attention to build genuine long-term value for customers. Successful CRM programs require cultural change, effective CRM project management, and employee engagement, leading to strategies that cultivate long-term relationships with customers, aided by the information gathered from CRM applications.

Simply put, companies need to *treat their customers right*. Not only does this mean providing the products and services they want at competitive prices, but also it means providing support services and other offerings that add value and create customer satisfaction. Because customers are not all the same, firms must identify and segment their customers, then provide different sets of desired products and services to each segment. As noted CRM consultant Barton Goldenberg has been telling clients for years—a successful CRM initiative is 50 percent people, 30 percent process, and 20 percent technology.[14]

Thus, a successful CRM program is both simple and complex—it is simple in that it involves training users and treating customers right, to make them feel valued. It is complex in that it also means finding affordable ways to identify (potentially millions of) customers and their needs, and then designing customer contact strategies geared toward creating customer satisfaction and loyalty. Doing these things right will produce bottom line results.

The delivery services of online retailer Amazon, for example, are very simple for the consumer, although actually some very complicated CRM tasks take place behind the scenes. "I think what ensured that Amazon was a dotcom winner was being dedicated to the initial principle of focusing on the customer," says Ms. Rakhi Parekh, group product manager at Amazon.co.uk. "We started off by passing-on the cost advantage of the model to consumers, with low prices, then extended that to clever use of their data so that we could work out what else they might enjoy." Today, Amazon continues to search for better ways to serve not only their consumer-customers, but their merchant-customers as well. For example, Amazon plans to establish about 1,300 new distribution facilities near major cities in Europe starting in 2017. The facilities would function as "last-mile" centers that receive and store shipments prior to their final deliveries to nearby customers. Domino's Pizza is also doing interesting things today, with pizza delivery, as described in the nearby SCM Profile.

SCM Profile | **Domino's Pizza Wins over New Fans**

Domino's Pizza is a company that embraces technological change. In 2015, Dominos began allowing customers to order pizza by texting a pizza emoji. Then in November 2016, it delivered a pizza by drone to a customer in New Zealand, claiming that it was faster and safer. In 2017, it announced use of an artificial intelligence (AI) technology that allows customers to order a pizza using their voices on phones, computers, or virtual assistants like Amazon's Alexa.

Domino's has been developing the AI platform for years, as part of a continuous strategy to enhance its customers' experiences and make ordering pizza easier than ever. They constantly tinker and innovate throughout their entire business, to help please customers.

An interesting note about Domino's is that its stock was worth just $3 in November 2008 compared to $180 in April 2017. Part of the reason for this turnaround is because customers are less interested in sitting down for a meal and more interested in takeout. Customers want to order food and get it quickly and cheaply. Domino's is using AI and even delivery drones for this purpose.

The idea behind the AI platform is that customers will no longer have to scroll through a bunch of pages. By using a voice-controlled AI, customers can just say what kind of pizza they want, making it a much faster and easier process. But technology is only one factor creating Domino's recent success. They have also improved food quality. As a result, the chain has managed to win over new fans.[15]

KEY TOOLS AND COMPONENTS OF CRM

A number of elements are required for the development of effective CRM initiatives and these include segmenting customers, predicting customer behaviors, determining customer value, personalizing customer communications, automating the sales force, and managing customer service capabilities. Each of these elements is discussed in detail below.

Segmenting Customers

One of the most basic activities in CRM is to **segment customers**. Companies group customers in varieties of ways so that customized communications and marketing efforts can be directed to specific customer groups. Efforts to up-sell and cross-sell can be directed to some groups, while efforts to discourage further purchases might be made to others. The global recession in 2009, for instance, may have changed some customer preferences, which in turn changed how firms segmented and marketed to these segments. Anything with the potential to change buying habits will eventually result in a different form of segmentation.

Customer segmentation can occur based on sales territory or region, preferred sales channel, profitability, products purchased, sales history, demographic information, desired product features, and service preferences, just to name a few. Analyzing customer information can tell companies something about customer preferences and the likelihood of customers responding to various types of **target marketing** efforts. By targeting specific customer segments, firms can save money by avoiding marketing efforts aimed at the wrong customers. Using target marketing, firms can also avoid becoming a nuisance to customers, which could drive them to competitors. JetBlue's target customer, for example, is the low budget traveler that wants a comfortable yet affordable solution to flying. They are typically a younger audience that likes to be reached through social media channels and expects quick responses from the company. That audience comes through in their target marketing effort in the medium they use (Twitter, for instance), and the words "fly like a boss, pay like an intern," and even the name of the Twitter handle (@JetBlueCheeps).[16]

Permission Marketing

An extension of target marketing is **relationship marketing** or **permission marketing**. The idea is to let customers select the type and time of their communications with organizations. These days, consumers are bombarded with thousands of commercial messages each day in every form of communication imaginable. The general consensus is that there are simply far too many ads, consumers ignore most of them, and no one is really trying to do anything to reduce them. On the contrary, the advertising industry seems forever on the lookout for new ways to introduce commercial messages.

One example of new advertising is **mobile marketing**, or placing advertising messages on mobile phones. Users opt-in to get all of their services on cell phones, including advertising. "Text messaging is an essential component of any integrated mobile marketing plan," said James Citron, CMO and co-founder of Mogreet. "Text marketing is accessible by 98 percent of U.S. cell phone users and yields the highest open rate within mobile marketing."[17] One form of mobile marketing is the use of quick response codes, or **QR codes**. It involves using the camera function on a smart phone and installing a QR code reader on the phone. Consumers worldwide are using their mobile phones while in-store to compare prices, scan quick response codes, and make purchases. This fusion of mobile and physical is in line with the general omnichannel trend that has formed on the global retail market. The Asia-Pacific region is one of the global leaders in terms of using mobile phones for online shopping. Over half of these online shoppers made purchases using mobile devices. In China, the number of mobile shoppers has grown to more than 200 million, while in India the share of mobile shoppers in the cities increased from just over 20 percent to more than a half.[18]

Thus in permission marketing, customers choose to be placed on (opt-in) and then taken off (opt-out) of text, e-mail, or traditional mailing lists for information about goods and services. It is becoming possible on websites, for consumers to specify exactly what they are interested in, when they want information, what type of information they want, and how they want it communicated. This kind of customer self-segmenting requires sophisticated software capabilities to track individual customers and their interaction preferences as well as the capability to update these preferences over time. With this capability, firms can better design multiple, parallel marketing campaigns around small, specific segments of their customer base, automate portions of the marketing process, and simultaneously free up time previously spent manually managing the marketing process. Facebook, LinkedIn, and Instagram, for example, allow users to create their own customized webpages that potential consumers choose to visit. Because visitors to these pages are self-selecting, this essentially amounts to permission marketing. This enables companies to identify interested consumers, engage them in dialogues, and market goods and services to them. As of 2017, Coca-Cola had more than 104,000,000 Facebook fans and about 1,000,000 followers on LinkedIn worldwide, while Nike had over 70,000,000 followers on Instagram.

Cross-Selling

Cross-selling occurs when customers are sold additional products as the result of an initial purchase. The initial purchase allows the seller to segment the customer. E-mails to customers from Amazon.com describing other products purchased by people who purchased the same product a customer just bought is an attempt at cross-selling. If the additional products or services purchased are even more profitable than the original purchase, this can provide significant add-on profits for the firm. In addition, if firms are successful at cross-selling the right products at the right time to the right customers, then customers perceive this as individualized attention, and it results in more satisfied and loyal customers.

When Bank of America acquired Merrill Lynch in 2009 for $50 billion, a number of cross-selling opportunities arose, since its wealth management employees could view each customer's savings and checking accounts along with their investment portfolios. One year later, these cross-selling opportunities were bearing fruit—global wealth management business had increased for Bank of America and profit margins were in excess of 20 percent—significantly higher than industry averages.[19] Sometimes though, aggressive cross-selling can lead to mis-selling, as Wells Fargo exhibited in 2016. As many as 2 million phantom accounts and credit cards were created for clients without their knowledge. And the purpose was clear: to inflate sales numbers, hit targets, and boost bonuses. More than 5,000 staff lost their jobs over the affair. Wells Fargo was fined $185 million and billions of dollars were wiped off its market value, demoting it from its rank as the world's most valuable lender.[20]

Predicting Customer Behaviors

By understanding customers' current purchasing behaviors, future behaviors can be predicted. Using data mining software and customer behavior analytics allows firms to predict which products customers are likely to purchase next and how much they would be willing to pay. In this way, companies can revise pricing policies, offer discounts, and design promotions to specific customer segments. Sheldon Gilbert, the creator of Proclivity, a behavior predicting software used by New York-based Proclivity Systems, knows all about you—your favorite color, how many times you added that flat screen TV to your online shopping cart without buying it, and what you like to do in your spare time. Sheldon explains, "Every time you click a link, it's a request for information you're making to a server. We can then mine the data stored on the servers to create a profile of a person's likes and dislikes or proclivities." LayerRx, a Proclivity company, allows pharmaceutical companies to sell digital ads, for instance, to cardiologists researching myocarditis or virologists researching zika.[21] Along with determining what customers might purchase next, another desirable CRM activity is **customer defection analysis**.

Customer Defection Analysis

Reducing customer defections (also referred to as **customer churn**) is another component of managing long-term customer relationships. And it can pay handsomely as well. According to Harvard Business School research, a 5 percent improvement in customer retention can result in a 75 percent increase in profits.[22] Knowing which customers have quit purchasing and why can be very valuable information for organizations. Recent research has found that the top three reasons for customer defections are—changes in customer needs; significant drop in product quality/customer service; and the competition offers better prices or deals.[23] Not only can these customers be approached to encourage a return to the business, but also the customer churn knowledge gained can be used to reduce future defections. "If I've got an 80 percent satisfaction rate, the focus needs to be on the 20 percent of dissatisfied customers," says Bob Furniss, president of CRM consultancy Touchpoint Associates of Tennessee. "If I can understand what's occurring in the 20 percent, then my impact is much more profound than being satisfied with the satisfaction rate."[24]

Offers of money, phones, or free minutes from telephone service companies are examples of efforts to regain customers who have defected to another phone service. In some cases though, organizations may actually *want* some customers (the unprofitable ones) to defect. By determining the value or profitability of each of the defecting customers, firms can design appropriate policies for retaining or regaining some customers as well as policies to discourage additional purchases from other customers (also termed *firing customers*). In some department stores, for instance, customers who repeatedly return merchandise are at some point given only store credit instead of cash. Businesses sometimes refer to these customers as *vampire customers* (as in they "bleed the company dry").

By monitoring purchase histories, firms can see if this type of discouragement makes customers quit returning merchandise.

Customer Value Determination

Until recently, determining **customer value** or **customer profitability** was difficult for most CRM systems. Today though, by integrating with ERP systems, capturing customer profitability information is possible. However, improper use of this information can cause poor decisions to be made. For instance, some customers that are unprofitable now, may become profitable later. A health club, for instance, may have some unmarried members who rarely make other purchases at the club but frequently visit and use the facility. While this type of member might be seen as unprofitable, it is likely that if these members are satisfied with the club, they will tell others; and at some point they may marry and upgrade to a family membership. Thus, it is necessary to determine **customer lifetime value** (CLV) such that appropriate benefits, communications, services, or policies can be directed toward (or withheld from) customers or customer segments.

Unless a firm has knowledge of customer profitability, they may be directing sizeable resources catering to customers who are actually unprofitable. For instance, in a study published a few years ago by consultant and database marketing author Arthur Middleton Hughes, he described how Boston-based Fleet Bank's marketing staff was working hard trying to retain customers who were actually losing money for the bank. In fact, half of Fleet's customers were deemed unprofitable, with the bottom 28 percent gobbling up 22 percent of the bank's total annual profits. (Fleet has since merged with Bank of America.)[25] Calculating CLV is based on a projection of a customer's lifetime purchases, the average profit margin on the items purchased, and the net present value of the customer's projected profits. Thus, the CLV can be calculated using the net present value of an annuity as shown here:

$$\text{NPV}_A = P\left[\frac{1-(1\ +\ i)^{-n}}{i}\right]$$

where

A = customer A
P = average annual profit, or (annual sales $\times$ profit margin)
i = annual discount rate
n = expected lifetime in years

Example 10.1 illustrates this calculation.

Example 10.1   Calculating Customer Lifetime Value

The Nevada Seed Company sells grass seed and drought-tolerant plant seeds to area plant nurseries. They have decided to project the lifetime value of each of their nursery customers in order to design individualized grass and plant seed promotions. Their top two customers have the following characteristics:

	AVG. ANNUAL SALES	AVG. PROFIT MARGIN	EXPECTED LIFETIME
Nursery A:	$22,000	20%	5 years
Nursery B:	$16,000	15%	15 years

Using a discount rate of 8 percent, and treating the average sales figures as annuities, the present value of the two nursery lifetime values is:

$$\text{NPV}_A = P\left[\frac{1-(1\ +\ i)^{-n}}{i}\right] = \$22,000(.2)\left[\frac{1-(1+0.08)^{-5}}{0.08}\right] = \$4,400\left(\frac{0.319}{0.08}\right) = \$17,568$$

$$\text{NPV}_B = P\left[\frac{1-(1\ +\ i)^{-n}}{i}\right] = \$16,000(.15)\left[\frac{1+(1+0.08)^{-15}}{0.08}\right] = \$2,400\left(\frac{0.684}{0.08}\right) = \$20,542$$

Based on these calculations, Nursery B is deemed more important because of the higher expected lifetime value.

Estimating customers' total lifetime purchases can also help to focus resources on managing the right customers. Consider two business customers, for example, one with purchases of $2 million per year and the other with annual purchases of $1 million. At first glance, the first customer might seem more valuable; however, if that customer's total purchases from all suppliers for similar products is $3 million whereas the second firm's total purchases of similar products is $20 million, then the second firm suddenly has much more potential for additional sales and should be managed with that potential in mind.

Personalizing Customer Communications

Knowledge of customers, their behaviors, and their preferences allows firms to customize communications aimed at specific groups of customers. Referring to customers by their first name, or suggesting services used in the past communicates value to the customer and is likely to result in greater levels of sales. The Ritz-Carlton Hotel, for instance, profiles its customers in order to provide the accommodations each person prefers on subsequent visits.

CRM software that can analyze a customer's **clickstream**, or how they navigate a website, can tailor a website's images, ads, or discounts based on past usage of the site. Website businesses may also send personalized e-mails, for instance, with incentives to lure customers back, if it has been a while since their last purchase. A quick-change oil and lube shop might send a postcard to a customer's address every ninety days, reminding them it's time for an oil change while offering a discount on the next visit. On the same card, they may also offer discounts on other services that the customer has used in the past, such as a radiator flush, a tune-up, or a tire-rotation. With time, this customization capability improves, as the firm learns of additional services, products, and purchasing behaviors exhibited by various customers.

Event-Based Marketing

Another form of personalized communication comes with the ability to offer individual promotions tied to specific events. Banks, for example, may try to market automated mortgage payment services to all of their customers who have recently applied for and received a home mortgage loan. The same bank might offer home improvement loans to customers once their mortgages reach an age of five years. The idea with **event-based marketing** (also referred to as trigger-based or event-driven marketing) is to offer the right products and services to customers at just the right time. When entertainment venues or restaurants ask for the birth dates of their customers as they purchase tickets or meals, for instance, they can direct future discounts to occur on days they are likely to be celebrating. Or, when bank customers call to determine the payout on an existing home mortgage, this indicates the customer is considering a different bank—an event-based tactic might be to transfer the caller to a special customer save group at the call center. With large volumes of customers, event-based promotion strategies are impossible without computer automation, so event-based marketing capabilities tend to be popular requirements among firms purchasing CRM systems.

Automated Sales Force Tools

Sales force automation (SFA) products are used for documenting field activities, communicating with the home office, and retrieval of sales history and other company-specific documents in the field. Today, sales personnel need better ways to manage their accounts, their business opportunities, and their communications while away from the office. To supply these capabilities, firms have been using CRM tools since the early 1990s to help management and sales personnel keep up with the ever-more complicated layers of information that are required as the number of customers and prospects increase. When field sales personnel have ready access to the latest forecasts, sales, inventory, marketing plans, and account information it allows more accurate and timely decisions to be made in the field, ultimately increasing sales force productivity and improving customer service capabilities.

Jonel Engineering's cloud-based sales force analytics tool, Sales Insight, harnesses mobile computing power to enable sales teams to score more wins and attract new business opportunities. Bidding and forecasting functions are tightly coupled with powerful analytics tools that quickly identify key market trends impacting service levels and overall customer performance. A four-dimensional analytical model ranks customers based on profit, payment, productivity, and ease of doing business, providing sales managers a holistic view of how servicing a specific customer impacts the bottom line. "Our goal is to take sales force automation to the next level," says Jonel President Mike Lawson.[26]

Sales Activity Management

These tools are customized to each firm's sales policies and procedures and offer sales personnel a sequence of pages/activities guiding them through their sales processes with each customer. These standardized steps assure the proper sales activities are performed and also put forth as a uniform sales process across the entire organization. The use of a **sales activity management system** reduces errors, improves sales force productivity, and boosts customer satisfaction. Along with the prescribed sales steps, field sales reps can be reminded of key customer activities as they are needed, generate mailings for inactive customers, be assigned tasks by management, and generate to-do lists. "Nearly every sales leader I meet would like to increase the productivity of their sales teams—but they struggle to identify which activities and behaviors will make a difference," said Jim Benton, co-founder of California-based ClearSlide, a sales engagement platform provider. A recent report states that on average, sales managers have less than 20 percent of their time available to help sales reps sell, and fewer than 60 percent of sales reps achieve their sales quota plans.[27]

Sales Territory Management

Sales territory management systems allow sales managers to obtain current information and reporting capabilities regarding each sales person's activities on each customer's account, total sales in general for each sales rep, their sales territories, and any ongoing sales initiatives. Using these tools, sales managers can create sales teams specifically suited to a customer's needs, generate profiles of sales personnel, track performance, and keep up with new leads generated in the field. Territories can be based on geography or customer types and are used to promote effective usage of the sales team to maximize sales opportunities, provide superior customer service, and expand existing customer relationships. Poorly planned sales territories, for example, can reduce face-time for sales personnel, resulting in lower sales.

Lead Management

Using a **lead management system** allows sales reps to follow prescribed sales tactics when dealing with sales prospects or opportunities, to aid in closing the deal. These applications can generate additional steps as needed to help refine the deal closing and negotiation process. During this process, sales personnel can generate product configurations and price quotes directly, using laptops or handheld devices remotely linked to the firm's server. In addition, leads can be assigned to field sales personnel as they are generated, based on the requirements of the prospect and the skill sets of the sales reps. Thus, lead management capabilities should result in higher deal closing success rates in less time. Another common characteristic allows managers to track the closing success of sales personnel and the future orders generated by each lead. As a matter of fact, an insurance study in 2016 found that insurance companies with lead management systems sold 13 percent more policies per household compared to companies without this system.[28]

Knowledge Management

Sales personnel require access to a variety of information before, during, and after a sale including information on contracts, client and competitor profiles, client sales histories, corporate policies, expense reimbursement forms, regulatory issues and laws, sales presentations, promotional materials, and previous client correspondence. Easy access to this information enables quick decision-making, better customer service, and a better-equipped and more productive sales staff. When sales and other skilled personnel leave an organization, years of accumulated knowledge walk out the door with them, unless a system is in place to capture this information for further use. A **knowledge management system** (KMS) gives the organization this capability.

Once knowledge is stored in a KMS, it must be readily accessible through a variety of devices, including smartphones and tablets. Electronic devices are necessary for communication in an increasingly digitalized world. Knowledge management systems should also be linked to other applications that support various business processes and workflows. A KMS captures, stores, recalls, and improves corporate knowledge. Lessons learned as well as documented work processes should both be linked to the KMS. The nearby SCM Profile describes the Atlantic States company's use of a KMS.

Managing Customer Service Capabilities

A key objective for any CRM initiative is the ability to provide good customer service. In fact, with any process dealing with the customer, a primary objective is always to provide adequate levels of customer service. But what does customer service actually mean? In Chapter 7, customer service was discussed in terms of safety stock and managing inventory. In Chapter 9, customer service was tied to delivering goods on time. And as mentioned earlier in this chapter, customer service can also mean answering customers' questions and having disputes or product and service problems resolved appropriately and quickly. Thus, many definitions of customer service can be found. As a matter of fact, numerous customer service rankings exist and are published each year. Unfortunately, complaints about shoddy customer service abound in many organizations today and this represents one area where organizations can create real competitive advantage, if customer service processes are designed and operated correctly. The next segment defines customer service and discusses several elements of customer service.

Customer Service Defined

One **customer service** definition covers most of the elements mentioned above and that is the **Seven Rs Rule**.[30] The seven Rs stand for having the *right* product, in the *right* quantity, in the *right* condition, at the *right* place, at the *right* time, for the *right* customer, at the *right* cost. In logistics parlance, for instance, a **perfect order** occurs when all seven Rs are

SCM Profile

Atlantic States KMS

New Jersey-based Atlantic States Cast Iron Pipe has been in operation since 1856, but the facility is not old fashioned according to senior vice president Dale Schmelzle. "Atlantic States has become a 'knowledge management' driven foundry," he said. In the past few years, Atlantic States has adopted and implemented a knowledge management system (KMS) to help the employees make good business decisions.

Atlantic States set about programming new charts and dashboards for its KMS to be used on the plant floor and in managers' offices to provide a visual representation of the data in the system. Its digital dashboards provided the real-time indicators the company needed. These included the following:

Open Work Orders: Keeping work orders in control helps reduce machine downtime, reduces part cost, and reduces safety risks. Managers can click on their department and view at a glance where they stand with their work orders.

Actual Cost by Ton: This provides real-time expenses against the budget. Departments can look at their financial budget goals and what's available for the month.

Sales and Shipped Tons: This shows by customer, what has been sold and what has been shipped. It allows the company to gauge sales and, at a glance, determine the presence of bottlenecks.

Top 10 Scrap Types by Percentage: Iron scrap can cost the company millions. The casting department and plant management look at this chart to see which casting machines are performing poorly.

Production Equipment Performance: This chart reports what each machine is producing and which machines are up and running. It helps sales and shipping determine which orders are being filled.

Direct Charge Spent Today: Reports what Atlantic States has spent for the day. When reducing a budget, the first step is to reduce spending.

Each scorecard tells users how the plant is doing for that hour, day, and week. "The nice thing about our dashboards is that we can drill down," said Jason Trimmer, plant operations manager. "If we want to know the number of plant work orders by department, we can drill down to see the detail of each work order. Our dashboards will show you key data at a glance." Atlantic States has found that the digital dashboards have motivated employees to be part of the solution to issues in the plant. They also have provided real cost savings.[29]

satisfied. This customer service definition can be applied to any service provider or manufacturer and for any customer. A misstep in any of the seven areas results in lower levels of customer service. Consequently, competitive advantage can be achieved by creating an organization which routinely satisfies the seven Rs.

Organizational performance measures are often designed around satisfying some of the seven Rs. For example, reducing stockouts to 1 percent means that customers get the product or service they want 99 percent of the time and having an on-time delivery performance of 97 percent means that customers get their orders at the right time 97 percent of the time. Other customer service measures are typically designed to measure *flexibility* (responding to changes in customer orders), *response* (responding to requests for information), *recovery* (the ability to solve customer problems), and *post-sales support* (providing operating information, parts, equipment, and repairs). In the airline industry, customer service is measured using frequencies of lost or damaged baggage, bumped passengers, canceled flights, on-time flights, and customer complaints. In North America, Alaska Airlines, Delta, and Virgin America were the top-rated air carriers in terms of customer service in 2017, while United, American, and Frontier were rated the worst, according to the annual Airline Quality Report.[31]

Providing award-winning services to customers keeps them returning, however this also comes at a cost. Firms must consider the costs of providing good customer service (such as faster transport, greater safety stock levels, more service provider training and better comforts) as well as the benefits (keeping customers' future profit streams). In organized supply chain relationships, firms often work together in determining (and paying for) adequate customer service, because the long-term costs of poor customer service can be substantial.

Customer service elements can be classified as **pretransaction**, **transaction**, and **posttransaction elements** as defined below.

- *Pretransaction elements*: These customer service elements precede the actual product or service purchase; examples are customer service policies, the organization's service structure, and the service system's flexibility.
- *Transaction elements*: These elements occur during the sale of the product or service and include the order lead time, the order processing capabilities, and the distribution system accuracy.
- *Posttransaction elements*: These elements refer to the after-sale services and include warranty repair capabilities, complaint resolution, product returns, and operating information.

To provide high levels of service and value to customers, firms seek to continually satisfy the seven Rs while also developing adequate customer service capabilities before, during, and after the sale. Call centers have been used in many organizations to improve customer service and supply chain performance and this topic is discussed next.

Call Centers

Call centers or **customer contact centers** have existed for many years, and some organizations have used these effectively to satisfy and keep customers loyal, while others have seen these as a necessary cost of doing business and viewed these as a drain on profits. As call centers became automated, customer service representatives were able to quickly see how similar questions were answered in the past, and resolve problems more quickly, resulting in greater call center effectiveness. Call center systems can categorize calls, determine average resolution time, and forecast future call volumes. These automated systems can reduce call center labor costs and training times, and improve the overall productivity of the staff, while improving customer service levels.

Within the past ten years, most call centers implemented virtual queuing systems, and most callers see this as a convenient call center characteristic. The virtual queue allows callers to request a callback from an agent without losing their place in the phone queue, which frees up callers' time, reduces caller frustration, and also reduces call center toll charges for keeping callers on hold. More recently, call centers have created interfaces with mobile applications to further enhance the customer experience. When a mobile customer can't complete his or her transaction, the application automatically forwards the entire history of the customer's mobile session to the contact center. The contact center then places the customer in a virtual queue and sends the customer a notice of when an agent will call.

The customer has the option of either taking the callback as scheduled or rescheduling it to a more convenient time. Either way, there are no wasted cell minutes. The agent also knows what steps the customer has already gone through and was attempting to do, when the issue popped up. When the call to the customer is made, the agent knows the entire transaction context, who the customer is, and their purchase history.[32]

Aside from solving customer problems, call centers today are also viewed increasingly as a source of revenue for the firm. In fact, a survey of managers at U.K. and U.S. in-house call centers revealed that 60 percent viewed their call centers as profit centers. Today, call center staff are expected to pursue cross-sell and up-sell opportunities. Additionally, 86 percent of the managers stated that reps needed a broader range of skills to deliver these revenues. "With more and more consumers opting out of direct marketing (telephone, mail, and e-mail), companies are realizing that they need to take advantage of every customer interaction; not only to serve the customers' needs, but also to engage with them individually, build relationships, and extend the customer lifetime value through effective up-sell and cross-sell," says Mark Smith, executive vice president at Portrait Software, a CRM software provider.[33]

While the practice of call center outsourcing has been around several decades, in the latter 1990s and the 2000s outsourcing call centers to offshore companies really exploded. The growth of the Internet, a boom in telecommunications capacity, cheap foreign labor, and education systems in areas like the Philippines, India, and Pakistan which encouraged the development of an English-speaking workforce all acted to create a perfect environment for the offshoring of call centers (along with other types of businesses). Today though, with the move toward onshoring and reshoring, this trend is reversing. Security issues are also hastening this trend. In 2015, for example, AT&T was fined $25 million for a customer data breach in their Mexico call center after two employees confessed to accessing customer information and reselling it to strangers.[34]

Measuring Customer Satisfaction

Measuring customer satisfaction remains somewhat of a tricky proposition. Customers are frequently given opportunities to provide feedback about a product, service, or organization through customer feedback cards placed at cash registers or on tables. Customer surveys are also provided with purchased products or shown on firm websites. In most cases though, the only time these forms are filled out is when customers are experiencing a problem. Given this, companies still can find valuable uses for the information. Responses can be analyzed and used to find solutions for the most commonly occurring problems. In CRM applications, customer satisfaction surveys can be personalized to fit specific customer segments, and responses can be matched to respondents' profiles to provide the company direction on improving its communication and service capabilities for various groups of customers. The design of the surveys themselves can be a particular problem. In some cases, surveys don't ask the questions customers want to answer. On many website surveys, customers are more often asked about the design of the website instead of how the firm is performing or what the customer may be happy or unhappy about.

On the other hand, actually talking with and listening to customers, and then taking action based on what customers are saying lets customers know the firm is completely engaged. Domino's Pizza, for example, profiled earlier, completely redesigned its product after listening to unflattering customer comments. As a result, customers were happier, and Domino's stock price went from $33 per share at the start of 2012 to $180 per share in 2017. According to new product development expert and author Don Adams, many companies are designing a new product, testing it with some potential customers, and then measuring their success by watching sales. Instead, companies should initiate feedback from customers prior to designing products. "There's no substitute for respectful dialogue with customers," says Adams.[35]

In this section of the chapter, the common elements necessary for successful CRM programs were reviewed. Many of these involve the use of technology and software. But having numerous software applications does not necessarily guarantee CRM success. A number of other factors come into play before, during, and after programs are implemented that must be adhered to, in order to give the firm and its CRM program a good chance of finding and keeping profitable customers. The next section will discuss this very important aspect of CRM.

DESIGNING AND IMPLEMENTING A SUCCESSFUL CRM PROGRAM

Designing and then implementing a CRM program can be a real challenge, because it requires an understanding of and commitment to the firm's customers, adherence to CRM goals, knowledge of the tools available to aid in CRM, support from the firm's top executives and the various departments that will be using the CRM tools, and a continuous awareness of customers' changing requirements. Poor planning is typically the cause for most unsuccessful CRM initiatives, because of the temptation to start working on a solution or to purchase several CRM applications before understanding the problem. The firm must first answer this question: *What are the problems a CRM program is going to solve?* This must involve employees from all functional groupings across the firm, as well as input from the firm's key customers. Putting together a sound CRM plan will force the organization to think about CRM needs, technology alternatives, and the providers that sell them. Selecting the right tools and providers is an important step, but should not occur until a CRM plan is completed.

Aside from creating a CRM plan and getting the firm's employees to buy-in to the idea and uses of CRM tools, managers must also consider any existing CRM initiatives implemented in piecemeal fashion across the firm. Integrating new and existing applications into one enterprise-wide initiative should be one of the primary objectives of the CRM implementation process. Additionally, the firm must decide on specific performance outcomes and assessments for the program and provide adequate training to the CRM application users.

Creating the CRM Plan

Putting together a solid plan for a CRM project is crucial both as an aid to purchasing and implementing CRM applications and to obtain executive management approval and funding for the project. The plan should include the objectives of the CRM program, its fit with corporate strategy, new applications to be purchased or used, the integration with or replacement of existing methods or legacy CRM systems, the requirements for personnel, training, policies, upgrades, and maintenance, and the costs and time frame for implementation. Once this document is completed, the firm will have a roadmap for guiding the purchase and implementation process.

The objectives of any CRM initiative should be customer-focused. Examples might include increasing sales per customer, improving overall customer satisfaction, more closely integrating the firm's key customers with internal processes, or increasing supply chain responsiveness. These will vary somewhat based on the overall strategic focus of the firm. Once these objectives are in place, tactical goals and plans can be instituted at the functional level, consistent with the CRM objectives. Finally, tactical performance measures can be used to track the ongoing performance of the CRM program. This performance will serve to justify the initial and ongoing costs of the program. For example, Illinois-based Vibrant Credit Union upgraded their CRM system recently, with an eye toward improving service while also leveraging sales opportunities with its 41,000 members. "We see CRM as allowing us to create better and deeper relationships with our members," explains president/CEO Matt McCombs. "Our goal is to have a complete picture of what our members look like, identify the opportunities or struggles they've had, and create a better experience for them. We measure everything on depth of relationship, primarily services per household, total deposits per household, total loan dollars per household, and specific overall product penetration levels per household. Our goals are very aggressive in increasing these metrics."[36]

Involving CRM Users from the Outset

In order to get acceptance of a new CRM initiative, employee involvement and support is required. This comes about by enlisting the help of everyone affected by the initiative from the very beginning. Employees need to understand how the CRM program will affect their jobs before they will buy-in to it. Creating a project team with members from sales, customer service, marketing, finance, and production, for instance, will tremendously aid in the selection, training, use, and acceptance of the CRM program. The team can contact CRM application providers and collect information regarding capabilities and costs, and they can also collect baseline or current customer service, sales, complaint, and other meaningful performance information. The team should also be heavily involved in evaluating and selecting the CRM applications and then implementing and integrating the applications in each department. As the implementation process continues, closely monitoring system performance will keep users convinced of its value and keep everyone committed to its success.

Quite a bit of research has been conducted to study CRM implementations and most have found a direct relationship between program success and employee involvement. Several researchers in New Zealand, for instance, talked with managers at three banks that had implemented CRM programs several years earlier. Two of the banks had failed to focus on employee buy-in while the third bank introduced a new sales culture to complement its CRM project, to win employee support. Eventually, the third bank's CRM system proved to be much more successful. In another example, Beene Garter, a Michigan area accounting firm, designed an internal contest to "sell" CRM to its employees. "Teams were assigned 'homework' on client records and the software tracked who entered updates," says Den Ouden of Beene Garter. "The contest mirrored components of the Olympics and was called 'Go for the Gold' to tie into the software name, GoldMine," she adds. Their success was remarkable. Users' attitudes about the CRM project changed from anxiety associated with entering all the data, to familiarity which created easy adoption and continuous use.[37]

Selecting the Right Application and Provider

Once the organization has completed its plan for CRM, it should have a fairly good idea of what they are going to do and which activities will require automation or technology. The job then becomes one of finding an appropriate application and determining how much customization will be required to get the job done. Finding the best application and supplier can be accomplished a number of ways including:

- visiting a CRM-oriented tradeshow
- using a CRM consulting firm
- searching CRM or business publications such as *Customer Magazine, Call Center Helper*, and *Inside Supply Management*
- using the knowledge of internal IT personnel, who already know the market, and
- searching the many CRM supplier directories and websites.

Firms should seek help from a number of these alternatives, and internal IT personnel should be viewed as internal consultants for the application and the supplier identification and selection process. Firms must analyze and compare the various products available. In her CRM handbook, Dychè recommends comparing the following software characteristics:[38]

- integration and connection requirements (the hardware, software, and networking capabilities)
- processing and performance requirements (the volume of data and number of users it can support)
- security requirements
- reporting requirements (preformatted and customized reporting capabilities)
- usability requirements (ability for users to customize the software, display graphics, and print information)
- function-enabling features (workflow management, e-mail response engine, predictive modeling capabilities), and
- performance capabilities (response times for various queries).

Comparing these CRM capabilities should narrow the list of qualified vendors substantially. When finally selecting a supplier for the application, one of the primary criteria for firms to consider is the support available from the application provider. Vendors offering implementation and after-sale user support that meet the needs of the firm should be valued more highly than other vendors. Suppliers offering free trial usage to verify their products' capabilities is another element that needs to be considered. Finally, cost and contract negotiations should be carefully considered.

Integrating Existing CRM Applications

In most firms, CRM systems are not one single product, but rather a suite of various applications that have been implemented over time. One of the biggest mistakes made is that departments across the firm implement various CRM applications without communicating these actions to other departments. Eventually, these systems will interfere with each other, as they communicate with the same customer, sending confusing and irritating signals that can chase customers away quickly.

Customer contact mechanisms need to be coordinated so that every CRM application user within the firm knows about all the contact activity for each customer. Today, this lack of integration is leading to real problems as call centers and sales offices seek to please and retain customers by adopting customer loyalty programs, customer-tracking mechanisms, and various customer contact mechanisms like Twitter and Facebook, without making this information widely known and available within the firm. Additionally, multiple stand-alone CRM applications throughout the company result in duplication of effort, incompatible formats, wasted money, and disgruntled customers. Compatible CRM modules are needed that are linked to one centralized database or **data warehouse** containing all customer information. Thus, from one database, users in the organization can retrieve information on a customer's profile, purchase history, promotion responses, payment history, web visitations, merchandise returns, warranty repairs, and call center contacts.

By integrating CRM information obtained throughout the firm, managers can analyze the information and make much more customer-focused decisions. Using predictive models and statistical analyses, firms can identify customers most likely to purchase certain products, respond to a new promotion, or churn. As the number of customers grow, however, their transactions and the desire to analyze all of this information is referred to as **big data analytics**. While analyzing large amounts of data has been around a long time (in the 1950s people analyzed data by hand from spreadsheets), today the process is extremely fast and can analyze much more data for quick decisions. The ability to analyze data today and make quick decisions is amazing—retailer Macy's adjusts pricing in near-real time for 73 million items, based on demand and inventory; Walmart.com uses text analysis, machine learning, and even synonym mining to produce relevant search results, which has improved online purchase completions by 10 to 15 percent; and the Los Angeles and Santa Cruz police departments have taken an algorithm used to predict earthquakes, tweaked it and started feeding it crime data, which results in predictions of where crimes are likely to occur down to 500 square feet. Los Angeles has seen a 33 percent reduction in burglaries and a 21 percent reduction in violent crimes in areas where the software is being used. And finally, who can forget the story of hedge fund manager Mike Burry (made famous in the Christian Bale movie "The Big Short") who was able to read the data pertaining to the subprime mortgage loans prior to 2008 and see the devastating effect they were going to have on the world's economy.[39]

Establishing Performance Measures

Performance measures linked to CRM program objectives (and customers) allow managers to monitor the progression of their systems in meeting objectives. It also serves to keep everyone excited and informed about the benefits of a well-designed program and will identify any implementation or usage problems as they occur, allowing causes to be found and solutions to be implemented quickly.

At the organizational level, performance measures should concentrate on areas deemed strategically important, such as CRM program productivity, new customers added, or sales generated from the CRM program. Some examples of these measures are listed in Table 10.1. Note that the performance measures cover the customers, the CRM program itself, and the users. Additionally, all of the metrics should be transparent and easy to measure. At the user level, other more tactical performance measures should be developed and tracked, supporting the firm-wide strategic measures. Linking performance measures in this way will give the firm the best chance of a successful program implementation and continued management of the program into the future.

Training for CRM Users

Another important step in the implementation process is to provide and require training for all of the initial system users and then provide ongoing training as applications are added or as other personnel begin to see the benefits of the CRM system. Training can also help convince key users such as sales, call center, and marketing personnel of the benefits and uses of CRM applications. Training is one area crucial to CRM program success.

Table 10.1	CRM Program Performance Measures		
PERFORMANCE MEASUREMENT TYPE	**DEPARTMENT OR USER-LEVEL PERFORMANCE MEASURES**		
	FIELD SALES	**CALL CENTER**	**MARKETING**
Customer Loyalty	1. % customer repurchases 2. avg. # repurchases 3. # customer referrals	1. # customer product information requests 2. # customer praises	1. % existing customers responding to promotions 2. # customer referrals
Customer Satisfaction	1. avg. # customer visits to resolve problem 2. # field service visits per customer	1. # complaints per customer 2. % first call resolution	1. % customers responding more than once to promotions 2. # customers engaged using social contacts
Average Sales Revenue per Customer	1. # sales quotas met 2. % repeat visits resulting in sales	1. sales per customer call 2. cross-sales and up-sales per customer call 3. % calls converted	1. # website/social visits per customer 2. website/social purchases per customer
CRM Productivity	1. % sales quotas met 2. # new leads generated 3. % new leads closed	1. avg. caller time 2. # complaints resolved 3. sales/call/hr. 4. transactions/agent/hr.	1. # segment catalogs produced 2. # promotional e-mails sent 3. # marketing campaigns 4. avg. campaign response rate
CRM User Satisfaction	1. sales rep. satisfaction score	1. call center agent satisfaction score	1. user satisfaction score
CRM User Training	1. hrs. training per year per rep. 2. # CRM applications trained per rep.	1. hrs. training per year per agent 2. # CRM applications trained per agent	1. hrs. training per year per user 2. # CRM applications trained per user

Unfortunately, in a survey conducted by *Customer Relationship Management* magazine, 43 percent of the respondents said their user training "needed improvement."[41] Unless the users are shown the personal gains they'll receive for taking time to learn the software and its capabilities, the CRM applications will most likely go unused or underused. Karen Ainley, product manager at U.K.-based CRM software developer Sage, emphasizes that shortcuts in training can ultimately prove costly. "The perception that CRM is so easy to use that you don't need training is a fallacy. By dismissing the need for training in the hope that users will simply 'learn on the job' and adapt their way of working, companies really are limiting the software's potential."[42]

Training managers and users in the key customer contact areas can also help the firm decide what customizations to the CRM applications are required, before the system is put into use. This is particularly important for larger firms where supply chains and the sales and marketing processes are complex. In many cases, CRM system implementation means that other systems already in place will be phased out or merged with the new system. Training can help personnel decide how best to phase out old systems and phase in the new ones. CRM consultant Barton Goldenberg suggests that firms should create a training profile for each of its CRM system users to provide training before, during, and after the implementation in one or more of these areas: computer literacy training, business process training, CRM application training, remedial training, and new user training.[43]

TRENDS IN CRM

According to the editors at CRM Magazine, the four emerging trends in CRM today are ease of use, personal value creation, continuous connectivity, and small data.[44] These topics will be discussed next.

Ease of Use

CRM solutions must become more intuitive, as users demand easy-to-understand interfaces similar to a number of popular consumer websites. This will eliminate the need for much of the training involved when implementing CRM applications. CRM users must be able to perform simple tasks like creating a lead, adding an interaction pertaining to a lead, or generating a report easily and quickly within the system. Easy-to-use CRM applications empower users and will enhance the adoption of CRM products. According to Virginia-based Capterra, a business software review company, Teamgate, is the highest rated user-friendly CRM software. The cloud-based system provides clear graphs and visual representations, making it easy to gain various insights. Its smart reporting capability is a handy tool to make tactical and strategic sales decisions. The software is compatible with Android, iOS, and Windows phone devices and integrates with Google apps and other third-party apps.[45]

Personal Value Creation

Collecting large volumes of data from a CRM system won't necessarily make salespeople more productive. Users will determine the system's value based on the useful information and insights it brings to their jobs every day. Successful CRM solutions will be measured by the personal value brought to users. According to FinancesOnline, an independent review platform for B2B, SaaS, and financial solutions, HubSpot CRM is one of the highest rated and value-enhancing CRM solutions. One reason is that the basic platform is free. Because it's free, HubSpot CRM is popular among freelancers and small businesses, but it is also a powerful lead-generation tool for larger enterprises. It won FinancesOnline's Expert's Choice Award for 2017.[46]

Continuous Connectivity

In today's digital age, the best CRM applications will become much more integrated into the daily work lives of users. Users need to access CRM information anytime and anyplace using their smartphones, tablets, and desktops. The top CRM systems must deliver continuous connectivity, enabling quick decision-making. Today's cloud CRM applications offer access using a web browser. Users can log in to the CRM system, simultaneously, from any Internet-enabled computer or device. Often, cloud CRM applications provide users with mobile apps to make it easier to use the CRM on smartphones and tablets. Teamgate and Hubspot, mentioned above, are both cloud applications.

Small Data

Recently, the use of big data analysis to improve sales has been the subject of much discussion (as evidenced by our earlier discussion in this and previous chapters). With CRM, the emphasis needs to be on **small data**. Small data is the data that was around before big data. It can bring CRM users meaningful insights, for instance, about one customer's next likely purchase or provide a demographic analysis of customers that bought a specific good or service. According to Paula Tompkins, the founder and CEO of Michigan-based ChannelNet, a digital marketing company, better use of small data will make CRM more successful. While categorizing all the data at one time would be overwhelming, it is better to define content data scope based on a customer journey map aligned to a specific business need. A customer journey map will identify what data are most important to customers and deepen an understanding of each customer. According to Paula, a customer journey map is akin to walking the distance in a customer's shoes—from the first hello to the contractual end of the financial relationship. The goal is simple: Use small data to learn about the customer.[47]

SUMMARY

In this chapter, we introduced and discussed the elements of CRM, its place within the field of supply chain management, the requirements for successful CRM program implementation, and the current trends in CRM. As we learned in this chapter, customer relationship management is really all about listening to customers, learning about customers, and treating customers right. For as long as there have been businesses, some firms have been very successful at keeping customers satisfied and coming back, while others have not. For the past ten or fifteen years though, both the level of competition in the market place as well as available computer technology and software capabilities have been increasing quite dramatically. Thus, we have seen a shift in CRM toward use of technology, software, and the Internet to better analyze, segment, and serve customers with the objective of maximizing long-term customer profitability.

Firms today are learning how to combine many channels of customer contact to better serve customers, resulting in better customer satisfaction and more sales. Though many traditional CRM applications are expensive, firms can use a structured approach to design an appropriate plan and then analyze and select the right applications and vendors to implement a successful CRM program. Cloud-based CRM applications have also become a major consideration in the development of many firms' CRM efforts.

KEY TERMS

big data analytics, 401

call centers, 396

clickstream, 392

cross-selling, 389

customer churn, 390

customer contact centers, 396

customer defection analysis, 390

customer lifetime value, 391

customer profitability, 391

customer relationship management, 386

customer service, 394

customer value, 391

data warehouse, 401

event-based marketing, 392

knowledge management system, 394

lead management system, 393

mobile marketing, 389

perfect order, 394

permission marketing, 389

posttransaction elements, 396

pretransaction, 396

QR codes, 389

relationship marketing, 389

sales activity management system, 393

sales force automation, 392

sales territory management systems, 393

segment customers, 388

Seven Rs Rule, 394

small data, 403

target marketing, 388

transaction, 396

DISCUSSION QUESTIONS

1. Define the term *customer relationship management* and what has impacted the way companies view CRM over the past fifteen or twenty years.

2. How does the actual practice of CRM differ from the use of CRM software?

3. Why have so many CRM efforts failed? Can you cite a personal example of a good or bad CRM effort?

4. Describe why CRM is so important in managing supply chains. What do firms with good CRM programs do? Can you cite an example aside from the ones mentioned in this chapter?

5. What is *segmenting customers* and why is it perhaps the most important activity in CRM? What do firms typically do with the segments of customers?

6. Define these terms: permission marketing, cross-selling, and churn reduction.

7. How would an analysis of customer defections help the firm become more competitive?

8. Why is the determination of customer lifetime value important?

9. Pick a specific company near your residence and describe how they could personalize their communications with you, the customer.

10. Describe several ways that CRM applications can increase the effectiveness and productivity of a firm's sales force.

11. How does *your definition* of customer service compare to the *Seven Rs Rule*?

12. Describe some businesses in your area providing good customer service, then list some providing poor customer service.

13. Describe the types of customer service that come before, during, and after the sale. Why are they important to CRM?

14. Are call centers good or bad for the firm? What has been your experience with call centers?

15. Do you think call center outsourcing negatively affects customer service? Explain.

16. Could self-service websites be used in place of call centers? Explain.

17. How should customer satisfaction be measured at a bank? A restaurant? A manufacturing firm? A retailer?

18. Do you think CRM applications unnecessarily invade customers' privacy? Explain.

19. Describe the steps necessary for designing and implementing a successful CRM program.

20. What is the most common mistake made when designing and implementing a CRM program?

21. How do you think CRM performance should be measured? Suggest several performance measures for a specific company.

22. What sort of problems can occur with a firm's existing or legacy CRM applications?

23. What do *big data* and *big data analytics* refer to?

24. Why is CRM program user training so important? How could the training requirement be minimized?

25. How can firms help to assure the privacy and security of their customers' information and data?

26. How do various social media impact an organization's CRM methods? Should firms use social media for attracting new customers?

27. What do you think the true value of social CRM is?

28. What is *cloud computing* and what are its advantages for CRM?

29. What is the difference between on-demand computing, the software-as-a-service model, and cloud computing?

30. What is small data? What does it have to do with CRM?

ESSAY AND PROJECT QUESTIONS

1. Go to the International Customer Management Institute's website: www.icmi.com and look at several news stories. Describe a new development in call center usage or technology.

2. Identify an on-demand Internet CRM provider and see if you can determine what is "free" and what is not.

3. Search on the term "call center technology" and describe a few of the latest uses of technology in call centers.

4. What are some of the latest developments in Internet privacy laws?

5. Identify some of this year's best and worst customer service providers. Have you dealt with any of these companies? If so, describe your service experience.

PROBLEMS

1. From the information given below, rank the customers in terms of their lifetime value.

	AVG. ANNUAL SALES	AVG. PROFIT MARGIN	EXPECTED LIFETIME
Customer A:	$ 2,500	17%	8 years
Customer B:	$ 4,000	12%	6 years
Customer C:	$ 1,200	30%	12 years

Use a discount rate of 6 percent and treat the average annual sales figures as annuities. Should any of these customers be fired?

2. A tree provider to plant nurseries is trying to use customer lifetime value to determine the value of its customers. Two customers are shown below. Use customer lifetime value to determine the importance of each customer. Use an 8 percent discount rate. What do you recommend?

	AVG. ANNUAL SALES	AVG. PROFIT MARGIN	EXPECTED LIFETIME
Customer A:	$ 21,500	20%	10 years
Customer B:	$ 14,000	10%	6 years

CASES

1. Polly's Sweet Treats and Drinks*

Iris Rice has managed Polly's Sweet Treats and Drinks for ten years. The owner, Mamie Hammond, essentially gave Iris full control about seven years ago. Mamie had established Polly's almost thirty years ago and has been in semiretirement for about the last five years. Mamie is considering selling the store and is giving Iris first choice. Iris is extremely excited about the prospect of owning her own business. However, Iris wants to expand the offerings and ultimately increase the number of locations.

*Written by Rick Bonsall, D. Mgt., McKendree University, Lebanon, IL. The people and institution are fictional and any resemblance to any person or any institution is coincidental. This case was prepared solely to provide material for class discussion. The author does not intend to illustrate either effective or ineffective handling of a managerial situation.

Iris asked Mamie if she could have one year to investigate how changes will be received by customers. Although excited, Iris is also very nervous about being an owner. It is one thing to manage a business owned by someone else and another to own it yourself. Mamie reflected on how she felt when she started Polly's. Mamie wanted Polly's to stay successful and would like it to grow as well. Iris was an excellent manager; therefore, Mamie believed Iris would be an excellent owner. Consequently, Mamie thought it was worth the time to let Iris make some changes and build her confidence.

Polly's Sweet Treats and Drinks has a variety of customers. Although Iris has never officially put them in any specific categories, now that she may be the owner, she began thinking along those lines. Polly's opened at 11 a.m. and closed at 8 p.m. Much of the lunch crowd is comprised of young mothers with children in school, on up to senior citizens. Around 3 p.m., the complexion of the crowd changes. It becomes dominated by teenagers. This made sense since school let out around 3 p.m. As 6 p.m. approached, Iris noticed that families were the predominate group.

Currently, the menu consisted of dessert-like food such as cakes, pies, tarts, muffins, doughnuts, and other pastries. The drinks were a variety of sodas that included diet and caffeine-free drinks. Polly's also served a variety of hot and cold teas, hot and cold coffees, as well as milk, hot chocolate, milk shakes, and frozen drinks.

Although Polly's Sweet Treats and Drinks has been in business for about thirty years and it still has a strong customer base, Iris is concerned about the future. Iris believes that for her to eventually expand and add new stores she will need a new menu. Iris thinks that she will have to expand the menu to include things beyond sweet treats and drinks. She is thinking about adding sandwiches and possibly a single blue plate special for those who may want a "full-course" type meal.

Iris has a Bachelor's degree in business. The one point that her favorite professor drilled into her was that you need data to make effective decisions. Once you collected the data you had to analyze it, then use it to drive your decisions. Currently, Iris has no data except for her casual observations of what is happening in the store from 11 a.m. to 8 p.m. In order to make the best decisions for Polly's Sweet Treats and Drinks, Iris understood she needed to collect some data. She could not assume that the changes she felt were necessary were the changes the customers would accept.

She talked it over with Mamie. Mamie's concern was that since such a variety of customers visited Polly's it would be a challenge to fulfill all their likes. Plus, many people liked the store as it was. They had visited it as children and now brought their kids there. Would they lose customers or gain them if changes were made? After much discussion Mamie and Iris agreed that they needed more information about what their customers liked and didn't like.

Discussion Questions

1. Iris Rice is planning to take a huge step toward changing Polly's Sweet Treats and Drinks' business strategy. What does she need to do to collect the type of data she'll require to make an effective decision? Explain what you would do if you were her. What would be your plan? Be specific.

2. Assume Iris moves forward with her plan to change the menu. This could alter the current customer base. Advise her on actions she should take to address customer defections. Explain how the actions will benefit her and potentially prevent customer defections.

3. The case suggests that many of Polly's Sweet Treats and Drinks' customers are from the same community. Parents came there as children and are now bringing their children there. Would you recommend that Iris use social CRM? Why or why not?

©2019 Cengage Learning

2. Perfection Call Center*

Perfection Call Center performs customer service activities for several different companies, large and small. Although the current clients are very satisfied, new business has been hard to obtain. Therefore, the board of directors recently hired Tim Roy as the new director of Perfection Call Center. His primary responsibility is to grow the business.

Tim is very familiar with call centers. He has worked in one or been associated with one most of his professional life. He decided that before he did anything else, he needed to observe how things were going in Perfection and understand its strengths and weaknesses. The professionalism of the call center personnel was beyond reproach. Tim listened in on call after call from different operators and found them to be polite, knowledgeable, and solution-oriented.

Tim's next task was to meet with clients and obtain a thorough understanding of how they felt about Perfection. As he talked with senior people from each client company, Tim discovered that everyone was extremely happy. In fact, Tim would even go as far as to declare that the clients were delighted with the services they received from Perfection.

To Tim's tremendous surprise, he discovered that Perfection Call Center did not collect very much performance data. In addition, he found out that most of the current clients had started with Perfection in its early days of operation; consequently, the relationship between them and Perfection had gradually grown very strong over the years. The result was a customer base that trusted Perfection to naturally do an outstanding job for them.

Unfortunately, potential new clients were not as trusting. They wanted to see proof that Perfection Call Center was as good as they claimed. What historical data did they have that illustrated past customer satisfaction? More importantly, what type of reports would they provide new customers to demonstrate they were meeting their expectations? Tim Roy now saw the problem. Perfection Call Center was extremely good at what it did; however, besides testimonials from current clients, they could not prove it.

Discussion Questions

1. Does Tim's conclusion make sense to you, that is, do you agree with it? What specific information could Perfection Call Center provide moving forward that would demonstrate to new clients that Perfection was meeting expectations?

2. Tim also discovered that Perfection Call Center had an outdated call center system. He decided to request a major update from the board of directors. The issue is that Tim was brought in to raise revenues through new clients, not to increase expenses

*Written by Rick Bonsall, D. Mgt., McKendree University, Lebanon, IL. The people and institution are fictional and any resemblance to any person or any institution is coincidental. This case was prepared solely to provide material for class discussion. The author does not intend to illustrate either effective or ineffective handling of a managerial situation.

with new systems. Develop an argument for Tim that highlights the benefits of upgrading the call system. Explain how it can drive customer satisfaction, which potentially drives new business.

3. Besides providing the usual customer problem resolution services, Tim believes there are other services that his call center could provide that would enhance his clients' revenue streams, and through its contract enable Perfection to trigger bonuses based on those increased revenues. What type of additional services could Perfection provide that addresses this point? Explain how those services would potentially enhance Perfection's clients' revenue, thus their own.

©2019 Cengage Learning

3. Burley's Biscuits, Beef, and Veggies*

Bob Burley and his brother Buford ran the best restaurant in Dallas, Texas. Many out-of-towners would visit Dallas and go to Burley's Biscuits, Beef, and Veggies for a good wholesome meal. One thing that Bob and Buford had going for them in a town as active as Dallas was that their restaurant was open 24/7. This was especially important for all the big game days. No matter what the professional sport was, thousands flocked to the city to watch their favorite team.

Bob and Buford were living high on the hog, but they weren't the type to take anything for granted. They knew they had the best food in the area and the service was second to none. However, in-between major sports events and other activities such as concerts, the restaurant wasn't always filled to capacity. A full restaurant with people wanting and waiting to get in was what Bob and Buford desired.

The Burley brothers discussed what to do at great length. There had to be some way to entice people out of their homes and into the restaurant every day of the week. Bob and Buford hoped that whenever a family decided to go out to eat the first place that would cross their mind was Burley's Biscuits, Beef, and Veggies.

Jose Sanchez was a close friend of the Burley brothers. Jose owned a marketing firm and one of Jose's specialties was customer relationship management (CRM). One day, Jose heard the brothers talking about ways they could fill the restaurant. Jose interrupted and starting asking them about their CRM program. Bob and Buford told Jose they didn't have one. They weren't clear on what exactly a CRM program was. Jose explained that it simply meant building and maintaining profitable long-term customer relationships. Jose asked how many customers were return customers. Although they had a lot of people they saw over and over again in the restaurant, neither Bob nor Buford knew the specific number. Jose then stated the obvious—the Burley brothers had to develop and implement a CRM program if they wanted to achieve their dream of nonstop business.

Discussion Questions

1. We know from the case that Bob and Buford have customers from many different segments. They could segment them by sports, business people, regulars, breakfast, lunch, or dinner crowd. How should Jose explain to the Burleys the advantages of

*Written by Rick Bonsall, D. Mgt., McKendree University, Lebanon, IL. The people and institution are fictional and any resemblance to any person or any institution is coincidental. This case was prepared solely to provide material for class discussion. The author does not intend to illustrate either effective or ineffective handling of a managerial situation.

segmenting customers? What types of customer relationship management activities should they implement that would drive business to the restaurant? Explain how those CRM activities would help.

2. Bob is excited about implementing social CRM. Buford is against using social CRM. Who do you agree with and why?

3. As part of their CRM initiative, Buford wants to utilize the "Seven Rs Rule." Can this truly be part of their CRM program or is it just a nice sounding "slogan"? Explain whether or not it can help as part of the CRM program.

©2019 Cengage Learning

ADDITIONAL RESOURCES

Barnes, J. G., *Secrets of Customer Relationship Management*. New York, NY: McGraw-Hill, 2001.

Bergeron, B., *Essentials of CRM: A Guide to Customer Relationship Management*. New York, NY: John Wiley & Sons, 2002.

Bloomberg, D. J., S. LeMay, and J. B. Hanna, *Logistics*. Upper Saddle River, NJ: Prentice Hall, 2002.

Dychè, J., *The CRM Handbook: A Business Guide to Customer Relationship Management*. Upper Saddle Rivear, NJ: Addison-Wesley, 2002.

Fitzsimmons, J., and M. Fitzsimmons, M., *Service Management for Competitive Advantage*. New York, NY: McGraw-Hill, 1994.

Lawrence, F. B., D. F. Jennings, and B. E. Reynolds, *eDistribution*: Mason, OH: South-Western, 2003.

Metters, R., K. King-Metters, and M. Pullman, *Successful Service Operations* Management, Mason, OH: South-Western, 2003.

END NOTES

1. Wardley, M., "Worldwide CRM Applications Software Forecast, 2016–2020: Cloud-Based ApplicationsIncrease in Penetration Mix," August 2016, https://www.idc.com/getdoc.jsp?containerId=US41645115

2. Bernier, P., "Come Together, Right Now, over Me: Companies Get Acquisitive About the Customer Experience," *Customer* 32(1), 2014: 8–9.

3. Bernier, P., "CRM: It's Getting Better All the Time," *Customer* 32(4), 2014: 8,10,12.

4. Miller, J., "How to Conquer a CRM Monster," *CIO* December 8, 2016: 1.

5. http://www.crmsearch.com/crm-software-market-share.php

6. http://www.superoffice.com/blog/crm-software-statistics

7. Dychè, J., *The CRM Handbook: A Business Guide to Customer Relationship Management*, Upper Saddle River, NJ: Addison-Wesley, 2002.

8. Bergeron, B., *Essentials of CRM: A Guide to Customer Relationship Management*, New York, NY: John Wiley & Sons, 2002.

9. Ragins, E., and A. Greco, "Customer Relationship Management and e-Business: More than a Software Solution," *Review of Business* 24(1) (2003): 25–30.

10. Anonymous, "Does CRM Really Work?" *The Financial Brand.com* September 11, 2015: 1.

11. Vella, J., and A. Caruana, "Encouraging CRM Systems Usage: A Study among Bank Managers," *Management Systems* Review 35(2), 2012: 121–133.

12. Sebring, S., "CRM Mistakes," *Credit Union Management* 40(1), 2017: 18–21.

13. Dickie, J., "Fueling the CRM Engine," *Customer Relationship Management* 11(4), 2007: 10.

14. Goldenberg, B., "Your People Are Half the Battle," *Customer Relationship Management* 14(4), 2010: 6.

15. Eastwood, G., "How Domino's Pizza Is Using AI to Enhance the Customer Experience," *CIO* March 3, 2017: 1.

16. https://blog.hubspot.com/blog/tabid/6307/bid/33749/7-Companies-That-Totally-Get-Their-Buyer-Personas.aspx#sm.0001xmpj5yz80efoyst18pubqxrv5

17. Anonymous, "Mogreet Lists 7 Goals for Boosting Mobile Marketing in 2014," *Entertainment Close–Up* January 27, 2014: 1.

18. Anonymous, "Research and Markets; Asia-Pacific M-Commerce Snapshot 2015," *Investment Weekly News* April 25, 2015: 74.

19. Hintze, J., "A Wealth of Progress," *USBanker* 120(4), 2010: 32–33.

20. Jenkins, P., "Crimes, Misdemeanours and Cross-Selling," *FT.com* September 19, 2016: 1.

21. https://www.proclivitysystems.com

22. Nadeem, M., "How e-Business Leadership Results in Customer Satisfaction and Customer Lifetime Value," *The Business Review, Cambridge* 6(1), 2006: 218–224.

23. http://www.mpellsolutions.com/customer-defections

24. Bailor, C., "Not Fade Away," *Customer Relationship Management* 11(2), 2007: 22–26.

25. Collieer, S., "Another Way to Look at '*Member Value*'," *Credit Union Magazine* 73(1), 2007: 9A.

26. Anonymous, "Jonel Programs Mobile Device-Ready, Sales Force Analytics Tool," *Concrete Products* 119(4), 2016: 60.

27. Anonymous, "ClearSlide and LevelEleven Announce Partnership: Sales Activity Management System Now Integrates with Sales Engagement Platform Leader," *PR Newswire* October 5, 2016: 1.

28. Satter, M., "Tech Helps Sell Policies, But Doesn't Retain Customers," *Benefits Selling. Breaking News* May 11, 2016: 1.

29. Rankis, N., "Knowledge Management Using Digital Dashboards," *Modern Casting* 104(9), 2014: 40–43.

30. Shaprio, R. D., and J. L. Heskett, *Logistics Strategy: Cases and Concepts*, St. Paul, MN: West Publishing Co., 1985.

31. https://www.forbes.com/sites/grantmartin/2017/04/10/americas-best-airlines-2017/#2e0e0c501f29

32. Finneran, M., and B. Herrington, "Excelling at Mobile Customer Service," *Customer* 31(2), 2012: 42.

33. Terney, J., "Survey: Call Centers Now Profit Centers," *Multichannel Merchant* December 21, 2010: 1.

34. http://www.tmcnet.com/channels/call-center-management/articles/419851-5-call-center-security-tips-protecting-customer-data.html

35. Anonymous, "Lessons from the Domino's Turnaround," *Restaurant Hospitality* 94(6), 2010: 30.

36. Franklin, D., "Implementing a CRM System," *Credit Union Management* 38(8), 2015: 24–27.

37. Shum, P., L. Bove, and S. Auh, "Employees' Affective Commitment to Change: The Key to Successful CRM Implementation," *European Journal of Marketing* 4211/12 (2008): 1346–1371; Lassar, W., S. Lassar, and N. Rauseo, "Developing a CRM Strategy in Your Firm," *Journal of Accountancy* 206(2), A2008: 68–73.

38. Dychè, J., *The CRM Handbook: A Business Guide to Customer Relationship Management*, Upper Saddle River, NJ: Addison-Wesley, 2002.

39. http://searchcio.techtarget.com/opinion/Ten-big-data-case-studies-in-a-nutshell and http://dataconomy.com/2017/01/7-mistakes-big-data-analysis

40. Stockford, P., and J. Staples, "Contact Center Metrics That Matter," *Customer* 31(11), 2013: 44–45; Hughes, A., "How to Measure CRM Success," www.dbmarketing.com/articles

41. Dickie, J., "Don't Confuse Implementation with Adoption," *Customer Relationship Management* 13(5), 2009: 10.

42. Davey, N., "CRM Training's Most Common Calamities," *MyCustomer.com* September 19, 2011: 1–10.

43. Goldenberg, B., "A CRM Initiative's Bermuda Triangle," *Customer Relationship Management* 11(5), 2007: 10.

44. Keenan, M., "4 CRM Trends for 2016," *CRM.com* January 6, 2016, http://www.destinationcrm.com/Articles/Web-Exclusives/Viewpoints/4-CRM-Trends-for-2016-108394.aspx

45. See www.teamgate.com

46. See www.financesonline.com and www.hubspot.com

47. Tompkins, P., "Reinventing the Mortgage Customer Experience," *Mortgage Banking* 76(7), 2016: 72–76.

Chapter 11

GLOBAL LOCATION DECISIONS

Looking forward, value chains disrupted by evolving technologies, such as digitalization, automation and 3D printing, will significantly impact how companies invest and how they define a competitively advantaged location.

—IBM Institute for Business Value[1]

McDonald's has been extraordinary at site selection; it was a pioneer in studying the best places for retail locations. One of the things it did is study very carefully where sprawl was headed.

—Eric Schlosser, author, "Fast Food Nation"[2]

Globalization continues to reshape the international economy. For many organizations, global expansion can have a tremendous positive impact on both top and bottom line. For others, expanding or relocating a business may be a matter of survival, as they face increasing pressure from foreign competitors.

—Greg Wiebe, Partner, KPMG LLP[3]

Learning Objectives

After completing this chapter, you should be able to

- Explain the impact of global location decisions on a supply chain.
- Identify the factors influencing location decisions.
- Understand the impact of the regional trade agreements on location decisions.
- Use several location evaluation models.
- Understand the advantages of business clusters.
- Explain the impact of sustainable development on facility location.

Chapter Outline

Introduction

Global Location Strategies

Critical Location Factors

Facility Location Techniques

Business Clusters

Sustainable Development and Facility Location

Additive Manufacturing and Its Impact on Facility Location

Summary

Amazon's Global Logistics Facilities Network

Jeff Bezos founded Amazon.com in 1995. Amazon's corporate mission is "to be Earth's most customer-centric company, where customers can find and discover anything they might want to buy online."[4] The company's global operations are in Australia, Brazil, Canada, China, France, Germany, India, Italy, Japan, Mexico, Netherlands, Spain, and United Kingdom. In 2016, Amazon's total net sales amounted to $136 billion with sellers from more than 130 countries fulfilling orders to customers in 185 countries.[5]

The early belief in electronic commerce was that millions of customers could be served without requiring the infrastructure of a Sears or Walmart. Today, online retailers are finding that without their own warehouses and shipping capabilities, customer service could suffer. The objective was to improve logistics and reduce shipping times to customers. The company currently has logistics facilities including fulfillment centers/distribution centers (DCs), pantry/fresh food DCs, sortation centers, delivery stations, and Prime Now hubs in twenty-five U.S. states. Logistics facilities in Europe are located in Czech Republic, France, Germany, Italy, Poland, Slovakia, Spain, and the United Kingdom. In Asia, the fulfillment centers are found in China, India, and Japan. Amazon also has logistics facilities in Canada, Mexico, and Brazil. With 214 logistics facilities in the United States exceeding 89.1 million square feet with 149 logistics facilities outside of United States exceeding 50.3 million square feet of space, Amazon is able to enhance its supply chain capabilities.[6] By strategically locating its logistics facilities and improving operations, Amazon is able to provide faster service globally.

Currently, Amazon uses third-party logistics companies such as UPS, FedEx, and DHL for delivery. However, Amazon's extensive logistics facilities network and early success with Prime Now to offer third-party delivery suggests that Amazon has the capability to provide comprehensive third-party services. According to a Baird Equity Research report, "Amazon may be the only company with the fulfillment/distribution density and scale to compete effectively with global UPS/FedEx/DHL."[7]

INTRODUCTION

Locating a facility is an important decision affecting the efficiency and effectiveness of managing supply chains, the level of service provided to customers, and a firm's overall competitive advantage. A supply chain is a network of facilities and the location of production facilities, offices, distribution centers, and retail sites determines the efficient flow of goods to and from these facilities. Once a decision on locating a facility is made, it is costly to move or shut down that facility. Thus, facility location has a long-term impact on the supply chain and must be an integral part of a firm's supply chain strategy. With increased globalization and investments in technology infrastructure, faster transportation, improved communications, and open markets, companies can locate anywhere in the world—previously thought to be impossible. Amazon.com has shown that by strategically locating its logistics facilities and improving operations, the company is able to provide faster service globally (see the opening SCM Profile).

It would appear that easy access to global markets and corporate networks makes the role of location less important as a source of competitive advantage. However, successful business clusters in areas such as Silicon Valley, Wall Street, the California wine region, and the Italian leather fashion center show that location still matters. The existence of business clusters in many industries provides clear evidence that innovation and successful competition are concentrated geographically. Dr. Michael Porter suggests that the immediate business environment is just as important as the issues impacting companies internally, in affecting location decisions.[8] Business clusters are discussed in detail later in this chapter.

Global location decisions involve determining the location of the facility, defining its strategic role, and identifying markets to be served by the facility. For example, Honda's global location strategy of building cost-effective manufacturing facilities in areas that best meet the requirements of local customers has served the company well. Honda's "Small Born" manufacturing strategy is to start small and expand production as local demand increases. This approach allows the company to be efficient and profitable, even when production volumes are low. Honda's first auto plant in the United States was built in Marysville, Ohio. Then the company added a second factory in East Liberty, Ohio. As demand for Honda automobiles continued to increase, Honda opened a facility to assemble the Odyssey minivans in Alabama and an auto plant producing Civic GX Natural Gas Vehicles in Indiana. Honda's Ridgeline trucks, which were built previously in Canada, are today produced in the Alabama plant. Toyota, Nissan, Mercedes, BMW, Volkswagen, Kia Motors, and Hyundai have also built assembly plants in the United States to cater to the local automobile markets.

GLOBAL LOCATION STRATEGIES

Global location decisions are made to optimize the performance of the supply chain and be consistent with the firm's competitive strategy. According to IBM Institute for Business Value's 2016 Global Location Trends annual report, "Companies continue to internationalize and seek opportunities around the world, despite growing uncertainty about several key economies and the future political commitment to globalization. As part of this, companies have altered investment patterns and many countries are playing different roles in global value chains."[9] A firm competing on cost is more likely to select a location that provides a cost advantage. For instance, Amazon.com, as discussed in the chapter-opening SCM Profile, locates logistics facilities in areas that will minimize logistics and inventory costs. Many toy manufacturers have also moved their factories to Vietnam, Thailand, or China because of cost advantages provided by these countries.

A firm that competes on speed of delivery, such as the FedEx Corporation, uses the hub-and-spoke approach to location determination. FedEx's first and largest hub in the United States is in Memphis, Tennessee. This site has 48 miles of conveyer belts, the capacity to sort 1.3 million packages, and has 7,000 people. About 150 to 160 trunk aircrafts and 130 trucks arrive at the Memphis International Airport every night. The objective is to have each container delivered from vehicle to sorting hub in under 30 minutes. The belts convey 180,000 items an hour through the scanner.[10] Planes land at the rate of one every ninety seconds. In addition to the SuperHub in Memphis, FedEx has six main hubs in the United States in Oakland, California; Newark, New Jersey; Fort Worth, Texas; Indianapolis, Indiana; Anchorage, Alaska; and Miami, Florida (serving Latin America). International main hubs are in Toronto, Canada; Dubai, UAE; Paris, France; Cologne, Germany; Osaka, Japan; Guangzhou, China; and Singapore.[11] Each of the hubs has been picked for its central location and easy access to customers.

To get the most out of foreign-based facilities, managers must treat these plants as a source of competitive advantage. These foreign facilities have a strategic role to perform. Professor Kasra Ferdows of Georgetown University suggests a framework consisting of six strategic roles depending on the strategic reason for the facility's location and the scope of its activities:[12]

- *Offshore factory*: An **offshore factory** manufactures products at low cost with minimum investment in technical and managerial resources. These products tend to be exported. An offshore factory imports or locally acquires parts and then exports all of the finished products. The primary objective is simply to take advantage of low labor costs. For example, in the early 1970s, Intel built a labor-intensive offshore factory to produce simple, low-cost components in Penang, Malaysia.

- *Source factory*: A **source factory** has a broader strategic role than an offshore factory with plant management heavily involved in supplier selection and production planning. The source factory's location is dictated by low production cost, fairly developed infrastructure, and availability of skilled workers. Hewlett-Packard's plant in Singapore started as an offshore plant in 1970 but with significant investments over a ten-year period was able to become a source factory for calculators and keyboards.[13]

- *Server factory*: A **server factory** is set up primarily to take advantage of government incentives, minimize exchange risk, avoid tariff barriers, and reduce taxes and logistics costs to supply the regional market where the factory is located. An example would be Coca-Cola's international bottling plants, each serving a small geographic region.

- *Contributor factory*: The **contributor factory** plays a greater strategic role than a server factory by getting involved in product development and engineering, production planning, making critical procurement decisions, and developing suppliers. In 1973, Sony built a new server factory in Bridgend, Wales. By 1988, the factory was involved in the design and development of many of the products it produced and now serves as a contributor factory in Sony's global manufacturing network.[14]

- *Outpost factory*: The **outpost factory** is set up in a location with an abundance of advanced suppliers, competitors, research facilities, and knowledge centers to get access to the most current information on materials, components, technologies, and products. Since the facility normally produces something, its secondary role can be that of a server or an offshore factory. For example, Lego still produces molds and toys in Denmark, Germany, Switzerland, and the United States in spite of the higher manufacturing cost.[15] Lego's factories serve as outpost facilities with access to research facilities, institutions of higher learning, and sophisticated suppliers of plastic materials.

- *Lead factory*: A **lead factory** is a source of product and process innovation and competitive advantage for the entire organization. It translates its knowledge of the market, competitors, and customers into new products. In the early 1970s, both Intel and Hewlett-Packard established offshore factories in Southeast Asia. Over time, the strategic roles of these factories were upgraded to that of lead factories.

CRITICAL LOCATION FACTORS

One of the most challenging tasks as a company grows, relocates, or starts up, is where to position assets strategically to create a long-term competitive advantage. Some of the questions and concerns that need to be addressed for each potential location are:

- What will be the reaction of shareholders, customers, competitors, and employees?
- Where is the target market located?
- Will the location provide a sustainable competitive advantage?
- What will be the impact on product or service quality?
- Can the right people be hired?
- What will be the effect on the supply chain?
- What is the projected cost?
- What will be the impact on delivery performance?
- How will the market react?
- Is the transfer of people necessary, and, if so, are employees willing to move?

There are basically three levels of location decisions: the global market or country selection, the subregion or state selection, and the community and site selection. The process starts with an analysis of the market region of the world that bears a strategic interest to the organization, and, eventually, a country is targeted. Once the country is selected, the focus shifts to finding a subregion or state within the country that best meets the company's location requirements. Finally, the community and site for the facility are selected. The weighted-factor rating model, which is discussed later in this chapter, can be used to make a location decision at each of the levels we have mentioned. Table 11.1 lists a number of factors affecting each of the three levels of location decisions and a discussion of each of these factors follows.

Table 11.1 Important Factors in the Location Decision Process			
LOCATION FACTOR	COUNTRY	REGION/STATE	COMMUNITY
Regional trade agreements—trade barriers, tariff, and import duties	X		
Competitiveness of nations—economic performance, government efficiency, business efficiency and infrastructure	X		
Government taxes and incentives	X		
Currency stability	X		
Environmental issues	X	X	X
Access and proximity to markets	X	X	X
Labor issues	X	X	X
Access to suppliers	X	X	X
Transportation issues	X	X	X
Utility availability and cost	X	X	X
Quality-of-life issues	X	X	X
State taxes and incentives		X	X
Right-to-work laws		X	X
Local taxes and incentives			X
Land availability and cost			X

Regional Trade Agreements and the World Trade Organization

An understanding of regional trade agreements and the **World Trade Organization** (WTO) is critical to the facility location decision process because of their impact on tariffs, costs, and the free flow of goods and services. The WTO is the successor to the General Agreement on Tariffs and Trade (GATT), which was responsible for setting up the multilateral trading system after World War II. Today, the WTO is the "only global international organization dealing with the rules of trade between nations. Its main function is to ensure that trade flows as smoothly, predictably, and freely as possible."[16] The WTO has 164 members and its goal is to help producers of goods and services, exporters, and importers conduct their business. Other functions include administering the WTO agreements, providing a forum for trade negotiations, handling trade disputes, monitoring national trade policies, providing technical assistance and training programs for developing countries, and cooperating with other international organizations.

There are 423 regional trade agreements under the WTO in force today.[17] Examples of the better-known regional trade agreements are the **European Union (EU)**, the **North American Free Trade Agreement (NAFTA)**, the **Southern Common Market (MERCO-SUR)**, the **Association of Southeast Asian Nations (ASEAN)**, and the **Common Market for Eastern and Southern Africa (COMESA)**. Several of these are discussed here:

- *The European Union (EU)*: Set up after World War II, the European Union was officially launched on May 9, 1950, with France's proposal to create a European federation consisting of six countries—Belgium, Germany, France, Italy, Luxembourg, and the Netherlands. A series of accessions in 1973 (Denmark, Ireland, and the United Kingdom), 1981 (Greece), 1986 (Spain and Portugal), 1995 (Austria, Finland, and Sweden), 2004 (Czech Republic, Estonia, Cyprus, Latvia, Lithuania, Hungary, Malta, Poland, Slovenia, and Slovakia), 2007 (Bulgaria and Romania), and 2013 (Croatia) has resulted in a total of twenty-eight member states. Currently, the EU has five candidate countries—Iceland, Montenegro, Serbia, Republic of Macedonia, and Turkey.[18] Two highlights of the EU are the establishment of the single market in 1993 and the introduction of the euro notes and coins on January 1, 2002. The EU has a population of 508 million inhabitants, third largest after China and India and with combined GDP of more than 14,600 billion Euros. In 2015, Greece became the first country to default on an IMF loan payment. EU member countries then provided bailout aid to Greece to enable the country to service its debt obligations. In 2016, British citizens voted to exit the European Union. The United Kingdom has to invoke an agreement called Article 50 of the Lisbon Treaty to leave the EU, giving the two sides two years to agree on the terms of the split.

- *The North American Free Trade Agreement (NAFTA)*: This trade agreement among the United States, Canada, and Mexico was implemented on January 1, 1994. NAFTA created the world's largest free trade area, currently with over 450 million people and GDP of more than US$20 trillion.[19] Many tariffs were eliminated with an immediate effect, while others were phased out over periods ranging from five to fifteen years. According to the Office of the US Trade Representative, "U.S. exports to Canada and Mexico support more than three million American jobs and U.S. trade with NAFTA partners has unlocked opportunity for millions of Americans by supporting Made-in-America jobs and exports."[20] In addition, Canada and Mexico are two of the United States' largest export markets and these countries buy more Made-in-America goods and services than any other countries in the world.

- *The Southern Common Market (MERCOSUR)*: This economic and political agreement among Argentina, Brazil, Paraguay, Uruguay, and Venezuela was formed in March 1991 with the signing of the Treaty of Asuncion. The agreement was created with the goal of forming a common market/customs union between the participating countries and was based on economic cooperation between Argentina and Brazil that had been in place since 1986. After Paraguay was suspended in 2012 for violating the Democratic Clause of Mercosur, Venezuela was added as a full member but was suspended on December 1, 2016. Associate members include Bolivia, Chile, Colombia, Ecuador, Peru, and Suriname. The total population of the member states is more than 307 million.[21]

- *The Association of Southeast Asian Nations (ASEAN)*: This association was created in 1967 in Bangkok, Thailand, and is comprised of the ten countries in the Southeast Asian region—Brunei, Cambodia, Indonesia, Laos, Malaysia, Myanmar, Philippines, Singapore, Thailand, and Vietnam. The primary objective of ASEAN is "to accelerate the economic growth, social progress, and cultural development in the region through joint endeavors in the spirit of equality and partnership in order to strengthen the foundation for a prosperous and peaceful community of Southeast Asian Nations."[22]

- *Common Market for Eastern and Southern Africa (COMESA)*: COMESA was established in 1994 to "be a fully integrated, internationally competitive regional economic community with high standards of living for all its people ready to merge into an African Economic Community."[23] The mission of COMESA is to "Endeavour to achieve sustainable economic and social progress in all member states through increased co-operation and integration in all fields of development particularly in trade, customs, and monetary affairs, transport, communication and information, technology, industry and energy, gender, agriculture, environment and natural resources."[24] COMESA has nineteen member states, a population of over 492.5 million, GDP per capita of $1,335, and annual imports of around US$183 billion with exports of US$95 billion and forms a major market for both internal and external trading.[25] The member countries are Burundi, Comoros, D.R. Congo, Djibouti, Egypt, Eritrea, Ethiopia, Kenya, Libya, Madagascar, Malawi, Mauritius, Rwanda, Seychelles, Sudan, Swaziland, Uganda, Zambia, and Zimbabwe.

Competitiveness of Nations

A nation's competitiveness (in international trade) is defined by the Organization of Economic Cooperation and Development (OECD) as "a measure of a country's advantage or disadvantage in selling its products in international markets."[26] There are two competing sources for national competitiveness rankings. One is the *World Competitiveness Yearbook* published annually by the Swiss business school IMD and the other is *The Global Competitiveness Report*, prepared by the World Economic Forum (WEC). According to Arturo Bris, director IMD Competitiveness Center and professor of Finance, "There is no single nation in the world that has succeeded in a sustainable way without preserving the prosperity of its people. Competitiveness refers to such an objective: it determines how countries, regions, and companies manage their competencies to achieve long-term growth, generate jobs and increase welfare. Competitiveness is therefore a way towards progress that does not result in winners and losers: when two countries compete, both are better off."[27] Since the two organizations use different criteria for their rankings, the lists vary somewhat. The rankings from both publications are shown in Table 11.2.

Table 11.2	International Competitiveness Ranking	
RANKING	2016–17 GLOBAL COMPETITIVENESS REPORT (WEC)	2016 WORLD COMPETITIVENESS YEARBOOK (IMD)
1.	Switzerland	Hong Kong
2.	Singapore	Switzerland
3.	USA	USA
4.	Netherlands	Singapore
5.	Germany	Sweden
6.	Sweden	Denmark
7.	United Kingdom	Ireland
8.	Japan	Netherlands
9.	Hong Kong	Norway
10.	Finland	Canada
11.	Norway	Luxembourg
12.	Denmark	Germany
13.	New Zealand	Qatar
14.	Taiwan	Taiwan
15.	Canada	United Arab Emirates
16.	United Arab Emirates	New Zealand
17.	Belgium	Australia
18.	Qatar	United Kingdom
19.	Austria	Malaysia
20.	Luxembourg	Finland

Sources: http://www3.weforum.org/docs/GCR2016-2017/05FullReport/TheGlobalCompetitivenessReport2016-2017_FINAL.pdf; and https://www.imd.org/uupload/imd.website/wcc/scoreboard.pdf

IMD's *World Competitiveness Yearbook* features sixty-one economies and provides businesses with the basic information on location decisions. There are 327 criteria, which are broadly grouped into four competitiveness factors:[28]

- *Economic Performance* (five subfactors): "Macro-economic evaluation of the domestic economy, international trade, international investment, employment, and prices."

- *Government Efficiency* (five subfactors): "Extent to which government policies are conducive to competitiveness: public finance, fiscal policy, institutional framework, business legislation, and societal framework."

- *Business Efficiency* (five subfactors): "Extent to which the national environment encourages enterprises to perform in an innovative, profitable, and responsible manner: productivity and efficiency, labor market, finance, management practices, and attitudes and values."

- *Infrastructure* (five subfactors): "Extent to which basic, technological, scientific, and human resources meet the needs of business: basic infrastructure, technological infrastructure, scientific infrastructure, health, and environment and education."

The yearbook provides an analysis of the data collected and ranks nations according to their abilities to create and maintain an organization's competitiveness. Data from the report can be used to compare countries globally, to see five-year trends, to understand strengths and weaknesses, and to examine factors and subfactors. In addition, businesses can use the yearbook to determine investment plans and assess locations for new operations. The **United States** was ranked third in 2016, behind Hong Kong and Switzerland.

The World Economic Forum defines competitiveness as "the set of institutions, policies, and factors that determine the level of productivity of an economy."[29] Their Global Competitiveness Report examines 138 economies in the 2016–2017 report and uses what the Forum describes as their "12 Pillars of Competitiveness" to determine the rankings. These are briefly described below.

The World Economic Forum's 12 Pillars of Competitiveness

1. Institutions—the legal and administrative framework.

2. Infrastructure—the transportation, telecommunications, and power networks.

3. Macroeconomic environment—the stability of the macroeconomic environment is important for business and includes issues such as fiscal deficits, inflation rates, unemployment, and GDP growth rates.

4. Health and primary education—investment in health services and quantity and quality of basic education.

5. Higher education and training—amount of secondary, tertiary, vocational, and on-the-job training in the workforce.

6. Goods market efficiency—overall environment for exchange of goods.

7. Labor market efficiency—the environment for male and female workers.

8. Financial market development—how resources are channeled to businesses.

9. Technological readiness—how readily the economy adapts to new technologies.

10. Market size—the availability of domestic and international markets for firms.

11. Business sophistication—the quality of the overall business networks and quality of individual firms' operations and strategies.

12. Innovation—overall support for innovative activities.

The top five countries according to the Global Competitiveness Report for 2016–2017 are Switzerland, Singapore, United States, Netherlands, and Germany. The criteria covered in the World Competitiveness Report represent issues that organizations would like to know about before making a country location decision. All things equal, a country with a higher competitiveness ranking would provide a better business climate for locating a facility than another country that is listed as less competitive.

In yet another competitiveness ranking, the global audit and tax service KPMG's *Competitive Alternatives* study examines business competitiveness in 111 cities and 10 countries—Australia, Canada, France, Germany, Italy, Japan, Mexico, the Netherlands, the United Kingdom, and the United States.[30] The study analyzes twenty-six major cost factors such as labor, facility, income taxes, other taxes, transportation, cost of capital, utilities, and incentives across seven business-to-business segments and twelve significant manufacturing sectors. The report helps organizations to identify and compare potential locations for relocation or starting new operations internationally. While the study is limited to ten countries, it nonetheless provides a useful guide for organizations considering locating in these countries. For 2016, the lowest-cost country ranking is as follows: (1) Mexico,

(2) Canada, (3) Netherlands, (4) Italy, (5) Australia, (6) France, (7) United Kingdom, (8) Germany, (9) Japan, and (10) United States. The United States, due to the strong dollar, is considered a high cost business location compared to its peers.

Government Taxes and Incentives

Government incentives, business attitude, economic stability, and taxes are important location factors. Several levels of government must be considered when evaluating potential locations. At the federal level, a *tariff* is a tax imposed by the government on imported goods to protect local industries, support the country's balance of payments, or raise revenue. Thus, countries with high tariffs discourage companies from importing goods into the country. At the same time, high tariffs encourage multinational corporations to set up factories to produce locally. However, membership in the WTO requires countries to open up their markets and to reduce the tariffs imposed on imported goods. Regional trade agreements such as NAFTA, MERCOSUR, and EU also serve to reduce tariffs among member nations to promote the free movement of goods. Many countries have set up *foreign trade zones* (FTZs) where materials can be imported duty-free as long as the imports are used as inputs to the production of goods that are eventually exported. If the goods are sold domestically, no duty is paid until they leave the free trade zones.

In the United States, forty-one states have a broad-based personal income tax and forty-six states have a corporate income tax. For example, Nevada is a business-friendly state that does not have a corporate income tax, state personal income tax, corporate franchise tax, or inventory tax. Companies such as Amazon.com have taken advantage of this by setting up warehouses in Nevada. The other states that do not have an individual income tax are Alaska, Florida, South Dakota, Texas, Washington, and Wyoming.[31] New Hampshire and Tennessee have a limited income tax on individuals. These two states tax dividends and interest. Location incentives at the state and local government levels are also important.

Currency Stability

One factor that impacts business costs and consequently location decisions is instability in currency exchange rates. Any organization involved with international business will be subjected to the risk of currency fluctuation. The discussion in the nearby SCM Profile on international business location costs shows how the strong U.S. currency affects the U.S. ranking in terms of location costs. For example, Amazon.com is exposed to foreign exchange rate fluctuations and risks associated with its international operations as presented in its 2016 10-K report as shown here: [32]

Foreign Exchange Risk
During 2016, net sales from our International segment accounted for 32% of our consolidated revenues. Net sales and related expenses generated from our internationally-focused websites, and from www.amazon.ca and www.amazon.com.mx (which are included in our North America segment), are primarily denominated in the functional currencies of the corresponding websites and primarily include Euros, Japanese Yen, and British Pounds. The results of operations of, and certain of our intercompany balances associated with, our internationally-focused websites and AWS (Amazon Web Services) are exposed to foreign exchange rate fluctuations. Upon consolidation, as foreign exchange rates vary, net sales and other operating results may differ materially from expectations, and we may record significant gains or losses on the

remeasurement of intercompany balances. For example, as a result of fluctuations in foreign exchange rates during 2016, International segment net sales decreased by $489 million in comparison with the prior year.

Environmental Issues

How the environment is managed has a significant impact on human health. The inability to dispose of solid and hazardous waste, plus the presence of illegal waste, contributes to high incidences of diseases such as hepatitis A and amebiasis. Global warming, air

SCM Profile   International Business Location Costs[33]

Competitive Alternatives has been providing information on business location costs focusing on cities and countries in North America and mature market economies in Europe and Asia Pacific since 1996. The 2016 report provides a comprehensive guide for comparing business costs in more than 100 cities in ten countries, covering twelve manufacturing sector operations and seven distinct business service operations. The study uses twenty-six location-sensitive cost factors categorized as labor costs, facility costs, transportation costs, utility costs, cost of capital, taxes other than income, income taxes, and incentives. The United States is used as the baseline for the study. The major cost factors as reported in *Competitive Alternatives* are shown below:[34]

- Labor costs represent the largest category of location-sensitive cost factors for all industries examined. For service operations, labor costs typically range from 72 to 86 percent of location-sensitive costs, while for manufacturing operations the typical range is from 40 to 57 percent.

- Facility costs represent the next significant cost factor. For service operations, office lease costs represent 4 to 15 percent of total location-sensitive costs. For those manufacturing operations that lease their facilities, industrial lease costs range from 2 to 5 percent of location-sensitive costs. For manufacturing operations that own their facilities, facility costs are capitalized but impact the cost of capital (interest on debt and depreciation of buildings).

- Transportation costs are only assessed for manufacturing operations, reflecting the costs of moving finished goods to markets. For the manufacturing firms examined, transportation costs represent 6 to 21 percent of total location-sensitive costs.

- Utility costs represent up to 7 percent of location-sensitive costs. Electricity and natural gas costs are more significant for manufacturers than for nonmanufacturers.

- Costs of capital include both depreciation and interest. These are major cost items for manufacturers, ranging from 11 to 25 percent of location-sensitive costs. Capital-related costs are much less significant for service operations, at 0 to 8 percent of location-sensitive costs.

- Taxes include income, property, transaction, and other business taxes. Collectively, taxes typically represent 3 to 16 percent of total location-sensitive costs for the service operations examined and 10 to 18 percent for manufacturing operations.

Overall, the top three countries with the lowest business costs are Mexico, Canada, and Netherlands. The United States is ranked tenth due to the strong U.S. dollar, which has constrained U.S. competitiveness.

pollution, and acid rain are issues that are increasingly being debated as the price to pay for industrialization. Millions of people live in cities with unsafe air and with asthma cases at an all-time high. In response to rising environmental concerns, the Clinton Administration negotiated the North American Agreement on Environmental Cooperation (NAAEC) as a supplementary environmental agreement to NAFTA. The key objectives of the agreement are to "foster the protection and improvement of the environment in the territories of the parties for the well-being of present and future generations" and "promote sustainable development based on cooperation and mutually supportive environmental and economic policies."[35] The agreement provides a framework for the three NAFTA countries to conserve, protect, and enhance the North American environment and to effectively enforce the environmental laws.

With trade liberalization, there is a need for environmental cooperation. The WTO agreement makes direct reference to sustainable development and the desire to protect and preserve the environment. WTO members recognize that "their relations in the field of trade and economic endeavor should be conducted with a view to raising standards of living, ensuring full employment and a large and steadily growing volume of real income and effective demand, and expanding the production of and trade in goods and services, while allowing for the optimal use of the world's resources in accordance with the objective of sustainable development, seeking both to protect and preserve the environment and to enhance the means for doing so in a manner consistent with their respective needs and concerns at different levels of economic development."[36]

Consumers and nongovernment agencies are now pressuring multinationals to be more environmentally conscious. Global organizations are assessing their total environmental footprints by focusing on carbon and life-cycle analysis. The life-cycle approach looks beyond just the carbon footprint since it focuses on a cradle-to-grave analysis of how products and services affect the environment. Walmart, for example, has a program to assist suppliers in managing their energy and materials usage and carbon emissions and now companies such as Procter & Gamble, IBM, and Pacific Gas & Electric have adopted this approach.

Access and Proximity to Markets

Initially, many companies outsourced their manufacturing to China because of its cost competitiveness. However, as China's per capita income continues to rise, more and more companies are indicating that their main reason for being in China is to have access to the local markets rather than for export reasons. As such, many companies are now expanding into China not only to take advantage of the lower costs but also to access the local market. Likewise, Honda is a global company that aims to build plants in locations that best satisfy the needs of local customers. Honda has assembly plants in the United States, Japan, Malaysia, China, and Indonesia, to name a few markets where Honda sells its vehicles.

In the service industry, proximity to customers is even more critical. Few customers will frequent a remotely located gas station or a supermarket if another more accessible alternative is available. Similarly, fast-food restaurants are well situated next to busy highway intersections to take advantage of heavy traffic areas. Walmart's early supercenters were located in predominantly rural markets to avoid direct competition with major discount stores in large metropolitan areas. Many regional chains, such as Jamesway, Bradlees, Caldor, Venture, and Hills, went out of business because they were not competitive with larger and more efficient chains such as Walmart and Target. More recently, Walmart has changed its location strategy to include urban locations in the west and northeast regions of the United States. In China, Walmart's location strategy has focused more on downtown areas, where most of the customers are located. McDonald's, for example, is looking for the next big urban sprawl which indicates where their customers are likely going to be.

Ashley Furniture Industries, the largest home furnishings manufacturer, decided a few years earlier to build a new plant in Advance, North Carolina, reversing the trend to move manufacturing to China. Ashley recognizes that speed in meeting customer demands is becoming more critical. The company is further expanding that facility by 1 million square feet to enhance its ability to serve consumers and retail customers along the East Coast, particularly in the Southeast.[37] While the company still sources items such as glass and mirrors globally, larger and heavier components and upholstery are made in the United States.

Amazon.com has performed quite well in meeting customers' needs quickly. In this era of instant gratification and fast turnaround on product delivery, many companies are finding out that it is better to manufacture their products domestically. Ford is another manufacturer that has moved manufacturing of its F-650 and F-750 trucks from Mexico to an assembly plant in Avon Lake, Ohio. As a result, shipping costs are reduced due to proximity to market and manufacturing quality has improved. One of the reasons that Fuyao Glass Industry Group moved its plant from China to Ohio is to be close to its customers. Fuyao is a Chinese auto glass supplier with 20 percent of the global market share. "For our customers, they had the expectations that you will be located close to them for supply chain stability," Fuyao chairman Cao Dewang (aka Cho Tak Wong) said. "If you ship from China, it is subject to all sorts of disruptions such as weather or shipping company delays."[38]

Labor Issues

Issues such as labor availability, productivity, and skill; unemployment and underemployment rates; wage rates; turnover rates; labor force competitors; and employment trends are key labor factors in making facility location decisions. Mexico has long competed on cheap labor but cannot continue to depend on this source of competitive advantage because of the emergence of lower labor cost countries like China. While China's labor cost is low compared to many countries, inflation and high economic growth has contributed to a sharp increase in wages there. Consequently, the apparel industry, which depends heavily on cheap labor, is beginning to see a shift in production from the "textile hub" in southern China to Vietnam or Cambodia because of the comparatively cheaper labor cost there. According to Cao Dewang, chairman of Fuyao Glass Industry Group, "Wage and transportation costs are getting higher in China. Compared with four years ago, labor wages [in China] today have tripled. Meanwhile, transportation in the U.S. costs the equivalent of less than one yuan ($0.15) per kilometer, while road tolls [in China] are higher."[39]

Although it is true that low labor cost is an important factor in making location decisions, sustainable competitive advantage depends on productive use of inputs and continual product and process innovations. Singapore is an example of a country that first relied on cheap labor to attract foreign direct investments. Over time, Singaporeans were able to increase the level of worker skills and develop human resource capabilities. The country moved from a producer of low-cost goods to one making high value-added products.

Access to Suppliers

Many firms prefer locations close to suppliers because of material availability and transportation cost reasons. The proximity of suppliers has an impact on the delivery of materials and, consequently, the effectiveness of the supply chain. Japanese electronics makers are finding that China is a better place to set up manufacturing facilities even though it means the cost to transport finished products to the U.S. market is higher. The reason is that a high proportion of components needed to make finished electronic products are made in China. Apple's iPhones, for example, are produced by Foxconn in China.

Utility Availability and Cost

The availability and cost of electricity, water, and gas are also important location considerations. In economically emerging countries, it is not unusual that the supply of electricity has not kept pace with the high speed of development, resulting in work stoppages due to electrical outages. Even developed countries, such as the United States, are not immune to energy problems, although for different reasons. The largest blackout in U.S. history occurred in 2003, with more than 50 million people without power in the Northeast, Midwest, and parts of Canada. The primary cause of the blackout was a software problem in the control room of the FirstEnergy Corporation in Ohio. Energy experts are concerned with the weakness of the U.S. power grid and predict that the United States could be one big catastrophic event away from a total meltdown in the country.

In heavy industries, such as steel and aluminum mills, the availability and cost of energy are critical considerations. The concern for companies is to have the power available when needed, at an affordable price. Consequently, areas such as upstate New York, the Tennessee Valley, and parts of Canada, which provide low-cost power, are gaining in location popularity because of their plentiful energy supply. With the explosive growth in energy-intensive industries such as machinery, auto, and steel, demand for electricity has outpaced the generation capacity in China and the country has experienced power shortages in the past. However, the power generated by the completed Three Gorges Dam Project, the world's largest hydropower complex, will help meet China's rapidly growing energy needs. With an increasing number of manufacturing facilities being added in China, the country must continue to invest in clean power-generating plants. China today is the world's largest producer of solar power. However, due to the sheer size of China, solar energy represents only 1 percent of the country's energy output.[40]

Quality-of-Life Issues

Quality of life can be defined as "general well-being of individuals and societies."[41] So what exactly are the issues affecting quality of life? While there is no definitive agreement on a set of **quality-of-life factors**, the Chamber of Commerce in Jacksonville, Florida, has annually prepared a report on the overall quality of life in the metropolitan area based on a comprehensive set of factors, which include the following:[42]

- *Achieving Educational Excellence*: Performance in terms of high-school graduation rates, college entrance test scores, teacher salaries, student–teacher ratios, and number of degrees awarded at universities and higher-education institutions provides an indicator of the quality of the education system.

- *Growing a Vibrant Economy*: Performance indicators such as net employment growth, new housing starts, and the unemployment rate show the economic health of the community. The economy must also be sufficiently diverse to allow for long-term careers for both spouses.

- *Preserving the Natural Environment*: Performance indicators include an air-quality index, average daily water use, and the amount of recycled waste diverted from landfills. A viable recycling program and clean air indicate a community's commitment to a green environment and the future health of the community.

- *Promoting Social Well-being and Harmony*: Performance indicators include whether racism is a problem, number of births to single mothers, volunteerism rate, and homeless survey count. A community where people and organizations contribute time and money to helping others in need shows a happy, affluent, and caring environment.

- *Enjoying Arts, Culture, and Recreation*: Performance measures include the public and private support for the arts, number of public performances and events, and library circulation. A community that offers choice in terms of cultural, entertainment, recreational, and sporting activities is a more attractive location than one that offers fewer of these options.

- *Sustaining a Healthy Community*: Performance indicators include the infant mortality rate, number of people without health insurance, cancer death rate, suicide rate, and new HIV cases. The ability to access good, affordable medical care provides residents with peace of mind and determines whether the community is a desirable place to live.

- *Maintaining Responsive Government*: Performance measures in this category include voter turnout, satisfaction rate with city services, number of neighborhood organizations, and a diverse and representative government. In the current economic situation, many state and local governments in the United States have been struggling to balance their budgets due to a slow growth economy and are considering cutting services and increasing taxes. This, in turn, will tend to negatively impact the quality of life.

- *Moving Around Efficiently and Safely*: This factor can be measured by indicators such as the average commute time to work, bus ridership, number of airport passengers, and the motor vehicle accident rate. If the roads are constantly jammed with traffic, this causes huge losses of productive time. The ability to travel easily within the area and to other locations affects the quality of life of the residents.

- *Keeping the Community Safe*: Performance indicators here include violent crime rate, percentage of people who feel safe in their neighborhood, people reporting being victims of crime, and the murder rate. In the United States, there has been a trend toward suburban living because of the perception of safer neighborhoods and, therefore, a better place to live. While there has been a decline in murders in Mexico's ongoing brutal drug war, the number of kidnappings is increasing and, as a result, vigilante militias taking justice into their own hands are on the rise.[43] Thus, the presence of crime could frighten off firms considering locating in Mexico.

Right-to-Work Laws

In the United States today, there are twenty-four states with **right-to-work laws**: Alabama, Arizona, Arkansas, Florida, Georgia, Idaho, Indiana, Iowa, Kansas, Louisiana, Mississippi, Nebraska, Nevada, North Carolina, Michigan, North Dakota, Oklahoma, South Carolina, South Dakota, Tennessee, Texas, Utah, Virginia, and Wyoming. A right-to-work law "secures the right of employees to decide for themselves whether or not to join or financially support a union."[44] In the last few decades, there has been a shift in the U.S. auto industry to the South, with assembly plants built in Tennessee, South Carolina, and

Alabama, all of which are right-to-work states. Dubbed the *Southern Auto Corridor*, this cluster represents a new era in U.S. auto manufacturing. The trend to locate in the sunny, incentive-friendly, nonunionized South will most likely continue to grow.

Land Availability and Cost

As land and construction costs in most big cities continue to escalate, the trend is to locate in the suburbs and rural areas. Suburban locations can be attractive because of the cost and wide choice of land, available workforce, and developed transportation network. As mentioned earlier, when Honda first decided to set up a factory in the United States, it located in Marysville, a small town about 40 miles from Columbus, Ohio. Affordable land near the highway was readily available and Honda could draw its workforce from several communities around Marysville. Similarly, when Honda built its assembly plant in Alabama to meet the increased demand for its Odyssey minivans and sport utility vehicles, the site was located in Lincoln, 40 miles east of Birmingham. When Honeywell decided to move its manufacturing facility in Phoenix, Arizona, to China, the decision was to go to Suzhou, a city about 30 miles from Shanghai. Although the Pudong industrial zone in Shanghai was an attractive site, Suzhou had lower land and labor costs, which were deemed important decision factors.

While we have observed many U.S. manufacturers moving overseas to find cheaper production locations, a Chinese billionaire moved his operations to the United States. According to Cao Dewang, chairman of Fuyao Glass, "a combination of cheap land, reasonable energy prices and other incentives means that, despite higher manufacturing costs, he can still make more money by making glass in the U.S. than by exporting Chinese-made panes to the U.S. market."[45] Fuyao Glass invested more than $1 billion to open two U.S. factories in Moraine, Ohio and Plymouth, Michigan. The glass maker was able to acquire the former General Motors assembly plant in Ohio that had been vacant since late 2008 for $15 million and secured more than $10 million in tax credits and infrastructural enhancements from Ohio.[46]

FACILITY LOCATION TECHNIQUES

Two techniques that are commonly used by organizations to assist in making global location decisions are described here: the weighted-factor rating model and the break-even model. The two techniques are discussed below.

The Weighted-Factor Rating Model

The **weighted-factor rating model** is a method commonly used to compare the attractiveness of several locations along a number of quantitative and qualitative dimensions. Selecting a facility location using this approach involves the following steps:

1. Identify the factors that are considered important to the facility location decision.
2. Assign weights to each factor in terms of their relative importance. Typically, the weights sum to 1.
3. Determine a relative performance score for each factor considered. Typically, the scores vary from 1 to 100, although other scoring schemes can be used.
4. Multiply the factor score by the weight associated with each factor and sum the weighted scores across all factors.
5. The location with the highest total weighted score is the recommended location.

Since the factors, the individual weights, and the scores are subject to interpretation and bias by the analyst, it is highly recommended that a team approach be used when performing this type of analysis. Ideally, the team should include representatives from marketing, purchasing, production, finance, and transportation, and possibly a key supplier and customer impacted by the location.

Determining the scores for each factor can include several intermediate steps. Comparing a labor cost score, for instance, might include determining an acceptable wage scale, along with insurance, taxes, and training costs and any other associated labor costs for each potential location. Then the total labor costs can be compared and translated into the final labor cost scores for each location by assigning the lowest-cost location the maximum score and then assigning the other locations a score based on their respective labor costs. Example 11.1 illustrates the use of the weighted-factor location model.

Example 11.1   The Weighted-Factor Location Model

The following factors have been identified as critical to making a location decision among three countries—China, Singapore, and Indonesia. A group of functional managers has determined the factors, weights, and scores to be used in the analysis.

IMPORTANT LOCATION FACTORS	FACTOR WEIGHTS (SUM TO 1)	CHINA SCORES (1–100)	SINGAPORE SCORES (1–100)	INDONESIA SCORES (1–100)
Labor cost	0.20	100	40	90
Proximity to market	0.15	100	60	80
Supply chain compatibility	0.25	80	80	60
Quality of life	0.30	70	90	60
Stability of government	0.10	80	100	50

To determine where the new facility should be located, the weighted scores for the three countries are calculated as follows:

China = 0.20(100) + 0.15(100) + 0.25(80) + 0.30(70) + 0.10(80) = 20 + 15 + 20 + 21 + 8 = 84.
Singapore = 0.20(40) + 0.15(60) + 0.25(80) + 0.30(90) + 0.10(100) = 8 + 9 + 20 + 27 + 10 = 74.
Indonesia = 0.20(90) + 0.15(80) + 0.25(60) + 0.30(60) + 0.10(50) = 18 + 12 + 15 + 18 + 5 = 68.

Based on the total weighted score, China would be the recommended country in which to locate the new facility.

The Break-Even Model

The **break-even model** is a useful location analysis technique when fixed and variable costs can be determined for each potential location. This method involves the following steps:

1. Identify the locations to be considered.
2. Determine the fixed cost for each facility. The components of fixed cost are the costs of land, property taxes, insurance, equipment, and buildings.
3. Determine the unit variable cost for each facility. The components of variable cost are the costs of labor, materials, utilities, and transportation.
4. Construct the total cost lines for each location on a graph.
5. Determine the break-even points on the graph. Alternatively, the break-even points can be solved algebraically.
6. Identify the range over which each location has the lowest cost.

Example 11.2 illustrates the use of the break-even model.

Example 11.2   The Break-Even Model

Three locations have been identified as suitable candidates for building a new factory. The fixed and unit variable costs for each of three potential locations have been estimated and are shown in the following table.

LOCATION	ANNUAL FIXED COST ($)	UNIT VARIABLE COST ($)
A	500,000	300
B	750,000	200
C	900,000	100

Given a forecasted demand of 3,000 units per year, the best location can be found by first plotting the three total cost curves, represented by

$$TC_A = 500,000 + 300Q$$
$$TC_B = 750,000 + 200Q$$
$$TC_C = 900,000 + 100Q$$

The three curves are shown in Figure 11.1.

Next, the break-even point between location A and location B is determined:

$$TC_A = TC_B$$
$$500,000 + 300Q = 750,000 + 200Q$$
$$100Q = 250,000 \text{ and then } Q = 2,500 \text{ units.}$$

This indicates that producing less than 2,500 units per year would be cheaper at location A (when the lower fixed cost predominates), while producing more than 2,500 units per year would be cheaper at location B (when the lower variable cost predominates).

Next, the break-even point between location B and location C is determined:

$$TC_B = TC_C$$
$$750,000 + 200Q = 900,000 + 100Q$$
$$100Q = 150,000 \text{ and then } Q = 1,500 \text{ units.}$$

This indicates that producing less than 1,500 units per year would be cheaper at location B, while producing more than 1,500 units per year would be cheaper at location C.

Finally, the break-even point between location A and location C is determined:

$$TC_A = TC_C$$
$$500,000 + 300Q = 900,000 + 100Q$$
$$200Q = 400,000 \text{ and then } Q = 2,000 \text{ units.}$$

This indicates that producing less than 2,000 units per year would be cheaper at location A, while producing more than 2,000 units per year would be cheaper at location C.

Based on the cost curves shown in Figure 11.1, location C has the lowest total cost when producing the forecasted quantity of 3,000 units per year. If, however, the annual demand forecast was 1,000 units, then location A would be preferred. From Figure 11.1, it can be seen that location B would never be the preferred location when comparing the costs of all three sites simultaneously.

BUSINESS CLUSTERS

Over the last decade, a number of trends have dramatically impacted the facility location process. Markets are increasingly globalized due to the liberalization of trade, technological advances, and increased demand from many regions of the world. Countries compete against one another for foreign direct investment. Having the necessary information to compare countries across a multitude of factors will help managers make better location decisions. Today, more **business clusters** are being created globally. Research parks and special economic/industrial zones serve as magnets for business clusters.

Figure 11.1	Break-Even Graph

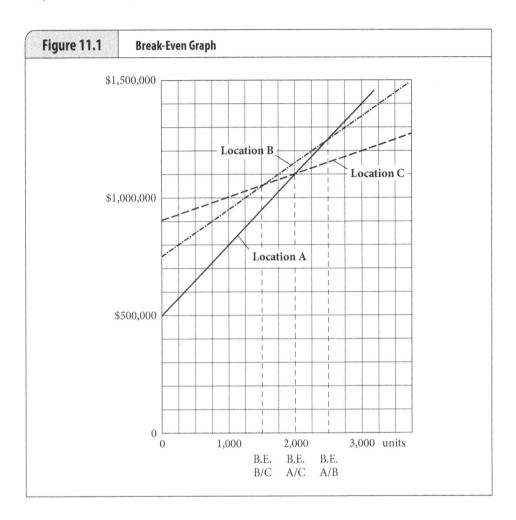

The concept of business clusters represents a new way of thinking about location decisions, challenges conventional logic on how companies should be configured, and provides a different approach to organizing a supply chain. As such, what exactly are these *business clusters*? According to Michael Porter, "clusters are geographic concentrations of interconnected companies and institutions in a particular field. Clusters encompass an array of linked industries and other entities important to competition."[47] Locating research and development, component manufacturing, assembly operations, marketing, and other associated businesses in one area can improve the supply chain, technology sharing, and information sharing.

There are different types of business clusters. First is the high-tech clusters such as Silicon Valley in California, East London Tech City in England, and Paris-Saclay. Another is the factor endowment clusters, which are created due to a competitive advantage arising from a geographic location.[48] Examples are the vineyards of Napa and Sonoma in California, Burgundy and Champagne in France, and Lombardy in Spain where good grapes can grow in the sunny countryside. Then we have the knowledge-service clusters that we find in many developing countries defined as "geographic concentrations of lower-cost technical and analytical skills serving rising global demand for commoditized knowledge services"[49] such as software engineering and other IT-based services. In developing countries, we also see the creation of low-cost manufacturing clusters involving auto production, electronics, and textiles. These clusters are typically well supported by foreign companies. A discussion of three of these countries follows:

- *Mexico*: Mexico has long been a hotbed for electronic manufacturers, with many located in cities such as Tijuana, Mexicali, Tecate, Chihuahua, Saltillo, Reynosa, and Guadalajara. Examples of major global companies operating in Mexico are IBM, Motorola, Hewlett-Packard, Siemens, Ericsson, Samsung, LG Electronics, Sony, and Panasonic. With NAFTA, goods can be exported duty-free to North America, allowing Mexico to become an electronics manufacturing center for the Americas. Mexico, for example, produces nearly one-quarter of the world's television receivers.

- *Taiwan*: Taiwan, dubbed the "Silicon Island" by *Forbes*, is a leading manufacturer of computer hardware and has the largest global market share for motherboards, modems, and scanners. Intel and Compaq are two major investors in Taiwan, due partly to the large pool of engineers possessing technical degrees.

- *India*: India is a major player in the software industry and country of choice for customized software development. India has the world's third-largest pool of scientific and technical personnel. India also provides a significant cost advantage due to its low labor cost. Companies such as IBM, Microsoft, Oracle, and Motorola have built facilities in India's silicon valleys—Bangalore, Hyderabad, and Mumbai.

There are many reasons why clusters are successful. One is the close cooperation, coordination, and trust among clustered companies in related industries. Another reason is the fierce competition for customers among rival companies located in the cluster. Companies are more productive in their operations because of access to the local supplier base, information, and technology. Companies are able to recruit from the local pool of skilled and experienced workers, thus reducing hiring costs. Due to the intensity of competition within the business cluster, peer pressure, and constant comparison among rivals, companies tend to respond quicker to customer needs and trends. Clusters thus provide the competitive environment that promotes increasing innovation and profitability.

Not all clusters are successful. For example, Michigan suffered through plant closings and employee layoffs in the auto industry due to the industry's overreliance on gas-guzzling auto designs and the oil shock in the 1970s. The groupthink mentality among the cluster participants of General Motors, Ford, and Chrysler in Detroit made it more difficult for individual companies to try new ideas and see the need for radical innovation in fuel economy automobile designs.

SUSTAINABLE DEVELOPMENT AND FACILITY LOCATION

The World Commission on Environment and Development (the Brundtland Commission) defines **sustainable development** as "development that meets the needs of the present without compromising the ability of future generations to meet their own needs."[50] Sustainable development is important because what we do today will affect future generations. The critical issues in sustainable development are energy consumption/production, air pollution, and climate change. These issues are strongly related to one another and need to be considered in an integrated manner and linked to economic, social, and environmental policies. As such, sustainable development will need fundamental changes in values and principles that influence development strategies and innovation. The increased global consumption of fossil fuels has increased global warming. In addition, prices of crude oil have continued to rise as demand has increased. More expensive oil translates to increased cost of production of goods and delivery of services. Ultimately this is affecting supply chain costs. This calls for the development of cleaner, more fuel-efficient and affordable energy technologies as well as renewable energy technologies.

It is clear that industrial development is the engine for economic growth and eradicating poverty in emerging countries. However, resource efficiency and technology innovation are opportunities for reducing cost and increasing competitiveness and employment, issues that are central to managing an effective supply chain. Air pollution has serious impacts on human health, environment, and the economy. A related issue is climate change and preserving the world's ecosystem. Due to the importance of climate change, most countries joined an international treaty, the United Nations Framework Convention on Climate Change (UNFCCC) "…to begin to consider what can be done to reduce global warming and to cope with whatever temperature increases are inevitable."[51] A few years earlier, two groups of scientists reported that global warming caused by greenhouse gases has led to destabilization of the ice sheet in the West Antarctic glaciers. A recent report based on the new science of phenology (calendar record of first bud, first flower, first nesting behavior, and first migrant arrivals) confirms that a sedge species in Greenland is springing to life twenty-six days earlier than a decade ago.[52] Many places in the United States are seeing an earlier spring. According to Dr. Jake Weltzin, a USGS ecologist and national director of the USA National Phenology Network, "While these earlier springs might not seem like a big deal—and who among us doesn't appreciate a balmy day or a break in dreary winter weather—they pose significant challenges for planning and managing important issues that affect our economy and our society."[53]

Another project with environmental implications is the Keystone XL pipeline, which is projected to move heavy oil sands oil from Alberta, Canada to the U.S. Gulf Coast. Environmentalists have been fighting to stop this controversial project because of the impact that processing this Canadian heavy oil might have on climate change and public health in the event of oil spills. Supporters of the project argue that jobs will be created and that the Alberta oil will be extracted and transported to markets whether the Keystone XL pipeline is built or not. The project has stirred years of heated debate. U.S. President Trump has revived the Keystone XL Pipeline and Dakota Access Pipeline projects after they were rejected by former President Obama. Currently, oil companies are processing this oil and moving it using trucks and trains, which are also argued to be creating high levels of greenhouse gases, along with oil spills.

A similar term, **green development**, has been used to describe environment-friendly development. The difference between green development and sustainable development is that green development "prioritizes what its proponents consider to be environmental sustainability over economic and cultural considerations."[54] An example would be the installation of a state-of-the-art waste treatment plant with very high maintenance cost in a poor country. Due to the high maintenance cost, the ideal plant from an environmental standpoint may not be sustainable and likely will be shut down. From a sustainable development perspective, it would be acceptable to have a less effective environmental technology but one that can be maintained by the users of the equipment. When decision-makers consider both economic and social issues in addition to environmental concerns, then sustainable development is more logical.

ADDITIVE MANUFACTURING AND ITS IMPACT ON FACILITY LOCATION

New technology developed recently may well change the landscape for manufacturing (see the nearby SCM profile on reshoring of shoe manufacturing in the United States). **Additive manufacturing** or **3D printing** is a "process of making a three-dimensional solid object of virtually any shape from a digital model."[59] The technology was first developed by MIT, funded by grants from the Office of Naval Research and the National Science Foundation. Production using a 3D printer involves laying down a very thin layer of stainless steel or ceramic powder and using liquid binder to fuse the different layers to form the final product. The technology is applicable to a wide range of industries such as defense, aerospace, automotive, medical, and metals manufacturing. Initially, 3D printing was used for rapid prototyping, but new developments make it possible for use in actual production. Benefits of additive manufacturing include shorter lead times, mass customization, reduced parts count, more complex shapes, parts on demand, efficient material use, and lower energy consumption. The National Additive Manufacturing Innovation Institute (NAMII) in Youngstown, Ohio, has been rebranded to America Makes, which is "the nation's leading and collaborative partner in AM (additive manufacturing) and 3DP

SCM Profile | Reshoring of Shoe Manufacturing in the United States

Adidas and Reebok, two of the major suppliers of running shoes, have plans to open plants in the United States to make these high-performing shoes. Reebok is a wholly owned subsidiary of Adidas since 2005. Adidas is looking at building a SpeedFactory plant in Atlanta, similar to the one in Germany. Meanwhile, Reebok is also launching a new facility in Lincoln, Rhode Island, to make the new Reebok Liquid Speed running shoes. This is the branding strategy adopted by Adidas and Reebok to join the "made in the US" movement. Bill McInnis, head of future at Reebok said, "Getting faster and closer to the consumer is 100% what we are after. If you can take out shipping and [making] molds that take time to formulate, it moves you closer to the consumer."[55] New Balance, another shoe manufacturer, makes or assembles more than 4 million pairs of athletic shoes per year in the United States.[56]

The Adidas plant will be operating in the second half of 2017, with expected production of 50,000 pairs of shoes in 2017 and increasing eventually to 500,000 pairs. Meanwhile, Reebok is looking to change the way shoes are being made. It is no surprise that Reebok intends to use 3D printing to produce the Liquid Speed running shoes. According to Bill McInnis, head of development for Reebok, "Every shoe from every brand is created using molds—an expensive, time-consuming process. With Liquid Factory, we wanted to fundamentally change the way that shoes are made, creating a new method to manufacture shoes without molds."[57] The production process involves using proprietary liquid resin from BASF to create the outer sole by building one layer at a time. McInnis said, "The Liquid Factory process is very flexible in that each machine can be used to create as many different concepts as imagination allows—it's programming, not molds. Scaling up is a matter of installing more Liquid Factory machine setups. The local manufacturing also gets us much closer to the consumer in terms of speed to market."[58] Reebok is expected to initially manufacture 300 pairs of these shoes, which will sell for about $189 a pair. Reebok's Liquid Factory is an example of how technological innovations can bring manufacturing back to the United States.

(3D Printing) technology research, discovery, creation, and innovation. Structured as a public-private partnership with member organizations from industry, academia, government, nongovernment agencies, and workforce and economic development resources, [the organization is] working together to innovate and accelerate AM and 3DP to increase [the] nation's global manufacturing competitiveness."[60]

Digital dentistry is one growth area for the technology where dentists use 3D printers to build teeth, dentures, braces, and implants in-house. Joseph DeSimone, CEO of Carbon 3D, explained that "dentists can now print a tooth in 6.5 minutes."[61] In digital dentistry, there is no need to make physical impressions. Dentists can use intraoral scanners to provide a full view of the anatomy of the mouth, jaws, and teeth and allow accurate models to be built by 3D printers that fit with high accuracy, minimum discomfort, and beautiful cosmetics. 3D printers enable on-site production at the dental clinics, which is faster, more economical, and predictable than ordering the implant from an outside vendor.

The affordability of 3D printers could keep businesses from going overseas for their manufacturing needs or bring manufacturing back to the United States (see the nearby SCM profile on reshoring of shoe manufacturing in the United States). Another aspect of 3D printing is speed. For example, Reebok is building the Liquid Factory in Rhode Island that uses 3D Printing to make shoes. Bill McInnis, head of future at Reebok, explains, "One of the most exciting things about Liquid Factory is the speed. We can create and customize the design of shoes in real time, because we're not using molds—we're simply programming a machine. Liquid Factory is not just a new way of making things, it's a new speed of making things."[62]

A small business or an entrepreneur (such as a dentist) can now afford to have its own little factory. However, major companies are experimenting with 3D printers, which will likely move the technology closer to the mainstream market and make the technology even more affordable. Shown below are two prime examples of major companies using 3D printers to create new products, improve old ones, and improve their business processes:

- **General Electric**
  General Electric, the world's largest manufacturer, is an early adopter of 3D printing. They have recently introduced the "brilliant factory" concept, which is "a sophisticated factory that combines lean manufacturing, advanced and additive manufacturing with advanced software analytics to enhance productivity."[63] Manufacturing has evolved from the Industrial Revolution where the assembly line was introduced. Today, with the emergence of 3D printing, we are seeing more and more innovations in the manufacturing industry. According to Philippe Cochet, SVP & chief productivity officer, General Electric, "Additive manufacturing, or 3D printing, is another piece that was in its infancy just ten years ago, but represents an enormous area of opportunity for manufacturing. Additive technologies allow us to create parts with precision and efficiency to a degree previously unheard of, create new types of parts that were previously impossible to produce, and reduce waste during production by using only the raw materials needed. These advancements will swing the pendulum back to domestic sourcing in the United States."[64]

- **Boeing**
  The airline company was an early adopter of 3D printing technology. It has been reported that Boeing has more than 20,000 3D printed plastics parts used in their

aircraft. Recently, Boeing announced they have hired the Oxford Performance Materials Company to make 600 3D-printed parts for its Starliner space taxis. "Oxford's parts will help Boeing lower costs and save weight on each seven-seat capsule, compared with traditional metal and plastic manufacturing," said Larry Varholak, president of Oxford's aerospace business.[65] The Guinness World Records has certified that the world's largest 3D-printed object measuring 17.5 feet long, 5.5 feet wide, and 1.5 feet tall is a wing trim that will be used in the forthcoming Boeing 777X airplane. The 3D object is made by the Oak Ridge National Laboratory, one of Boeing's research partner in the United States.

SUMMARY

Facility location decisions can provide organizations with a competitive advantage and, therefore, must be an integral part of their overall strategic plans. The effectiveness of a supply chain is greatly influenced by facility locations. Increased globalization and improved technologies have resulted in a variety of options for companies to locate their facilities. Today, companies must consider a number of factors when analyzing potential locations; several comparison methods are available when considering the country, region, and community for a facility location. Business clusters often provide for strong business development, collaboration, growth opportunities, and improved supply chain management. The existence of successful clusters suggests that innovation and competition are concentrated geographically. China today represents an attractive location for many of the world's top companies due to its inexpensive labor and huge market. There has been much discussion about sustainable development and the greening of the supply chain and its effect on global location decisions. Finally, emerging technologies such as additive manufacturing or 3D printing will have a major impact on how companies view manufacturing and where they locate production facilities.

KEY TERMS

3D printing, 434

additive manufacturing, 434

Association of Southeast Asian Nations (ASEAN), 418

break-even model, 429

business clusters, 430

Common Market for Eastern and Southern Africa (COMESA), 418

contributor factory, 416

European Union (EU), 418

green development, 433

lead factory, 416

North American Free Trade Agreement (NAFTA), 418

offshore factory, 416

outpost factory, 416

quality-of-life factors, 426

right-to-work laws, 427

server factory, 416

source factory, 416

Southern Common Market (MERCOSUR), 418

sustainable development, 432

weighted-factor rating model, 428

World Trade Organization, 418

DISCUSSION QUESTIONS

1. What is the impact of facility decisions on a supply chain?

2. Why is demand management important for effective supply chain management?

3. What are business clusters? Provide several examples of business clusters in a variety of countries. What are the advantages of clustering?

4. What are the factors influencing facility location?

5. Discuss the major regional trade agreements in Asia, Africa, Europe, Latin America, and North America.

6. What is the World Trade Organization and what is its role in world trade?

7. What are the critical factors in making community and site decisions?

8. Discuss Walmart's location strategy.

9. Discuss Amazon's global facilities network.

10. Define *quality of life*. Why is quality of life an important factor in facility location? Is the set of quality-of-life factors used by the Chamber of Commerce in Jacksonville, Florida, a good one? Please explain.

11. What is a right-to-work state? What are the advantages or disadvantages of doing business in a right-to-work state?

12. Why is China an attractive location for many businesses?

13. What are the challenges of doing business in China?

14. Discuss the six strategic roles of a foreign facility.

15. What is sustainable development, and why is this policy important to a country and the world at large?

16. What is the difference between green development and sustainable development?

17. Explain why 3D printing may lead to a revival of manufacturing in the United States.

18. Provide examples of major U.S. companies that are using 3D printing and explain why they are reshoring their manufacturing back to the United States?

ESSAY/PROJECT QUESTIONS

1. Go to the website of IMD—World Competitiveness Yearbook at http://reports.weforum.org/global-competitiveness-index/#topic=data. Select any region of the world such as Africa and Middle East, Americas, Asia and Pacific, and Europe and Eurasia. Prepare a report showing the regional highlights and include a performance overview of selected countries in the region.

2. Go to the World Economic Forum website at http://www.weforum.org/. Select "Initiatives" from the top menu. Then select "Shaping the Future of Production." Based on the articles presented in the website, prepare a report discussing how emerging technologies will transform production systems, business models, and sustainability.

3. Go to the website of the World Trade Organization at www.wto.org. Click on the menu item "Documents, data, and resources" and select the option on "Economic research." Under "Publications" select the latest World Trade Report. Explain the key findings of the report and the changing landscape of international trade and the emergence of global value chains.

4. Go to the website of the U.S. Commercial Service at https://www.export.gov/ccg. First, select a country you wish to study. Based on the country commercial guide, prepare an assessment of the suitability of the country for doing business in the particular industry you wish to study.

5. Go to the website http://www.reshorenow.org/ and prepare a report on why U.S. companies should move manufacturing back to the United States.

PROBLEMS

1. The Soft Toys Company has collected information on fixed and variable costs for four potential plant locations.

LOCATION	ANNUAL FIXED COST ($)	UNIT VARIABLE COST ($)
A	200,000	50
B	300,000	45
C	400,000	25
D	600,000	20

a. Plot the total cost curves for the four plant locations on a single graph.

b. Find the break-even points and determine the range of demand for which each location has a cost advantage.

c. The sales manager predicts that demand will be 30,000 units. Which facility is best for the predicted demand?

2. The Budapest Company has identified four locations to set up a new production facility. They have determined the fixed and variable costs associated with each location as follows:

LOCATION	ANNUAL FIXED COST ($)	UNIT VARIABLE COST ($)
Pittsburg	10,000	5
Atlanta	30,000	4
Miami	60,000	3
Houston	70,000	6

a. Plot the total cost curves for the three plant locations on a single graph.

b. Find the break-even points and determine the range of demand for which each location has a cost advantage. Which city has no cost advantage at all?

c. Which plant location is best if demand is (i) 40,000 and (ii) 15,000 units?

3. Fastbuy is looking to open up a new fulfillment center as part of their expanding network to meet faster delivery needed for their prime customers in California. To assist the company in deciding where to locate this new fulfillment center, three sites have been identified with the information shown below.

CRITICAL LOCATION FACTORS	FACTOR WEIGHT (SUM TO 1)	MORENO VALLEY SCORES (1–100)	ONTARIO SCORES (1–100)	SAN BERNARDINO SCORES (1–100)
Labor availability	0.20	85	90	70
Proximity to market	0.25	100	80	80
Supplier base	0.20	90	100	90
Taxes	0.10	80	70	80
Utilities	0.10	75	85	75
Transportation	0.15	90	75	85

Which site would be ideal for the fulfillment center?

4. The Bruhaha Brewery is planning to build another brewery for the expanding U.S. market. The company has identified five critical location factors and their relative weights. The scores for each of the three potential sites are shown in the following table. Which site should be selected for the new brewery?

CRITICAL LOCATION FACTORS	FACTOR WEIGHT (SUM TO 1)	COLUMBUS SCORES (1–100)	LAS VEGAS SCORES (1–100)	SPOKANE SCORES (1–100)
Labor cost	0.15	70	90	50
Proximity to market	0.25	100	90	80
Supplier base	0.20	80	100	70
Quality of life	0.30	90	60	60
Taxes	0.10	60	80	90

CASES

1. Quigley Global Transportation*

Queenie Quigley is a very successful entrepreneur. She grew up in an ocean port city and loved the sea. Her father was a commercial fisherman and often took her with him during the summer. Her love for the sea triggered an interest in international shipping. Queenie knew that an ocean transportation business would provide services that would always be needed and she eventually created a large, successful ocean transportation company.

Queenie understands that her transportation company has to be located at major shipping ports to get the best contracts. Often her clients want to board the ship and look around to see how their cargo will be handled and stored. While those types of clients are not frequent shippers, they are willing to pay a premium price to ensure their goods get to the distant locations undamaged. A brief tour aboard one of the Quigley Global Transportation vessels appears to instill confidence and trust.

Quigley Global Transportation currently has ships stationed in the following ports— Hong Kong; Rotterdam, Netherlands; Los Angeles, USA; New York-New Jersey, USA; Santos, Brazil; and Ambarli, Turkey. These ports were rated as number 5, 11, 19, 23, 39, and 48 out of the top 50 worldwide in 2015.* Queenie believes her selection of these ports was a crucial factor in her company's success. As the old adage goes, it is all about location, location, location. These ports gave Quigley Global Transportation a set of locations that enabled her company to serve all major areas of the world—North America, South America, Europe, the Middle East, and Asia. However, Queenie knew there were still many opportunities for business if she could expand into other major ports.

One key criterion was the 20-foot equivalent unit or TEU. The TEU is a common unit of measure, even though it is an inexact unit of measure. The unit basically describes the common shipping container that is 20 feet × 8 feet × 8 feet. Ports are rated by the volume shipped through them each year, in millions of TEU. Obviously, from the perspective of potential business Queenie's company could obtain, total TEU handled per year is her number one criterion for selecting the next port. In the past, Queenie's expansion strategy was based on opportunities that gained her access to a major continent. She had sought out contracts that she knew would lead to a foothold in a port. However, now that Quigley Global Transportation was on solid footing, Queenie wants to develop selection criteria that are more robust. She decided to use the weighted factor rating model as her selection tool for the next port. She is still convinced that TEU should be the number one criterion. Although she has four other factors shown in the table below, Queenie has not decided on their importance. Queenie thought if she looked at her current ports through that criterion it would help her decide on how to weight the criteria going forward.

*Written by Rick Bonsall, D. Mgt., McKendree University, Lebanon, IL. The people and institution are fictional and any resemblance to any person or any institution is coincidental. This case was prepared solely to provide material for class discussion. The author does not intend to illustrate either effective or ineffective handling of a managerial situation.

COUNTRY	PORT RANKING BY TEU (1 = BEST)	EASE OF DOING BUSINESS BY COUNTRY[†]	GDP GROWTH BY COUNTRY—2016[‡]	GETTING CREDIT BY COUNTRY[†]	ENFORCING CONTRACT BY COUNTRY[†]
Brazil	39	123	−3.3%	101	37
Hong Kong, China	5	4	1.4%	20	21
Netherlands	11	28	1.7%	82	71
LA, USA	19	8	1.6%	2	20
NY, USA	23	8	1.6%	2	20
Turkey	48	69	3.3%	82	33

Discussion Questions

1. Queenie has a very challenging task ahead of her. As stated, she didn't use any selection system for the first six ports except that she secured a contract with a client and then built that into a foothold in that port. Queenie wants a more effective selection system moving forward. Her first criterion is still TEU and she plans to weight it at 30 percent on a scale of 0–100%. No two criterions can have the same weighting; Queenie wants some sort of distinction between each one. What is your recommendation for weighting the other four criteria? Why did you weight each one as you did? Explain the logic of your weighting.

2. Queenie wants to expand her business into Africa. Based on her initial analysis there are no ports large enough in many African countries to make them viable by themselves. However, transporting goods from another port to African ports would be a sound business move. Queenie had her staff provide a list of five ports that could be used to serve Africa. Using the recommendation you provided Queenie for the weighting-factor model and the chart below, select the best port for Quigley Global Transportation.

COUNTRY	PORT RANKING BY TEU (1 = BEST)	EASE OF DOING BUSINESS BY COUNTRY	GDP GROWTH BY COUNTRY—2016	GETTING CREDIT BY COUNTRY	ENFORCING CONTRACT BY COUNTRY
United Arab Emirates	44	28	2.3%	101	25
Sri Lanka	28	110	5.0%	118	116
Saudi Arabia	36	147	1.2%	82	105
Malta	49	132	4.1%	139	58
Spain	33	85	3.1%	62	29

3. Review the locations of the ports listed in question 2 (the World Fact Book[‡] can help). Keeping the TEU as criterion number 1, which of the other criteria would you change to enhance the selection process? Think in terms of the African question. What factors would be better criteria from a business and supply chain perspective? Explain your reasoning.

©2019 Cengage Learning

[†]http://www.worldshipping.org/about-the-industry/global-trade/top-50-world-container-ports; World Bank Doing Business, www.doingbusiness.org

[‡]World Fact Book, https://www.cia.gov/library/publications/the-world-factbook/index.html

2. Pittman's Fireplaces*

Percy Pittman recently took over the family business. Pittman's Fireplaces has been in business since 1922. It was started by Percy's grandfather and then passed on to Percy's father. The business has thrived. They install fireplaces throughout the United States. In addition to the fireplaces, Pittman's Fireplaces sells all the accessories you can imagine to make your fireplace the centerpiece of your room.

Percy wants to take the business to the next level and go international. The reputation of Pittman's Fireplaces is excellent. They have installed many fireplaces in the homes of diplomats who are representing their countries in the United States. Furthermore, many international businessmen who keep homes in New York, Los Angeles, Chicago, and other large U.S. cities have purchased Pittman's fireplaces and accessories.

As Percy ruminates about how to proceed with his business expansion, he considers the following points. One, he would need to consider labor. What skills must a worker have and what skills can Pittman train them on? Another consideration is wages. Percy believes in paying a fair wage for a fair days work; however, labor costs are a huge expense in any business. Materials are another critical factor for Pittman's Fireplaces. Percy sources the finest wood, marble, granite, and other types of stonework for their fireplaces. The final consideration is the local environmental laws. Pittman's Fireplaces sells gas-burning fireplaces, wood-burning fireplaces, and electric fireplaces. The rules, regulations, and laws are often different in cities, counties, and states. Percy assumes he will encounter the same situation in foreign countries.

Percy decides he will investigate three countries—United Kingdom, Germany, and Finland. His initial criteria for his weighted factor model are labor costs, weather (cold winters), environmental laws, and trade agreements with the United States. However, as Percy continues to ponder the best factors, he isn't yet sure which are the best ones to use as location selection criteria. The wrong set of criteria could result in selecting the wrong country for his foreign expansion.

Discussion Questions

1. Percy is investigating several tools to help him make his decision as to which country he should expand into first. He thinks that these tools may also guide him in deciding which specific factors he should use to evaluate the three countries— United Kingdom, Germany, and Finland. Percy is reviewing both the 2016 Global Competitiveness Report and the 2016 World Competitiveness Yearbook. Clearly, in both documents the three countries are rated significantly different. Obviously, this is a critical decision for the future of Pittman's Fireplace. As a businessperson what is your opinion regarding the two references Percy should use? Explain your answer.

2. Percy has decided that he will not have more than five factors as part of his weighted factor model. Currently, he is thinking of four factors—labor costs, weather, environmental laws, and trade agreements with the United States. However, when he was originally pondering the situation he thought along these lines—labor-skill set, labor wages, material sourcing, and environmental laws. Based on the case, do you believe the final four are the absolute best four for Percy to select, or should he go with his original four, or some different ones? Explain why you agree or disagree with him. Justify your views either way. In addition, what should be the fifth factor?

*Written by Rick Bonsall, D. Mgt., McKendree University, Lebanon, IL. The people and institution are fictional and any resemblance to any person or any institution is coincidental. This case was prepared solely to provide material for class discussion. The author does not intend to illustrate either effective or ineffective handling of a managerial situation.

3. Assume that Percy has selected Finland as the best location to begin his international expansion. Now, Percy begins to put costs together. He forecasted 7,000 fireplaces per year. Calculate the breakeven points for the three countries. Should Percy still go with Finland or should he select another country? If the forecast was 5,000 should Percy ignore the weighted factor model? Explain why or why not.

LOCATION	ANNUAL FIXED COST ($)	UNIT VARIABLE COST ($)
Finland	$550,000.00	$180.00
Germany	$450,000.00	$200.00
United Kingdom	$400,000.00	$220.00

©2019 Cengage Learning

3. O'Leary Management Solutions*

Mary O'Leary is an extremely successful management consultant. Mary worked for several large corporations in various roles before starting her consulting business. Mary's forte is using long-established management concepts and applying them in innovative ways.

Consequently, Mary is a much sought-after consultant. As the years have passed, Mary has hired other very talented people and trained them in her approach.

Currently, O'Leary Management Solutions is located in New York. However, her company of consultants travels all over the United States. At last count, they consulted in thirty-two states on a routine basis. Technology helps limit some of the travel. Conferences calls, e-mail, and transferring files using the cloud all help O'Leary work closely with their clients, while being efficient with their own time management.

As Mary reviews her company's current status and looks toward its future she wonders if it is time to open a second office location. Although technology helps, Mary is a big believer in hands-on consulting. Mary's experience tells her that meeting people face to face, when trying to find a solution to their issues, is crucial. That is getting more and more difficult to do, particularly in states closer to the west coast.

Mary plans to address this idea with her staff, but in the meantime, she did some personal brainstorming about what factors she should consider when choosing a second location. Her employees were all high powered, highly educated, successful people, many who have families. All enjoy their time off, although they don't get much of that. Although government regulations weren't a big concern, taxes for her company and employees were. Mary felt it was best to think long term and anticipate further growth, such as what new states could be future markets. One key marketing factor for Mary is being located in the high rent section of the business district. This is as important as her employees being well groomed and well dressed. First impressions often sealed the deal.

Mary eventually decides that opening a second office is a must. Mary schedules a meeting with her staff for next Thursday and plans to explain why they are opening another office and share her thoughts about the selection criteria. Also, she plans to get their feedback on what would be the best location selection criteria since some of them will have to move there.

*Written by Rick Bonsall, D. Mgt., McKendree University, Lebanon, IL. The people and institution are fictional and any resemblance to any person or any institution is coincidental. This case was prepared solely to provide material for class discussion. The author does not intend to illustrate either effective or ineffective handling of a managerial situation.

Discussion Questions

1. The textbook lists eleven major community factors to use as selection criteria for choosing a location. Mary realizes that all factors are important; however, eleven are too many because it waters down the effect of each factor's weight. Therefore, Mary wants no more than five major factors. Based on the information in the case, which factors should Mary and her staff choose? Explain why the specific factors you picked are pertinent to Mary's company.

2. Building on question 1, weight the five factors you choose for O'Leary Management Solutions. Mary has expressed that she does not want any two factors with the same weight. Explain why you rated them as you did, that is, why one criterion is more or less important than another.

3. Mary is thinking that quality of life may be one of the factors they should pick. However, it is much too general a term to be a good indicator of the best location. Therefore, Mary believes it would be best to create a weighed factor rating matrix just for quality of life. Each location can be looked at through that specific criteria as well and the score each receives can then put inputted into the broader selection matrix. There are nine quality-of-life factors listed in the textbook. This time, Mary wants no more than four for this subweighted factor rating analysis. Which four would you recommend and why? How would you weight them and why?

©2019 Cengage Learning

END NOTES

1. "Global Location Trends 2016 Annual Report," IBM Institute for Business Value; https://www-01.ibm.com/common/ssi/cgi-bin/ssialias?htmlfid=GBE03760USEN

2. Locations Quotes, BrainyQuote; https://www.brainyquote.com/quotes/quotes/e/ericschlos528614.html?src=t_locations

3. Senger, E., "The Pros and Cons of Business Clusters," HSBC Global Connections; https://globalconnections.hsbc.com/canada/en/articles/pros-and-cons-business-clusters

4. Amazon.com on Facebook; https://www.facebook.com/pg/Amazon/about/

5. 2013 Amazon.com Annual Report; http://phx.corporate-ir.net/phoenix.zhtml?c=97664&p=irol-proxy

6. "Amazon Global Fulfillment Center Network," MWPVL International; http://www.mwpvl.com/html/amazon_com.html

7. Kim, E., "Latest Data Shows Where Amazon Might Be Headed Next—And It Should Terrify UPS and FedEx (AMZN)," *Business Insider*, October 19, 2015; http://www.businessinsider.com/amazon-logistics-facilities-update-2015-10

8. Porter, M., "Clusters and the New Economics of Competition," *Harvard Business Review*, November–December 1998.

9. Global Location Trends—2016 Annual Report, IBM Institute for Business Value, July 2016; https://www-01.ibm.com/common/ssi/cgi- bin/ssialias?htmlfid=GBE03760USENom/services/us/gbs/thoughtleadership/gltr2016/

10. "Behind the scenes at the FedEx Memphis Hub," FedEx Small Business Center; https://smallbusiness.fedex.com/fedex-hub-behind-the-scenes.html

11. "About FedEx," FedEx; http://about.van.fedex.com/our-story/global-reach/

12. Ferdows, K., "Making the Most of Foreign Factories," *Harvard Business Review*, March–April 1997: 73–88.

13. Ibid.

14. Ibid.

15. Ibid.

16. "What Is the WTO?" http://www.wto.org/english/thewto_e/whatis_e/whatis_e.htm

17. Evolution of Regional Trade Agreements in the World, 1948–2016; https://www.wto .org/english/tratop_e/region_e/regfac_e.htm

18. "The European Union at a Glance, Member States of the EU"; http://europa.eu/abc/ european_countries/index_en.htm

19. Amadeo, K., "Advantages of NAFTA," The Balance, February 13, 2017; https://www .thebalance.com/advantages-of-nafta-3306271

20. "North American Free Trade Agreement (NAFTA)," Office of the United States Trade Representative; http://www.ustr.gov/trade-agreements/free-trade-agreements/ north-american-free-trade-agreement-nafta

21. MERCOSUR; http://en.wikipedia.org/wiki/Mercosur

22. Association of South East Asian Nations (ASEAN); http://asean.org/asean/ about-asean/

23. (COMESA Vision and Mission; http://www.comesa.int/comesa-vision-and-mission/

24. COMESA Vision and Mission; http://www.comesa.int/comesa-vision-and-mission/

25. Common Market for Eastern and Southern Africa (COMESA); http://www.uneca .org/oria/pages/comesa-common-market-eastern-and-southern-africa

26. "Glossary of Statistical Terms," OECED; http://stats.oecd.org/glossary/detail .asp?ID=399

27. "IMD World Competitiveness Center," IMD; http://www.imd.org/wcc/

28. World Competitiveness Methodology and Principles of Analysis; http://www.imd.org/ uupload/imd.website/wcc/methodology.pdf

29. "The Global Competitiveness Report 2016–2017," World Economic Forum; http://www3.weforum.org/docs/GCR2016-2017/05FullReport/ TheGlobalCompetitivenessReport2016-2017_FINAL.pdf

30. "Competitive Alternatives: KPMG's Guide to International Business Locations Costs," KPMG, 2016 Edition; https://www.competitivealternatives.com/reports/ compalt2016_report_vol1_en.pdf

31. Bell, K., "7 States That Don't Have a State Income Tax (And Two That Don't Tax Wage Income)," ABC News; http://abcnews.go.com/Business/states-income-tax-us/ story?id=21490926#

32. 2016 Amazon.com Form 10-K; http://services.corporate-ir.net/SEC.Enhanced/ SecCapsule.aspx?c=97664&fid=14806946

33. "Competitive Alternatives," KPMG's Guide to International Business Location Costs, 2016 Edition, KPMG; https://www.competitivealternatives.com/reports/compalt2016_report_vol1_en.pdf

34. North American Agreement on Environmental Cooperation: Part One Objectives; http://www.cec.org/about-us/NAAEC

35. "Competitive Alternatives," KPMG's Guide to International Business Location Costs, 2016 Edition, KPMG; https://www.competitivealternatives.com/reports/compalt2016_report_vol1_en.pdf

36. "Sustainable Development," WTO; https://www.wto.org/english/tratop_e/envir_e/sust_dev_e.htm

37. Craver, R., "Ashley Expanding Davie Workforce by 454 Jobs," *Winston-Salem Journal*, October 13, 2015; http://www.journalnow.com/news/local/ashley-expanding-davie-workforce-by-jobs/article_29d2b44e-06d1-5333-a75b-5a8c28aca1d5.html

38. "Fuyao Glass Investing $1 Billion in U.S. Factories: Chairman," *Reuters*, October 7, 2016; http://www.reuters.com/article/us-fyg-usa-idUSKCN1262M0

39. "Meet the Chinese Billionaire Who's Moving His Manufacturing to the U.S. to Cut Costs," *Fortune.com*, December 21, 2016; http://fortune.com/2016/12/22/us-china-manufacturing-costs-investment/

40. Chang, L., "China Is Now the World's Largest Solar Power Producer," Digital Trends, February 5, 2017; http://www.digitaltrends.com/cool-tech/china-solar-energy/

41. "Quality of Life," Wikipedia; http://en.wikipedia.org/wiki/Quality_of_life

42. Indicators—Quality of Life Progress Report, Jacksonville Community Council Inc.; www.jcci.org/jcciwebsite/pages/indicators.html

43. "Mexico's Drug War Leads to Kidnappings, Vigilante Violence," *Time*; http://world.time.com/2014/01/17/mexico-drug-war-kidnapping/

44. "Right-to-Work States"; www.nrtw.org/rtws.htm

45. Lui, K., "Meet the Chinese Billionaire Who's Moving Manufacturing to the U.S. to Cut Costs," Fortune.com, December 21, 2016; http://fortune.com/2016/12/22/us-china-manufacturing-costs-investment/

46. Lui, K., "Meet the Chinese Billionaire Who's Moving Manufacturing to the U.S. to Cut Costs," Fortune.com, December 21, 2016; http://fortune.com/2016/12/22/us-china-manufacturing-costs-investment/

47. Porter, M., "Clusters and the New Economics of Competition."

48. "Business Cluster," Wikipedia; https://en.wikipedia.org/wiki/Business_cluster

49. Manning, S., "New Silicon Valleys or a New Species? Commoditization of Knowledge Work and the Rise of Knowledge Services Clusters," *Research Policy*, 42, 2013: 379–390; https://en.wikipedia.org/wiki/Business_cluster

50. Report of the World Commission on Environment and Development: Our common future; http://www.un-documents.net/our-common-future.pdf

51. The United Nations Framework Convention on Climate Change; http://unfccc.int/2860.php

52. Radford, T., " Spring Moving Forward at Record Rate," *Climate News Network*, March 1, 2017; http://climatenewsnetwork.net/spring-moving-forward-record-rate/

53. Radford, T., " Spring Moving Forward at Record Rate," *Climate News Network*, March 1, 2017; http://climatenewsnetwork.net/spring-moving-forward-record-rate/

54. "Sustainable Development"; http://en.wikipedia.org/wiki/Sustainable_development

55. Kell, J., "Reebok Is Bringing Some of Its Shoemaking Back to U.S." *Fortune*, October 20, 2016; http://fortune.com/2016/10/20/reebok-new-shoe-manufacturing/

56. "Does New Balance Manufacture Shoes in United States?" New Balance FAQs; https://support.newbalance.com/hc/en-us/articles/213335077-Does-New-Balance-Manufacture-Shoes-In-The-United-States-

57. Raleigh, P., and R. Miel, "Adidas, Reebok to Ramp up Manufacturing in U.S.," *European Rubber Journal and Plastic News*, December 9, 2016; http://www.rubbernews.com/article/20161209/NEWS/311289998/adidas-reebok-stride-toward-u-s-manufacturing

58. France-Presse, A., "Reebok Reshores Shoe Manufacturing, Though Still at a Small Scale," *Industry Week*, October 24, 2016; http://www.industryweek.com/global-economy/reebok-reshores-shoe-manufacturing-though-still-small-scale

59. 3D Printing, Wikipedia; http://en.wikipedia.org/wiki/3D_printing

60. America Makes; https://www.americamakes.us/about/overview

61. Quito, A., "Dentists Will Soon Be Able to 3D Print You a New Tooth in Minutes," *Quartz*, March 28, 2015; https://www.americamakes.us/about/overview

62. Wright, I., "Can 3D Drawing Bring Shoe Manufacturing Back to America?" *Engineering.com*, October 24, 2016; http://www.engineering.com/AdvancedManufacturing/ArticleID/13488/Can-3D-Drawing-Bring-Shoe-Manufacturing-Back-to-America.aspx

63. Brilliant Factory: Boosting Productivity by Re-imagining the Way We Design, Manufacture and Service Products, GE; https://www.ge.com/stories/brilliantfactory

64. Cochet, P., "Viewpoint: From Assembly Line to 'Digital Thread,' the Factory of the Future is Here," *Boston Business Journal*, October 7, 2016; http://www.bizjournals.com/boston/news/2016/10/07/viewpoint-from-assembly-line-to-digital-thread-the.html

65. Scott, A., "Boeing's Space Taxis to Use More Than 600 3D-Printed Parts," *Science News*, Reuters, February 3, 2017; http://www.reuters.com/article/us-boeing-space-exclusive-idUSKBN15I1HW

Chapter 12

SERVICE RESPONSE LOGISTICS

UnionPay launched Mobile QuickPass together with commercial banks and major mobile phone manufacturers worldwide. It covers mobile phone brands including Huawei, ZTE, and Apple, and supports multiple payment channels. UnionPay will take advantage of its network and technology to accelerate the launch of Mobile QuickPass overseas, and to deliver secure and convenient cross-border payment experience to cardholders. It is also important for UnionPay to expand Cloud QuickPass on a global scale.

—*Cai Jianbo, CEO of UnionPay International*[1]

We just don't have enough service capacity. With all the vehicles that we've sold over the last five to seven years, the retailers need to invest their profits in expansion.

—*Tom Doll, Subaru of America President*[2]

Learning Objectives

After completing this chapter, you should be able to

- Understand how supply chain management for services differs from supply chain management for manufacturers.
- Define service response logistics and describe all of its elements.
- Understand the importance of service layouts and perform a layout analysis using several techniques.
- Describe the strategies for managing capacity, wait times, distribution, and quality in services.
- Understand queuing system design issues and calculate queue characteristics.
- Use various techniques for managing customers' perceived waiting times.
- Understand the different distribution channels available for services.
- Define service quality and describe how to measure and improve it.

Chapter Outline

Introduction

An Overview of Service Operations

Supply Chain Management in Services

The Primary Concerns of Service Response Logistics

Summary

SCM Profile | Mexpress International Creates Quick Cross-border Service

Road feeder trucking services have always been a vital link in the airfreight supply chain, but one that is often invisible, as cargo is transported from one airport to another, or to the point of delivery. Along the U.S.–Mexico border, California-based Mexpress International has built its business on the cross-border, airport-to-airport road feeder service, using bonded less-than-truckload (LTL) and full-truckload (FTL) trucking, to offer next-day air and second-day air solutions. Mexpress moves each trailer across the border from one truck to another without breaking down the load. "Since we handle air cargo originating in Europe/Asia, we have to present the USA inbound documents to customs and border patrol, to make the transfer," says company president Carlos Duron.

Mexpress' bonded services have expanded rapidly in Mexico because many airports lack the infrastructure to handle air cargo shipments, and, given their distance from the country's main international airport in Mexico City, lack direct connectivity with cargo airports in Asia and Europe. Thus, much of the international freight destined for smaller cities in Mexico first touches the ground in Los Angeles (LAX) or Dallas (DFW) and then moves to Mexico by air or road. According to Duron, "oftentimes, freight on pallets arriving from international destinations, in the bellies of wide body aircraft, simply does not fit on the smaller interline planes traveling to smaller airports, so the freight must be consolidated and flown to Mexico City or Guadalajara, and then trucked to its final destination, or simply carried to the final destination by Mexpress." Mike Gamel, chairman and head of sales, claims that Mexpress' FTL service from LAX or DFW to smaller Mexican cities "beats the airfreight process to these locations by at least one day."

Mexpress developed its bonded trucking operations as a solution to clearing customs at the border. Initial approval of the program required collaboration with Hacienda, Mexico's internal revenue service, and the Mexican customs authority, to obtain the bonded Mexican trucking authority. Once seen as an obstacle to the customs-free border crossing, Mexican customs and local maquiladora associations are now some of the greatest proponents of Mexpress service expansions. After clearing customs at the destination airport, Mexpress cargo traditionally changed hands for last-mile delivery. Now, however, the company is offering customers the option of having Mexpress handle the entire process, including last-mile delivery. "The program has been in the works for about a year now," according to Gamel. "It is the result of growing cross-border e-commerce demand," he added. "Our customers kept asking for this service, because their clients—ecommerce e-tailers, manufacturers, as well as freight forwarders—kept pushing for it."[3]

INTRODUCTION

While most of the concepts of supply chain management discussed up to this point in the text can be applied to service organizations, this chapter introduces and discusses supply chain management concepts suited particularly to services and the service activities of manufacturers. Service firms differ from manufacturers in a number of ways including the tangibility of the end product, the involvement of the customer in the production process, the assessment of product quality, the labor content contained in the end products, and facility location considerations. Many services are considered **pure services**, offering few, if any tangible products to customers. Examples are consultants, lawyers, entertainers, and stockbrokers. Other services may offer end products containing a tangible component such as restaurants, repair facilities, transportation providers, and public warehouses. Most manufacturers, on the other hand, have tangible products with a relatively small service component that might include maintenance, warranty repair, and delivery services, along with customer call centers.

In most services, customers are either directly or indirectly involved in the production of the service itself. In this sense, services are said to provide **state utility**, meaning that services do something to things that are owned by the customer (such as transport and store their supplies, repair their machines, cut their hair, and provide their healthcare). Managing the interactions between service firms and their customers while the service is being performed is the topic of this chapter and is of paramount importance to the ultimate success of service organizations.

To generate initial and repeat customer visits, service firms must be located near their customers, they must know what their customers want, and they must be able to satisfy these needs quickly and in a cost-effective manner. This requires service firms to adequately hire, train, and schedule service representatives; to acquire technologies and equipment to aid in the provision of services; and to provide the right facility, network, and procedures to continually satisfy customers. Problems or mistakes that occur during the delivery of services most likely mean an increase in service delivery time, a reduction in customer satisfaction, lower perceived service quality, and lost current and future sales.

The important role services play in the global economy is becoming more evident today as developed countries become increasingly service oriented and as the Internet creates global "e-preneurs" whose businesses exist solely on the Internet. Service jobs are replacing those in manufacturing as productivity gains in manufacturing mean fewer laborers are needed to make the same volume of products. In the United States, for instance, services accounted for about 78 percent of the nation's gross domestic product (GDP) in 2014, which is up from 76 percent in 2006. In the United Kingdom, services provided about 80 percent of GDP; in France, 79 percent; and in Japan, 73 percent. In contrast, for underdeveloped countries like Afghanistan, Cambodia, Ethiopia, and Indonesia, services accounted for 54, 42, 43, and 45 percent of GDP, respectively. The country with the highest service percent of GDP in 2014 was Hong Kong at 93 percent, and the country with the lowest was Congo at 26 percent.[4]

Successful firms today are busy identifying and improving the customer-desired service elements in their product offerings, in order to provide better value through attention to these elements. These efforts are at the heart of service operations and the topic of service response logistics. Let's first review service operations in general and then move on to discuss service response logistics in particular.

AN OVERVIEW OF SERVICE OPERATIONS

Services include organizations such as retailers, wholesalers, transportation and storage companies, healthcare providers, financial institutions, schools, real-estate companies, government agencies, hotels, and consulting companies. Since the 1950s, the ratio of services to manufacturing and agriculture in terms of its share of the U.S. workforce has been increasing quite dramatically, and it is extremely likely that current university graduates entering the job market will be employed in some service role. In the United States and other developed economies, as the population has generated more wealth, they have continued to demand more services. In 1960, for example, Americans were spending about 46 percent of their personal consumption income on services. Today, Americans spend more than 67 percent on services.[5]

On the other hand, India, the world's second largest emerging economy (after China), has experienced a continued growth of their service sector. Their economy has shifted away from an agrarian economy toward a more service-oriented economy, which has improved the standard of living in India and boosted domestic consumption. This has helped to bolster overall productivity and competitiveness of companies in India, creating higher-value jobs. Services now account for about 52 percent of India's GDP.[6] Multinational restaurant chains are moving into India rapidly. Yum! Brands Inc., owner of Taco-Bell, KFC, and Pizza Hut, has expanded rapidly in India, from 230 at the end of 2009, to 677 in 2017. Dominos Pizza is also expanding in India with 1,127 stores in 2017, and is planning more.[7]

Some of the differences between goods and services are listed below:

- Services *cannot be inventoried*. Typically, services are produced and consumed simultaneously—once an airliner has landed, or surgical operations are performed, or legal advice is given, customers have "consumed" the service. For this reason, services often struggle to find ways to utilize their employees during low-demand periods and to serve customers effectively during busy periods.

- Services are often *unique*. High-quality service providers with well-trained and motivated employees have the capability of customizing services to satisfy each customer—insurance policies, legal services, and even fast-food services can be uniquely designed and then delivered to customers. Thus, hiring and training become important issues for satisfying individual customer needs.

- Services have *high customer—server interactions*. Services often require high levels of server attention, whether it means delivering purchased products to a specific location at the buyer's facility, analyzing data, answering customer questions, resolving complaints, or repairing machinery. Many services today are finding ways to automate or standardize their service products, or to utilize customers to provide some of the service, to reduce costs and improve productivity. For instance, the past few years have seen a rapid growth in automated, self-serve services such as purchasing goods online, performing checkout services at grocery stores, and completing one's taxes.

- Services are *decentralized*. Service facilities must be decentralized because of their inability to inventory services and because of competition. Therefore, finding good, high-traffic locations is extremely important (even Internet-based services must locate their advertisements where they will be easily seen by people using search engines).

Thus, services, whether they are stand-alone organizations or departments in goods producing firms, must be managed in ways that will take into account these various service characteristics. A number of service elements are discussed next.

Service Productivity

The basic measure of productivity is shown by the following formula:

$$\text{Productivity} = \frac{\text{Outputs produced}}{\text{Inputs used}}$$

where service outputs produced might be customers served, the number of services performed, or simply sales dollars, and inputs might be shown as labor hours or labor dollars (for a **single-factor productivity** measure). Alternately, inputs can be shown as the sum of labor, material, energy, and capital costs (for a **multiple-factor productivity** measure). The productivity measures used in an organization might be based on manager preferences or industry standards. Further, firms measure productivity to gauge their successes in employee training, equipment or technology investments, and cost-reduction efforts.

Productivity and its growth over time are commonly used indicators of a firm's (or a country's) economic success. For most services, automation can be a troublesome issue when calculating productivities, and the labor content per unit of output can be quite high relative to manufactured goods. These two things can lead to a declining productivity growth rate as a nation's economy becomes less manufacturing oriented and more services oriented. In the United States, the nonfarm labor productivity growth rate has declined from about 2.8 percent per year in the 1950s to about 1.2 percent per year today.[9] Because of this growth in services, service productivity now drives the advanced economies around the world, and this caused a major disruption in standards of living after the economic recession of 2008. The nearby SCM Profile discusses this problem in the United Kingdom.

This productivity growth problem has been termed **Baumol's disease**, named after noted U.S. economist William Baumol. In the 1960s, he and his colleague, William Bowen, argued that productivity growth tends to be low in service-oriented economies. And, in fact, this effect was realized in the United States from the mid-1970s through the mid-1990s as productivity growth averaged a relatively low 1.5 percent per year. Since the mid-1990s, however, productivity growth in the United States has been up and down, leading to other theories such as the **Walmart effect**, which postulates that the booming growth

SCM Profile — Service Productivity Drives Economies

Lawyers, accountants, and management consultants are at the heart of the UK's productivity growth problem, explaining almost a quarter of the UK's shortfall since 2008. Financial Times research shows that the stagnation of productivity growth since the global economic crisis is largely explained by just four sectors—professional services, telecommunications and computing, banking and finance, and manufacturing. The sectors, which played an important role in improving national output per worker before the financial crisis, have now lost their sparkle.

The drop in productivity growth is the most pressing problem in the global economy and it is deeper in Britain than any other member of the Group of Seven leading economies. The Office for National Statistics stated that the absence of productivity growth in the years since 2007 was unprecedented in the postwar period.

Productivity in professional services has stalled for many reasons including corporate reluctance to fire staff even as business dried up in the recession and subsequent new hires taking time to become more productive. The lack of productivity growth since 2008 explains a weakness in living standards, since productivity growth is the ultimate driver of higher incomes.

For many decades before the financial crisis of 2008, the United Kingdom's annual productivity growth averaged 1.75 percent. Professional services though—lawyers, accountants, and management consultants—averaged 3.8 percent between 1997 and 2008. Since the crisis, productivity has been flat at a level slightly below the 2008 peak, confounding forecasters in the Bank of England and Office for Budget Responsibility who have repeatedly forecasted that productivity growth would resume the 1.75 percent per year level.[8]

in information technology has allowed many big-box retailers such as Walmart to realize large productivity growth rates. Today, some economists are even saying that Baumol's disease has been "cured."[10] A service productivity example appears in Example 12.1.

Example 12.1   Productivity at the Ultra Ski Shop

The Ultra Ski Shop rents snow skis for fifteen weeks each year and employs five people. The owner wants to track productivity performance measures using the data shown below.

INPUTS AND OUTPUTS	2015
Skis rental revenue	$66,000
Labor cost	$10,800
Lease payments	$24,000
INPUTS AND OUTPUTS	**2016**
Skis rental revenue	$69,500
Labor cost	$11,600
Lease payments	$24,500

Single-factor productivities

2015:   Labor productivity = $66,000 sales/$10,800 = 6.11 sales $ per labor $
Lease productivity = $66,000/$24,000 = 2.75 sales $ per lease $

2016:   Labor productivity = $69,500 sales/$11,600 = 5.99 sales $ per labor $
Lease productivity = $69,500/$24,500 = 2.84 sales $ per lease $

Multiple-factor productivities

2015: $66,000 sales/[$10,800 + $24,000] = 1.90 sales $ per input $

2016 $69,500 sales/[$11,600 + $24,500] = 1.93 sales $ per input $

Labor productivity grew from 2015 to 2016 by (5.99 − 6.11)/6.11 = −0.02 = −2%. Lease productivity grew from 2015 to 2016 by (2.84 − 2.75)/2.75 = 0.033 or 3.3%. Multiple-factor productivity grew by (1.93 − 1.90)/1.90 = 0.016 or 1.6%. Ultra management should look into why labor cost grew faster than ski revenue from 2015 to 2016.

In services with high labor costs, there is often a desire to reduce labor costs to improve productivity (since labor cost is considered a productivity input). This can lead companies to relocate to lower labor cost areas, outsource jobs to other, lower cost service providers, or lay off workers. These can be risky strategies, since relocating can create added and unforeseen costs, outsourcing reduces managerial control, and reducing the workforce can adversely affect morale, service quality, and service availability.

Other strategies for increasing service productivity attack the numerator of the productivity equation. One example is the use of technology or automation to increase outputs. Adam Fein, president of Pennsylvania-based Pembroke Consulting, states, "In the warehouse, the productivity improvements from wireless networks come from substituting technology for potentially error-prone human activities such as order processing, inventory control, or picking." Productivity improvements can also be realized through better education and training, which can ultimately impact both inputs and outputs in the productivity equation. Hallmark Consumer Services, a U.K. logistics company, purchased a warehouse management software (WMS) application and then provided their warehouse employees with the necessary training to operate the system. "The training cost us £7,500 and the productivity gains alone were £7,000 our first year," says Chris Hall, managing director of Hallmark. "The WMS software was an investment of £20,000 and will have paid for itself in less than three years on labor savings alone."[11]

Improving service productivity can be quite challenging because of the desire in many cases for customized, labor-intensive services and because of the difficulty of assessing service quality (for instance, was the car fixed properly? Was the client properly defended? Was the hired comedian funny?). A complete discussion of service quality appears later in the chapter.

Global Service Issues

The growth and export of services are occurring everywhere as world economies improve and the demand for services increases. Even during the global recession a few years ago, a number of services were finding ways to stay competitive and expand. Just a few examples include—the expansion of Florida-based ZeroChaos, a workforce solutions provider, to the Nordic and European regions. "The Swedish market and the Nordic region remain attractive for expansion," says Harold Mills, CEO of ZeroChaos. "The exceptional market stability and nearly 5 percent GDP growth has provided numerous opportunities for our growth initiatives," he added. Small business funding specialist firm Bibby Financial Services of the United Kingdom expanded its presence in the Asia Pacific region by launching their Hong Kong and New Zealand operations in 2011, followed by opening a first location in Singapore in 2012. "Our overarching goal is to support the funding requirements of a greater number of small- and medium-sized businesses across the globe, and this latest venture will ensure we continue to develop our flexible trade finance packages," said CEO Simon Featherstone. U.K.-based deVere Group, a financial advisory service, started opening another 100 locations worldwide in 2011. "This is part of deVere's continued geographic expansion initiative to increase our presence in key growth markets and support our global growth strategy," said CEO Nigel Green.[12]

Successfully managing services as they expand into foreign markets involves a number of issues:

- *Labor, facilities, and infrastructure support.* Cultural differences, education, and expertise levels can prove to be problematic for firms unfamiliar with local human resources. Firms must also become adept at locating the most appropriate support facilities, suppliers, transportation providers, communication systems, and housing.

- *Legal and political issues.* Local laws may restrict foreign competitors, limit use of certain resources, attach tariffs to prices, or otherwise impose barriers to foreign services. Some countries require foreign companies to form joint ventures with domestic business partners.

- *Domestic competitors and the economic climate.* Company managers must be aware of their local competitors, the services they offer, their pricing structures, and the current state of the local economy. Firms can devise competitive strategies by modifying their services to gain a local or regional competitive advantage.

- *Identifying global customers.* Perhaps most importantly, managers must find out where potential global customers are, through use of the Internet, foreign government agencies, trading partners, or foreign trade intermediaries. Once potential customers are identified, managers can begin modifying their service products to meet the needs of these customers.

More on global service expansion can be found later in the chapter.

Service Strategy Development

Manufacturing and service organizations use one or more of the three generic competitive strategies: cost leadership, differentiation, and focus.[13] Each of these is briefly discussed below in relation to services.

Cost Leadership Strategy

Using a **cost leadership strategy** often requires a large capital investment in automated production equipment and significant efforts in the areas of controlling and reducing costs, doing things right the first time, standardizing services, and aiming marketing efforts at cost-conscious consumers. Walmart has been successful using its strategy of everyday low prices to attract and keep customers. It offers products at a cheaper price than its competitors, rather than using promotions. Walmart is able to achieve this due to its large quantity purchases and its highly efficient supply chain. Other examples include McDonald's, Ikea, and Southwest Airlines.[14]

Differentiation Strategy

Implementing a **differentiation strategy** is based on creating a service that is considered unique. The uniqueness can take many forms including customer service excellence (Ritz-Carlton hotels), brand image (the Google logo and its variations for holidays), variety (Best Buy's merchandise), and use of technology (Southwest Airlines' ticketing website and their "ding" notifications). Differentiation strategies are often created as the result of companies listening to their customers. Services are beginning to engage customers more effectively through various touch-points such as the phone, store locations, catalogs, social media, and online sites. New York-based Citigroup is well-known for its social media savvy. "Money is a highly sensitive topic," says Michelle Peluso, Citigroup's global consumer chief marketing and Internet officer. "One of the things social media allows us to do is to listen in to hear what people say about our brand, our competitors, our industry, products and services, and our people."[15] Differentiation does not necessarily mean higher costs and prices; it merely refers to the ability of the service company to offer unique elements in their service products. In many cases, though, it may mean the customer is willing to pay more for the service. Advertisements, logos, awards, and company reputations all play a part in creating the perception of uniqueness among a service's potential customers.

Focus Strategy

A **focus strategy** refers to a service that can effectively serve a narrow target market or niche better than other firms trying to serve an entire market. Companies specializing in these market niches can provide customized services and expertise to suit the specific needs of these customers. For instance, a neighborhood hobby shop is more likely to serve the needs of hobby enthusiasts than a big-box retailer like Carrefour or Walmart, even though they might sell some of the same merchandise. Within each market niche, firms can then exhibit characteristics of differentiation or cost leadership. Florida-based French Fry Heaven, a gourmet French fry restaurant, started in 2011 and sells many types of French fries and potatoes. They have found success serving this narrow fast-food niche. Their mission is: To serve the best fries on earth, be everywhere people are hungry, leave you with a smile on your face, and make a significant positive impact on the world! Today they are expanding nationwide with locations in Arizona, Ohio, Texas, and New Jersey.[16]

The Service Delivery System

Customers actually purchase a bundle of attributes when purchasing services, including the *explicit service* itself (storage and use of your money at a bank), the *supporting facility* (the bank building, drive-up tellers, and website), *facilitating goods* (the deposit forms, monthly statements, and coffee in the lobby), and *implicit services* (the security provided, friendly atmosphere in the bank, privacy, and user-friendliness of the website). Successful services deliver this bundle of attributes in a cost-conscious manner, while still satisfying customer requirements. Service managers define their companies' **service bundles** and then design the most effective delivery system.

Service delivery systems fall along a continuum with mass-produced, low customer contact systems at one extreme (such as ATMs) and highly customized, high customer contact systems at the other (such as an expensive beauty salon). Many delivery system designs seek to physically separate high-contact (front-of-the-house) operations from low-contact (back-of-the-house) operations to allow use of various management techniques to maximize performance of each area (such as in a restaurant). **Back-of-the-house operations** tend to be managed as manufacturing centers, where the emphasis is on maximizing quality outputs while achieving economies of scale. Technical people are hired for specific well-defined tasks, and technology is employed to increase productivity. On the other hand, **front-of-the-house operations** are characterized by hiring front-line service providers with good public relations skills, taking good care of customers, and giving employees the power and resources to solve customers' problems quickly and effectively.

Hospitals provide good examples of organizations characterized by a clear separation of high-contact and low-contact services. Administrative offices, labs, drug storage, laundry, and food preparation, for instance, are low-contact, back-of-the-house operations in a hospital. Managing these elements of the hospital service bundle can make a tremendous difference in profitability. No customer contact exists, so the emphasis is on materials management, space utilization, automation, and technical skills. However, patient care, prescription services, emergency room, and other high-contact services directly involve patients in the delivery of services. In these cases, customer−server interactions must be managed so that customers get what they need in an effective way.

Auditing the Service Delivery System

The service bundle delivery system should be audited periodically to assess the system's ability to meet customer expectations in a cost-effective way. Monitoring customer complaints, talking to and observing customers, and tracking customer feedback using customer comment cards and website comment forms (as well as looking at the bottom line) are ways to continually monitor the service delivery system. **Walk-through service audits** can be used to observe service system attributes from the time customers initially encounter the service until they leave. Several tools have been developed and used for this purpose including service system surveys to be completed by managers, employees, and/or customers, and service process maps (as discussed in Chapter 8). The objective of the service audit is to identify service system problems or areas in need of improvement.

Service Location and Layout Strategies

Good locations provide barriers to entry and competitive positioning for services as well as generate high levels of demand. Once a location has been secured, firms can begin to consider layout strategies that help to maximize customer service, server productivity, and service efficiencies. Since location strategies and analysis models were discussed in Chapter 11, only a brief discussion of location considerations is included here, followed by the design of service layouts.

Location Strategies

Location decisions are extremely important for most services because they have a significant impact on customer visits and, consequently, the long-term profits of the company (How likely is it that customers would visit a clothing store, for instance, in an otherwise abandoned shopping center?). Location selection is viewed as a moderate- to long-term decision because of the typically high costs of construction, remodeling, and relocation. (Note: Here, it is assumed that service locations are permanent structures, although some services actually are not bound by this assumption, as with a small legal office renting space in an office building or a music teacher who visits customers' homes.)

Global market opportunities, global competitors, and technological and demographic changes contribute to the importance of a good location. In all location evaluations, it is desirable to consider a number of relevant factors to reduce reliance on managers' personal preferences and intuition. Although intuition can certainly be a valuable location analysis tool, many disastrous location decisions have been made on the basis of intuition and not much more. For example, one-time Las Vegas gambler, entrepreneur, and self-proclaimed "Polish maverick" Bob Stupak built the 1,149-foot Stratosphere Hotel and Casino, which opened in a rundown neighborhood on the fringes of the famous Las Vegas Boulevard or "the Strip" in 1996. Within just a few months, the hotel was in financial trouble, partly because of the lack of foot traffic in the area. Stupak defaulted on payments to the bondholders who had put up the construction funds, and corporate raider Carl Icahn subsequently bought the bonds for $82 million (much less than half their original value). He assumed control of the hotel in 1998. His company then sold this and three other Nevada casinos to Goldman Sachs Group's Whitehall Street Real Estate Fund in 2008 for a profit of over $1 billion.[17]

A number of location analysis models can be used as aids in the location decision, and these include the weighted-factor location model, the location break-even model, and the center-of-gravity model (refer to Chapter 11 for use of these models).

Layout Strategies

Service layout strategies work in combination with location decisions to further support the overall business strategies of differentiation, low cost, or market focus. Office layouts tend to be departmentalized to allow specialists to share resources; many retailers like U.K.-based Tesco PLC also tend to be departmentalized to assist customers in finding items to purchase, whereas others may have centers throughout the store to entice customers to try things out and buy on impulse; commercial airliner layouts segment customers, reduce the time to restock and service the galleys and lavatories, and allow for fast passenger boarding and exit (at least in theory!); casino layouts are designed to get customers in quickly and then keep them there by spacing out the attractions; and self-serve buffet restaurant layouts are designed to process customers quickly. Warehouse layouts consider matching the products handled to the specific layout required (as discussed in the nearby SCM Profile). These are just a few examples, and many service layouts use multiple layout strategies. As customer preferences, products, technologies and service strategies change, layouts also tend to change. Several specific service layout design tools are illustrated below.

SCM Profile — Warehouse Layout Considerations

Although a warehouse management solution (WMS) is a crucial tool, common mistakes can make it challenging to maintain a successful warehouse operation even when a WMS is being used. Common problems include failure to put in place an efficient warehouse layout best suited to the products being handled and lack of knowledge of the inventory on hand.

It may sound like a simple concept, but having a logical warehouse layout is paramount to the success of any warehouse solution. Think of a warehouse like an easy-to-navigate system where each section is clearly defined. Most warehouses store product materials in bins that are scattered throughout the warehouse floor, which makes it challenging to find a product's location and causes delays and errors in product shipment. To avoid this, companies can establish a naming convention for bins so warehouse staff can find things quickly and easily, thus creating a logical sequence to bring people to where they need to be. Name the bins and lay out the warehouse in such a way that when someone looks at a bin tag, they will know how to find the bin.

How well the staff knows the inventory on hand will also help determine the warehouse layout and ultimate success of the WMS. Place higher moving products near picking lanes that are close to shipping areas, place bulk areas in a location to facilitate bin replenishment, and determine logical areas for items that require cage, cooler, and vault storage. Be aware of how products are moving so that locations can periodically be rearranged in the warehouse as needed.[18]

Departmental Layouts That Reduce Distances Traveled

Service layouts can be designed to reduce the travel times of customers or service workers when moving from one area to another. An example of a layout where this might be a primary consideration would be a health clinic. The waiting area is located in front where customers enter, and the examination rooms are located nearby. The doctors' offices might be centrally located, whereas the lab, storage, and x-ray rooms might be located farther to the back of the clinic away from most of the patients. A primary consideration is how far nurses, doctors, and patients have to walk to reach the various areas within the clinic. The objective would be to place high-traffic volume departments close to each other to minimize the total distances traveled by everyone per day. Example 12.2 illustrates a design tool for this type of layout.

Departmental Layouts That Maximize Closeness Desirability

Designing service layouts to place certain desirable pairs of departments closer to one another is another useful type of layout analysis tool and is often used for retail or office layouts. Here, the importance is placed on the relationships between various departments. In a convenience store, for instance, it would be extremely important to have the cashier close to the entrance and the cold food items in the back, close to the cold storage areas and the rear loading doors of the store. In an office setting, it might be desirable to have the receptionist close to the office entrance and the file room, with the managers close to the conference room. For each department pair, a **closeness desirability rating** is determined, with the objective being to design a layout that maximizes an overall desirability rating for the entire facility. Example 12.3 illustrates this concept. It should also be noted that it can be advantageous to use both of the analyses illustrated in Examples 12.2 and 12.3 for a given layout problem; in this way, the evaluation team could consider the best layout from both a distance traveled and closeness desirability perspective.

Example 12.2　Layout of Thompson Health Clinic

The Thompson Health Clinic wants to see whether there is a better layout that will reduce the time doctors and nurses spend walking throughout the clinic. The existing layout is shown below, along with the number of trips and the distances between each department.

Existing Layout

Storage (F)	Doctor's offices (C)	Exam rooms (B)		Lobby & waiting area (A)
Nurses (E)	Lab & x-ray (D)			

Interdepartmental Doctors' and Nurses' Trips/Day

	B	C	D	E	F
A	55	0	0	50	0
B		40	15	40	0
C			15	60	10
D				30	0
E					18

Distances between Departments (meters)

	B	C	D	E	F
A	20	40	40	60	60
B		20	20	40	40
C			10	20	20
D				20	20
E					10

To analyze the existing layout, the total distance traveled per day is calculated as follows:

$$\text{Total distance traveled} = \sum_{i=1}^{n}\sum_{j=1}^{n} T_{ij}D_{ij}$$

where n = number of departments
　　　i,j = individual departments
　　　T_{ij} = number of trips between departments i and j
　　　D_{ij} = distance from department i to department j

The objective is to find the layout resulting in the lowest total distance traveled per day. For the layout shown above, we find:

Total distance traveled per day = 55(20) + 50(60) + 40(20) + 15(20) + 40(40) + 15(10) + 60(20) + 10(20) + 30(20) + 18(10) = 9,130 meters

From the layout and the trips and distances shown, it can be seen that the nursing station should be closer to the lobby and waiting area, closer to the exam rooms and closer to the doctors' offices. This can be accomplished by switching departments E and D (nurses and lab/x-ray). This also creates a trade-off, since now departments C, B, and A will all be farther from department D. To calculate the new total distance traveled per day, the distance table must be modified as shown below. The asterisks denote changes made to the table.

Distances between Departments

	B	C	D	E	F
A	20	40	60*	40*	60
B		20	40*	20*	40
C			20*	10*	20
D				20	10*
E					20*

The new total distance can then be calculated as follows:

Total distance traveled per day = 55(20) + 50(40) + 40(20) + 15(40) + 40(20) + 15(20) + 60(10) + 10(20) + 30(20) + 18(20) = 7,360 meters

This is a better layout (not necessarily the best) and only one of a large number of potential layouts. The layout distance improvement is $\frac{9,130 - 7,360}{9,130} = 0.193$ or 19.3%. Typically a number of layouts are evaluated as shown here, until either the lowest-total-distance layout or some other reasonable alternative lower-distance layout is found.

Example 12.3   Closeness Desirability Rating for an Office Layout

Existing Office Layout

File room (F)	Engineering offices (C)	Marketing offices (B)	Secretary & waiting area (A)
Purchasing (E)	President's office (D)	Conference room (H)	Copy room (G)

Desirability Ratings

	B	C	D	E	F	G	H
A	2	0	−1	2	2	3	−1
B		0	2	1	1	0	3
C			2	2	0	0	1
D				1	−1	−1	3
E					3	1	2
F						3	1
G							0

The desirability ratings are based on a (−1 to 3) scale, where −1 = undesirable, 0 = unimportant, 1 = slightly important, 2 = moderately important, and 3 = very important. To calculate the score for the above layout, we count the closeness desirability score only when departments are adjacent to each other. For this layout:

$$\text{Closeness desirability score} = (A/B{:}2) + (A/H{:}{-}1) + (A/G{:}3) + (B/C{:}0) + (B/H{:}3) + (C/F{:}0) + (C/D{:}2) + (D/E{:}1) + (D/H{:}3) + (E/F{:}3) + (G/H{:}0) = 16 \text{ points}$$

Note that department pairs are not counted twice and are also not counted if only the corners are touching. To find a better layout, we could place the department pairs with a rating of 3 adjacent to each other, and place adjacent pairs with a rating of −1 such that they are not adjacent. For instance, the file room (F) could be moved adjacent to the copy room (G), and the conference room (H) could be moved farther away from the secretary and waiting area (A).

The new layout might look like this:

New Office Layout

President's office (D)	Engineering offices (C)	Marketing offices (B)	Secretary & waiting area (A)
Purchasing (E)	Conference Room (H)	File room (F)	Copy room (G)

The closeness desirability score for the new layout shown above would then be:

$$\text{Closeness desirability score} = (A/B{:}2) + (A/F{:}2) + (A/G{:}3) + (B/C{:}0) + (B/H{:}3) + (B/F{:}1) + (C/D{:}2) + (C/E{:}2) + (C/H{:}1) + (D/E{:}1) + (E/H{:}2) + (H/F{:}1) + (F/G{:}3) = 23 \text{ points}$$

On the basis of this analysis, it can be concluded that the second layout is better; like the previous example, though, there are many potentially good layouts, so a number of those should be evaluated prior to selecting the most appropriate one.

SUPPLY CHAIN MANAGEMENT IN SERVICES

In many respects, service-producing organizations are like goods-producing organizations: Both make purchases and therefore deal with suppliers; incur order costs and inventory carrying costs; and transport, count, store, and assess the quality of their purchased inventories. For some services, purchased items are part of the service provided and are extremely important sources of competitive advantage (as with a retailer or restaurant), whereas for others, this may be a less important concern (e.g., law offices and barber shops). Service firms also purchase **facilitating products** such as computers, furniture, and office supplies that are not part of the services sold but rather consumed inside the firm, and these materials must also be managed. Table 12.1 shows some typical transportation, warehousing, and inventory considerations at several different types of services.

In other respects, though, service firms are unlike goods-producing organizations, in that services typically deal with the end customers in their supply chains, whereas most goods-producing firms deal with wholesalers, distributors, other manufacturers, or retailers. In other words, service products are typically not passed on to customers further down a distribution channel. Thus, any goods that are delivered as part of the service are typically consumed or used by the immediate customers.

Service firms also interact closely with their customers, and the services performed in many cases contain higher labor content than manufactured products. Customers probably have no idea what resources or facilitating goods were used to deliver the services they purchase; rather, customers' primary concerns are with the service itself and the way it is delivered. For this reason, the distribution elements of interest to services revolve around customers and how they are being served. A good example of this can be found in the transportation industry. When shippers want things moved, they want the move performed at a specific time, delivered to a specific place, delivered on time, and performed as economically as possible. Most large transportation companies today have sophisticated information systems to allow customers to track deliveries as well as determine the best combination of warehousing, transportation mode, port-of-entry, routing, pricing, and consolidation.

One of the latest automated transportation elements is autonomous trucks. Taken together with double 53-foot trailers or triple 28-foot trailers, autonomous trucks could lead to a sizable reduction in logistics costs. Automating transportation though, comes with

Table 12.1	Transportation, Warehousing, and Inventory Considerations in Services	
SERVICES	**TRANSPORTATION**	**WAREHOUSING AND INVENTORY**
Banks	• Movements of checks, coins/cash among branches and operations centers • Movement of checks to cities with federal reserve processing centers	• Office supplies and coins/cash • Furniture and computers • Files
Hospitals	• Movement of medical supplies to stockrooms • Transfers of patients • Movement of medical records, test results, and films among units	• Surgical/medical supplies • Pharmaceutical supplies • Office furniture • Medical equipment
Telephone Cos.	• Inbound transportation of switches, parts and equipment to warehouses • Transportation of construction equipment and supplies to job sites • Routing of consumer products to retail outlets	• Parts, equipment, consumer products • Repair truck parts and equipment • Construction supplies

Adapted from Drazen, E. L., R. E. Moll, and M. F. Roetter, *Logistics in Service Industries*. Oak Brook, IL: Council of Logistics Management, 1991: 24–26.

more challenges and if successful, may reduce transportation jobs. "Robust autonomous technology [need to be] capable of dealing with variable weather conditions, invisible lane markings, hackers, communication system disruptions," says John Larkin, managing director of investment banking firm Stifel Capital Markets. "Taken alone, autonomous trucks operating on the interstate highway system would likely eliminate the persistently challenging driver shortage and might destroy highway-to-rail intermodal conversion economics."[19]

Service Quality and Customers

The satisfaction or perceived level of quality a customer experiences with regard to the service is of paramount concern to most services. The concept of service quality includes many elements, and these can change over time—recently, for example, customers of many businesses include sustainability as an element in their definitions of service quality. Food waste in restaurants is one place where sustainability can add to service quality. "Approximately 4 to 10 percent of food purchased by restaurants is wasted before reaching the consumer," claims New York-based Grace Communications Foundation, whose mission is to increase public awareness of the relationships among food, water, and energy. "Drivers of food waste at restaurants include oversized portions, inflexibility of chain store management, and extensive menu choices. On average, diners leave 17 percent of their meals uneaten and 55 percent of edible leftovers are left at the restaurant. This is partly due to the fact that portion sizes have increased significantly over the past 30 years, often being two to eight times larger than USDA or FDA standard servings," the foundation notes.[20]

Service quality assessments vary based on both the tangible and intangible elements of the services supplied and the satisfaction of the customers receiving the services. Call centers that fail to satisfy customers, for example, provide opportunities for improvement in service quality. With respect to call centers, the "gold standard" of service quality is their first call resolution score or the percent of callers whose problem is solved on their first call. Companies like Canada-based Service Quality Measurement Group survey call center customers and then identify what call centers with the highest first call resolution score are doing right. These best practices are then communicated to their call center clients.[21]

All the elements of supply chain management including supplier selection, transportation, warehousing, process management, quality assessment, distribution, and customer service hold strategic importance for the long-term success of service organizations. While the previous sections have discussed many of these elements, the remainder of this chapter is devoted to the portion of supply chain management of greatest concern to service organizations and the service arms of goods-producing companies—namely, the activities associated with the production and delivery of the actual service.

THE PRIMARY CONCERNS OF SERVICE RESPONSE LOGISTICS

Service response logistics is defined as the management and coordination of the organization's activities that occur while the service is being performed.[22] Managing these activities often means the difference between a successful service experience and a failure. The four primary activities of concern in service response logistics are the management of service capacity, waiting times, distribution channels, and service quality. Since a service cannot be inventoried, managing service capacity enables the firm to meet variable demand—perhaps, the most important concern of all services. When demand variability cannot be adequately

met, the firm must resort to managing queues or waiting times to keep customers satisfied. Demand management tactics also play a role in the service firm's ability to satisfy varying levels of demand. Customer waiting times are closely related to the customer's view of
service quality and, ultimately, customer satisfaction. Since services usually must be decentralized to attract customers while providing adequate service delivery times, use of various
distribution channels also becomes important to the delivery of service products. Each of
these service elements is discussed in detail in the following sections.

Managing Service Capacity

Service capacity is most often defined as the number of customers per day the firm's
service delivery systems *are designed to serve*, although it could also be some other period
of time such as customers per hour or customers per shift. Capacity measures can be stated
somewhat differently too, depending on the service industry standard—for instance, airline companies define capacity in terms of available seat miles per day. Most services desire
to operate with some excess capacity, to reduce the likelihood of having queues and long
waiting times develop. For service employees dealing directly with customers, service
capacity is largely dependent on the number of employees providing the services and the
equipment they use in these activities.

Since service outputs can't be inventoried, firms are forced to either turn away customers when demand exceeds capacity, make customers wait in line, or hire additional personnel. Since hiring, training, supervising, and equipping service personnel are quite costly (in
many cases 75 percent of total operating costs), the decision of how many service personnel to hire greatly affects costs, productivity, and ultimately sales and profits. Ideally, firms
want enough service capacity (or service personnel) to satisfy variable demand, without
having too much excess (and costly) capacity. This can be a tricky proposition if demand
varies erratically throughout the day, week, or month, as is typical in a great many services.
So an important part of a service manager's job is to forecast demand for various segments
of time and customer service processes, and then provide enough capacity to meet the
forecasted demand. The nearby SCM Profile describes an Internet tool designed by Mopar
to manage service capacity at Fiat Chrysler dealerships.

When things work out right, a service operates at an optimal **capacity utilization**.
Capacity utilization is defined as:

$$\text{Capacity utilization} = \frac{\text{Actual customers served per period}}{\text{Capacity}}$$

As utilization approaches (and sometimes even exceeds) 1.0 or 100 percent, services
become more congested, service times increase, wait times increase, and the perceived
quality of service deteriorates. With utilization close to 1.0, even a slightly greater than
average service time for several customers can cause queues to become very long (some
readers may recall, for instance, waiting one or two hours beyond an appointment time to
see a busy doctor). Thus, an optimal utilization would leave some level of capacity unutilized (perhaps 15 to 25 percent depending on the volatility of demand), so that variations
in service times and customer demand won't severely affect customer wait times. In the
trucking industry, the recent economic recession caused a dramatic decrease in trucking
capacity, as some companies went out of business while others reduced drivers and equipment to reduce costs. Today, most trucking companies are reporting high utilizations with
no capacity reserves, and new truck purchases have only covered replacement needs. There
was also a shortage of about 50,000 drivers in the United States at the end of 2016.[24]

SCM Profile | Mopar Gets Service Capacity Right

Mopar, the parts and service organization with Fiat Chrysler Automobiles (FCA), is introducing a new software application to assist FCA U.S. dealerships prepare for and predict the best service capacity strategies. Mopar's Service Capacity Analyzer is an online tool that helps dealers to assess, plan, and implement changes to the number of technicians, technician hours, and service bays to better service customers. "Providing a great customer experience is at the core of what we do," said Pietro Gorlier, president and CEO of Mopar. "That is why this year alone we have supported the addition of more than 1,300 technicians, 700 service advisors, and 500 service bays in our dealer network, which overall is well ahead of our targets. Now, the new Mopar Service Capacity Analyzer offers dealerships a 'road map' to more efficiently utilize these resources by forecasting customer needs out to 2018 based on dealer-specific parameters."

The company said that the algorithm-based Service Capacity Analyzer allows dealers to adjust physical capacity metrics such as number of technicians/service advisors, technician available hours, and stall numbers, to match projected service lane traffic. The dealer can create scenarios and evaluate the changes needed to reach the optimum level of service. Mopar said that it also offers tools to help dealerships implement service capacity changes. They are launching a new Service Capacity Guidebook as part of the Service Capacity Analyzer to assist dealers in seizing existing opportunities while avoiding the pitfalls of a crowded service lane. "The customer journey is about Mopar partnering with our dealers to ensure that we have the tools, the people, and the plan to continue to serve those who drive us," said Gorlier.[23]

The two most basic strategies for managing capacity are to use a **level demand strategy** (when the firm utilizes a constant amount of capacity regardless of demand variations) or a **chase demand strategy** (when the amount of capacity is allowed to vary with demand). When a level demand strategy is used, the firm is required to use **demand management** or **queue management** tactics to deal with excess customers. When a chase demand strategy is used, effective plans must be in place to utilize, transfer, or reduce service capacity when there is excess available and to develop or borrow capacity quickly when demand exceeds capacity. Capacity management techniques that are useful when demand exceeds available service capacity are discussed next, followed by a discussion of capacity management when service capacity exceeds demand.

Capacity Management When Demand Exceeds Capacity

An initial observation might be to simply let customers wait, or hire workers when demand exceeds existing capacity and then lay them off when capacity exceeds demand. Most likely, though, firms would like to avoid these options because of the expenses of finding, hiring, training, and supervising new workers; the loss of current and future business when people wait too long in queues; as well as the expense and damage to the firm's reputation when laying off workers. Instead, a number of other methods can be employed to minimize the costs of hiring and laying off workers and the cost of letting customers wait in line. These methods include cross-training and sharing employees, using part-time employees, using customers, using technology, using employee scheduling strategies and, finally, using demand management techniques to smooth or shift demand. Each of these methods is discussed next.

Cross-training and Sharing Employees

Have you ever been waiting in line to pay for items at a retail store and thought to yourself, "Why don't they use some of these other workers that are just standing around to ring up customers' purchases?" Many service firms, though, do make wide use of this employee-sharing strategy. Quite often in many service firms, some processes are temporarily overutilized while other processes remain under- or unutilized. Rather than hiring someone to add capacity to the overutilized processes, progressive firms have adequately hired and cross-trained workers to be proficient in a number of different process functions. Thus, when demand temporarily exceeds service capacity in one area, creating a customer queue, idle workers can quickly move to that process to help serve customers and reduce the time customers spend waiting in a queue.

By sharing employees among a number of processes, firms create the capability to quickly expand capacity as demand dictates while simultaneously minimizing the costs of having customers wait or hiring and laying off workers. This type of resource sharing arrangement can occur in almost any type of organization, from retailers to banks, hospitals and universities.

Using Part-time Employees

Use of part-time employees is also seen as a low-cost way to vary capacity. The hourly wages and costs of fringe benefits are typically lower than those of full-time employees. Firms use full-time employees to serve that stable portion of daily demand, while scheduling part-timers for those historically busy periods (such as lunch and dinner times, holidays, weekends, or busy seasons). Part-time employees can also be used to fill in during the vacation periods, off days, and sick days of full-time employees. Laying off part-time employees during slower periods is also viewed as more acceptable to the permanent full-time workforce and is somewhat expected by the part-time employees.

Using Customers

As the need to contain costs and improve productivity and competitiveness continues, firms are finding that customers themselves can be used to provide certain services, as long as it is seen by customers as value enhancing. The benefits of self-service include faster service, more customized service, and lower prices, since firms need fewer employees. The benefits for the companies include lower labor costs and additional service capacity. In this sense, customers are "hidden employees," allowing the firm to hire fewer workers and to vary capacity to some extent as needed. The trade-off for customers is that they expect to pay less for these services, since they are doing some of the work. This includes services like bagging groceries, filling soda cups, and filing taxes.

In other cases, though, customers might actually pay the same or more for the service, as when using self-checkout at grocery stores or using 24-hour automated teller machines, if customers perceive the work they perform as saving time or providing some other benefits. Thus, if firms can identify service process jobs that customers can perform, if they can provide process directions that are easy to understand and learn, and if they can adequately satisfy customers who are being asked to perform the work, then using customers as service providers creates yet another method for managing capacity. U.K.-based Photo-Me International, which owns 27,000 self-service photo booths in 17 countries, and 2,000 self-service launderettes, operates solely with the self-service concept.[25]

Using Technology

Providing technological assistance in the form of computers, software applications, or other equipment to service company personnel can improve the ability of servers to process customers, resulting in more service capacity, faster service completion times, better service quality, and the need for fewer employees. Voice-activated telephone response systems, online banking, purchasing, selling, and comment systems and field sales software applications are just a few examples of technology helping the provision of services. Some forms of technology may completely replace the need for sales or other types of customer service personnel as in the case of Amazon.com and other online retailers. Advances in software capabilities and cloud computing have also allowed services to share use of expensive software systems like reservation systems and property management systems, which greatly improve productivity while reducing labor and software development costs. Retailers are also increasingly using workforce management solutions to create a better customer experience, while ensuring the right associates are available at the right place and the right time. Workforce management solutions align workforce schedules with demand forecasts and enterprise initiatives, such as promotions and markdowns.[26]

Technology can also enable service standardization—providing the service exactly the same way every time, as with automated teller machines or ticketing machines. In many cases, service standardization is viewed as a high-quality characteristic by customers seeking specific, periodic services. Standardization allows services to be accessed anywhere at any time, without the need for relearning the service process.

Using Employee Scheduling Policies

As mentioned briefly above, properly scheduling workers allows firms to adjust capacity to accommodate varying demand. Businesses forecast demand in short-time increments during the day and then convert the demand to staffing requirements for each period, given the average service capabilities for workers. The problem of assigning workers to shifts is complicated by the number of hours each day and the number of days each week the business is open, the timing of days off and consecutive days off, and employee shift preferences. The objective of worker scheduling is to adequately serve customers with the minimum number of employees, while also assigning equitable work shifts to employees. Employee scheduling software is available to provide managers with multiple scheduling solutions to this problem.

Use of part-time workers, as stated earlier, makes scheduling easier and is illustrated in Example 12.4. In the example, the manager uses full-time workers for the base-level requirement for the five-day week, while using part-timers to fill out the requirements each day.

Example 12.4   Workforce Scheduling at Rose Plumbing Supply

The manager of Rose Plumbing Supply has determined his workforce requirement as shown below for the five-day workweek. Given these requirements, Bill sees that he needs two full-time employees working all five days, resulting in the part-time requirements as shown (found by subtracting two from each workday requirement). To satisfy these requirements with the fewest number of part-time employees, he begins by assigning part-timer no. 1 to the maximum number of workdays (Monday, Thursday, and Friday). Part-timer no. 2 is assigned to the maximum number of workdays remaining (Monday and Friday). Then part-timers 3 and 4 are assigned to the remaining workday (Friday).

	MONDAY	TUESDAY	WEDNESDAY	THURSDAY	FRIDAY
Workers Required	4	2	2	3	6
Full-time Workers	2	2	2	2	2
Part-time Workers	2	0	0	1	4
Part-timer No. 1	1			1	1
Part-timer No. 2	1				1
Part-timer No. 3					1
Part-timer No. 4					1

Using Demand Management Techniques

Even when accurate forecasting and good capacity management techniques are used, there are many occasions when demand exceeds available capacity. As stated earlier, forcing customers to wait in line for a long period of time may result in lost current and future business and damage to the firm's reputation. Organizations can try to reduce demand during busy periods using several short-term **demand management** techniques. These include raising prices during busy periods to reduce demand and shift it to less busy periods, taking reservations or appointments to schedule demand for less busy periods, discouraging undesirable demand through use of screening procedures and marketing ads, and segmenting demand to facilitate better service (examples include use of first-class and economy-class seating, and use of express and regular checkout stations). These tactics are combined with the capacity management techniques discussed earlier to provide the firm with the ability to better serve customers. The next section describes capacity management techniques for periods when service capacity exceeds demand.

Capacity Management When Capacity Exceeds Demand

When capacity exceeds demand, the firm is faced with the problem of how to utilize excess capacity. Too much excess capacity means higher fixed costs, resulting in higher prices for the services provided, and may also affect customers' perceptions of quality (readers may recall their own quality perceptions when walking into a mostly deserted restaurant at peak dinner hours). Besides the obvious long-term solution of laying workers off and reducing location size, firms may be able to find other uses for service capacity or use demand management techniques to stimulate demand.

Finding Other Uses for Capacity

One way to utilize excess capacity is to develop additional service products. Periodic lack of demand might be particularly troublesome for services with seasonal demand such as hotels, airlines, and ski resorts. For these services, management may try to develop service products that the firm can provide during their characteristically slow periods. This might include airlines partnering with resorts to provide vacation packages during off-peak seasonal periods, hotels booking business conferences during slow periods, or ski resorts designing mountain bike trails or building cement luge runs for summer use. Firms can also make use of cross-training to shift or transfer employees to other areas temporarily needing more capacity. For instance, swimming pool builders might train and then use their construction workers to build pool enclosures during the winter months. In an interesting use of excess electricity capacity, Canada is gearing up for handling the electricity demand for electric cars, estimated to be a total of 500,000 units by 2020. Currently, Canada's hydro, coal, natural gas, and nuclear power sources go largely unused during nighttime hours, and this power can't easily be turned off. It thus becomes wasted power. Consequently, Canada is developing smart electricity meters to charge users drastically cheaper rates for power usage during off-peak hours, which will allow electric cars to be cheaply recharged at night. "We have the resources and the electricity," says Al Cormier, executive director of the not-for-profit organization Electric Mobility Canada. "We should take advantage of this opportunity."[27]

Using Demand Management Techniques

When capacity exceeds demand, demand management techniques can be used to stimulate demand. These include lowering prices during off-peak periods, as in early-bird dinner specials or mid-week hotel rates, as well as designing aggressive marketing campaigns for use during slow business periods. Gatwick airport in the United Kingdom, for example, eliminated its landing fees during the slow winter months to encourage more use of the airport during this period. This strategy increased passenger traffic by 3.3 percent in 2011, compared to the year earlier, when the policy was not in effect.[28]

Managing capacity in services thus involves techniques to adjust capacity and either stimulate or shift demand to match capacity to demand. When an oversupply or undersupply of capacity exists, service times, waiting times, cost, and service quality all suffer, all of which ultimately impact the competitiveness of the firm. The second concern in service response logistics is discussed next—managing queue times.

Managing Queue Times

Queue times are frequently encountered every day by consumers including waiting at checkout counters, waiting for a table at a restaurant, and waiting on hold on the cellphone. Ideally, service managers would like to design **queuing systems** such that customers never have to wait in a queue; however, the cost of maintaining enough excess service capacity to handle peak demand and unexpectedly high levels of demand is simply too expensive. Thus, managers use information they have about their customers as well as their service employees to design adequate queuing systems and then couple this with management of customers' perceived waiting times to minimize the negative impact of waiting in line. Many businesses have resorted to using text messaging to reduce queue lengths and wait times. The nearby SCM Profile discusses the use of text messaging for services.

| SCM Profile | Text Messages Help Reduce Wait Times |

Missed appointments on the UK's National Health Service (NHS) are a continual struggle for the facility and are costing the country billions each year, but automated SMS appointment reminders (text messages) are helping to reduce these losses. "The NHS has been slow to adopt appointment reminders, but they're beginning to get on board with it now," says Alex Kinch, CEO of next-generation telecoms operator Ziron. "Sending someone a text 24 hours before their doctor or dentist appointment, reminding them when and where it is and what to do if they want to cancel, is saving an awful lot of money."

Another problem for consumers is home-delivery services. Amazon, for example, is starting to implement SMS services more heavily to minimize customer waiting times. "They are starting to send SMS on the morning of delivery, telling the consumer 'we'll be with you between 10 and 11am'," says Kinch.

But perhaps most important is the finance industry's use of text messaging services: "Every time I make a financial transaction, I get an SMS from my bank telling me what transaction has been made," says George Fraser, VP of EMEA at CSG International. "The idea of having a confirmation after every single transaction is very reassuring." And this is starting to become the norm for consumers worldwide. While SMS is being adopted rapidly in Europe, many U.S. consumers are still charged not only to send but also to receive SMS messages, and this could be a major deciding factor behind the slow uptake in the country. "You don't really want people to be constantly sending you a stream of messages if you're paying every time," says Kinch.[29]

Good queue management consists of the management of *actual waiting time* and *perceived waiting time*. To accomplish this, managers must consider a number of issues:

- What is the average arrival rate of the customers?
- In what order will customers be serviced?
- What is the average service rate of the service providers?
- What is the average service time requirement of customers?
- How are customers' arrival and service times distributed?
- How long will customers actually wait in a queue before they either leave or lower their perceptions of service quality?
- How can customers be kept in line even longer without lowering their perceptions of service quality?

Answers to these questions will allow the firm to adequately design a queuing system that will provide acceptable service to most customers while minimizing the service system cost and the cost of lost and disgruntled customers. Properly thought-out and designed queuing systems decrease waiting times and subsequently the need for further managing waiting times; however, occasionally, waiting time management tactics must be utilized to decrease perceived waiting times. The design of queuing systems is discussed first, followed by a discussion of managing perceived waiting times.

Queuing System Design

The four types of queuing system configurations are shown in Figure 12.1. The most appropriate queuing system depends on the volume of customers to be served, the willingness of customers to wait in a queue, the physical constraints imposed by the service structure, and the number and sequence of services to be performed. The outputs from various queuing systems that managers need to compare are the average number of customers in the queue and in the system, the average waiting time in the queue and in the system, and the average server utilization (the "system" includes the actual service time). As alluded to earlier, the primary elements of all queuing systems are the *input process*, the *queue characteristics*, and the *service characteristics*. These elements are discussed next, along with several applications.

The Input Process

Customer arrivals are referred to here as the **demand source**. The size of the demand source can be considered either infinite or finite. Many situations (along with the examples covered later) assume an unlimited or infinite demand source such as customers arriving at a retail outlet, whereas other situations have a finite-sized demand source, such as ticketed customers showing up for a concert at an arena.

Customers also arrive at a service according to an **arrival pattern**. When students show up for a scheduled class, this is an example of a known or *deterministic interarrival time*. In many cases as in a retail establishment, customers show up in a random pattern, and the *Poisson distribution* (named after the nineteenth-century French mathematician Siméon Denis Poisson) is commonly used to describe these customer arrivals. Using the Poisson distribution, the probability of x-customers arriving within some time period, T, is expressed as:

$$P_{x(T)} = \frac{e^{-\lambda T}(\lambda T)^x}{x!}$$

where λ = average customer arrivals in time period T
e = 2.71828 (natural log base)
T = time period in hours (usually assumed to be 1)
$x!$ = x factorial = $x(x-1)(x-2)...(1)$

| Figure 12.1 | Queuing System Configurations |

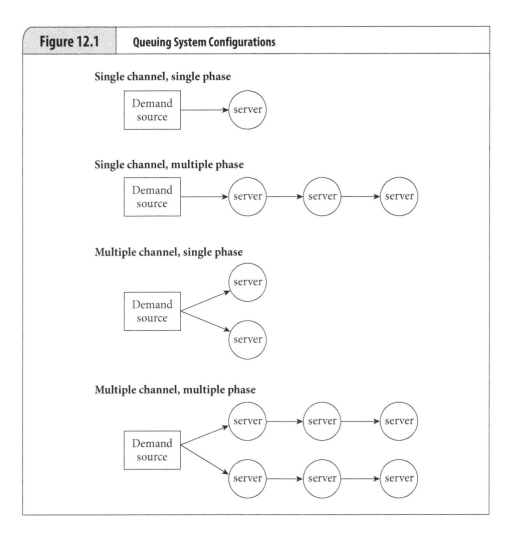

Single channel, single phase

Single channel, multiple phase

Multiple channel, single phase

Multiple channel, multiple phase

Example 12.5 illustrates the use of this formula.

Example 12.5　Arrivals per Hour at Jay's Quick Lube Shop

Jay's Quick Lube Shop can service an average of four cars per hour with a partial crew of three employees, and the owner Jay is interested in calculating the probability they can handle all the customers on Saturdays with the partial crew, instead of his usual full crew of five. Given an average arrival rate of three customers per hour on Saturdays, he uses the Poisson distribution to calculate the probabilities of various customer arrivals per hour, shown below.

NUMBER OF ARRIVALS, x	$P(x \text{ for } T = 1 \text{ hour}) = \dfrac{e^{-3}3^{x}}{x!}$	CUMULATIVE PROBABILITY
0	0.0498	0.0498
1	0.1494	0.1992
2	0.2240	0.4232
3	0.2240	0.6472
4	0.1680	0.8152

By summing the probabilities for each of the arrival levels, Jay figures that he can handle the demand per hour approximately 82 percent of the time. Conversely, he figures that approximately 18 percent of the time, demand per hour will be greater than four customers, causing queues to develop.

If we assume the number of arrivals per time period is Poisson distributed with a mean arrival rate of λ, then the interarrival time (time between arrivals) is described by the negative exponential distribution, with a mean interarrival time of $1/\lambda$ (so if the mean arrival rate is 10 per hour, then the mean interarrival time is (60 minutes/10 arrivals), or 6 minutes/arrival).

Most queuing models assume that customers stay in the queue once they join it. In other words, customers do not exhibit **balking** (refusing to join the queue once they see how long it is) or **reneging** (leaving the queue before receiving the service). Though most people have done this at one time or another, queuing analysis becomes much more complex when these arrival characteristics are allowed.

The Queue Characteristics

Queuing models generally assume the length of a queue can grow to an infinite length, although for some situations this is not appropriate (e.g., people with tickets waiting to enter a concert). Queuing configurations can contain single or multiple queues (e.g., the single winding queue at Wendy's vs. the multiple queues at some McDonald's). Another queue characteristic is the **queue discipline**. The discipline describes the order in which customers are served. The most common queue discipline is first-come-first-served, although other examples include most-needy-first-served (in emergency rooms) and most-important-first-served (a VIP queue at a nightclub).

Virtual Queues

Technology is impacting queuing systems such that **virtual queues** are becoming more commonplace. Customers' places in the queue are tracked by a computerized system that allows them to roam the premises until their hand-held monitor lights up. This reduces balking and reneging while allowing customers to make better use of their time. For instance, the Lavi Industries' Qtrac system registers customers via their smartphone or computer, then lets customers know their expected waiting time. Customers are continuously updated. In hospitals in Shanghai, waiting patients can input their cell phone numbers into a computer system that sends them a text message when they become fifth in line, allowing them to leave without fear they will miss an appointment.[30]

Increasingly, companies are allowing queue-jumping, which can happen invisibly in virtual queues. Call centers, for example, can prioritize callers in a telephone queue once they have been identified. Additionally, customers willing to pay extra can in many cases jump queues. Banks, airlines, and credit card companies have elite call centers, and some doctors give patients priority if they pay extra. U.K.-based Accesso operates hand-held devices (called Q-bots) and smartphone apps (called Q-smart) that allow theme park visitors in twenty theme parks worldwide, to reserve a spot in line. A premium option allows visitors to jump the queues.[31]

The Service Characteristics

Services can be provided either by a single server or by multiple servers that act in series or in parallel. Multiple servers acting in parallel is referred to as a **multiple-channel queuing system**. Multiple servers acting in series is referred to as a **multiple-phase queuing system**. Figure 12.1 shows these queuing configurations.

The *single-channel, single-phase* configuration is the most basic. For standard distribution patterns of customer arrival and service times, the formulas to evaluate this type of system are very straightforward. An example is the one-person retail shop (such as a comic book shop or gift shop). The *single-channel, multiple-phase* queuing system is the next configuration shown. For this system, customers all contact the same servers, but receive more than one service and encounter a queue at each service. An example of this type of service is a dentist's office where customers are checked-in by a receptionist, get their teeth cleaned by a dental hygienist, get their teeth x-rayed by a dental assistant, and then get a dental exam by a dentist. For each service, longer-than-average service times by the preceding customer or during one phase of the service can mean waiting line buildups within the entire system. The third configuration shown is the *multiple-channel, single-phase* system. Customers enter the system, receive one service from any one of a number of servers, and then exit. Examples of this are retailers' checkout stands or banks' teller windows. These systems can have queues at each channel or one winding queue where all channels receive customers from one line. The final configuration shown is the *multiple-channel, multiple-phase* queuing system. In this example, customers all receive more than one service in sequence from more than one set or channel of servers. An example here might be a large medical clinic where patients are checked in by one of several assistants, have their vital signs recorded by one of several nurses, and receive a medical consultation and service by one of several doctors.

Another characteristic of a service are the times required to complete each of the services provided. For each phase in the system, service times are described by a mean time and a probability distribution. Frequently, the negative exponential distribution is used to describe the randomness of service time distributions. To determine the probability that the service time, t, will be less than or equal to some specified time, T, the following formula can be used:

$$P(t \leq T) = 1 - e^{-\mu T}$$

where $e = 2.71828$ (natural log base)
$\mu =$ the average service rate

Example 12.6 illustrates the use of this formula for calculating the probability of completing service within a specified time period.

For single-channel systems, the average arrival and service rates can be used to calculate average capacity utilization, by dividing the customer arrival rate by the customer service rate. For example, if the arrival rate is three per hour and the service rate is four per hour, then the average capacity utilization is 75 percent. Although, as can be seen in Example 12.5, there will likely be times when utilization for periods during the day approaches or

---

Example 12.6   Service Times at Jay's Quick Lube Shop

Jay's Quick Lube Shop can service an average of four customers per hour, or one customer every fifteen minutes, with a crew of three service personnel. The average customer arrival rate on Saturdays is three customers per hour, or one customer every twenty minutes. Jay is interested in calculating the probability that actual service time, t, will be within a specific time period, T, and he develops a chart showing these probabilities below, using the negative exponential distribution.

SPECIFIC TIME PERIOD	$P(t \leq T \, hrs) = 1 - e^{-4T}$
15 min (0.25 h)	$1 - e^{-4(0.25)} = 0.6321$
20 min (0.33 h)	$1 - e^{-4(0.33)} = 0.7329$
30 min (0.5 h)	$1 - e^{-4(0.5)} = 0.8647$
40 min (0.67 h)	$1 - e^{-4(0.67)} = 0.9314$
45 min (0.75 h)	$1 - e^{-4(0.75)} = 0.9502$

Thus, Jay thinks that about 73 percent of the time, they will be able to service a customer in less than or equal to twenty minutes.

exceeds 100 percent. Now that all of the important elements of queuing systems have been reviewed, various applications of the models can be discussed and these are presented next.

Queuing System Applications

When using queuing models, managers collect arrival rate and service rate data by observing over time how many customers actually arrive for service and how many customers are actually served. Depending on the service, it may take a number of days or weeks to compile meaningful information. Presented below are applications of the single-channel, single-phase queuing model and the multiple-channel, single-phase queuing model. These are meant only to be introductory applications. Examples for the other queuing systems and applications can be quite complicated and are beyond the scope of this text. Interested readers are encouraged to examine management science or operations research texts for more advanced treatments of this topic. Several references are provided at the end of the chapter for this purpose.

A Single-Channel, Single-Phase Queuing System Application

This is the most widely used and simplest of all queuing systems. The assumptions for the system are:

- Customers come from an infinite population and are Poisson distributed over time.
- Customers are served in first-come-first-served sequence.
- No balking or reneging occurs.
- Service times are distributed according to the negative exponential distribution.
- The average service rate is greater than the average arrival rate.

The symbols and equations used to determine the operating characteristics for the single-channel, single-phase queuing model are:

λ = average arrival rate
μ = average service rate
ρ = average server utilization = λ/μ
L_s = expected number of customers in the system = $\lambda/(\mu-\lambda)$
L_q = expected number of customers in the queue = $\lambda^2/[\mu(\mu-\lambda)] = L_s - \lambda/\mu$
W_s = expected waiting time in the system = $1/(\mu-\lambda) = L_s/\lambda$
W_q = expected waiting time in the queue = $\lambda/[\mu(\mu-\lambda)] = L_q/\lambda$
P_n = probability that there are n units in the queuing system = $(\lambda/\mu)^n(1-\lambda/\mu)$

Example 12.7 illustrates the calculations of operating characteristics for a single-channel, single-phase service.

A Multiple-Channel, Single-Phase Queuing System Application

All of the assumptions shown above still apply for the multiple-channel, single-phase system, except that the number of servers is now greater than one, and the queuing system consists of multiple servers serving customers from multiple queues. The operating characteristics of this queuing system are as follows:

λ = average arrival rate
$s\mu$ = average service rate, where s = number of service channels

Example 12.7   Operating Characteristics for Kathy's Sewing Shop

Kathy's Sewing Shop can serve about five customers per hour. For the past two weeks Kathy has kept track of the customer arrival rate, and the average has been four customers per hour. Kathy is interested in calculating the operating characteristics for her store. So she asks one of her customers, a business student at the local university, to help her. The student provides the following information:

$\lambda = 4$ customers per hour

$\mu = 5$ customers per hour

$\rho = 4/5 = 0.8$ or 80% utilization

$L_s = \lambda/(\mu-\lambda) = 4/(5-4) = 4$ customers

$L_q = L_s - \lambda/\mu = 4 - 4/5 = 3.2$ customers

$W_s = L_s/\lambda = 4/4 = 1$ hour $= 60$ minutes

$W_q = L_q/\lambda = 3.2/4 = 0.8$ hours $= 48$ minutes

Kathy also wants to know how likely it will be that more than four customers will be in her shop at one time. So the student thinks about this and decides to determine the probabilities of zero, one, two, three, and four customers in the shop, and then subtract their sum from 1. So she provides the following information:

For $n = 0$ $P_0 = (4/5)^0(1-4/5) = 0.200$

$n = 1$ $P_1 = (4/5)^1(1-4/5) = 0.160$

$n = 2$ $P_2 = (4/5)^2(1-4/5) = 0.128$

$n = 3$ $P_3 = (4/5)^3(1-4/5) = 0.102$

$n = 4$ $P_4 = (4/5)^4(1-4/5) = 0.082$

For $n > 4$ $P_{n>4} = 1 - (P_0+P_1+P_2+P_3+P_4) = 1- (0.2+0.16+0.128+0.102+0.082) = 1 - 0.672 = 0.328$

So Kathy can expect that there will be more than four people in her shop about 33 percent of the time.

Kathy can also purchase a barcode scanner with an automated cash register that will increase her service rate to ten customers per hour. She wants to know how this will change the average wait time in the queue and in the system. The student then shows her the very significant change this will make:

$L_s = \lambda/(\mu-\lambda) = 4/(10-4) = 0.67$ customers

$W_q = \lambda/[\mu(\mu-\lambda)] = 4/[10(6)] = 0.067$ hours $= 4$ minutes

$W_s = 1/(\mu-\lambda) = 1/6$ hour $= 10$ minutes

ρ = average server utilization $= \lambda/s\mu$

P_0 = probability of zero customers in the system

$$= \cfrac{1}{\displaystyle\sum_{n=0}^{s-1} \cfrac{(\lambda/\mu)^n}{n!} + \cfrac{(\lambda/\mu)^s}{s!}\left[\cfrac{1}{1-(\lambda/s\mu)}\right]}, \text{ for } s\mu > \lambda$$

P_n = probability of n customers in the system $= P_0\dfrac{(\lambda/\mu)^n}{n!}$, for $n \leq s$, or

$\qquad = P_0\dfrac{(\lambda/\mu)^n}{s!s^{n-s}}$, for $n > s$

L_q = !expected number of customers in the queue $= p_0\dfrac{(\lambda/\mu)^s(\lambda/s\mu)}{s!(1 - \lambda/s\mu)^2}$

L_s = expected number of customers in the system $= L_q + \lambda/\mu$

W_q = expected waiting time in the queue $= L_q/\lambda$

W_s = expected waiting time in the system $= W_q + 1/\mu$

Example 12.8 extends the single-channel, single-phase shop, to the two-channel, single-phase shop, for comparison purposes.

> ### Example 12.8   Operating Characteristics for Kathy's Expanded Sewing Shop
>
> Kathy's Sewing Shop has decided to hire a second worker and buy a second checkout stand with cash register for the shop. Both Kathy and the second worker can serve five custome rs per hour and the average arrival rate is four customers per hour. Kathy again wants to know all of the operating characteristics of the new configuration. Once again, her student-customer helps her out:
>
> $\rho = 4/10 = 0.4$, or 40 % utilization
>
> $$P_0 = \cfrac{1}{\cfrac{(4/5)^0}{0!} + \cfrac{(4/5)^1}{1!} + \cfrac{(4/5)^2}{2!}\left(\cfrac{1}{1-(4/10)}\right)} = \frac{1}{1 + 0.8 + 0.32(1.67)} = \frac{1}{2.33} = 0.428$$
>
> $$L_q = \frac{(4/5)^2(4/10)}{2(1-4/10)^2}(0.428) = 0.152 \text{ customers}$$
>
> $L_s = 0.152 + 4/5 = 0.952 \text{ customers}$
> $W_q = 0.152/4 = 0.038 \text{ hours, or } 2.28 \text{ minutes}$
> $W_s = 0.038 + 0.2 = 0.238 \text{ hours, or } 14.28 \text{ minutes}$
>
> Note that because of the mean service time and distribution differences, having a two-channel, two-queue system serving customers with an average service rate of five customers per hour per channel is not the same as having a one-channel, one-queue system that serves at a rate of ten customers per hour.

Managing Perceived Waiting Times

The final topic of discussion in managing queue times management of **perceived waiting times** (sometimes, customers perceive the wait time to be much longer or shorter than it really is). Even though an admirable job may be done designing a queuing system, there are still likely to be times when demand exceeds the queuing system's capacity (recall the two-hour wait in a doctor's office mentioned earlier). For these time periods, service firms must have other tools at their disposal to influence customers' perceptions of the waiting times. In a well-known paper written on the topic of waiting time, noted professor and author Dr. David Maister presented some very interesting observations. These are discussed below.

First and Second Laws of Service:[32]

Law #1: Satisfaction = perception − expectation

When customers expect a certain level of service and then perceive the service they actually received to be higher, they will be satisfied. Conversely, when customers' service expectations are higher than their perceptions once the service has been completed, they are unsatisfied.

Law #2: It's hard to play catch-up ball

If customers start out happy when the service is first encountered, it is easy to keep them happy. If they start out disgruntled or become that way during the service, it is very difficult to turn things around.

Service law #1 is interesting in that expectations and perceptions are not necessarily based on reality. For example, customer expectations are formed based on previous experiences, marketing campaigns, signs, information from other people, and the location, while customer perceptions can be affected during the service encounter by a friendly server, mood music, visually pleasant surroundings, and a host of other things. A common practice coming out of law #1 is to "under-promise and over-deliver." Service law #2 is good for firms to remember when they are trying to improve service. Investments in service improvements might best be placed at the initial contact or early stages of the service to make sure the service encounter gets off to a good start.

Firms can manage both customer expectations and perceptions by observing and understanding how they are affected when customers wait for service. Waiting time management techniques resulting from this understanding include keeping customers occupied, starting the service quickly, relieving customer anxiety, keeping customers informed, grouping customers together, and designing a fair waiting system.[33] Each of these is briefly discussed next.

Keeping Customers Occupied

Firms can benefit by keeping customers occupied while waiting in line. This is why magazines, televisions, and toys for children are often seen in office waiting areas. Other attention-keepers such as music, windows, mirrors, or menus to look at keep customers' minds off the passage of time. In amusement parks such as Disneyland where long lines can be a big problem, customers waiting in line might get entertained by Mickey Mouse, a mime, or a juggler, for instance. All these techniques try to lessen the perceived passage of time and influence customer satisfaction with the waiting experience. At Illinois-based Abt Electronics, the store's merchandise pickup area is a hub for customer activity. Abt has made it an emblem of the store's personality as well as a way to keep customers occupied during their wait for a TV or iPad. "We have a Wall of Fame there that's an interesting history of the store; nothing to do with product, just photos of a lot of famous people who've shopped there," says Billy Abt, copresident. "And that's always changing; if new people are added, we move some of the older celebrities up to the lunchroom. There is also what amounts to an appliance museum of sorts with ringer washers from the 1930s, old refrigerators with the motors on top, TVs from the 1950s, and one of the first Macintosh computers. Also added for customers' distraction three years ago were two LCD commercial screens that display a map of the Greater Chicago area, so that all of Abt's deliveries for the day can be shown. Customers find it interesting to see how many different neighborhoods we go to on an average day, and it's fun for them to find theirs," he said.[34]

Starting the Service Quickly

Giving waiting customers menus, forms to complete, drinks from the bar, or programs to read all act to give customers the impression the service has started. When firms acknowledge receipt of an order via telephone, mail, or e-mail, this is another example of beginning the service. If organizations can design preprocess activities that begin quickly once a customer encounters a queue, this will act to keep customers occupied and make long waits seem much shorter. The London-based Carphone Warehouse (CPW), a mobile phone retailer, has turned to Facebook and Twitter to engage customers quickly and keep them satisfied. They have found it allows them to address complaints more quickly, offer quick feedback on problems, and to positively impact customer satisfaction. If a customer wants to know whether a certain city has a retail location, CPW can tweet a link to the store; if a customer wants to know how to remove a SIM card, CPW can tweet the solution.[35]

Relieving Customer Anxiety

Customer anxiety is created in many waiting situations; for example, when customers are afraid they've been forgotten, when they don't know how long their wait is going to be, when they don't know what to do, or when they fear they've entered the wrong queue. Managers need to observe customers, learn what is likely causing their anxieties, and then develop plans for relieving them. These plans might include simply having employees reassure customers, announcing how much longer a caller on hold is likely to wait, announcing the lateness of a plane yet to arrive, or using signs to direct customers to the correct line.

Keeping Customers Informed

Managers can derail customer anxieties before they even begin by giving customers information as their preprocess and in-process waits progress. When receptionists tell patients that their doctor is thirty minutes behind schedule, when pilots tell passengers that the plane is waiting to be cleared for gate departure, when work crews place a flashing sign on the road warning drivers to expect delays during a certain period of time, and when amusement parks place signs in the queue telling customers the waiting time from that point forward, this information makes waiting customers much more patient because they know that a delay will occur and the reasons for the delay. Consequently, they are much more willing to stay in line, remain satisfied, and complete the service.

Grouping Customers

Customers generally prefer waiting together in queues, rather than waiting alone. Customers act to alleviate their own and others' anxieties, fears, and problems while waiting in line by talking to each other, sharing concerns, and helping out if possible. This sense of togetherness reduces perceived waiting times and may even add enjoyment to the waiting experience. Managers should think of ways to create or encourage group waiting instead of solo waiting such as closer seating, single queues instead of multiple queues, and use of numbered tickets or virtual queues so people don't have to physically stand in the queue.

Designing a Fair Waiting System

"Taking cuts" or queue-jumping is something that can cause significant irritation to others already waiting, particularly if it is seen as unfair. In an emergency room, most people waiting will likely accept that others coming into the queue later might be taken care of first (this queue discipline would be most-critical-first-served). Alternately, taking cuts in a long queue at a retail store or amusement park could result in grumbling and shouting from those already waiting (recall our earlier discussion about virtual queues removing some of these problems). Whenever the queue discipline is something other than first-come-first-served, managers need to be aware of the potential problems this causes and take steps to reduce the feeling of unfairness, or segment customers such that the queue discipline is not obvious. Examples include physically separating customers such as in first-class versus economy-class seating on airplanes, taking names and group sizes at a restaurant while concealing the list, and putting up signs like "six items or less" at retail checkout stands. In many cases, customers will understand and accept the reasons for using a particular queue discipline if they are informed of it. The next concern of service response logistics is the management of distribution channels.

Managing Distribution Channels

This next topic within service response logistics describes several distribution channels and strategies a service can use to deliver their services and products to customers. Table 12.2 lists a number of distribution alternatives for a retailer, a bank, an auto repair facility, and a university. Many of these distribution alternatives are the traditional ones everyone is used to seeing; however, services today are experimenting with other, nontraditional

Table 12.2	Service Distribution Channels
SERVICE	**DISTRIBUTION CHANNEL**
Retailer	• Freestanding • Mall • Internet • Mail order
Bank	• Main office/headquarters • Freestanding branches • Sites in malls • Sites in retail locations • ATMs • Internet • Cellphone
Auto Repair Business	• Freestanding • Attached to a large retailer • Franchised outlets • Mobile repair van
University/College	• Public • Private • Specialized/general • Traditional/adult education • Main campus • Branches • Internet • Day/evening • Television

distribution channels as customer preferences and habits, demographics, technology, and competition change.

Some distribution channels have revolutionized the way services do business. For instance, ATMs, debit cards, and the Internet have completely changed the financial services industry; many customers almost never set foot inside a bank or stockbroker's office. Today, many people have come to expect these things, and services have responded.

Other distribution strategies have arisen because new technologies made them possible, and because customers were asking for them. In the grocery industry, Amazon.com's grocery delivery service AmazonFresh has been operating since 2007 and promises same-day and next-day delivery of groceries (depending on when the order is placed) to customers in Seattle, parts of California, New York City, and Philadelphia. Even though grocery home-delivery businesses have failed in the past, materials handling technologies such as robotics and refrigerated totes, Amazon's mobile app, and the deep pockets of Amazon.com give it a good chance of succeeding.[36] Several of the distribution channel alternatives and issues facing services today are discussed next.

Eatertainment, Entertailing, and Edutainment

As service distribution concepts change, new words have been coined to describe these concepts. **Eatertainment** is the combination of restaurant and entertainment elements. Many of these services incorporate elements of local culture or history into their design themes and offer the capabilities of eating, drinking, entertainment, and shopping all in one venue. For over thirty years, fast food restaurants like McDonald's and Burger King have incorporated children play areas in their restaurants, and Chuck E. Cheese restaurants are another example of the eatertainment concept that's been around for a while. A newer example combines entertainment with classy food and drink options—the Royal Palms Shuffleboard Club opened in Brooklyn, NY, in 2014. This 17,000-square-foot venue has turned a pastime favored by seniors into the next craze for young adults. The club features ten shuffleboard courts, craft beer, trendy cocktails, and food-truck dining. There's an indoor bay for food trucks, which change nightly, and two 27-foot bars serving drinks like you would get on vacation in the tropics, as well as standard bar offerings including craft beers on tap. You can also play board games at the cabana tables and there's nightly DJ music, tiki bands, and even bingo nights.[37]

Entertailing refers to retail locations with entertainment elements. Many shopping malls are designed today to offer entertainment such as ice skating, rock climbing, and amusement park rides. Since opening in 1992, Bloomington, Minnesota's Mall of America boasts 4.2 million square feet of enclosed area, a theme park, an aquarium, a Lego play area, a mini-golf park, a flight simulator center, 500+ retailers, over 400 events per year, and 11,000 employees. The Body Shop in London is a prototype for a new "experience-based" store. The retailer, with 3,000 locations in more than 65 countries, is testing the new entertailing model that includes information and conversation areas designed to encourage customers to linger as they flow through the store. Shoppers can receive hand massages while listening to stories at the "story table" and test a variety of products for sale, including ointments, lotions, and makeup. "We found that the average amount of time a consumer spends in our prototype stores has doubled, from an average of five minutes to more than ten. This shows a depth of interaction and communication we have witnessed," says Sophie Gasperment, CEO of Body Shop International.[38]

Museums, parks, radio shows, movies, and a host of service providers are also getting into the act with **edutainment** or **infotainment** to attract more customers, create a learning experience, and increase revenues. Edutainment combines learning with entertainment to appeal to customers looking for education along with play. In the United States, state and national park employees entertain and inform tourists with indigenous animal lectures and shows or campfire stories in the evenings. For many years, documentary movies have been shown to educate and entertain, and radio shows like the U.K. radio soap opera *The Archers* have been educating its audience (in this case, on agricultural matters). Theme parks, such as Legoland in San Diego, offer attractions that combine fun and education aimed at the two- to twelve-year-old audience.[39]

Franchising

Franchising allows services to expand quickly into dispersed geographic markets, protect existing markets, and build market share. When the owners have limited financial resources, franchising is a good strategy for expansion. Franchisees are required to invest some of their own capital, while paying a small percentage of sales to the franchisor in return for the brand name, start-up help, advertising, training, and assistance in meeting specific operating standards. Many services such as fast-food restaurants, accounting and tax businesses, auto rental agencies, beauty salons, clothing stores, ice cream shops, motels, and other small service businesses use franchising as a strategy for growing and competing.

Control problems are one of the biggest issues in franchising. Franchisors periodically perform financial and quality audits on the franchisees along with making frequent visits to facilities to assure that franchisees are continuing to comply with operating standards of the company. The idea of control, however, is something that some new franchisors are experimenting with. The Massachusetts-based Wings Over franchise chain, for instance, lets franchisees make changes to their stores in order to lend an element of uniqueness to each restaurant. Harold Tramazzo and Patrick Daly created a wings delivery business at the University of Massachusetts in 1999. Finding a fairly different, yet desirable niche, the company thrived, and today there are about thirty Wings Over stores, primarily located on the Eastern side of the United States. The franchise in Boston is called Wings Over Boston and has a citrus chipotle sauce among others; several in North Carolina offer dry rub sauces; and in college towns, many Wings Over restaurants don't open until 4:00 p.m., and they close at 3:00 or 4:00 a.m. This gives franchisees the flexibility to compete with local businesses.[40]

The **microfranchise** is another type of franchising concept and is seen as a good way for economically disadvantaged people to make a living. It offers ready-made, low-risk starter jobs for people with little or no education and little available capital, while giving established companies additional distribution avenues. Drishtee, for example, is an India-based microfranchise. Their small kiosks can be seen in over 1,900 rural Indian villages serving about 2 million customers. Drishtee sells basic healthcare, financial, educational, and retail products and services. The kiosks can earn the franchisees about $30 per month in profits.[41]

International Expansion

The search for larger and additional markets has driven services to expand globally. Since the world today has become essentially borderless because of the Internet and other communication mediums, more freedom of movement, greater use of common currencies, and the expansion that has already taken place, services today compete in a global economy.

Global service expansion most likely means operating with partners who are familiar with the region's culture, markets, suppliers, competitors, infrastructure, and government regulations. For instance, when McDonald's opened its first restaurant in Moscow in 1990, an entire food supply chain had to be designed and implemented. McDonald's had to train farmers to produce the type and quality of crops needed to supply the business and then find buyers for the excess food the farmers produced (e.g., Moscow hotels and embassies). By the way, over 30,000 people showed up for the grand opening.[42]

China's service sector is emerging as a key driver of the Chinese economy—the service sector has now surpassed agriculture in terms of contribution to annual GDP, and is growing annually by about 13 percent. Consequently, many foreign services are looking to become involved in Chinese markets. For instance, Chinaco Healthcare, the very successful Tennessee-based hospital chain, opened its first hospital in the Chinese city of Cixi in 2014. They are operating the CHC International Hospital in a joint venture with the municipal government of Cixi. "Until 2009, the hospital industry was a nonchanging industry," says Sheldon Dorenforest, founder of Dorenforest China Healthcare Group. Today though, "the growth is unlimited. The opportunity is so great, investors are saying, now is the time," he adds.[43]

Exposure to foreign currency exchange rate fluctuations can also pose a problem for expanding service firms, requiring them to use financial hedging strategies to reduce exchange rate risk. Firms can operate in several different countries to offset currency problems, since economic downturns in one country can often be offset by positive economic conditions in other countries.

Language barriers, cultural problems, and the varying needs of different regional cultures also must be addressed when expanding. Local management must be allowed to vary services, signage, and accompanying products to suit local tastes. Restaurants, for instance, typically add local favorites to menus to increase acceptability. Companies must become familiar with language translations in order to properly change the wording on signs and advertisements to increase readability and understanding. The Coca-Cola name in China, for example, was initially rendered as "ke-kou-ke-la" on thousands of signs before it was found that the meaning of the phrase was either "bite the wax tadpole" or "female horse stuffed with wax" depending on the regional dialect. Coke personnel eventually studied 40,000 characters to find the phonetic equivalent "ko-kou-ko-le," which translates into "happiness in the mouth." Similarly, Japan's second-largest tourist agency, Kinki Nippon Tourist Co., felt compelled to change its U.S. name after they began getting requests from American customers for unusual sex-oriented trips.[44]

Internet Distribution Strategies

Internet-based "dot com" companies exploded on the scene during the latter part of the 1990s, pushing the NASDAQ to historic highs and promising to enrich anyone with an idea, good or bad, for a website that could generate revenues on the Internet. E-commerce was touted as the coming trillion-dollar revolution in retailing. But as it turned out, most of the dot com companies of that era are gone today. Still, online retailing is growing faster than traditional brick-and-mortar retailing. In the fourth quarter of 2016, e-commerce accounted for $102.7 billion of U.S. retail sales, or approximately 8.3 percent of total U.S. retail sales for the quarter. This reflects an increase of 53 percent, for example, from the 2013 fourth quarter. E-commerce sales are growing by about 14 percent per year while total retail sales are growing by about 4 percent per year.[45]

One of the primary advantages of the Internet is its ability to offer convenient sources of real-time information, integration, feedback, and comparison shopping. Individual consumers use Internet search engines to look for jobs, find and communicate with businesses, find the nearest movie theater, find products, sell things, and barter goods. And they can do all this in the privacy of their homes. Globally, approximately 2 + trillion online Google searches occurred in 2016, for example.[46] Businesses, too, use the Internet to communicate, find, and then purchase items from suppliers, and sell or provide goods and services to individual consumers and other businesses. Today, most businesses either have a website or are building one. Many individuals also have their own websites, since domain names can easily be purchased. Many retailers today sell products exclusively over the Internet (a *pure strategy*), while others use it as a supplemental distribution channel (a *mixed strategy*).

The **pure Internet distribution strategy** can have several distinct advantages over traditional brick-and-mortar services. Online companies can become more centralized, reducing labor, capital and inventory costs while using the Internet to decentralize their marketing efforts to reach a vastly distributed audience of business or individual consumers. Amazon.com falls into this category. Today, though, the **mixed Internet distribution strategy** of combining traditional retailing with online retailing seems to be emerging as the stronger business model. Firms such as JCPenney sell items in retail outlets and also from Internet and store catalogs. Customers can either pick up their purchases at the store or have them delivered. Southwest Airlines was the first airline to establish a home page on the Internet, and by the end of 2016, approximately 80 percent of its passenger revenue was generated by online bookings via their industry leading website, www.southwest.com.[47]

Developing good customer service capabilities can be challenging, however. JCPenney representatives, for instance, must be able to perform customer service functions over the Internet, in-person, and via mail and telephone. Companies are addressing this problem by developing sophisticated **customer contact centers**. These centers integrate their websites and traditional call centers to offer 24/7 support where customers and potential customers can contact the firm and each other using telephone, e-mail, chat rooms, and e-bulletin boards. These contact centers allow firms to serve a large number of geographically dispersed customers with a relatively small number of customer service agents.

Just as services have to be concerned with managing service capacity and queues, firms must also invest in designing the necessary distribution channels to compete in today's marketplaces. The final element of the service response logistics discussion affects all elements of the service itself and the way it is distributed, and that is the management of service quality. Although this topic was initially addressed in Chapter 8, the quality management topics geared strictly toward services need further discussion, and this topic is presented below.

Managing Service Quality

The fourth and final topic area in service response logistics is the management of service quality. For services, quality occurs during the service delivery process and typically involves interactions between a customer and service company personnel. In other words, service quality is closely tied to customer satisfaction. Customer satisfaction with the service depends not only on the ability of the firm to deliver what customers want, but also on the customers' perceptions of the quality of service received. When customer expectations are met or exceeded, the service is deemed to possess high quality, and when expectations are not met, the perception of quality is poor (recall Maister's first law of service). Thus, service quality is highly dependent upon the ability of the firm's employees and service systems to meet or exceed customers' *varying* expectations. Because of the variable nature of customer expectations, perceptions, and happiness, services must continually be monitoring their service delivery systems using the tools described in Chapter 8 while concurrently observing, communicating with, and surveying customers to adequately assess and improve quality.

The Five Dimensions of Service Quality

Some of the most highly quoted studies of service quality are those done by Drs. Parasuraman, Zeithaml, and Berry.[48] Surveying customers of a number of different services and situations, they identified **five dimensions of service quality** generally used by customers to rate service quality—reliability, responsiveness, assurance, empathy, and tangibles. Reliability was consistently reported in their study as the most important quality dimension. The five dimensions are defined below.

- *Reliability*: consistently performing the service correctly and dependably.
- *Responsiveness*: providing the service promptly or in a timely manner.
- *Assurance*: using knowledgeable, competent, courteous employees who convey trust and confidence to customers.
- *Empathy*: providing caring and individual attention to customers.
- *Tangibles*: the physical characteristics of the service including the facilities, servers, equipment, associated goods, and other customers.

Using their survey, the three researchers were able to identify any differences occurring between customer expectations in the five dimensions listed above and customer perceptions of what was actually received during the service encounter. These differences were referred to as service quality "gaps," and can thus be used in actual situations to highlight areas in need of service improvement. What this research shows is that organizations should develop specific, measurable criteria relating to the five service quality dimensions and then collect data using customer comment cards and mailed or e-mailed surveys of customer satisfaction regarding each of the quality dimensions. This will allow managers to measure overall service quality performance. Table 12.3 presents criteria that might be used in each of the five quality dimensions. Obviously, these would vary by industry, products, and company. When weaknesses or gaps are encountered in any of the performance criteria, managers can institute improvements in the areas indicated.

World-class service companies realize they must get to know their customers, and they invest considerable time and efforts gathering information about customer expectations and perceptions. This information is used to design services and delivery systems that satisfy customers, capture market share, and create profits for the firm. These organizations understand that one of the most important elements affecting long-term competitiveness and profits is the quality of their goods and services relative to their competitors. South African Airways (SAA) was honored in 2016 by Global Traveler magazine as, "Best Airline in Africa." The magazine recognized the airline for its consistent high-quality service that keeps it in the world-class category and best in the region for the thirteenth consecutive year. SAA also received honorable mentions for Best Airline for Onboard Service, Best Airline for Flight Attendants, and Best Airport Lounges. "We are truly honored to, once again, receive this award and be distinguished by the readers of Global Traveler as Africa's top airline. These are discerning international business travelers and their recognition of SAA serves as a validation of our efforts to continually enhance our product and deliver world-class service," said Todd Neuman, executive vice president, the Americas, for South African Airways.[49]

Recovering from Poor Service Quality

There will undoubtedly, from time to time, be occasions when an organization's products and services do not meet a customer's expectations. In most cases, quick recovery from these service failures can keep customers loyal and coming back, and may even serve

Table 12.3	Examples of Service Quality Criteria
SERVICE QUALITY DIMENSIONS	**CRITERIA**
Reliability	• billing accuracy • order accuracy • on-time completion • promises kept
Responsiveness	• on-time appointment • timely callback • timely confirmation of order
Assurance	• skills of employees • training provided to employees • honesty of employees • reputation of firm
Empathy	• customized service capabilities • customer recognition • degree of server−customer contact • knowledge of the customer
Tangibles	• appearance of the employees • appearance of the facility • number of customers at facility • quality of equipment and other goods used

as good word-of-mouth advertising for the firm, as customers pass on their stories of good service recoveries. Most importantly, when service failures do occur, firms must be able to recover quickly and forcefully to satisfy customers. This involves empowering front-line service personnel to identify problems and then provide solutions quickly and in an empathetic way.

Good services offer guarantees to their customers and empower employees to provide quick and meaningful solutions when customers invoke the guarantee. In the United States, the great majority of retailers offer money-back guarantees if customers are not satisfied and about half offer low-price guarantees where customers are refunded the price difference for a period of time after purchase.[50] In many cases, quick solutions to service problems are designed into service processes and become part of a service firm's marketing efforts. Firms that anticipate where service failures can occur, develop recovery procedures, train employees in these procedures, and then empower employees to remedy customer problems can assure they have the best service recovery system possible.

SUMMARY

Services constitute a large and growing segment of the global economy. Managing the supply chains of services is thus an important part of an overall competitive strategy for services. Since service customers are most often the final consumers of the services provided, successfully managing service encounters involves managing productive capacity, managing queues, managing distribution channels, and managing service quality. These four concerns are the foundations of service response logistics and were the primary focus of this chapter.

Service companies must accurately forecast demand, design capacity to adequately meet demand, employ queuing systems to serve customers as quickly and effectively as possible, utilize distribution systems to best serve the firm's customers, and then take steps to assure service quality and customer satisfaction throughout the service process. Provided that managers have selected a good location, designed an effective layout, hired, trained, and properly scheduled service personnel, and then employed effective service response logistics strategies, firms and their supply chains should be able to maintain competitiveness, market share, and profitability.

KEY TERMS

arrival pattern, 470

back-of-the-house operations, 457

balking, 472

Baumol's disease, 453

capacity utilization, 464

chase demand strategy, 465

closeness desirability rating, 459

cost leadership strategy, 456

customer contact centers, 482

demand management, 465

demand source, 470

differentiation strategy, 456

eatertainment, 479

edutainment, 480

entertailing, 480

facilitating products, 462

five dimensions of service quality, 483

focus strategy, 456

franchising, 480

front-of-the-house operations, 457

infotainment, 480

level demand strategy, 465

microfranchise, 481

mixed Internet distribution strategy, 482

multiple-channel queuing system, 472

multiple-factor productivity, 453

multiple-phase queuing system, 472

perceived waiting times, 476

pure Internet distribution strategy, 482

pure services, 450

queue discipline, 472

queue management, 465

queue times, 469

queuing systems, 469

reneging, 472

service bundles, 457

service capacity, 464

service delivery systems, 457

service layout strategies, 458

service response logistics, 463

single-factor productivity, 453

state utility, 451

virtual queues, 472

walk-through service audits, 457

Walmart effect, 453

DISCUSSION QUESTIONS

1. Is your university a pure service? Explain.

2. Why is the service sector in the United States and other highly developed economies growing more rapidly than the manufacturing sector?

3. Describe the primary differences between goods and service firms.

4. Using the formula for productivity, describe all the ways that firms can increase productivity. Which of these ways might be considered risky?

5. Describe several single- and multiple-factor productivity measures that could be used at your university.

6. Define Baumol's disease and the Walmart effect and how they affect service-oriented economies like the United States.

7. Discuss the primary issues in the management of global services.

8. What sorts of problems must services overcome as they expand into foreign markets?

9. What are the three generic strategies that services use to compete? Give examples.

10. When a service competes using a cost leadership strategy, does this mean the service is low quality? Explain.

11. When customers purchase a service, they are actually getting a bundle of service attributes. List and describe these attributes using a car-rental agency, a convenience store, and a radio station.

12. How would you characterize your university's service delivery system?

13. Provide some examples of front-of-the-house and back-of-the-house service operations.

14. What are some things service firms can do to monitor customer satisfaction?

15. Why are service locations so important?

16. What strategy do you think was used in selecting the location of your university? Could there be a better location?

17. Discuss the principal design objectives for service layouts.

18. How do supply chain management activities differ between services and manufacturing companies? In what ways are these activities alike?

19. What are the four concerns of service response logistics?

20. Define service capacity and provide three examples of it that were not listed in the text.

21. What is the capacity of your class' classroom?

22. Define capacity utilization. What is an ideal utilization? Can utilization ever be greater than 100 percent? Explain.

23. Describe how you would use a level and a chase demand capacity utilization strategy. Which one does your university use?

24. What are some alternatives to hiring and laying off workers to vary service capacity as demand varies?

25. Can customers be used to provide extra service capacity? Explain.

26. Describe some demand management techniques that are used when demand exceeds capacity and when capacity exceeds demand. Your university has periods of time when both of these situations exist. What do they do?

27. How can firms make use of excess capacity?

28. What are the two elements managers must pay attention to, when managing queues, to maximize customer satisfaction?

29. What are the primary elements to consider when designing any queuing system?

30. What type of queuing system configuration is used at a restaurant? A car dealer? At Zappos?

31. Define the terms "balking" and "reneging." How could a firm minimize them?

32. What is a virtual queue? When might one be used?

33. What type of queuing system does a three-channel, four-phase system refer to?

34. What are the advantages and disadvantages of increasing the number of channels?

35. What queue discipline is used to register students at your university? What about seating patrons at a fancy nightclub?

36. Explain and give examples of Maister's first and second laws of service. Use your personal experiences.

37. If your firm has designed an effective queuing system, why is it still necessary to practice waiting time management on some occasions?

38. What are the distribution channel alternatives for a weather service? A souvenir shop? A marriage counselor? How about your university?

39. What is a microfranchise? Would these be good for a developing country? For the United States?

40. What is edutainment? Does your university use it? How?

41. Describe the important issues in the international expansion of services.

42. Describe and give examples of a pure Internet distribution strategy and a mixed Internet distribution strategy. Find your examples on the Internet.

43. How is service quality related to customer service and satisfaction?

44. Describe the five dimensions of service quality for a dentist's office, how performance in these dimensions might be measured, and how recoveries might be handled for failures in each of the service quality dimensions.

45. Can recovery from a poor service quality incident be a good thing? Explain.

ESSAY/PROJECT QUESTIONS

1. Search the Internet for additional examples of eatertainment, entertailing, and edutainment, and describe them in a report.

2. Search the Internet for examples of microfranchising and report on several.

3. Search the Internet for the terms "McDonald's carbon footprint" or "McDonald's green initiatives," and write a report on this firm's efforts.

4. Write a paper on Walmart's location and layout strategies in the United States and other countries.

5. Search for examples of virtual queuing systems and report on several of these, explaining how they work.

PROBLEMS

1. For the previous month, the Bichsel Lounge served 1,500 customers with very few complaints. Their labor cost was $3,000; material cost was $800; energy cost was $200;

and the building's lease cost was $1,500. They were open twenty-six days during the month, and the lounge has twenty seats. They are open six hours per day, and the average customer stay is one hour.

a. Calculate the single-factor productivities and the overall multiple-factor productivity. How could they improve the productivity?

b. Calculate the monthly capacity and the capacity utilization.

2. The Iarussi Legal Aide office assisted 126 people in June 2013, with a staff labor cost of $3,240. In June 2014, the office provided assistance to 145 people with a labor cost of $3,960. What was their productivity growth over this one-year period?

3. The Valentine Ski Company makes top-of-the-line custom snow skis for high-end ski shops and employs fifteen people. Chris, the owner, wants to track several productivity performance measures using the data shown below.

FINANCIAL INFORMATION	2017 RESULTS
Net sales	$205,000
Cost of goods sold (purchased items)	$32,000
Net income after taxes	$28,200
Current assets	$68,000
Current liabilities	$22,000
Avg. inventory value	$4,500
Inputs and Outputs	
Skis produced	1,000
Labor hours	10,800
Lease payments	$24,000

a. Calculate the labor productivity, lease productivity, and material productivity.

b. Calculate the multiple-factor productivity. If the multiple-factor productivity for 2016 was 0.004 skis/dollar, then what was the productivity growth from 2016 to 2017?

4. For the office layout shown below and the accompanying trip and distance matrices, determine the total distance traveled per day. Find another layout that results in a lower total distance traveled per day.

Management (1)	Production (2)	Engineering (3)	Reception (4)
Files (5)	Accounting (6)	Purchasing (7)	Sales (8)

Interdepartmental Trips per Day

	(2)	(3)	(4)	(5)	(6)	(7)	(8)
(1)	6	5	2	1	7	6	15
(2)		12	4	5	2	10	5
(3)			2	9	2	10	8
(4)				18	12	4	2
(5)					0	0	0
(6)						6	14
(7)							6

Distances between Departments (meters)

	(2)	(3)	(4)	(5)	(6)	(7)	(8)
(1)	15	30	45	10	20	35	50
(2)		15	30	20	10	20	35
(3)			15	40	20	10	20
(4)				60	50	30	10
(5)					10	30	50
(6)						20	40
(7)							20

5. For the office layout shown in problem 4, determine the closeness desirability rating using the rating table below. Treat the hallway as if it doesn't exist (i.e., the production and accounting departments touch each other). Can you find a more desirable layout? How could you use both the total distance traveled and the closeness desirability in assessing the layout alternatives? Can you find a layout resulting in relatively good scores using both types of criteria?

Closeness Desirabilities between Departments

	(2)	(3)	(4)	(5)	(6)	(7)	(8)
(1)	2	2	−1	0	1	3	3
(2)		3	0	0	0	3	1
(3)			0	2	0	2	3
(4)				3	1	2	2
(5)					2	2	1
(6)						0	2
(7)							1

6. Corner's Cat Care needs help in her grooming business as shown below for the five-day workweek. Determine a full- and part-time work schedule for the business using the fewest number of workers.

	MONDAY	TUESDAY	WEDNESDAY	THURSDAY	FRIDAY
Workers Required	2	3	3	4	5

7. Given an average service rate of twelve customers per hour, what is the probability the business can handle all the customers when the average arrival rate is ten customers per hour? Use the Poisson distribution to calculate the probabilities for various customer arrivals.

8. With an average service rate of twelve customers per hour and an average customer arrival rate of ten customers per hour, calculate the probability that actual service time will be less than or equal to six minutes.

9. Theresa can handle about ten customers per hour at her one-person comic book store. The customer arrival rate averages about six customers per hour. Theresa is interested in knowing the operating characteristics of her single-channel, single-phase queuing system.

10. How would Theresa's queuing system operating characteristics change for the problem above if she added another cashier and increased her service rate to twenty customers per hour?

CASES

1. Daisy Perry*

Daisy Perry is the repair shop supervisor at one of the largest automotive dealerships in Phoenix, Arizona. Daisy has been working on cars since she was twelve years old, for more than twenty-five years. She began by helping her father repair racecars; he raced cars as a hobby. After her graduation from high school, Daisy attended a technical school to earn her Automotive Service Excellence (ASE) certification.

Early in her career Daisy moved around from auto maker to auto maker to get as much experience as she could. Daisy has worked on all types of cars, from traditional family vans to sporty high-performance cars. Because of her experience at different dealerships, Daisy has an excellent reputation throughout Phoenix, so much so, that some customers actually switched brands when Daisy moved on to another dealership. Daisy was ready to go out on her own and open an all-purpose automotive repair shop.

Opening her own business required a lot of thought. Daisy had many things to consider, for example, layout, location, type of strategy, productivity, capacity, and customer waiting time, to name just a few. Daisy began to jot down some of the things she believed were important to include in her business.

One critical feature of the business is to have ASE-certified mechanics. In addition to the certification, Daisy wanted her mechanics to look professional. They would wear coveralls with her company logo and their name. She planned to give each mechanic five sets of clothing and to provide each a personal locker to keep them in. She would have a laundry service clean them so there would always be a clean set available to start each workday.

Daisy knew that customers like freebies so she planned to offer a free oil change after every fifth one. Although the type of warranty depended on the work completed and the parts provided, at a minimum, Daisy planned to provide a thirty-day warranty on all work. In addition, the invoices would contain itemized charges, with no hidden costs. Prior to any repairs, the customer would receive a quote. If for some reason the repairs were more extensive than originally thought, Daisy would contact the customer and provide a revised quote before the work continued.

*Written by Rick Bonsall, D. Mgt., McKendree University, Lebanon, IL. The people and institution are fictional and any resemblance to any person or any institution is coincidental. This case was prepared solely to provide material for class discussion. The author does not intend to illustrate either effective or ineffective handling of a managerial situation.

The waiting room would have Wi-Fi, sufficient electrical outlets to charge electronic devices, magazines to read, a TV to watch, and drink and snack machines. The waiting room would be in the center of the facility with windows looking out to all the work bays. This allowed the customer to watch the repairs and see the care given to their vehicles. Each work bay would contain state-of-the-art equipment.

One challenge Daisy was concerned about was scheduling. She believed that once she opened the doors many of her current and past customers would bring her their business. Scheduling, if business is strong, will not be an issue. However, if there are periods, whether seasonal or otherwise, where there are too many mechanics on shift, it will be difficult to manage. ASE-certified mechanics are not interested in part-time work. A forty-hour per week job is expected and easy to find. Using part-time employees as a safety valve to balanced demand and capacity does not seem an option.

As Daisy reviewed her list, she felt that there were still many unanswered questions. However, Daisy felt reasonably confident since she effectively ran the repair shop at the dealership for the last five years. Daisy had many friends in the business and decided to share her list with several of them and get feedback.

Discussion Questions

1. Daisy decided that the main thing she should focus on is customer satisfaction. She believed that if you did that then you'd address all the other items since they drive customer satisfaction. Evaluate Daisy's list of things she believed were necessary for her business. Explain which items support the five dimensions of service quality. Has Daisy missed any of the five service quality dimensions? If so, which one(s)?

2. Which service strategy is Daisy planning to implement? Provide specifics that support your selection. Do you believe this is the best strategy? Should she consider one of the other two?

3. Daisy's concern about scheduling during nonpeak periods is a serious problem. She cannot risk alienating her ASE-certified mechanics by cutting their hours because they can easily find other work. Assume the following: after the first year, Daisy determines the nonpeak periods. There are very few times; however, she believes they will be consistent year after year, meaning the same general timeframe. Explain to Daisy what options or initiatives she can use to increase demand since cutting hours is not an option.

©2019 Cengage Learning

2. Designing a Call Center for an Express Logistics Service Provider*

E-commerce has been growing drastically in Thailand, and it provides an opportunity for an express logistics service. Bangmod is a leading logistics service provider, with headquarters based in Thailand. Its core business includes integrated logistics, international freight forwarding, and express and supply chain solutions. The company focuses mainly on express logistics service in order to serve the high demand of e-commerce shipments. Many of the e-commerce entrepreneurs employ Bangmod

*Written by Watcharapoj (Jack) Sapsanguanboon, Graduate School of Management and Innovation, King Mongkut's University of Technology, Thailand. The people and institution are fictional and any resemblance to any person or any institution is coincidental. This case was prepared solely to provide material for class discussion. The author does not intend to illustrate either effective or ineffective handling of a managerial situation.

across a wide spectrum of industries including fashion and lifestyle, cosmetics, supplement foods and beverages, and pharmaceutical. Due to its growing customer base, Bangmod has decided it needs to also provide services through a call center, to better serve customers countrywide. Bangmod's desire is to deliver customer products faster and more cost-effective than anyone else.

Bangmod offers domestic express services throughout Thailand including coverage of all provinces and cities, offering same-day delivery to three-day economy services. By understanding and anticipating customer express service needs, Bangmod helps create real value for their customers' business, ensuring delivery to customers in a smooth, cost-efficient manner. Customers normally request services from Bangmod's field sales personnel, but managers believe a lot of missed sales opportunities exist. Various service options are offered to serve different needs as follows:

- **Same-day delivery**—Immediate pickup and door-to-door delivery in the shortest possible timeframe.

- **Next-day delivery before 9:00 a.m.**—Nationwide door-to-door delivery by 9:00 a.m. on the next business day.

- **Next-day delivery before 12:00**—Nationwide door-to-door delivery by 12:00 noon on the next business day.

- **Next-day delivery before 17:00**—Nationwide door-to-door delivery by 17:00 on the next business day.

- **Three-day economy delivery**—Nationwide domestic delivery by the end of the next three business days.

- **Value-added services**—A wide range of value-added services are also available upon request, including home delivery, repacking, e-commerce, web tracking, web booking, onsite services, hold at location, cash-on-delivery, invoice return, delivery by appointment, and more.

Discussion Questions

1. Do you think a call center would benefit Bangmod at this point? What benefits could it provide?

2. From the case, identify items of importance in terms of designing the call center and rank them in terms of importance.

3. Discuss the important issues for managing the daily center operations, including queuing management, facilitating products, and service quality for Bangmod.

©2019 Cengage Learning

3. Benevolence Children Hospital*

Benevolence Children Hospital has grown steadily over the last decade. They have been fortunate to receive several large sums of charitable donations. This has enabled them to recently add a new surgical wing. This wing is actually a completely new service the hospital is providing. In the past, children were sent to other area hospitals for

*Written by Rick Bonsall, D. Mgt., McKendree University, Lebanon, IL. The people and institution are fictional and any resemblance to any person or any institution is coincidental. This case was prepared solely to provide material for class discussion. The author does not intend to illustrate either effective or ineffective handling of a managerial situation.

surgery. Now, Benevolence Children Hospital can provide surgical services specializing in children's needs.

The new surgical wing has come at the perfect time because the population of Widow Creek has grown exponentially in the past three years. Unfortunately, the hospital wasn't prepared for the volume of surgeries. Although they have the physical capacity, for example, operating rooms, staff, recovery rooms, etc., they have fallen short on customer care.

When Meredith Webb, Benevolence's CEO, read all the complaints concerning the surgical services she saw two glaring issues. When she correlated the complaints to the five service quality dimensions she knew about, Meredith believed that they were weak in responsiveness and empathy. Customers had no complaints with reliability, such as billing. Nor did they have issues with assurance, as in surgeons' skills. The tangibles, such as employee appearance and facility appearance, were always given high ratings.

As Meredith examined the data and talked with the families of the patients she began to understand the root cause of their complaints. Communications were poor. Parents didn't feel that they were kept informed in a timely manner about their children's surgeries. Their perception was that a lot of time passed before any updates were provided. Also, if they had a complaint or a compliment, they didn't know who specifically to name. Since they were extremely stressed because their child was having surgery, they didn't always remember which staff member they interacted with. Meredith talked with her senior staff and they concluded that in many ways the problem was similar to managing queue times. Many of the same emotions and reactions people felt when in a queue were similar to what waiting families were experiencing.

Discussion Questions

1. Obviously, hospital personnel wear nametags to identify themselves. However, in the case above, the families are not remembering who they interact with because they are stressed. Recommend a solution that guarantees to eliminate this issue; thus, improve the families' sense of connection to those caring for their children.

2. What actions do you recommend the hospital take to increase the feeling of customized service, thus enhancing empathy? Hint: Think about what restaurants and/or airlines do to enable better communications.

3. Besides the actions or initiatives taken to solve the specific problems mentioned in questions 1 and 2, what additional things can the hospital do to manage perceived waiting times and the issues they cause?

©2019 Cengage Learning

ADDITIONAL RESOURCES

Anderson, D., D. Sweeney, and T. Williams, *An Introduction to Management Science*. Mason, OH: South-Western, 2003.

Davis, M., N. Aquilano, and R. Chase, *Fundamentals of Operations Management*. New York: McGraw-Hill, 1999.

Drazen, E., R. Moll, and M. Roetter, *Logistics in Service Industries*. Oak Brook, IL: Council of Logistics Management, 1991.

Fitzsimmons, J., and M. Fitzsimmons, *Service Management for Competitive Advantage*. New York: McGraw-Hill, 1994.

Heizer, B., and B. Render, *Principles of Operations Management.* Upper Saddle River, NJ: Prentice Hall, 2001.

Markland, R., S. Vickery, and R. Davis, *Operations Management.* Mason, OH: South-Western, 1998.

Metters, R., K. King-Metters, and M. Pullman, *Successful Service Operations Management.* Mason, OH: South-Western, 2003.

Rodriguez, C., *International Management: A Cultural Approach.* Mason, OH: South-Western, 2001.

Taha, H. A., *Operations Research: An Introduction.* Upper Saddle River, NJ: Prentice Hall, 2003.

Taylor, B., *Introduction to Management Science.* Upper Saddle River, NJ: Prentice Hall, 2002.

END NOTES

1. Anonymous, "UnionPay International Accelerates Mobile QuickPass Expansion Overseas," *China Business Newsweekly* March 22, 2016: 193.

2. Walsworth, J., "Subaru Says Dealers Falling Behind on Service: Sales Gains Outpace Departments' Capacity," *Automotive News* 91(6775), 2017: 23.

3. Kauffman, C., "Mexpress Feeder Service Hungry for Expansion," *Air Cargo World* 19(4), 2016: 16.

4. http://data.worldbank.org/indicator/NV.SRV.TETC.ZS?view=chart&year_high_desc=false

5. McCully, C., "Trends in Consumer Spending and Personal Saving, 1959-2009," *Survey of Current Business* 91(6), 2011: 14−23; and see https://www.bls.gov/cex/

6. Same as endnote #1.

7. See http://www.yum.com/company and http://www.dominos.co.in/store-location

8. Giles, C., F. Giugliano, and S. O'Connor, "Professional Services at Heart of UK Productivity Problem," *FT.com* April 19, 2015: 1.

9. https://www.bls.gov/lpc/prodybar.htm

10. Blackstone, B., "Is Productivity Growth Back in Grips of Baumol's Disease?" *Wall Street Journal* August 13, 2007: A2.

11. Pollitt, D., "Warehouse Team Develops IT Skills One Stage at a Time," *Training & Management Development Methods* 23(3), 2009: 525−530.

12. Anonymous, "ZeroChaos Continues Growth and Expansion," *Economics & Business Week* August 13, 2011: 1366; Zafar, A., "deVere Unveils Global Expansion Plan," *Financial Advisor* November 12, 2011: 1; Anonymous, "Bibby Financial Services Continues Global Expansion," *The Secured Lender* 68(10), 2012: 14−15.

13. Porter, M., *Competitive Strategy: Techniques for Analyzing Industries and Competitors.* New York: The Free Press, 1980.

14. http://smallbusiness.chron.com/examples-cost-leadership-strategy-marketing-12259.html

15. Melone, L., "Tiptoeing into Social Media," *Computerworld* 47(2), 2013: 26−28.

16. http://www.frenchfryheaven.com/locations

17. Ainlay, T., and J. Gabaldon, *Las Vegas: The Fabulous First Century.* Mt. Pleasant, SC: Arcadia Publishing, 2003; Land, B., and M. Land, *A Short History of Las Vegas.* Reno: University of Nevada Press, 2004; http://www.golflink.com/about_4669_history-stratosphere-hotel-las-vegas.html; https://www.reviewjournal.com/news/icahn-sells-southern-nevada-casinos; http://www.nytimes.com/2007/04/23/business/worldbusiness/23iht-icahn.4.5406280.html

18. Scioscia, J., "Optimizing Warehouse Management," *Pharmaceutical Technology* 38(2), 2014: 54.

19. Kilcarr, S., "Ten Transportation Trends to Watch in 2017," *Fleet Owner*, January 6, 2017: 1.

20. Krummert, B., "Three Tools Aid in Slashing Food Waste," *Restaurant Hospitality*, November 16, 2016: 1.

21. https://www.sqmgroup.com/about-sqm-group

22. Drazen, E. L., R. E. Moll, and M. F. Roetter, *Logistics in Service Industries*. Oak Brooks, IL: Council of Logistics Management, 1991: 34.

23. Anonymous, "Mopar Introduces Service Capacity Analyzer," *Wireless News* August 28, 2015: 1.

24. https://www.trucks.com/2016/06/14/truck-driver-shortage-self-inflicted

25. http://www.photo-me.co.uk/about-us/who-we-are

26. Anonymous, "Labor Management: Automated Solutions Take Center Stage," *Chain Store Age* 89(3), 2013: 25.

27. Li, H., "Charging Cars for Pennies," *Canadian Business* 82(19), 2009: 24; and http://www.cbc.ca/news/technology/canada-electric-cars-electricity-system-1.3526558

28. Jacobs, R., "Gatwick Beats Rival in Battle for Passengers," FT.com November 29, 2011: 1.

29. Hedges, L., "The SMS Renaissance," *Capacity Magazine* July 1, 2014: 1.

30. http://qtrac.lavi.com/virtual-queuing; and Anonymous, "Lavi Industries Inc.," *Marketing Weekly News* March 27, 2010: 200; Anonymous, "North Asia Office Carat China, Shanghai," *Media* December 17, 2009: 36.

31. http://accesso.com/news/accesso-acquired-by-lo-q; and Morris, J., "The Waiting Game," *Management Today* January 2013: 44−47.

32. Maister, D., "The Psychology of Waiting Lines," In J. A. Czepiel, M. R. Solomon, and C. F. Surprenant, eds., *The Service Encounter*. Lexington, MA: Lexington Books, D.C. Heath & Co., 1985.

33. Ibid.

34. Klosek, N., "Counter Offensives," *Dealerscope* 55(11), 2013: 24, 26, 28.

35. Petouhoff, N., "The Social Customer Economy," *Customer Relationship Management* 14(3), 2010: 14. Also see www.carphonewarehouse.com

36. Andel, T., "Can Amazon Succeed at Grocery Delivery?" *Modern Materials Handling* 62(9), 2007: 15. Also see their website: http://fresh.amazon.com

37. https://www.whitehutchinson.com/news/lenews/2015/june/article104.shtml

38. Anonymous, "The Body Shop Tests 'Entertailing' in Britain," www.retailcustomerexperience.com, May 2012; www.mallofamerica.com/about

39. See http://www.bbc.co.uk/programmes/b006qpgr/features/about for more on *The Archers*; see http://kidstvmovies.about.com/od/theelectriccompany/fr/ElectricCor.htm for more on The Electric Company

40. See www.wingsover.com

41. See www.drishtee.org and http://nextbillion.net/drishtee-rural-health-franchising

42. Byrne, H., "Welcome to McWorld," *Barron's* 74(35), 1994: 25−28; and http://englishrussia.com/2015/01/30/first-mcdonalds-in-soviet-union-biggest-launch-event-in-the-world

43. Kutscher, B., "Eastern Opportunities: HCA Founders Look to Nascent Chinese Market," *Modern Healthcare* 43(5), 2013: 20−21.

44. Hoffman, G., "On Foreign Expansion," *Progressive Grocer* 75(9), 1996: 156.

45. https://www.census.gov/retail/mrts/www/data/pdf/ec_current.pdf

46. http://searchengineland.com/google-now-handles-2-999-trillion-searches-per-year-250247

47. Rooney, K., "Consumer-Driven Healthcare Marketing: Using the Web to Get up Close and Personal," *Journal of Healthcare Management* 54(4), 2009: 241−251; also see www.swamedia.com/channels/Corporate-Fact-Sheet/pages/corporate-fact-sheet

48. See, for instance, Parasuraman, A., V. A. Zeithaml, and L. L. Berry, "SERVQUAL: A Multiple-Item Scale for Measuring Consumer Perceptions of Service Quality," *Journal of Retailing* 64(1), 1988: 12−40; Parasuraman, A., V. A. Zeithaml, and L. L. Berry, "Conceptual Model of Service Quality and Its Implications for Future Research," *Journal of Marketing* 49, Fall 1985: 41−50.

49. Anonymous, "South African Airways Named Best Airline in Africa by Global Traveler Magazine," *Journal of Transportation* December 31, 2016: 107.

50. McWilliams, B., and E. Gerstner, "Offering Low Price Guarantees to Improve Customer Retention," *Journal of Retailing* 82(2), 2006: 105.

PART 5

Integration Issues in Supply Chain Management

Chapter 13   Supply Chain Process Integration

Chapter 14   Performance Measurement Along Supply Chains

Chapter 13

SUPPLY CHAIN PROCESS INTEGRATION

Some end users have no idea how vulnerable a lot of the physical security systems installed on their networks are. And there are rarely any assurances run against physical security systems or scanning for evolving risks. End users will have to start asking manufacturers for cyber protections, and regulated industries [such as those with high compliance requirements from the DoD] will likely be the first to switch.

—Andrew Lanning, cofounder of Integrated Security Technologies and chairman of the PSA Cybersecurity Advisory Committee[1]

When the customer has a valid claim, we need to remedy those problems quickly. You have to have a method internally for making sense of the types of things, whatever the hiccups are in the supply chain.

—Joanne Longo, G-lll Apparel Group Ltd.[2]

Learning Objectives

After completing this chapter, you should be able to

- Discuss the overall importance of process integration in supply chain management.
- Describe the advantages of, and obstacles to, process integration.
- Understand the important issues of internal and external process integration.
- Understand the role played by information systems in creating information visibility along the supply chain.
- Describe the various processes requiring integration along the supply chain.
- Understand the various causes of the bullwhip effect and how they impact process integration.
- Discuss the various issues associated with supply chain risk and security.

Chapter Outline

Introduction

The Supply Chain Management Integration Model

Obstacles to Process Integration along the Supply Chain

Managing Supply Chain Risk and Security

Summary

SCM Profile | Integrating Processes Helps Companies Save Costs, Improve Service

Process integration has been shown to be an important factor over the years, in making companies more successful. Companies in different sectors around the world have paired with each other to achieve new supply chain efficiencies.

For example, the collaboration between Ford and GM dealers in the United States—Schneider Logistics was optimizing a Ford dealer's parts supply chain when it noticed an overlap between Ford's and GM's suppliers and dealers. The dealerships were located in groups and many suppliers were grouped as well. Sharing these parts networks brought significant cost savings through better asset utilization and increased volumes to Ford and GM because the two dealer distribution networks agreed to share their parts networks and order schedules.

In another example, U.S. food company Land O'Lakes was shipping a number of empty truck trailers along the eastern seaboard. Working with Nistevo.com, an online logistics matchmaker, it was able to partner with other companies with similar transportation schedules. On one specific route, General Mills was sending its products from point A to point B on a similar schedule as Land O'Lakes was sending its products from point B to point A. Both were deadheading back with empty trailers. The two companies were thus able to synchronize loads and reduce empty miles, saving Land O'Lakes' over $2 million per year.

U.S. personal care company Kimberly-Clark integrated processes with a number of companies across Europe to capture cost savings from their extensive distribution networks. Kimberly-Clark found that it shared a number of shipping lanes with Unilever in the Netherlands. After setting up a joint logistics plan, the two companies worked with Hays Logistics to set up a new warehouse where both could store their products. Unilever and Kimberly-Clark then worked with customers to receive orders the same day. Customers benefited because they were able to order twice as frequently with the same shipping costs. Kimberly-Clark was able to reduce inventory cycles, improve service levels, and reduce its holding costs. Eventually about 93 percent of Kimberly-Clark's product volume in the Netherlands was moved by shared deliveries. Kimberly-Clark also collaborated with Kellogg's in the United Kingdom. Kellogg's products were sent from a northern facility to London where they were cross-docked and shipped in smaller quantities with Kimberly-Clark's products to customers in southern England. The process quickly became permanent, and Kellogg's eventually also began to cross-dock Kimberly-Clark products in the northern England. Both companies achieved significant benefits from this relationship.[3]

INTRODUCTION

The ultimate goal in supply chain management is to create value for the services and products provided to end customers, which, in turn, provides benefits to the firms in the supply chain network. To accomplish this, firms in the supply chain must integrate their process activities internally and then with their trading partners. Throughout this text, the integration of key business processes along the supply chain has been a recurring theme. The term **process integration** (also sometimes called process collaboration) means sharing information and coordinating resources to jointly manage a process or processes. We have been introducing and discussing the various processes and issues concerning this time-consuming and somewhat daunting task throughout the text and have been alluding to the idea that key processes must somehow be coordinated, shared, or integrated among the supply chain members. In this chapter, some of these issues will be revisited and refined.

Additionally, the advantages, challenges, methods, and tools used to achieve process integration both within organizations and among their trading partners will be discussed. Today, process integration remains a significant problem for many organizations. In fact, the global process integration software market is expected to grow by about $100 billion from 2017 to 2021, due in part to internal and external integration problems that organizations are having.[4] Since process integration between departments is considered to be the necessary foundation for successful external integration between trading partners, it can then be understood that problems with internal integration have made external integration even more difficult to achieve.

Specifically, this chapter discusses the key business processes requiring integration, the impact of integration on the bullwhip effect, the importance of internal and external process integration in supply chain management, issues of supply chain risk and security that come about as information is shared and products are moved significant distances, and the important role played by information technology (IT) when integrating processes.

External process integration can be an extremely difficult task because it requires proper training and preparedness, willing and competent trading partners, trust, compatible information systems, potentially a change in one or more organizational cultures, and, as mentioned above, successful internal process integration. The benefits of collaboration and information sharing between trading partners can be significant: reduced supply chain costs, greater flexibility to respond to market changes, and fewer process problems, which means less supply chain safety stock, higher quality levels, reduced time to market, and better utilization of resources. It is hoped that this chapter will allow readers to recall and consider all of the previous chapters' topics, their contributions to successful supply chain management, and the means by which information sharing and process integration must occur to make supply chain management a success.

THE SUPPLY CHAIN MANAGEMENT INTEGRATION MODEL

Figure 13.1 presents a supply chain integration model, starting with the identification of key trading partners, the development of supply chain strategies, aligning the strategies with key process objectives, developing internal process performance measures, internally integrating these key processes, developing external supply chain performance measures for each process, externally integrating key processes with supply chain partners, extending process integration to second-tier supply chain participants, and then, finally, reevaluating the integration model periodically. Each of the elements in the model is discussed next.

Identify Critical Supply Chain Trading Partners

For each of the focal firm's products and services, it is important to identify the critical or **key trading partners** that will eventually enable the successful sale and delivery of end products to the final customers. Over time, companies identify these trading partners through successful business dealings—suppliers that have come to be trusted and that provide a large share of the firm's critical products and services; and repeat, satisfied customers that buy a significant portion of the firm's products. As the focal firm moves

| Figure 13.1 | The Supply Chain Integration Model |

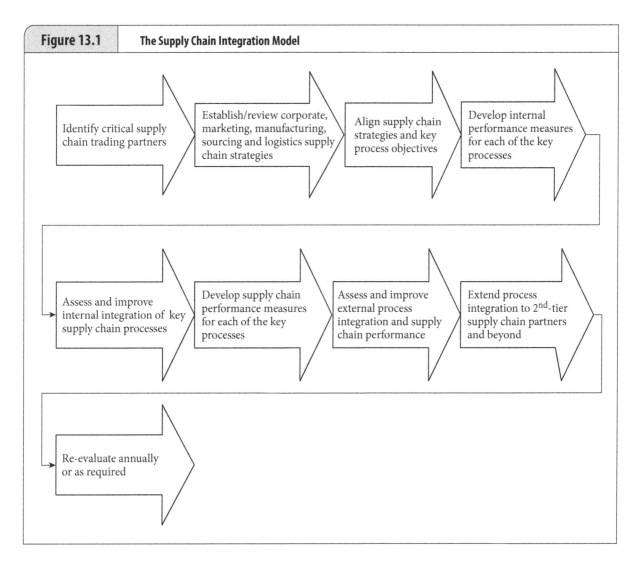

out to second- and third-tier suppliers and customers, trading partner numbers increase quite dramatically, which can greatly complicate integration efforts. Identifying only the first-tier primary trading partners allows the firm to concentrate its time and resources on managing important process links with these companies, enabling the larger supply chain to perform better. Including nonessential and minor supporting businesses will most likely prove counterproductive in terms of successful supply chain management. In a landmark supply chain article by Drs. Lambert, Cooper, and Pagh, they define primary or key trading partners as "all those autonomous companies or strategic business units who actually perform operational and/or managerial activities in the business processes designed to produce a specific output for a particular customer or market."[5]

Depending on where within a supply chain the focal firm is physically located (close to its key suppliers, close to end-product customers, or somewhere in between), the structure of the network of primary trading partners will vary. Mapping the network of primary trading partners is something that should be done to help the firm decide which businesses to include in its supply chain management efforts. For instance, a firm with a large number of key suppliers and customers might limit the number of integrative processes, leading to fewer second-tier relationships as well. Coordinating processes with its key suppliers was seen as so important to IBM, for example, that in 2006 it moved its global procurement headquarters to Shenzhen, China, from the United States. Then, after six successful years in Shenzhen, IBM again moved its procurement headquarters to Budapest, Hungary. IBM had made sizeable investments in African growth markets and created a new procurement center in Ghana, so moving the procurement headquarters closer to suppliers in Eastern Europe and Africa allowed IBM to share its expertise and accelerate business with clients in those areas.[6]

Review and Establish Supply Chain Strategies

On an annual basis, management should identify the basic supply chain strategies associated with each of its trading partner's goods and services. If an end product is competing based on quality, then supply chain members should also be using strategies consistent with delivering high-quality products at competitive price and service levels. Product strategies should then translate into internal functional policies regarding the types of parts purchased and suppliers used, the manufacturing processes employed, the designs of goods and services, the warranty and return policies offered, and potentially the amount of outsourcing employed. In each of these areas, policies should be geared toward supporting the overall strategy of the supply chain.

Similarly, if end products are competing based on sustainability, then strategies and functional policies among each of the supply chain participants must be consistently aimed at achieving favorable environmental impacts or carbon footprints as intermediate goods and services are purchased, produced, and moved along the supply chain. Supply chain sustainability has become an important issue today as organizations seek better ways to compete. In 2012, for example, global food maker General Mills commissioned a study of its environmental dependence on natural resources across its supply chains and found that nearly two-thirds of greenhouse gas emissions and 99 percent of water use occurred outside its own operations—in the growth of raw materials and preparation of ingredients that General Mills uses to produce its products. Consequently, General Mills designed a sourcing plan to improve the sustainability of raw materials it uses and to manage the impact of water usage across its supply chains.[7]

Align Supply Chain Strategies with Key Supply Chain Process Objectives

Once the primary strategy has been identified for a supply chain's end product, managers need to identify the important processes linking each of the supply chain trading partners and establish process objectives to assure that resources and efforts are effectively deployed within each firm to support the end-product strategy. The key processes and the methods used to integrate and manage process links among supply chain partners will vary based on the internal structure of each firm, the prevailing economic conditions in the marketplace, the degree to which **functional silos** exist in any of the trading partners and the nature of existing relationships within each supply chain. In some cases, it may be best to integrate only one key process with one trading partner, while with other partners, more processes would be integrated.

Based on the research of Lambert, Cooper, and Pagh, eight processes have been identified as important in supply chains. These **key supply chain processes** are shown in Table 13.1. A **process** can be defined as a set of activities designed to produce a product or

Table 13.1	The Eight Key Supply Chain Business Processes[9]
Customer Relationship Management	Identifying key customer segments, tailoring product and service agreements to meet their needs, measuring customer profitability and firm's impact on customers.
Customer Service Management	Providing information to customers such as product availability, shipping dates, and order status; administering product and service agreements.
Demand Management	Balancing customer demand with the firm's output capacity; forecasting demand and coordinating with production, purchasing, and distribution.
Order Fulfillment	Meeting customer requirements by synchronizing the firm's marketing, production, and distribution plans.
Manufacturing Flow Management	Determining manufacturing process requirements to enable the right mix of flexibility and velocity to satisfy demand.
Supplier Relationship Management	Managing product and service agreements with suppliers; developing close working relationships with key suppliers.
Product Development and Commercialization	Developing new products frequently and getting them to market effectively; integrating suppliers and customers into the process to reduce time to market.
Returns Management	Managing used product disposition, product recalls, packaging requirements; and minimizing future returns.

service for an internal or external customer. Simply put, a process is how work gets done. A discussion of each of these eight key processes follows.

Customer Relationship Management

The **customer relationship management process** provides the firm with the structure for developing and managing customer relationships. As discussed in Chapter 10, key customers are identified, their needs are determined, and then products and services are developed to meet their needs. Over time, relationships with these key customers are solidified through the sharing of information; the formation of cross-company teams to improve product design, delivery, quality, and cost; the development of shared goals; and, finally, improved performance and profitability for the trading partners along with agreements on how to share these benefits. The firm should monitor the impact of customer relationship management (CRM) efforts in terms of both the financial impact of these efforts and with customer satisfaction. Over time, CRM has come to be associated with software applications to aid the CRM process. In fact, in 2013, Microsoft was granted a patent for extending a "CRM eventing framework" to a cloud computing environment.[8]

Customer Service Management

The customer service management process is what imparts information to customers while also providing ongoing management of any product and service agreements between the firm and its customers. Information can be offered through a number of communication channels including websites, personal interactions, information system linkages, and printed media. Objectives and policies are developed to assure proper distribution of products and services to customers, to adequately respond to product and delivery failures and complaints, and to utilize the most effective means of communication to coordinate successful product, service, and information deliveries. The process also includes methods for monitoring and reporting customer service performance, allowing firms to understand to what extent their management efforts are achieving their process objectives.

Demand Management

The **demand management process** is what balances customer demand and the firm's output capabilities. The specific demand management activities include forecasting demand and then utilizing techniques to vary capacity and demand within the purchasing, production, and distribution functions. Various forecasts can be used, based on the time frame, the knowledge of the forecaster, the ability to obtain point-of-sale information from customers, and the use of forecasting models contained in many ERP systems. The next step is to determine how to synchronize demand and productive capacity. As discussed in Chapters 5, 6, and 12, a number of effective techniques exist to smooth demand variabilities and increase or decrease capacity when disparities exist between demand and supply. Contingency plans must also be ready for use when demand management techniques fail or when forecasts are inaccurate. Performance measurement systems can prove quite useful here to increase the accuracy of forecasts and to track the success of various demand management activity implementations. After a terrible explosion at a Georgia-based Imperial Sugar refinery destroyed 60 percent of the plant's capacity in 2008, Imperial Sugar was able to rely on its demand management software to show everyone from production to sales, in real time, what could be delivered to which customers using available inventories. "It was our saving grace," said CIO George Muller.[10]

Order Fulfillment

The **order fulfillment process** is the set of activities that allows the firm to fill customer orders while providing the required levels of customer service at the lowest possible delivered cost. Thus, the order fulfillment process must integrate the firm's marketing, production, and distribution plans to be effective. More specifically, the firm's distribution system must be designed to provide adequate customer service levels, and their production system must be designed to produce at the required output levels, while marketing plans and promotions must consider the firm's output and distribution capabilities. Related order fulfillment issues are the location of suppliers, the modes of inbound and outbound transportation used, the location of production facilities and distribution centers, and the system used for entering, processing, communicating, picking, delivering, and documenting customer orders. The nearby SCM Profile discusses the automated order fulfillment capabilities in some warehouses.

The order fulfillment process must integrate closely with customer relationship management, customer service management, supplier relationship management, and returns management to assure that customer requirements are being met, customer service levels are being maintained, suppliers are helping to minimize order lead times, and customers are getting undamaged, high-quality products. A 2013 survey of U.S. consumers and supply chain managers highlighted the importance of effective order fulfillment—89 percent of the consumers said they would likely shop at a different retailer if an order was delivered late, and 54 percent of the supply chain mangers said that fulfillment issues have had a negative impact on their firms' revenues and profitability over the past few years.[12]

Manufacturing Flow Management

The **manufacturing flow management process** is the set of activities responsible for making the actual product, establishing the manufacturing flexibility required to adequately serve markets, and designing the production system to meet cycle-time requirements. To be effective, manufacturing flow management activities must be interfaced with demand management and customer relationship management processes, using customer requirements as inputs to the process. As customers and their requirements change, so too

SCM Profile | Automated Order Fulfillment

Automated inventory control solutions provide advanced data-capture capabilities and traceability for finished goods and raw materials. Michigan-based Lowry Solutions offers its inventory control data collection system to streamline the movement of raw materials and finished goods. "Warehouse inventory movement information is captured right as the work is being performed," says Paul Rakowicz, vice president of software development. The system automatically enforces first-in, first-out (FIFO) protocol.

The Perfect Pick system, available from NJ-based OPEX Corp., is engineered to simplify order fulfillment. A Perfect Pick aisle is comprised of modular, high-density racking along with a fleet of robotic delivery vehicles, iBOTs, which can access every storage location within their aisle—both horizontally and vertically.

iBOTs deliver inventory directly to a workstation located at one or both ends of the aisle. This direct interface eliminates the need for conveyor systems, elevators, or lifts. Perfect Pick's traffic control software monitors the position of all iBOTs in the aisle and directs their movement to ensure operational efficiency.

Operators follow text and visual prompts on a screen located at their workstation, which directs picking and putting operations. When the operator indicates that the final pick or put is complete, the next tote is driven into position for the next sequence. Upon delivery, the iBOT tilts for ergonomic positioning.

Looking ahead, experts envision a connected warehouse in which automated equipment collects data from various other devices. Autopositioning technology will connect operators, equipment, and warehouse management systems in this brave new automated world.[11]

must the supply chain and the manufacturing flow processes change to maintain a firm's competitiveness. As was shown in Chapter 8, the flexibility and rapid response requirements in many supply chains result in the firm's use of lean systems in order to continue to meet customer requirements.

Manufacturing flow characteristics also impact supplier requirements. For instance, as manufacturing batch sizes and lead time requirements are reduced, supplier deliveries must become smaller and more frequent, causing supplier interactions and supplier relationships to potentially change. The importance of an adequate material requirements planning (MRP) system should become evident here, as customer requirements must be translated into production capabilities and supplier requirements. As with other processes, a good set of performance metrics should also be utilized to track the capability of the manufacturing flow process to satisfy demand.

Supplier Relationship Management

The **supplier relationship management process** defines how the firm manages its relationships with suppliers. As was discussed in Chapters 2, 3, and 4, firms in actively managed supply chains seek out small numbers of the best-performing suppliers and establish ongoing, mutually beneficial, close relationships with these suppliers in order to meet cost, quality, and/or customer service objectives for key materials, products, and services. For nonessential items, firms may use reverse auctions, bid arrangements, or catalogues to select suppliers. Activities in this process include screening and selecting suppliers, negotiating product and service agreements, managing suppliers, and then monitoring supplier performance and improvement. Some companies may have a cross-functional team to manage suppliers' progress toward meeting the firm's current and long-term requirements and establishing records of performance improvement over time, while other suppliers may be managed little or not at all, depending on supply chain, company, or product requirements. Supplier relationship management personnel routinely communicate with production personnel to obtain feedback on supplier and purchased item performances, and with marketing personnel for customer satisfaction feedback. Additionally, suppliers are frequently contacted for new product development and performance feedback purposes.

Product Development and Commercialization

The **product development and commercialization process** is responsible for developing new goods and services to meet changing customer requirements and then getting these products to market quickly and efficiently. In actively managed supply chains, customers and suppliers are involved in the new product development process to assure that products conform to customers' needs and that purchased items meet manufacturing requirements. Activities in the product development and commercialization process include methods and incentives for generating new product ideas; the development of customer feedback mechanisms; the formation of new product development teams; assessing and selecting new product ideas based on financial impact, resource requirements, and fit with existing manufacturing and logistics infrastructure; designing and testing new product prototypes; determining marketing channels and rolling out the products; and, finally, assessing the success of each new product introduction. Successful new product development requires inputs from external customers and suppliers, and from internal manufacturing, marketing, and finance personnel.

More and more, big data analyses are being relied upon to develop new products. One of the pioneers in use of big data is the retail industry. An athletic shoemaker like Nike might use big data to predict the hot sneaker model for the year—big data analysis combines internal corporate data with other information from web-browsing patterns, sneaker industry advertising, and social media perceptions. In another example, by analyzing their vast amount of search histories, Google noticed an above-average search demand for the word "flu," and some pharmaceutical company paid Google a nice sum of money for that predictive information. In yet another example, British Airways (BA) launched a program called "Know Me" that aims to get the most out of its customer data. BA marketers are able to make better decisions about how they interact with their customers, through knowing and understanding passenger needs at a deeper level.[13]

Returns Management

The **returns management process**, discussed in Chapter 9, can be extremely beneficial for supply chain management in terms of maintaining acceptable levels of customer service and identifying product improvement opportunities. Returns management activities include environmental compliance with substance disposal and recycling, writing operating and repair instructions, troubleshooting and warranty repairs, developing disposition guidelines, designing an effective reverse logistics process, and collecting returns data. Returns management personnel frequently communicate with customers and personnel from customer relationship management, product development and commercialization, and supplier relationship management during the returns process.

One of the goals of returns management is to reduce returns. This is accomplished by communicating return and repair information to product development personnel, suppliers, and other potential contributors to any returns problems, to guide the improvement of future product and purchased item designs. Logistics services may also be included in the returns feedback communication loop. In a recent reverse logistics survey by the Massachusetts-based business consultants Aberdeen Group, the companies best at reverse logistics were found to have a few things in common, including a standardized returns and repair process, the ability to recover costs from suppliers, real-time information reporting, and multichannel visibility.[14]

For each of the eight processes identified above, objectives or goals must be developed to help guide the firm toward its supply chain strategy. Additionally, consistent objectives within each functional area of the firm, for each process, help to integrate the processes internally, as well as focus efforts and firm resources on the supply chain strategy. For instance, if the supply chain strategy is to compete using low pricing, marketing objectives for the customer relationship management process might be to find cheaper delivery alternatives, develop vendor-managed inventory (VMI) accounts, and automate the customer order process. Production objectives might be to develop bulk packaging solutions consistent with the modes of transportation and distribution systems used, to increase mass production capabilities, and to identify the lowest total cost manufacturing sites for specific products, while purchasing objectives might be to identify the cheapest materials and components that meet specifications and to utilize reverse auctions whenever possible. Firms should similarly progress through each of the key processes using teams of employees, suppliers, and customers to help develop process objectives.

Develop Internal Performance Measures for Key Process Effectiveness

As alluded to in each of the key processes above (and to be discussed at greater length in Chapter 14), procedures and metrics must be in place to collect and report internal performance data for the eight key processes. Thus, prior to measuring and comparing performance with their supply chain partners, firms must first build good internal performance measurement capabilities across functions. This can prove troublesome given that in recent surveys of experts in performance measurement systems, about 56 percent of performance measurement implementations fail.[15] Successful performance measures need to create a consistent emphasis on the overall supply chain strategy and the corresponding process objectives. To ensure that processes are supporting the overall supply chain strategy, performance should be continuously monitored using a set of metrics designed for each process.

Continuing the discussion from the previous section where competing based on low price was the supply chain strategy, performance measures for the customer relationship management process would need to be designed for each of the firm's functional areas. The responsibility for designing these measures can also be assigned to the teams developing objectives for each of the functional areas. Since the objectives in this case are cost driven, the performance measures should reflect this as well. For the customer relationship management process, performance measures in marketing might be the average delivery cost, the number of new VMI accounts, the average cost of ordering and carrying inventories for the new VMI accounts, and the number of new automated order systems over the period of time studied. For production, performance measures might be the average packaging cost per order, the average daily output capability for each product, and the average unit cost per order. For purchasing, the performance measures for the customer relationship management objectives might be the average purchasing cost for each of the items purchased and the percentage of time that reverse auctions were used over the period of time studied. Performance measures would similarly be designed for each of the key processes and their corresponding functional objectives. In this way, firms have the capability to track the progress toward meeting each of the objectives for the key processes.

Assess and Improve Internal Integration of Key Supply Chain Processes

Successful supply chain management requires process coordination and collaboration internally between employees in the firm's functional areas as well as externally between the firm and its trading partners. Achieving process integration within the firm requires a transition from the typical functional silos to one of teamwork and cooperation across business functions. Internal integration has been shown to provide significant benefits for the firm. In a survey of 500 U.S. organizations, for instance, good interdepartmental relationships were found to result in reduced cycle times and fewer stockouts.[16] To achieve internal integration, personnel must have management support, resources, and empowerment to make meaningful organizational changes to foster the type of cooperation necessary to support the overall supply chain strategy. The formation of cross-functional teams to develop the key process objectives and accompanying performance measures is a good starting point in achieving internal process integration.

The primary enabler of integration, though, is the firm's ERP system. In Chapter 6, the importance and capabilities of ERP systems were described, along with some of the various software applications or modules that are used today. ERP systems provide a view of the entire organization, enabling decision-makers within each function to have information regarding customer orders, production plans, work-in-process and finished goods inventory levels, inbound and outbound goods in-transit, purchase orders, purchased item inventories, and financial and accounting information. ERP systems thus link business processes and facilitate communication and information sharing between the firm's departments. Since the key business processes overlay each of the functional areas, the firm eventually becomes process oriented rather than functionally oriented as ERP systems are deployed. It is this visibility of information across the organization that allows processes to become integrated within the firm.

To assess the current state of internal integration, firms should first develop an understanding of their **internal supply chains**. Internal supply chains can be complex, particularly if firms have multiple divisions and global organizational structures. Thus, firms should assess the makeup of the teams used in setting process objectives and designing performance measures—do they include representatives from each of the organization's divisions or business units? These cross-functional teams should adequately represent the firm's internal supply chain. For example, during the global economic downturn in 2009, internal integration was impacted as companies trimmed staff and transferred workers to cut costs. Managers then turned to team-based games to get employees working together again. "Many employees have been shifted into new job roles because of layoffs, and employers are using team-based business games to train workers in their new responsibilities and to increase their retention of new knowledge," says Elizabeth Treher, CEO of Minnesota-based The Learning Key. "Team-based business games result in better knowledge retention, provide focused, memorable learning and a more enjoyable learning atmosphere than traditional methods," Treher adds.[17]

Once the firm has an understanding of its internal supply chain, it can begin to assess the level of information access across functional boundaries. Does the firm have a single company-wide ERP system linking the functional areas? Are all of the firm's **legacy systems** linked to its ERP system? How easy is it to extract the information needed to make effective decisions? Are centralized **data warehouses** being used to collect data from the various divisions of the firm? Firms that are successfully integrating key business processes are using global ERP systems and data warehouses to make better, informed decisions.

Data warehouses store information collected from ERP and legacy systems in one location, such that users can extract information as needed, analyze it, and use it to make decisions.

A globally linked ERP system allows the firm to use a common database from which to make product, customer, and supplier decisions. Information is captured once, reducing data input errors; information is available in real time, eliminating delays throughout the organization as information is shared; and, finally, information is visible throughout the organization—all transactions taking place can be seen and accessed by everyone on the system. As the firm moves away from legacy systems and toward a fully integrated ERP system, as cross-functional teams are created to link key processes to supply chain strategies, and as process performance is monitored and improved, the firm will become more focused on managing the key supply chain processes in an integrated fashion.

Develop Supply Chain Performance Measures for the Key Processes

As described earlier for internal performance measures, the firm should also develop external performance measures to monitor the links with trading partners regarding the key supply chain processes. And, as with the design of internal performance measures, teams composed of members from primary trading partners should be created to design these measures to be consistent with overall supply chain strategies.

Continuing with the low-cost supply chain strategy example, trading partners should monitor a number of cost-oriented performance measures that are averaged across the member firms for each of the key supply chain processes. For the customer relationship management process, examples might include the average delivery cost, rush order cost, VMI carrying cost, finished-goods safety stock costs, returned order costs, and spoilage costs. Inbound and outbound logistics costs, in particular, have come under much greater scrutiny over the past few years, due to the rising cost of fuel. From 2001 to 2015, for example, gasoline prices increased by more than 130 percent in the United States.[18] Fuel prices have thus placed increased pressure on trading partners to find cheaper ways to transport goods in a timely fashion, and this can be particularly problematic for supply chains following a low-cost strategy. External performance measures should align with internal performance measures, but may vary based on purchasing, production, distribution, customer service, and other variations across the participating firms. The topic of external performance measures is discussed further in Chapter 14.

Assess and Improve External Process Integration and Supply Chain Performance

Over time, firms eliminate poor-performing suppliers as well as unprofitable customers while concentrating efforts on developing beneficial relationships and strategic alliances with their remaining suppliers and customers. Building, maintaining, and strengthening these relationships is accomplished through use of external process integration. As process integration improves among supply chain partners, so too does supply chain performance. As a matter of fact, in a study published in 2014, supply chain process integration was found to be *the most significant predictor* of firm's competitive position.[19] When firms have achieved a reasonably good measure of internal process integration, they are ready to move on to externally integrating key supply chain processes with trading partners.

Trading partners must be willing to share sales and forecast information, along with information on new products, expansion plans, new processes, and new marketing campaigns in order to ultimately satisfy end customers and maximize profits for all supply chain members. As with internal process integration, the teams formed to design and organize process performance measures should be viewed as a key resource for external process integration. These teams can set and revise supply chain process objectives, and the type of information that must be shared to achieve the objectives. Once the performance metrics are designed for each of the processes, they can be monitored to identify lack of process integration and supply chain weaknesses. Firms should thus periodically communicate levels of process performance and integration to their trading partners and collaborate on methods to improve both.

Once again, the way information is communicated plays an extremely important role in external process integration. Today, connecting buyers and suppliers via the Internet is the way supply chains are becoming integrated. More generally termed **knowledge management solutions**, Internet applications tied to desktop applications enable real-time collaboration and flow of information between supply chain partners, the ability to "see" into suppliers' and customers' operations, faster decision-making, and the collection of supply chain performance metrics.

Supply chain communication capabilities must deal with handling the flows of goods and information between companies, negotiating and executing contracts, managing supply and demand problems, making and executing orders, and handling financial settlements, all with a high level of security. California-based home textile retailer Anna's Linens uses an Internet portal solution to communicate with over 100 of its key vendors and distributors. The system has enabled Anna's to make opportunistic purchases from other retail closures and immediately interpret global trends using real-time visibility within its supply chain.[20]

Extend Process Integration to Second-Tier Supply Chain Partners

As supply chain relationships become more trusting and mature, and as the supply chain software used to link supply chain partners' information systems evolves and becomes more widely used and relied upon, the tendency will be to integrate processes to second-tier partners and beyond. Today, supply chain software suppliers are developing systems that integrate more easily with other applications, allowing trading partners to exchange ever more complex or detailed information on contracts, product designs, forecasts, sales, purchases, and inventories. Using these linkages, companies can, in real time, work with suppliers and customers to compare design ideas, forecasts, and order commitments; determine supply/demand mismatches; and analyze supplier performance.

Every major software developer today is trying to make its supply chain applications easier to integrate with existing systems and gather data anywhere along a firm's supply chain. One development is the **radio-frequency identification tag (RFID)**, discussed in Chapters 7 and 9. These microchip devices can be attached to pallets or cases to relay information on the products' whereabouts as they move through a supply chain. Thus, a firm's supply chain system can access real-time inventory information and instigate a replenishment order as inventories are drawn down. RFID tags have a number of applications, several of which are described in the nearby SCM Profile.

SCM Profile RFID Tags Used for Theft and Temperature Control

With tag readers positioned inside a truck trailer, RFID tags can be read and reported in real time. The information can indicate items that were loaded at origin; if some tags do not respond after two hours it helps identify a cargo loss problem, which might result from goods being delivered to the wrong destination, or a cargo theft problem.

California-based Intelleflex Corp. is one company offering a temperature-monitoring RFID tag that can be read from 100 meters. Placing the tags throughout a load of perishables, for instance, the tags can record and report temperature variations across the load. This ability to monitor down to the pallet or container level can reduce product waste.

In one example, using tags placed in pallets of fruit coming from the field, the temperatures of the different pallets were monitored and recorded as the fruit was loaded, and during transport to the packing house. The temperatures of the pallets of fruit varied based on time of day when they were harvested and loaded and other factors. Using the data collected on the temperatures, the shelf life of the different pallets of fruit could be estimated. It was found that 70 percent of the fruit maintained an optimal shelf life of fourteen days or more based on the conditions at harvest and during transport. The other 30 percent of the load had dropped below the optimal fourteen days. Thus, instead of a first-in-first-out approach, the shipper was able to use a first-expiry-first-out approach so the fruit that had the shorter estimated shelf life was prioritized and shipped to closer distribution centers.[21]

The prices of RFID tags vary greatly depending on whether they are *active* or *passive.* **Passive RFID tags** don't contain a power source, require power from a tag reader, and cost from $0.05 to $1.00 each, depending on purchase volume, packaging, and how the tag is made. **Active RFID tags** draw power from an internal battery and are priced in the $10 to $70 range depending on the volume required and battery type. Both are finding applications. The passive variety are placed on pallets, cases, and even units of product and are used in many retail and warehousing environments. In retail environments, passive RFID usage is on the rise. In a study by Atlanta-based management consulting firm Kurt Salmon in 2014, 34 percent of respondents had either implemented or were currently implementing or piloting passive RFID tags. In their 2016 study, RFID usage had more than doubled to 73 percent. Part of the reason for the significant growth in RFID is that the technology is delivering significant results. One standout measure is inventory accuracy. Inventory accuracy is the most widely used RFID metric, and Kurt Salmon found an average of inventory accuracy improvement of 25.4 percent when using RFID. Even more interesting was that retailers reported that lack of inventory accuracy accounted for an average loss of 8.7 percent of total sales.[22]

The much more costly active tags are being used, for example, to track the whereabouts of expensive equipment in a hospital or for identification of fleet vehicles and shipping containers in and out of a facility. The U.S. Marines also use active tags to track container loads on international shipments. The Marines' vision is to have tags talk directly to logistics databases via network access points that will then communicate information to other locations via satellite.[23]

Prior to the development of these supply chain applications, integrating processes beyond first-tier suppliers and customers was somewhat more difficult and time-consuming. As discussed in Chapter 4, firms can develop relationships with some of their second-tier suppliers and then insist that their direct suppliers use these suppliers. They can also work closely with their key direct suppliers to solve second-tier supplier problems and help them, in turn, better manage *their* direct suppliers. To stay on the competitive edge, firms today must use a combination of information system linkages and old-fashioned customer and supplier teamwork to identify and manage second-tier relationships along the supply chain.

Reevaluate the Integration Model Annually

In light of the dramatic and fast-paced changes occurring with the development of supply chain communication technologies and the frequent changes occurring with new products, new suppliers, and new markets, trading partners should revisit their integration model annually to identify changes within their supply chains and to assess the impact these changes are having on integration efforts. New suppliers may have entered the scene with better capabilities, more distribution choices, and better resources. Or perhaps the firm may be redesigning an older product, requiring different purchased components or supplier capabilities. Alternatively, the firm may be moving into a new foreign market, potentially requiring entirely different supply chains. These examples are common and should cause firms to reevaluate their supply chain strategies, objectives, processes, performance measures, and integration levels.

OBSTACLES TO PROCESS INTEGRATION ALONG THE SUPPLY CHAIN

A number of factors can impede external process integration along the supply chain, causing loss of visibility, information distortion, longer cycle times, stockouts, and the bullwhip effect, all of which contribute to higher overall costs and reduced customer service capabilities. Managers must try to identify these obstacles and take steps to eliminate them to improve profitability and competitiveness for a supply chain's members. Table 13.2 summarizes these obstacles. Each of these is discussed next.

Table 13.2	Obstacles to Supply Chain Integration
Silo Mentality	Failing to see the big picture, and acting only in regard to a single department within a firm or a single firm within a supply chain.
Lack of Supply Chain Visibility	The inability to easily share or retrieve trading partner information in real time, as desired by supply chain participants.
Lack of Trust	Unwillingness to work together or share information because of the fear that the other party will take advantage of them or use the information unethically.
Lack of Knowledge	Lack of process and information system skills and lack of knowledge regarding the benefits of SCM among management and other employees, within the firm and among partners.
Activities Causing the Bullwhip Effect:	
• Demand forecast updating	Using varying customer orders to create and update forecasts, production schedules, and purchase requirements.
• Order batching	Making large orders for goods from suppliers on an infrequent basis to reduce order and transportation costs.
• Price fluctuations	Offering price discounts to customers, causing erratic buying patterns.
• Rationing and shortage gaming	Allocating short product supplies to customers, causing them to increase future orders beyond what they really need.

The Silo Mentality

Too often, firms do not consider the impact of their actions on their supply chains and long-term competitiveness and profitability. An "I win, you lose" **silo mentality** can be evidenced when using the cheapest (or hungriest) suppliers, paying little attention to the needs of customers, and assigning few resources to new goods and services designs. Particularly with firms involved in global supply chains, silo mentalities can crop up as a result of cultural differences. The U.K. auto firm Rover is a case in point. In the 1980s, Rover formed a partnership with Japan-based Honda to provide products for its new model program. The arrogance of Rover managers and a lack of a learning culture at Rover prevented it from realizing any benefits from the partnership. Later, when the German firm BMW bought Rover, communications with German managers and political infighting were even worse. The managerial problems that surfaced when Chrysler and Daimler-Benz got together, which ultimately led to the dissolution of that partnership, were similar.[24]

Eventually, lack of internal or external collaboration will create quality, cost, delivery timing, and other customer service problems that are detrimental to supply chains. In fact, Mr. Wayne Bourne, vice president of logistics and transportation at electronics retailer Best Buy, noted in an interview that the most significant obstacle to overcome in supply chain management was the silo mentality that exists in some companies.[25]

Internally, the silo effect might be found between personnel of different departments. The transportation manager, for instance, may be using rail transportation to minimize transportation costs against the wishes of the firm's sales manager. Delivery inconsistencies caused by continued use of the cheapest transportation providers might be deteriorating customer satisfaction and leading to a loss of customers.

To overcome these and other silo mentalities, firms must strive to align supply chain goals and their own goals and incentives. Functional decisions must be made while considering the impact on the firm's overall profits and those of the supply chain members. Performance reviews of managers should include the ability of their department to integrate processes internally and externally and meet overall supply chain goals. Outside the firm, managers must work to educate suppliers and customers regarding the overall impact of their actions on their supply chains and the end customers. This should be an important part of the supply chain partnership creation and management process. Additionally, suppliers should be annually evaluated and potentially replaced if their performance vis-à-vis supply chain objectives does not improve. California-based Sutter Health, a network of physicians, hospitals, and other healthcare providers, has long believed integration among all departments is the best and most efficient way to deliver care to patients. In fact, in a study by Dartmouth Medical School's Center for the Evaluative Clinical Sciences, Sutter's hospitals, physicians, home care, and hospice services were found to represent a national benchmark.[26]

Lack of Supply Chain Visibility

Lack of **information visibility** along a supply chain is frequently cited as a common process integration problem. In global supply chains, information visibility is particularly important. Product safety standards, trade agreements, and security requirements are changing almost daily, making information visibility critical for importers, shippers, and logistics providers. If trading partners have to carve out data from their information systems and then send it to one another where it then has to be uploaded to other systems prior to the data being shared and evaluated, the extra time and data transfer errors can mean higher inventories, higher costs, longer response times, and lost customers. "Visibility into inventory allows a company to do a better job accessing that inventory to fulfill a customer order, change transportation routes, and balance supply and demand using market conditions. But before that can happen, a business needs data from a number of different channels and processes: its warehouses, its stores, its finished goods supplier or manufacturer as well as freight forwarders, 3PLs, and local carriers. If these data cannot be consolidated and rationalized, a business is failing to exploit significant business value," says Scott Fenwick, senior director of product strategy at business consultant Manhattan Associates.[27]

Today, connectivity and visibility are becoming much easier with the use of **cloud-based communication platforms**. Cloud systems provide greater visibility, ensure faster time to market, and offer faster response to changing market dynamics and demands. Another key benefit to the use of cloud-based communications is speed. Customers and suppliers can be up and running in minutes to days, not months to years. California-based Del Monte Foods, one of the largest producers, distributors, and marketers of branded food and pet products for the U.S. retail market, enhanced its global supply chain operating platform by using a cloud-based service. Del Monte automated its inventory and document management processes with its international suppliers using a cloud-based system hosted by GT Nexus.[28]

As businesses expand their supply chains to accommodate foreign suppliers and markets, and as outsourcing of manufacturing and logistics services continues, the need to use systems that provide real-time information to trading partners increases. "It's not good enough to just take the order," says Beth Enslow of Massachusetts-based research company Aberdeen Group. "Now you have to provide a continuous stream of information about its status, feasibility, and total cost to customers and partners throughout the world. You don't want customers receiving unexpected transportation expenses or delays in shipments—or worse, receiving them without you knowing about it."[29]

RFID tags, as mentioned earlier, can be used to improve information visibility in supply chains. With the right equipment, users can determine the exact location of any product, anywhere in a supply chain, at any time. An RFID tag attached to an automobile seat or engine, for example, can be used to gather and exchange work-in-process data. Or, when a shipment of flowers drops below a safe temperature, an RFID system can alert packers to pull those cartons and send them to a closer destination. When a thief tries to break into a shipping container, an RFID-controlled monitor can send an alert to company representatives. These are all applications of RFID technology. "When you have bad data, you make bad decisions," says Kaushal Vyas, director of product development at Georgia-based Infor, a business software provider. "You must be able to source and mine data from all the different places in real time, so you can focus on the exceptions that you need to manage in order to boost your performance."[30]

Lack of Trust

Successful process integration between trading partners requires trust, and as with the silo mentality and lack of information visibility, lack of trust is seen as a major stumbling block to process integration in supply chains. Trust develops over time between trading partners, as each organization follows through on promises made to the other firms. Even though this sounds cliché, relationships employing trust result in a win-win or win-win-win situation for the participants.

Unfortunately, old-fashioned company practices and purchasing habits don't change overnight. Until managers understand that it is in their firms' best interests to trust each other and collaborate, supply chain management will be an uphill battle. Organizations such as the medical treatment innovator Mayo Clinic build a collaborative culture by hiring professionals with collaborative attitudes and a common set of deeply held values regarding care for patients. At computing giant IBM, CEO Sam Palmisano transformed an extremely hierarchical culture based on individualism to one of collaboration by organizing online, town hall-type meetings involving tens of thousands of IBM employees and dozens of trading partners. Collaborative projects resulted from these meetings. IBM reinforced collaboration with "thanks awards," which are T-shirts, backpacks, and other similar gear emblazoned with the IBM logo and given by IBM employees.[31]

Some useful advice for creating collaboration and trust is summed up nicely in an article appearing in *CIO* magazine, a business journal for IT and other business executives. They recommended six ways of "getting to yes":[32]

1. *Start small*—Begin by collaborating on a small scale. Pick a project that is likely to provide a quick return on investment for both sides. Once you can show the benefits of trust and collaboration, then move to larger projects.

2. *Look inward*—The necessary precondition for establishing trust with outside partners is establishing trust with internal constituents. Break down the barriers to internal communication and integration.

3. *Gather 'round*—The best way to build trust is to meet face-to-face, around a table. Listen to objections, find out the agendas, and spring for lunch. Then do it all over again as people leave and as management changes.

4. *Go for the win-win*—Collaboration is a new way of doing business where the biggest companies don't bully their partners, but instead help create an environment that optimizes business for all supply chain members.

5. *Don't give away the store*—No one has to share all of their information. Some information should remain proprietary. The simple exchange of demand, purchase, and forecast information goes a long way.

6. *Just do it*—One of the best ways to build trust is to simply start sharing information. If all goes well, then success breeds trust, allowing partners to progress to bigger things.

Lack of Knowledge

Companies have been slowly moving toward collaboration and process integration for years, and it is just within the past few years that technology has caught up with this vision, enabling process integration across extended supply chains. Getting a network of firms and their employees to work together successfully, though, requires managers to use subtle persuasion and education to get their own firms and their trading partners to do the right things. The cultural, trust, and process knowledge differences in firms are such that firms successfully managing their supply chains must spend significant time influencing and increasing the capabilities of their own employees as well as those of their trading partners.

Training of supply chain partner employees is also known as **collaborative education** and can result in more successful supply chains and higher partner returns. As technologies change, as outsourcing increases, and as supply chains are expanded to foreign sources and markets, the pressure to extend software and management training to trading partners increases. As Rick Behrens, senior manager of supplier development at Boeing Company's Integrated Defense Systems unit, explains, "We look at our suppliers as an extension of Boeing. So since we invest heavily in training and education of our employees, why wouldn't we invest in education and development for our suppliers?" Farm and construction equipment manufacturer John Deere, for example, has established a global learning and development center specifically for training its key suppliers.[33]

Change and information sharing can be threatening to people; they may fear losing control or losing their job, particularly if outsourcing accompanies process integration. Additionally, as firms construct their supply chain information infrastructure, they may find themselves with multiple ERP systems with various software applications that all need to be integrated both internally and externally. Thus, firms must realize that people using the systems should be involved early on in terms of the purchase decision, the implementation process, and training.

For all organizations, successful supply chain management requires a regimen of ongoing training. When education and training are curtailed, innovation cannot occur, and innovation fuels supply chain competitiveness. Poor decision-making and other human errors can have a rippling effect in supply chains, causing loss of confidence and trust, and a magnification of the error and correction cost as it moves through the supply chain. Industry trade shows, conferences, and expos such as the Sensors Expo and Conference, the Annual Institute for Supply Management Conference, or the GSI Connect Conference can also be valuable sources of learning, exchanging ideas, and gathering new information about supply chain management.[34]

Activities Causing the Bullwhip Effect

As discussed in Chapter 1 of this text, the **bullwhip effect** can be a pervasive and expensive problem along supply chains and is caused by a number of factors that supply chain members can control. Recall that even though end item demand may be relatively constant, forecasts of trading partner demand, additions of safety stock, and the corresponding orders to suppliers as they are traced back up the supply chain can become amplified, causing what is termed the bullwhip effect. These amplified demand levels cause problems with capacity planning, inventory control, and workforce and production scheduling, and ultimately result in lower levels of customer service, greater overall levels of safety stock, and higher total supply chain costs. In an early publication on the bullwhip effect, Dr. Hau Lee and his associates identified four major causes of the bullwhip effect. More recently, Dr. Lee commented that the economic downturn a few years ago caused a number of bullwhips to again emerge, but that firms could still "tame the bullwhip" with hard work, understanding the causes of demand, gaining visibility, and investing in *collaboration* with partners.[35] The causes of the bullwhip effect and the methods used to counteract it are discussed below.

Demand Forecast Updating

Whenever a buying firm places a purchase order, its supplier uses that information as a predictor of future demand. Based on this information, suppliers update their demand forecasts, which then impact orders placed with their suppliers. If lead times grow between orders placed and deliveries, then safety stocks also grow and impact purchase orders as well, which adds to the bullwhip effect. Thus, fluctuations are magnified as orders vary from period to period, and as the review periods change, causing frequent **demand forecast updating**. These are major contributors to the bullwhip effect.

One solution to this problem is for the buyer to make its actual demand data available to its suppliers. (Recall from Chapter 5 that this activity is part of a collaborative planning, forecasting, and replenishment effort.) Better yet, if all point-of-sale data are made available to the upstream tiers of suppliers, all supply chain members can then update their demand forecasts less frequently, using actual demand data. This real demand information also tends to reduce safety stocks among supply chain members, generating even less variability in supply chain orders. Thus, the importance of supply chain information visibility can again be seen.

Using the same forecasting techniques and buying practices also tends to smooth demand variabilities among supply chain members. In many cases, buyers allow some of their suppliers to observe actual demand, create a forecast, and determine their resupply schedules—a practice known as vendor managed inventory (discussed in Chapters 3 and 4). This practice can generally reduce inventories substantially.

Reducing the length of the supply chain can also lessen the bullwhip effect by reducing the number of occasions where forecasts are calculated and safety stocks are added. Examples of this are Drugstore.com, Amazon.com, and other firms that bypass distributors and resellers and sell directly to consumers. Firms can thus see actual end-customer demand, resulting in much more stable and accurate forecasts.

Finally, reducing the lead times from order to delivery will lessen the bullwhip effect. For example, developing just-in-time ordering and delivery capabilities results in smaller, more frequent orders being placed and delivered, which more closely matches supply to demand patterns, thus decreasing the need for safety stocks.

Order Batching

In a typical buyer–supplier scenario, demand draws down existing inventories until a reorder point is reached wherein the buyer places an order with the supplier. Inventory levels, prior delivery performance, and the desire to order full truckloads or container loads of materials may cause orders to be placed at varying time intervals. Thus, the supplier receives an order of some magnitude; then at some indeterminate future time period, another order is received from the buyer, for some quantity potentially much different in size from the prior order. This causes the supplier to hold extra safety stock. Thus, **order batching** tends to amplify demand variability, which creates greater use of safety stock, again causing the bullwhip effect.

Another type of order batching can occur when salespeople need to fill end-of-quarter or end-of-year sales quotas, or when buyers desire to fully spend budget allocations at the end of their fiscal year. Striving to meet sales quotas and making excess purchases to spend budget money causes erratic surges in consumption and production, causing, you guessed it, the bullwhip effect. If the timing of these surges is the same for many of the firm's customers, the resulting bullwhip effect can be severe.

As with forecast updating, more information visibility and frequent and smaller order sizes will reduce the order batching problem. When suppliers know that large orders are occurring because of the need to spend budgeted monies, for instance, they will not revise forecasts based on this information. Further, when using automated or computer-assisted order systems, order costs are reduced, allowing firms to order more frequently. To counteract the need to order full truckloads or container loads of an item, firms can order smaller quantities of a variety of items from a supplier, or use a freight forwarder to consolidate small shipments, to avoid the high unit cost of transporting at less-than-truckload or less-than-container load quantities.

Price Fluctuations

When suppliers offer special promotions, quantity discounts, or other special discounts, these pricing fluctuations result in significant **forward buying** activities on the part of buyers, who "stock up" to take advantage of the low-price offers. Forward buying can occur between retailers and consumers, between distributors and retailers, and between manufacturers and distributors due to pricing promotions at each stage in a supply chain, all contributing to erratic buying patterns, lower forecast accuracies, and consequently the bullwhip effect. If these pricing promotions become commonplace, customers will stop buying when prices are undiscounted and buy only when the discount prices are offered, even further contributing to the bullwhip effect. To deal with these surges in demand, manufacturers may have to vary capacity by scheduling overtime and undertime for employees, finding places to store stockpiles of inventory, paying more for transportation, and dealing with higher levels of inventory shrinkage as inventories are held for longer periods.

The obvious way to reduce the problems caused by fluctuating prices is to eliminate price discounting among a supply chain's members. Manufacturers can reduce forward buying by offering uniform wholesale prices to their customers. Many retailers have adopted this notion, termed **everyday low pricing (EDLP)**, while eliminating promotions that cause forward buying. Similarly, buyers can negotiate with their own suppliers to offer EDLP. Big box retailer Target, for example, did not have a great year financially, in 2016. In a conference call following the release of its weaker-than-expected financial results for fiscal 2016, Brian Cornell, Target's CEO explained, "We spent a lot of time looking at the changes we had made following the [data breach of 2013], and we were very promotional, and that promotional intensity has continued. In 2017, you will see us getting back to our roots, getting back to establishing everyday low pricing in those essential categories."[36]

Rationing and Shortage Gaming

Rationing can occur when demand exceeds a supplier's finished goods available—in other words, the supplier might allocate units of product in proportion to what buyers ordered. Thus, if the supply on-hand is 75 percent of total demand, buyers would be allocated 75 percent of what they ordered. When buyers figure out the relationship between their orders and what is supplied, they inflate their orders to satisfy their real needs. This strategy is known as **shortage gaming**. Of course, this further exacerbates the supply problem, as the supplier and, in turn, its suppliers, struggle to keep up with these higher demand levels. When, on the other hand, production capacity eventually equals demand and orders are filled completely, orders suddenly drop to less than normal levels as the buying firms try to unload their excess inventories. This has occurred occasionally in the United States and elsewhere around the world—for instance, with gasoline supply shortages, and in 2012 with Hostess Twinkies. As soon as consumers think a gasoline shortage is looming, demand suddenly increases as people top off their tanks and otherwise try to stockpile gasoline, which itself creates a deeper shortage. In December 2012, when Hostess Brands entered Chapter 7 liquidation, it set off a period of mass panic as fans of Twinkies, Ding Dongs, and other Hostess baked goods flew off shelves.[37] When these types of shortages occur due to shortage gaming, suppliers can no longer discern their customers' true demand, and this can result in unnecessary additions to production capacity, warehouse space, and transportation costs.

One way to eliminate shortage gaming is for sellers to allocate short supplies based on the demand histories of their customers and not their customers' orders. In that way, customers are essentially not allowed to exaggerate orders. And once again, the sharing of capacity and inventory information between a manufacturer and its customers can also help to eliminate customers' fears regarding shortages and eliminate gaming. Also, sharing future order plans with suppliers allows suppliers to increase capacity if needed, thus avoiding a rationing situation.

Thus, it is seen that a number of decisions on the part of buyers and suppliers can cause the bullwhip effect in supply chains. When trading partners use the strategies discussed above to reduce the bullwhip effect, the growth of information sharing, collaboration, and process integration occurs along supply chains. Firms that strive to share data, forecasts, plans, and other information can significantly reduce the bullwhip effect.

MANAGING SUPPLY CHAIN RISK AND SECURITY

As supply chains grow to include more foreign suppliers and customers, there is a corresponding growth in supply chain disruptions caused by weather and traffic delays, infrastructural problems, political problems, and fears of, or actual, unlawful or terrorist-related activities. For example, in just the last few years there have been civil rights protests across the United States, major flooding in Beijing, China, the ransomware cyberattacks that hit dozens of countries across Europe, Asia, and the United States, typhoon Nepartak in Taiwan and China, earthquakes in the Philippines, and numerous commercial airline crashes and suicide bombings. Besides the obvious impact on life and limb, these events add elements of financial, reputation, and customer service risk to global supply chains and the need for enhanced planning, change management, and security to mitigate that risk.

So, while lengthening supply chains may have resulted in cheaper labor and material costs, better product quality, and greater market coverage, it has also resulted in higher security costs and greater levels of risk, potentially leading to deteriorating profits and customer service levels. Managing risk and security along the supply chain is discussed in detail below.

Managing Supply Chain Risk

Recall from Chapter 1 that **supply chain risk** is defined as the likelihood of an internal or external event that disrupts supply chain operations, causing potential reductions in service levels, product quality, and sales, along with an increase in costs. According to the Chartered Institute of Procurement & Supply Risk Index, powered by Dun & Bradstreet, global supply chain risk is increasing, which has been a trend since the global recession in 2009. "The fourth quarter of 2015 was dominated by non-economic news, such as the Paris terror attacks and the continued refugee inflows into Europe, combined with the increased political resistance and sometimes controversial measures aimed at curtailing these inflows," explained Oana Aristide, acting global leader at Dun & Bradstreet. These and other indicators point to the fact that as more and more firms penetrate new and emerging markets, supply chain risk, particularly in these areas, is increasing.[38]

Information technology advances, for example, have made cyberattacks more and more common. "Obviously, hackers and intruders can also affect the availability of a system, and that can come from any angle," says Thomas Srail, senior vice president at FINEX North America, a risk advisement service. Linda Conrad, director of strategic business risk for Zurich Global Corporate, says the effect from hackers getting access to companies' data along their supply chains can cause the loss of the data itself, reputation damage, regulatory issues, and fines. Zurich's disruption database shows that 52 percent of supply chain disruptions in a one-year period resulted from information technology or communications outages between buyer and supplier.[39]

Tom Ridge, the former governor of Pennsylvania, former secretary of Homeland Security in the United States and now CEO of risk management consulting firm Ridge Global, says that supply chains need to be vetted down to the second, third, and fourth tiers. No multinational firm ". . . can afford to let anybody in the supply chain, no matter how far removed, and view risk less seriously than it does," he says. The 2010 BP oil disaster in the Gulf of Mexico is a good example. Transocean was the oil rig operator, a supplier for BP in this case. Based on the finger-pointing in that disaster, Transocean was at least partially responsible for the explosion, rig destruction, worker deaths, and oil well blowout. If communication and due diligence can break down as badly as it did between BP and one of its primary direct suppliers, consider the potential financial, reputation, and customer service risks posed by the many second- and third-tier suppliers.[40]

A number of steps have been suggested for managing supply chain risk, and several good examples exist that highlight successful supply chain risk management. Table 13.3 describes a number of risk management activities, and they are discussed next.

Increase Safety Stocks and Forward Buying

If the firm fears a supply disruption, it may choose to carry some level of safety stock to provide the desired product until a suitable substitute supply source can be found. If the purchased item is readily available from other sources, the desired level of safety stock may be relatively small. On the other hand, if the item is scarce, if the supply disruption is likely to be lengthy, or if the firm fears a continued and lengthy price increase, it may decide to purchase large quantities of product, also known as forward buying. Safety stocks and forward buying should only be viewed as temporary solutions since they can dramatically increase inventory carrying costs, particularly for firms with large numbers of purchased items.

In some cases, though, forward buying may be viewed as the only short-term solution for managing risk. In 2006, many organizations opted to stockpile the influenza drug Tamiflu to prepare for a potential avian influenza pandemic, since shortages of the drug worldwide had already been experienced. In the United States, for example, 300 firms along with the federal government itself had already been engaged in significant stockpiling by the summer of 2006. After that period, as supplies of antiviral drugs increased, the practice of forward buying decreased.[42]

Table 13.3	Activities Used to Manage Supply Chain Risk[41]
RISK MANAGEMENT ACTIVITY	**DESCRIPTION**
Increase safety stocks and forward buying	Can be costly. A stopgap alternative.
Identify backup suppliers and logistics services	Can create ill will with current partners; requires additional time and relationship building.
Diversify the supply base	Use of suppliers from geographically dispersed markets to minimize the impacts of disruptions.
Utilize a supply chain IT system	Collection and sharing of appropriate information with supply chain partners.
Develop a formal risk management program	Identifies potential disruptions and the appropriate response.

Identify Backup Suppliers and Logistics Services

Another very simple strategy for guaranteeing a continuous supply of purchased items and logistics services is to identify suppliers, transportation and warehousing services, and other third-party services to use in case the preferred supplier or service becomes unavailable. This topic was discussed in relation to the use of sole or single sources in Chapter 2. The disadvantage of this strategy is that it requires additional time to find and qualify sources and to build trusting relationships. Additionally, this strategy may tend to damage existing supplier or logistics provider relationships. The backup source may see limited value in the relationship if they are providing only a small percentage of total demand; their price for the goods or services will likely be higher, and the existing firm may view the use of backup companies as a signal that their "piece of the pie" will continue to shrink. Additionally, use of multiple sources may allow proprietary designs or technologies to be copied, creating further risk.

Backup or **emergency sourcing** and multiple sourcing, though, may be a sound strategy in specific cases. During the 2002 U.S. West Coast dockworker strikes, airfreight capacity quickly ran out, causing freight rates to skyrocket and firms to be unable to quickly move freight. Companies that had already entered into contracts for emergency airfreight service, though, were able to maintain operations during the port disruptions.[43] Sainsbury's, a U.K. supermarket chain, uses multiple suppliers for the many products it buys as part of its business continuity plan, established in response to events such as the Irish Republican Army's bombing campaigns in the 1990s, the Y2K computer bug, a 2001 fuel shortage, and various foot-and-mouth cattle disease outbreaks in the United Kingdom. Additionally, Sainsbury's works closely with key suppliers to ensure that they, too, have business continuity plans.[44]

Diversify the Supply Base

Madagascar, one-time provider of half of the world's vanilla supply, saw cyclone Hudah destroy 30 percent of its vanilla bean vines in 2000. Additionally, a political problem in Madagascar caused its primary port to be closed for many weeks in 2002. These two events caused vanilla prices to skyrocket for an extended period of time until growers in Madagascar and other countries could increase their production. Buyers with vanilla supply contracts in multiple countries were able to avoid some of this pricing problem. Eventually, the market for vanilla became more diversified, creating a situation whereby vanilla buyers today have multiple vanilla sources outside of Madagascar.[45] The supply of liquid natural gas, LNG, is at risk, since much of the supply of LNG comes from production plants in Arabian Gulf countries and Russia. LNG consumers are thus busy trying to diversify their purchases of LNG from other countries such as Norway, Algeria, and Libya. Further, new plans for construction of LNG shipping and receiving facilities, additional LNG vessels, and LNG regasification facilities will eventually allow for diversification of LNG supply and transportation services.[46] An earthquake and tsunami in Japan in 2011 halted automobile and parts production at a number of the country's manufacturing plants. In India, for example, Suzuki and Honda production and retail facilities had to cease operations for a time, since their Japanese parent companies and parts suppliers sustained damage from the tsunami.[47]

In all of the examples above, concentrating purchases with one supplier was seen as increasing supply risk, while purchasing the same or similar products from geographically dispersed suppliers could have the effect of spreading and hence reducing the risk of supply disruptions from political upheavals, weather-related disasters, and other widespread supply problems. Buyers, though, must also consider the impact of a geographically dispersed supply base on other supply chain risks. While potentially reducing the risk associated with geographic supply disruptions, the use of suppliers in multiple countries exposes buyers to additional political, customs clearance, exchange rate, and security risks.

Utilize a Supply Chain IT System

Chapter 6 discussed the importance of supply chain communication and information systems. As firms geographically expand their supply chains, they find customs clearance requirements and paperwork becoming increasingly complicated. Complying with these regulations requires information and data visibility among supply chain participants and involvement by all key supply chain partners. Accurate data transmissions can aid in the reduction of stockouts and the bullwhip effect caused by forecasting and order inaccuracies and late deliveries, which also pose significant risks and costs to supply chains.

Information systems should be designed to help mitigate supply chain risk. As stated by Julian Thomas, head of the supply chain advisory department at global auditing and advisory firm KPMG, "Risk should be on the agenda and as you build your systems, you need to put in place systems to monitor and evaluate risk continuously."[48] Farm and ranch equipment retailer Tractor Supply, headquartered in Tennessee, is a good example of a firm making use of information technologies to support flexible and quick decision-making to reduce risk. For example, they use an on-demand transportation management system (TMS), an ERP system, and a voice-picking solution for their distribution centers. "In 2005, transportation capacity was really tight after Hurricane Katrina hit, but the way our TMS is configured we have the ability to escalate carrier service from low-cost to high-cost providers and sometimes when all the carriers in a market were taken, we had to take carriers in from another market," says Mike Graham, vice president of logistics at Tractor Supply. "We also have the flexibility within our DC network to react quickly if there is an event and move stores from one DC to another."[49] In the nearby SCM Profile, Jabil Circuit describes the design and use of its supply chain disruption platform.

Develop a Formal Risk Management Program

By far the most proactive risk management activity is to create a formal risk management plan encompassing the firm and its supply chain participants. Risk management should become an executive-level priority. Potential risks should be identified and prioritized, and appropriate responses should be designed that will minimize disruptions to supply chains. Additionally, mechanisms should be developed to recover quickly, efficiently, and with minimal damage to the firm's reputation and customer relationships. Finally, performance measures need to be developed to monitor the firm's ongoing risk management capabilities. "Risk happens," says Dr. Kate Vitasek, supply chain faculty member at the University of Tennessee. "Plan for it. Collaborate with your partners in the supply chain to mitigate and eliminate it, and don't bury your head in the sand."[51]

A supply chain risk management office should be created to oversee and coordinate the firm's risk management efforts. The risk manager provides guidance and support to department managers, is the interface between the firm and its trading partner risk managers, and possesses the knowledge to adequately identify, prioritize, and provide a plan to reduce risks. In 2005, Tractor Supply, for example, developed a disaster recovery plan as part of its overall risk management strategy. One year later, its Waco, Texas, distribution center was struck by a tornado in the evening, leaving 2 to 3 inches of water standing in the facility and product scattered across the landscape for miles. By the time logistics VP Mike Graham made it to his office the next day, plans were already in place to repair the damage, and within several hours all of the customers served by the Waco distribution center were linked to other facilities. "We did not miss a delivery the following week and May is actually a peak season for us," said Mr. Graham.[52]

SCM Profile — Jabil's Supply Chain Risk Platform

In 2012, the logistics and supply team at Florida-based manufacturer Jabil Circuit started thinking about how it could make its global supply chain more efficient by protecting against supply chain disruptions while products and information flowed from supplier to manufacturer to distributor to end user. Realizing that Excel spreadsheets weren't going to cut it, Jabil set out to build a supply chain risk platform, by tapping the collective knowledge of its managers and employees and exploring the functional areas contributing to its overall supply chain.

Within three months, the company had a product that was proving its worth across five key areas: revenue, profitability, cash flow, working capital, and service levels. The platform enabled advanced planning and helped Jabil Circuit identify changes in demand and then adjust operations accordingly. The company was able to more efficiently utilize and allocate inventory. Based on this information, Jabil invested millions to build the second version on a commercial platform.

To date, the company has been able to reduce its inventory costs by more than $300 million, or 13 percent and improve its customer service levels by 20 percent, by proactively protecting against supply chain disruptions. The platform also lets customers optimize Jabil's significant manufacturing and distribution footprint to minimize their own total costs.

Following the 2015 explosions at the container storage station at the Port of Tianjin in China, for example, Jabil quickly identified which of its suppliers were within a 150-mile radius of the explosions. Using its supply chain visibility platform, the company could view in-transit inventories and the potential impact of supply disruptions. "We had all of this information within minutes and immediately started working on alternative sourcing strategies," says Fred Hartung, vice president of supply chain and global logistics for Jabil "whereas with most companies, it takes about three to four weeks to fully understand that picture."[50]

Richard Sharman, a partner in KPMG's risk advisory services group, offers his advice for developing risk management plans—"Companies almost need to ask themselves the stupid questions to think about the full spectrum of business risks, and how they would manage them," he says. Another consideration is to know who the firm is doing business with, to assure they are using an appropriate labor force, complying with product safety guidelines, and generally using practices that fit with the firm's reputation. "Know your partner. There is no substitute for that," says Brian Joseph, partner at global business consultant PricewaterhouseCoopers.[53] When outsourcing to firms in foreign locales, it is also necessary to have adequate quality controls in place, and require suppliers to report periodically to the firm to ensure their products meet design requirements.

Managing Supply Chain Security

As supply chains become more global and technologically complex, so does the need to secure them. **Supply chain security management** is concerned with reducing the risk and impacts of intentionally created disruptions in supply chain operations including product and information theft and activities seeking to endanger personnel or sabotage supply chain infrastructure. The crash of Pan Am Flight 103 in Lockerbie, Scotland, in 1988 not only tragically illustrated the weaknesses of airline security systems at the time but also exposed the dependency of entire supply chains on each member's security capabilities.

Pan Am's security processes did not fail in permitting a bomb onto Flight 103—it was actually Malta's Luqa Airport's security system that allowed the luggage carrying the bomb into the baggage handling system that eventually led to the luggage being flown on an aircraft to London where it was then placed aboard Flight 103.[54] In the United States, the attacks of September 11, 2001, were a wakeup call to many businesses to begin assessing their needs for supply chain security systems. Prior to that time, most executives were aware that their operations might be vulnerable to security problems; however, most firms (as well as governments) chose to put off improving security practices.

The notion that a supply chain is only as secure as its weakest link is illustrated in the Pan Am example above. It is therefore necessary today for firms to manage not only their own security but also the security practices of their supply chain partners. Supply chain security, though, is an extremely complex problem—security activities begin at the factory where goods are packaged and loaded, and then include the logistics companies transporting goods to ports, the port terminals and customs workers, the ocean carriers, the destination ports and customs workers, additional transportation companies, distribution centers and workers, and the final delivery companies. And integrating all of these participants are various information systems that also need to be protected.

Security management collaboration should include, for example, contractual requirements for secure systems, "standards of care" for movement and storage of products as they move along the supply chain, and the use of law enforcement officials or consultants in security planning, training, and incident investigation. James G. Liddy, internationally recognized expert on security, CEO of Virginia-based security firm Liddy International, and the son of famous Watergate burglar and talk-show host G. Gordon Liddy, says, "Focus on what your real vulnerabilities are and have in place a safety-and-preparedness plan for all hazards. When you enhance your safety procedures and integrate them into your security you create efficiencies."[55] Table 13.4 describes four increasing levels of supply chain security system preparedness, and these are discussed below.

Basic Initiatives

At the most basic level, security systems should include procedures and policies for securing offices, manufacturing plants, warehouses, and other physical facilities and additionally should provide security for personnel, computing systems, and freight shipments. Managers should consider use of security badges and guards, conducting background checks on applicants, using antivirus software and passwords, and using shipment-tracking technologies.

Table 13.4	Supply Chain Security System Response[56]
LEVEL OF SECURITY SYSTEM RESPONSE	**DESCRIPTION**
Basic initiatives	Physical security measures, personnel security, standard risk assessment, basic computing security, continuity plan, freight protection.
Reactive initiatives	Larger security organization, C-TPAT compliance, supply base analysis, supply continuity plan, limited training.
Proactive initiatives	Director of security, personnel with military or government experience, formal security risk assessment, advanced computing security, participation in security groups.
Advanced initiatives	Customer/supplier collaboration; learning from the past; formal security strategy; supply chain drills, simulations, and exercises; emergency control center.

Today, cargo theft is one of the biggest problems facing global supply chains, and some of the basic security approaches can be used to reduce this threat. Global loss estimates are tagged at $10 billion to $30 billion per year. And technology and lack of downside risk have enabled thieves to be more sophisticated and daring than ever before. Stolen goods can be moved to a warehouse, off-loaded, repackaged, remanifested, and placed on another vehicle before the theft is even discovered and reported. The existence of online marketers and auction sites even further facilitates the movement and sale of stolen merchandise.[57] Food and beverage items are frequently being targeted by cargo thieves, according to U.S. cargo consulting firm CargoNet. In terms of the most stolen types of products, food and beverages topped the list in 2016, with the electronics industry running a close second. The average monetary loss is more than $200,000. One reason foodstuffs are being stolen more frequently is that they are easy to resell, especially in the case of brand-name products, and their resale value is very high, around 70 cents on the dollar.[58]

Corruption is another potential problem organizations must begin to manage. Transparency International, a global group leading the fight against corruption, annually publishes its Corruption Perceptions Index to publicize the degree of corruption existing in a number of countries. The scale ranges from 0 (highly corrupt) to 100 (no corruption). The index combines multiple surveys of public sector employees' perceptions of the level of corruption in their countries. In 2016, the global average score was an alarmingly low 43. The United Kingdom, Japan, and the United States ranked tenth, eighteenth, and twentieth, respectively. Denmark, New Zealand, and Finland continue to be the top-rated countries, while North Korea, South Sudan, and Somalia were at the bottom of the 176-country list. More countries declined than improved from 2015, showing the urgent need for committed action to thwart corruption. "In too many countries, people are deprived of their most basic needs and go to bed hungry every night because of corruption, while the powerful and corrupt enjoy lavish lifestyles with impunity," says José Ugaz, chair of Transparency International.[59]

Reactive Initiatives

Reactive security initiatives represent a somewhat deeper commitment to the idea of security management compared to basic initiatives, but still lack any significant efforts to organize a cohesive and firm-wide plan for security management. Many firms in this category, for example, implemented security systems in response to the terrorist attacks of September 11, 2001. These initiatives include becoming Customs-Trade Partnership Against Terrorism (C-TPAT) compliant, assessing suppliers' security practices, developing continuity plans for various events, and implementing specific training and education programs.

C-TPAT compliance refers to a partnership among U.S. Customs, the International Cargo Security Council (a U.S. nonprofit association of companies and individuals involved in transportation), and Pinkerton (a global security advising company, headquartered in New Jersey), whereby companies agree to improve security in their supply chain in return for "fast lane" border crossings at both the U.S./Canadian and U.S./Mexican borders. This includes conducting self-assessments of the firm's and its partner facilities and updating security policies to meet C-TPAT security requirements, and then completing a C-TPAT application. As of the end of 2016, there were about 11,400 C-TPAT-certified companies. U.S. Customs and Border Protection states that nonparticipants are about six times more likely to receive a security-related container inspection at U.S. border crossings.[60] The U.S. government is currently working with other countries to implement similar programs.

A number of other government initiatives also fall into the reactive category, such as the "10+2" or Importer Security Filing rule that requires a 48-hour notice for all ocean shipping containers coming into the United States and the Certified Cargo Screening Program (CCSP) regarding all air cargo loaded onto planes in the United States—starting in 2010, all air cargo originating in the United States must be screened the same way as passenger luggage.[61]

Proactive Initiatives

Proactive security management initiatives venture outside the firm to include suppliers and customers, and also include a more formalized approach to security management within the firm. Security activities occurring among firms in this category include the creation of an executive-level position such as director of corporate security; the hiring of former military, intelligence, or law enforcement personnel with security management experience; a formal and comprehensive approach for assessing the firm's exposure to security risks; the use of cyberintrusion detection systems and other advanced information security practices; the development of freight security plans in collaboration with 3PLs; and the active participation of employees in industry security associations and conferences. Home Depot, for example, uses a computer risk modeling approach to assess its supply chains' vulnerabilities and design appropriate security measures. "We look at 35 global risk elements and one of those is threat of terrorism," explains Benjamin Cook, senior manager for global trade service for Home Depot. "We use that technique to help us roll out a strategy that is most appropriate to the country we are sourcing from."[62]

Massachusetts-based life insurance company MassMutual wanted to ensure the security of its IT system, spread across a dozen applications, including its website as well as the 12 million business and individual customer accounts it managed. It named a vice president of information security to direct its information security efforts, and it put in place a fifty-person security group that included an internal consulting team with specific security item experts, an engineering team that supported firewalls, a security assurance team that analyzed security monitoring devices, and a team responsible for identity management. Finally, it purchased a security management software application to help its security team quickly assess and prioritize risks. It creates an aggregate risk score for each application and system it uses to determine which risks need to be addressed first.[63]

Advanced Initiatives

Firms with advanced security management systems are recognized as industry leaders with respect to their security initiatives. Activities within this category include full collaboration with key suppliers and customers in developing quick recovery and continuity plans for supply chain disruptions, consideration of past security failures of other firms in developing a more comprehensive and effective security system, the design of a complete supply chain security management plan that is implemented by all key trading partners, the undertaking of exercises designed to train participants and test the resilience of the supply chain to security disruptions, and the use of an emergency control center to manage responses to unexpected supply chain disruptions.

Industry security leaders, such as Michigan-based Dow Chemical, see supply chain security as simply good business. According to Henry Ward, director of transportation security and safety at Dow, "We view security as one of the steps we take to make sure we remain a reliable supplier of goods to the marketplace." Dow's efforts to improve supply chain visibility and security led to a 50 percent improvement in the time it takes to identify and resolve trade transit problems, and a 20 percent inventory reduction at receiving terminals. Dow uses RFID and a global positioning system (GPS) to track large intermodal containers as they move from North America to Asia. Dow also sees collaboration with governments and its supply chain partners as crucial to its success. "We take an integrated approach to supply chain security, which means we look at it holistically," says Ward.[64]

As described in this final section, supply chain participants are pulled by opposing objectives—one is to reduce supply chain costs and improve freight handling speed to improve competitiveness and profits; the other is to manage the risk and cost of security breaches. Unfortunately, as supply chains venture into countries in search of cheaper suppliers or new markets, or make logistics changes to reduce transit times, the security risks grow. Managers and government representatives understand the problem much better, though, today than ten years ago, and hopefully, this is leading to better management of risk and security.

SUMMARY

In this chapter, the topic of integrating processes within the firm and among supply chain partners was discussed, including the steps required to achieve internal and external process integration, the advantages integration, as well as the obstacles to overcome. Process integration should be considered the primary means to achieving successful supply chain management and it is the one thing firms struggle with most when setting out to manage their supply chains. Without the proper support, training, tools, trust, and preparedness, process integration most likely will be impossible to ever fully achieve.

The supply chain integration model provides the framework for integrating processes first within the firm and then among trading partners, and this model served as the foundation of the chapter. The role played by performance measures in assessing and improving integration was also discussed. Finally, a discussion of supply chain risk and security management outlined the need for firms and their trading partners to collaborate in developing effective strategies for assessing the risk of supply chain disruptions and implementing solutions.

KEY TERMS

active RFID tags, 514

bullwhip effect, 519

cloud-based communication platforms, 517

collaborative education, 518

C-TPAT compliance, 528

customer relationship management process, 506

data warehouses, 511

demand forecast updating, 519

demand management process, 507

emergency sourcing, 524

everyday low pricing (EDLP), 521

forward buying, 521

functional silos, 505

information visibility, 516

internal supply chains, 511

key supply chain processes, 505

key trading partners, 503

knowledge management solutions, 513

legacy systems, 511

manufacturing flow management process, 507

order batching, 520

order fulfillment process, 507

passive RFID tags, 514

process integration, 502

process, 505

product development and commercialization process, 509

radio-frequency identification tag (RFID), 513

rationing, 521

returns management process, 509

shortage gaming, 521

silo mentality, 516

supplier relationship management process, 508

supply chain risk, 522

supply chain security management, 526

DISCUSSION QUESTIONS

1. What does process integration mean and why is it difficult to achieve?

2. What makes a supplier or customer a key or primary trading partner? Describe why it is important to begin supply chain management efforts with only these key companies.

3. Describe the linkage between supply chain strategies and internal functional strategies and policies.

4. How do functional silos prevent process integration?

5. What are the eight key supply chain business processes and why are they important when managing supply chains?

6. What is the difference between the customer service management process and the customer relationship management process?

7. Do you think customer service has improved over the years for retailers? Cite some examples.

8. What sort of demand management techniques would an exclusive restaurant use when demand exceeds its capacity? What about McDonald's?

9. Is it necessary to have internal performance measures for each of the supply chain business processes? Why or why not?

10. Which should come first—internal process integration or external process integration? Why?

11. Explain the differences between process integration, coordination, and collaboration.

12. Why is an ERP system important for both internal and external process integration? What other IT considerations are there?

13. Think of some supply chain (external) performance measures for several of the eight key supply chain business processes, assuming the overall strategy is superior customer service. What if the overall strategy is sustainability?

14. What is an internal supply chain? Do some firms not have any?

15. What are knowledge management solutions and how can they support a firm's supply chain integration efforts? Give some examples.

16. How do organizations extend process integration to second-tier suppliers and customers?

17. How can RFID tags help to enable external process integration?

18. What is the difference between active and passive RFID tags?

19. Why is lack of trust an obstacle to supply chain management? How can we overcome this obstacle?

20. Why is visibility so important when integrating processes?

21. Define the bullwhip effect and describe how it impacts supply chain integration, or how integration impacts the bullwhip effect.

22. What is cloud-based supply chain management and how might it impact process integration?

23. What is the difference between supply chain management and supply chain process integration?

24. Define the term "collaborative education" and explain what this has to do with supply chain management.

25. Describe an incidence either personally or at work where you have been involved in shortage gaming.

26. What is order batching and is this something that will reduce the bullwhip effect? Why or why not?

27. Why should reducing the length of the supply chain also reduce the bullwhip effect?

28. What is everyday low pricing and how does it impact the bullwhip effect?

29. Have you ever experienced rationing and/or shortage gaming? Please describe an instance.

30. What is the difference between supply chain risk management and supply chain security management? Which do you think is most important?

31. What do most small businesses do to reduce supply chain risk? Could they do something more effective?

32. In Chapters 3 and 4, it was explained how some firms were successfully single- or sole-sourcing. Doesn't this increase supply chain risk?

33. What types of supply chains are most likely to be impacted by risk and security problems? Why?

34. Which is more important—risk management or security management?

35. List some steps firms can take to reduce supply chain risk and increase security.

36. What is C-TPAT and which companies would benefit most from using it?

37. Explain why supply chain process management is so important to the success of supply chain trading partners.

ESSAY/PROJECT QUESTIONS

1. Go to the Institute for Supply Management website, www.ism.ws, and find the listing for the latest ISM Annual International Supply Management Conference. Then find the Conference Proceedings, and report on a paper that was presented regarding a topic covered in this chapter.

2. Find a company online that is successfully using internal and/or external process integration and report on its experiences.

3. Find the websites of several supply chain security and risk assessment firms and report on their specialties and management experience.

4. Search on the term "Customs-Trade Partnership Against Terrorism" or "C-TPAT," and write a paper on the history of C-TPAT and how it is being used today.

5. Search on the term "supply chain security problems" and write a report on several current problems and how they are being addressed.

CASES

1. 3D Printing: Will Additive Manufacturing Solve the Bullwhip Effect?*

Precision Parts (PP) was a traditional machine shop producing OEM parts for the construction equipment industry until 2017 when they began a transition to an additive manufacturer using state-of-the-art 3D printing. Early last year, two of Precision Parts' customers representing 35 percent of their revenue and 47 percent of their profit notified PP that orders for their industrial grade fasteners would be reduced by almost 75 percent. Both manufacturing companies explained a shift in their supplier pool as part of the reevaluation of parts supplier-partners in their second-tier integration efforts. Fortunately, the industrial fastener sales team had been working with Crane-Tech Manufacturing (C-TM) to include Precision Parts as one of their primary

*Written by Brian Hoyt, PhD, Professor of Management, Ohio University. This case was prepared solely to provide fictional material for class discussion. The author does not intend to illustrate either effective or ineffective handling of a managerial situation.

parts suppliers. Crane-Tech Manufacturing uses industrial fasteners for their OEM processes (crane equipment used in the construction industry) and for the aftermarket parts used for repair and replacement. The contract would triple orders and make up about 90 percent of the lost revenue. The contract was contingent on Precision Parts addressing the following requirements: collaborate in cost reduction practices in parts, inventory, and transportation; maintain adequate inventory of OEM parts and aftermarket parts for equipment sold in past 20 years; be responsive to on-demand order batches; and reduce lead times for parts.

In 2016, Precision Parts invested in three HP multijet fusion 4200 3D printers averaging $200,000 per printer. Each printer could produce the entire Precision Parts fastener line using digital designs and plastic materials. PP's R&D will field test and approve products for all required product specifications starting with products that Crane-Tech Manufacturing purchases. Precision Parts will be locating the three HP 3D printers in strategic decentralized locations in proximity to the three largest C-TM manufacturing facilities.

3D printing is an additive manufacturing process that produces three-dimensional objects from a digital file. A 3D printed item is manufactured by laying down successive layers of materials until the computer-generated designed product is produced. Materials used in 3D printing are much more diverse than metal machining and includes metals (aluminum, gold, silver, steel, etc.), ceramics, porcelain, plastic, acrylics, sandstone, and many other materials. 3D printing uses less material inputs and reduces material waste. 3D printed products can also use alternative materials and designs (i.e., honeycomb) that reduce weight and raw material costs. 3D printing can redesign parts to consolidate part and subassembly components. 3D printing design capability eliminates the need to develop and produce tooling required in more traditional machining operations. 3D printing's digital design and single-piece efficiencies are not negatively cost impacted at low production volumes. Lead times for low-volume 3D parts are significantly less than traditional machined parts with the quick cycle time from design to produced part. Make-to-order parts with quick changeovers will reduce labor costs and storage and handling as WIP and finished goods inventories become unnecessary. Waste at any time in the process can be recycled when 3D printing uses heat-processed recyclable plastics.

Crane-Tech Manufacturing invited Precision Parts to submit a bid to be approved in their Elite Supplier Program. Precision Parts' bid would focus on the key advantages to C-TM if they contracted with an additive manufacturer. PP would produce make-to-order parts that can be ordered, designed, produced, and shipped within three days and delivered next day if the digital design file is submitted with the order. Precision Parts will commit to a lead time of one-day production plus one-day delivery when an order from Crane-Tech Manufacturing is placed with notification dates ten days, three days, and one day before the parts need to be delivered to a C-TM facility. Industry lead-time standards are four weeks for CNC machined parts. Precision Parts' make-to-order capability will enable PP to produce newly designed parts for new equipment models. PP's additive manufacturing can produce parts for discontinued equipment (old models) as needed, rather than storing these in inventory. This feature will reduce the risk of obsolescence and replace the need to maintain adequate inventories for old equipment. Precision Parts' 3D printed parts can be used in prototypes and collaborative R&D with Crane-Tech Manufacturing, replacements for broken or worn machine parts, and as needed for production runs by C-TM's OEM facilities.

Discussion Questions

1. What are the challenges and benefits for Crane-Tech Manufacturing if they use Precision Parts' 3D printing capability to improve production of equipment and aftermarket parts orders for its customers?

2. How much warehouse space expansion should C-TM add to include the new 3D printed parts used for aftermarket sales?

3. Will the supply chain partnership with Precision Parts improve Crane-Tech Manufacturing's sustainable competitive advantage in the construction equipment and aftermarket parts industries?

©2019 Cengage Learning

2. Managing Supply Chain Security*

Warehouse Security Professionals (WSP) provides private security guards for warehouses, construction sites, and commercial properties. WSP has grown from a New England-based private security firm with 250 security guards to providing over 10,000 highly trained private security personnel on sites across the United States within just the last five years. Early in this rapid growth period, WSP was forced to address high turnover and costly liability insurance issues. With turnover almost twice the industry average and liability insurance costs increasing yearly, WSP developed a proprietary background check system named Secure Check. Secure Check uses an extensive screening process that includes application reviews and text analysis, interviews, criminal background checks, general background checks including social media searches, and integrates other streams of data that develop a "Best Performer Profile" using big data analytics. The initial impact of Secure Check for WSP was the improved quality of their new hires including advanced technology skills in monitoring and protection.

WSP's success in reducing turnover, employee theft, and insurance claims using Secure Check developed into a new revenue stream for WSP. They began marketing Secure Check to their existing customer base of warehouses, construction companies, and commercial and industrial complexes. The marketing team for Secure Check has recently been focusing on selling Secure Check to large manufacturers of consumer electronic products whose extensive supply chains include logistics and transportation, warehousing, wholesalers, third-party logistics firms, and retailers.

One consumer product manufacturer, Global Electronics (G-E), is developing their supply chain integration planning to integrate employee background check procedures across their supply chains as identified in their key process objectives for managing supply chain security. With the help of WSP's Secure Check implementation team, Global Electronics has developed internal performance security measures of turnover, theft, and insurance claim losses. They will use the next six months to assess and improve their internal integration for security measures. Upon completion of G-E's internal application of Secure Check, they will develop external supply chain security performance measures for their first-tier suppliers. As part of the assessment and improvement of supplier partners' security performance, Global Electronics will offer Secure Check to meet compliance with the new security performance targets.

---

*Written by Brian Hoyt, PhD, Professor of Management, Ohio University. This case was prepared solely to provide fictional material for class discussion. The author does not intend to illustrate either effective or ineffective handling of a managerial situation.

Secure Check uses a process for collecting background information and makes use of an interactive algorithm-based model. The predictive modeling uses company specific information and data streams from a variety of sources, recommends the appropriate background check level as well as detailed information to be collected, and reports the best performer profile representing the ideal candidate. The basis for Secure Check is twofold: Secure Check is first a security risk detector for screening in human resources for a supply chain partner. The second purpose for using Secure Check is to facilitate the hiring of best performing candidates. The system provides direction as to who not to hire as well as which candidate in the remaining pool is the best fit to hire. Secure Check reduces the risk of a "failed hire" and a "bad hire." The failed hire is an aborted hire (i.e., a final candidate does not accept the position or does not make it through the probation period) or a hire that leaves before full performance expectations are realized. The associated lost costs include increased unemployment taxes, supplementary costs for overtime or contingency workers, additional promotion, recruitment, and hiring costs, drug testing and background check fees, and orientation, training, certification, and on-boarding costs. The bad hire is an employee hired who does not meet performance expectations. Associated costs for a bad hire include reduced productivity and quality of work, increases in training and overtime costs, and increased supervision costs. More significant costs that a bad hire may cause include lost time accidents (employee and others), customer property loss, and theft or other illegal activities that contribute to increased legal and insurance costs.

Both Warehouse Security Professionals and Global Electronics have calculated the average cost of a failed hire to be approximately 25–30 percent of salary and a bad hire to be almost 130 percent of salary. To mitigate the failed and bad hire risks, Secure Check inputs information about the position including risk factors (employee and customer safety, insurance and liability issues, etc.), skills (technical), and any legislative requirements including job-relatedness of conviction, time since conviction, and evidence of rehabilitation.

Discussion Questions

1. Identify the levels of security system response Global Electronics is trying to address by collaborating with Warehouse Security Professionals and with the integration of Secure Check. Explain how the use of Secure Check would meet the level objectives.

2. What challenges will Global Electronics incur in integrating the use of Secure Check throughout its supply chain?

3. What advice would you offer to Warehouse Security Professionals to advance their supply chain security portfolio of products and services?

©2019 Cengage Learning

3. Supply Chain Integration of Third-Party Logistics Providers*

Bobcat Logistical Solutions (BLS) is a third-party logistics service provider (3PL) serving the Ohio market (Columbus, Cincinnati, and Cleveland) as a noncontract partner with a broker that serves food and beverage processors and distributors including direct relationships with large food and beverage shippers. BLS owns a fleet of trucks used to

---

*Written by Brian Hoyt, PhD, Professor of Management, Ohio University. This case was prepared solely to provide fictional material for class discussion. The author does not intend to illustrate either effective or ineffective handling of a managerial situation.

serve the "spot" markets. Spot markets are the final destinations for food and beverage deliveries to grocery stores, institutions with large food service operations (public and private school systems, colleges and universities, prisons, etc.), franchised and independent restaurants, and large entertainment venues. Large shippers use 3PLs in spot markets when they need extra capacity or when major weather events keep large truck capacities off the road. Brokers usually act as intermediaries to utilize their carrier networks (including BLS) so shippers can deliver product to market. The largest food and beverage shipper in the United States has been challenged with three severe winters in a row along with natural disasters (hurricanes, tornadoes, floods) unlike any consecutive three-year period before. As the economy has grown, carriers who were not building assets during the recession now suffer from capacity limitations. During these severe conditions of the last three years, the use of 3PLs exploded, doubling the truck movements handled across the United States as compared to nonpeak capacity requirements.

Bobcat Logistical Solutions has experienced steady growth over the last five years, averaging 10 percent revenue growth each year. BLS has also taken advantage of the recent increase in spot markets with significant market share gains within its strategic group of 3PLs. The growth funded strategic initiatives for BLS included adding trucks to the fleet, purchasing warehouse space in key locations, integrating innovative electronic logging devices into all vehicles ahead of government mandates, and establishing a stable driver pool by collaborating with a specialized veterans recruiting and placement firm.

The increased ownership in warehouse space has established an effective distribution center model that has differentiated Bobcat Logistical Solutions from other 3PLs and brokers in their capability to handle freight. Using state and local tax incentives, BLS has been a leader in improving sustainability by reducing fuel consumption, electric bills, and greenhouse gas emissions. BLS has been working with a local university on a software project to develop a proprietary warehouse management system (WMS) to improve operations of the 24/7 distribution center using RFID technology, and to improve carbon footprints to meet sustainability targets. The WMS has added value by providing data directing changes in four areas:

1. Operating efficiencies with energy reduction gains—Inventory movement analysis displays opportunities to reduce energy costs by cycling conveyer belts off during idle times and managing lighting with sensors that switch off lights in empty rack areas.

2. Partner with energy utilities—Data on energy use provide opportunities to work with local utility companies to purchase off-peak rates and make equipment scheduling adjustments.

3. Picking route scheduling—Material movement scheduling can produce routes that are more efficient, save energy, and improve labor efficiencies. Efficient routing can reduce forklift usage in both numbers of forklifts needed and utilization of existing equipment, saving fuel costs, and reducing emissions. Well-organized picking routes in the warehouse eliminate unnecessary travel when using a WMS picking system rather than order-based picking (pick one order at a time).

4. Reduce packaging costs—Information from the WMS can aid in reducing packaging materials by optimizing the size of the box and amount of packing materials, maximizing cube in trucks, and minimizing damage to goods.

While the increased utilization of 3PLs increased capacity to reach spot markets, the increased cost of adding broker fees and 3PL capacity has negatively influenced budgets for the large food shippers that Bobcat Logistical Solutions serves. The large food shippers across the country are resetting strategic initiatives as it relates to using Brokers and 3PLs. They need to reduce exposure to volatile spot markets, increase service consistency, more accurately forecast capacity, and reduce added or unbudgeted costs of using spot market brokers and 3PLs. Many large food and beverage shippers are setting new broker/3PL network targets with drastic cuts to the total number of brokers and 3PLs used. This initiative seeks to reign in the costs of added margins of brokers and 3PLs, geographic overlaps, and inconsistent service. A second approach for some shippers includes developing a stronger network with asset-based 3PL carriers. This initiative focuses on strategic partnerships with a smaller number of brokers who work with asset-based 3PLs or directly with the 3PLs. These partnerships are generally contract based so that volume will be optimized and product handling and capacity secured. The most desirable 3PL partners will be in important spot markets and be more technology-based providers. A third initiative for a few of the larger food and beverage shippers involves connecting with 3PLs who have been active in mergers or acquisitions of 3PLs in strategic geographic regions of the country. Partnering with these 3PLs provides many advantages: expanded scale of warehousing operations, broadened service offerings, expanded geographic coverage, more assets and/or technology, new management talent, new customers, more market share, greater knowledge in a targeted industry, and in some instances, reduced need for broker networks.

A large food and beverage manufacturer has approached BLS as part of their supply chain integration management effort. Midwest Food and Beverage Transportation (MFBT) is extending the process integration beyond their largest food and beverage shippers to second-tier supply chain partners and has targeted several 3PLs.

Discussion Questions

1. Identify and briefly explain the key items that Bobcat Logistical Solution's proposal should include to secure the 3PL contract with Midwest Food and Beverage Transportation's supply chain integration efforts.

2. What are the advantages for Bobcat Logistical Solutions to be part of this potential relationship?

3. What are the advantages for Midwest Food and Beverage Transportation to partner with Bobcat Logistical Solutions as an integrated second-tier supply chain member?

4. What are the potential risks?

©2019 Cengage Learning

ADDITIONAL RESOURCES

Chopra, S., and P. Meindl, *Supply Chain Management: Strategy, Planning, and Operation*. Upper Saddle River, NJ: Prentice Hall, 2001.

Croxton, K. L., S. J. Garcia-Dastugue, D. M. Lambert, and D. S. Rogers, "The Supply Chain Management Processes," *International Journal of Logistics Management* 12(2), 2001: 13–36.

Handfield, R. B., and E. L. Nichols, *Supply Chain Redesign: Transforming Supply Chains into Integrated Value Systems*. Upper Saddle River, NJ: Financial Times Prentice Hall, 2002.

Lambert, D. M., M. C. Cooper, and J. D. Pagh, "Supply Chain Management: Implementation Issues and Research Opportunities," *International Journal of Logistics Management* 9(2), 1998: 1–19.

Simchi-Levi, D., P. Kaminsky, and E. Simchi-Levi, *Designing and Managing the Supply Chain*. New York: McGraw-Hill/Irwin, 2003.

END NOTES

1. Meyer, C., "When Cyber Met Physical: It's Time to Evaluate Your Security System's Cyber Risks," *Security* 54(4), 2017: 36–38.

2. Shappell, B., "Steve Savino: Extending Credit's Role by Breaking Down Barriers," *Business Credit* 116(3), 2014: 14–15, 17–19.

3. Saenz, M., R. Gupta, and C. Makowski, "Finding Profit in Horizontal Collaboration," *Supply Chain Management Review* 21(1), 2017: 16–22.

4. Anonymous, "Research and Markets—Global System Integration Market Value of USD 387.85 Billion by 2021—Trends, Technologies & Opportunities Report 2016-2021," *PR Newswire Europe* November 22, 2016: 1.

5. Lambert, D., M. Cooper, and J. Pagh, "Supply Chain Management: Implementation Issues and Research Opportunities," *International Journal of Logistics Management* 9(2), 1998: 1–19.

6. Siu, S., "CargoSmart Ltd.," *Journal of Commerce* January 8, 2007: 1; and http://www-03.ibm.com/procurement/proweb.nsf/contentdocsbytitle/United+States~IBM+Chief+Procurement+Officer+transition+to+Budapest,+Hungary?OpenDocument&Parent=Supplier+letters

7. Andel, T., "General Mills Releases Its Sustainable Supply Chain Strategy," *Material Handling & Logistics* April 30, 2013: 1.

8. Anonymous, "Microsoft Corporation—Patent Issued," *Marketing Weekly News* October 12, 2013: 465.

9. These processes are discussed in detail in Lambert, D. M., M. C. Cooper, and J. D. Pagh, "Supply Chain Management: Implementation Issues and Research Opportunities," *International Journal of Logistics Management* 9(2), 1998: 1–19; and in Croxton, K. L., S. J. Garcia-Dastugue, and D. M. Lambert, "The Supply Chain Management Processes," *International Journal of Logistics Management* 12(2), 2001: 13–36.

10. Overby, S., "Managing Demand after Disaster Strikes," *CIO* 23(9), 2010: 1.

11. Lorenzi, N., "Warehouse Management Solutions," *Snack Food & Wholesale Bakery* 106(4), 2017: 64, 66.

12. Andel, T., "Many Retailers Not Ready for Holiday Order Fulfillment," *Material Handling & Logistics* November 21, 2013: 1.

13. Borkowsky, M., and B. Walther, "The Next Big Thing," *Air Transport World* 51(6), 2014: 34.

14. Dutton, G., "Reverse Logistics: Money Tree or Money Pit?" *World Trade* 23(7), 2009: 28–32.

15. Haywood-Sullivan, M., and N. Stuart, "Does Functional Experience Impair Cross-pollination of the Balanced Scorecard?" *Management Accounting Quarterly* 17(4), 2016: 34–44.

16. Wilding, R., "Playing the Tune of Shared Success," *Financial Times* November 10, 2006: 2.

17. Anonymous, "Companies Are Using Team-Based Business Games to Increase Productivity," *CPA Practice Management Forum* 6(5), 2010: 22.

18. https://energy.gov/eere/vehicles/fact-915-march-7-2016-average-historical-annual-gasoline-pump-price-1929-2015

19. Mellat-Parast, M., and J. Spillan, "Logistics and Supply Chain Process Integration as a Source of Competitive Advantage: An Empirical Analysis," *International Journal of Logistics Management* 25(2), 2014: 289–314.

20. Wilson, M., "A Blanket Solution," *Chain Store Age* 86(1), 2010: 39.

21. Trunick, P., "Auto ID: Getting Comfortable with RFID," *Material Handling & Logistics* March 18, 2015: 1.

22. http://www.kurtsalmon.com/en-us/Retail/vertical-insight/1628/Kurt-Salmon-RFID-in-Retail-Study-2016

23. See, for instance, www.rfidinc.com, www.rfidjournal.com; Andel, T., "RFID: The Only Thing Passive About the Marines," *Modern Materials Handling* 62(8), 2007: 61; Fink, R., J. Gillett, and G. Grzeskiewicz, "Will RFID Change Inventory Assumptions?" *Strategic Finance* 89(4), 2007: 34–39; and Joch, A., "'Active' Assistance," *Hospitals & Health Networks* 6(3), 2007: 36–37.

24. Lester, T., "Masters of Collaboration—How Well Do U.K. Businesses Work Together," *Financial Times* June 29, 2007: 8.

25. Trunick, P., "It's Crunch Time," *Transportation & Distribution* 43(1), 2002: 5–6.

26. Anonymous, "Robert Reed on Hospital-Physician Integration," *Healthcare Financial Management* 64(6), 2010: 30.

27. Fenwick, S., "Why Supply Chain Visibility Matters," *Manufacturing Business Technology* July 29, 2015: 1.

28. Anonymous, "Del Monte Looks to the Cloud for Inventory Visibility," *Material Handling & Logistics* May 4, 2011: 1.

29. Beasty, C., "The Chain Gang," *Customer Relationship Management* 11(10), 2007: 32–36.

30. Field, A., "Sound the Alarm," *Journal of Commerce* May 7, 2007: 1.

31. Maccoby, M., "Creating Collaboration," *Research Technology Management* 49(6), 2006: 60–62.

32. Paul, L., "Suspicious Minds: Collaboration Among Trading Partners Can Unlock Great Value," *CIO* 16(7), 2003: 74–82.

33. Maylett, T., and K. Vitasek, "For Closer Collaboration, Try Education," *Supply Chain Management Review* 11(1), 2007: 58.

34. Information about these annual conferences can be found at www.sensorsexpo.com, www.ism.ws, and www.gs1us.org

35. Lee, H., V. Padmanabhan, and S. Whang, "The Bullwhip Effect in Supply Chains," *Sloan Management Review* 38(3), 1997: 93–102; Lee, H., "Taming the Bullwhip," *Journal of Supply Chain Management* 46(1), 2010: 7.

36. Hamstra, M., "Target Invests in Price, Small Formats, Online Fulfillment," *Supermarket News* March 1, 2017: 1.

37. Hines, A., "Twinkie Shortage Shows Hostess Fans Went a Little Crazy Over Bankruptcy," *Huffington Post Business* November 16, 2012, found at: http://www.huffingtonpost.com/tag/twinkies-shortage

38. Anonymous, "Global Supply Chain Risk Increasing," *Material Handling & Logistics* March 18, 2016: 1.

39. Zolkos, R., "Cyber Exposures Threaten Supply Chain Risk Management," *Business Insurance* 47(26), 2013: 4–29.

40. Anonymous, "A BP Lesson: Supply-Chain Risk," *Institutional Investor* June 2010: 1.

41. Field, A., "How 'Free' Is Free Trade?" *Journal of Commerce* December 18, 2006: 1–3; Kline, J., "Managing Emerging Market Risk," *Logistics Management* 46(5), 2007: 41–44; Swaminathan, J., and B. Tomlin, "How to Avoid the Risk Management Pitfalls," *Supply Chain Management Review* 11(5), 2007: 34–43.

42. Esola, L., "Employers Questioned on Pandemic Drug Plan," *Business Insurance* 40(49), 2006: 4–5.

43. Swaminathan, J., and B. Tomlin, "How to Avoid the Risk Management Pitfalls," *Supply Chain Management Review* 11(5), 2007: 34–43.

44. Anonymous, "Supply Disruption Discussed," *Business Insurance* 37(22), 2003: 17.

45. Swaminathan, J., and B. Tomlin, "How to Avoid the Risk Management Pitfalls," *Supply Chain Management Review* 11(5), 2007: 34–43.

46. Anonymous, "Supply Diversity Cuts Risk Exposure," *Oil & Gas Journal* 105(17), 2007: 65–68.

47. Tieman, R., "It's About Common Sense," *Financial Times* September 10, 2007: 5; Chauhan, C., "Importer of Japanese Automobiles, Spare Parts to Stop," *The Economic Times Online* March 13, 2011: 1.

48. Tieman, R. (See note 50.)

49. Anonymous, "Flexing Supply Chain Muscle," *Chain Store Age* 83(9), 2007: 10A.

50. McCrea, B., "Jabil: Automating Supply Chain Decision-Making," *Logistics Management* 55(9), 2016: 40–42, 44.

51. Shacklett, M., "What to Do About Risk," *World Trade* 26(10), 2013: 22–27.

52. See note 52.

53. Felsted, A., "Lessons from Barbie World," *Financial Times* September 10, 2007: 1.

54. Rice, J., "Rethinking Security," *Logistics Management* 46(5), 2007: 28; Knowles, J., "The Lockerbie Judgments: A Short Analysis," *Case Western Reserve Journal of International Law* 36(2/3), 2004: 473–485.

55. Terreri, A., "How Do You Balance Shipment Speed with a Secure Supply Chain?" *World Trade* 19(11), 2006: 18–22.

56. Rice, J., "Rethinking Supply Chain Security," *Logistics Management* May 1, 2007.

57. Anderson, B., "Prevent Cargo Theft," *Logistics Today* 48(5), 2007: 37–38.

58. Kilcarr, S., "Brand 'Damage' a Side Effect of Cargo Theft Issue, Expert Says," *Fleet Owner* October 29, 2013: 1; and https://www.ajot.com/news/cargonets-2016-cargo-theft-trend-analysis

59. Information found at www.transparency.org

60. See, for example, the website www.cargosecurity.com/ncsc/education-CTPAT.asp; and https://www.cbp.gov/border-security/ports-entry/cargo-security/c-tpat-customs-trade-partnership-against-terrorism

61. See https://www.securecargo.org/content/what-certified-cargo-screening-program-ccsp-0

62. Terreri, A., "How Do You Balance Shipment Speed with a Secure Supply Chain?"

63. Greenemeier, L., "MassMutual Gets Control of Its Security Data," *InformationWeek* September 17, 2007: 108–109.

64. Michel, R., "Profit from Secure Supply Chains," *Manufacturing Business Technology* 24(11), 2006: 1.

Chapter 14

PERFORMANCE MEASUREMENT ALONG SUPPLY CHAINS

Through services such as ICMA Insights, which combines industry-leading analytics with one of the largest repositories of U.S. local government performance metrics, we can apply comparative performance tools across vast numbers of local governments and apply predictive analytics to some of the more complex service delivery issues of our time.

—**Bob O'Neill, executive director, International City/County Management Association (ICMA)**[1]

If we're using blood pressure as a performance measure, we should do it correctly. Let's figure out the best way to do it, standardize that method, and then have all physicians do it the same way for three years. Reward improvement and guard against "gaming." Do a couple of important things well rather than measuring for its own sake. That way, we would at least get people's blood pressure under better control. That would be a good use of performance measurement.

—**Robert Berenson, MD, a fellow at the Urban Institute in Washington, DC**[2]

Learning Objectives

After completing this chapter, you should be able to

- Discuss why managers need to assess the performance of their firms as well as their supply chains.

- Discuss the merits of financial and nonfinancial performance measures.

- List, describe and calculate a number of traditional and world-class performance measures.

- Describe how the balanced scorecard and the supply chain operations reference models work.

- Describe how to design a supply chain performance measurement system.

Chapter Outline

Introduction

Viewing Supply Chains as a Competitive Force

Traditional Performance Measures

World-Class Performance Measurement Systems

Supply Chain Performance Measurement Systems

The Balanced Scorecard

The SCOR Model

Summary

SCM Profile | Clayton Missouri's Use of Performance Scorecards

The St. Louis suburb of Clayton, Missouri, demonstrates how a smaller city can excel in performance management. Clayton has received a certificate of excellence in performance management from the ICMA Center for Performance Analytics each year since 2011.

Internally, Clayton fosters a culture that embraces performance management. Orientation for new city staff includes a meeting with city manager Craig Owens, who describes the city's performance management strategies. "We are indeed passionate about demonstrating value," he says. Owens also meets annually with employees to review the three elements of the organization's culture: team pride, quality services, and high value. The quality services element focuses heavily on benchmarking and emphasizes the city's strong performance.

The city has formally collected performance data using scorecards for more than eight years. At the start of the annual data collection cycle each year, an e-mail alerts staff members that the data collection period has begun. At least quarterly, Owens reviews performance data with department heads, and performance results are discussed as part of performance evaluations for employees.

The city conducts an annual community survey covering forty-five measures that are surveyed across more than thirty cities in Kansas and Missouri. The 2014 survey, for example, showed that Clayton rated above the national and Kansas/Missouri averages on all forty-five measures.

The city has developed an Exceptional City Services Scorecard showing resident satisfaction; cost and revenue measures; police, fire, and EMS response times; employee training hours; and facility use. It is published in the city's budget book, summarizing historical and current performance data along with goals for the fiscal year. The scorecard also captures results from an internal employee engagement survey.

In the final analysis, Clayton has embraced performance management by instilling it as a value throughout the organization; ensuring the accurate collection and verification of data from residents and local government operations; sharing results publicly; comparing performance with benchmark cities; and using the results to continuously improve services.[3]

INTRODUCTION

This chapter discusses the role and importance of performance measurements for both the firm and its supply chains. The old adage "you can't improve what you aren't measuring" is certainly true for firms as well as their supply chains. In fact, for over ten years, the global business research firm Gartner has published a ranking of the world's most successful supply chains. For 2016, the top three are Unilever, followed by McDonald's and Amazon. Firms with the best supply chains create hierarchies of precise performance measures at the execution level combined with a distillation of meaning at the strategic level. These organizations realize that strategic goals at the top will only succeed if there is a clear path to performance measures at the transaction level to identify execution problems.[4] While several types of performance measures have been discussed or suggested in earlier chapters of this textbook, firms need to develop an entire system of meaningful performance measures to become and then remain competitive, particularly when managing supply chains is one of the imperatives.

Performance measurement systems vary substantially from company to company. For example, many firms' performance measures concentrate solely on the firm's costs and profits. While these measures are certainly important, managers must realize that making decisions while relying on financial performance alone gives no indication of the underlying causes of financial performance. Designing standards and then monitoring the many activities or processes indirectly or directly impacting financial performance can provide much better information for decision-making purposes.

Indeed, during the recession in 2009 as global demand for goods and services languished, personnel relied on their supply chain management skills to drive costs out of their supply chains to improve profitability. According to a survey of global business managers, three of the activities receiving the most attention during this period were purchasing, logistics, and performance measurement.[5] Always the supply chain innovator, Walmart, for instance, decided to purchase up to 80 percent of its private label merchandise directly from manufacturers, saving billions of dollars.[6] Supply chain leaders are working closely with their trading partners to seek out and eliminate non-value-creating activities while identifying new customer requirements and turning these into product and service attributes. And, supporting and guiding these activities are good performance measurement systems.

Even for companies like Walmart (which by the way is a long-time member of the annual Top 25 Supply Chains published by Gartner and was ranked number 16 on the 2016 list) that rely on low prices to attract customers, cost performance alone is not enough to guarantee success without assuring that products are also available when needed and at acceptable levels of quality. Attaining world-class competitive status requires managers to realize that making process decisions to create or purchase products and services customers want, and then to distribute them in ways that will satisfy customers, requires careful monitoring of cost, quality, and customer service performance among all key supply chain trading partners. Achieving adequate performance and then continually improving on those measures are what firms aim toward. Using an adequate system of performance measures allows managers to pursue that vision.

Unfortunately, many firms and their supply chains today are not adequately measuring process performance. According to a survey of Canadian manufacturing firms, for instance, only about 50 percent of the firms had even moderately well-developed performance measurement systems. And in another survey of business technologists, about 75 percent said their firms mainly relied on their suppliers to furnish them with inbound performance information.[7] In other cases, organizations are busy measuring everything in sight, and in so doing, they make poor measurements, measure the wrong things, and measure things that only make the firm look good—actions that can sometimes lead to misstatements and restatements, loss of confidence, and even prove dangerous (Enron and Worldcom come to mind here). Managers need to realize the importance of creating a good, true set of performance measures, and this is the objective of the chapter.

When managing supply chains, assessing the performance of several tiers of suppliers and customers further complicates an already formidable performance measurement problem. With supply chains, performance measurement systems become much larger and are complicated by varied relationships, trust, and interactions. Performance at the end-customer level depends on the collective performance among the primary trading companies within a supply chain. Thus, performance measures must be visible and communicated to all participating members of the supply chain while managers collaborate to achieve results that allow firms to plan ahead, create value, and realize benefits. Indeed, it is likely that some member costs will be higher than otherwise would be the case to permit supply chains to offer what end customers want. It is only through cooperation and shared planning and benefits that an effective supply chain-wide performance measurement system can be designed and implemented.

This chapter will discuss the basics of performance measurement including cost-based and other traditional measurements, and then move on to discuss the more effective measurement systems typical of world-class organizations. From there, the discussion will move into measuring the performance of supply chains. Finally, the balanced scorecard and the SCOR model methods of performance measurement, which are being utilized effectively in supply chain settings, will be presented and discussed.

VIEWING SUPPLY CHAINS AS A COMPETITIVE FORCE

The eventual and ultimate goal of supply chains is to successfully deliver products and services to end customers. Traditionally, to meet customer service requirements, trading partners might simply load their retail shelves, warehouses, and factories with large quantities of finished goods. Today, though, this strategy would ultimately lead to inventory carrying costs and product prices so high that the firms would no longer be competitive. For companies to be successful, supply chain customers and end-product users must be satisfied. Thus, firms must invest time and effort understanding supply chain partner and end-customer requirements, and then adjust or acquire supply chain competencies to satisfy the needs of these customers. To obtain the resources to accomplish these tasks, top managers must become involved and support the firm's improvement efforts. Ultimately, well-designed performance measurement systems integrated among key trading partners must be implemented to control and enhance the capabilities of these firms and the related supply chains.

Understanding End Customers

As discussed in Chapter 10, companies segment customers based on their service needs and then design production and distribution capabilities to meet each segment's needs. In other words, instead of taking a one-size-fits-all approach to product design and delivery, firms and their supply chains need to look at each segment of the markets they serve and determine the needs of those customers. Companies consider customer segment needs such as:

- the variety of products required,
- the quantity and delivery frequency needed,
- the product quality desired,
- the level of sustainability sought, and
- the pricing of products.

Obviously, depending on the range of customers the company and its supply chains serve, there will be multiple customer segments and requirements. Computer maker Dell, for example, a leader in social marketing and support, integrates Twitter data to allow brand managers and support teams to actively track what's being said in tweets. The data can be codified to show microsegments of customers who are, for example, frequent visitors to coffee shops during their work day, commute ninety minutes or more, fly internationally during the week, stay in business hotels, are passionate about football, are eco-savvy, and watch a lot of TV.[8]

Understanding Supply Chain Partner Requirements

Once firms understand end customers' needs, the next step is determining how their supply chains can best satisfy those needs. Supply chain strategies must consider the potential trade-offs existing among the cost, quality, sustainability, and service requirements mentioned above. For instance, supply chain responsiveness (meeting due date, lead-time, and quantity requirements while providing high levels of customer service) can come at a cost. To achieve the desired level of responsiveness, companies along the supply chain may also have to become more responsive, potentially requiring investments in additional capacity and faster transportation. Likewise, supply chain quality or reliability may require investments in newer equipment, better technology, and higher-quality materials and components among participants in supply chains.

Conversely, increasing supply chain efficiency (enabling lower prices for goods) creates the need among supply chain partners to make adjustments in their purchasing, production, and delivery capabilities that will lower costs. This may include using slower transportation modes, buying and delivering in larger quantities, and/or reducing the quality of the parts and supplies purchased. Ultimately, firms within supply chains must collaborate and decide what combination of customer needs their supply chains can and should provide, both today and in the long term. For example, in 2016, California-based ResMed, a global sleep disorder equipment manufacturer, needed to trim supply chain costs. It targeted two fairly simple ways to improve efficiency— moving more of its shipping volume from air to sea freight, and increased manufacturing volumes in lower cost plants.[9]

Adjusting Supply Chain Member Capabilities

Supply chain members can audit their capabilities and those of their trading partners to determine if what they do particularly well is consistent with the needs of the end customers and other supply chain members. Some companies may be well positioned to supply the desired levels of cost, quality, and customer service performance, while others may not be as well positioned. Matching or adjusting supply chain member capabilities with end-customer requirements can be a very difficult task, particularly if the communication and cooperation levels among companies are not excellent, or if companies are serving multiple supply chains and customer segments requiring different sets of capabilities.

In many cases, a dominant company within the supply chain (e.g., Walmart) can use its buying power to leverage demands for suppliers to conform to its supply chain requirements. As customer tastes and competition change over time, supply chain members can reassess and redesign their strategies for meeting end-customer requirements and remaining competitive. Use of the Internet as a marketplace, for instance, has become a significant part of many firms' competitive strategies, allowing them to offer much greater product variety and convenience than ever before.

Matching supply chain capabilities to end-customer requirements means that firms and their supply chain partners must be continually reassessing their performance with respect to these changing end-customer requirements. This brings us back to the importance of performance measures and their ability to relay information regarding the performance of each member within the supply chain, along with the performance of the supply chain vis-à-vis the end customers. Now, more than ever before, successful supply chains are those that can continue to deliver the right combinations of cost, quality, sustainability, and customer service, as customer needs change. Weaknesses in any of

SCM Profile | **McDonald's Supply Chain Sustainability Efforts**

McDonald's supply chain ties together many local and regional supply chains using strategic frameworks and policies and its Worldwide Supply Chain department. For issues related to sustainability, a global management structure was created in 2007 called the Sustainable Supply Steering Committee (SSSC). The SSSC guides McDonald's toward a more sustainable flow of supplies. McDonald's buyers of beef and potatoes, for example, include sustainability initiatives in their purchasing strategies.

McDonald's announced plans in 2015 to stop using eggs from chickens raised in cages in the United States and Canada, over the following ten years, after facing pressures from animal-rights advocates to make its supply chain more humane. "Our customers are increasingly interested in knowing more about their food and where it comes from," says Mike Andres, president of McDonald's USA. McDonald's said it would "listen, learn, and collaborate with stakeholders from farm to the front counter" to move its supply chain toward more sources of sustainable beef. McDonald's created the Global Roundtable for Sustainable Beef with several stakeholders to draft principles and guidelines for sustainable beef.

The company buys over 3 billion pounds of potatoes per year. "If we can find a variety that . . . with less inputs, water or whatever, that's something we're looking for. To date, there are not a lot of varieties that perform consistently enough. The mainstay is the Russet Burbank which provides the best taste, but has some substantial limitations—it takes a long time to mature/grow, requires huge quantities of water, and is vulnerable to rots and disease," says Mitch Smith, director, U.S. Quality Systems and Agricultural Products at McDonald's. Finally, bags of lettuce have the oxygen sucked out of them and replaced with nitrogen. This gives McDonald's fourteen days of a fresh supply. "We have to have a very tight-knit distribution network," says Smith.[10]

these areas can mean loss of competitiveness and profits for all supply chain members. Today, the best supply chain performers are more responsive to customer needs, quicker to anticipate changes in the markets, and much better at controlling costs, resulting in greater supply chain profits. The nearby SCM Profile describes McDonald's efforts to make their supply chain more sustainable. The next section discusses traditional performance measures.

TRADITIONAL PERFORMANCE MEASURES

Most performance measures used by firms today continue to be the traditional cost-based and financial statistics reported to shareholders in the form of annual report, balance sheet, and income statement data. This information is relied upon by potential investors and shareholders to make stock transaction decisions and forms the basis for many managers' performance bonuses. Unfortunately, financial statements and other cost-based information don't necessarily reflect the underlying performance of the productive systems of an organization. As readers might recall with the fraudulent practices at firms like Texas-based energy company Enron, Mississippi-based long-distance phone company WorldCom, and New York-based Bernard Madoff Investment Securities, cost and profit information can be hidden or manipulated to make performance seem far better than reality.

As an example, Enron claimed revenues of $111 billion in 2000. That year, *Fortune* magazine named Enron "America's Most Innovative Company." The very next year, high-profile managers left the company, Enron declared bankruptcy, and its fraudulent corporate and accounting practices became public, and by 2004, Enron had become one of the costliest bankruptcy cases in U.S. history. Thousands of employees lost everything, executives ended up in jail, and the Arthur Andersen accounting company, associated with Enron during this period, was dissolved.[11]

As illustrated above, decisions that are made solely to make the firm look good don't necessarily mean the firm is performing well or will continue to perform well in the future. Business success depends on a firm's ability to turn internal competencies into products and services that customers want, while providing desired environmental, quality, and customer service levels at a reasonable price. Financial performance measures, while important, cannot adequately capture a firm's ability to excel in various process areas.

Use of Organization Costs, Revenue, and Profitability Measures

These might at first glance seem to be useful types of performance measures, but several problems are associated with using costs, revenues, and profits to gauge a firm's performance. Windfall profits that occur when prices rise due to sudden demand increases or supply interruptions, as has been the case at different times in the oil industry, are one example. When sudden oil price increases occur, airlines and other transportation companies suddenly experience much higher costs and reductions in profits, while oil companies see suddenly rising profits. In 2012, for example, Exxon Mobil reported the highest profits in the world—$44.9 billion, while Royal Dutch Shell posted the highest sales—$481.7 billion. Exxon Mobil was also number one in profits in 2009 and 2011, while slipping to number two in 2010 and 2013. Moving to 2015, Exxon Mobil was again number two and Chevron was number five. Several other oil companies also frequently make the top ten.[12] Similarly, many tourist destinations such as Las Vegas saw dramatic declines in visitor volumes during the 2008 to 2010 economic recession, causing hotels and theme parks to report much lower occupancies and profits during this period. Beginning in 2008, for instance, Las Vegas saw plunges in visitor volume, gaming revenues, occupancies, and average daily room rates for the first time since the Las Vegas Convention and Visitors Authority began tracking the numbers in 1970. Hotels laid off over 25,000 workers while several resorts filed for bankruptcy.[13] Thus, profits, as described here, were not necessarily the result of something the firms did or did not do particularly well; they were caused for the most part by uncontrollable environmental conditions. In other words, changes in cost and profit statistics, in many cases, may not accurately reflect the true capabilities of the firm.

Another problem with the use of costs, revenues, or profits as performance measures is the difficulty in attributing any financial contributions to the various functional units or underlying processes of the organization. Many departments and units are interdependent and share costs, equipment, labor, and revenues, making it extremely difficult to split out costs and revenues equitably. Additionally, using costs alone as a departmental or business unit performance measure can result in actions that actually hurt the organization. For example, rewarding the purchasing department for minimizing its purchasing costs might cause increased new product return rates and warranty repairs due to low-cost but poor-quality part purchases. Minimizing transportation costs might also look great on financial reports but may result in late deliveries and lower customer service levels, causing a loss of customers. Finally, the practice of allocating overhead costs based on a department's percentage of direct labor hours causes managers to waste time trying to reduce direct labor hours to lower overhead cost allocations when, today, direct labor accounts for only a small fraction of total manufacturing costs. In essence, these overhead costs merely get transferred somewhere else in the firm, leaving the organization no better off and perhaps in worse shape due to the loss of valuable labor resources.

Use of Performance Standards and Variances

Establishing standards for performance comparison purposes can be troublesome and particularly when the standards are unrealistic, damaging to an organization. Establishing output standards like 1,000 units/day or productivity standards like 10 units/labor hour creates a goal that can drive employees and managers to do whatever it takes to reach these goals, even if it means producing shoddy work or "cooking the books." When performance expectations are not met, perfectly good products, employees, or departments can be branded as losers. Additionally, once goals are actually reached, there is no further incentive to keep improving.

When standards are not reached, a **performance variance** is created, which is the difference between the standard and actual performance. When organizations hold managers up to performance standards that then create performance variances, managers can be pressured to find ways to make up these variances, resulting in decisions that may not be in the long-term best interests of the firm. Decisions like producing to make an output quota regardless of current finished goods inventory levels, or purchasing unneeded supplies just to use up department budgets, are examples of things that can happen when performance standards are applied without considering the true benefits to the organization. When applied at the functional level, standards can reinforce the idea of **functional silos**. Departments are then assessed on meeting their performance standards instead of optimizing firm or supply chain performance.

Productivity and Utilization Measures

Overall, **total productivity measures** such as:

$$\frac{\text{outputs}}{\text{costs of (labor + capital + energy + material)}}$$

and **single-factor productivity measures** such as:

$$\frac{\text{outputs}}{\text{costs of labor}}$$

while potentially useful, have the same problems as the use of costs and profits for performance measures. These measures, while allowing firms to view the impact of one or any number of the firm's inputs (e.g., the cost of labor) on the firm's outputs (e.g., units produced), do not allow the firm to determine the actual performance of any of the resources behind these elements. Decisions made to increase productivity may prove to actually increase a firm's costs and reduce quality or output in the long term, ultimately reducing productivity. For example, a business unit might be tempted to produce at output levels greater than demand to increase productivity, which also increases inventories and inventory carrying costs. Or managers might be inclined to lay off workers and buy the cheapest materials to decrease input costs and thus maximize their productivity without considering the impact on the firm's quality, customer service, and employee morale. In these ways, productivity measures can prove to be damaging. Example 14.1 provides a look at calculating productivity and the problems that can arise when making decisions based solely on productivity.

Example 14.1   Productivity Measures at Ultra Ski Manufacturing

The Ultra Ski company makes top-of-the-line custom snow skis for high-end ski shops as well as its own small retail shop and employs fifteen people. The owner has been adamant about finding a way to increase productivity because her sales have been flat for the past two seasons. Given the information shown below, she has calculated the annual single-factor and total productivity values as:

Labor productivity = 1,000 skis/10,800 hours = 0.093 skis per labor hour
Material productivity = 1,000 skis/$18,000 = 0.056 skis per dollar of materials
Lease productivity = 1,000 skis/$24,000 = 0.042 skis per lease dollar

INPUTS AND OUTPUTS	LAST YEAR
Skis produced	1,000
Labor hours	10,800
Materials purchased	$18,000
Lease payments	$24,000

She calculates the company's total productivity by multiplying the labor hours by its average wage of $17 per hour and finds:

Total productivity = 1,000 skis/[10,800($17) + $18,000 + $24,000]
                   = 0.0044 skis per dollar

So the owner figures that she can get some great improvements in productivity by finding a low-cost supplier, moving to a cheaper location, and laying off six workers (reducing her workforce by 40 percent), making the new single-factor productivities:

Labor productivity = 1,000 skis/10,800(0.6) hours = 0.154 (a 66 percent increase)
Material productivity = 1,000 skis/$12,000 = 0.083 (a 48 percent increase)
Lease productivity = 1,000/$18,000 = 0.056 (a 33 percent increase)

and the new total productivity:

Total productivity = 1,000 skis/[10,800($17)(.6) + $12,000 + $18,000]
                   = 0.0071 skis per dollar (a whopping 61 percent increase!)

Consequently, the owner decided to make the changes for the coming year. Unfortunately, they went out of business in six months due to poor-quality materials, a bad location, and overworked, low-morale employees.

Labor and machine utilization can be shown as:

$$\frac{\text{actual units produced}}{\text{standard output level}} \quad \text{or} \quad \frac{\text{actual hours utilized}}{\text{total hours available}}$$

These performance measures, when used as performance goals, can encourage the firm, for instance, to reduce labor levels until everyone is overworked, causing queues of work or customers to develop, morale to suffer, and quality and customer service levels to erode. Additionally, when using the measures discussed above, there is a tendency to continue producing and adding to inventory just to keep machines and people busy. Less time is spent doing preventive maintenance, training, and projects that can lead to greater performance and profits in the future. While it is obviously beneficial to meet demand and keep labor costs at optimal levels, maximizing utilization can prove to be expensive for firms.

Thus, the emphasis on overall performance in terms of generalized criteria such as the firm's financial, productivity, or utilization characteristics does not tell the entire story. While it certainly is important for firms to possess financial strength and high levels of productivity and factory utilization, these measures do not reveal in detail the firm's underlying process performance. Using general and internally focused measures like these does not give many clues as to specific problems that may exist or how to go about solving those problems. Managers are left to guess which types of actions are needed and have no way of knowing if any corrections made actually had the intended effect. What is needed is a set of detailed performance measures throughout the organization and extending to supply chain partners that are consistent with firm and supply chain strategies, allow managers to find root causes of performance failures, and, finally, lead managers to reasonable problem solutions.

Traditional performance measures also tend to be short-term oriented. To maximize profits in the upcoming quarter, for instance, firms may focus considerable efforts on delaying capital investments, selling assets, denying new project proposals, outsourcing work, and leasing instead of purchasing equipment. These actions, while reducing short-term costs, can also significantly reduce a firm's ability to develop new products and remain competitive. New product research, new technology purchases, new facilities, and newly trained people all enhance the capabilities of the firm and position it to keep up with ever-changing customer requirements, but these things all initially worsen the performance measures discussed above. Without this infusion of ideas and capital expenditures though, firms will ultimately perform poorly.

On the other hand, world-class organizations understand that long-term competitive advantage is created when strategies are geared toward continually meeting and exceeding customer expectations of product and service cost, quality, deliverability, flexibility, and sustainability. These firms know that investments to improve capabilities in these areas will eventually bear fruit and position them to be successful in the long term. Effective performance measurement systems link current operating characteristics to these long-term strategies and objectives. Peoria, Arizona, for example, a city with a population of about 170,000 sitting just northwest of Phoenix, has been using performance measures for years and has won numerous awards for its efforts. Their most effective programs have used performance measures along with program descriptions and goals to tell a story. Many of the city's programs also incorporate satisfaction surveys to measure the extent to which outcomes are valued by customers. They benchmark performance with some 150 other cities in the Phoenix, Arizona area and across the United States.[14]

WORLD-CLASS PERFORMANCE MEASUREMENT SYSTEMS

Businesses respond to increased competitive and marketplace pressures by developing and maintaining a distinctive competitive advantage, which creates the need to develop effective performance measurement systems linking firm strategies and operating decisions to customer requirements. Performance criteria that guide a firm's decision-making to achieve strategic objectives must be easy to implement, understand, and measure; they must be flexible and consistent with the firm's objectives; and they must be implemented in areas that are viewed as critical to the creation of value for customers. The nearby SCM Profile, for example, describes the World Bank's use of performance measures to improve its procurement efforts.

An effective performance measurement system should consist of the traditional financial information for external reporting purposes along with tactical-level performance criteria used to assess the firm's competitive capabilities while directing its efforts to attain other desired capabilities. In short, good performance helps firms attain their goals. A good performance measurement system should include measures that *assess what is important to customers*. In a survey of manufacturing and service company executives, for example, researchers found that in firms with successful lean and Six Sigma programs, there was use of a wider variety of both financial and nonfinancial performance measures.[16]

> ### SCM Profile | World Bank Group Improves Procurement Using Performance Measures
>
> The World Bank Group (WBG) in Washington, DC, has more than 140 global offices. Its procurement department consists of fifty people based in DC and twenty in Chennai, India, and it manages more than $1.6 billion of annual spend. With a mission to provide goods and services globally to developing countries at optimal quality and minimal total costs, it initiated a three-year program of improvement in 2012.
>
> Initially, WBG completed a comprehensive organizational analysis and benchmarked the department against leading public and private sector organizations. This highlighted performance gaps, and these gaps formed the basis of an improvement plan. Six opportunities for improvement were identified: organizational design and alignment, procurement framework and process, procurement planning and oversight, category management, procurement systems and tools, and performance measurement.
>
> With respect to performance measurement, scorecards and metrics were implemented including cycle times, savings targets, and qualitative performance measures. These measurements increased visibility and transparency of the procurement process, which led to enhanced planning, innovation, and collaboration between internal stakeholders and procurement teams by 2015. A procurement scorecard using twenty-seven areas and linked back to strategic objectives was created for continuous monitoring by senior management. Stakeholder engagement in the process led to broad management support and ownership outside the procurement division, creating sustained and improved collaboration between procurement and client divisions.[15]

Developing World Class Performance Measures

Creating an effective performance measurement system involves the following steps:[17]

- Identify the firm's strategic objectives.
- Develop an understanding of each functional area's set of requirements for achieving the strategic objectives.
- Design and document performance measures for each functional area that adequately track each required capability.
- Assure the compatibility and strategic focus of the performance measures to be used.
- Implement the new performance monitoring system.
- Identify internal and external trends likely to affect firm and functional area performance over time.
- Periodically reevaluate the firm's performance measurement system as these trends and other environmental changes occur.

In this way, world-class firms establish strategically oriented performance criteria among each of their functional areas, using the categories of quality, cost, customer service, and perhaps sustainability, and then revisit these measures as problems are solved, competition and customer requirements change, and as supply chain and firm strategies change.

For instance, the San Diego Zoo in California, a world-class leader in conservation, audits among other things, its own waste-recycling performance. The zoo initially became interested in waste recycling and other conservation efforts in response to customer and employee suggestions. Today, it recovers over 90 percent of all waste generated within the facility, an improvement of 10 percent since 2013. The Zoo composts 2.6 tons of food scraps annually. Zoo patrons' eating utensils, plates, bowls, and cups are also compostable. Even to-go boxes are made from recycled plastic containers. Additionally, it found that most of the unrecycled waste was compostable. As a result, new programs including the zoo's sister location, Safari Park, have been developed that include composting to further improve its waste recovery performance.[18]

Table 14.1 lists a number of world-class performance measures that might be used in different functional areas of the firm to satisfy strategic objectives, enhance the value of the firm's products and services, and increase customer satisfaction. As firms become more proactive in managing their supply chains, performance measures must be incorporated into this effort. The next section discusses performance measurement in a supply chain setting.

Table 14.1	World-Class Performance Measures
CAPABILITY AREAS	PERFORMANCE MEASURES
Quality	1. Number of defects per unit produced and per unit purchased
	2. Number of product returns per units sold
	3. Number of warranty claims per units sold
	4. Number of suppliers used
	5. Lead time from defect detection to correction
	6. Number of workcenters using statistical process control
	7. Number of suppliers that are quality certified
	8. Number of quality awards applied for; number of awards won
Cost	1. Scrap or spoilage losses per workcenter
	2. Average inventory turnover
	3. Average setup time
	4. Employee turnover
	5. Average safety stock levels
	6. Number of rush orders required for meeting delivery dates
	7. Downtime due to machine breakdowns
Customer Service	*Flexibility*
	1. Average number of labor skills
	2. Average production lot size
	3. Number of customized services available
	4. Number of days to process special or rush orders
	Dependability
	1. Average service response time or product lead time
	2. Percentage of delivery promises kept
	3. Average number of days late per shipment
	4. Number of stockouts per product
	5. Number of days to process a warranty claim
	6. Average number of hours spent with customers by engineers
	Innovation
	1. Annual investment in R&D
	2. Percentage of automated processes
	3. Number of new product or service introductions
	4. Number of process steps required per product

SUPPLY CHAIN PERFORMANCE MEASUREMENT SYSTEMS

Performance measurement systems for supply chains must effectively link supply chain trading partners to achieve breakthrough performance in satisfying end users. At the local or interfirm level, performance measures similar to the ones presented in Table 14.1 are required for high-level performance. In a collaborative supply chain setting, these measures must overlay the entire supply chain to ensure that firms are all contributing to the supply chain strategy and the satisfaction of end customers. In successful supply chains, members jointly agree on appropriate supply chain performance measures. The focus of the system should be on value creation for end customers, since customer satisfaction drives sales for all of the supply chain's members.

While challenging to implement, the best managed supply chains are indeed pulling it off. In a major study by the Massachusetts-based Performance Measurement Group that looked at firms and their supply chains from 1995 to 2000, the top supply chain performers were found to be leading the way in terms of responsiveness and reliability performance, and total supply chain costs. In a 2008 survey of 287 companies and their supply chains conducted by Connecticut-based AMR Research, the most successful supply chains were found to be more centralized, integrated, global, and focused on measuring performance. And finally, in a ranking of the "Top 25" supply chains compiled each year since 2004 by business research firm Gartner, one of the common characteristics is a focus on measurements that matter; measures that will improve operational results.[19]

Supply Chain Environmental Performance

Environmental sustainability has been a recurring theme throughout this textbook, and as consumers, governments, and business leaders begin to address the need for protecting the environment and reducing greenhouse gas emissions, the demand for products and services will change, along with regulations impacting how supply chains operate. As a result, supply chain performance must begin to include assessments of environmental performance. The Hilton Union Square Hotel in San Francisco, for example, has been using sustainability measures for some time now. "We require our hotels to set annual targets for energy reduction. Each site has to implement improvement projects and use our corporate responsibility performance measurement system, which tracks over 200 sustainability metrics," says Tristam Coffin, sustainable facilities coordinator. "We've seen over $550 million saved through efficiency projects and our company is the first international hospitality group to receive ISO 50001 certification for energy management."[20]

Green supply chain management (GSCM) is the objective of an effective supply chain environmental performance system. The reach of GSCM extends across the organization and its trading partners, and includes the processes involved in purchasing, manufacturing, and materials management, distribution, and reverse logistics. GSCM promotes the sharing of environmental responsibility along the supply chain in each of these areas such that environmentally sound practices predominate, and adverse impacts to global environments are minimized.[21] Perhaps, the world's largest GSCM initiative is being implemented by Walmart—its goals are to be supplied 100 percent by renewable energy, to produce zero waste, and to sell products that sustain health and the environment. By 2011, 80.9 percent of its physical waste in the United States was recycled, and that this was worth some $231 million to its bottom line, due to recycling revenues and other cost avoidance. By the end of 2013, Walmart had eliminated 7.6 million metric tons (MMT) of greenhouse gas emissions. It also implemented other projects that eliminated 18 MMT of greenhouse gas emissions by the end of 2015. In 2011, Walmart began to integrate a supplier sustainability index into its business by scoring vendor product offerings in terms of sustainability. It has developed scorecards to help its purchasing agents evaluate products in this way.[22]

The design of an effective green supply chain performance system should be discussed by all key supply chain members and be compatible with existing performance monitoring systems. As discussed in earlier chapters, the ISO 14000 environmental management standards, typically associated with one organization's environmental compliance, can be a good starting point for building a green supply chain strategy among supply chain partners. Today, trading partners all realize that green supply chains are not only becoming a requirement but also are providing cost savings, additional profits, and cheaper prices to supply chain members and end-product customers. For these reasons, use of environmental sustainability assessments is a common practice.

Today, software is available that enables companies to analyze the **carbon footprints** of their supply chains and then evaluate design configurations and various options for reducing total carbon emissions. In many cases, this will also mean lower costs. A number of software suppliers are extending their existing software applications to measure and optimize areas such as transportation and inventory management, with explicit considerations for greening the supply chain. Several examples include carbonfootprint.com, thinkstep.com, and carbontrust.com.

To achieve the type of performance alluded to in this chapter, specific measures must be adopted by supply chain trading partners such that performance can be further aligned with supply chain objectives. A number of these are listed below.[23]

1. *Total Supply Chain Management Costs*: the costs to process orders, purchase materials, purchase energy, comply with environmental regulations, manage inventories and returns, and manage supply chain finance, planning, and information systems. Leading supply companies are spending from 4 to 5 percent of sales on supply chain management costs, while the average company spends about 5 to 6 percent.

2. *Supply Chain Cash-to-Cash Cycle Time*: the average number of days between paying for raw materials and getting paid for product, for the supply chain trading partners (calculated by inventory days of supply plus days of sales outstanding minus average payment period for material). This measure shows the impact of lower inventories on the speed of cash moving through firms and the supply chain. Top supply chain companies have a cash-to-cash cycle time of about thirty days, which is far less than the average company. These trading partners no longer view "slow paying" as a viable strategy.

3. *Supply Chain Production Flexibility*: the average time required for supply chain members to provide an unplanned, sustainable 20 percent increase in production. The ability for the supply chain to quickly react to unexpected demand spikes while still operating within financial targets provides tremendous competitive advantage. One common supply chain practice is to maintain stocks of component parts locally for supply chain customers to quickly respond to unexpected demand increases. Average production flexibility for best-in-class supply chains is from one to two weeks.

4. *Supply Chain Delivery Performance*: the average percentage of orders for the supply chain members that are filled on or before the requested delivery date. In the top-performing supply chains, delivery dates are being met from 94 to 100 percent of the time. For average firms, delivery performance is approximately 70 to 80 percent. Updating customers on the expected delivery dates of orders is becoming a common e-service for many supply chains.

5. *Supply Chain Perfect Order Fulfillment Performance*: the average percentage of orders among supply chain members that arrive on time, complete and damage-free. This is quickly becoming the standard for delivery performance and represents a significant source of competitive advantage for top-performing supply chains and their member companies.

6. *Supply Chain e-Business Performance*: the average percentage of electronic orders received for all supply chain members. In 1998, only about 2 percent of all firms' purchase orders were made over the Internet. By 2007, for example, office supply retailer Staples said that 90 percent of its orders came in electronically. Additionally, use of e-procurement can save up to 90 percent of the administrative costs of ordering.[24] Today, supply chain companies are investing heavily in e-based order-receipt systems, marketing strategies, and other forms of communication and research using the Internet.

7. *Supply Chain Environmental Performance*: the percentage of supply chain trading partners that have become ISO 14000 certified; the percentage of supply chain trading partners that have created a director of environmental sustainability; the average percentage of environmental goals met; the average number of policies adopted to reduce greenhouse gas emissions; and the average percentage of carbon footprints that have been offset by sound environmental practices. While these performance indicators may certainly vary by supply chain and industry, the measures here will provide a good starting point for collaboration on supply chain environmental performance.

When combined with the world-class performance measures of Table 14.1, the measures shown above can help trading partners align themselves with supply chain strategies, creating competencies that lead to dominant positions in their markets. In fact, according to a financial analysis of the leading supply chain management companies and their closest competitors for the period 2004–2007, the analysis conclusively shows that the leading supply chain companies do, in fact, outperform their peers in most financial measures—even when accounting for other factors such as size and financial leverage. The leading supply chain companies also showed greater stock returns and economic value added, over the 2004–2007 timeframe.[25]

THE BALANCED SCORECARD

The **balanced scorecard (BSC)** approach to performance measurement was developed in 1992 by Drs. Robert Kaplan and David Norton and representatives from a number of companies as a way to align an organization's performance measures with its strategic plans and goals. The BSC thus allowed a firm to move away from reliance on merely financial measures, which effectively improved managerial decision-making.[26]

Also referred to as simply **scorecarding**, the BSC has become a widely used model with some 80 percent of large U.S. businesses either using it or having previously used it and a smaller but growing percentage of European businesses using it. Many companies have reported notable successes with the use of the BSC including Mobil Oil, Tenneco, Brown & Root, AT&T, Intel, Allstate, Ernst & Young, and KPMG Peat Marwick.[27] According to Shell Canada's human resource director John Hofmeister, "It gives us better and better alignment (between all operating units) and focuses attention on what's important and on results. In addition, the group's reward structure is linked directly to the scorecard."[28] Scorecarding is becoming popular among city municipalities as well, as described in the chapter-opening SCM Profile.

There are some indications, though, that BSC use can be problematic, expensive, and even unsuccessful. Research from the U.S.-based benchmarking company Hackett Group indicated that while 82 percent of its company database reportedly used scorecards, only 27 percent of the systems were considered "mature." They concluded that most companies were having difficulty taking BSC from concept to reality. John McMahan, senior advisor at Hackett Group, said, "Most companies get very little out of scorecards because they haven't followed the basic rules that make them effective." For example, in the United States, the average number of measures used is very high and often confusing 132, while Kaplan and Norton suggest use of 20 to 30 measures.[29] Additionally, consultants are used in many cases to help map the organization's strategy and its effect on performance, and to assist in selecting performance measures. Further, information systems may have to be modified, sometimes at great expense, to supply the information necessary for the scorecards. Other weaknesses in the BSC include its inability to show what one's competitors are doing; exclusion of employee, supplier, and alliance partner contributions; and its reliance on top-down measures.[30]

Nevertheless, the BSC is widely used in helping organizations track performance and identify areas of weakness. Performance scorecards are designed to provide managers with a formal framework for achieving a balance between nonfinancial and financial results across both short-term and long-term planning horizons. The BSC framework consists of four perspectives as shown in Figure 14.1:

- *Financial Perspective*—measures that address revenue and profitability growth, product mix, cost reduction, productivity, asset utilization, and investment strategies. Traditional financial measures are typically used.

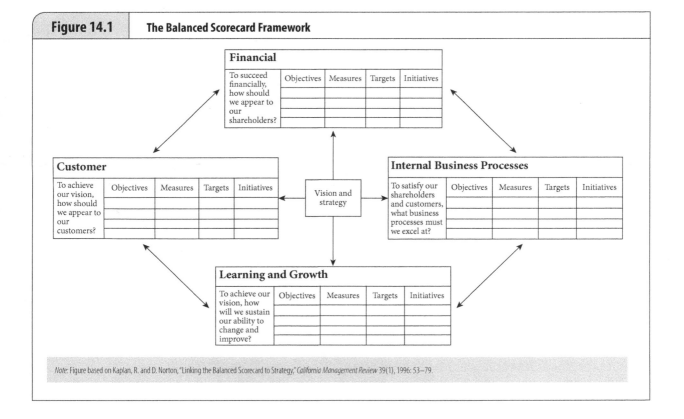

| Figure 14.1 | The Balanced Scorecard Framework |

Note: Figure based on Kaplan, R. and D. Norton, "Linking the Balanced Scorecard to Strategy," *California Management Review* 39(1), 1996: 53–79.

- *Internal Business Process Perspective*—focuses on performance of the most critical internal business processes of the organization including quality, new product development, flexibility, innovative elements of processes, and time-based measures.

- *Customer Perspective*—measures that focus on customer requirements and satisfaction including customer satisfaction ratings, reliability and responsiveness, customer retention, new customer acquisition, customer-valued attributes, and customer profitability.

- *Learning and Growth Perspective*—measures concentrating on the organization's people, systems, and external environment and including retaining and training employees, enhancing information technology and systems, employee safety, and health and environmental sustainability issues.

These perspectives are all linked together using performance measures within each of the four areas. Measurements are developed for each goal in the organization's strategic plan and include both outcome measures and the performance drivers of those outcomes. In doing this, senior managers can channel the specific set of capabilities within the organization toward achieving the firm's goals. A properly constructed scorecard should support the firm's strategy and consists of a linked series of measures that are consistent and reinforcing. By developing suitable performance measures in each of the perspectives, firms can detect problem areas before they become significant, trace the problem to its root causes, and make improvements to alleviate the problem.

The process of developing a BSC begins with defining the firm's strategy. Once that strategy is understood and agreed upon by senior managers, the next step is to translate the strategy's goals into a system of relevant performance measures. Each of the four perspectives in the BSC require four to seven performance measures, resulting in a scorecard with about two dozen measures relating to one single strategy. As alluded to above, the potential for failure does exist if firms are not clear about what they are hoping to achieve and are not focused on ensuring that the best scorecards with the right performance measures linked to firm strategies are used.

The BSC can also be utilized by firms in a collaborative supply chain setting by expanding the internal perspective of the scorecard to include interfunctional and partnership perspectives that characterize the supply chain. In this way, for instance, the firm's employees are motivated to view their firm's performance vis-à-vis the success of the entire supply chain. Supply chain–oriented performance measures, such as the ones described earlier, can thus be added to the more internally focused measures traditionally used in a balanced scorecard to help the firm as well as its supply chains meet their objectives.

Balanced scorecards are being used in the government and healthcare sectors, too, with many positive outcomes. One example is the U.S. Economic Development administration (EDA). The EDA used the BSC to help develop its world-class performance measurement system. After adoption of the BSC approach, it aligned the organization around a common set of goals, improved the quality of its investments, enhanced efficiencies, and created higher-quality jobs.[31]

Web-Based Scorecards

Today, a number of software applications are available to help design scorecards, which link via the web to a firm's enterprise software system. Web-based balanced scorecard applications are also sometimes referred to as **performance dashboards**. They enable users to retrieve data easily from enterprise databases and also enable wide access by users at many locations, while providing desired security features. Performance dashboards are being used to track "big picture" corporate objectives as well as core process performance and more tactical, detailed data. Use of these web-based dashboards allows managers to see real-time progress toward organizational milestones and helps to ensure that decisions remain in sync with the firm's overall strategies.

Virtually all accounting applications, for example, provide BSC capabilities, including applications offered by Microsoft, SAP, IBM, and Oracle. Performance dashboard applications are becoming commonplace these days. For example, the U.S. Department of Veterans Affairs uses performance dashboards to give its IT employees a visual representation of its effectiveness in solving problems for customers. Some of the top supply chain companies use dashboards to compare team performances and find that this motivates teams to perform better. American energy company ConocoPhillips uses performance dashboards at a number of its oil and gas wells to let well operators know when plunger-lift operating cycles must be adjusted to eliminate fluid buildups that restrict the flow of gas. Using these dashboards has allowed production to increase by about 30 percent. The U.S. Environmental Protection Agency (EPA) uses state dashboards and comparative maps that provide the public with information about the performance of state and EPA enforcement and compliance programs across the country. "Transparency and access to information at all levels helps to drive improvements in environmental performance," says Cynthia Giles, assistant administrator for the EPA's Office of Enforcement and Compliance Assurance.[32]

THE SCOR MODEL

One of the more recognized methods for integrating supply chains and measuring performance is use of the supply chain operations reference (SCOR) model developed in 1996 by supply chain consulting firms Pittiglio, Rabin, Todd & McGrath and AMR Research. These firms also founded the Texas-based Supply Chain Council (SCC) to oversee the SCOR model, a nonprofit global organization with a current membership of over 1,000 profit and nonprofit organizations on six continents. In 2014, APICS, the global supply chain management association, merged with the SCC and formed APICS SCC. Today, APICS SCC manages the SCOR model, while providing education opportunities for its members.[33]

The SCOR model helps to integrate the operations of supply chain members by linking the delivery operations of a seller to the sourcing operations of a buyer. Starting in 2013, members could obtain a professional certification in knowledge and methods of the SCOR model, termed as SCOR-P endorsement. Also new in 2013, was the SCOR model's new process category, ENABLE, as shown in the model in Figure 14.2.[34]

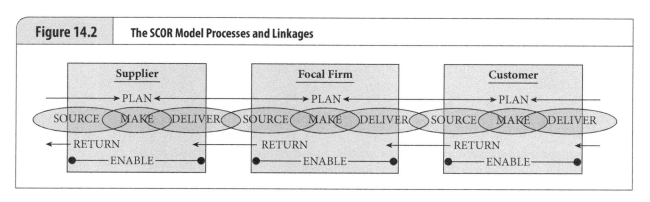

| Figure 14.2 | The SCOR Model Processes and Linkages |

The SCOR model is used as a supply chain management diagnostic, benchmarking, and process improvement tool by manufacturing and service firms in a variety of industries around the globe. Some of the notable firms to have success using the SCOR model include Intel, IBM, 3M, Cisco, Siemens, and Bayer. Striving for the best telecommunications supply chain, Alcatel (now Alcatel-Lucent), for example, used SCOR metrics following the economic downturn of 2001 to measure and benchmark its performance. Major improvements were realized in delivery performance, sourcing cycle time, supply chain management cost, and inventory days of supply.[35] Cisco set out to revamp its supply chain in 2005 using the SCOR model as a way to monitor its growing global footprint. It eventually appointed a vice president responsible for the SCOR model's functions.[36] In 2010, German semiconductor manufacturer Infineon used the SCOR model to build an agile and adaptable supply chain. Hundreds of employees, customers, suppliers, and production partners were involved in the eighteen-month project. Results included improved flexibility and reduction of total finished goods inventory levels, leading to improved shareholder confidence and stock price. Finally, in 2017, APICS, in partnership with JD.com, a Chinese ecommerce company, will help establish the JD Supply Chain Academy within JD University, a supply chain talent development center and e-commerce supply chain research center. APICS and JD.com will also collaborate to cross-reference the SCOR model with the JD.com database in order to develop a specific SCORmark Omni Channel Benchmark for China.[37]

The SCOR model separates supply chain operations into six process categories: plan, source, make, deliver, return, and enable, as described below:[38]

- *PLAN*—Demand and supply planning including balancing resources with requirements; establishing/communicating plans for the supply chain; management of business rules, supply chain performance, data collection, inventory, capital assets, transportation, and regulatory requirements.

- *SOURCE*—Sourcing stocked, make-to-order, and engineer-to-order products including scheduling deliveries, receiving, verifying, and transferring product, authorizing supplier payments, identifying and selecting suppliers, assessing supplier performance, and managing incoming inventory and supplier agreements.

- *MAKE*—Make-to-stock, make-to-order, and engineer-to-order production execution including scheduling production activities, producing, testing, packaging, staging, and releasing product for delivery, finalizing engineering for engineer-to-order products, managing work-in-process, equipment, facilities, and the production network.

- *DELIVER*—Order, warehouse, transportation, and installation management for stocked, make-to-order, and engineer-to-order product including all order management steps from order inquiries and quotes to routing shipments and selecting carriers, warehouse management from receiving and picking to loading and shipping product, invoicing customer, managing finished product inventories, and import/export requirements.

- *RETURN*—Returns of purchased materials to suppliers and receipt of finished goods returns from customers including authorizing and scheduling returns, receiving, verifying, and disposition of defective or excess products, return replacement or credit, and managing return inventories.

- *ENABLE*—The processes associated with establishing, maintaining, and monitoring information, relationships, resources, assets, business rules, compliance, and contracts required to operate supply chains. Enable processes support the design and management of the planning and execution processes of supply chains.

The SCOR model also uses five categories of performance attributes as shown in Table 14.2.[39] Implementing the SCOR model is no simple task. It requires a significant investment of time and open communications within the firm and among supply chain partners. In 2017, the 12th version of SCOR will be released. It will include updates to maturity models, best practices, and terminology. "The new version of SCOR is incorporating many emerging drivers of supply chain success such as big data, omni-channel, and automation to keep SCOR at the forefront of supply chain," says APICS CEO Abe Eshkenazi. "SCOR has been the leader in addressing, improving, and communicating supply chain business performance for the last twenty years, and it's our intent to maintain SCOR's position as the cross-industry, global standard."[40]

The SCOR model is designed to enable effective communication, performance measurement, and integration of processes between supply chain members. A standardized reference model helps management focus on management issues, serving internal and external customers, and instigating improvements along the supply chain. Using the SCOR software, virtually any supply chain can be configured, evaluated, and benchmarked against best practices, leading to continuous improvements and sustainable competitive advantage for the supply chain's participating members.

SCORmark is one of the newest tools of the APICS SCC, which allows member firms to benchmark performance against peer companies using a benchmarking portal at the APICS SCC website. Members have access to confidential benchmarking based on the SCOR model metrics. Companies generally use SCOR-based benchmarking to:

- set reasonable performance goals based on the SCOR model,
- calculate performance gaps against a global database, and
- develop company-specific roadmaps for supply chain competitive success.

This has greatly reduced the time normally taken by firms to perform a benchmarking study—from months to weeks and, in some cases, days. The SCORmark portal removes cost barriers for members to obtain accurate and timely benchmark reports.

Table 14.2	SCOR Performance Categories and Attributes
PERFORMANCE CATEGORY	**PERFORMANCE ATTRIBUTE**
Reliability	1. On-time delivery performance
	2. Order fill rates
	3. Order accuracy rates
Responsiveness	1. Order lead times or speed
Agility	1. Response times for unforeseen events
	2. Production flexibility
Cost	1. Supply chain management and logistics costs
	2. Cost of goods sold
	3. Warranty and returns processing costs
Asset Management	1. Cash-to-cash cycle time
	2. Inventory days of supply
	3. Asset turns

SUMMARY

Measuring the performance of companies and their supply chains is critical for identifying underlying problems and keeping end customers satisfied in today's highly competitive, rapidly changing marketplaces. Unfortunately, many firms have adopted performance measurement systems that measure the wrong things and are thus finding it difficult to achieve strategic goals and align their goals with those of the other supply chain members and the supply chain as a whole. Good performance measures allow firms to improve their processes, making their supply chains better as well.

Financial performance, while important to the firm and its shareholders, is argued to provide too little information regarding the firm's underlying ability to provide products and services that satisfy customers. Thus, measures that say something about the firm's quality, productivity, flexibility, and customer service capabilities have begun to be used successfully in many organizations. World-class organizations realize how important it is to align strategies with the performance of their people and processes, and performance measurement systems give these firms a means for directing efforts and firm capabilities toward what the firm is trying to do over the long haul—meet strategic objectives and satisfy customers.

As was discussed throughout the chapter, performance measurement systems should be a mix of financial, nonfinancial, quantitative, qualitative, process-oriented, environmentally oriented, and customer-oriented measures that effectively link the actions of the firm to the strategies defined by its executive managers. Firms actively managing their supply chains have an added layer of performance measurement requirements—measures must be added that link the operations of member firms as well as linking the actions of the firms to the competitive strategies of the supply chain. Several performance measurement models were presented and discussed in the chapter that have been successfully used in supply chains to monitor and link supply chain members' performance—namely, the balanced scorecard and the supply chain operations reference models.

KEY TERMS

balanced scorecard (BSC), 557

carbon footprints, 556

environmental sustainability, 555

functional silos, 550

green supply chain management (GSCM), 555

performance dashboards, 559

performance variance, 550

scorecarding, 557

single-factor productivity measures, 550

total productivity measures, 550

DISCUSSION QUESTIONS

1. Walmart's success is due to its low prices. Why would they need to monitor anything except price performance?

2. Do you think there is a relationship between performance measurement and a firm's competitiveness and profitability? Explain.

3. Why would IKEA be interested in sustainability performance measures?

4. What do customers have to do with good performance measures?

5. How should performance measures be viewed from a supply chain perspective?

6. In building supply chain competencies, what are the trade-offs that must be considered?

7. What risk do managers take when they view their firm's performance solely in financial terms?

8. List some of the traditional performance measures, and describe their value in today's competitive climate.

9. Discuss the use of performance standards and performance variances. Do schools and universities use them? How can they be damaging to the organization?

10. How can performance standards create functional silos?

11. What is the difference between a total productivity measure and a single-factor productivity measure? Provide an example.

12. List some single-factor and multiple-factor productivity measures for a restaurant, a quick-change oil garage, and an overnight delivery service.

13. Using the basic formula for productivity, (outputs)/(inputs), what are all the ways that productivity can be increased?

14. What is the productivity growth rate right now in the United States? Explain why it is as low as it is.

15. What are the advantages and disadvantages of using labor utilization as a performance measure? Do these same arguments apply to machine utilization?

16. How could you increase labor productivity without increasing labor utilization?

17. Using the formulas provided for utilization, calculate the utilization of your classroom.

18. What do you think a good labor utilization would be for a factory? A restaurant? Why?

19. How do world-class performance measures differ from, say, financial performance measures?

20. Using the steps suggested for developing performance measures, create several world-class performance measures for a hotel's front-desk area, maintenance department, and room service personnel.

21. How should a firm extend its performance measures to include other supply chain members?

22. What are demand-driven supply networks, and what role do performance measures play in these networks?

23. How can you create performance measures for an entire supply chain?

24. Why should supply chains begin using green performance measures? Provide some examples of green supply chain performance measures. How would these differ from green performance measures for one firm?

25. What is a carbon footprint, and how can firms reduce theirs? How could you measure the carbon footprint for a supply chain?

26. What is perfect order fulfillment? Cash-to-cash cycle time?

27. Describe the four perspectives of the balanced scorecard. How is this model different from a set of world-class performance measures?

28. What are the steps in developing a balanced scorecard?

29. What are some weaknesses of the BSC?

30. How is a scorecard different from a dashboard?

31. What are the six process categories of the SCOR model, and which one do you think is the most important?

32. In what ways is the BSC similar to the SCOR model? Different from the SCOR model?

33. Which model do you think is best suited to measure supply chain performance—the BSC or the SCOR? Why?

34. How is SCORmark beneficial for member organizations?

PROBLEMS

1. Cindy Jo's Hair Salon is concerned about its rising costs of supplies, energy, and labor, so it is considering investing in better equipment, which hopefully will reduce the time required to perform most hairstyles as well as result in better perceived quality by its customers. It predicts that the added investment will increase output levels as well as reduce energy costs, since some of the new equipment (hair dryers) use less electricity. Using the following information, determine the current and expected single-factor and total productivity measures. What is the percentage change in total productivity? What other items should be considered before making this capital investment? Do you think the increase in output will overcome the capital costs?

INPUTS AND OUTPUTS	CURRENT (THIS YEAR)	EXPECTED (NEXT YEAR)
Hairstyles per week	250	300
Labor costs per week	$960	$1,010
Energy costs per week	$400	$350
Material costs per week	$300	$325
Capital investment	$0	$12,000

2. For the four months shown, calculate the monthly labor productivities and the monthly productivity growths.

	MARCH	APRIL	MAY	JUNE
Units produced	1,260	1,340	1,293	1,324
Labor hours	328	332	321	318

3. Calculate the single-factor productivities and the total productivity given the information below.

OUTPUT	INPUTS
325,000 units Sales price = $1,249.00/unit	6,400 labor hours @ $15.00 per hour Material cost = $40,625,000 Utilities cost = $4,400

ESSAY/PROJECT QUESTIONS

1. Using data obtained from the U.S. Bureau of Labor Statistics website (www.bls.gov), write a report on labor productivity in the United States compared to several other countries listed.

2. Find a company using sustainability performance measures to assess its own company as well as their suppliers, and write an essay on this company and their performance measures.

3. Pick a company from Gartner's annual listing of the Top 25 Supply Chains (see their listing at http://www.gartner.com/technology/supply-chain/top25.jsp), and discuss the performance measures it uses.

4. Find current examples of firms that are using balanced scorecards and the SCOR model, and report on their success.

CASES

1. Production Labor Sourcing for Supply Chain Management*

Over 75 percent of U.S. manufacturers have been reported to outsource some of their business functions. A shift in offshore outsourcing has returned some business activities to the United States even as cost reduction pressure still challenges most U.S. businesses. Brook Medical Supplies (BMS), a manufacturer of medical supplies and ambulatory kits, recently ended outsourcing operations overseas as a competitive measure to improve quality and reduce costs. BMS instead selected a cost reduction project that outsourced semiskilled labor locally. The labor-sourcing approach reduced overall costs below the offshore program, while maintaining complete oversight of product quality. The positive results in cost reduction prompted BMS to expand the labor-sourcing initiative beyond its production positions. BMS now uses labor sourcing for semiskilled labor in its material handling (shipping and receiving), staging (tow motor drivers), maintenance, and waste handlers without displacing any existing employees by moving them to other departments in the plant. With the responsibility to hire, train, and supervise this group of semiskilled laborers, BMS has been able to increase efforts in core areas of increased quality, efficiencies, and product improvement.

Stor-Pak Distribution Center handles 90 percent of BMS' New England distribution, including assembly and kitting for their drug testing kits. In addition to their customer–supplier relationship, Stor-Pak partners with BMS as a Best in Class and benchmarking mentoring through a national association of U.S. manufacturers and distribution centers. As part of BMS' supply chain management integration efforts, they have recommended to Stor-Pak that they evaluate alternatives to expanding their labor force with permanent employees. Stor-Pak is evaluating three alternatives including hiring permanent warehouse employees, contracting with temporary employment agencies for expanded labor, and contracting with a specialized labor-sourcing company similar to the contract BMS secured for their production and warehousing operation. Stor-Pak has been gathering internal data on labor costs for permanent employees and has a large pool of temporary employment agencies that responded to their RFP. Only one proposal was submitted that was identified as a specialized labor-sourcing company.

Bethel Consulting Services (BCS) is a third-party labor-sourcing company with expertise in screening, selection, training, and supervision of semiskilled warehouse associates. BCS presents a "company within a company" or vendor onsite service with competencies in training for warehouse positions in material handling, pick and pack, assembly and kit making that reduces the learning curve time and improves quality of work. Their proprietary competency-based hiring system and onsite supervision result in lower tardiness, turnover, and safety issues. BCS' specialized staffing system starts

---

*Written by Brian Hoyt, PhD, professor of management, Ohio University. This case was prepared solely to provide fictional material for class discussion. The author does not intend to illustrate either effective or ineffective handling of a managerial situation.

with an assessment of required skills and activities of the warehouse operation and then drafts standard operating procedures (SOPs) for training and performance evaluations. Their data and performance-based system allows performance incentives for BCS employees and gain sharing opportunities for contract partners.

BCS has data necessary for developing a business case that warehouses and distribution centers can use to present contracting with a specialized labor-sourcing company. The business case compares BCS cost and performance measures to hiring permanent employees and contracting through temporary agencies. The business case presents data reporting productivity gains and a reduction of overall labor cost by 20–40 percent. The data reports an increased quality of work (reduced errors in storage and retrieval, assembly, and kit making), improved performance measures (picking and packing efficiencies), and improved safety (reduced liability and claims). The BCS system will allow distribution customers to redirect efforts in supervising semiskilled labor to supervising skilled labor and focusing on core competencies and other lean cost saving priorities.

Discussion Questions

1. How could contracting with Bethel Consulting Services advance Stor-Pak's position as a world-class supply chain partner for Brook Medical Supplies and other customers?

2. What cost advantage perspective should Stor-Pak use to determine the differences between using a traditional temp agency versus a third-party labor source provider such as Bethel Consulting Services?

3. If the reduced costs projected by Bethel Consulting Services are realized, will there still be any risks for Stor-Pak in bringing in a third-party labor source company such as BCS?

©2019 Cengage Learning

2. Warehouse and Distribution Center Robotics*

Rack and Shelving Manufacturing (RSM) is an 85-year-old U.S. niche pallet rack and shelving manufacturer. RSM sells to volume resellers, direct to manufacturers with warehousing, warehouse distribution centers, and to small end users through B2B e-commerce. Major fluctuations of steel pricing, poor inventory management, and labor issues with a local union at its largest manufacturing facility have put RSM at a financial crossroad. RSM, recognized as a high-quality manufacturer with a limited product line, has small market share in the growing storage equipment industry sector. Recently, the shelving lines have been updated to accommodate innovations in the pick, pack, and ship fulfillment centers. The pallet rack line (Pallets Plus) is a standard selective rack system featuring two upright frames and shelf beams inserted between the frames. Their high-quality rack is one of the most flexible (easy-to-configure racking to all layouts) and compared to more complex pallet rack systems including drive through racking and roller racks is economical with quick access to pallets. The Pallets Plus rack system is ideal for manufacturing or warehouse storage with a broad array of items but

*Written by Brian Hoyt, PhD, professor of management, Ohio University. This case was prepared solely to provide fictional material for class discussion. The author does not intend to illustrate either effective or ineffective handling of a managerial situation.

moderate-to-low turnover volume. Innovation of the Pallets Plus line has not been introduced to the market for over ten years. The growth in the rack storage sector is intently focused on optimizing warehouse cubic feet with high-density racking systems that facilitate high number of items and high turnover volume. These rack systems, while significantly more expensive than the selective Pallets Plus rack system, increase the productive use of warehouse floor space by 60–75 percent more than selective systems.

Rack and Shelving Manufacturing attended the most recent ProMat tradeshow in Chicago, organized by the Material Handling Industry of America. The ProMat tradeshow is an international showcase of material handling, supply chain and logistics solutions in North America. The industry event offers productivity solutions and information by highlighting the products and services of leading material handling and logistics providers. At the ProMat show RSM was looking for direction relative to their next new product in pallet systems. They decided to "leapfrog" the existing high-density pallet systems (i.e., drive through, roller racks, and pallet flows) and partner with a technology firm that manufactures warehouse-specific automated guided vehicles (AGVs). RSM is now focusing on building a new pallet rack and shelving product line that will meet all the specifications for automated storage technology's (AST) warehouse robotics line.

Rack and Shelving Manufacturing's new technology partner Automated Storage Technology is a leader in automated storage and retrieval systems (AS/RS). They were one of the first to test AGVs and with several generations of innovations now have a prototype for a fully robotic forklift. Similar to RSM, automated storage technology has evolved from systems associated with large pallet racks to automation and robotics associated with "pick, pack, and ship" fulfillment centers. AST's AGV technology supports pick up, carry, and drop-off loads for manufacturing plants, warehouses, and distribution centers. The guidance technologies and navigation technologies are laser-guided for self-driving material handling vehicles similar to self-driving cars. AST uses a laser and light-based navigation that scans the facility to gather data to construct a detailed map of the facility floor. The reference map can then be used to navigate any route. The AGV system is a smart technology that can plan and follow its own route similar to how an auto GPS will re-route the map once the car deviates from the original mapped route. Operators can drag and drop instructions to direct the vehicle's pickups and drop-offs. AST is developing a navigation system that will allow warehouse/inventory management to control a fleet of AGVs using apps on mobile devices such as tablets, phones, and laptops.

Rack and Shelving Manufacturing is investing in a strategy where they identify and occupy a niche in the future of warehouse storage and retrieval. They must position themselves as the first to control this niche with their partnership with AST that positions the new RSM pallet and storage systems as essential to the process of automated storage and retrieval (AGV and AS/RS). The pricing strategy for the premium price of the new pallet and shelving products is based on the very small percentage of cost of the entire automated (i.e., self-guided pallet trucks) warehouse system and design. The niche is small enough and unattractive to rivals at first and Rack and Shelving Manufacturing can grow along with the projected growth of the high-tech warehouse.

Discussion Questions

1. Defend Rack and Shelving Manufacturing's new product development strategy of tying new rack and shelving products to automated storage technology's AGV/robotic innovation cycles.

2. How will product manufacturers and supply chain partners benefit in their efforts to adopt high-performance supply chain measures by using RSM and AST AGV equipment and storage racks?

3. What risks do RSM and AST face that may alter (quicken or slow down) the pace of the adoption of warehouse robotics in the warehouse, storage, and logistics sectors?

Note: For pallet rack descriptions, see Rack Manufacturers Institute/Material Handling Institutes SIG's (www.mhi.org). Students should also visit the ProMat tradeshow website at www.ProMatshow.com. General information on robotics for warehousing can be found at www.dcvelocity.com.

©2019 Cengage Learning

3. The Balanced Scorecard Approach*

PJ Express (PJEx) is one of the largest privately owned New England business-to-consumer (B2C) carriers specializing in "last-mile" deliveries. PJEx is a company with new leadership, but also with a two-year drop in sales and profits, and recently was contacted by a more successful competitor as an acquisition target. The overnight shipments to residential consumers have increased competitive pressures as UPS, FedEx, and Amazon have moved into smaller, Tier 2 distribution hubs. Profits for all carriers of consumer products have been squeezed as major retailers have established a "free shipping" benefit that is not going away after peak shipping seasons (i.e., cyber week and holidays).

The PJEx executive team is led by a new CEO who left FedEx Ground after leading a successful turnaround of an acquired carrier. The success was attributed to a focused strategy using the balanced scorecard (BSC) framework. The CEO was selected in part because of his success in using the BSC and because PJEx had just recently committed to using the BSC performance measurement framework to align with its three-year turnaround strategic plan. Last year, PJEx charged four teams with developing perspectives for the BSC framework—the financial perspective team, the internal business process perspective team, the customer perspective team, and the learning and growth perspective team. To accelerate the strategic turnaround effort, the learning and growth (L&G) perspective team contracted with a BSC consulting company, balanced scorecard systems (BSS). BSS is a strategic planning consulting group specializing in the logistics and transportation industry using the BSC approach. The L&G team efforts are much farther along than the other teams and BSS has presented a first draft of the learning and growth measures.

A partial L&G scorecard focused on improving organizational capacity performance and includes:

Objectives:

a. Establish a learning organization effort.

b. Improve training effectiveness.

Measures:

a. Add organizational learning components: observe, capture, store, access, disseminate, and evaluate.

b. Increase percent of Six Sigma program—Green Belts (by 45 percent), Black Belts (by 20 percent), and Master Black Belts (by 15 percent).

*Written by Brian Hoyt, PhD, professor of management, Ohio University. This case was prepared solely to provide fictional material for class discussion. The author does not intend to illustrate either effective or ineffective handling of a managerial situation.

Targets:

a. Develop knowledge management system (KMS).

b. Build high-performance improvement teams (HPT).

Initiatives:

a. Benchmark—learning new concepts from external sources and internal sources on KMS.

- Plan—assess where new knowledge is needed as related to key performance indicators.
- Find—locate a department/division (internal) or organization (external) that performs our identified process (KMS) better for comparison.
- Observe—monitor performance of benchmarked KMS and note differences in performance.
- Analyze—determine causes for differences in performance.
- Adapt—select best practices from benchmarked organization and modify for our KMS.
- Improve—integrate our new learning into other process improvements.

b. Transition to project-based training delivery for Six Sigma content.

- Analyze department training needs—determine the number and level of qualified "belts" to have all employees engaged in HPT.
- Analyze training task—produce a detailed description of skills required at Green Belt, Black Belt, and Master Black Belt levels.
- Develop training objective measures—measures in quality tool knowledge, statistical analysis, improvement process, and improvement experiment design.
- Organize training content—secure training materials and subject matter experts in Six Sigma, DMAIC, and belt requirements.
- Determine training methods—project-based training methodology where training occurs while teams are involved in actual HPT improvement projects.
- Select training resources—secure Six Sigma guidebooks.
- Complete training plan.
- Deliver training pilot.
- Assess training pilot, make adjustments, and submit to HR for KMS inclusion.

The transition with the new executive management team is certain to have some impact on PJEx's recent strategy and planning activities. The new CEO has indicated in preliminary discussions that he would be driving the balanced scorecard initiative based on his previous experience and success with BSC. A growing number of employees have been critical in open discussion meetings initiated and delivered by the new executive team. A common complaint in these meetings is that PJEx has introduced several similar companywide programs in the past that have had limited success but huge organizational investments of time and money including total quality management, LEAN management, Six Sigma/Black Belt, just in time (JIT), constraint theory (TOC), etc. All of the previous programs started out with positive results but efforts, measures of effectiveness, and eventually support and commitment waned. In addition, the manufacturing group assigned the internal business processes perspective (IBP) of BSC is presenting an alternative to the BSC all together as an effort to achieve the new management turnaround goals. The IBP group is proposing a shift to the Baldrige Award framework.

Discussion Questions

1. Should the learning and growth team sever its relationship with balanced scorecard systems before the new CEO presents the new BSC plan? Develop a Pro/Con response that the learning and growth team could present to the BSC steering committee.

2. What advice can you provide the new executive team for their next organizational meeting that addresses the staying power of BSC?

3. Is the Baldrige approach that the manufacturing group is presenting an alternative to the BSC or can it run parallel?

©2019 Cengage Learning

ADDITIONAL RESOURCES

Kaplan, R. S., and D. P. Norton, "Linking the Balanced Scorecard to Strategy," *California Management Review* 39(1), 1996: 53–79.

Evans, J. R., and W. M. Lindsay, *The Management and Control of Quality*. Mason, OH: South-Western, 2002.

Metters, R., K. King-Metters, and M. Pullman, *Successful Service Operations Management*. Mason, OH: South-Western, 2003.

Nicholas, J. M., *Competitive Manufacturing Management*. New York: McGraw-Hill, 1998.

Wisner, J. D., and S. E. Fawcett, "Linking Firm Strategy to Operating Decisions through Performance Measurement," *Production and Inventory Management Journal* 32(3), 1991: 5–11.

END NOTES

1. Young, G., "Decades of Leadership," *Public Management* 97(11), 2015: 15–17.

2. Burns, J., "MIPS: The 'Death Knell' for Small Practices?" *Medical Economics* 93(4), 2016: 32, 34–36.

3. Moore, B., "Excellence in Performance Management," *Public Management* 97(11), 2015: 26–28.

4. http://www.gartner.com/newsroom/id/3323617

5. Poirier, C., M. Swink, and F. Quinn, "Progress Despite the Downturn," *Supply Chain Management Review* 13(7), 2009: 26.

6. Biederman, D., "The Customer Is King, Again," *Journal of Commerce* May 10, 2010: 1.

7. Henri, J., "Are Your Performance Measurement Systems Truly Performing?" *CMA Management* 80(7), 2006: 31–35; Biddick, M., "Time for a SaaS Strategy," *InformationWeek* January 18, 2010: 27–30.

8. Woodcock, N., N. Broomfield, G. Downer, and M. Starkey, "The Evolving Data Architecture of Social Customer Relationship Management," *Journal of Direct, Data and Digital Marketing Practice* 12(3), 2011: 249–266.

9. Beaulieu, L., "ResMed's Flow Gen Sales Blow Up," *HME News* 21(9), 2015: 20–21.

10. Anonymous, "Mitch Smith—Director, U.S. Quality Systems, Agricultural Products, McDonald's Corporation," *Boardroom Insiders Profiles*, Boardroom Insiders, Inc., January 9, 2017: 1.

11. Fusaro, P., and R. Miller, *What Went Wrong at Enron: Everyone's Guide to the Largest Bankruptcy in U.S. History*. Hoboken, NJ: Wiley, 2002.

12. Found at *CNN Money*: http://money.cnn.com/magazines/fortune/fortune500/2010/index.html, and https://www.usatoday.com/story/money/personalfinance/2015/10/24/24-7-wall-st-most-profitable-companies/74501312

13. Stoessel, E., "Reaching New Heights," *Lodging Hospitality* 67(4), 2011: 1.

14. See Christensen, P., and K. Gregory, "Becoming a Data-Driven Organization: City of Peoria, Arizona," *Government Finance Review* 26(2), 2010: 57–59; and http://transformgov.org/en/Article/107738/Valley_Benchmark_Cities_Releases_FY_201415_Data_Trends_Report

15. Cook, B., "Making Good," *Supply Management* 20(5), 2015: 32–34.

16. Debusk, G., and C. Debusk, "Characteristics of Successful Lean Six Sigma Organizations," *Cost Management* 24(1), 2010: 5–10.

17. Adapted from Nicholas, J. M., *Competitive Manufacturing Management*. New York: McGraw-Hill, 1998; and Wisner, J., and S. Fawcett, "Linking Firm Strategy to Operating Decisions Through Performance Measurement," *Production and Inventory Management Journal* 32(3), 1991: 5–11.

18. Hae, E., and D. Ballou, "Raising the Recycling Rate at World-Class Zoo," *BioCycle* 50(10), 2009: 31–33. Also see p. 4 in http://www.sandiego.gov/environmental-services/pdf/geninfo/news/2013RecyclingAwardFS.pdf, and https://www.sandiego.gov/sites/default/files/legacy/environmental-services/pdf/recycling/ro/SanDiegoZooGlobal.pdf

19. Geary, S., and J. Zonnenburg, "What It Means to Be Best in Class," *Supply Chain Management Review*, July 2000: 42–50; Aquino, D., and K. O'Marah, "What Makes a Modern Supply Chain Professional?" *Supply Chain Management Review* May 2009: 12–13; Hofman, D., and S. Aronow, "The Supply Chain Top 25 Raising the Bar," *Logistics Management* 51(9), 2012: 54–64.

20. Anonymous, "Hilton Has Room to Improve with Plug Loads and LEDs," *Buildings* 110(8), 2016: 20.

21. Hervani, A., M. Helms, and J. Sarkis, "Performance Measurement for Green Supply Chain Management," *Benchmarking* 12(4), 2005: 330–354.

22. Editorial staff, "Green Supply Chain News: Walmart's Vast Efforts and Progress in Sustainability," found at http://www.thegreensupplychain.com/news/12-04-18-1.php, April 18, 2012; http://corporate.walmart.com/global-responsibility/environment-sustainability/sustainability-index-leaders-shop

23. Adapted from Geary, S., and J. P. Zonnenburg, "What It Means to Be Best in Class," *Supply Chain Management Review* July 2000: 42–50.

24. Varmazis, M., "What to Look for in Online Office Supply Catalogs," *Purchasing* 136(11), 2007: 33.

25. Swink, M., R. Golecha, and T. Richardson, "Does Supply Chain Excellence Really Pay Off?" *Supply Chain Management Review* 14(2), 2010: 14.

26. See, for example, DeBusk, G., and A. Crabtree, "Does the Balanced Scorecard Improve Performance?" *Management Accounting Quarterly* 8(1), 2006: 44–48; Kaplan, R. S., and D. P. Norton, "The Balanced Scorecard—Measures That Drive Performance," 70(1), 1992: 71–79; Lester, T., "Measure for Measure, the Balanced Scorecard Remains a Widely Used Management Tool," *Financial Times* October 6, 2004: 6; and Lawson, R., W. Stratton, and T. Hatch, "Scorecarding in the Public Sector: Fad or Tool of Choice?" *Government Finance Review* 23(3), 2007: 48–52.

27. Chow, C. W., D. Ganulin, K. Haddad, and J. Williamson, "The Balanced Scorecard: A Potent Tool for Energizing and Focusing Healthcare Organization Management," *Journal of Healthcare Management* 43(3), 1998: 263–280.

28. Lester, T., "Measure for Measure, the Balanced Scorecard Remains a Widely Used Management Tool."

29. Lester, T., "Measure for Measure, the Balanced Scorecard Remains a Widely Used Management Tool."

30. Alsyouf, I., "Measuring Maintenance Performance Using a Balanced Scorecard Approach," *Journal of Quality in Maintenance Engineering* 12(2), 2006: 133–143.

31. Bush, P., "Strategic Performance Management in Government: Using the Balanced Scorecard," *Cost Management* 19(3), 2005: 24–31.

32. Anonymous, "New Look at State Enforcement of Regs," *Pollution Engineering* 45(3), 2013: 14–15; Blanco, E., "Seeing Is Believing: Harnessing the Power of Visualization," *Supply Chain Management Review* 17(5), 2013: 10–11; Henschen, D., "Drilling Down into Big Data," *InformationWeek* September 9, 2013: 15–17; Mayor, T., "IT Takes on Bureaucracy," *Computerworld* 47(10), 2013: 24–26.

33. Interested readers can visit http://www.apics.org/about/overview/about-apics-scc

34. McCrea, B., "Certification: The Career Enhancer," *Supply Chain Management Review* 16(4), 2012: S3–S11; Anonymous, "SCOR Model Enhances How Supply Chains Are Enabled," *Material Handling & Logistics* December 4, 2012: 1.

35. Taken from the online proceedings of the Supply-Chain World—Latin America 2002 conference, Mexico City, Mexico (www.supplychainworld.org/la2002/program.html).

36. Harbert, T., "Why the Leaders Love Value Chain Management," *Supply Chain Management Review* 13(8), 2009: 12–16.

37. Anonymous, "SCC Names Supply Chain Excellence Winners," *Material Handling & Logistics* November 1, 2010: 1. Also see Anonymous, "APICS Joins Forces with JD.com, Forms Corporate Advisory Board," *Manufacturing Close-Up* April 17, 2017: 1.

38. For more information, see www.supply-chain.org

39. For more information, see www.supply-chain.org. Also see, Myerson, P., "How Do You Know If Your Supply Chain Is Lean Enough?" *Material Handling & Logistics* July 9, 2012: 1; Georgise, F., K. Thoben, and M. Siefert, "Adapting the SCOR Model to Suit the Different Scenarios: A Literature Review & Research Agenda," *International Journal of Business and Management* 7(6), 2012: 2–17.

40. http://www.mmh.com/article/apics_to_update_industry_recognized_scor_model_in_its_20th_year

Appendix 1

Areas Under the Normal Curve

This table gives the area under the curve to the left of x for various Z scores or the number of standard deviations from the mean. For example, in the figure, if $Z = 1.96$, the value .97500 found in the body of the table is the total shaded area to the left of x.

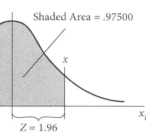

Shaded Area = .97500

Z	.00	.01	.02	.03	.04	.05	.06	.07	.08	.09
.0	.50000	.50399	.50798	.51197	.51595	.51994	.52392	.52790	.53188	.53586
.1	.53983	.54380	.54776	.55172	.55567	.55962	.56356	.56749	.57142	.57535
.2	.57926	.58317	.58706	.59095	.59483	.59871	.60257	.60642	.61026	.61409
.3	.61791	.62172	.62552	.62930	.63307	.63683	.64058	.64431	.64803	.65173
.4	.65542	.65910	.66276	.66640	.67003	.67364	.67724	.68082	.68439	.68793
.5	.69146	.69497	.69847	.70194	.70540	.70884	.71226	.71566	.71904	.72240
.6	.72575	.72907	.73237	.73536	.73891	.74215	.74537	.74857	.75175	.75490
.7	.75804	.76115	.76424	.76730	.77035	.77337	.77637	.77935	.78230	.78524
.8	.78814	.79103	.79389	.79673	.79955	.80234	.80511	.80785	.81057	.81327
.9	.81594	.81859	.82121	.82381	.82639	.82894	.83147	.83398	.83646	.83891
1.0	.84134	.84375	.84614	.84849	.85083	.85314	.85543	.85769	.85993	.86241
1.1	.86433	.86650	.86864	.87076	.87286	.87493	.87698	.87900	.88100	.88298
1.2	.88493	.88686	.88877	.89065	.89251	.89435	.89617	.89796	.89973	.90147
1.3	.90320	.90490	.90658	.90824	.90988	.91149	.91309	.91466	.91621	.91774
1.4	.91924	.92073	.92220	.92364	.92507	.92647	.92785	.92922	.93056	.93189
1.5	.93319	.93448	.93574	.93699	.93822	.93943	.94062	.94179	.94295	.94408
1.6	.94520	.94630	.94738	.94845	.94950	.95053	.95154	.95254	.95352	.95449
1.7	.95543	.95637	.95728	.95818	.95907	.95994	.96080	.96164	.96246	.96327
1.8	.96407	.96485	.96562	.96638	.96712	.96784	.96856	.96926	.96995	.97062
1.9	.97128	.97193	.97257	.97320	.97381	.97441	.97500	.97558	.97615	.97670
2.0	.97725	.97784	.97831	.97882	.97932	.97982	.98030	.98077	.98124	.98169
2.1	.98214	.98257	.98300	.98341	.98382	.98422	.98461	.98500	.98537	.98574
2.2	.98610	.98645	.98679	.98713	.98745	.98778	.98809	.98840	.98870	.98899
2.3	.98928	.98956	.98983	.99010	.99036	.99061	.99086	.99111	.99134	.99158
2.4	.99180	.99202	.99224	.99245	.99266	.99286	.99305	.99324	.99343	.99361
2.5	.99379	.99396	.99413	.99430	.99446	.99461	.99477	.99492	.99506	.99520
2.6	.99534	.99547	.99560	.99573	.99585	.99598	.99606	.99621	.99632	.99643
2.7	.99653	.99664	.99674	.99683	.99693	.99702	.99711	.99720	.99728	.99736
2.8	.99744	.99752	.99760	.99767	.99774	.99781	.99788	.99795	.99801	.99807
2.9	.99813	.99819	.99825	.99831	.99836	.99841	.99846	.99851	.99856	.99861
3.0	.99865	.99869	.99874	.99878	.99882	.99886	.99889	.99893	.99896	.99900
3.1	.99903	.99906	.99910	.99913	.99916	.99918	.99921	.99924	.99926	.99929
3.2	.99931	.99934	.99936	.99938	.99940	.99942	.99944	.99946	.99948	.99950
3.3	.99952	.99953	.99955	.99957	.99958	.99960	.99961	.99962	.99964	.99965
3.4	.99966	.99968	.99969	.99970	.99971	.99972	.99973	.99974	.99975	.99976
3.5	.99977	.99978	.99978	.99979	.99980	.99981	.99981	.99982	.99983	.99983
3.6	.99984	.99985	.99985	.99986	.99986	.99987	.99987	.99988	.99988	.99989
3.7	.99989	.99990	.99990	.99990	.99991	.99991	.99992	.99992	.99992	.99992
3.8	.99993	.99993	.99993	.99994	.99994	.99994	.99994	.99995	.99995	.99995
3.9	.99995	.99995	.99996	.99996	.99996	.99996	.99996	.99996	.99997	.99997

Appendix 2

Answers to Selected End-of-Chapter Problems

CHAPTER 2

1. 8%
3. a. Gross profits increase by $50,000; b. Profits before taxes increase by $50,000
5. $500,000
7. b. COGS = $18,375,000 Avg. Inv. = $243,417; c. Turnover = 75.49
9. a. Breakeven quantity, Q = 60,000 units; cost at breakeven point = $1,025,000
   b. Make option is cheaper; cost savings = $2,555,000 − $2,375,000 = $180,000
11. $27.45, delivery, quality, and volume flexibility, among others

CHAPTER 3

1. The weighted score is 87.25. Supplier is classified as a certified vendor.

CHAPTER 4

34. 50,000 second-tier suppliers. Alternately, 2000 second-tier suppliers.

CHAPTER 5

2. a. 1.622 = Jan 2017 forecast for alpha = 0.3; 1.832 = Jan 2017 forecast for alpha = 0.5
   b. MAD = 0.307 for alpha = 0.3; MAD = 0.253 for alpha = 0.5
4. a. F = 5954.5 + 56.99X
   b. F = 6695.5
6. a. 3-month FJan = 86,667; 4-month FJan = 72,500; 5-month FJan = 68,000
   b. F13 = 81,941.4
8. Tracking signal1 = RSFE1/MAD1 = 2.576; Tracking signal2 = RSFE2/MAD2 = −0.533

CHAPTER 6

1. a.   Chase production strategy

MONTH	JAN	FEB	MAR	APR	MAY	JUN
Demand	2,000	3,000	5,000	6,000	6,000	2,000
Production	2,000	3,000	5,000	6,000	6,000	2,000
Ending inventory	0	0	0	0	0	0
Workforce	20	30	50	60	60	20

b. Level production strategy

MONTH	JAN	FEB	MAR	APR	MAY	JUN
Demand	2,000	3,000	5,000	6,000	6,000	2,000
Production	4,000	4,000	4,000	4,000	4,000	4,000
Ending inventory	2,000	3,000	2,000	0	−2,000	0
Workforce	40	40	40	40	40	40

(−2000 indicates backlog of 2,000 in May.)

4. ATP: D

WEEK		1	2	3	4	5	6	7	8
MODEL B									
MPS	BI = 20	20	0	20	20	0	20	20	20
C C Orders		10	10	10	10	10	0	0	10
ATP: D		20	0	10	0	0	20	20	10

6. POR = 120 in week 2
8. POR_D = 30 in week 1, 30 in week 5; POR_E = 14 in week 1, 11 in week 2, 6 in week 3, 8 in week 4; POR_F = 60 in week 2
10. POR_{LV} = 120 in week 2 and 20 in week 3

CHAPTER 7

1. 13.7 times
3. EOQ = 1,000 units
   Annual holding cost = $7,500, Annual order cost = $7,500
   Total annual inventory cost = $15,000
8. a. Optimal order quantity = 151 units
   b. Annual purchase cost = $25,200,000.00
   c. Annual holding cost = $405,888.00
   d. Annual order cost = $2,980.13
   e. Total annual inventory cost = $25,608,868.13
11. a. Daily demand =100 units
    b. Optimal lot size = 750 units
    c. Highest inventory = 600 units
    d. Annual product cost = $2,880,000
    e. Annual holding cost = $7,200
    f. Annual setup cost = $7,200
    g. Total annual inventory cost = $2,894,400
    h. Length of a production period = 1.5 days
    i. Length of each inventory cycle = 7.5 days
    j. Rate of inventory buildup during the production cycle = 400 units/day
    k. The number of inventory cycles per year = 48 times
12. Safety stock = 117.6 units, Statistical reorder point = 767.6 units
14. Safety stock = 1,470 units, Statistical reorder point = 4,470 units
19. a. 500 units; b. $100,000; c. $1,000; d. $1,000; e. $102,000; f. 83.33 units;
    g. 10 orders; h. 36 days; i. cost curves versus order quantity
22. There is no economic manufacturing quantity for this problem because the annual demand of 500,000 units is larger than the annual production rate of 360,000 (1,000 × 360) units.

CHAPTER 8

2. $T = 64/(14.375) = 4.45$ hrs or 4 hrs and 27 minutes
4. a. $D = 75$ parts/hr
   b. Can double containers, reduce T to 2 hrs, or increase C to 30
6. 125 defects
8. a. variable data
   b. $UCL_x = 31.2$; $LCL_x = 23.6$; $UCL_R = 11.9$; $LCL_R = 0$
10. a. $\overline{P} = 0.1167$; b. $\sigma_p = 0.1015$; c. $UCL = 0.42$, $LCL = 0$; d. Yes
12. a. $\overline{c} = 0.733$
   b. $UCL = 3.3$; $LCL = 0$

CHAPTER 9

2. a. S2 = 22,045 units for 9 warehouses
   b. S2 = 25,456 units for 12 warehouses
   c. 22.5% increase from 6 to 9; 41.4% increase from 6 to 12

CHAPTER 10

1. $NPV_A = \$2,639$; $NPV_B = \$2,362$; $NPV_C = \$3,018$

CHAPTER 11

2. c. If demand is 40,000 units, then it is cheaper to produce at the Miami plant.
4. The Columbus site has the highest total weighted score (84.5) and is the selected site.

CHAPTER 12

1. a. Single-factor productivities: labor—0.5 customers/labor\$; material—1.875 customers/material\$; energy—7.5 customers/energy\$; building—1 customer/ lease\$.
   Multifactor productivity—0.272 customers/total\$.
   They could improve productivity by improving capacity utilization, possibly increasing the number of hours they are open or adding seats.
   b. Capacity = 3,120 customers per month. Utilization = 0.48 or 48%
4. Distance traveled = 5,545 m/day; you could put Depts. 4 and 5 closer together (switch 5 and 8), so the new distance = 3,805 m/day.
5. 13 points; try switching Depts. 5 and 8 = 18 points
6. Two full-time and three part-time workers to fill the requirements.
8. Probability = 0.7
9. $L_s = 1.5$ customers; $L_q = 0.9$ customers

CHAPTER 14

1. Current total productivity = 250/\$ 1,660 = 0.151 haircuts/dollar
   Expected total productivity = 300/\$ 1,685 = 0.178 haircuts/dollar (an 18% increase)
3. Labor = 4228 \$/labor\$
   Material = 9.992 \$/mat'l\$; Utility = 92,256 \$/utility\$
   Total = 9.967 \$/input\$

Glossary

80/20 rule   A theory originating from Pareto analysis, which suggests that most of a firm's problem "events" (80 percent) are accounted for by just a few (20 percent) of the problems; can also be applied to other areas, such as ABC inventory control, which says that 80 percent of the inventory dollars come from 20 percent of the inventory items.

A

ABC inventory control system   A useful technique for determining which inventories should be managed more closely and which others should not (A-items are the most important).

ABC inventory matrix   A diagram that illustrates whether a firm's physical inventory matches its inventory usage. It is derived by plotting an ABC analysis based on inventory usage classification on the vertical axis and an ABC analysis based on physical inventory classification on the horizontal axis.

acceptance sampling   In purchasing, it is a statistical screening technique that can be used to determine whether or not a shipment will be accepted, returned to the supplier or used for billback purposes when defects are fixed or units are eliminated by the buyer.

active RFID tags   An RFID tag that is equipped with an onboard power supply to power the integrated circuits and broadcast its signal to the tag reader.

additive manufacturing or 3D printing   A process of making a three-dimensional solid object of virtually any shape from a digital model.

aggregate production plan (APP)   A long-range production plan; it sets the aggregate output rate, workforce size, utilization, inventory and backlog levels for a plant.

air carriers   For-hire airlines.

airline security   Protection that is provided for airlines against terrorist attacks and other illegal activities.

analytic SRM   A method that allows the company to analyze the complete supplier base.

arrival pattern   The frequency with which customers arrive at a business.

assignable variations   Process variations that can be traced to a specific cause. Assignable variations are created by causes that can be identified and eliminated and thus become the objective of statistical process control efforts.

Association of Southeast Asian Nations (ASEAN)   An economic and geopolitical organization created in 1967 that today comprises the following countries in the Southeast Asian region: Brunei, Cambodia, Indonesia, Laos, Malaysia, Myanmar, the Philippines, Singapore, Thailand and Vietnam. The primary objective of ASEAN is to promote economic, social and cultural development of the region through cooperative programs.

attribute data   Yes/no kinds of data. These indicate the presence of some attribute such as color, satisfaction, workability or beauty (for instance, determining whether or not a car was painted the right color, if a customer liked the meal, if the lightbulb worked or if the dress was pretty).

available-to-promise (ATP) quantity   The uncommitted portion of a firm's planned production. It is used to promise new customer orders.

B

back-of-the-house operations   Those services that do not require customer contact.

backward vertical integration   Acquiring upstream suppliers.

balanced scorecard (BSC)   A management system developed in the early 1990s by Robert Kaplan and David Norton that helps companies to continually refine their vision and strategy. The balanced scorecard uses a set of measures to provide feedback on internal business performance in order to continually improve strategic performance. Also referred to as scorecarding.

balking   Refusing to join a queue once it is seen how long it is.

barter   The complete exchange of goods and/or services of equal value without the exchange of currency. The seller can either consume the goods and/or services or resell the items.

Baumol's disease   A productivity growth problem named after noted U.S. economist William Baumol in the 1960s. For most services, automation can be a troublesome issue, and the labor content per unit of output can be quite high relative to manufactured goods. These two things can lead to a declining productivity growth rate as a nation's economy becomes less manufacturing oriented and more service oriented.

benchmarking   The practice of copying what other businesses do best; studying how things are done well in other firms to potentially make use of the same methods.

best-of-breed solution   An ERP system that picks the best application or module for each individual function.

bid   When suppliers respond to a buyer's invitation to bid, with an offered price for specific services or goods.

big data analytics   As the number of customers grows for large businesses, their transactions and the desire to analyze all of this information also grows, which requires big data analytics.

big data   Collections of data sets that are too large and complex to be processed by traditional database management tools or data processing software applications.

bill of materials (BOM)   An engineering document that shows an inclusive listing of all component parts and assemblies making up the final product.

billback penalty   A fee charged back to the supplier for services or products not received by the customer.

blank check purchase order   A small value purchase order with a signed blank check attached, usually at the bottom of the purchase order.

blanket order release   A form used to release a specific quantity against a prenegotiated blanket purchase order.

blanket purchase order   A purchase order that covers a variety of items and is negotiated for repeated supply over a fixed time period, such as quarterly or yearly.

break-even analysis   A tool for computing the cost-effectiveness of sourcing decisions when cost is the most important criterion. Several assumptions underlie the analysis: (1) all costs involved can be classified as either fixed or variable cost, (2) fixed cost remains the same within the range of analysis, (3) a linear variable cost relationship exists, (4) fixed cost of the make option is higher because of initial capital investment in equipment, and (5) variable cost of the buy option is higher due to supplier profits.

break-even model   A useful location analysis technique when fixed and variable costs can be determined for each potential location.

bullwhip effect   A term referring to ineffective communication between buyers and suppliers and infrequent delivery of materials, combined with production based on poor forecasts along a supply chain that results in either too little or too much inventory at various points of storage and consumption. Simply, it causes an amplification of the variation in the demand pattern along the supply chain.

business clusters   According to Dr. Michael Porter, "clusters are geographic concentrations of interconnected companies and institutions in a particular field. Clusters encompass an array of linked industries and other entities important to competition."

business cycle   Alternating periods of expansion and contraction in economic activity.

business ethics   The application of ethical principles to business situations.

business metrics   Business performance measures.

business process reengineering (BPR) or reengineering   The radical rethinking and redesigning of business processes to reduce waste and increase performance.

Buy American Act   Legislation mandating that U.S. government purchases and third-party purchases that utilize federal funds must buy domestically produced goods, if the price differential between the domestic product and an identical foreign-sourced product does not exceed a certain percentage amount.

C

C charts   Counts the number of defects per unit of output.

call centers or customer contact centers   Customer service departments that integrate all of the methods customers can use to contact a business, including telephone, mail, comment cards, email, and website messages and chat rooms.

capacity requirements planning (CRP)   A short-range capacity planning technique that is used to check the feasibility of the material requirements plan.

capacity utilization   The actual customers served per period divided by capacity.

capacity   The output capabilities of a firm's labor and machine resources.

carbon footprints   A firm's or supply chain's total carbon emissions.

cause-and-effect diagrams   Also called fishbone diagram or Ishikawa diagram. A method that is used to aid in brainstorming and isolating the causes of a problem. Typically there are four causes of problems (the 4-Ms).

cause-and-effect forecasting   A forecasting method that uses one or more factors (independent variables) that are related to demand to predict future demand.

centralized purchasing   A single purchasing department, usually located at the firm's corporate office, makes all the purchasing decisions, including order quantity, pricing policy, contracting, negotiations, and supplier selection and evaluation.

centralized warehousing system   Fewer warehouses means that outbound transportation costs will be higher.

centralized/decentralized purchasing structure   A hybrid purchasing structure that is centralized at the corporate level but decentralized at the individual business unit level.

chase demand strategy   A strategy that is used when the amount of capacity varies with demand. See also chase production strategy.

chase production strategy   A production strategy that adjusts output to match the demand pattern during each production period.

check sheets   A tool that allows users to determine the frequencies of specific problems.

Civil Aeronautics Act of 1938   Legislation that promoted the development of the air transportation system, air safety, and airline efficiency by establishing the Civil Aeronautics Board to oversee market entry, establish routes with appropriate levels of competition, develop regional feeder airlines and establish reasonable rates. The Civil Aeronautics Administration was also established to regulate air safety.

class rates   The transportation rates based on the particular class of the product transported; some products have higher published class rates than others. Rates are based on an evaluation of four transportation characteristics: density, stowability, handling and liability.

clickstreams   A record of the items that a specific customer clicks on when visiting a website.

closed-loop MRP   An MRP-based manufacturing planning and control system that incorporates aggregate production planning, master production scheduling, material requirements planning and capacity requirements planning.

closeness desirability rating   A scale used to rate how desirable it is to have two departments close together. The objective is to design a layout that maximizes the desirability rating for the entire facility.

cloud computing   When shared resources and other information are made available to users over the Internet, usually for a subscription fee. It allows small businesses, for example, to make use of sophisticated software without actually making the purchase; also termed on-demand computing.

cloud-based communication platforms   An internet-based platform that provides greater visibility, ensures faster time to market, and offers faster response to changing market dynamics and demands.

cloud-based forecasting   Using supplier-hosted or software-as-a-service (SaaS) advanced forecasting applications that are provided to companies on a subscription basis.

coal slurry   Pulverized coal that is suspended in water.

cold chains   Refer to temperature controlled transportation, transfers, and warehousing.

collaborative education   Providing training for supply chain partner employees.

collaborative negotiations/integrative or win–win negotiations   The process that occurs when both sides work together to maximize the joint outcome, or to create a win-win result; also referred to as integrative negotiations.

collaborative planning, forecasting, and replenishment (CPFR)   According to the Council of Supply Chain Professionals, "CPFR seeks cooperative management of inventory through joint visibility and replenishment of products throughout the supply chain. Information shared between suppliers and retailers aids in planning and satisfying customer demands through a supportive system of shared information. This allows for continuous updating of inventory and upcoming requirements, essentially making the end-to-end supply chain process more efficient. Efficiency is also created through the decrease expenditures for merchandising, inventory, logistics, and transportation across all trading partners."

co-managed inventories   A somewhat more collaborative form of VMI; can also refer to JIT II buyer and supplier reach an agreement regarding how information is shared, order quantities, when an order is generated, and the delivery timing and location.

commodity rates   Rates that apply to minimum quantities of specified products that are shipped between two specified locations.

common carriers   Transportation providers that offer services to all shippers at published rates between designated locations.

Common Market for Eastern and Southern Africa (COMESA)   A customs union established to foster economic growth among the member countries of Burundi, Comoros, D. R. Congo, Djibouti, Egypt, Eritrea, Ethiopia, Kenya, Libya, Madagascar, Malawi, Mauritius, Rwanda, Seychelles, Sudan, Swaziland, Uganda, Zambia, and Zimbabwe.

consolidation warehouses   Warehouses that collect large numbers of LTL shipments from nearby regional sources of supply, then deliver in TL or CL quantities to a manufacturer.

consumer's risk   The risk assumed when a buyer accepts a shipment of poor-quality units because the sample did meet the acceptance standard; this results in a type-II error.

container-on-flatcar (COFC)   A form of intermodal transportation; standardized shipping containers are transported via rail flatcar, and they can also be placed on a truck chassis or on an ocean-going container ship.

continuous review system   An inventory management system where the physical inventory levels are counted on a continuous or daily basis.

contract carriers   For-hire carriers that are like common carriers but are not bound to serve the general public. They serve specific customers under contractual agreements.

Contracts for the International Sale of Goods (CISG)   A set of rules established by the United Nations to govern the international transactions in goods.

contributor factory   A manufacturing facility that plays a greater strategic role than a server factory by getting involved in product development and engineering, production planning, making critical procurement decisions and developing suppliers.

control charts   A method that monitors process variabilities and then collects and plots sample measurements of the process over time. The means of these sample measures are plotted on the control charts.

corporate social responsibility (CSR)   The practice of business ethics.

cost leadership strategy   Competing based on a low cost strategy.

cost-of-service pricing   A pricing strategy used when carriers desire to establish prices that vary based on their fixed and variable costs.

counterpurchase   A trade arrangement whereby the original exporter either buys or finds a buyer to purchase a specified quantity of unrelated goods and/or services from the original importer.

countertrade   A global sourcing process in which goods and/or services of domestic firms are exchanged for goods and/or services of equal value or in combination with currency from foreign firms. This type of arrangement is sometimes used by countries where there is a shortage of hard currency or as a means to acquire technologies.

critical-to-quality (CTQ) characteristics   Those characteristics related to customers and their service or product requirements that are critical to achieving customer satisfaction.

crossdocking   A continuous replenishment logistics process at a distribution center, where incoming goods are sorted and/or consolidated, and then shipped out to their final destinations, without the need to store the goods. Cross-docking generally takes place within 24 hours, sometimes less than an hour, after shipment arrivals and is used to replenish high demand inventories.

cross-selling   Purchasing that occurs when customers are sold additional products as the result of an initial purchase.

C-TPAT compliance   A partnership among U.S. Customs, the International Cargo Security Council, and Pinkerton (a global security advising company), whereby companies agree to improve security in their supply chain in return for "fast lane" border crossings at both the U.S./Canadian and U.S./Mexican borders.

customer churn The rate at which customers leave or stop using a firm.

customer defection analysis Information that analyzes why customers stop using a particular business.

customer lifetime value (CLV)/customer value or customer profitability Assigning a profit figure to each customer by summing the margins of all the products and services purchased over time, less the cost of marketing to and maintaining that customer, such as the costs of direct mail and sales calls and the service costs for each customer. Additionally, the firm forecasts future purchased quantities, profit margins, and marketing costs for each customer, discounts these back to the current date and then adds this projected profit quantity to the current profit amount. Also known as customer value or customer profitability.

customer relationship management process Provides the firm with the structure for developing and managing customer relationships.

customer relationship management Managing a firm's customer base such that customers remain satisfied and continue to purchase goods and services. Sometimes it also refers to CRM software applications.

customer service The provision of information, help, and/or technical support to customers in a way that meets or exceeds customer expectations.

customs brokers Global logistics intermediaries that move international shipments through customs for companies as well as handle the necessary documentation required to accompany the shipments.

Customs-Trade Partnership Against Terrorism program (C TPAT) A partnership between U.S. Customs, the International Cargo Security Council (a U.S. nonprofit association of companies and individuals involved in transportation) and Pinkerton (a global security advising company, headquartered in New Jersey), whereby companies agree to improve security in their supply chain in return for "fast lane" border crossings.

cycle counting A commonly used technique in which physical inventory is counted on a periodic basis to ensure that physical inventory matches current inventory records.

D

data warehouse Information system structures used to store data that was collected from the various divisions of the firm.

decentralized purchasing Individual, local purchasing departments, such as at the plant level, make their own purchasing decisions.

decentralized warehousing system Used when faster delivery service is required. As the number of warehouses used increases, the system becomes more decentralized.

decentralized/centralized purchasing structure A hybrid purchasing structure that is decentralized at the corporate level but centralized at the individual business unit level.

deep-sea transportation Ocean-going water carriers. The development and use of supertankers and containerships are examples.

defects per million opportunities (DPMO) A Six Sigma quality metric.

demand forecast updating When buyers place purchase orders, suppliers use this information to revise their demand forecasts.

demand management process The steps used for balancing customer demand and the firm's output capabilities.

demand management A set of activities that range from determining or estimating the demand from customers through converting specific customer orders into promised delivery dates to help balance demand with supply.

demand source That part of the input process that deals with customer arrivals.

demand time fence A firmed planning segment that is used with the MRP application; it usually stretches from the current period to a period several weeks into the future.

Department of Defense (DOD) A major public buyer within the United States government.

Department of Transportation Act Legislation that created the Department of Transportation (DOT) in 1966 to coordinate the executive functions of all government entities dealing with transportation related matters.

dependent demand The internal demand for parts based on the demand of the final product in which the parts are used.

differentiation strategy A business approach that is based on creating a product or service that is considered unique. Usually associated with high quality.

direct costs Costs that are directly traceable to the unit produced, such as the amount of materials and labor used to produce a unit of the finished good.

direct offset A form of countertrade that usually involves coproduction, or a joint venture, and exchange of related goods and/or services.

distribution center A warehouse that performs break-bulk activities and then forms outbound specific product assortments that are then shipped to the customer.

distribution network The organization of a distribution system that ensures successful product delivery.

distribution requirements plan (DRP) A time-phased finished goods inventory replenishment plan in a distribution network.

Distribution requirements planning (DRP) The time-phased net requirements from central supply warehouses and distribution centers. It links production with distribution planning by providing aggregate time-phased net requirements information to the master production schedule.

distributive negotiations A negotiating objective that seeks an outcome that primarily favors the interests of one side.

E

early supplier involvement (ESI) Involving key suppliers during the product design and development stage to take advantage of their knowledge and technologies.

eatertainment The combining of restaurant and entertainment elements.

economic manufacturing quantity (EMQ) or production order quantity (POQ) model A variation of the classic EOQ model, used to determine the most economical number of units to produce.

economic order quantity (EOQ) model The classic independent demand inventory system that computes the optimal order quantity to minimize total inventory costs.

economies of scale A theory stating that the cost per unit decreases as the number of units purchased, produced or transported increases.

edutainment or infotainment The combining of learning with entertainment to appeal to customers looking for substance along with play.

efficient consumer response (ECR) developed by a U.S. grocery industry task force charged with making grocery supply chains more competitive. Point-of-purchase transactions at grocery stores were forwarded via computer to distributors and manufacturers, allowing the stores to keep stocks replenished while minimizing the need for safety stock inventories.

electronic data interchange (EDI) A computer-to-computer exchange of business documents such as purchase orders, order status inquiries and reports, promotion announcements and shipping and billing notices.

electronic product code (EPC) A widely used RFID standard managed by EPC global, Inc.

emergency sourcing The act of maintaining a backup source of supply available to provide purchased items when the primary source has temporarily become unavailable.

empty miles The trucks that return empty after their delivery; these return journeys cause big energy wastes.

enterprise resource planning (ERP) A packaged business software system that lets a company automate and integrate the majority of its business processes, share common data and practices across the enterprise and produce and access information in a real-time environment.

entertailing The combining of retail locations with entertainment elements—such as offering ice skating, rock climbing and amusement park rides at a shopping mall.

environmental management system (EMS) The practices put in place by a firm to try to reduce environmental waste and improve environmental performance.

environmental sustainability The need to continually protect the environment and reduce greenhouse gas emissions.

equipment setups The steps required to prepare production equipment for the next product to be produced.

ethical and environmental certifications certifying companies according to ethical and environmental requirements. A number of certifying agencies can be used, such as the New York-based Rainforest Alliance and Trans-Fair USA.

ethical and sustainable sourcing Purchasing from suppliers that are governed by environmental sustainability and social and ethical practices.

ethical sourcing The practice of purchasing from suppliers that are governed by social and ethical practices.

Ethical Trading Initiative (ETI) An alliance of organizations seeking to take responsibility for improving working conditions and agreeing to implement the ETI Base Code, a standard for ethical practices for the firms and its suppliers.

European Union (EU)   A European international trade organization designed to reduce tariff and nontariff barriers among member countries. Set up after the Second World War, the EU was officially launched on May 9, 1950, with France's proposal to create a European federation consisting of six countries: Belgium, Germany, France, Italy, Luxembourg, and the Netherlands. A series of accessions resulted in a total of 28 member states in 2013. Most recently, the EU has added Iceland, Montenegro, Serbia, Republic of Macedonia and Turkey.

event-based marketing   A marketing strategy that offers the right products and services to customers at the right time.

everyday low pricing (EDLP)   The elimination of price discounting and offering wholesale prices to customers. Helps reduce the bullwhip effect.

exception rates   Published rates that are lower than class rates for specific origin-destination locations or volumes.

exempt carriers   For-hire carriers that are exempt from the regulations of services and rates. They transport certain exempt products such as produce, livestock, coal, garbage, or newspapers.

expediting   The act of contacting the supplier to speed up an overdue shipment.

F

facilitating products   Products such as computers, furniture, and office supplies that are not part of the services sold but rather are consumed inside the firm and must also be managed.

fair trade products   A product manufactured or grown by a disadvantaged producer in a developing country that receives a fair price for its goods.

Federal Acquisition Regulation (FAR)   The primary set of rules issued by the U.S. government to govern the process through which the government purchases goods and services.

Federal Acquisition Streamlining Act (FASA)   A federal act signed by President Clinton in October 1994 to remove many restrictions on government purchases that do not exceed $100,000.

Federal Aviation Act of 1958   Legislation that replaced the Civil Aeronautics Administration with the Federal Aviation Administration (FAA) and gave the FAA authority to prescribe air traffic rules, make safety regulations and plan the national airport system.

five dimensions of service quality   Five categories used by customers to rate service quality: reliability, responsiveness, assurance, empathy, and tangibles.

five-Ss   Five Japanese words, coming originally from Toyota, that relate to industrial housekeeping. The idea is that by implementing the five-Ss, the workplace will be cleaner, more organized and safer, thereby reducing processing waste and improving productivity.

Five-Why   When something is found to be missing or out of place, the solution should be to repeatedly ask "why?" until the root (or most basic) cause is found and corrected. Until

why is asked five times, the root cause has probably not been identified.

fixed costs   Costs that are independent of the output quantity.

fixed order quantity models   Independent demand inventory models that use fixed parameters to determine the optimal order quantity to minimize total inventory costs.

flow diagrams/process diagrams/process maps   Tools that use annotated boxes representing process action elements and ovals representing wait periods, connected by arrows to show the flow of products or customers through the process. These tools are the necessary first step to evaluating any manufacturing or service process.

FOB destination pricing   A price quotation that includes transportation to the buyer's location when products are purchased from a supplier.

FOB origin pricing   A price quotation in which the buyer may decide to purchase goods and provide the transportation to the shipping destination; in this case, the supplier quotes are lower.

focus strategy   A business approach incorporating the idea that a firm can serve a narrow target market or niche better than other firms that are trying to serve a broad market.

follow-up   A proactive act to contact the supplier to ensure on-time delivery of the goods ordered.

forecast bias   A measure of the tendency of a forecast to be consistently higher (negative bias) or lower (positive bias) than the actual demand.

forecast error   The difference between actual demand and the forecast.

foreign freight forwarders   Service providers that move goods for companies from domestic production facilities to foreign customer destinations, using surface and air transportation and warehouses. They consolidate small shipments into larger TL, CL or container shipments, decide what transportation modes and methods to use, handle all of the documentation requirements and then disperse the shipments at their destination.

foreign-trade zones (FTZs)   Secure sites within the U.S. under the supervision of the U.S. Customs Service. These are where materials can be imported duty-free as long as the imports are used as inputs to production of goods that are eventually exported.

forward buying   When buyers stock up to take advantage of low price offers.

forward vertical integration   Acquiring downstream customers.

franchising   A business practice that allows services to expand quickly in dispersed geographic markets, protect existing markets and build market share. Franchisees are required to invest some of their own capital, while paying a small percentage of sales to the franchiser in return for the brand name, start-up help, advertising, training and assistance in meeting specific operating standards.

Free and Secure Trade program (FAST)   A U.S. Customs' security program; the overall goal is to ensure the security of international supply chains and international trucking in particular. To participate in FAST, motor carriers must become C-TPAT certified and their commercial drivers must complete an application and undergo a background check.

freight brokers   Legally authorized intermediaries that bring shippers and transportation companies (mainly truckers) together.

front-of-the-house operations   Operations that are involved with interactions with customers, such as front desk operations.

functional products   MRO items and other commonly purchased items and supplies. These items are characterized by low profit margins, relatively stable demands and high levels of competition.

functional silos   Departments in a firm that are only concerned with what is going on in their department and not what is in the best interests of the firm.

G

general freight carriers   The carriers transporting the majority of goods shipped in the U.S.; includes common carriers.

General Services Administration (GSA)   A U.S. federal agency that is responsible for most federal purchases. It is based in Washington, D.C., and has 11 regional offices throughout the U.S.

global sourcing   Purchasing from non-domestic suppliers.

global supply chains   Supply chains with foreign trading partners.

global trade management systems   Software that enables shippers and carriers to submit the correct import/export documents as goods are moved between countries.

green development   The implementation of environmentally friendly development.

green purchasing   A practice aimed at ensuring that purchasing personnel include environmental considerations and human health issues when making purchasing decisions; also termed green sourcing and sustainable procurement.

green reverse logistics programs   Systems that focus on reducing the environmental impact of certain modes of transportation used for returns, reducing the amount of disposed packaging and product materials by redesigning products and processes, and making use of reusable totes and pallets.

green supply chain management (GSCM)   An organizational approach that extends the concept of green logistics to include activities related to environmentally responsible product design, acquisition, production, distribution, use, reuse and disposal by partners within the supply chain.

H

high-speed trains   Passenger trains that typically average 70 miles per hour or greater.

holding or carrying costs   The costs incurred for holding inventory in storage.

horizontal collaboration   Two or more companies cooperating at the same level on a certain activity to realize benefits they could not achieve independently.

hybrid purchasing organization   A firm that uses either a centralized–decentralized or decentralized–centralized purchasing structure.

I

ICC Termination Act of 1995 Legislation that eliminated the Interstate Commerce Commission.

implosion When demand information is gathered from a number of field distribution centers and aggregated in the central warehouse, and eventually passed onto the manufacturing facility.

import broker or sales agent A firm that is set up to import goods for customers for a fee. An import broker does not take title to the goods.

import merchant A firm that imports and takes title to the good, and then resells them to a buyer.

incoterms (International Commercial Terms) A uniform set of rules created by the International Chamber of Commerce to simplify international transactions of goods with respect to shipping costs, risks and responsibilities of the buyer, seller and shipper.

indented bill of materials Indentations are used to present the level number within the bill of materials; also known as the multilevel bill of materials.

independent demand The demand for final products and service parts. It has a demand pattern that is affected by trends, seasonal patterns and general market conditions.

indirect costs Those costs that cannot be traced directly to the unit produced and are synonymous with manufacturing overhead.

indirect offset A form of countertrade that involves an exchange of goods and/or services unrelated to the initial purchase.

industrial buyers Buyers with a primary responsibility of purchasing raw materials for conversion purposes.

information visibility The degree that information is communicated and made available to various constituents, typically on the Internet.

innovative products Newly developed products characterized by short product life cycles, volatile demand, high profit margins and relatively less competition.

intermediate or medium-range planning horizon A planning horizon that covers six to eighteen months.

intermediately positioned strategy A location strategy that places warehouses midway between the sources of supply and the customers.

intermodal marketing companies (IMCs) Companies that act as intermediaries between intermodal railroad companies and shippers.

intermodal transportation Two or more modes of transportation that combine to deliver a shipment of goods.

internal control An internal operational system that prevents, for example, abuse of purchasing funds.

internal supply chains An organization's network of internal suppliers and internal customers. Internal supply chains can be complex, particularly if the firm has multiple divisions and organizational structures around the globe.

inventory turnover ratio or inventory turnovers A widely used measure to analyze how efficiently a firm uses its inventory to generate revenue.

inventory turnover The number of times a firm's inventory is utilized and replaced over an accounting period, such as a year.

inventory visibility The ability of supply chain companies to see inventory quantities of the various members, typically using the Internet.

invitation for bid (IFB) A request for qualified suppliers to submit bids for a contract. Suppliers are asked to bid, given certain opening and closing dates of the bid. The basis for awarding a contract is preset and binding.

ISO 14000 A family of international standards for environmental management developed by the International Organization for Standardization (ISO).

ISO 9000 A series of management and quality assurance standards in design, development, production, installation and service developed by the International Organization for Standardization (ISO).

J

just-in-time (JIT) Originally associated with Toyota managers like TaiichiOhno and his kanban system, JIT encompasses continuous problem solving to eliminate waste. Today it is also referred to as lean or lean thinking.

K

kaizen blitz A rapid improvement event or workshop, aimed at finding big improvements.

kaizen ways to reduce supplier delivery and quality problems, solve movement problems, visibility problems, machine breakdown problems, machine setup problems, and internal quality problems.

kanban A Japanese word for "card"; it is a visual tool used in lean production.

keiretsu relationships partnership arrangements between Japanese manufacturers and suppliers.

key supply chain processes The eight processes that are most important to integrate in the supply chain.

key trading partners Suppliers that have come to be trusted and that provide a large share of the firm's critical products and services; and repeat, satisfied customers that buy a significant portion of the firm's products.

knowledge management solutions A system that uses Internet applications tied to desktop applications that enable real-time collaboration and flow of information between supply chain partners.

knowledge management system A system that is able to capture the accumulated knowledge of experienced sales staff and other skilled personnel if they leave an organization.

L

lag capacity strategy A reactive approach that adjusts capacity in response to demand.

lead capacity strategy A proactive approach that adds or subtracts capacity in anticipation of future market condition and demand.

lead factory A source of product and process innovation and competitive advantage for the entire organization.

lead management system A tool that allows sales reps to follow prescribed sales tactics when dealing with sales prospects or opportunities, to aid in closing the deal with a client.

lean layouts Arrangements that reduce wasted movements of workers, customers and/or work-in-process (WIP), and achieve smooth product flow through the facility.

lean production system Also known as a pull system, where parts are placed in standardized containers, and kanbans exist for each container.

lean production/lean manufacturing/lean thinking Organizing work and analyzing the level of waste existing in operating machinery, warehouses and systems to fit a lean process flow. The goals are to reduce production throughput times and inventory levels, cut order lead times, increase quality and improve customer responsiveness with fewer people and other assets.

Lean Six Sigma/Lean Six A new term used to describe the melding of lean production and Six Sigma quality practices.

lean supply chain relationships The relationships that occur when the focal firm, its suppliers and its customers begin to work together to identify customer requirements, remove waste, reduce cost and improve quality and customer service.

lean warehousing When warehousing, crossdocking, packaging and freight consolidation is offered to companies who are looking to increase speed and reduce costs as much as possible to compete.

legacy MRP system A broad label used to describe an older information system that usually works at an operational level to schedule production within a single facility.

legacy systems A firm's existing software applications.

less-than-truckload (LTL) carriers Carriers that move small packages or shipments taking up less than one truckload; the shipping fees are higher per hundred weight (cwt) than TL fees, since the carrier must consolidate many small shipments into one truckload, then break the truckload back down into individual shipments at the destination for individual deliveries.

level demand strategy A theory for managing capacity that occurs when a firm utilizes a constant amount of capacity regardless of demand variations.

level production strategy Using a constant output rate and capacity while varying inventory and backlog levels to handle the fluctuating demand pattern.

leveraging purchase volume The concentration of purchase volume to create quantity discounts, less-costly volume shipments and other more favorable purchase terms.

line haul rates The charges for moving goods to a nonlocal destination; these can be further classified as class rates, exception rates, commodity rates and miscellaneous rates.

linear trend forecast A forecasting method in which the trend can be estimated using simple linear regression to fit a line to a time series of historical data.

logistics brokers Legally authorized intermediaries that bring shippers and transportation companies (mainly truckers) together.

logistics   The practice of moving and storing goods to meet customer requirements for the minimum cost.

long-range planning horizon   A planning horizon that covers a year or more.

M

make or buy decision   A strategic one that can impact an organization's competitive position. It is obvious that most organizations buy their MRO and office supplies rather than make the items themselves.

make-to-order manufacturing firms   Firms that make custom products based on orders from customers, resulting in long lead times and higher unit costs.

make-to-stock   Firms that typically emphasize immediate delivery of off-the-shelf, standard goods at relatively low prices compared to the chase strategy.

manufacturing cells or work cells   Cells that are designed to process similar parts or components, saving duplication of equipment and labor as well as centralizing the area where units of the same purchased part are delivered.

manufacturing flow management process   The set of activities responsible for making the actual product, establishing the manufacturing flexibility required to adequately serve the markets, and designing the production system to meet cycle time requirements.

manufacturing resource planning (MRP-II)   An outgrowth and extension of the original closed loop MRP system.

market positioned strategy   A location strategy that places warehouses close to customers, to maximize customer service and to allow the firm to generate transportation economies by using inbound TL and CL deliveries to each warehouse location.

master production schedule (MPS)   A medium range production plan that is more detailed than the aggregate production plan.

match or tracking capacity strategy   A moderate strategy that adjusts capacity in small amounts in response to demand and changing market conditions.

material requirements plan (MRP)   A software application that has been available since the 1970s; it performs an analysis of the firm's existing internal conditions and reports back what the production and purchase requirements are for a given finished product manufacturing schedule.

Material requirements planning   Use of the MRP.

material requisition (MR)   An internal document initiated by the material user to request materials from the warehouse or purchasing department.

maximize competition   The competition that is designed for ensuring the purchases of goods and services that are in strict compliance with statutes and policies, public procurement procedures.

merchants   Firms that buy goods in large quantities for resale purposes. Wholesalers and retailers are examples of merchants.

microfranchise   A type of franchising concept that offers ready-made, low-risk starter jobs to people with no education and little available capital while giving established companies additional distribution avenues.

micro-purchases   Government purchases of less than $2,500.

miscellaneous rates   Contract rates that are negotiated between two parties involving shipments containing a variety of products (in the typical case, the rate is based on the overall weight of the shipment).

mixed Internet distribution strategy   The combining of traditional retailing with Internet retailing.

mobile marketing   An advertising technique that places advertising messages on mobile phones.

Motor Carrier Act of 1935   Legislation that brought motor carriers under ICC control, thus controlling entry into the market, establishing motor carrier classes of operation, setting reasonable rates, requiring ICC approval for any mergers or acquisitions, and controlling the issuance of securities.

motor carriers   Trucks; the most flexible mode of transportation, accounting for almost one third of all U.S. for-hire transportation.

muda   A Japanese word meaning waste or anything that does not add value.

multiple regression forecast   A forecast technique using multiple regression.

multiple-channel queuing system   A system in which multiple servers act in parallel.

multiple-factor productivity   Inputs that can be represented by the sum of labor, material, energy and capital costs.

multiple-phase queuing system   A system in which multiple servers act in series.

N

naïve forecast   A forecasting approach where the actual demand for the immediate past period is used as a forecast for next period's demand.

natural variations   Variations that are random and uncontrollable with no specific cause; also termed environmental noise or white noise.

near field communication (NFC)   A secure form of data exchange between an NFC tag or Android-powered device with another Android-powered device. NFC is a specialized subset of RFID technology.

negotiated pricing   Transportation pricing that is agreed upon by both parties.

nontariff barriers   Import quotas, licensing agreements, embargoes, laws, and other regulations imposed on imports and exports.

non-vessel operating common carriers (NVOCC)   Carriers that operate very similarly to international freight forwarders but normally use scheduled ocean liners.

North American Free Trade Agreement (NAFTA)   Legislation that began on January 1, 1994, and will eventually remove most barriers to trade and investment among the U.S., Canada and Mexico.

O

Ocean Shipping Reform Act of 1998   Legislation that eliminated the requirement for ocean carriers to file rates with the Federal Maritime Commission.

offset   An exchange agreement for industrial goods and/or services as a condition of military- related export. It is also commonly used in the aerospace and defense sectors.

offshore factory   A firm that manufactures products at low cost with minimum investment in technical and managerial resources in low labor cost countries, then exports all of its finished goods.

open-end purchase order   A purchase order that covers a variety of items and is negotiated for repeated supply over a fixed time period, such as quarterly or yearly. Additional items and expiration dates can be renegotiated in an open-end purchase order.

opportunities for a defect to occur (OFD)   The number of activities or steps in a product wherein a defect could occur. Used in the DPMO calculation.

option overplanning   Raising the final requirements of component parts beyond 100 percent in a super bill of materials to cover uncertainty.

order batching   A type of inventory control that occurs when small orders are combined into one large order. This amplifies demand variability and adds to the use of safety stock, creating the bullwhip effect.

order costs   Direct variable costs associated with placing an order with a supplier.

order fulfillment process   The set of activities that allows a firm to fill customer orders while providing the required levels of customer service at the lowest possible delivered cost.

Original equipment manufacturers (OEM)   The companies that make the final products.

outpost factory   A manufacturing facility that is set up in a location with an abundance of advanced suppliers, competitors, research facilities and knowledge centers to get access to the latest information on materials, components, technologies and products.

outsource   The process that occurs when a firm purchases materials or products instead of producing them in-house.

P

P charts   Monitors the percent defective in each sample.

Pareto analysis   A graphic technique that prioritizes the most frequently occurring problems or issues. The analysis recommends that problems falling into the most frequently occurring category be assigned the highest priority and managed closely.

Pareto charts   A useful method for organizing applications of data in many formats; based on the work of Vilfredo Pareto, a nineteenth-century economist.

Pareto principle   Refers to the observation that 20 percent of something is typically responsible for 80 percent of the results.

part families   similarly processed parts in a manufacturing cell.

passive RFID tags   RFID tags that are without an internal power source and require power from a tag reader.

payment bonds   Bonds posted by the bidders to protect the buyer against any third-party liens not fulfilled by the successful bidder.

perceived waiting times   An aspect of queue management that occurs when customers think the wait time is much longer or shorter than it really is.

perfect order   An order that did arrive on time, complete and damage free.

performance bonds   Bonds posted by the bidders to guarantee that the work done by the successful bidder meets specifications and is completed in the time specified.

performance dashboards   Web-based balanced score-card applications.

performance variance   The difference between the standard and actual performance.

periodic review system   A review of physical inventory at specific points in time.

petty cash   A small cash reserve maintained by a midlevel manager or clerk.

piggyback service   A type of intermodal transportation involving the loading of shipping containers or truck trailers on a rail flatbed car; also known as container-on-flat-car (COFC) and trailer-on-flat-car (TOFC).

pipeline carriers   One of the five modes of transportation; carries oil, natural gas, coal slurry and other liquids/gases.

place utility   A situation that is created when customers get things delivered to the desired location.

planned order releases   The bottom line of an MRP part record. It designates when the specific quantity is to be ordered from the supplier or to begin being processed. These quantities also determine the gross requirements of the dependent or "children" parts going into this higher level part or product.

planning factor   A calculation showing the number of units of a specific component required to make one unit of a higher-level part.

planning time fence   A period typically stretching from the end of the firmed segment to several weeks farther into the future; also known as the tentative segment.

poka-yoke   Error- or mistake-proofing.

posttransaction costs   Costs are incurred after the goods are in the possession of the company, agents, or customers.

posttransaction elements   Customer service activities that occur after a sale.

pretransaction costs   Costs that are incurred prior to order and receipt of the purchased goods.

pretransaction elements   Customer service activities that occur before a sale.

price break point   The minimum quantity required to receive a quantity discount.

private carrier   A form of transportation owned by a company, such as a fleet of trucks, which is used to ship that company's goods only.

private warehouses   Warehouses that are owned by the firm storing the goods.

process integration   The sharing of information and coordinating resources to jointly manage a process.

process   A set of steps to accomplish a task or get work done.

procurement credit cards or corporate purchasing cards (P-cards)   Credit cards with a predetermined credit limit, usually not more than $5,000 depending on the organization, issued to authorized personnel of the buying organization to make low-dollar purchases.

producer's risk   The risk that occurs when a buyer rejects a shipment of good-quality units because the sample quality level did not meet the acceptance standard.

product development and commercialization process   The development of new products to meet changing customer requirements and then getting these products to market quickly and efficiently.

product family   A group consisting of different products that share similar characteristics, components or manufacturing processes.

product positioned strategy   A location strategy that places warehouses close to the sources of supply, to enable the firm to collect various goods and then consolidate these into TL or CL quantities for shipment to customers.

production kanban   A visual signal such as a light, flag or sign that is used to trigger production of certain components.

production strategy   Consists of a chase, level, or mixed strategy.

profit-leverage effect   A purchasing performance measure that calculates the impact of a change in purchase spend on a firm's profit before taxes, assuming gross sales and other expenses remain unchanged.

public procurement or public purchasing   The management of the purchasing and supply management function of the government and nonprofit sector, such as educational institutions, charitable organizations and the federal, state and local governments.

public warehouses   An independent warehouse that is operated as a for-profit business.

pull system   An operating system where synchronized work takes place only upon authorization from another downstream user in the system rather than strictly to a forecast. JIT systems or lean systems are typically referred to as pull systems.

purchase order (PO)   A contractual commercial document issued by the buying firm to a supplier, indicating the type, quantities and agreed prices for products or services that the supplier will provide to the buying firm.

purchase requisition   An internal document initiated by the material user to request the purchasing department to buy specific goods or services.

purchase spend   The money a firm spends on goods and services.

purchasing spend   The amount of money purchasing has spent on materials, supplies, and services in a period.

pure Internet distribution strategy   Selling goods or services strictly over the Internet.

pure services   Services that offer few, if any, tangible products to customers.

Q

QR codes   A form of mobile marketing that involves the use of the camera function on a smart phone and installing a QR (quick response) code reader on the phone.

qualitative forecasting methods   Forecasts based on opinions and intuition.

quality-of-life factors   Those issues that contribute to "a feeling of well-being, fulfillment or satisfaction resulting from factors in the external environments."

quantitative forecasting methods   Forecasts based on mathematical models and relevant historical data.

quantity discount model or price-break model   A variation of the classic EOQ model, wherein purchase price is allowed to vary with the quantity purchased.

queue discipline   The order in which customers are served.

queue management   A demand management strategy that is used to deal with excess customers.

Queue times   The time that people or goods have spent waiting in line.

queuing systems   The processes used to align, prioritize and serve customers.

quick response (QR)   "Developed by the U.S. textile industry in the mid-1980s as an offshoot of JIT and was based on merchandisers and suppliers working together to respond more quickly to consumer needs by sharing information, resulting in better customer service and less inventory and waste."

R

R chart   Used to track sample ranges, or the variation of the measurements within each sample.

radio frequency identification (RFID)   A technology that enables huge amounts of information to be stored on chips (called tags) and read at a distance by readers, without requiring line-of-sight scanning.

radio-frequency identification tag (RFID)   The chips used to store information about a specific product or carton using RFID.

rail carriers   Trains or railroads.

Railroad Revitalization and Regulatory Reform Act   Commonly known as the 4-R Act; this legislation was passed in 1976 and made several regulatory changes to help the railroads.

Railway Passenger Service Act   Legislation passed in 1970 that created Amtrak.

rationing   A strategy that can occur when demand exceeds a supplier's finished goods available. In such cases, the supplier may allocate product in proportion to what buyers ordered.

real-time location systems (RTLSs)   WiFi-enabled radio frequency identification (RFID) tags used on rail cars to allow tracking of rail cars (and their assets) in real-time.

Reed-Bulwinkle Act   Legislation passed in 1948 that gave groups of carriers the ability to form rate bureaus or conferences wherein they could propose rate changes to the ICC.

relationship marketing or permission market-ing   An extension of target marketing; letting customers select the type and time of communication with organizations.

reneging   Leaving a queue before receiving the service

reorder point (ROP)   The lowest inventory level at which a new order must be placed to avoid a stockout during the order cycle time period.

request for proposal (RFP)   A formal request for a project or product proposal issued by the buyer to qualified suppliers. The use of RFPs allows the supplier to develop part specifications based on their own knowledge of the materials and technology needed.

request for quotation (RFQ)   A formal request for pricing from a supplier; commonly used when the purchasing requirements are clear.

resource requirements planning (RRP)   A long range capacity planning module that is used to check whether aggregate resources are capable of satisfying the aggregate production plan.

return on assets (ROA)/return on investment (ROI)   A financial ratio of a firm's net income in relation to its total assets.

returns management process   A process that manages product returns. This can be extremely beneficial for supply chain management in terms of maintaining acceptable levels of customer service and identifying product improvement opportunities.

reverse logistics/returns management   Returning products, warranty repairs, and recycling or disposing items. Also referred to as returns management.

rewarding suppliers   Giving suppliers more business when their performance is deemed to be excellent.

rights and duties   A theory stating that some actions are right in themselves without regard for the consequences.

right-shoring   The combining of on-shore, near-shore and far-shore operations into a single, flexible, low-cost approach to supply chain management.

right-to-work laws   State legislation that provides employees with the right to decide whether to join or support a union financially.

risk pooling   The relationship between the number of warehouses, inventory and customer service; it can be explained intuitively as follows: when market demand is random, it is very likely that higher-than-average demand from some customers will be offset by lower-than-average demand from other customers. As the number of customers served by a single warehouse increases, these demand variabilities will tend to offset each other more often, thus reducing overall demand variance and the likelihood of stockouts.

road trains   Trucks pulling more than two trailers; these are commonly seen in Australia where trucks are used instead of railroads in low population areas.

root causes   The most significant/potential cause of a problem that impacts the process.

ROROs   Roll-on-roll-off containerships that allow truck trailers and containers to be directly driven on and off the ship, without use of cranes.

rough-cut capacity plan (RCCP)   A plan that is used to check the feasibility of the master production schedule.

S

sales activity management system   Software tools that give sales personnel a sequence of activities guiding them through their sales processes with customers. These standardized steps assure the proper sales activities are performed and also put forth a uniform sales process across the entire organization.

sales force automation (SFA)   Software products used for documenting field activities, communicating with the home office, and retrieval of sales history and other company-specific documents in the field.

sales order   A supplier's offer to sell goods and services at the supplier's terms and conditions. The sales order becomes a legally binding contract when accepted by the buyer.

sales territory management systems   Software applications that allow sales managers to obtain current information and reporting capabilities regarding each salesperson's activities on each customer's account, total sales in general for each sales rep, their sales territories and any ongoing sales initiatives.

scorecarding   A performance measure design technique such as the Balanced Scorecard that uses the scorecard model.

sealed bids   A bid for business by a supplier in response to an invitation for bid sent by a buyer. The bid is kept sealed until all bids are received, whereupon they are opened and the low bidder is typically awarded the purchase contract.

second-tier customers   A customer's customers.

second-tier suppliers   A supplier's suppliers.

segment customers   Placing customers in a behavioral class, such as males/females, age brackets and profitability, so as to better design marketing campaigns for each segment.

server factory   A manufacturing facility that is set up primarily to take advantage of government incentives, minimize exchange risk, avoid tariff barriers and reduce taxes and logistics costs to supply the regional market where the factory is located.

service bundles   A group of attributes that are offered to customers when purchasing services, including the explicit service itself, the supporting facility, facilitating goods and implicit services. Successful services are designed to deliver this bundle of attributes in the most efficient way, while still satisfying customer requirements.

service capacity   The number of customers per day that a firm's service delivery systems are designed to serve, although it could also be some other period of time such as customers per hour or customers per shift.

service delivery systems   A continuum of services that may range from mass-produced, low-customer-contact systems at one extreme (such as ATMs) to highly customized, high customer-contact systems at the other (such as expensive beauty salons).

service layout strategies   A method that works in combination with location decisions to further support the overall business strategies of differentiation, low cost or market focus. Office layouts tend to be departmentalized; commercial airliner layouts segment customers; casino layouts are designed to get customers in quickly and then keep them there by spacing out the attractions; and self-serve restaurant buffet layouts are designed to process customers quickly.

service level   The in-stock probability.

service response logistics   The management and coordination of an organization's activities that occur while the service is being performed.

setup costs   The costs associated with setting up machines and equipment to produce a batch of product; the term is often used in place of order costs.

Seven Rs Rule   Having the right product, in the right quantity, in the right condition, at the right place, at the right time, for the right customer, at the right cost.

seven wastes   A concept that encompasses things such as excess wait times, inventories, material and people movements, processing steps, variabilities and any other non-value-adding activity.

shippers' associations   Nonprofit membership cooperatives that make domestic or international arrangements for the movement of members' cargo.

Shipping Act of 1984   Legislation that allowed ocean carriers to pool or share shipments, assign ports, publish rates and enter into contracts with shippers.

shortage gaming   A strategy that occurs when buyers figure out the relationship between their orders and what is supplied, and they then tend to inflate their orders to satisfy their real needs.

short-range planning horizon   A planning horizon that covers a weekly, daily, or hourly basis.

sigma drift   A theory that assumes process variations will grow over time, as process measurements drift off target.

silo effect/silo mentality   An I-win-you-lose organizational issue that causes a firm to be reactive and short-term-goal oriented. At this stage, no internal functional integration is occurring.

simple moving average forecast   A method that uses historical data to generate a forecast; it works well when the demand is fairly stable over time.

simplification   A reduction of the number of components, supplies, or standard materials used in a product or process.

single integrator solution   An ERP system that uses all the desired applications from the same vendor.

single sourcing   "Refers to the deliberate practice of concentrating purchases of an item with one source from a pool of viable suppliers."

single-factor productivity measures   The output measure divided by a single input measure, such as labor cost.

Six Sigma quality management   A commitment by the firm's top management to help the firm identify customer expectations and excel in meeting and exceeding those expectations.

Six Sigma   A system that stresses a commitment by top management to enable a firm to identify customer expectations and excel in meeting and exceeding those expectations. A type of TQM method devised by Motorola.

small data   The data that was around before big data, or data that is 'small' enough for human comprehension.

sole sourcing   Refers to the situation when the supplier is the only available source.

source factory   A manufacturing facility that has a broader strategic role than an offshore factory, with plant management heavily involved in supplier selection and production planning.

Southern Common Market (MERCOSUR) A regional trade agreement among Argentina, Brazil, Paraguay and Uruguay, formed in March 1991.

specialized carriers Carriers that transport liquid petroleum, household goods, agricultural commodities, building materials and other specialized items.

square root rule A rule suggesting that the system average inventory (impacted by adding or deleting warehouses) is equal to the old system inventory times the ratio of the square root of the new number of warehouses to the square root of the old number of warehouses.

Staggers Rail Act of 1980 Legislation aimed at improving finances for the rail industry.

state utility A situation that occurs when services do something to things that are owned by the customer, such as transport and store their supplies, repair their machines, cut their hair or provide their healthcare.

statistical process control (SPC) A method that allows firms to visually monitor process performance, compare the performance to desired levels or standards and take corrective steps quickly before process variabilities get out of control and damage products, services and customer relationships.

stockless buying or system contracting An extension of the blanket purchase order.

strategic alliance development Improving the capabilities of key trading partners.

strategic partnerships A close working relationship that develops among trading partner relationships.

strategic sourcing Strategically managing a firm's external resources and services to improve cost, quality, delivery, performance and competitive advantage.

strategic supplier alliances The creation of partnerships with key suppliers.

subcontracting The process of entering into a contractual agreement with a supplier to produce goods and/or services according to a specific set of terms and conditions.

super bill of materials Another type of bill of materials that is useful for planning purposes.

supplier certification Defined by the Institute of Supply Management as "an organization's process for evaluating the quality systems of key suppliers in an effort to eliminate incoming inspections."

supplier development The efforts of a buying firm to improve the capabilities and performance of specific suppliers to better meet its needs.

supplier evaluation Determining the current capabilities of suppliers.

supplier management One of the most crucial issues within the topic of supply management— getting suppliers to do what the buyer's firm wants them to do.

supplier relationship management (SRM) Accenture defines SRM as "the systematic management of supplier relationships to optimize the value delivered through the relationship over their life cycle."

supplier relationship management process A process by which the firm manages its relationships with suppliers.

supply base or supplier base Refers to the list of suppliers that a firm uses to acquire its materials, services, supplies, and equipment.

supply base rationalization, supply base optimization, or supply base reduction Getting rid of poorly performing suppliers.

Supply chain analytics Tools that harness data from internal and external sources to produce breakthrough insights that can help supply chains reduce costs and risk.

supply chain management (SCM) The integration of key business processes regarding the flow of materials from raw material suppliers to the final customer.

supply chain performance measurement Determining the performance of an entire supply chain.

supply chain risk The likelihood of an internal or external event that disrupts supply chain operations, causing potential reductions in service levels, product quality, and sales, along with an increase in costs.

supply chain security management A method that is concerned with reducing the risk of intentionally created disruptions in supply chain operations including product and information theft and activities seeking to endanger personnel or sabotage supply chain infrastructure.

supply chain sustainability Meeting the needs of current supply chain members without hindering the ability to meet the needs of future generations in terms of economic, environmental, and social challenges.

Supply chain visibility The ability of suppliers, manufacturers, business partners, and customers to know exactly where products are, at any point in the supply chain.

supply chain A network of trading partners that make products and services available to consumers, including all of the functions enabling the production, delivery and recycling of materials, components, end products and services

supply management The identification, acquisition, access, positioning and management of resources the organization needs or potentially needs in the attainment of its strategic objectives.

surety bonds Bonds posted by bidders to ensure that the successful bidder will accept the contract.

sustainability A commitment to environmental responsibility.

sustainable development A development that meets the needs of the present without compromising the ability of future generations to meet their own needs.

sustainable sourcing A process of purchasing goods and services that takes into account the long-term impact on people, profits, and the planet.

system nervousness A situation where a small change in the upper-level production plan causes a major change in the lower-level production plan.

T

target marketing Targeting specific customer segments, with respect to promotional efforts.

tariff An official list or schedule showing the duties, taxes or customs imposed by a host country on imports or exports.

the 4 M's The standard classifications of problem causes and represent a very thorough list for problem–cause analyses. In almost all cases, problem causes will be in one or more of these four areas: Material, Machine, Methods, and Manpower.

third-party logistics providers (3PLs) For-hire outside agents that provide transportation and other services including warehousing, document preparation, customs clearance, packaging, labeling and freight bill auditing.

third-party logistics services For-profit logistics companies.

three P's Refers to people, planet, and profit.

Tier-1 suppliers A company's direct suppliers.

Tier-2 suppliers The suppliers' suppliers of a company.

Tier-3 suppliers The suppliers' suppliers' suppliers of a company.

time fence system Separates the planning horizon into two segments: a firmed and a tentative segment.

time series forecasting A prediction technique based on the assumption that the future is an extension of the past and that historical data can thus be used to forecast future demand.

time utility A state of well-being that is created when customers get products delivered at precisely the right time, not earlier and not later.

total cost of ownership (TCO) or total cost of acquisition Considers the unit price of the material, payment terms, cash discount, ordering cost, carrying cost, logistical costs, maintenance costs and other more qualitative costs that may not be easy to assess.

total productivity measures A measure of total outputs divided by total inputs.

total quality management (TQM) A focus on the customer, performance measurement, and formal training in quality control methods. Six Sigma embodies an organizational culture wherein everyone from CEO, to production worker, to frontline service employee is involved in quality assessment and improvement.

Toyota Production System A methodology created by Toyota Motor Company in the 1950s. The idea is to make the best use of an organization's time, assets and people in all processes in order to optimize productivity. Also known as JIT and lean production.

tracking signal A tool used to check the forecast bias.

trading companies A firm that puts buyers and sellers from different countries together and handles all of the export/import arrangements, documentation and transportation for both goods and services.

trailer-on-flatcar service or TOFC service Railroads that offer flatcars used to carry truck trailers.

transaction costs Costs include the cost of the goods/services and cost associated with placing and receiving the order.

transaction elements Activities that occur during the sale of a product or service.

transactional SRM A system that enables an organization to track supplier interactions such as order planning, order payment and returns. The volume of transactions involved may result in independent systems maintained by geographic region or business lines. Transactional SRM tends to focus on short-term reporting.

Transportation Act of 1920   Legislation that instructed the ICC to ensure that rates were high enough to provide a fair return for the railroads each year.

Transportation Act of 1940   Legislation that further extended the Interstate Commerce Act of 1887, establishing ICC control over domestic water transportation.

Transportation Act of 1958   Legislation that established temporary loan guarantees to railroads, liberalized control over intrastate rail rates, amended the rule of rate making to ensure more intermodal competition and clarified the differences between private and for hire motor carriers.

transportation brokers   Legally authorized intermediaries that bring shippers and transportation companies (mainly truckers) together.

transportation deregulation   The laws that seek to reduce government regulation in the transportation industry, allowing market forces to dictate services offered.

transportation intermediaries   For-hire agencies that bring shippers and transportation providers together.

transportation management systems   Software applications that allow firms to select the best mix of transportation services and pricing to determine the best use of containers or truck trailers, to better manage transportation contracts, to rank transportation options, to clear customs and to track fuel usage, product movements and carrier performance.

transportation regulation   The laws that protect consumers in areas of transportation monopoly pricing, safety and liability.

transportation security   Protection that is provided to transportation companies against unlawful activities such as terrorism.

Transportation Worker Identification Credential (TWIC)   A transportation security initiative for transportation workers mandated by the Maritime Transportation Security Act of 2002 and the Safe Port Act of 2006.

travel card   P-cards can be used to pay for meals, lodging, and other traveling expenses, thus eliminating the need

to process travel expenses in advance for the user. This type of P-card is commonly called a travel card.

traveling requisition   A material requisition that is used for materials and standard parts that are requested on a recurring basis.

triple bottom line   A broad term that includes protecting the environment and some aspects of social responsibility, as well as financial performance.

truckload (TL) carriers   For-hire trucks that move shipments that take up one full truckload.

Type-I error   When a process is mistakenly thought to be out of control and an improvement initiative is undertaken unnecessarily.

Type-II error   When a process is thought to be exhibiting only natural variations and no improvement is undertaken, even though the process is actually out of control.

U

U.S. Baldrige Quality Award   Legislation enacted in 1987, named in honor of Malcolm Baldrige, President Ronald Reagan's Secretary of Commerce, that seeks to recognize U.S. companies for service or product quality.

Uniform Commercial Code (UCC)   Legislation that governs the purchase and sale of goods.

utilitarianism   A theory that maintains an ethical act creates the greatest good for the greatest number of people.

V

value engineering   Designing better quality and cost savings into the products originally.

value-of-service pricing   A strategy that allows carriers to price their services at competitive levels the market will bear.

variable costs   Expenses that vary as a function of the output level.

variable data   Measurable data, such as weight, time and length (as in the weight of a box of cereal, the time to serve a customer or the length of a steel girder).

vendor managed inventory (VMI)   A progressive partner-based approach to controlling inventory and reducing supply chain costs. Customers provide information to the

key supplier, including historical usage, current inventory levels, minimum and maximum stock levels, sales forecasts and upcoming promotions, who then takes on the responsibility and risk for planning, managing and monitoring the replenishment of inventory. The supplier may even own the inventory until the product is sold.

virtual queues   A queuing system in which customers' places in the queue are tracked by a computerized system that allows customers to roam the premises until their names are called.

W

walk-through service audits   A method of monitoring a service system that is performed by management and covers service system attributes from the time customers initially encounter the service until they leave.

Walmart effect   A theory postulating that the booming growth in information technology has allowed many big-box retailers such as Wal-Mart to realize large productivity growth rates.

warehouse management systems   Software applications facilitating the proper storage and movement of inventory and minor manufacturing such as assembly or labeling activities within the warehouse, and movement of shipments onto the transportation carrier.

waste elimination   Includes reducing excess inventories, material movements, production steps, scrap losses, rejects, and rework.

water carrier   A carrier using ships for transportation.

weighted-factor rating model   A method commonly used to compare the attractiveness of several locations along a number of quantitative and qualitative dimensions.

World Trade Organization (WTO)   The only international organization dealing with the rules of trade between nations. Its functions include administering the WTO agreements, providing a forum for trade negotiations, handling trade disputes, monitoring national trade policies, providing technical assistance and training programs for developing countries and cooperating with other international organizations.

Y

yokoten   A Japanese term meaning "across everywhere." In lean terminology, it is used to mean the sharing of best practices.

Author Index

A

Arnseth, Lisa, 37

B

Blackstone, J. H., 193

C

Champy, James, 12
Cochet, P., 435
Cooper, M., 504, 505
Covey, Stephen R., 85, 86

D

Deming, W. E., 279, 297
Drazen, E. L., 462
Drucker, Peter, 12
Dychè, J., 400

F

Fenwick, S., 517
Ferrell, Krista, 37
Finstad, Ryan, 90
Fisher, Martin, 120
Fleenor, G., 231
Fogarty, D. W., 193

G

Goldenberg, B., 387, 402

H

Hammer, Michael, 12
Hoffmann, T. R., 193
Hoover, E. M., 355

J

Jones, D., 282

K

King, A., 292

L

Lambert, D., 504, 505
Lee, H., 519
Lenox, M., 292
Lewis, Jordan, 84

M

Maister, D., 476
Moll, R. E., 462

N

Nadella, S., 183

O

O'Reilly, T., 145

P

Padmanabhan, V., 519
Pagh, J., 504, 505
Pate, P., 183
Pinchot, Gifford, 117
Porter, M., 415

R

Roetter, M. F., 462
Roos, D., 282

S

Shaw, Arch W., 12

T

Tompkins, P., 403

U

Uchneat, J., 164

V

Vitasek, Kate, 129
Vora, Manu, 7

W

Whang, S., 519
Womack, J., 282

Subject Index

Note: Figures, tables, and examples are indicated by page numbers including f, t, and e.

A

Abbott Diagnostics Longford, 295
ABC inventory control system, 237–242
  classification, 238–239, 239e, 239t, 241e
ABC inventory matrix, 240–242, 241f
Aberdeen Group, 510, 517
ABP Group, 90
Abt Electronics, 477
acceptance sampling, 315
Accesso, 472
accounting and finance, ERP module, 217
Acela Express, 339
Ackermans, 167
active RFID tags, 243, 514
adaption, in supplier relationships, 90
additive manufacturing, 434–436
Adidas, 434
advanced security management
  initiatives, 529–530
AFS Technologies, 168
aggregate production planning (APP),
  185–191
  chase production strategy, 187–189,
    188t, 189f
  defined, 187
  level production strategy, 189–190,
    190f, 190t
  mixed production strategy, 191
air carriers, 332, 339–340
airline security, 344
air pollution, 433
Alaska Airlines, 396
Alibaba Group, 351
Allstate, 557
Aloha Airlines, 334
Alpha Comm Enterprises, 356
Amazon.com, 4, 350, 387, 389, 414, 422,
  425, 467, 479, 482, 520
Amazon Kindle, 120
American Airlines, 334, 348
American Express, 51
American Institute for Shippers'
  Associations (AISA), 360
American Railcar Industries, 363
America West Airlines, 334
AMR Research, 99, 560
Amtrak, 335, 338

analytic SRM, 99–100
Angoss Software, 168
Anheuser-Busch, 23, 117
Annual Survey of Manufactures, 39, 40,
  41t
AP Moller-Maersk Group, 362
APP. *see* aggregate production planning
  (APP)
Apple, 4
Applied Materials Inc., 125
The Archers, 480
Ariens, 359
Armstrong, Elmer, 26
arrival pattern, 470
Arthur Andersen, 549
Ashley Furniture Industries, 425
assignable variations, 309
Association for Operations Management
  (APICS), 7, 132
Association of Southeast Asian Nations
  (ASEAN), 419
Atlantic States Cast Iron Pipe, 395
Atlas Planning Suite, 165
AT&T, 397, 557
attribute data, 309
  control charts, 311–314
ATV Corporation
  aggregate production plan for, 187,
    187e, 188t
  bill of materials for, 195, 196f
  distribution requirements plan for,
    207e
  hypothetical ERP transaction for, 211e
  master production schedule, 191t, 192
  mixed production strategy, 191
  MRP example at, 201e
  super bill of materials for, 197–198,
    198f
automated inventory control solutions,
  508
automobile supply chain, 6
available-to-promise (ATP) quantity,
  192–195
  discrete, 193–195, 194t
average range, 309
Avercast, LLC, 167
Aviation and Transportation Security
  Act, 2011, 344

B

back-of-the-house operations, 457
backup suppliers, 523t, 524
backward vertical integration, 52
balanced scorecard (BSC) approach,
  557–559, 558f, 569–570
balking, 472
Bank of America, 389, 390
Barbies, 296
Baril, Oliver, 16
barter, 67
basic security initiatives, 527–528, 527t
Baumgartner, Buford, 76
Baumol's disease, 453
Beene Garter, 399
The Beer Game, 28–31
Behrens, Rick, 518
benchmarking, 131–133
Benchmarking Partners, Inc., 164
Benevolence Children Hospital, 493–494
Benton, Jim, 393
Bernard Madoff Investment Securities,
  548
best-of-breed solution, 213
Bexon, Richard, 384
Bezos, Jeff, 414
bid, 68
big data, 22, 246–247
big data analytics, 401
billback penalty, 131
bill of materials (BOM), 46, 195–198
  for ATV, 195, 196f
  defined, 195
  indented, 196–197, 197t
  super, 197–198, 198f
Blakester's Speedy Pizza, 293e
blank check purchase order, 52
blanket order release, 52
blanket purchase order, 52
Blommer Chocolate Co., 119
Blue Yonder, 22
BMG, 359
BMW, 516
BNSF Railway, 342, 357
Boatwright, Bernie, 76
Bobcat Logistical Solutions (BLS),
  536–538
Bodek, Norman, 281

Body Shop International, 480
Boeing, 6, 97, 435–436, 518–519
BOM. *see* bill of materials (BOM)
Bombardier Inc., 338
Bosch, 90
Bourne, Wayne, 516
BP oil disaster, 523
Brandenburg, Basil, 76
Braniff, 348–349
breakbulk, 351
break-even analysis, 56, 57f
break-even model, 429, 430e, 431f
break-even point, 56–57
Bridgestone Americas, 119
British Airways (BA), 509
Brook Medical Supplies (BMS), 566–567
Brower, David, 117
Brown & Root, 557
Brussels, Inc., 260e
BSC (balanced scorecard) approach,
    557–559, 558f
buffer stock, 235
bullwhip effect, 10, 148, 185, 515t, 519
Burger King, 480
Burgess, Chris, 169
Burley's Biscuits, Beef, and Veggies,
    409–410
business clusters, 430–432
business cycle, 150
business ethics, 113
Business Excellence Inc., 7
Business Forecasting, 165
Business Forecast Systems, Inc. (BFS), 165
business process reengineering (BPR), 12
Buy American Act, 70
buyer–supplier relationships, 8, 14, 15
    interpersonal relationships in, 85
buying
    decision, 53
    reasons for, 53–55

C

Cainiao, 351
call centers, 396–397, 463, 492–493
Cao Dewang, 425, 428
capacity
    defined, 205
    in resource planning, 185
    strategies, 206
capacity management, 464–469
    capacity exceeds demand, 468
    cross-training, 466
    demand exceeding capacity, 465
    demand management techniques, 468
    part-time employees, 466
    scheduling policies, 467, 467e
    sharing employees, 466
    technology, 466–467

capacity planning, 205–206
capacity requirements planning (CRP),
    206
capacity utilization, 464
Capterra, 403
Carbon 3D, 435
carbon footprints, 556
CargoNet, 528
Carnival Cruise Lines, 335
Carphone Warehouse (CPW), 477
Carrefour, 456
carrying costs, 236
Casey Publishing Co., 314
Cathay Solutions, 90
cause-and-effect diagrams, 306–307, 308f
cause-and-effect forecasting, 150,
    156–158
    multiple regression forecasting, 157–158
    simple linear regression forecast, 157,
        157f, 158e
C charts, 314
CeeJay Lightbulb Co., 313e, 314f
Center for Advanced Purchasing Studies
    (CAPS), 132
centralized/decentralized purchasing
    structure, 64
centralized purchasing, 63–64
centralized warehousing system, 352–354
Cerny, Lou, 369
certification programs, 15
Certified Cargo Screening Program
    (CCSP), 529
change management, 85–86
ChannelNet, 403
Chartered Institute of Procurement &
    Supply (CIPS), 132
Chartered Institute of Procurement &
    Supply Risk Index, 522
chase demand strategy, 465
chase production strategy, 187–189, 188t,
    189f
check sheets, 305, 306f
China
    rail network, 339
    RFID technology usage in, 246
    sustainability approach, 119
    Walmart's location strategy, 425
Chinaco Healthcare, 481
China National Institute for Standards,
    294
CHRISTUS Health, 131
Chrysler, 57, 62
Chuck E. Cheese, 480
Citigroup, 456
Citron, James, 389
Civil Aeronautics Act of 1938, 347
Civil Aeronautics Administration, 347
CJ Steels, 10

class rates, 343
Clayton, Missouri, 544
ClearSlide, 393
clickstream, 392
Clinton, Bill, 68
closed-loop MRP, 198
closeness desirability rating, 459
cloud-based communication platforms,
    517
cloud-based forecasting, 167–169
cloud computing, 212
CLX Logistics, 341
Coalition for Responsible Transportation
    (CRT), 362
coal slurry, 341
Coca-Cola, 389, 416, 482
Coffin, Tristam, 555
cold chains, 352
Cole, Dave, 278
collaborative education, 518
collaborative negotiations, 129, 130t
collaborative planning, 10, 161–164
collaborative planning, forecasting, and
    replenishment (CPFR), 161–164
comanaged inventories, 126
commitment, and supplier relationships,
    85, 90
commodity rates, 343
common carriers, 335
Common Market for Eastern and
    Southern Africa (COMESA), 419
communications, 5
    customers, 392
    lines of, 86
    in supplier relationships, 90
    technologies, 5
Companies and Markets, 352
Competitive Alternatives (KPMG), 421,
    423
competitive force, supply chain as,
    546–548
competitiveness, of nations, 419–421,
    420t
confidentiality, 86
ConocoPhillips, 560
consolidation warehouses, 350
consumer's risk, 315
container-on-flatcar (COFC), 342
Continental Airlines, 334
continuous review system, 261, 262–263
contract carriers, 335
contracting, 39
Contracts for the International Sale of
    Goods(CISG), 67
contributor factory, 416
control charts, 308, 311t
    attribute data, 311–314
control system, 186f

Con-way, 341
Cook, Benjamin, 529
Cooper, M. C., 504, 505
Cornell, Brian, 521
corporate purchasing cards, 51
corporate social responsibility (CSR), 114
corruption, 528
Corruption Perceptions Index, 528
cost leadership strategy, 456
cost-of-service pricing, 342
costs, 554t
    carrying, 236
    direct, 236
    facility location, 423
    fixed, 236
    holding, 236
    indirect, 236
    inventory, 235–236
    labor, 423
    order, 236
    organization, 549–550
    setup, 236
    sunk, 236
    supply chain, 10e
    transaction, 87
    transportation, 354, 423
    utility, 423, 426
    variable, 236
Council of Supply Chain Management
    Professionals (CSCMP), 7, 162
counterpurchase, 67
countertrade, 66, 67
Covey, Stephen R., 85, 86
Cox Machine, 284
Crabtree Electronics, 272–273
creativity, in supplier relationships, 90
critical-to-quality (CTQ) characteristics,
    303
Crosby, Philip, 298, 299t
crossdocking, 350
cross-selling, 389–390
cross-training, 466
Cruz, Johnny, 324
C-TPAT compliance, 528
currency stability, 422–423
customer behaviors, 390–391
customer churn, 390–391
customer contact centers, 396–397, 482
customer defection analysis, 390
customer lifetime value (CLV), 391–392
customer profitability, 391
customer relationship management
    (CRM), 13, 218, 384–385
    application, selection of, 399–400
    components, 388–398
    customer behaviors, 390–391
    customer service capabilities,
        managing, 394–398

customer value determination,
    391–392
    defined, 386–387
    designing and implementing, 398–402
    integrating applications, 400–401
    involving users from the outset, 399
    performance measures linked to, 401,
        402t
    personalizing customer
        communications, 392
    plan, creating, 398–399
    process, 506, 506t
    sales force automation (*see* sales force
        automation (SFA))
    segmenting customers, 388–390
    tools, 388–398
    trends in, 402–403
    users, training for, 401–402
Customer Relationship Management
    (magazine), 402
customers
    anxiety, relieving, 477–478
    communications, 392
    end, 546
    firing, 390
    grouping, 478
    informing, 478
    keeping occupied, 477
    segmentation, 388–390
    service quality and, 463
    surveys, 149–150
    vampire, 390
customer satisfaction, 397–398
customer service, 554t
    call centers, 396–397
    customer satisfaction, 397–398
    defined, 394–396
    managing capabilities, 394–398
customer service management, 506, 506t
customer value determination, 391–392
customs brokers, 366
Customs-Trade Partnership Against
    Terrorism program (C-TPAT),
    365–366
Cyber Logic Systems, 26–27, 106–107
cycle counting, 237, 238
cyclical variations, as time series
    component, 150

D

dabbawalas, Mumbai, 294
Daisy Perry, 491–492
Dallas Cowboys, 335
data control charts
    C charts, 314
    P charts, 311, 312–314, 314f
Datalliance, 126
data warehouses, 401, 511–512

DB Schenker, 362
Deaconess Health System, 304
Dean Vanwinkle Enterprises, 139–141
decentralized/centralized purchasing
    structure, 64
decentralized purchasing, 63, 64
decentralized warehousing system, 352,
    353–354
deep-sea transportation, 340
Deere & Company, 15
defects per million opportunities
    (DPMO), 293
    for Blakester's Speedy Pizza, 293e
    Six Sigma metrics, 293t
Dell, 546
Del Monte Foods, 517
Deloitte, 8, 9, 150
Delphi Automotive, 57
Delphi method, 149
Delta Airlines, 334, 348, 349, 396
demand forecasting
    accuracy, 159–161, 160e
    cloud-based, 167–169
    collaborative planning, forecasting,
        and replenishment, 161–164
    importance of, 147–148
    software, 165–167
    techniques of (*see* forecasting
        techniques)
    websites, 164–165
demand forecast updating, 515t, 519–520
demand management, 17, 465
    process, 506t, 507
    techniques, 468–469
Demand Solutions, 164
demand source, 470
demand time fence, 192
Deming, W. Edwards, 279, 297, 298t
departmental layouts, 459
Department of Defense (DOD), 68
Department of Transportation Act, 347
dependent demand, 196, 198, 234
DeSimone, Joseph, 435
deterministic interarrival time, 470
Deutsche Post DHL Group, 356
deVere Group, 455
DHL, 414
DHL Global Forwarding, 360
DHL Supply Chain, 356
differentiation strategy, 456
digital dentistry, 435
Diners Club, 51
direct costs, 236
direct offset, 67
Disneyland, 477
distribution centers, 350, 351
    RFID and, 245
    robotics, 567–569

distribution channels, 478–483, 479t
  eatertainment, 479–480
  edutainment, 480
  entertailing, 480
  franchising, 480–481
  international expansion, 481–482
  internet distribution strategies,
    482–483
distribution network, 18–19
distribution requirements planning
  (DRP), 186, 206–207
distributive negotiations, 129
DMAIC improvement cycle, 303–304, 303f
Domino's Pizza, 387, 388, 397, 452
Dow Chemical, 529–530
Downey College, 323
Drishtee, 481
Drug Quality and Security Act (DQSA),
  212
Drugstore.com, 520
Drug Supply Chain Security Act
  (DSCSA), 212–213
Dun & Bradstreet, 522

E

early supplier involvement (ESI), 58,
  125–126
  vendor managed inventory, 126
eatertainment, 479–480
e-commerce, 13, 482, 492
economic manufacturing quantity
  (EMQ) model, 252–257
economic order quantity (EOQ) model,
  247–251
  assumptions of, 247–248
  calculation at Las Vegas Corporation,
    249e
  deriving, 248–251
  physical inventory with, 251f
  and total costs, 250
economies of scale, 54
EcoPorts, 362
EcoTransIT World, 362
Edison Awards, 120, 121t
edutainment, 480
efficient consumer response (ECR), 277
80/20 rule, 238, 306
Eiji Toyoda, 278, 279
electronic data interchange (EDI), 47, 208
electronic product code (EPC), 243–244,
  244f
Elite Collision Centers, 280
emergency sourcing, 524
emission scandal (Volkswagen), 91
employees
  cross-training, 466
  hidden, 466
  part-time, 466

scheduling policies, 467, 467e
  sharing, 466
empty miles, 361
Enron, 548, 549
enterprise resource planning (ERP), 13,
  17, 184, 186, 511–512
  advantages of, 216
  development of, 209–211
  disadvantages of, 217
  generic, 210f
  growth of, 211–212
  hypothetical transaction, 211e
  implementation of, 213–216
  software applications, 217–218
  and supply chain management, 215
entertailing, 480
Environmental Management System
  (EMS), 94
Environmental Protection Agency, 362
environmental sustainability
  in logistics, 361–362
  supply chain and, 555–557
EPCglobal, Inc., 243, 243t
e-procurement, 47–50, 98
equipment setups, 287
Ernst & Young, 22, 557
ethical and environmental certifications,
  124
ethical and sustainable sourcing, 16
ethical and sustainable supplier
  certifications, 123–124
ethical sourcing, 113–115
  initiatives, 123–125
  strategies, development of, 120–123, 121t
Ethical Trading Initiative (ETI), 115
  Base Code, 115, 116t, 122
ethics
  business, 113
  code of, 132–133
European Union (EU), 65–66, 94, 114,
  353, 418
event-based marketing, 392
everyday low pricing (EDLP), 521
exception rates, 343
exempt carriers, 335
expediting, order, 47
explosion, in MRP, 200
EXPO Logistics, 337
exponential smoothing forecasting,
  153–154, 155e, 155f
Export Trading Company Act, 1982, 367
Export Trading Company Affairs
  (ETCA), 367
external certifications, 93–95
  ISO 9000, 94
  ISO 14000, 94–95
external process integration, 512–513
Exxon Mobil, 549

F

Facebook, 389
facilitating products, 462
facility location, 414–415
  access to suppliers, 425–426
  additive manufacturing and, 434–436
  business clusters, 430–432
  competitiveness of nations, 419–421,
    420t
  costs, 423
  critical factors, 416–428, 417t
  currency stability, 422–423
  environmental issues, 423–424
  foreign exchange risk, 422–423
  global strategies, 415–416
  labor issues, 425
  land availability and cost, 428
  proximity to customers, 424–425
  quality-of-life factors, 426–427
  right-to-work laws, 427–428
  sustainable development, 432–433
  taxes and incentives, 422
  techniques (*see* facility location
    techniques)
  trade agreements, 418–419
  utility availability and cost, 426
  World Economic Forum, 421–422
  World Trade Organization, 418
facility location techniques
  break-even model, 429, 430e, 431f
  weighted-factor rating model,
    428–429, 429e
Fairtrade Foundation, 115
Fairtrade International, 115
fair trade products, 115
Fair Trade USA, 115, 124
FCA US, 82
Featherstone, Simon, 455
Federal Acquisition Regulation (FAR), 67
Federal Acquisition Streamlining Act
  (FASA), 68
Federal Aviation Act of 1958, 347
Federal Aviation Administration (FAA),
  347
Federal Maritime Commission, 349
Federal-Mogul, 93
FedEx Corporation, 23, 339, 414
FedEx Freight, 337
Ferdows, Kasra, 415
Fiat Chrysler, 8
FinancesOnline, 403
finished goods, 235
Finstad, Ryan, 90
firing customers, 390
firmed planned order, 200
firmed time fence system, 192
First and Second Laws of Service,
  476–477

FirstEnergy Corporation, 426
first-tier customers, 6
first-tier suppliers, 6
fishbone diagrams, 306–307, 308f
Fitz-Simmons Consultants, 138–139
five dimensions of service quality,
    483–484
Five-Ss, 283–284, 283t
Five-Why, 283
fixed costs, 236
fixed order quantity models, 247
Fleet Bank, 391
Florin, Daniel, 8
flow diagrams, 305, 305f
FOB destination pricing, 343
FOB origin pricing, 343
focal firm, 6
focus strategy, 456
follow-up, order, 47
Ford, Henry, 279
Ford Motor Co., 23, 82, 278, 425, 502
    Aligned Business Framework, 83
    One Ford program, 82
    supplier relationship management
        at, 82
forecast bias, 159
forecast error, 159
forecasting, 10, 161–164
    accuracy, 159–161, 160e
    cloud-based, 167–169
    demand (see demand forecasting)
    exponential smoothing, 153–154, 155e,
        155f
    linear trend, 155–156, 156e
    multiple regression, 157–158
    naïve, 151
    simple linear regression, 157, 157f, 158e
    simple moving average, 151–152, 152e,
        152f
    software, 165–167
    techniques of (see forecasting
        techniques)
    time series, 151–156
    websites, 164–165
    weighted moving average, 153, 153e,
        154f
forecasting techniques, 148–158
    qualitative, 148, 149–150
    quantitative, 148, 150–158
Forecast Pro TRAC, 165, 166
Forecast Pro Unlimited, 165
Forecast Pro XE, 165
ForecastX Wizard, 165, 166
foreign exchange risk, 422–423
foreign freight forwarders, 366–367
foreign-trade zones (FTZs), 367, 422
Foreign-Trade Zones Board, 367
Forest Stewardship Council (FSC), 123

Forrester, Nora, 105
forward buying, 521, 523, 523t
forward vertical integration, 52
4 M's, 306
4-R Act, 348
Fox, Connie, 137–138
Fox's Furniture Division, 227–228
Fragrance Du Bois, 122
Free and Secure Trade program (FAST),
    365–366
free trade zones, 367
freight brokers, 360
freight forwarders, 360
French Fry Heaven, 456
Frontier Airlines, 334
front-of-the-house operations, 457
functional products, 120
functional silos, 505, 550
Furniss, Bob, 390
Fuyao Glass Industry Group, 425, 428

G

Gamel, Mike, 450
Gartner, Inc., 4, 365, 385
Gasperment, Sophie, 480
Gatepoint Research, 126
Genco, 369
General Agreement on Tariffs and Trade
    (GATT), 65, 418
General Electric (GE), 17, 304, 435
general freight carriers, 337
generally accepted accounting principles
    (GAAP), 238
General Mills, 362, 364, 505
General Motors (GM), 6, 83, 279, 298,
    502
General Services Administration (GSA),
    68
geographical specialization, 235
GHG Protocol standards, 124
Gilbert, Sheldon, 390
Global Competitiveness Report, 419
Global Electronics (G-E), 535
global location decisions. see facility
    location
global logistics, 365–368
    freight security, 365–366
    intermediaries, 366–367
Global Reporting Initiative, 119
global sourcing, 64–67
    countertrade, 67
    defined, 64
    potential challenges for, 66–67
    reasons for, 66–67
global supply chains, 19
global trade management (GTM)
    systems, 362–363, 365
Goldman Environmental Prize, 117

goods vs. services, 452
Google, 150, 247, 294, 482, 509
Gore, Al, 117
Gorlier, Pietro, 465
Grace Communications Foundation, 463
Graham, Mike, 525
Granger Laws, 345
Grant, Lenwood, 84
Grebson Manufacturing, 10, 10e
Green, Nigel, 455
Green Belt Movement, 117
green development, 433
Greenhalgh, Leonard, 85
Greenhut, Melvin, 355
green purchasing, 70, 117
green reverse logistics programs, 370
green supply chain management
    (GSCM), 555
Greyhound, 335
gross domestic product (GDP), 66, 451
gross requirement, in MRP, 199

H

Hackett Group, 558
Hall, Carl, 126
Hallmark Consumer Services, 454–455
Halo, 169
Hammerstein University, 176–177
Hardin, Ed, 131
Harpert Store, 260
Hawaiian Airlines, 334
Hayley Girl Soup Co., 310, 310e, 311
Hazardous Materials Transportation Act,
    1972, 347
Hedge, John, 83
HELP, 344
Hershey Co., 119
Hess Corp., 280
Hewlett Packard (HP), 86, 358, 416
hidden employees, 466
high-speed trains, 338
Hill, Greg, 280
Hilton Union Square Hotel, 555
holding costs, 236
Home Depot, 529
Homeland Security Act, 2002, 344
Honda Motor Company, 52, 82, 83, 424,
    428
    facility location, 415
    partnership with Rover, 516
Honeycutt Warehouse and Shipping
    Corporation, 376–377
Honeywell, 428
    Six Sigma Plus program, 96
Honeywell Safety Products (HSP), 165, 166
Hoover, Edgar, 355
horizontal collaboration, 361
Hormel Food Corporation, 97–98

horsemeat scandal, 90
HubSpot CRM, 403
Hudson's Bay, 122
Hughes, Arthur Middleton, 391
human resource management, 218
hybrid purchasing organization, 64
Hyperloop, 339
Hyperloop One, 338
Hyundai, 8

I

IBM, 298, 424, 505, 518
ICC Termination Act of 1995, 349
Imperial Sugar refinery, 507
implosion, 207e
import broker, 65
import merchant, 65
incentives, 422
An Inconvenient Truth (documentary), 117
incoterms, 67
Incoterms 2010, 67
indented bill of materials, 196–197, 197t
independent demand, 196, 198, 234
India, 432
    GDP, 452
    as service-oriented economy, 452
indirect costs, 236
indirect offset, 67
industrial buyers, 39
information exchange, 5
information sharing, 86
information visibility, 515t, 516–517
infotainment, 480
Infotrends, 387
in-house production, reasons for, 55–56
innovative products, 120
Instagram, 389
instantaneous replenishment, 252
Institute for Supply Management (ISM),
    7, 39, 91, 117, 132, 146, 148
Institute of Business Forecasting &
    Planning (IBF), 164
in-stock probability, 258
integration elements, supply chain
    management, 20–21
integrative negotiations, 129
Integrity Interactive Corp., 124
Intel, 557
Intel, Supplier Continuous Quality
    Improvement (SCQI) program, 96, 97
Intelleflex Corp., 514
interdependence, in supplier
    relationships, 90
intermediaries, transportation, 360–361
intermediately positioned strategy, 355
intermediate operations planning, 185
intermodal marketing companies
    (IMCs), 361

intermodal transportation, 341–342
internal control, 44
internal supply chains, 511
International Commercial Terms, 67
international expansion, 481–482
International Institute of Forecasters
    (IIF), 164
International Motor Vehicle Program
    (IMVP), 279
International Organization for
    Standardization (ISO), 94, 123
international purchasing. *see* global
    sourcing
Internet-based electronic purchasing
    system, 49f
interpersonal relationships, 85
Interstate Commerce Act of 1887, 345,
    347
Interstate Commerce Commission (ICC),
    341, 345, 346–348
inventory
    costs, 235–236
    functions of, 235
    investment, 233t
    management, 17
    models (*see* inventory models)
    physical, 251f
    projected on-hand, 200
    service considerations in, 462t
    setup time reduction and, 287–288
    tracking software, 12
    types of, 235
    zombie, 369
inventory investment, 236–237
    total revenue/total assets *vs.*, 233t
inventory management, 231–274
    ABC inventory control system, 237–242
    concepts and tools of, 234–247
    continuous review system, 261,
        262–263
    dependent demand, 234
    independent demand, 234
    inventory costs, 235–236
    inventory investment, 236–237
    inventory models (*see* inventory
        models)
    periodic review system, 261, 263
    radio frequency identification, 242–247
    statistical reorder point, 257–261
inventory models, 247–263
    economic manufacturing quantity
        model, 252–257
    economic order quantity model,
        247–251
    fixed order quantity models, 247
    quantity discount model, 251–252,
        253e, 254e
    statistical reorder point, 257–261

inventory turnover, 42–44, 236
inventory turnover ratios, 43–44,
    236–237, 237t
inventory visibility, 17
invitation for bid (IFB), 68
Ishikawa diagrams, 306–307, 308f
ISM Report on Business, 146, 148, 232
ISO 9000, 94, 123, 302–303
ISO 9001, 94
ISO 14000, 94–95, 123, 302–303

J

Jabil Circuit, 526
Jaeger Industrial Solutions, 105
Jaguar Land Rover, 8
Jay's Quick Lube Shop, 471e, 473e
J.B. Hunt, 341
JCPenney, 482
JetBlue, 388
Joe Gibbs Racing (JGR), 184
John Galt Solutions, 165–166
Jonel Engineering, 393
Joseph, Brian, 526
Journal of Supply Chain Management, 132
Juran, Joseph, 299
jury of executive opinion, 149
JustEnough, 166–167
just-in-time (JIT) strategy, 12, 277

K

Kaiser Permanente, 117
kaizen, 291
kaizen blitz, 291
kanbans, 279, 289
Kaplan, Robert, 557, 558
Kathy's Sewing Shop, 475e, 476e
Kawasaki Motors Corp. U.S.A., 358
keiretsu relationships, 277
Kennedy, Ted, 348
Keyes, Jessica, 387
key performance indicators, 89–90
Keystone XL pipeline, 341, 433
key supply chain process, 506t
    customer relationship management
        process, 506
    customer service management, 506
    defined, 505
    demand management process, 507
    internal integration of, 511–512
    manufacturing flow management
        process, 507–508
    order fulfillment process, 507
    product development and
        commercialization process, 509
    returns management process, 509–510
    supplier relationship management
        process, 508–509
key trading partners, 503–505

Kifer, Ron, 125
Kimberly-Clark, 502
Kimble Chase Life Science, 364
Kinch, Alex, 469
Kinki Nippon Tourist Co., 482
Knight, Phil, 115
knowledge, lack of, 515t, 518–519
knowledge management solutions, 513
knowledge management system (KMS), 394, 395
Konica Minolta, 114
Korn Ferry International, 357
KPMG, 421, 525, 526, 557
Kraft, 6
Kuantan ATV Inc., 60–61e

L

"laboratory point of view," 12
labor costs, 423
lag capacity strategy, 206
Lambert, D. M., 504, 505
Lamb's Automotive Supplies, 271–272
Lam Research, 125
Land O' Lakes, 362, 502
Las Vegas Sands Corp. (LVS), 237
law office's supply chain, 6
Lawson, Mike, 393
LayerRx, 390
layout strategies, 458
lead capacity strategy, 206
lead factory, 416
lead management system, 393–394
lean, elements of, 281–291, 282t
    waste elimination, 281–284
lean layouts, 285–286
lean manufacturing, 277
lean production, 17, 277
    and Toyota Production System, 278–280
lean Six Sigma, 295, 296
lean supply chain relationships, 284–285
lean systems, and environment, 292
lean thinking, 277, 280
    and supply chain management, 281
lean warehousing, 355–356
The Learning Key, 511
legacy material requirements planning systems, 208–209
legacy systems, 511
Lego, 416
less-than-truckload (LTL) carriers, 336–337, 350
level demand strategy, 465
level production strategy, 189–190, 190f, 190t
leveraging purchase volume, 63
Lewis, Jordan, 84
Liddy, James G., 527

Liddy International, 527
linear trend forecast, 155–156, 156e
line haul rates, 343
lines of communication, 86
LinkedIn, 389
Liquid Factory, 435
location. *see also* facility location
    strategies, 457–458
    warehouses, 354–355
logistics. *see* transportation
    defined, 333
    environmental sustainability in, 361–362
    global (*see* global logistics)
    goal of, 18
    place utility and, 333
    reverse (*see* reverse logistics)
    and supply chain management, 12–13, 18–20, 356–361
    time utility and, 333
logistics brokers, 360
logistics management software applications, 362–365
    global trade management systems, 362–363, 365
    transportation management systems, 362, 363
    warehouse management systems, 362, 363–364
London, Inc., 259e
Lone Wild boar Corporation, 257e, 258f
long-range operations planning, 185
loss of visibility, 199, 203
lot size, 200, 288f
lowest-priced bidder, 68
low-level coding, in MRP, 200
Lowry Solutions, 508
Lush Fresh Handmade Cosmetics, 114

M

Maathai, Wangari, 117
Macy's, 401
Madagascar, 524
Mailplus, 169
maintenance, repair, and operating supplies (MRO supplies), 235
make/buy decision, 52
make-to-order manufacturing firms, 189
make-to-stock manufacturing firms, 190
Malcolm Baldrige National Quality Award, 300–301t, 300–302
Malfliet, Ellen, 130
management standards, 302–.303
Managing Strategic Relationships (Greenhalgh), 85
manual purchasing system, 43–46, 44f
    material requisition, 45–46
manufacturing cells, 286

manufacturing flow management process, 506t, 507–508
manufacturing planning, 186f
manufacturing resource planning (MRP-II), 186, 208–209, 218
marketing, event-based, 392
market positioned strategy, 355
Marks & Spencer, 246
Mars, 119
Martin Fisher, 120
Maryann Franklin Industries (MFI), 137–138
MassMutual, 529
MasterCard, 51
master production schedule (MPS), 186, 191–195
    available-to-promise quantities, 192–195, 194t
    time fence, 192
match capacity strategy, 206
material requirements planning (MRP), 12, 17, 46, 186, 198–205
    benefit of, 199
    closed-loop, 198
    computation, example of, 201, 201e
    defined, 198
    terms used in, 199–200
material requisition (MR), 45–46
materials management, RFID and, 245
Mattel, 368
maximize competition, 68
Mayo Clinic, 518
McAdam, Jim, 18
McCombs, Matt, 399
McDonald's, 4, 425, 480, 481, 548
McInnis, Bill, 434
McKenna, Tom, 18
McMahan, John, 558
McMillon, Doug, 118
mean absolute deviation (MAD), 159
mean absolute percentage error (MAPE), 159
mean square error (MSE), 159
medium-range operations planning, 185
Mehring, Peter, 352
Memphis Light, Gas and Water Division (MLGW), 127
Mendoza, Rhonda, 26–27
merchants, 39
Merrill Lynch, 389
Mesa Airlines, 334
Metcam, 124–125
Metro Group, 246
Mexico, 432
Mexpress, 450
MHI, 8, 9
microfranchise, 481
micro-purchases, 68

Microsoft, 385
Middleton Fine Furniture, 78–79
Mills, Harold, 455
miscellaneous rates, 343–344
Mitsubishi Corporation, 112
mixed Internet distribution strategy, 482
mixed production strategy, 191
mobile marketing, 389
Mobil Oil, 557
Mogreet, 389
monitoring, supplier relationships, 89–90
Mopar, 465
Motor Carrier Act of 1935, 347
motor carriers, 332 , 336–337, 349
Motorola, 17, 292, 294
muda, 279
Muilenburg, Dennis, 97
Muller, George, 507
multiple-channel, multiple-phase
    queuing system, 473
multiple-channel, single-phase queuing
    system, 473, 474–475, 476e
multiple-factor productivity, 453
multiple regression forecasting, 157–158
Musk, Elon, 338, 339
mutual benefits and needs, supplier
    relationships, 85

N

naïve forecast, 151
NAMU Travel Group, 384
National Additive Manufacturing
    Innovation Institute (NAMII), 434
National Association of Purchasing
    Management (NAPM), 146
National Health Service (NHS), 469
National Institute of Standards and
    Technology (NIST), 300
National Motor Freight Classification
    (NMFC), 343
National Motor Freight Traffic
    Association (NMFTA), 343
nation's competitiveness, 419–421, 420t
natural variations, 309
near field communication (NFC), 242–243
negotiated pricing, 343
Nelson, Dave, 84
Nestlé, 119, 130, 168
net requirement in MRP, 199, 200
NetSuite SuiteCloud system, 169
NFT, 364
Nielsen, Erling, 362
Nike, 115, 130–131, 389, 509
Nissan, 82
Nistevo.com, 362, 502
nontariff barriers, 65
non-vessel operating common carriers
    (NVOCCs), 367

North American Agreement on
    Environmental Cooperation
    (NAAEC), 424
North American Free Trade Agreement
    (NAFTA), 65, 365, 368, 418, 424,
    432
Northwest Airlines, 334
Norton, David, 557, 558
Novellus, 125

O

objectives, in supplier relationships,
    84–85
Ocean Shipping Reform Act of 1998, 349
offset, 67
offshore factory, 416
Ohmae, Kenichi, 83
Olam, 112
Old Dominion Freight, 337
O'Leary Management Solutions, 443–444
O'Neill, Eileen, 117
open-end purchase orders, 52
operations planning, 185–186
OPEX Corp., 508
opportunities for a defect to occur
    (OFD), 293
option overplanning, 198
Oracle, 13, 215, 217, 385
order batching, 515t, 520
order costs, 236
order fulfillment process, 506t, 507
order intervals, 52
organizational cultures, 8
organization costs, 549–550
Organization of Economic Cooperation
    and Development (OECD), 419
original equipment manufacturers
    (OEM), 59
Ortega, Alvin, 175–176
Osterloh, Rick, 150
Ouden, Den, 399
Out of the Crisis (Deming), 297
outpost factory, 416
outsourcing, 47, 53
    information technology, 54
    products and services, 124–125
    reasons for, 53–55
overall mean, 309
Owen Poole, 228
Owens, Craig, 544

P

Pacific Gas & Electric, 424
Pagh, J. D., 504, 505
Palmisano, Sam, 518
Pan Am, 526–527
Parekh, Rakhi, 387
parent, in MRP, 199

Pareto analysis, 238
Pareto charts, 305–306, 307f
Pareto Principle, 306
part families, 286
partner requirements, supply chain, 547
partnerships, and supply chain
    management, 13
passive RFID tags, 243, 514
payment bonds, 68
P-cards, 51
P charts, 311, 312–314, 314f
PearlChain, 130
Pearson Bearings Co., 10, 10e
pegging, in MRP, 200
Peluso, Michelle, 456
Pembroke Consulting, 454
Penske Logistics, 18
People Express, 349
perceived waiting times, 476–478
Perfection Call Center, 408–409
perfect order, 394–395
Perfect Pick system, 508
performance bonds, 68
performance dashboards, 559
performance measurement systems
    supply chain, 555–557
    traditional, 548–552
    world-class, 552–554, 554t
performance metrics, suppliers, 87–89,
    88–89t
performance standards, 550
performance variance, 550
periodic review system, 261, 263
permission marketing, 389
personal relationships, 85, 90
Peterson, Keith, 169
petty cash, 52
Photo-Me International, 466
physical inventory, 251f, 255f
piggyback service, 342, 361
Pinchot, Gifford, 117
pipeline carriers, 333, 340–341
Pittiglio, 560
Pittman's Fireplaces, 442–443
PJ Express (PJEx), 569–570
place utility, 333
planned order receipt, in MRP, 200
planned order releases, 46, 199, 200
planning factor, 195–196, 200
Planning Perspectives, Inc., 83
planning time fence, 192
poisson distribution, 470
poka-yoke, 279
Polaroid, 294
Polly Pockets, 296
Polly's Sweet Treats and Drinks, 406–408
Ponnudurai, Mohan, 15
Porter, Michael, 415, 431

Portrait Software, 397
posttransaction costs, 87
posttransaction elements, 396
Pratt & Whitney, 15, 296–297
prenumbered purchase orders, 44
PrePass, 344
pretransaction costs, 87
pretransaction elements, 396
price-break model, 251–252
price break point, 252
price fluctuations, 515t, 521
PricewaterhouseCoopers, 526
pricing, transportation
    cost-of-service pricing, 342
    FOB destination pricing, 343
    FOB origin pricing, 343
    negotiated pricing, 343
    rate categories, 343–344
    terms of sale, 343
    value-of-service pricing, 342–343
private carrier, 336
private warehouses, 350–351
proactive security management
        initiatives, 529
process, defined, 505–506
process diagrams, 305
process integration, 20, 502
process maps, 305
Proclivity, 390
Procter & Gamble, 4, 126, 163, 424
procurement, 39–40
    electronic systems, 47–50
    in government and nonprofit agencies
        (see public procurement/
        purchasing)
    state, 69
procurement credit cards, 51
producer's risk, 315
product development and
        commercialization process, 506t, 509
product family, 187
production kanban, 289–290
production order quantity (POQ) model,
        252–257
productivity, 452–455
    example, 454e
    and global economy, 453
    measures, 452–453, 551e
    multiple-factor, 453
    single-factor, 453
product positioned strategy, 355
profitability measures, 549–550
profit-leverage effect, 41–42, 42t
projected on-hand inventory, in MRP, 200
Project RAND, 149
public procurement/purchasing, 67–70
    characteristics of, 68–70
    defined, 67
public warehouses, 351–352

pull system, 289, 289f
purchase orders (POs), 44
    blank check, 52
    blanket, 52
    defined, 47
    duplicate, 44
    open-end, 52
    prenumbered, 44
    sample, 48f
    small-value, 50–51
purchase requisition, 45, 46f
purchase spend, 41
purchasing, 38
    centralized, 63–64
    decentralized, 63, 64
    goals of, 40
    green, 117
    industrial buyers, 39
    merchant, 39
    organization, 63–64
    process (see purchasing process)
    profit-leverage effect, 41–42, 42t
    terms, history of, 39–40
Purchasing Managers Index (PMI), 146
purchasing process, 44–53
    e-procurement, 47–50
    manual purchasing system, 43–46, 44f
purchasing spend, 120
pure Internet distribution strategy, 482
pure services, 450

Q

Q-bots, 472
QR codes, 389
Q-smart, 472
qualitative forecasting methods, 148,
        149–150
    customer surveys, 149–150
    Delphi method, 149
    jury of executive opinion, 149
    sales force composite, 149
quality, 58, 554t
    defined, 292
    Six Sigma, origins of, 292–295
Quality Handbook (Juran), 299
Quality Is Free (Crosby), 298
quality of life
    defined, 426–427
    factors, 426–427
Quality without Tears (Crosby), 298
quantitative forecasting methods, 148,
        150–158
    cause-and-effect forecasting, 150,
        156–158
    time series forecasting (see time series
        forecasting)
quantity discount model, 251–252, 253e,
        254e
queue discipline, 472

queue management, 465
queue time management, 469–470
    beginning service quickly, 477
    customer anxiety, relieving, 477–478
    fairness and, 478
    grouping customers, 478
    keeping customers informed, 478
    keeping customers occupied, 477
    perceived waiting times, 476–478
    queuing systems (see queuing systems)
queuing systems
    applications, 474–475
    characteristics, 472
    defined, 469
    design, 470–472, 471f
    input process, 470, 472
    service characteristics, 472–474
    virtual queues, 472
quick response (QR), 277
Quigley Global Transportation, 440–441
Quincy Snodgrass Enterprises, 174–175

R

Rabin, 560
Rack and Shelving Manufacturing (RSM),
        567–569
radio frequency identification (RFID), 17,
        364, 513
    active tags, 243, 514
    barcode *vs.*, 243
    components of, 244, 245f
    global implementation and challenges,
        246
    and inventory management, 242–247
    passive tags, 243, 514
    and supply chain automation, 244–245
rail carriers, 332, 337–339
Railroad Revitalization and Regulatory
        Reform Act, 1976, 348
Railsponsible initiative, 16
Railway Passenger Service Act, 1970, 347
random variations, as time series
        component, 150–151
rationing, 515t, 521–522
raw materials, 235
Raytheon, 84, 128
R chart, 309–311
reactive security initiatives, 527t, 528–529
real-time location systems (RTLSs),
        337–338
Redcat Racing, 359
Reebok, 114, 434
Reed-Bulwinkle Act, 1948, 347
reengineering, 12
*Reengineering the Corporation: A
    Manifesto for Business Revolution*
    (Hammer and Champy), 12
regional trade agreements, 418–419
relationship marketing, 389

reliability, in supplier relationships, 90
Renault, 8, 23
reneging, 472
reorder point (ROP), 257
repackaging, 351
replenishment, 10, 161–164
request for proposal (RFP), 47
request for quotation (RFQ), 47
ResMed, 547
resource planning, 185
resource requirements planning (RRP), 205
responsive bid, 68
retailing industry, 13
retail store, RFID and, 245
return on assets (ROA), 42
return on investment (ROI)., 42
returns management, 368, 506t, 509–510. *see also* reverse logistics
revenue measures, 549–550
reverse logistics, 6, 368–370
   defined, 368
   and environment, 370
   impact on supply chain, 369–370
rewarding suppliers, 130–131
Rhyan, Travis, 23
Ridge, Tom, 523
rights and duties, 114
right-shoring, 366
right-to-work laws, 427–428
Risk International Services, 19
risk pooling, 353–354, 354e
Ritz-Carlton Hotel, 392
RJW Transport, 341
road trains, 337
root causes, 307
ROROs, 342
rough-cut capacity plan (RCCP), 206
Rover, 516
Royal Dutch Shell, 549
Royal Palms Shuffleboard Club, 480
RSM McGladrey, 15
running sum of forecast errors (RSFE), 159
Ryan International, 334

S

S. Bacher, 167
safety stock, 200, 235, 258f, 353
Sakichi Toyoda, 278
sales activity management system, 393
sales agent, 65
sales force automation (SFA), 392–394
   knowledge management system, 394
   lead management system, 393–394
   sales activity management system, 393
   sales territory management systems, 393
sales force composite, 149

Sales Insight, 393
sales order, 47
sales territory management systems, 393
samples, 309
San Diego Zoo, 553–554
SAP, 13, 215, 217, 385
   Supplier Relationship Management application, 99
SAS Forecast Server, 167
scheduled receipt, in MRP, 200
Schmelzle, Dale, 395
SCM. *see* supply chain management (SCM)
scorecarding, 557
SCOR (supply chain operations reference) model, 560–562, 560f, 562t
sealed bids, 68
seasonal variations, as time series component, 150
Seawise Giant, 340
second-tier customers, 9, 10
second-tier partners, 513–515
second-tier suppliers, 9, 10
Sedam, Scott, 281
Sedlak Management Consultants, 369
segment customers, 388–390
   cross-selling, 389–390
   permission marketing, 389
self-diagnosis method (SDM) checklist, 362
server factory, 416
service bundles, 457
service capacity
   defined, 464
   management, 464–469
service delivery systems, 457
service level, 258
service parts, 234
service quality
   and customers, 463
   five dimensions of, 483–484
   managing, 483–484
   poor, recovering from, 484–485
service response logistics, 463–464
services
   cross-border, 450
   delivery systems, 457
   in global economy, 451
   global issues, 455
   goods *vs.,* 452
   layout strategies, 458, 460–461e
   location strategies, 457–458
   overview of, 451–452
   productivity, 452–455, 454e
   pure, 450
   state utility, 451
   strategy development, 456

   supply chain management in, 462–463, 462t
setup costs, 236
setup time reduction, inventory and, 287–288
Seven Rs Rule, 394
seven wastes, 282, 283t
shared vision, in supplier relationships, 84–85
Sharman, Richard, 526
Sharp's Sandwich Shop, 269–271, 321–322
Shaw, Arch W., 12
Shelton, Ruby, 374–375
shippers' associations, 360–361
Shipping Act of 1984, 349
shortage gaming, 515t, 521–522
short-range planning horizons, 185
sigma drift, 293
silo mentality, 515t, 516
simple linear regression forecast, 157, 157f, 158e
simple moving average forecast, 151–152, 152e, 152f
simplification, of materials and components, 52
single-channel, multiple-phase queuing system, 473
single-channel, single-phase queuing system, 472–473, 474, 475e
single-factor productivity, 453
   measures, 550
single integrator approach, 213–214
single sourcing, 62
Six Sigma, 277
   Crosby's contributions, 298, 299t
   Deming's contributions, 297, 298t
   DMAIC improvement cycle, 303–304, 303f
   elements of, 297–304
   ISO 9000, 302–303
   ISO 14000, 302–303
   Juran's contributions, 299, 299t
   Malcolm Baldrige National Quality Award, 300–301t, 300–302
   quality, origins of, 292–295
   statistical tools of (*see* statistical tools, of Six Sigma)
   and supply chain management, 295–297
   training levels, 304, 304t
Six Sigma quality management, 17
small batch production scheduling, 288–290
small data, 403
small dollar value, 51
SmartWay, 362
Smith, Mark, 397

social media, 456
software-as-a-service (SaaS), 167
sole sourcing, 62
Some Problems in Market Distribution
    (Shaw), 12
S-One Holdings, 359
Sony, 416
source factory, 416
sourcing function, assessing and
    improving, 133–134
South African Airways (SAA), 484
Southern Air, 334
Southern Common Market
    (MERCOSUR), 419
Southwest Air, 335, 349
Southwest Airlines, 482
S&P 500, 114, 119
SpaceX, 338
Sparta Systems, 15
specialized carriers, 337
Spin Master, 148
SPX, 127
square root rule, 353
stability, in supplier relationships, 90
Staggers Rail Act of 1980, 349
Starbucks, 281
state procurement, 69
state utility, 451
statistical process control (SPC), 307–315
    acceptance sampling, 315
    attribute data control charts, 311–315
    R chart, 309–311
    samples, 309
    supply chain management and, 315
    variations, 309
    x-bar chart, 309–311
statistical reorder point, 257–261
    with constant demand and
        probabilistic lead time, 260
    with probabilistic demand and
        constant lead time, 258–260
    with probabilistic demand and lead
        time, 261
statistical tools, of Six Sigma, 305–315
    cause-and-effect diagrams, 306–307,
        308f
    check sheets, 305, 306f
    flow diagrams, 305, 305f
    Pareto charts, 305–306, 307f
    statistical process control (*see* statistical
        process control (SPC))
stockless buying, 52
strategic alliance agreements, 129–130
strategic alliance development, 127–130
strategic alliance organization process,
    127t
strategic partnerships, 16
strategic sourcing, 113

strategic supplier alliances, 123
Sturm, Jacklyn, 97
subcontracting, 55
sunk costs, 236
super bill of materials, 197–198, 198f
Supplier Advisory Council (SAC), 84, 128
supplier certification, 15
    defined, 91–92
    external certifications, 93–95
    implementation of, 92
Supplier Continuous Quality
    Improvement (SCQI) program
    (Intel), 96, 97
supplier development, 47
    defined, 95
    seven-step approach, 95–96
Supplier Ethical Data Exchange (Sedex),
    125
supplier evaluation, 15, 91–95
    weighted criteria, 92–93
supplier management, 15
supplier partnership, defined, 83
supplier performance
    metrics, 87–89, 88–89t
    rewarding, 130–131
supplier recognition programs, 97–98
supplier relationship management (SRM),
    14, 98–100
    defined, 98
    at Ford Motor Co., 82
    process, 506t, 508–509
    at Raytheon, 84
    software, companies offering, examples
        of, 98t
supplier relationships, 83
    capabilities, 86–87
    change management, 85–86
    commitment and top management
        support, 85
    continuous improvement, 89
    at Cyber Logic Systems, 106–107
    information sharing, 86
    lines of communication, 86
    monitoring, 89–90
    mutual benefits and needs, 85
    performance metrics, 87–89, 88–89t
    personal relationships, 85
    shared vision and objectives, 84–85
    trust building, 84
supplier(s)
    capacity, 59
    communication capability, 59
    multiple, reasons favoring, 62–63
    number of, usage for purchased item,
        59, 62–63
    reliability, 59
    selection of, 58–59
    single, reasons favoring, 62

supplier scorecard, 93e
supply base, 523t, 524–525
supply base optimization, 124
supply base rationalization programs, 124
supply base reduction, 124
supply chain, 5–9
    automation, radio frequency
        identification and, 244–245
    boundaries, 8–9
    as competitive force, 546–548
    costs, 10e
    and environmental sustainability,
        555–557
    generic, 6f
    impact of reverse logistics on, 369–370
    internal, 511
    IT systems, 523t, 525
    member capabilities, 547–548
    partner requirements, 547
    performance evaluation, 13
    performance measurement systems,
        555–557
    processes, 512
    process objectives, 505–510
    strategies, 505–510
supply chain analytics, 22
Supply Chain Council, 132
supply chain integration model, 503–505,
    504f
    obstacles to, 515–522, 515t
supply chain management (SCM), 218
    air carriers and, 332
    case study, 26–27
    client/server software, 13
    defined, 5–9
    foundations of, 14–21, 14t
    historic events in United States, 11f
    importance of, 9–11
    integration elements, 20–21
    integration model, 503, 504f
    lean thinking and, 281
    logistics and, 12–13, 18–20, 356–361
    motor carriers and, 332
    operations elements, 16–17
    origins of, 11–14
    partnerships and, 13
    pipeline carriers and, 333
    production labor sourcing for, 566–567
    rail carriers and, 332
    in services, 462–463, 462t
    Six Sigma and, 295–297
    statistical process control and, 315
    supply elements, 14–16
    trends in, 21–23
    water carriers and, 332
supply chain operations reference
    (SCOR) model, 560–562,
    560f, 562t

Supply Chain Operations Reference (SCORE) model, 132
supply chain performance measurement, 21
supply chain risk, 522–526
supply chain security management, 526–530, 527t
supply chain sustainability, 22–23
supply chain trading partners, 503–505
supply chain visibility, 23
supply management, 14–15, 39
   financial significance of, 41–44
   role in organization, 40–44
supply/supplier base, 57–58
surety bonds, 68
sustainability, 14, 117–118
sustainable development, 432–433
sustainable sourcing, 116–119
   initiatives, 123–125
   strategies, development of, 120–123, 121t
Sustainable Supply Steering Committee (SSSC), 547
Sutter Health, 516
system contracting, 52
system nervousness, 192

T

Taiichi Ohno, 279
Taiwan, 432
Target, 350, 351, 424, 521
target marketing, 388
tariff, 65
taxes, 422
Taylor, Mark, 19
Teen's Scene, 225–227
Tenneco, 557
10-4 Systems, 23
tentative segment time fence system, 192
terms of sale, 343
Terra Technology, 161
Tesco, 246
Tesla Motors, 120, 338
Texas Air, 349
text messages, 469
third-party logistics providers (3PLs), 13, 18, 356, 357–359, 536–538
   mode, 358
   outsourcing end-to-end supply chain management activities, 358
   selection, 358
   strategic alliances, 358–359
   supply base reduction, 358
Thomas, Julian, 525
Thompson's Boot Barn, 354e
3 Bees Buttermilk Corporation, 76
3D printing, 434–436, 533–535
Three Gorges Dam Project, 426

three P's, 118
tier-2 suppliers, 59
tier-3 suppliers, 59
time bucket, in MRP, 200
time fence system, 192
time series, components of, 150–151
time series forecasting, 150–156
   exponential smoothing, 153–154, 155e, 155f
   linear trend forecast, 155–156, 156e
   naïve forecast, 151
   simple moving average forecast, 151–152, 152e, 152f
   weighted moving average forecast, 153, 153e, 154f
time utility, 333
Todd & McGrath, 560
Tompkins, Paula, 403
top management support, and supplier relationships, 85
Torda, Theodore, 146
Toshiba Semiconductor Company, 100
total cost of acquisition, 58
total cost of ownership (TCO), 58, 59, 61f, 87, 89
total productivity measures, 550
total quality control (TQC), 279
total quality management (TQM), 12, 279, 293
Toyota, 17, 82, 83, 85
Toyota Production System, 278–280
tracking capacity strategy, 206
tracking signal, 159
trade agreements, 418–419
trade secrets, defined, 86
trading companies, 65, 367
trailer-on-flatcar (TOFC), 337, 342
transaction costs, 87
transaction elements, 396
Trans-Pacific Partnership (TPP), 365
Transparency International, 528
transportation. *see also* logistics
   air carriers, 339–340
   common carriers, 335
   contract carriers, 335
   costs, 354, 423
   deregulation, 345, 347–349, 348t
   exempt carriers, 335
   intermediaries, 360–361
   intermodal, 341–342
   legal forms of, 335–336
   modes of, 336–341
   motor carriers, 336–337
   objective of, 334–335
   pipeline carriers, 340–341
   pricing (*see* pricing, transportation)
   private carrier, 336
   rail carriers, 337–339

   regulation, 345–347, 346t
   security, 344
   service considerations in, 462t
   water carriers, 340
Transportation Act of 1920, 345, 346
Transportation Act of 1940, 347
Transportation Act of 1958, 347
transportation brokers, 360
transportation deregulation, 345, 347–349, 348t
transportation management systems (TMS), 362, 363
transportation regulation, 345–347, 346t
Transportation Worker Identification Credential (TWIC), 344
travel card, 51
traveling requisition, 45
Treadwell Distribution Centers, 375–376
Treher, Elizabeth, 511
trend variations, as time series component, 150
triple bottom line, 14
truck-load (TL) carriers, 336–337, 350
TrueNorth Development, 281
Truman, Harry, 68
Trump, Donald, 341, 365
Truong, Donnell, 104
trust, 515t, 517–518
trust building, and supplier relationships, 84, 90
Trusted Partners (Lewis), 84
TWA Airlines, 348
type-I error, 315
type-II error, 315

U

Uchneat, Jim, 163–164
Ultra Ski Manufacturing, 551e
Ultra Ski Shop, 454e
UN Global Compact, 22
Uniform Commercial Code (UCC), 47, 66–67
Unilever, 4, 116–117, 130
United Airlines, 334, 349
United Nations Framework Convention on Climate Change (UNFCCC), 433
UPS, 22, 23, 335, 342, 358, 370, 414
UPS Freight, 337
U.S. Baldrige Quality Award, 300–301t, 300–302
U.S. Census Bureau's Annual Survey of Manufactures, 9
U.S. Customs and Border Protection (CBP), 365, 367
U.S. Department of Transportation, 334
U.S. Economic Development administration (EDA), 559
U.S. Economic Espionage Act of 1996, 86

U.S. Environmental Protection Agency (EPA), 560
U.S. Food and Drug Administration (FDA), 213
U.S. Marines, 514
U.S. Securities and Exchange Commission (SEC), 40
US Airways, 334
UTC, 291
utilitarianism, 113
utility costs, 423, 426

V

value, in supplier relationships, 90
value engineering, 125
value-of-service pricing, 342–343
vampire customers, 390
variable costs, 236
variable data, 309, 310e
variable data control charts
    R chart, 309–311
    x-bar chart, 309–311
variance, performance, 550
variations, 309
vendor managed inventory (VMI), 126, 510
vendors, classification of, 93
Vibrant Credit Union, 399
Victaulic Co., 276
Vince's Market, 20
Virgin America, 396
virtual queues, 472
Visa, 51
visibility, information, 515t, 516–517
Volkswagen (VW), 8, 90–91, 279
Voluntary Interindustry Commerce Solutions (VICS) Association, 161
von Thünen, Johann Heinrich, 354–355
Vora, Manu, 7

W

Walk, Kip, 119
walk-through service audits, 457

Wallenius Wilhelmsen Logistics (WWL), 15
Wall Street Journal, 148
Walmart effect, 453–454
Walmart Stores, Inc., 17, 40, 126, 131, 163, 246, 336, 424, 456, 545, 555
    food sustainability initiative, 118
warehouse management systems (WMS), 362, 363–364, 459
Warehouse Security Professionals (WSP), 535–536
warehouses/warehousing
    centralized system, 352–354
    consolidation, 350
    decentralized system, 352, 353–354
    and distribution, 349–356
    importance of, 350–352
    lean, 355–356
    location, 354–355
    private, 350–351
    public, 351–352
    service considerations in, 462t
    types of, 350–352
Warner Electric, 285
waste elimination, 281–284
    Five-Ss, 283–284, 283t
    seven wastes, 282, 283t
water carriers, 332, 340
web-based scorecards, 559–560
Weber, Alfred, 355
weighted criteria evaluation system, 92–93
weighted-factor rating model, 428–429, 429e
weighted moving average forecast, 153, 153e, 154f
Wells Fargo, 390
Weltzin, Jake, 433
West Marine, 163
Whipple Logistics Company, 374–375
wholesaling industry, 13
Wings Over, 481
win–win negotiations, 129
Wolverton, Mark, 114

work cells, 286, 286f
workforce commitment, 291
work-in-process, 235
World Bank Group (WBG), 553
World Business Council on Sustainable Development (WBCSD), 124
world-class performance measurement systems, 552–554, 554t
WorldCom, 548
World Commission on Environment and Development, 432
World Competitiveness Yearbook, 419, 420
World Economic Forum, 421–422
World Fair Trade Organization, 115
World Resources Institute (WRI), 124
World Trade Organization (WTO), 65, 418, 424

X

x-bar chart, 309–311
Xerox, 57, 62
XL Screw Corp., 365

Y

Year 2000 Millennium Bug (Y2K bug), 211
yokoten, 281
Yoplait UK, 364
YRC Freight, 337
Yum! Brands Inc., 452

Z

Zappos, 370
Zara Espana, S.A., 147
ZeroChaos, 455
Ziegler, Frank, 77
Zimmer Biomet, 8
Ziron, 469
zombie inventory, 369
Zurich Global Corporate, 522